# POLITICAL CORRUPTION IN AMERICA

*An Encyclopedia of Scandals, Power, and Greed*

## Volume 2

# POLITICAL CORRUPTION IN AMERICA

*An Encyclopedia of Scandals, Power, and Greed*

Second Edition

**Volume 2**

Mark Grossman

Grey House
Publishing

| PUBLISHER: | Leslie Mackenzie |
| EDITORIAL DIRECTOR: | Laura Mars-Proietti |
| EDITORIAL ASSISTANT: | Jael Bridgemahon |
| MARKETING DIRECTOR: | Jessica Moody |

| AUTHOR: | Mark Grossman |
| COPYEDITOR: | Elaine Alibrandi |
| COMPOSITION & DESIGN: | ATLIS Systems |

Grey House Publishing, Inc.
185 Millerton Road
Millerton, NY 12546
518.789.8700
FAX 518.789.0545
www.greyhouse.com
e-mail: books @greyhouse.com

# CONTENTS

*Preface, xi*

*Introduction, xv*

## POLITICAL CORRUPTION IN AMERICA

*An Encyclopedia of Scandals, Power, and Greed*

Stars * indicate *See* listings that are cross-referenced to full articles.

Stars * indicate *See* listings that are cross-referenced to full articles.

Stars * indicate *See* listings that are cross-referenced to full articles.

Stars * indicate *See* listings that are cross-referenced to full articles.

**Primary Documents,** 501

Fifty-eight full-text articles from *The Washington Post, New York Times,* etc.

**Appendices**

**Chronology,** 679

**Bibliography,** 703

**Index,** 723

Stars * indicate *See* listings that are cross-referenced to full articles.

# PREFACE

"Scandal: disgrace, shame, discredit, or other ignominy brought upon a person or persons due to illicit or corrupt wrongdoing."

Oscar Wilde wrote that scandal is gossip made tedious by morality. In England, one form of defamation due to scandal or corruption was called *scandalum magnatum*, or "the slander of great men," usually reserved for the worst of all allegations. It is the scandal of political corruption, corruption that is perpetrated by men and women in elected and appointed offices, that is the focus of this work. Historian Edwin G. Burrows explained:

> Corruption in government—the betrayal of an office or duty for some consideration—is a familiar subject among American historians, but for several reasons the history of corruption as such is not. For one thing, corruption has never denoted a specific kind or form of misconduct, much less a specific crime. No one has ever gone to jail for it. It is essentially only an accusation that encompasses a large and shifting ensemble of determinate abuses—bribery, fraud, graft, extortion, embezzlement, influence peddling, ticket fixing, nepotism—not all of which have always been recognized as improper; some of which continue to be regarded as more consequential than others; most of which have been defined in different ways at different times; and each of which, arguably, deserves a quite different historical treatment.

Despite all this, a comprehensive history of the pervasiveness of corruption in American politics had yet to be written—until the First Edition of *Political Corruption in America* in 2003. Corruption, as a study of history, deals also with ethics, and how laws and ethics clash. From the Greek *ethika*, meaning "character," ethics encompass the principles or standards of human conduct, also sometimes called morals. The laws discussed herein set the boundaries of morality, both in the actual law and in the letter of the law, and the violation of them is considered "unethical." Historian Norman John Powell wrote:

> Political corruption has four principal meanings. The first is patently illegal behavior in the sphere of politics; bribery is a prime example. The second relates to government practices that, while legal, may be improper or unethical. To some people, patronage is such a practice—although, it should be noted, patronage can also serve democratic ends and can even be used to combat corruption. A third meaning involves conflicts of interest on the part of public officials—for example, the vote of a legislator who owns oil stock and casts his vote in favor of oil depletion allowances. James Madison made this point in *Federalist No. 10*: "No man is allowed to be a judge in his own cause, because his interest would certainly bias his judgment, and, not improbably, corrupt his integrity." The fourth meaning also has an ethical, rather than a legal, basis: It related to political behavior that is nonresponsive to the public interest. The Watergate scandals provide vivid examples of such corrupt behavior, but the classic formulation of this view

remains the one given by John E. E. Dalberg-Acton (Lord Acton): "Power tends to corrupt, and absolute power corrupts absolutely."

Writers from the beginning of America—even before it became a nation, when it was merely a series of colonies, firmly connected to Mother England—have railed against corruption, with disparate results. William Livingston wrote in the latter part of the eighteenth century: "No Man who has projected the Subversion of his Country will employ Force and Violence, till he has, by sowing the Seeds of Corruption, ripen'd it for Servility and Acquiescence: He will conceal his Design, till he spies an Opportunity of accomplishing his Iniquity by a single Blow." Englishman William Cobbett came to America, where he used the art of writing bitterly satirical pamphlets to rail against political corruption and social injustice. The issue of political corruption was also folded into many of the writings of some of America's best politicians: Daniel Webster explained, "Justice is the ligament which holds civilized beings and civilized nations together." Alexander Hamilton, writing in the *Federalist, No. 78*, penned, "[T]here can be but a few men in the society who will have sufficient skill in the laws to qualify them for the stations of judges. And making proper deductions for the ordinary depravity of human nature, the number must still be smaller of those who unite the requisite integrity with the requisite knowledge."

In the years since the end of the Second World War, more than fifty members of Congress have been indicted for various criminal offenses, although many of these have been acquitted. At the same time, however, Congress has imposed stricter and stricter ethics rules on its members, banning honoraria (monetary gifts for speeches) and other gift giving, and instituting rigid reporting standards for campaign contributions. In two rare instances since the end of the Civil War, two members have been expelled from the U.S. House of Representatives for corruption.

This book is not a history of all corruption in American political history—the sex scandals are not included, as the author believed from the outset that these were not scandals of corruption in the pure sense of the word. By the standards set up for use in this work, "political corruption" is defined as "the dishonest use of a position of elected power to gain a monetary advantage." Despite this clear definition, some scandals contained herein fall outside of this, but are included nonetheless: for instance, Watergate, or Iran-Contra, which are considered "political scandals," were used for gains or agendas other than monetary gain. It was also discovered that political corruption is not owned by any one party—included in the pages that follow are crooks who were Republicans, Democrats, and third-party members, and reformers who were Republicans, Democrats, and third-party members.

As well, this is not just a history of political corruption in America—it is also the history of reformers, and reform measures, and the laws and court cases that have come down to shape laws in this area. This work is also the history of how ethics has been treated in our nation's history. Senator Paul H. Douglas of Illinois, in discussing the ethics in government, stated in 1951, "[W]hen I once asked a policeman how some of his colleagues got started on the downward path, he replied, 'It generally began with a cigar.'" The state of ethics has radically changed: for instance, in 1832, Representative William Stanbery (D-OH) was censured by the entire House for saying that Speaker of the House Andrew Stevenson's eyes might be "too frequently turned from the chair you occupy toward the White House." However, in 1872, Representative James A. Garfield was not censured, despite admitting that he had illegally accepted stock in the Crédit Mobilier scandal; eight years later, Garfield was elected president of the United States. Mark Twain once wrote that "[t]here is no distinctly native American criminal class except Congress." How a century later his words still have effect is why this work exists.

Historians have been warning about the acidic effects of corruption upon the body politic for many years. In 1787 Scottish historian Alexander Tyler explained:

> A democracy cannot exist as a permanent form of government. It can only exist until the voters discover that they can vote themselves largesse from the public treasury. From that moment on, the majority always votes for the candidates promising the most benefits from the public treasury, with the result that a democracy always collapses over loose fiscal policy, always followed by a dictatorship.¢flldots The average age of the world's greatest civilizations has been two hundred years. These nations have progressed through this sequence: From bondage to spiritual faith; from spiritual faith to great courage; from courage to liberty; from liberty to abundance; from abundance to complacency; from complacency to apathy; from apathy to dependence; from dependence back again into bondage.

Tyler was writing about the fall of Athens some two millennia prior, but his words shine a light on any democracy and the pitfalls of allowing scandal and corruption to go unpunished.

In *The Federalist, No. 51*, James Madison explained, "If men were angels, no government would be necessary. If angels were to govern men, neither external nor internal controls on government would be necessary. In framing a government which is to be administered by men over men, the great difficulty lies in this: you must first enable the government to control the governed; and in the next place oblige it to control itself. A dependence on the people is, no doubt, the primary control on the government; but experience has taught mankind the necessity of auxiliary precautions."

## Preface to the Second Edition

When the First Edition of this work appeared in 2003, it was hailed as the consummate examination of the whole of American political corruption, from the beginnings of the nation to the present. What has changed since then? Little has, unfortunately, evidenced by the dozens of additional entries in this Second Edition. We continue to see politicians—of both parties—use the color of their office to swindle, steal, and simply bribe their way into either keeping power or making their office financially opportunistic for themselves and their cronies. The scandal surrounding super lobbyist Jack Abramoff, which brought down several members of Congress, as well as the scandals surrounding Reps. William Jefferson of Louisiana and Allan Mollohan of West Virginia, also serve to note that corruption continues even with increased ethics rules and even more scrutiny, both from ethics panels in the federal and state governments, as well as the press which now includes investigative journalists on blogs, or internet websites. The continuing scandal surrounding Illinois Governor Rod Blagojevich, which may bring down his entire administration, as well as that around the actions of New York Governor Eliot Spitzer, who resigned in March 2008 after his ties to a prostitution ring became known, paired with the conviction of Alabama Governor Don Siegelman, and Detroit Mayor Kwame Kilpatrick also prove that corruption is not just the purview of the federal government but occurs in states and cities across the nation.

But times, in one state anyway, may be a-changing. In 2008, the specter of corruption in the state of Louisiana abated as newly-elected Governor Bobby Jindal, the first Indian-American to be elected governor of a US state, pushed through that state's legislature a package of ethics and lobbying reforms that aims to change the way the state's legislators do business with lobbyists. In a state known for its corrupt leaders on both sides of the political aisle, Jindal's reforms make Louisiana, ironically, one of the toughest ethics-minded states in the nation. We can only hope that others will follow suit.

What we know for sure, is that corruption was part of the global political landscape since time immemorial. In researching this Second Edition of *Political Corruption in America*, the author discovered a report in *The New York Times* from 17 August 1936 detailing the discovery of cuneiform tablets in Mesopotamia, now modern Iraq, from 1500 BC, that disclosed how a Mayor Kushshiharbe of the city of Nuzi was tried for taking bribes, tax graft, and intimidation. It seems that every culture throughout history has had to wrestle with politicians who line their own pockets rather than do the peoples' business.

Teddy Roosevelt said, "Unless a man is honest we have no right to keep him in public life, it matters not how brilliant his capacity, it hardly matters how great his power of doing good service on certain lines may be... No man who is corrupt, no man who condones corruption in others, can possibly do his duty by the community." More recently, John Breaux, a US Representative (1971–1980) and later a US Senator from Louisiana, said, "I can't be bought, but I can be rented."

Laws may be passed to crack down on corruption, but in the end it is the diligence of the media and other politicians, as well as the people, to keep their elected representatives, be they local, state, or federal, in check ethically.

## Acknowledgments

I would like to thank the following people and institutions, without whose collections and valuable assistance this work would have remained an idea, and not the completed form that it has become: The Library of Congress, and all of the people who aided me during several trips there while I researched and wrote this work; The British Library in London, where I was able to copy many rare volumes dealing with British and American political corruption; Roger Addison in the Legislative Resource Center, Office of the Clerk of the House of Representatives, for his assistance in finding information on Representative "Bud" Shuster of Pennsylvania; The folks at the Oklahoma Department of Libraries, Archives and Records Division, for allowing me access to the Henry S. Johnston Papers, including the record of his impeachment; and the many others who assisted me with information, with photocopies, and with the guiding hand that any author tackling such a diverse and complicated subject always needs.

Finally, while it is impossible to document every instance of political corruption in American history—especially small or local cases, or those recorded by contemporary historians and since forgotten—I have done my best to unearth as many of these scandals as possible. All errors of fact and spelling are mine and mine alone.

*Mark Grossman*

Mark Grossman is the author of nine reference works and encyclopedias, such as the *Encyclopedia of Capital Punishment*, the *Encyclopedia of the United States Cabinet*, and the *Encyclopedia of World Military Leaders*. He is currently working on a bibliographic encyclopedia titled *The Speakers of the US House of Representatives*.

**References:** Burrows, Edwin G., "Corruption in Government" in *Encyclopedia of American Political History*, 3 vols. Jack P. Greene, ed. (New York: Charles Scribner's Sons, 1984), I:417; Douglas, Paul H., quoted in *Ethical Standards in Government*, U.S. Senate, Committee on Labor and Public Welfare, *Report of the Special Subcommittee on the Establishment of a Commission on Ethics in Government*, 82d Cong., 1st Sess. (1951), 44; Powell, Norman John, "Corruption, Political" in *Dictionary of American Biography*, 7 vols. (New York: Charles Scribner's Sons, 1976–1978), II:231.

# INTRODUCTION

This second edition of *Political Corruption in America: An Encyclopedia of Scandals, Power and Greed* is the first published by Grey House Publishing. The previous edition was published by ABC-CLIO in 2003. This second edition is heavy with new material and added features:

■ **Primary Documents**—160 pages that include 58 full-text articles from *The Washington Post, The New York Times, Chicago Tribune*, and more. Presented in chronological order, these reports begin in 1804, with the impeachment of John Pickering, and end in 2008, with the misconduct of Alabama governor Don Seigelman.

■ **New entries**—24 brand new, detailed biographies of those politicians whose scandalous stories have been brought to light since the publication of the First Edition, and the same rules apply—that is, no scandals of a strictly sexual nature, nor those whose subjects have not been indicted.

■ **Updated original entries**—including details on those criminals who have since died (in prison or elsewhere), those who

have been released, and those who are still fighting.

■ **Updated Chronology**—29 brand new listings for complete currency.

■ **Updated Bibliography**—23 brand new listings, including books, articles and government documents.

■ **New Appendix**—listing mayors in ethical trouble, for a total of nine appendices.

■ **More images**—63 additional images, for a total of 109 photographs and political cartoons.

■ **Now in two volumes**—with 250 more pages than the First Edition.

This Second Edition of *Political Corruption in America* has no equal. Each of the **288 Biographies** is carefully researched and expertly written, supported by *cross references*, a list of *References* and a wealth of supplemental material: **Primary Document** articles give "the rest of the story" for many individuals included in this work; **Nine Appendices** list politicians in a range of trouble from membership qualifications to investigations to convictions; up-to-date **Chronology** and **Bibliography**; and a detailed, multi-leveled **Index**.

# S

## Schenck, Robert Cumming (1809–1890)

United States representative from Ohio (1843–1851, 1863–1871), U.S. minister to Great Britain (1870–1876), accused, but later cleared, of using his office in London for financial gain. Born in Franklin, Ohio, on 4 October 1809, he attended rural schools before graduating from Miami University in Oxford, Ohio, in 1827. He served as a professor at the university for two years, after which he studied the law and was admitted to the state bar in 1833. He opened a practice in the town of Dayton, Ohio.

Schenck, a Whig, entered the Ohio state house of representatives in 1839 and served until 1843. In 1842 he was elected as a Whig to a seat in the U.S. House of Representatives, entering the Twenty-eighth Congress on 4 March 1843 and serving through the Thirty-first Congress. He served as chairman of the Committee on Roads and Canals. When David Tod, U.S. minister to Brazil, was recalled in early 1851, President Millard Fillmore named Schenck to succeed him. At the same time, Schenck was also accredited as the minister to Uruguay, to the Argentine Confederation, and to Paraguay. On 8 October 1853, after his successor, William Trousdale, had been selected, Schenck stated that he had been recalled, and he sailed for home.

*Robert C. Schenck (Library of Congress, Prints & Photographs Division, LC-DIG-cwpbh-04879)*

When the Civil War broke out in early 1861, Schenck volunteered for service and, entering the U.S. Army on 17 May 1861. He was given the rank of brigadier general of volunteers, eventually being promoted to major general, the rank he held until he resigned his commission on 3 December 1863. At that time, having again been elected to a seat in the U.S. House of Representatives, he left the field of battle to enter the political realm. This time, however, he was elected as a Republican, and he took his seat in the Thirty-eighth Congress, serving from 4 March 1863 until his resignation on 5 January 1871. He eventually served as chairman of the Committee on Ways and Means and chairman of the Committee on Military Affairs. As the chairman of the House Committee on Ways and Means, he earned the nickname "Poker Bob" because of his card playing.

In 1870 Schenck was defeated for reelection, and to award him for his service to the Republican Party President Ulysses S. Grant named Schenck to the post of minister to Great Britain. Grant had first named U.S. Senator Frederick T. Frelinghuysen of New Jersey, and then U.S. Senator Oliver T. Morton of Indiana to the position, but both men had declined. Schenck accepted and sailed to London, where he presented his credentials on 23 June 1871. While in London, Schenck picked up his card playing, achieving some notoriety when he penned a letter to an English duchess on how to play poker.

What got Schenck into trouble was his investment in the Emma Silver mine in Nevada. He decided to make money on the deal before the mine went broke, selling near worthless stock to unsuspecting British investors at the same time that he was supposed to be carrying out his official duties. It was later ascertained that Schenck had been paid more than £10,000 for the mine to use his name in its English advertisements. When the mine did indeed go bankrupt, the investors complained, and a congressional investigation, initiated by Representative Abram S. Hewitt (D-NY), was begun to look into the matter. Historian George Kohn writes, "Ultimately, Schenck was cleared of fraud charges, but his reputation had been badly stained. Both British and Americans accused him of using his dignified public position for personal gain. His dealings caused a British court to issue a writ against him, which he dodged by pleading diplomatic immunity. In May 1876, Schenck resigned and came home in shame, to be replaced as minister to Great Britain by Edwards Pierrepont, who had been Attorney General of the United States."

Schenck settled in Washington, D.C., where he practiced law for the remainder of his life. In 1880 he penned a book on card playing, entitled *Draw Poker*. He died in Washington on 23 March 1890, two weeks shy of his eighty-first birthday. He was buried in Woodland Cemetery in Dayton, Ohio.

**References:** Joyner, Fred B., "Robert Cumming Schenck, First Citizen and Statesman of the Miami Valley," *Ohio State Archaeological and Historical Quarterly*, 58 (July 1949), 286–297; "Robert C. Schenck: Humiliated Diplomat," in George C. Kohn, *Encyclopedia of American Scandal: From ABSCAM to the Zenger Case* (New York: Facts on File, 1989), 294–295; "Schenck, Robert Cumming," in Allen Johnson and Dumas Malone, et al., eds., *Dictionary of American Biography*, 10 vols. and 10 supplements (New York: Charles Scribner's Sons, 1930–1995), VIII, 427–428.

## Schmitz, Eugene Edward (1864–1928)

Mayor of San Francisco (1902–1907), convicted of numerous counts of graft and bribery in his operations of the city before and during the San Francisco earthquake of 1906. Schmitz remains somewhat obscure, despite being one of the most corrupt mayors in American history. Perhaps this corruption arises from the fact that little is known of his life before he assumed the mayorship. He was born in San Francisco on 22 August 1864, the son of pioneer parents. What little education he received has been lost to history, except that he apparently took up music at an early age; he became a drummer boy working in the Standard Theater in San Francisco. He rose to become president of the city Musicians' Union, and became the bandleader of the Columbia Theater orchestra in 1900.

Somehow, Schmitz's musical talent caught the eye of political leader Abraham Ruef, political boss of the city, and Ruef pushed Schmitz to run for mayor in 1901. The city was looking for a change. Despite many years of clean government under Mayor James Duval Phelan, mayor since 1897, a series of labor disputes had become violent. When Phelan used the police to crush a strike by the City Front Federation of Waterfront Workers against the Employers' Association, the unions formed the Union Labor Party to gain political power. Ruef, head of the city's Republican Party, moved to become head of the Union Labor group, and enlisted bandleader—and musical union member—Schmitz as the Union Labor candidate for mayor. Schmitz won easily over Phelan, becoming the first labor-backed candidate to win a major office in the United States. Historian Peter D'A. Jones writes,

"Handsome Gene" Schmitz was good-looking, and well-liked, and, although not "the smallest man mentally and meanest man morally" ever to be mayor, as one opponent claimed, he was easily ruled by Ruef. With each passing day, the links between the city administration and the underworld ramified, especially after the large electoral victory of 1905, after which the city began taking "tributes" from respectable businessmen.

By 1905 Schmitz and his administration were openly accused by several people of corruption, including taking kickbacks and brib-

ery. Attorney Francis J. Heney, who had been named by President Theodore Roosevelt to prosecute land frauds in Oregon (and had netted U.S. Senator John H. Mitchell), held a rally in San Francisco and denounced Schmitz and Ruef as corrupt. Despite this, Schmitz was easily reelected in 1905 over attorney John S. Partridge, the candidate of the Democrats and Republicans. Ruef, with Schmitz's backing, was given control of every department in the San Francisco municipal government.

At this point, former mayor Phelan joined with local business leader Rudolph Spreckels and Fremont Older, editor of the San Francisco *Evening Bulletin*, to call on Heney in December 1905 to open an investigation into the alleged corruption. Heney employed William J. Burns, founder of the U.S. Secret Service (which guards the president), to investigate. Heney and Burns worked in conjunction with San Francisco District Attorney William H. Langdon. Then the Great San Francisco Earthquake, striking on 18 April 1906, derailed the investigation. During the crisis Schmitz rose to the occasion, displaying great leadership to a torn and destroyed city. As soon as the emergency passed, however, Schmitz resumed his parade of graft, shaking down builders for a piece of the action to reconstruct the city. On 24 October 1906, D. A. Langdon announced that Heney would become deputy district attorney to investigate alleged graft and corruption in city government. Ruef and the Union Labor Party decried the selection; at a mass rally on 31 October, Ruef denounced Heney as "the Benedict Arnold of San Francisco," while other speakers called Schmitz "the peerless champion of the people's rights" and Ruef "the Mayor's loyal, able and intrepid friend." Schmitz, on a business trip in Europe, was replaced for a time by Supervisor James L. Gallagher as acting mayor. Gallagher, working with Ruef and Schmitz, decided to forestall the investigation, and on 25 October removed D. A. Langdon and Heney from office and appointed Ruef to investigate the alleged graft. The *San Francisco Call* printed, under a picture of Ruef, the words "This Man's Hand Grips the Throat of San Francisco."

Ruef moved to put an end to a grand jury, which had been empaneled to hear the charges. Ruef could not stop it, however, and Heney presented the evidence. On 7 November Schmitz and Ruef were indicted on charges of extorting kickbacks from brothels; members of the board of supervisors, testifying under grants of immunity, confessed to being in on the massive corruption scheme. During Schmitz's trial, the heads of the United Railroads (a labor union) were implicated in payoffs. Editor Older was kidnapped to shut him up, but was later released, and an ex-felon was paid to murder Heney in open court, shooting the prosecutor but merely wounding him in the jaw. (Heney was replaced for a time by a young attorney named Hiram W. Johnson, who rose to become governor of California and a U.S. senator.) Schmitz was convicted of several counts and sentenced to five years in prison. His conviction was ultimately reversed by an appellate court and by the state supreme court, and he ultimately never served any prison time, unlike Ruef. In 1915 and 1919 Schmitz ran again for mayor, losing both races. In 1916 he was elected to a seat on the city Board of Supervisors, where he served until 1925. Thereafter he was engaged in private business. Schmitz died of heart disease in San Francisco on 20 November 1928 at the age of sixty-four.

Historian Barnaby Conrad explained:

San Francisco cleared away not only the ruins of the fallen City Hall but the human rubble that had been in it, for the graft and corruption had reached heroic—if that's the word—proportions. Rudolph Spreckels financed an investigation of the appalling conditions to the tune of

$100,000, and was aided by his friend James Phelen and Fremont Older, editor of the *Call Bulletin*, who dedicated his newspaper to a crusade against the underworld. The rodents to be fumigated turned out to be Mayor Schmitz himself and his sly cohort, Abe Ruef. Prosecution was difficult because of lack of witnesses, who quite rightly feared for their lives if they testified. The trials were the most explosive ever held in San Francisco, with the house of the chief witness being dynamited, prosecuting attorney Francis J. Heney was shot in the jaw, and Fremont Older himself was kidnapped. The upshot was that in 1907 Schmitz was sentenced to San Quentin for five years, and in 1908 Ruef was convicted on 129 counts of civic graft and sentenced to a fourteen-year term.

Perhaps Schmitz has been "lucky" in his obscurity, mainly because his graft did not occur in New York or Chicago. Books on city bosses do not list him; even works on the history of graft and corruption in municipal situations do not even mention him.

**References:** Conrad, Barnaby, *San Francisco: A Profile With Pictures* (New York: Bramhall House, 1959); Hansen, Gladys, *San Francisco Almanac: Everything You Want to Know About the City* (San Francisco: Chronicle Books, 1975), 85–86; Hichborn, Franklin, *"The System" as Uncovered by the San Francisco Graft Prosecution* (San Francisco: Press of the James H. Barry Company, 1915), 18–21, 74–89, 370–373; "Indicted Mayor Gets Himself Into Japanese Controversy; Schmitz Advises School Board in Matter," *San Francisco Chronicle*, 1 February 1907, 1; Jones, Peter d'A., "Schmitz, Eugene E.," in Melvin G. Holli and Peter d'A. Jones, *Biographical Dictionary of American Mayors, 1820$–$1980: Big City Mayors* (Westport, CT: Greenwood Press, 1981), 320–321; San Francisco [Municipal Government], "Report on the Causes of Municipal Corruption in San Francisco, as Disclosed by the Investigations of the Oliver Grand Jury, and the Prosecution of Certain Persons for Bribery and other Offenses against the State; Schmitz Advises School Board in Matter," *San Francisco Chronicle*, 1 February 1907, 1; "William Denman, Chairman. Committee appointed by the Mayor, October 12, 1908. Reprinted with a Preface and Index of Names and Subjects by the California Weekly." (San Francisco: Rincon Publishing Co., 1910).

## Schumaker, John Godfrey (1826–1905)

United States representative from New York (1869–1871, 1873–1877), the subject of expulsion proceedings in the House in 1875 on allegations of corruption. He was born in the town of Claverack, New York, on 27 June 1826, and completed preparatory studies at the Lenox Academy (Massachusetts). He studied law and was admitted to the New York bar in 1847. That year he opened a practice. In 1853 he relocated to Brooklyn, New York, and continued his law practice. In 1856 he was named district attorney for Kings County (Brooklyn), serving until 1859 and in 1862 as corporation counsel for the city of Brooklyn (it became part of New York City in 1898), serving until 1864. In 1862 (and later 1867 and 1894) he served as a member of the New York state constitutional convention.

In 1868 Schumaker defeated Republican Henry S. Bellows to win a seat in the U.S. House of Representatives, representing New York's Second Congressional District. In 1870 he did not run for reelection. Although he had served as a Democrat, Schumaker jumped on board the liberal Republican movement and ran under that banner in 1872, defeating a Republican only identified as "Perry" to win another term to the House. He won reelection in 1874.

Although the cause has been lost to history, Schumaker was investigated for allegations of political corruption. (An examination of congressional records from the period does not turn up the charge or allegation.) At the same time, another representative, William S. King, was also investigated. Some light can be derived by the report of the committee, which held that:

> Your committee are of opinion that the House of Representatives has no authority to take jurisdiction of violations of law or offenses committed against a previous

*John G. Schumaker (Library of Congress, Prints & Photographs Division, LC-DIG-cwpbh-04386)*

Congress. This is purely a legislative body, and entirely unsuited for the trial of crimes. The fifth section of the first article of the Constitution authorizes "each house to determine the rules of its proceedings, punish its members for disorderly behavior, and, with the concurrence of two-thirds, expel a member." This power is evidently given to enable each house to exercise its constitutional function of legislation unobstructed. It cannot vest in Congress a jurisdiction to try a member for an offense committed before his election; for such offense a member, like any other citizen, is amenable to the courts alone.

Schumaker did not run for reelection in 1876 and returned to private life. He died in 1905, having slipped into obscurity.

**See also** King, William Smith

**References:** *Biographical Directory of the American Congress, 1774–1996* (Alexandria, VA: CQ Staff Directories, Inc., 1996); Schumaker and King report in House Report No. 815, 44th Congress, 1st Session (Washington, DC: Government Printing Office, 1876), 2.

## Seabury, Samuel (1873?–1958)

Noted jurist, head of the Seabury Commission that investigated and helped to bring down Mayor James J. "Jimmy" Walker of New York City. Born in New York City possibly in 1873, he was the great-grandson of the famed clergyman Samuel Seabury (1729–1796), and was named after him. Seabury was educated at the New York Law School and received his law degree from that institution. In 1906 he was elected as a justice to the New York Supreme Court and served until 1914, when he resigned to take a seat on the New York Court of Appeals. In 1916 he resigned that post to run as the Democratic candidate for governor of New York, but he was defeated by Governor Charles S. Whitman.

Ironically, Seabury had sat on the second trial in a case that had made Whitman governor—that of Charles Becker. Becker, a police sergeant, had been accused of participating in the murder-for-hire of gangster Herman "Beansie" Rosenthal in 1912. After Becker's first trial, in which he was convicted but the conviction was struck down on appeal, Seabury was named as the judge to oversee the second trial. Whitman was the prosecutor and obtained a second conviction before Seabury.

Samuel Seabury (Library of Congress, Prints & Photographs Division, LC-DIG-ggbain-23034)

Becker eventually died in the electric chair in 1916. After losing to Whitman in the election in 1916, Seabury then entered into a private law practice for the next two decades.

In 1930 New York Governor Franklin D. Roosevelt, faced with a growing scandal involving allegations of corruption in the magistrate courts of New York City, appointed Seabury as a special counsel to investigate. His inquiry, while not headline-grabbing, did result in the removal of two magistrates, three magistrates resigning, and a sixth running from the law. Impressed by his investigative skill, Roosevelt named Seabury in 1931 to be the special counsel for a state legislative committee "to investigate the affairs of New York City." After a period of investigation, Seabury, as counsel, called his first witness: New York Mayor Jimmy Walker. The New York Times later commented, "Seabury was a patient, shrewd and tenacious cross-examiner in connection with financial advantages that had accrued to the Mayor." In fact, in an unprecedented move, Governor Roosevelt presided over the hearings. Walker, known as the "Debonair Mayor," tried to use glib expressions and humor to overcome the evidence that Seabury had collected; instead, the charm offensive backfired, and Seabury's relentless questioning drove Walker to crack on the stand. On 1 August 1932, Walker returned to New York City and resigned, afterwards heading off to Europe. In early 1932, the play Face the Music debuted on Broadway. The play, composed by playwright Moss Hart and lyricist Irving Berlin, was aimed directly at the Walker administration and the Seabury investigation.

But Seabury was not finished: instead, he turned his sights on corruption in the operation of Tammany Hall, the leading political organization in New York City, one that controlled all patronage and other facets of city government. Starting with lower Tammany employees and working up to the more important ones, Seabury exposed the Tammany operation. Thomas A. Farley, sheriff of New York City, admitted on the stand that $100,000 that he had deposited in his account in 1928 "came out of a wonderful tin box." James A. McQuade, Register of King's County, could only say that he "borrowed" more than $510,000 in six years, but couldn't say from whom. Seabury's extensive investigation cast light on massive corruption that had been going on for years, unchallenged, in Tammany politics. Because of the investigation, an "anti-Tammany" candidate for mayor was named. Seabury himself vetoed Robert Moses and Major General John F. O'Ryan, selecting instead Fiorello La Guardia, who went on to victory in the 1933 election. La Guardia went on to serve as mayor from 1934 to 1945.

After the corruption investigation ended, Seabury was elected president of the New York Law Institute. The author of *New Federation* (1950), Seabury died in New York City on 7 May 1958. Despite the fact that he was one of the leading investigators into corruption in New York state in the twentieth century, his name is almost wholly forgotten.

**See also** Tammany Hall; Walker, James John

**References:** Dewey, John, ed., *New York and the Seabury Investigation: A Digest and Interpretation of the Reports by Samuel Seabury concerning the Government of New York City, Prepared by a Committee of Educators and Civic Workers under the Chairmanship of John Dewey* (New York: The City Affairs Committee of New York, 1933); Mitgang, Herbert, *The Man Who Rode The Tiger: The Life of Judge Samuel Seabury and the Story of the Greatest Investigation of City Corruption in this Century* (New York: Norton, 1979); Mitgang, Herbert. *Once Upon a Time in New York: Jimmy Walker, Franklin Roosevelt, and the Last Great Battle of the Jazz Age* (New York: Free Press, 2000); New York State Supreme Court, Appellate Division, *The Investigation of the Magistrates Courts in the First Judicial Department and the Magistrates Thereof, and of Attorneys-at-Law Practicing in Said Courts: Final Report of Samuel Seabury, Referee* (New York: The City Club of New York, 1932); Northrop, William Bacot, *The Insolence of Office: The Story of the Seabury Investigations* (New York and London: G. P. Putnam's Sons, 1932); "Samuel Seabury Dies on L. I. at 85," *New York Times*, 7 May 1958, 1; "Seabury Declares Walker is Not Worthy of Belief, Scores Legal Quibbling," *New York Times*, 4 August 1932, 1.

## Select Committee on U.S. National Security and Military/Commercial Concerns with the People's Republic of China

*See* Cox Report

## Senate Finance Committee Hearings 1997 (Thompson Committee)

Congressional investigation that examined campaign finance irregularities by the Democratic Party in the 1996 presidential campaign. During that election campaign, allegations of improper fundraising were advanced against the Democratic Party and its candidates for president and vice president, Bill Clinton and Albert Gore. These allegations reached a fever pitch that October, when it was alleged that foreign donors, prohibited by law from giving to American election campaigns, were nonetheless pumping funds into the Clinton/Gore campaign as well as the Democratic National Committee (DNC). On 14 October, the DNC acknowledged receiving more than $450,000 from an Indonesian couple, Arief Wiriadinata and his wife, both partners of a wealthy friend of Clinton, James Riady, head of the Lippo Group, an Indonesian banking concern with a branch in Arkansas, where Clinton was governor. Allegations also arose that a Buddhist temple with ties to Taiwan had raised funds during a visit by Gore the past April. Gore explained that he did not know the event was a fundraiser, even though he was warned by his staff in memos that funds would be raised, a violation of law. On 28 October, the DNC refused to release a preelection spending report showing the donors to their party; after an outcry, they relented two days later and released a partial list of donors. Clinton was reelected overwhelmingly on 7 November, but the controversy did not end there.

During his first postelection new conference, a reelected Clinton declared that alleged contributions from Indonesia had "absolutely not" influenced his policies toward Asia, and, at the same time, he called for congressional passage of the so-called McCain-Feingold campaign finance bill, introduced by Senator John McCain (R-Arizona) and Senator Russ Feingold (D-Wisconsin). The following day, DNC cochairman Don Fowler held his own press conference, in which he stated that "never has there been any desire, plan or intent to evade requirements of applicable laws and regulations.... In fact, we have tried to comply strictly with all relevant requirements." On 13 November, the Justice Department refused to honor a request from McCain for the appointment of an independent counsel to investigate DNC donations. By January, allegations of further wrongdoing by the Clinton campaign and the DNC prompted further calls from congressional Republicans for either the appointment of an independent counsel or a congressional investigation. When stories of "coffees," or meetings in the White House that were attended by Clinton and Gore in which fundraising calls were issued, a violation of law, became public, the potential scandal reached a fever pitch. In February, Clinton acknowledged that he had rewarded top donors to the DNC and his campaign with overnight stays in the Lincoln Bedroom in the White House.

On 11 March 1997, the U.S. Senate voted unanimously to authorize the Governmental Affairs Committee, headed by Senator Fred D. Thompson of Tennessee, to conduct "an investigation of illegal or improper activities in connection with 1996 Federal election campaigns"—a deadline of 31 December 1997 was imposed as a condition that the hearings not get out of hand. Starting in July and lasting through October in 33 total days of testimony, the committee heard direct testimony from more than 70 witnesses, with an additional 200 witnesses interviewed; 418 subpoenas were issued for testimony and documents, and more than 1.5 million documents were reviewed.

On the first day of the hearings, 8 July 1997, Senator Thompson gave an opening statement that outlined what he saw coming out of the hearings:

> On March 11 1997, the United States Senate voted 99–0 to authorize an investigation of illegal or improper activities in connection with the 1996 federal election campaigns.... Article One of our Constitution grants Congress its legislative powers. Implied within those powers is the right of Congress to conduct investigations with regard to matters that are of concern to this nation. Therefore, from time to time throughout our history when problems arise that raise grave questions about our government, Congress has carried out such investigations through congressional hearings such as the ones we begin today.
>
> These hearings serve two purposes. One purpose is to make determinations as to whether or not our laws should be changed or whether additional legislation is needed. The second purpose of hearings is to inform the American people as to how their government is operating—to pull back the curtain and give the American people an unfiltered review as to how their system is working.
>
> Within this broad outline, I believe it is important for us to remember what these hearings are and what they are not. First of all, they are not trials where people are prosecuted. They are not soap operas, designed to titillate. They are not athletic events where we keep a running score. Rather, these hearings are serious looks at how our system is working with a view toward making our system better.
>
> A lot of facts are already out on the public record. In fact, there has been an outpouring of information and

allegations in the media for the last several months. There has been so much troubling information that it is easy for the average citizen to get lost in the maze of competing stories. Therefore, we are tempted to look for one key witness or one document which will explain it all. However, the truth seldom emerges that way. Our obligation in these hearings is to take this virtual blizzard of information, add new facts, provide some depth and context, and pull the material together and present it in a comprehensible form. And at the end of the day, I'm convinced that the true picture will emerge.

The allegations before us are serious. They include illegal foreign contributions and other illegal foreign involvement in our political process, money laundering, influence peddling, violations of the Hatch Act—which prevents fundraising on government time or government property—violations of the Ethics in Government Act, violations of the conflict of interest laws, the improper use of the White House in fundraising activities and questions of whether our government's domestic and foreign policy was affected by political contributions.

These matters go to the basic integrity of our government and our electoral process and will constitute the first phase of our hearings.

There apparently was a systematic influx of illegal money in our presidential race last year. We will be wanting to know: Who knew about it? Who should have known about it? And was there an attempt to cover it up?

It has been pointed out that certain witnesses have fled the country or taken the Fifth Amendment. It has also been noted that we have a cutoff date of December 31. However, it should be remembered that we have much evidence available to us. And if anyone should unlawfully impede or misinform this Committee, there are criminal sanctions available.

Valuable information can be obtained in various ways. It seems that due to the fact these hearings are about to start, the White House has decided to release certain information before this Committee discloses it. Since information is being disclosed that the American people have long since been entitled to, we welcome being preempted. We expect that those under investigation will have cause to preempt us many times in the future.

When the first phase of our hearings is complete, we will begin the second phase, in which we will address the broader issues concerning our electoral process, including the role of soft money and the role of independent groups.

While most of the activities examined in the second phase are presumably legal, I believe that common practices in these areas by both parties are a far cry from the intent of Congress when it drafted our campaign finance laws after Watergate. I personally believe we can do much better than the campaign finance system we

have today. However, we cannot move forward unless we have accountability for the past. We cannot let calls for campaign finance reform be used as a shield to prevent examination of the violations of existing law. Otherwise, calls for reform will be viewed as merely partisan and the cause of reform will be harmed, not enhanced.

These hearings come at a time of economic prosperity, but at a time of increasing public cynicism about government. We now have less than half our people voting. I believe that part of this is due to what has happened to our political process, as evidenced by the matters before us. The American people see their leaders go to greater and more extreme lengths to raise unprecedented amounts of money for their political campaigns.

During its hearings, the committee was faced with several delays and obstructions. Despite the fact that the vote to authorize the hearings was bipartisan, the Democrats on the panel, led by Senator John Glenn (D-OH), orchestrated a campaign to denounce the hearings as one-sided and partisan, refusing at times to vote to issue subpoenas or to cooperate at all. In addition, twenty-three witnesses called before the committee asserted their Fifth Amendment rights against self-incrimination and refused to testify; nine additional witnesses refused to testify until the committee had granted them immunity from prosecution. Ten other witnesses, included Yah Lin "Charlie" Trie, a close friend of Clinton, Ted Sioeng, and Pauline Kanchanalak, fled the United States and refused to return or be interviewed. Another dozen foreign witnesses, including James Riady, also refused to be interviewed.

On 5 March 1998, the Senate Governmental Affairs Committee released its final report, a 1,100-page tome, on the campaign finance scandal. Writing in the report, the majority explained;

In mid-1995, the President and his strategists decided that they needed to raise and spend many millions of dollars over and above the permissible limits of the Presidential campaign funding law if the President were going to be reelected. They devised a legal theory to support their needs and proceeded to raise and spend $44 million in excess of the Presidential campaign spending limits.

The lengths to which the Clinton/Gore campaign and the White House-controlled Democratic National Committee were willing to go in order to raise this amount of money is essentially the story of the 1996 Presidential campaign scandal. The President and his aides demeaned the offices of the President and Vice President, took advantage of minority groups, pulled down all the barriers that would normally be in place to keep out illegal contributions, pressured policy makers, and left themselves open to strong suspicion that they were selling not only access to high-ranking officials, but policy as well. Millions of dollars were raised in illegal contributions, much of it from foreign sources. When these abuses were uncovered, the result was numerous Fifth Amendment claims, flights from the country, and stonewalling from the White House.

**See also** Campaign Finance Scandal 1996; Clinton, William Jefferson; Gore, Albert Arnold, Jr.

**References:** Baker, Peter, "White House Seeks To Protect Gore In Temple Inquiry," *Washington Post*, 3 September 1997, A1; Baker, Peter, and Susan Schmidt, "President Had Big Role in Setting Donor Perks," *Washington Post*, 26 February 1997, A1; *Final Report of the Investigation of Illegal or Improper Activities in Connection With 1996 Federal Election Campaigns, together with Additional and Minority Views* (Report of the Senate Governmental Affairs Committee, 105th Congress, 2nd Session, 1998), i; Gugliotta, Guy, "For Tamraz, Pursuit of Presidential Access Was Also Pursuit of American Dream," *Washington Post*, 19 September 1997, A7; Gugliotta, Guy. "Senate Campaign Probers Release Findings," *Washington Post*, 6 March 1998, A6; "'92 Democratic Fund-Raisers May Have Kept Cash: Almost $160,000 Went to Firms of Couple Guilty in Separate Scheme," *Washington Post*, 17 December 1997, A6; Suro, Roberto, "Reno Decides Against Independent Counsel To Probe Clinton, Gore," *Washington Post*, 3 December 1997, A1; "White House, in Its Thirst For Money, Took Control," *Washington Post*, 10 February 1998, A6; Woodward, Bob, "Gore Donors' Funds Used as 'Hard Money', Federal Restrictions Apply to Such Gifts," *Washington Post*, 3 September 1997, A1.

## Senate Select Committee on Ethics

United States Senate panel, established to oversee ethics in that legislative branch body. Under Article I, Section 5 of the U.S. Constitution, each house of Congress "may determine the Rules of its Proceedings, punish its Members for disorderly Behaviour, and, with the Concurrence of two thirds, expel a Member." However, the Senate and House did not establish formal rules for members to follow, or to discipline members, until the 1960s.

The move to establish these rules started in the 1950s, during hearings in the Senate into alleged corruption in the Reconstruction Finance Corporation, a government aid program created by President Herbert Hoover in 1930. Chaired by Senator J. William Fulbright of Arkansas, the conclusion of the hearings called for ethics rules to be incorporated into the Senate. Fulbright said on the Senate floor, "What should be done about men who do not directly and blatantly sell the favors of their offices for money and so place themselves within the penalties of the law? How do we deal with those who, under the guise of friendship, accept favors which offend the spirit of the law but do not violate its letter?" Fulbright offered a resolution calling for hearings into the creation of a code of ethics. Before a special subcommittee of the Senate Committee on Labor and Public Welfare, chaired by Senator Paul H. Douglas of Illinois, rules that had been advocated since 1951 by Representative Charles Edward Bennett of Florida, calling for "all Government employees, including officeholders" to adhere to a congressional ethics code, were presented for consideration. Douglas later said, "When is it proper to offer [gifts to] public officials and what is it proper for them to receive? A cigar, a box of candy, a modest lunch…? Is any one of these improper? It is difficult to believe so. They are usually a courteous gesture, an expression of good will, or a simple convenience, symbolic rather than intrinsically significant. Normally they are not taken seriously by the giver nor do they mean very much to the receiver. At the point at which they do begin to mean something, however, do they not become improper? Even small gratuities can be significant if they are repeated and come to be expected." Formal rules were established in 1958.

On 24 July 1964, following the famed case of Robert Gene "Bobby" Baker, who was the secretary to the Senate Majority Leader, the Senate adopted Resolution 338, which established the Senate Select Committee on Standards and Conduct with the power to "receive complaints and investigate allegations of improper conduct which may reflect upon the Senate, violations of law, and violations of rules and regulations of the Senate." As the new committee assembled to draft provisions for ethics rules, the Senate was forced to deal with ethics charges against Senator Thomas J. Dodd (D-CT). After Dodd was censured by the Senate for financial impropriety, the committee released new rules on 15 March 1968. On 1 March 1977, Congress enacted the Official Conduct Amendments of 1977, which revised and expanded not only the 1968 set of rules,

but the jurisdiction and authority of the select committee. At the same time, in 1977, the Senate Select Committee on Standards and Conduct was changed into the modern Senate Select Committee on Ethics.

This committee, the first to deal with the ethics issue, was charged with the responsibility to:

Receive complaints and investigate allegations of improper conduct which may reflect upon the Senate, violations of law, violations of the Senate Code of Official Conduct, and violations of rules and regulations of the Senate, relating to the conduct of individuals in the performance of their duties as Members of the Senate, or as officers of employees of the Senate, and to make appropriate findings of fact and conclusions with respect thereto;

Recommend, when appropriate, disciplinary action against Members and staff;

Recommend rules or regulations necessary to insure appropriate Senate standards of conduct;

Report violations of any law to the proper Federal and State authorities;

Regulate the use of the franking privilege in the Senate;

Investigate unauthorized disclosures of intelligence information;

Implement the Senate public financial disclosure requirements of the Ethics in Government Act;

Regulate the receipt and disposition of gifts from foreign governments received by Members, officers, and employees of the Senate;

Render advisory opinions on the application of Senate rules and laws to Members, officers, and employees...

*Senator Tom Dodd, standing at right, attends a 1967 Senate hearing that is investigating his alleged financial wrongdoings. (© Wally McNamee/CORBIS)*

The committee's rules have been expanded, most recently in 1995, with the enactment of the Gifts Rule, which restricts the acceptance by members of gifts. In 2000 a new set of rules established by the committee included those covering the Internet.

According to the standing rules of the U.S. Senate, the committee "investigates alleged misconduct of Senate members and employees, and also keeps senators and staff abreast of new rules and regulations of conduct."

**See also** Dodd, Thomas Joseph

**References:** Amer, Mildred, *The Senate Selection Committee on Ethics: A Brief History of Its Evolution and Jurisdiction* (Washington, DC: Congressional Research Service, 1993); "Ethical Standards in Government" *Report of the Special Subcommittee on the Establishment of a Commission on Ethics in Government*, Senate Committee on Labor and Public Welfare, 82nd Congress, 1st Session (1951), 23; "Study of Reconstruction Finance Corporation: Hearings Before a Subcommittee of the Senate Comm. on Banking and Currency" (81st Congress, 2nd Session, and 82nd Congress, 1st Session (1950–1951)); United States Senate, Select Committee on Ethics, *Senate Ethics Manual* (Washington, DC: Government Printing Office, 2000).

## Senate Select Committee on Standards of Conduct

*See* Senate Select Committee on Ethics

## Shepherd, Alexander Robey (1835–1902)

Territorial governor of the District of Columbia (1873–1874), known as "Boss" Shepherd for numerous acts of corruption of which he was accused but never found guilty. Shepherd remains a highly obscure figure. He was born in Washington, D.C., on 31 January 1835, and attended the schools of that city. Following his father's death, Shepherd left school and worked in odd jobs, most notably as a clerk, a carpenter's apprentice, and as a plumber's assistant. He eventually opened his own plumbing business and became a wealthy man. At the same time, he was involved in numerous real estate deals.

A Republican, Shepherd volunteered for service when the Civil War broke out and served in the military for three months before being elected to the Washington, D.C., Common Council. He served for three years, rising to the presidency of the council in 1862. Because Washington, D.C., at this time was a rundown and dirty city with unpaved roads, Shepherd took on the task of advocating a program of construction and modernization. In 1871 Shepherd was instrumental in establishing a territorial form of government for the district. Two years later, Shepherd was named governor of the Territory by President Ulysses S. Grant, replacing Henry D. Cooke. Historian Lowell Ragatz wrote:

> He quickly overshadowed his colleagues and won the name "Boss Shepherd" by assuming complete control. Imbued with the callous philosophy of a notoriously corrupt era and carried away by his enthusiasm, he spent millions beyond the legally authorized expenditures and hopelessly involved District finances. His custom of awarding contracts to friends in casual fashion without competitive bidding led to accusations that he was sharing in the spoils…. His recklessness and unscrupulous methods led to congressional investigation and the passage of the act of June 20, 1874, which replaced territorial government by commission rule. Grant thereupon named him commissioner, but the Senate refused to confirm the appointment, although he had been found innocent of dishonesty.

Hurt by the accusations made against him and the Senate's refusal to confirm him, Shepherd left Washington and moved to Mexico, where he went to work at a silver mine in Batopilas, Chihuahua. He died there of appendicitis on 12 September 1902 at the age of sixty-seven.

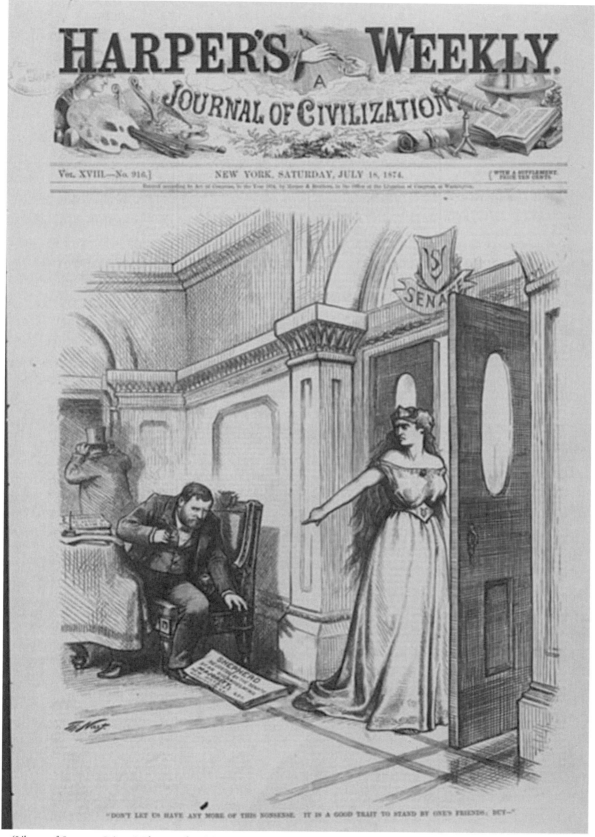

**References:** Ragatz, Lowell Joseph, "Shepherd, Alexander Robey," in Allen Johnson and Dumas Malone, et al., eds., *Dictionary of American Biography*, X vols. and 10 supplements (New York: Charles Scribner's Sons, 1930–1995), IX:77–78; "Shepherd, Alexander Robey," in Rossiter Johnson, ed., *The Twentieth Century Biographical Dictionary of Notable Americans: Brief Biographies of Authors, Administrators, Clergymen, Commanders, Editors, Engineers, Jurists, Merchants, Officials, Philanthropists, Scientists, Statesman, and Others who are Making American History,*10 vols. (Boston: Biographical Society, 1897–1904), IX; "Shepherd, Alexander Robey," in *The National Cyclopaedia of American Biography*, 57 vols. and supplements A-N (New York: James T. White & Company, 1897–1984), XIII:80–81.

## Shuster, Elmer Greinert "Bud" (1932– )

United States representative from Pennsylvania (1973–2001), rebuked by the House Ethics Committee for allegedly accepting improper gifts and favoring a lobbyist. Born in Glassport, Pennsylvania, on 23 January 1932, Shuster attended the public schools of Glassport before attending the University of Pittsburgh, from which he was awarded a bachelor of science degree in 1954, and Duquesne University in Pittsburgh, where he earned a master of business degree in 1960. He completed his education by earning a Ph.D. in economics and management from American University in Washington, D.C., in 1967. After receiving his degree from the University of Pittsburgh, Shuster entered the U.S. Army and served in the infantry and as a counter-intelligence agent from 1954 to 1956. When he finished his duty, Shuster returned to Pennsylvania and became involved in the then-infant computer industry, becoming vice president of RCA's Electronic Computer Division. Involved in the early installation of the UNIVAC, the world's first computer system, he left RCA to found his own computer software company.

A conservative Republican in politics, Shuster ran for a seat in the U.S. House of Representatives in 1972. Defeating Democrat Earl D. Collins, Shuster entered the House on 3 January 1973, representing the Ninth Pennsylvania District. Shuster would eventually serve fourteen terms, from the 93rd through the 106th Congress. A member of the House Transportation Committee, he would eventually become known as "The King of Asphalt" for helping to send millions of dollars to his home state to pave roads, one of which was named in his honor. During his tenure in Congress, Shuster became one of the leading authors of much of the transportation-related legislation in Congress, including the Surface Transportation Act of 1982, the Surface Transportation and Uniform Relocation Assistance Act of 1987, and the Intermodal Surface Transportation Efficiency Act of 1991 (ISTEA). This latter action completed the Interstate Highway System begun under the administration of President Dwight D. Eisenhower. In 1995, when Republicans took control of the House, Shuster became chairman of his committee, renamed the Committee on Transportation and Infrastructure. Three years later, Shuster introduced the Transportation Equity Act for the 21st Century, known as TEA-21. This legislation directed that funds collected for highway construction nationwide be dedicated specifically for that purpose.

Shuster got into ethical trouble starting in 1996. On 6 March of that year, Common Cause, a well-known political watchdog group, sent a letter to the chair of the House Committee on Standards of Conduct (known as the House Ethics Committee), asking for investigation into Shuster's dealings with Ann Eppard, a former Shuster chief of staff who left his employ to go to work as a lobbyist for some of the companies doing business before Shuster's committee. Eppard was also in criminal difficulty—on 9 April 1998 she was indicted by a grand jury in Boston for embezzling $27,500 from Shuster's campaign at the same time that she accepted $230,000 in illegal payments while working for Shuster to help in the passage of the "Big Dig" construction project in Boston. On 9 November 1997, the chairman of the committee, Representative Lamar Smith, a Republican, and ranking minority member, Representative Howard Berman, a Democrat, formed an investigative subcommittee to look into the allegations. Representatives Joel Hefley, a Republican, and Zoe Lofgren, a Democrat, were named to head the subcommittee.

On 1 November 1999, Eppard pled guilty in Boston to accepting illegal compensation from a lobbyist. On 26 July 2000, the investigative subcommittee of the House Committee on Standards of Conduct concluded that Shuster had violated House ethics rules and adopted a Statement of Alleged Violation. Presented with this statement, and a pending report, Shuster accepted the committee's findings. This 147-page report was released on 5 October 2000. In it, the committee explained that Shuster brought "discredit to the House of Representatives." In its letter to Shuster, the Committee explained:

By a unanimous vote on October 4, 2000, the Committee on Standards of Official Conduct, acting on behalf of the House of Representatives, voted to issue to you this Letter of Reproval. The Committee unanimously voted to adopt the Report of the Investigative Subcommittee concerning its investigation of the numerous allegations of misconduct lodged against you.

By your actions you have brought discredit to the House of Representatives.

On November 14, 1997, the Chairman and Ranking Minority Member of the Committee on Standards of Official Conduct established an Investigative Subcommittee pursuant to Committee Rule 17(c)(2) in the matter of Representative Bud Shuster. The Investigative Subcommittee's inquiry focused on the allegations in a complaint filed by the Congressional

Accountability Project and expanded to include an examination of whether your campaign committee violated House Rules and/or federal laws between 1993 and 1998. During the course of its inquiry the Investigative Subcommittee thoroughly investigated the allegations against you. The Investigative Subcommittee issued over 150 subpoenas, counsel interviewed approximately 75 witnesses and the Investigative Subcommittee deposed 33 witnesses. At the conclusion of the inquiry, the Investigative Subcommittee found substantial reason to believe that you had committed violations of House Rules within the Committee's jurisdiction. On July 26, 2000, the Investigative Subcommittee unanimously adopted a Statement of Alleged Violation finding that you engaged in a pattern of conduct that did not reflect creditably on the House of Representatives in violation of former Rule 43, clause 1, of the House of Representatives. As part of a negotiated settlement you admitted, under penalty of perjury, to the Statement of Alleged Violation. By voluntarily admitting to the Statement of Alleged Violation, you agreed that your conduct did not reflect creditably on the House of Representatives through five areas of conduct.

The Statement of Alleged Violation to which you admitted provides that your conduct did not reflect creditably on the House of Representatives in the following manner:

You engaged in a pattern and practice of knowingly allowing your former chief of staff to appear before or communicate with you in your official capacity, during the 12-month period following her resignation from your staff, in a manner that created the appearance that your official decisions might have been improperly affected.

You violated House Gift Rules by accepting expenses from two sources related to a trip to Puerto Rico with your family in December 1995 and January 1996.

You violated former House Rule 45 by authorizing and/or accepting the scheduling and advisory services of your former chief of staff on matters that were official in nature for approximately 18 months after she resigned from your congressional office.

While under your supervision and control, employees in your congressional office worked for your campaign committee to the apparent detriment of the time they were required to spend in your congressional office. While under your supervision and control employees of your congressional office performed services for your campaign in your congressional office.

Expenditures for "political meetings" and expenditures for transportation on chartered aircraft by your campaign committee combined with inadequate record-keeping practices to verify the legitimate campaign purposes of these expenditures, created the appearance that between 1993 and 1998 certain expenditures of your campaign committee may not have been attributable to bona fide campaign or political purposes.

Common Cause President Scott Harshbarger stated, "The sanction imposed today by the House Committee on Standards of Official Conduct upon Representative Bud Shuster (R-PA) makes crystal clear that he brought discredit to the House of Representatives by engaging in a staggeringly wide array of ethical violations. These include a problematic relationship with his former Chief of Staff, flagrant violations of the House Gift Rules, blurring of the lines between official staff and campaign staff, and misuse of campaign funds for apparent personal benefit.... The Letter of Reproval issued by the Committee also shows that Representative Shuster has displayed a cavalier and arrogant attitude toward these serious charges—a tone, according to the letter, of 'blame-shifting and trivializing of misconduct.' But the Committee's report also shows that Shuster escaped punishment for potentially more serious allegations involving special favors and possible quid-pro-quos."

Despite this action, Shuster was overwhelmingly reelected in November 2000 to another term. However, health concerns and a feeling by Shuster that he had "reached the pinnacle of my congressional career," led the fourteen-term congressman to announce on 4 January 2001 that he would resign from the House on 31 January. In May 2001, Shuster's son, William "Bill" Shuster, won a special election to fill his father's seat.

**References:** *Biographical Directory of the American Congress, 1774–1996* (Alexandria, VA: CQ Staff Directories, Inc., 1996); Pianin, Eric, "Veteran Lawmaker Shuster to Retire—'King of Asphalt' Cites Health Reasons," *Washington Post*, 5 January 2001, A4; Plungis, Jeff, "The Driving Force of Bud Shuster," *CQ Weekly*, 7 August 1999, 1914–1919; U.S. House of Representatives, Committee on Standards of Official Conduct, *In the Matter of Representative E. G. 'Bud'*

*Shuster: Report* (Washington, DC: Government Printing Office, 2000).

## Siegelman, Donald Eugene (1946– )

Governor of Alabama (1999–2003), indicted in 2004 for corruption while in office; convicted in 2006, he was sentenced to seven years in federal prison. Born in Mobile, Alabama, on 24 February 1946, he attended local schools before graduating from the University of Alabama in 1968 and the Georgetown University Law Center in Washington, D.C., in 1972. He also studied international law at the University of Oxford in the United Kingdom. Siegelman also served in the Alabama state Air National Guard (ANG), and, later, worked as an aide in the Washington, D.C., congressional office of Rep. Allard Lowenstein, Democrat of New York. Siegelman also worked as a Capitol Hill policeman during his time in law school.

Returning to Alabama, Siegelman began a political career that saw him elected to every major political office in the state: in 1978, he was elected as Secretary of State, serving until 1986, when he ran and was elected as state Attorney General, serving from 1987 to 1991. In 1994, he was elected lieutenant governor, serving until 1999; in 1998, he was elected governor, defeating the incumbent, Republican "Fob" James, 58% to 42%. Siegelman was reelected in 1998, but in 2002 was defeated by Republican Bob Riley. In 2006, Siegelman attempted a political comeback by running in the Democratic primary, but he was defeated by Lieutenant Governor Lucy Baxley, who was defeated in the general election by Riley.

According to the U.S. Department of Justice, while serving as governor, Siegelman became involved in widescale political corruption in Alabama. In 1999, U.S. attorneys in Alabama began a quiet investigation of Siegelman's ac-

*Donald E. Siegelman (AP Images / Rob Carr)*

tivities, although for two years nothing of substance occurred. It was not until 2001, when the Clinton administration ended and the Bush administration began, that a new U.S. attorney looked harder into the allegations. Finally, on 27 May 2004, as Siegelman prepared to run for governor in the 2006 race, the former governor was indicted on federal charges of bribery, racketeering, and mail fraud. When Siegelman's trial began, the judge overseeing the case threw out nearly all of the prosecution's evidence with prejudice (meaning that it could not be allowed in trial ever again against Siegelman), and the prosecutors were forced to drop nearly all of the charges against the former governor. Siegelman was acquitted of all of the remaining charges. However, on 26 October 2005, Siegelman and Richard M. Scrushy, the former CEO of HealthSouth, one of the nation's largest health care providers lo-

cated in Birmingham, Alabama, were both indicted by a federal grand jury on additional charges of bribery and mail fraud. Siegelman was charged along with his former chief of staff, Michael Hamrick, with violating the Racketeer Influenced and Corrupt Organizations (RICO) statute while governor, as well as obstruction of justice and bribery. At the same time, three persons tied to Siegelman pled guilty to corruption charges, including Siegelman's friend and confidant Clayton "Lanny" Young and former Alabama Department of Economic and Security Affairs Director Nick Bailey.

According to the U.S. Department of Justice, which led the investigation and indictment of Siegelman, "Siegelman is also charged with extortion for allegedly demanding payments from individuals under the threat of harming their business interests with the State of Alabama. Specifically, the indictment alleges that Siegelman demanded $100,000 and accepted $40,000 from one individual under the threat of harming that person's business with the Alabama Department of Transportation (ALDOT). Siegelman also allegedly demanded $250,000 from another individual under the same threat. The indictment also alleges that Siegelman, Hamrick, and others established a criminal enterprise in which official actions were exchanged for bribes. Specifically, the indictment alleges that then-HealthSouth Chief Executive Officer Richard M. Scrushy made two disguised payments totaling $500,000 to Siegelman in exchange for Siegelman's appointment of Scrushy to Alabama's Certificate of Need Review Board. Scrushy—initially named in a sealed indictment filed on 17 May 2005—is charged with bribery and mail fraud. Gary Mack Roberts, the former director of ALDOT, is charged in the indictment with honest services mail and wire fraud for his alleged role in influencing ALDOT actions on behalf of

Siegelman." This new indictment alleged that Siegelman was involved in criminal activity when he was lieutenant governor, and that the activity continued while governor.

While on trial, Siegelman protested his innocence and, at the same time, ran in the Democratic primary for governor which he lost on 6 June to Baxley by a vote of 60% to 36%. On 29 June 2006, the federal jury hearing his case found Siegelman and Scrushy guilty. U.S. District Judge Mark Fuller later sentenced Siegelman to seven years and four months in prison.

In 2007, a Republican lawyer in Alabama, Dana Jill Simpson, alleged that White House advisor Karl Rove was behind the case to get Siegelman indicted and removed from office. Later, however, Simpson contradicted claims made under oath that "Karl" was behind the prosecution. Despite the apparent controversy, as of this writing no evidence has ever been uncovered showing that Rove, or anyone in the White House, had anything to do with an investigation against Siegelman which began in 1999 under the Clinton administration.

See also Primary Documents, page 657.

References: Biographical information online at http://www.archives.state.al.us/lg_seigl.html; "Former Alabama Governor Don Siegelman, Others Indicted in Racketeering, Bribery and Extortion Conspiracy," News release of the U.S. Department of Justice, 26 October 2005, online at http://www.usdoj.gov/opa/pr/2005/October/05_crm_568.html; "Former Alabama Governor Don Siegelman, Former HealthSouth CEO Richard Scrushy Convicted of Bribery, Conspiracy and Fraud," News release of the U.S. Department of Justice, 29 June 2006, online at http://www.usdoj.gov/opa/pr/2006/June/06_crm_409.html.

## Sikes, Robert Lee Fulton (1906–1994)

United States representative from Florida (1941–1944, 1945–1979), reprimanded by the U.S. House of Representatives for financial misconduct, for which he eventually lost his seat. Sikes was born in the village of Isa-

bella, near the town of Sylvester, Georgia, on 3 June 1906, the son of Benjamin Fulton Sikes and Clara (née Ford) Sikes. Robert Sikes attended the public schools of the area before he entered the University of Georgia at Athens, which awarded him a bachelor of science degree in 1927. He later earned a master of science degree from the University of Florida at Gainesville in 1929, after which he entered the publishing business in Crestview, Florida. Through this business—and the running of two local newspapers, in Crestview and Valparaiso—Sikes gained important contacts and status in the community.

Sikes's political career began in Florida in 1935, when he was elected to that state's house of representatives, serving from 1936 until 1940. In 1940 he ran for a seat in the U.S. House of Representatives as a Democrat from the Third District of Florida. That seat had been held by Representative Millard Caldwell, who had retired. Sikes, being unopposed, was elected to the first of two terms. He would have been reelected in 1944, but on 19 October 1944 he resigned his seat to serve in the U.S. Army during World War II. He was allowed to run for his seat in the 1944 elections, however, and once again he was elected. He would hold the seat until his resignation in 1979.

Sikes became an important leader for the district he represented; one constituent referred to him as a "He Coon," a metaphor for the revered leader of a tribe of racoons, which were in abundance in West Florida when the first British and Spanish settlers arrived. It was a name that stuck, and his followers were called "He Coons." It also became the name of Sikes's autobiography. Sikes's praise was due mainly because of his leadership in bringing dollars to the area he represented for defense. Sikes was also a leader in helping to build the Apalachicola-Chattahoochee-Flint River system, which brought water to areas of Florida, Georgia, and Alabama. For this work he was popular among his constituents and his colleagues in Congress. But at the same time, Sikes was involved in financial dealings that would ultimately cause his downfall. As chairman of the House Military Construction Appropriations Subcommittee, Sikes had the power to push or resist lucrative military construction projects. On 28 April 1976, the House Committee on Standards of Official Conduct began an inquiry into conflict of interest allegations lodged against Sikes by Common Cause, the citizens' lobbying group that called for strict ethics rules in Congress. Common Cause alleged that Sikes, as chairman of the House subcommittee, had not reported the ownership of stock in Fairchild Industries Inc., a military contractor doing business before the subcommittee, as well as stock in the First Navy Bank at the Pensacola Naval Air Station in Pensacola, Florida, in violation of Rule 44 of the House Ethics rules. The group also charged that Sikes had sponsored legislation in the House in 1961 that removed restrictions on parcels of land in Florida for use in construction, despite the fact that Sikes had a financial interest in this land. On 12 May 1976, the panel voted nine to zero to initiate a "factual investigation" into the charges. Committee chairman John J. Flynt Jr. (D-GA) told reporters that "as far as he knew" it was the first such intensive investigation by the House committee charged with upholding ethics.

Following a comprehensive investigation, the committee voted ten to two on 21 July 1976 to approve a report prepared by investigators that recommended that the full House reprimand Sikes for financial misconduct only, despite the overwhelming evidence of violations of conflict-of-interest laws. All three charges made by Common Cause were proved; however, the panel held that Sikes's failure to

report the Fairchild stock did not appear to be "an effort to conceal" ownership, but deserved a reprimand nonetheless. The charges involving the land deals were cited as a conflict of interest, but no further action was called for. A fourth charge, alleging that Sikes voted for a fiscal 1975 military appropriations bill, which included $73 million for an aircraft contract with Fairchild, did not violate House rules because he had only a limited number of shares in the company, and such ownership did not disqualify him from voting on the matter.

On 29 July 1976, the House voted 381 to 3 to reprimand Sikes, the first time a sitting member had been so punished since Representative Adam Clayton Powell in 1969. Despite this punishment, Sikes won reelection in 1976. However, on 27 May 1978, he announced he would not be a candidate for reelection in that year's election. He left office on 3 January 1979. He retired to Crestview, Florida, where he remained until his death from pneumonia on 28 September 1994 at the age of eighty-eight.

References: "[The Case of] Robert L. F. Sikes," in *Congressional Ethics* (Washington, DC: Congressional Quarterly, 1980), 22; Sikes, Bob, *He-Coon: The Bob Sikes Story* (Pensacola, FL: Perdido Bay Press, 1984); United States Congress, *Biographical Directory of the United States Congress, 1774$–$1989: The Continental Congress, September 5, 1774, to October 21, 1788, and the Congress of the United States, from the First through the One Hundredth Congresses, March 4, 1789, to January 3, 1989, Inclusive* (Washington, DC: Government Printing Office, 1989).

## Simmons, James Fowler (1795–1864)

Rhode Island industrialist and U.S. senator (1841–1847, 1857–1862), who resigned his seat because of corruption. Born on his family's farm near the town of Little Compton, Rhode Island, on 10 September 1795, Simmons attended a private school in Newport, Rhode Island. In 1812 he moved to Providence, Rhode Island, and worked in various manufacturing concerns in both Rhode Island and Massachusetts. In 1822 he again moved, this time to a small town in New Hampshire that he renamed Simmonsville, and there he opened a yarn factory. Five years later, he relocated the factory to Johnston, Rhode Island.

In 1827 Simmons was elected to the New Hampshire state house of representatives, where he served until 1841. A Whig, Simmons was elected to the U.S. Senate, where he initially served from 4 March 1841 until 3 March 1847.

On 2 July 1862, Senator Joseph A. Wright, Unionist of Indiana, submitted a resolution calling for Simmons's expulsion. Wright claimed that Secretary of War Edwin M. Stanton had reported to him that Simmons had used his influence as a U.S. senator to try to obtain a war contract for two Rhode Island companies that had contributed to Simmons's election efforts—allegedly two $10,000 promissory notes, as well as a promise of some $500,000 in profits from the company if they got the contract. The matter was referred to the Senate Judiciary Committee—there was no Ethics Committee as of yet—which reported back to the Senate within a week. Historians Anne Butler and Wendy Wolff explain:

> The committee ascertained that an agent of a Rhode Island business firm approached Simmons and requested aid in procuring a government contract for the manufacture of 50,000 breech-loading rifles. Simmons corroborated the testimony of the agent, C. D. Schubarth, but insisted that the manufacturers' payments to him were not tied to a guarantee of government contracts. Simmons detailed the transactions with great frankness, expressing his complete astonishment at the charges and contending that he acted for the benefit of both his constituents and his government. Simmons cited the recent Union draft of 500,000 men, for whom the government had but 200,000 weapons. With such a critical shortage, Simmons assumed that the prompt delivery from a responsible firm could only aid the war

effort. The unabashed senator made no move to deny that he still held the promissory notes or that he expected them to be paid in full.

> In its July 14 report, the committee set forth Simmons's case in the most deferential terms, citing his age and honorable life, but ultimately found the senator's behavior entirely inexcusable.

However, because the Senate session was nearly ended, no action was taken on Simmons's case. Simmons was warned that once the Senate reconvened, he would be the subject of an expulsion resolution. Facing this, he resigned his seat on 15 August 1862, one of only a handful of senators to take such a step because of political corruption.

Simmons returned to Rhode Island and his manufacturing pursuits. He lived only two years after leaving the Senate, dying in Johnston, Rhode Island, on 10 July 1864 at the age of sixty-eight. His name, and his case, have slipped into obscurity.

**References:** *Biographical Directory of the American Congress, 1774–1996* (Alexandria, VA: CQ Staff Directories, Inc., 1996); Butler, Anne M; and Wendy Wolff, *United States Senate Election, Expulsion and Censure Cases, 1793–1990* (Washington, DC: Government Printing Office, 1995), 115–116.

## Small, Lennington "Len" (1862–1936)

Governor of Illinois (1921–1929), implicated in massive corruption in that state but acquitted by a jury. Born near Kankakee, Illinois, on 16 June 1862, Lennington Small, known as "Len," was the son of a doctor. He attended public schools and Northern Indiana Normal School. Little is known about his early life. A Republican, in 1901 Small was elected to a seat in the Illinois state senate, serving until 1905. He was elected state treasurer in 1904 and served until 1908. From 1908 until 1912 he served as assistant treasurer in charge of the United States Subtreasury in Chicago. In 1916 he was again elected Illinois state treasurer, serving from 1917 until 1921.

In 1920 Small captured the Republican nomination for governor and went on to defeat Democrat James H. Lewis by more than half a million votes out of 2 million cast. Assuming office on 10 January 1921, Small won a second term in 1924.

Almost from the start of his administration, Small was beset by allegations of massive corruption from his days as state treasurer from 1917 to 1921. It was during this period that Small worked with William "Big Bill" Thompson, mayor of Chicago and himself a corrupt politician. Small aided Thompson in keeping Chicago in the grips of the corrupt powers that had elected Thompson as mayor. Historian Jay Robert Nash explained, "Not long after taking office for the first time in 1921, [Small] was indicted for embezzling $600,000 during his previous term as state treasurer. Small was charged with depositing millions of dollars of state funds in a bank controlled by his friend, State Senator E. C. Curtis, and profited by the interest in 1917 when he was serving as state treasurer." Historian George Kohn adds, "The experience of undergoing judicial arraignment did not, however, deter Small. He found a way to circumvent the authority of the court. He teamed up with a notorious gunman, a lawyer turned crook, and a dishonorable union official to bribe and threaten members of the jury and their families. He was, in due course, acquitted."

Small was now free from embezzlement charges, but instead of remaining clean he decided to use the governor's office to sell pardons to the highest bidder. From the time of his acquittal until he left office, Small sold some 8,000 pardons—making him one of the most corrupt governors in American history. Working closely with Thompson in Chicago and Robert E. Crowe, the state's attorney for Cook County, Small would find convicts, have a third party approach them with the offer of a pardon, and then grant it for a fixed sum. Small would then split the fees with Crowe. One such parolee was Ignatz Potz, sentenced to death for killing a police officer. Small commuted his sentence in 1922 to life and in 1926 granted him a full pardon that released Potz from prison altogether. Small became known as "The Pardoning Governor of Illinois."

In 1928 Small actually tried to run for a third term. In what was called the "Pineapple Primary" (in which extremists from both sides set off bombs, nicknamed "pineapples," to force the other parties' voters away from the polls), Small and Crowe were defeated, despite having the financial and political backing of Mafia boss Al Capone. Small lost the Republican primary to Louis L. Emmerson, the Illinois secretary of state. Small ran for governor again in 1932, but lost to Democrat Henry Horner; he also ran in 1936, but lost the Republican nomination to C. Wayland Brooks. Shortly after the 1936 primary, Small died on his farm near Kankakee on 17 May 1936. He was buried in Kankakee. Although it is obvious that Small was indeed one of the most corrupt, if not the most corrupt, governor in American history, his name is almost wholly forgotten.

**See also** Thompson, William Hale

**References:** "Len Small: Pardoning Governor," in George C. Kohn, *Encyclopedia of American Scandal: From ABSCAM to the Zenger Case* (New York: Facts on File, 1989), 302; "Len Small," in Jay Robert Nash, *Encyclopedia of World Crime: Criminal Justice, Criminology, and Law Enforcement,* 4 vols. (Wilmette, IL: CrimeBooks, Inc, 1989), IV:2780; "Small, Lennington," in Robert Sobel and John Raimo, eds., *Biographical Directory of the Governors of the United States, 1789–1978*, 4 vols. (Westport, CT: Meckler Books, 1978), II:384–385.

*Frank L. Smith (Library of Congress, Prints & Photographs Division, LC-DIG-ggbain-39091)*

## Smith, Frank Leslie (1867–1950)

United States representative (1919–1921) and senator-elect (1926–1928) from Illinois, refused his seat in the U.S. Senate because of allegations of fraud and corruption in his campaign. Born in the village of Dwight, Illinois, on 24 November 1867, Frank Smith attended local public schools and for a time taught in local schools, although it does not appear that he ever received any secondary education or a degree. Branching out into private business pursuits, he entered the fields of insurance, real estate, banking, and agriculture. In 1894 he served as the village clerk for Dwight, apparently his first political position.

In 1904 Smith was nominated by the Republicans for the office of lieutenant governor of Illinois. However, although the Republican gubernatorial nominee, Charles S. Deneen, was elected easily, Smith was defeated by Democrat Lawrence Yates Sherman (1858–1939), former Speaker of the Illinois House of Representatives. Smith did serve, from 1905 to 1909, as the internal revenue collector for Illinois. Smith left office in 1909 and returned to private business, but ten years later was elected to a seat in U.S. House of Representatives, serving in the Sixty-sixth Congress from 4 March 1919 to 3 March 1921. In 1920 he gave up his seat to try for the Republican nomination for the U.S. Senate, but lost to William Brown McKinley. Again, he returned to his business pursuits. In 1921 Illinois Governor Lennington "Len" Small named Smith chairman of the Illinois Commerce Commission, where he served until 1926. In 1926 Smith ran for the U.S. Senate seat held by McKinley—who was seriously ill—and defeated Democrat George E. Brennan. On 7 December 1926, Senator McKinley died, and Governor Small named Smith to the vacancy, which expired on 3 March 1927.

Smith went to Washington, both as the appointed senator and as the senator-elect in his own right. As soon as he presented his credentials, protests were made to his taking his seat. These protests alleged that Smith had used "fraud and corruption" in his 1926 campaign for the U.S. Senate, and the case was sent to the Senate Committee on Privileges and Elections (now the Committee on Rules and Administration). After a lengthy inquiry into the 1926 contest, on 17 January 1928, the committee held that Smith not be allowed to take his seat because of corruption perpetrated by him and his supporters. On 19 January the Senate adopted this resolution, and the seat was declared vacant. Despite the fact that he had never served a single day in the U.S. Senate, Smith "resigned" on 9 February 1928. Otis F. Glenn, a Republican, was elected to take the vacant seat and he began his service on 3 December 1928.

Tarred by the scandal that cost him a seat in the U.S. Senate, Smith ran for a seat in the U.S. House of Representatives in 1930, but was unsuccessful. He served as a member of the Republican National Committee in 1932, then left politics altogether to return to his business pursuits, including serving as chairman of the board of directors of the First National Bank of Dwight, Illinois. Smith died in Dwight on 30 August 1950 at the age of eighty-two and was buried in Oak Lawn Cemetery in that city.

References: Wooddy, Carroll Hill, *The Case of Frank L. Smith: A Study in Representative Government* (Chicago: The University of Chicago Press, 1931).

## Smith, John (1735?–1824)

U.S. Senator from Ohio (1803–08), nearly expelled (and later resigned) from the Senate for his role in the conspiracy of Vice President Aaron Burr to separate several Western states from the Union and create a new nation. Little is known of his early life: he was born in either Virginia or Ohio about 1735. He prepared for the ministry, and for much of his life served as a pastor in various Baptist congregations in Ohio and Virginia until 1790. In that year, he is first recognized, serving in a Baptist church on the forks of the Cheat River in what is now West Virginia. In 1791 he moved to Columbia, Ohio, later a part of the city of Cincinnati, where he became a preacher and merchant. His gifts of public speaking brought him great notice, and in 1798 he was elected to the first of four terms in the Northwest Territorial legislature until 1803.

When Ohio was admitted as a state into the Union in 1803, the new state legislature moved to elect two men to the United States Senate. One of these men was John Smith, most likely for his actions in pushing state-hood. While in the Senate, from 1 April 1803 until 25 April 1808, he apparently made only one speech, spending most of his time engaged in private pursuits. These actions caused his downfall that occurred in 1808. Rumors of his ties with Vice President Aaron Burr's attempts to get several Western states to secede from the Union, as well as the obvious neglect of his senatorial duties, led to his being called by a grand jury in Frankfort, Kentucky, which was investigating Burr's actions. Fearing that he would be called before the panel, Smith fled to West Florida, where he waited until Burr was tried and acquitted. Smith's counsel in his case was Francis Scott Key, who later wrote "The Star-Spangled Banner." When he arrived back in Washington in January 1807, the U.S. Senate took up a call to investigate Smith's actions. Senator John Quincy Adams, Federalist of Massachusetts, chaired the committee that investigated whether to expel or censure Smith. Their report, released 31 December 1807, stated, "When a man whom his fellow citizens have honored with their confidence on the pledge of a spotless reputation has degraded himself by the commission of infamous crimes, which become suddenly and unexpectedly revealed to the world, defective, indeed, would be that institution which should be impotent to discard from its bosom the contagion of such a member." John Lowell, in writing to John Quincy Adams on his report on Smith, lambasted the future president, reminding him that "there are those amongst us who have not forgotten the report in the case of Senator Smith, where justice, so far from being sacred in her temple, was to be dragged from her seat to perform the polluting office of private revenge; where the snail-like pace of the common law seemed to be too tardy for thos

In 1844, Rep. Edward Junius Black of Georgia went before the House and spoke about the right of either house of Congress to expel certain members, citing specifically the Smith case. He said, "In 1807, when John Smith was the unhappy culprit, Mr. [John Quincy] Adams, as chairman of the committee to whom the case was referred, believed that the Senate might well entertain even the higher and more important question of expulsion, without 'depriving him of right secured by the constitution of the United States.' Hear him— for nothing can so fully illustrate his position in 1842, and his deliberate opinions in 1807, as to place them in contrast by quoting his own words. How curses will come home! Smith represented himself 'as solitary, friendless, and unskilled;' and intimated that his rights were about to be denied him by senators 'liable, so long as they held their offices, to have his case made their own.' The chairman, in his 'pride of place,' not dreaming that his own words were prophetic of his own future condition, replied: 'The committee are not unaware that, in the vicissitudes of human events, no member of this body can be sure that his conduct will never be made a subject of inquiry and decision before the assembly to which he belongs. They are aware that, in the course of proceeding which the Senate may sanction, its members are marking out a precedent which may hereafter apply to themselves. They are sensible that the principles upon which they have acted ought to have the same operation upon their own claims to privilege as upon those of Mr. Smith; the same relation to the rights of their constituents which they have to those of the legislature which he represents.'"

What John Smith did with the remainder of his life remains unknown; what is known is that he moved in 1812 to West Florida (now Louisiana), settling for a time in Pensacola, and later in St. Francisville, now in Louisiana. He died in St. Francisville on 30 July 1824.

**References**: Smith biography, courtesy of *The Biographical Directory of the United States Congress*, online at http://bioguide.congress.gov/scripts/biodisplay.pl?index=S000567; Cox, Isaac J., "Smith, John" in Allen Johnson and Dumas Malone, et al., eds. , *Dictionary of American Biography* (New York: Charles Scribner's Sons; X volumes and 10 supplements, 1930-95), IX:296-97; Wilhelmy, Robert W., "Senator John Smith and the Aaron Burr Conspiracy," *Cincinnati Historical Society Bulletin*, 28 (Spring 1970), 39-60; Pitcher, M. Avis, "John Smith, First Senator from Ohio and his Connections with Aaron Burr," *Archaeological and Historical Society Quarterly*, 45 (1936), 68-75; Lowell comments on Adams in John Lowell, "Remarks on the Hon. John Quincy Adams's Review of Mr. Ames's Works, with Some Strictures on the Views of the Author" (Boston: Printed by T.B. Wait and Co., 1809), 25; "Speech of Mr. Black, of Georgia, on the Right of Members to Their Seats in the House of Representatives. Delivered in the House of Representatives, February 12, 1844" (Washington: Printed at the Globe Office, 1844), 11.

## Special Prosecutor (Federal)
*See* Independent Counsel Statute

## Speech or Debate Clause of the U.S. Constitution

Section of the United States Constitution providing that legislators cannot he held criminally liable for words spoken on the floor of the U.S. House or U.S. Senate, which the Supreme Court has interpreted to protect "against inquiry into acts that occur in the regular course of the legislative process and into the motivation for those acts." Located in Article 1, Section 1, Clause 6, the clause reads, "They shall in all cases, except treason, felony and breach of the peace, be privileged from arrest during their attendance at the session of their respective Houses, and in going to and returning from the same; and for any speech or debate in either House, they shall not be questioned in any other place." Legislators under potential corruption charges have used this clause to shield themselves from inquiries into activities that involve their official duties.

The immunity for lawmakers from prosecution for speech pursuant to their legislative duties has its origins in the fight between the English Parliament and the king over control of the nation. During the reign of Richard II (1396–1397), one member of Parliament, Thomas Haxey, was thrown into prison and condemned to death for introducing a bill calling for the reduction of royal household expenditures. Richard was murdered before Haxey could be put to death, and his successor, Henry IV, set aside the judgment. When Henry VII threw Richard Strode, another member of Parliament, into prison in 1512 for trying to regulate the English tin industry, Parliament enacted a law annulling the judgment against Strode, releasing him from prison, and declaring null and void all future attempts by English monarchs to regulate the speech of members of Parliament. This law was followed by the monarchy until Charles I, in 1632, imprisoned Sir John Elliot, and William and Valentine Strode (no known relation to the aforementioned Richard Strode) for speaking against the Crown in Parliament. Elliot died in the Tower of London, and it was not until 1643 that the Strodes were released because Parliament had raised an army to fight the king. In 1689, as part of the English Bill of Rights, Parliament declared "that the Freedom of Speech, and Debates or Proceedings in Parliament, ought not to be impeached or questioned in any Court or Place out of Parliament."

The drafters of the Articles of Confederation were so concerned about this freedom that they incorporated into that document as Article V, "Freedom of speech and debate in Congress shall not be impeached or questioned in any court or place out of Congress." The Speech or Debate Clause was inserted into the Constitution without debate or dissent—James Wilson, one of the signers of the Constitution, penned, "In order to enable and encourage a representative of the public to discharge his public trust with firmness and success, it is indispensably necessary, that he should enjoy the fullest liberty of speech, and that he should be protected from the resentment of every one, however powerful, to whom the exercise of that liberty may occasion offence." James Madison, one of the framers of the Constitution, wrote in *Federalist No. 48*:

> It is agreed on all sides, that the powers properly belonging to one of the departments, ought not to be directly and completely administered by either of the other departments. It is equally evident, that neither of them ought to possess directly or indirectly, an overruling influence over the others in the administration of their respective powers. It will not be denied, that power is of an encroaching nature, and that it ought to be effectually restrained from passing the limits assigned to it. After discriminating therefore in theory, the several classes of power, as they may in their nature be legislative, executive, or judiciary; the next and most difficult task, is to provide some practical security for each against the invasion of the others. What this security ought to be, is the great problem to be solved.

This right is considered one of the most fundamental to the system of checks and balances, which is a major component of the American system of government. The clause has been used both by those claiming heroic causes and those who eventually fell in ignominy. The Speech and Debate Clause slowed an investigation into a committee that entered the Pentagon Papers into a hearing report, and also delayed a probe into wrongdoing by former House Ways and Means Chairman Dan Rostenkowski (D-IL). The Supreme Court has visited the issue of the use of the clause in five separate cases: *Kilbourn v. Thompson*, 103 U.S.

168 (1881); *Tenney v. Brandhove*, 341 U.S. 367 (1951); *United States v. Johnson*, 383 U.S. 169 (1966); *Dombrowsky v. Eastland*, 387 U.S. 82 (1967); and *Powell v. McCormack*, 395 U.S. 486 (1969). Justice Sandra Day O'Connor wrote in *Flanagan v. United States*, 465 U.S. 259 (1984), "Similarly, the right guaranteed by the Speech or Debate Clause is more than the right not to be convicted for certain legislative activities: it is the right not to 'be questioned' about them—that is, not to be tried for them." In *United States v. Helstoski*, 422 U.S. 477 (1971), Chief Justice Burger wrote that the clause's intent is "to preserve the constitutional structure of separate, coequal, and independent branches of government. The English and American history of the privilege suggests that any lesser standard would risk intrusion by the Executive and the Judiciary into the sphere of protected legislative activities." The right of the Senate to use its investigative powers under the clause, which fall under the power of a "legitimate legislative sphere," is absolute—so said the Court in *Eastland v. United States Servicemen's Fund*, 421 U.S. 491 (1975). However, in an earlier case, *United States v. Brewster*, 408 U.S. 501 (1972), the same Court held that the sole exception to the clause was an inquiry into alleged criminal conduct by a congressman or senator aside from his or her actions as a member of Congress.

**See also** *United States v. Brewster*

**References:** Andrews, James De Witt, ed., *The Works of James Wilson: Associate Justice of the Supreme Court of the United States and Professor of Law in the College of Philadelphia, Being his Public Discourses Upon Jurisprudence and the Political Science, Including Lectures and Professor of Law, 1790–1792*, 2 vols. (Chicago: Callaghan & Co., 1896), II:38; Elliot, Jonathan, ed., *The Debates in the Several State Conventions on the Adoption of the Federal Constitution, as Recommended by the General Convention at Philadelphia in 1787. Together with the Journal of the Federal Convention, Luther Martin's letter, Yates's Minutes, Congressional Opinions, Virginia and Kentucky Resolutions of '98–'99, and other Illustrations of the Constitution. Collected and Revised from Contemporary Publications, by Jonathan Elliott. Published under the Sanction of Congress*, Printed for the editor, 5 vols. (Washington, DC: Printed for the editor, 1836–1845), V:406; Farrand, Max, ed., *The Records of the Federal Convention of 1787*, 3 vols. (New Haven, CT: Yale University Press, 1911), II:246; *Flanagan v. United States*, 465 U.S. 259, 266 (1984); Great Britain, Public Record Office, *Calendar of State Papers: Domestic Series, of the Reign of William and Mary. Preserved in the Public Record Office. Edited by William John Hardy*, 5 vols. (London, Printed for His Majesty's Stationery Office by Eyre and Spottiswoode, 1895–1906), session 2, chapter 2; *Helstoski v. United States*, 442 U.S. 477, 491 (1979); "History of the Foundations of the Speech and Debate Clause," in Trevelyan, George Macaulay, *History of England* (New York: Longmans, Green, 1927), 335–336, *Tenney v. Brandhove*, 341 U.S. 367, 371 n.2, (1951); Jefferson, Thomas, *The Writings of Thomas Jefferson: Collected and edited by Paul Leicester Ford*, 10 vols., Paul Leicester Ford, ed. (New York: G.P. Putnam's Sons, 1892–1899), VIII:322; Lederkramer, David M., "A Statutory Proposal for Case-by-Case Congressional Waiver of the Speech or Debate Privilege in Bribery Cases," *Cardozo Law Review*, 3:3 (Spring 1982), 465–518.

## Star Route Frauds

Scandal in which bribes were given to postal officials in exchange for plum routes of mail sending and delivery. In the nineteenth century mail was delivered in the western and southern United States via the sale of postal routes to locals who could deliver the mail to rural areas at the lowest cost possible. Called "Star Routes" because an asterisk appeared next to them on official post office department documents, this program allowed for mail delivery to some of the most remote areas of the western United States. Mail was delivered by horse, buggy, and cart. Historian J. Martin Klotsche wrote that after the Civil War these routes sprang up. "In time," he explained, "the large unoccupied regions between the Pacific Coast and the 'jumping-off place' were filled in and by the [1870s] weekly, semi-weekly, and daily mails were being carried to what at one time had been considered inaccessible regions. So important had the 'star service' become that by 1880 the total annual transportation amounted to over 75 million miles."

In 1880 James A. Garfield, a member of the U.S. House of Representatives from Ohio, was elected president. As soon as he took office the following March, he discovered that the Star Route program was rife with massive fraud and corruption—a circle of officials, mostly in Garfield's own Republican party, had used the Star Route program to line their own pockets at the same time that services were either cut or nonexistent. It is estimated by some that approximately $4 million dollars was stolen from government coffers. He also discovered that the former postmaster general, John A. J. Creswell, had investigated these frauds in 1869 and 1870, but had dismissed all claims of corruption. A House committee investigation in 1872 looked into the matter, but no charges were brought forward.

Upon taking office and discovering the fraud, Garfield ordered Postmaster General Thomas Lemuel James to investigate the corruption. Garfield allegedly told James "Go ahead [and investigate]. Regardless of where or whom you hit, I direct you to probe this ulcer to the bottom and then to cut it out." He added that "the proposed investigation must be aimed at a system, and not at men ... that if the inquiry should disclose the fact that any person or persons had been guilty of corruption or fraud, that person or those persons must be handed over to the Department of Justice." Garfield also named William Cook, a criminal attorney, to aid James with any criminal prosecutions. In his own internal inquiry inside the Post Office Department, James discovered that the second assistant postmaster

general, Thomas J. Brady, was involved, and forced Brady's resignation. Brady had aided to increase compensation to Star Route contractors, many of whom were his friends. With Brady's ouster, the investigation centered on one of the contractors, former U.S. Senator Stephen W. Dorsey. Dorsey, who served in the U.S. Senate from Arkansas (1873–1879), also served as chairman of the Republican National Committee during the 1880 election and had been instrumental in Garfield's election. Letters later turned up showed that when Garfield was composing his cabinet, Dorsey expressed his dissatisfaction with several reformist members being named, most notably Thomas L. James in the Post Office Department. When Brady was forced out, Dorsey threatened in a letter to *The World* of New York that if he were targeted for prosecution he would name those officers of the party who were involved in the fraud, corruption that he said helped to carry Indiana for the Republicans in 1880.

On 2 July 1881, Garfield was shot by a crazed mental patient, and while he lingered over the summer the Star Route investigation slowly faded from the public. In 19 September 1881 Garfield succumbed to his wounds, and Vice President Chester Alan Arthur was sworn in as his successor. Dorsey, seeing Arthur as more pliable than Garfield, asked to meet with the new president, but was refused. In fact, Arthur's message to Congress in December called attention not only to the investigations but also to his push for reforms in the department.

On 4 March 1882, a federal grand jury in Washington, D.C., indicted seven men, including Brady and Dorsey, on charges of defrauding the government. The trial for the two men began on 1 June 1882. From the start, the prosecution was hampered by several factors—one was in the choice of one of the prosecutors, A. M. Gibson, who, it was later proved, had been paid $2,500 by one Star Route contractor. He was eventually removed from the case. Another factor was that the Star Route defense all pointed to a government conspiracy as the true cause of the prosecutions. The prosecution at trial presented 115 witnesses and more than 3,600 exhibits. When the jury returned with verdicts, two lower defendants were acquitted, two were found guilty, and for the rest there was a hung jury. The judge set aside the guilty verdicts, calling them "unreasonable." The men, including Dorsey and Brady, were retried in late 1882 and 1883, but all were found not guilty. Other cases around the country of lesser figures in the scandal also led to not guilty verdicts. To recover some of the funds stolen by those targeted, the government instituted numerous civil lawsuits, but local judges who sympathized with the defendants dismissed all of them—one as late as 1922. When the government attempted to prosecute alleged acts of bribery of jurors, only one went to a jury trial, and that case was dismissed by Grover Cleveland's Postmaster General, William F. Vilas. In total, of all the Star Route trials, only two lesser figures, Thomas McDevitt and Christian Price, were convicted on charges of defrauding the government and sent to prison. When the Democrats retook control of the House of Representatives in 1883, they opened an investigation into the frauds, but this investigation ended with no further prosecutions.

The Star Route frauds were a turning point in government corruption, leading to the passage of civil service reform. It also led to the wholesale repudiation of Republican rule in the 1884 elections.

See also Dorsey, Stephen Wallace; Ingersoll, Robert Green

References: Klotsche, J. Martin, "The Star Route Cases," *Mississippi Valley Historical Review*, XXII:3 (December 1935), 407–18; "Star Route Frauds," in George C.

Kohn, *Encyclopedia of American Scandal: From ABSCAM to the Zenger Case* (New York: Facts on File, 1989), 307; *Star Route Transportation of Mails*, House Report 1701, 47th Congress, 1st Session (1882), 1–6; *Testimony Relating to Expenditures in the Department of Justice. The Star-Route Cases*, House Miscellaneous Doc 38 (Part 2), 48th Congress, 1st Session (1884), 1–9.

## Starr, Kenneth Winston (1946– )

Solicitor General of the United States (1989–1993), independent counsel in the Whitewater and Monica Lewinsky investigations (1994–2000), the first independent counsel to bring impeachment charges against the focus of his investigation, President William Jefferson "Bill" Clinton. Starr was born in Vernon, Texas, on 21 July 1946, the son of a Baptist minister. He received his education in Texas, then earned a bachelor's degree from George Washington University in 1968, his master's degree in political science from Brown University in Rhode Island in 1969, and law degree from Duke University in 1973. Because of his family's poverty, Starr sold Bibles door to door to pay for his college education. After he received his law license, Starr went to work as a clerk for Judge David W. Dyer of the U.S. Court of Appeals for the District of Columbia Circuit. Two years later, Starr joined the Los Angeles, California, law firm of Gibson, Dunn & Crutcher. In 1977 he became an associate partner in the firm.

In 1975 Starr was appointed a law clerk to Supreme Court Chief Justice Warren E. Burger, a position he held for two years. He left his law firm to serve Burger, but, after leaving the Court, rejoined the firm as an associate partner. One of the partners of the firm was William French Smith, a close friend and confidante of former California Governor Ronald Reagan. In 1980 Reagan was elected president

*Kenneth Starr reading from the U.S. Constitution during the Clinton impeachment inquiry of the House Judiciary Committee. (© Reuters/CORBIS)*

and named Smith his attorney general. Starr, a conservative Republican, was named a counselor at the Department of Justice.

After only three years in Washington, Starr was named by Reagan to a seat on the U.S. Court of Appeals for the District of Columbia Circuit, one level below the U.S. Supreme Court. Sitting on that court with Starr were Antonin Scalia, who would one day sit on the U.S. Supreme Court, and Robert H. Bork, a former solicitor general who was named to the court by Reagan in 1987 but defeated in the Senate. Starr's conservative philosophy shone through in his decisions—including striking down an affirmative action plan for the District of Columbia—but his honesty and integrity earned him respect even among judges who disagreed with him.

In 1988 Reagan's vice president, George H. W. Bush, was elected president. He invited Starr to serve as his solicitor general, the chief government officer who argues the cases of the United States before the U.S. Supreme Court. Starr enjoyed his work on the Court of Appeals—often a stepping stone to a Supreme Court appointment—so he waited several days before accepting the offer. As solicitor general (1989–1993), Starr argued several important cases before the Supreme Court, most notably arguing that burning an American flag was an activity not protected by the First Amendment; as well, he penned briefs with a conservative outlook on such issues as abortion. Following the election of Bill Clinton in 1992, Starr left office and became a partner in the Washington office of the Chicago law firm Kirkland and Ellis. His clientele including numerous business interests.

On 5 August 1994, Starr came back into the public eye when a three-judge panel in Washington named him the new independent counsel to succeed Robert B. Fiske Jr. in investigating the Whitewater affair, a complicated land deal in Arkansas in which President Bill Clinton and his wife, Hillary, had been involved. Fiske was delving through allegations that the Clintons had used shady means to finance the land deal when the court decided that Starr should replace him. The decision sent shockwaves through the media: who was this man Starr, and why did the three-judge panel decide Fiske needed to be replaced? It became known that several Republican senators, most notably Lauch Faircloth of North Carolina, had written to the court complaining about Fiske's dilatory approach to the investigation. Starr took up his duties.

Starr first went to Arkansas to investigate Whitewater. (See the entry on Whitewater for the full information on this scandal.) He was later asked to look into such issues as the suicide of White House counsel Vincent W. Foster Jr. in 1993, and the 1993 firing of White House Travel Office employees. Starr got several convictions relating to Whitewater, most notably Arkansas Governor Jim Guy Tucker and the Clintons' Whitewater business partners Jim and Susan McDougal.

In January 1998 a former White House employee, Linda R. Tripp, brought to Starr several audio tapes. On these tapes, a former aide to Clinton, Monica Lewinsky, bragged that she had had a long-running affair with Clinton. The president was in the midst of a lawsuit brought by a former Arkansas worker, Paula Corbin Jones, in which it was alleged that Clinton asked for sexual favors from Jones and then retaliated against her when she resisted by hindering her career advancement. The U.S. Supreme Court had allowed her lawsuit to continue while Clinton was in office, and in January 1998 Clinton was deposed. Tripp's tapes implied that Lewinsky, asked by Jones's attorneys for information, was going to lie under oath in a deposition—and that Clinton had asked her to do it. Further, Lewinsky told of the destruction of evidence, again ordered by Clinton. Lewinsky said that she was being rewarded for her silence with a high-paying job arranged by Clinton's friend, civil rights advocate Vernon E. Jordan Jr. In investigating Whitewater, Starr had suspected that Jordan was the middleman between Clinton and Webster Hubbell, a former assistant attorney general and law partner of Hillary Clinton, when Hubbell was allegedly paid off to keep silent about Whitewater.

When the allegations of Clinton's affair with Lewinsky and his role in trying to buy her silence was uncovered, it exploded across the nation. Clinton denied all of the allegations in an angry speech, his wife went on national television and alleged that the whole scandal was part of some "right-wing conspiracy" to attack Clinton, and his political allies openly declared "war" on Starr. As the months of investigation followed, Starr doggedly followed uncovered evidence that Lewinsky did indeed have an affair with Clinton, and that the president had lied under oath before a grand jury. Starr, as part of his duties as an independent counsel, sent a referral report to the U.S. House of Representatives, demonstrating several crimes by Clinton that could lead to impeachment. Starr's report, laden with talk of sex and crimes by Clinton, was a national scandal in itself.

In December 1998 the U.S. House of Representatives impeached Clinton on three articles dealing with lying under oath and obstruction of justice. Starr thus became the first—and only—independent counsel to send a referral report to the House that led to impeachment articles being adopted. Clinton was tried in the Senate and acquitted on 12 February 1999, and Starr was seen as an overzealous prosecutor. He left the independent counsel's office in 2000 and returned to his law practice. He now serves as the dean of the Pepperdine University School of Law in Malibu, California. He occasionally attaches his name to cases that come before the U.S. Supreme Court, including trying to overturn the death penalty case of a man on Virginia's death row.

**References:** Labaton, Stephen, "Judges Appoint New Prosecutor for Whitewater; Ruling is Surprise," *New York Times*, 6 August 1994, A1; Lacayo, Richard, and Adam Cohen, "Inside Starr and His Operation, *Time*, 9 February 1998, 42–48; Manegold, Catherine S., "Kenneth Winston Starr: A Prosecutor Overnight," *New York Times*, 6 August 1994, 12; "Starr, Kenneth W.," in Clifford Thompson, ed., *Current Biography 1998* (New York: H. W. Wilson Company, 1998), 50–54.

# Sullivan, Timothy Daniel (1863–1913)

New York political boss, known as "Big Tim" and "The Big Feller," whose death in a strange accident left his place in history obscured. Sullivan was in fact two men: one who worked for the needy of New York, and the other who profited from his own corruption. Born in the rough Five Points section of New York City on 23 July 1862, he was the son of Daniel Sullivan, an Irish laborer, and Catherine Connelly. Daniel Sullivan had emigrated, as did his wife, from Ireland during the Potato Famine of the 1840s, and their son was born in a tenement in the Lower East Side of Manhattan. Timothy grew up in poverty, exacerbated when his father died in 1867, leaving his mother to care for four small children. When Catherine Sullivan remarried, her family's circumstances changed little as they moved to another ghetto. She did laundry, and one of Timothy Sullivan's sisters worked in a sweatshop. Sullivan himself started working at the age of seven, selling newspapers on corners. Four years later, when he finished grammar school, he left school and survived on the little education he had received. He earned a reputation as a hard fighter who defended the poorer newsboys.

In 1882, when Sullivan was twenty, he had saved enough money to purchase a saloon. As a member of the Whyos, one of the city's most notorious street gangs, Sullivan made his saloon a meeting place for the gang. However, Sullivan saw advancement in politics instead of street robbery, so in 1886 he ran for a seat in the state assembly, representing the Five Points area. As he had when he was younger, he made his name in politics by standing up for the rights of the poor and downtrodden. However, rumors surrounded him that Sullivan was knee deep—if not deeper—in massive corruption, including taking proceeds from prostitutes working the seedy streets of New York City. Daniel Czitrom wrote on Sullivan's defense to these charges:

On April 17, 1889, members of the New York State Assembly crowded around an obscure young colleague as he angrily and tearfully defended himself that he was the boon companion of thieves, burglars, and murderers. Timothy Sullivan had first been elected to represent the Five Points slum district of New York City in 1886, at the age of 23. His accuser was the formidable Thomas E. Byrnes, chief inspector of the New York police department, hero of a popular series of mystery novels, and the most famous detective in the nation. Sullivan had angered the inspector by opposing a bill that would have given the city police the power to jail on sight any person who had ever been arrested. After learning that his two saloons had been suddenly "pulled" for excise law violations and after reading Byrnes's denunciations of him in the New York press, Sullivan disregarded the advice of friends, rose on the assembly floor, and made what everyone agreed was an extraordinary response. "The speech," reported the *New York Herald*, "was given in the peculiar tone and language of a genuine Fourth Warder, and while was interesting in that respect to the countrymen, its tone was so manly that Tim gained much sympathy. If the Inspector's bill had come up today it would have been beaten out of sight."

As a member of the state assembly, Sullivan made a name for himself—one that lasts to this day—when he introduced a bill to make it a crime to carry a concealed weapon in the state. Still on the books, it is known as Sullivan's Law. One of the women who lobbied him for increased protection for female laborers was future Secretary of Labor Frances Perkins. Sullivan was an early advocate of the suffrage for women.

Despite his protestations of innocence, Sullivan was widely involved in a number of crooked schemes that netted his gang and Tammany Hall, whose backing he had, money and influence in the city wards they controlled. Historian Robert Jay Nash explained Sullivan's connections this way:

For most of the nineteenth century, the political fortunes of New York City were in the hands of a puissant ethnic-Irish cabal that came to be known as Tammany Hall. Through the usual blend of charity and patronage dispensed through the wards by the district leaders, the Tammany "Democracy," as corrupt and venal as it was, became an invincible political machine. It reached the height of its power around 1901, when "Big" Tim Sullivan, the swaggering boss of the Lower East Side, installed Tom Foley as the Tammany leader of the rebellious second district. To ensure the victory of this saloon keeper against the respected incumbent Paddy Divver, Sullivan brought in members of Paul Kelly's Five Points Gang to form a human chain around the polling places. Kelly's gang was composed mostly of Italians. The Irish residents of the Fourth Ward organized their own gang to do battle, but the heavily armed Italians drove them away from the polls, while Police Chief William Dovery and his men passively stood by. Devery was Sullivan's erstwhile "business" partner, who regulated (as opposed to suppressing) gambling and vice in the city.

Sullivan also involved himself in legitimate enterprises, such as theaters and vaudeville houses. However, he earned the name "the King of the Underworld."

His time in Albany done, in 1902 Sullivan ran as a Democrat for a seat in the U.S. House of Representatives. Elected, he served in the Fifty-eighth and Fifty-ninth Congresses (4 March 1903–27 July 1906), resigning before his second term was over because he was bored. He returned to the state senate in 1908 and 1910; in 1912 he was elected again to a seat in the U.S. House of Representatives, but never took it. It was at that time that he descended into madness, possibly brought on by syphilis. In January 1913 he was declared insane and committed to a sanitarium in Yonkers, New York, on 10 January 1913. However, he was later moved to his brother's home in East Chester, New York.

On 31 August 1913, Sullivan escaped from his brother's home. Meandering along the railroad tracks near what is today the Pelham Parkway in New York City, Sullivan wandered into the path of a train and was struck and killed. The train so disfigured him that he remained unidentified for days in the morgue before a policeman recognized him just before he was to be shipped to a potter's field. After a huge funeral attended by thousands of his supporters, Sullivan was buried in Calvary Cemetery in Long Island City, New York.

**References:** Baldwin, Peter C., "Sullivan, Timothy Daniel," in John A. Garraty and Mark C. Carnes, gen. eds., *American National Biography*, 24 vols. (New York: Oxford University Press 1999), 21:126–127; Czitrom, Daniel, "Underworlds and Underdogs: Big Time Sullivan and Metropolitan Politics in New York, 1889–1913," *Journal of American History*, 78:2 (September 1991), 536–558; "Sullivan, Timothy," in Jay Robert Nash, *Encyclopedia of World Crime: Criminal Justice, Criminology, and Law Enforcement*, 4 vols. (Wilmette, IL: CrimeBooks, Inc, 1989), IV:2876.

## Sulzer, William (1863–1941)

United States representative from New York (1895–1912), governor of New York (1913), impeached and removed from office because of numerous financial and other improprieties. Born on his father's farm near Elizabeth, New Jersey, on 18 March 1863, he was the second son of seven children of Thomas Sulzer, a German immigrant, and Lydia (née Jelleme) Sulzer. Of his siblings, two brothers eventually died in the Spanish-American War, and a third brother, Charles Augustus Sulzer (1879–1919), served as a territorial delegate from Alaska (1919). William Sulzer attended a country school near his home and when still young went to work on a ship sailing to South America. In 1877 his family moved to the Lower East Side of New York City, and Sulzer worked while he attended classes first at the Cooper Union and then at Columbia University. He studied law and in 1844 was admitted to the New York bar. He opened a practice in that city. He also went to work for the Tammany organization, the powerful political association that controlled jobs, patronage, and all other political services in New York City.

Five years after beginning his practice, Sulzer entered the political arena, running for and winning a seat in the New York state as-

*Sulzer impeachment committee. (Library of Congress, Prints &*
*Photographs Division, LC-DIG-ggbain-14103)*

sembly, representing the Lower East Side. He
served in this post for five years, rising to
serve as Speaker in 1893. In 1894 he gave up
his assembly seat to run for a seat in the U.S.
House of Representatives. Elected to the Fifty-
fourth Congress, he sat as chairman of the
Committee on Foreign Affairs and was a supporter of progressive causes, including the
passage of a graduated income tax. He was reelected eight times, serving until 1 January
1913.

In 1912 Sulzer was nominated by the Democratic Party of New York as their candidate for
governor. He ran in a crowded field that included Job E. Hedges, the Republican, and Oscar S. Straus (a former secretary of commerce
and labor), on the Independence League ticket. Despite his once having worked for the
Tammany organization, Sulzer was considered
a reformer, and the head of Tammany, Charles
F. Murphy, backed him only reluctantly. Sulzer campaigned as "The People's Governor."
On November 5, 1912, Sulzer was elected governor. Immediately, he angered Tammany by
denying that organization patronage in Albany
and ordering investigations into scandals in
state government offices that were run by
Tammany-backed appointees. An investiga-

tion into the Highway Department led to Sulzer's dismissal of the Democratic superintendent, C. Gordon Reel. However, Sulzer was bipartisan in his attacks on state government—
he demanded that the Republican warden of
Auburn prison be replaced with a Democrat.
When the state prison superintendent, Joseph
F. Scott, refused, Sulzer fired Scott for being
"inefficient, incompetent, derelict and neglect-
ful of duty." When the state legislature refused
to confirm several of Sulzer's appointees to
state positions, he initiated what some legislators called "a reign of terror" on the state. One
assemblyman, Anthony Griffin, wrote that
"until we destroy the Constitution, I will not
take the dictation of one man as to what I
shall do as a legislator…. [Sulzer is trying] to
usurp legislative functions." Griffin denounced
the governor as "Sulzer the First."

To fight Sulzer, the state legislature established a committee under the direction of state
Senator James J. Frawley, a friend of Tammany, to investigate how state government was
running. Historian Robert Wesser wrote:

Begun as a means of showing Sulzer "in his true light to
the voters," the Frawley inquiry accomplished much

*William Sulzer (Library of Congress, Prints & Photographs Division,*
*LC-DIG-ggbain-13966)*

more. First in private investigations, then in public hearings in July and August, the legislative snoopers unraveled a web of wrongdoing and chicanery that made a mockery of the governor's charges against the "crooks" and "grafters" of Tammany and its allies. They discovered that his widely publicized scrutiny of the prison department was a farce and a fraud. They heard testimony that he indirectly bargained with legislators for their support of his primary bill. They found that after the campaign of 1912 Sulzer had failed to report thousands of dollars as political contributions in violation of state law. Where had the money gone? The investigators learned that some of it went into Sulzer's personal account with the Farmers' Loan and Trust Company. Some of it also made it way into a secret investment account held by the New York brokerage firm of Fuller and Gray. Known as "number 100" on the company books, this account was used to purchase nearly $12,000 of stocks in a midwestern railroad. The stocks were delivered to Sulzer by a "bagman." The committee then heard testimony about the existence of a second investment account, this one with Harris and Fuller, and designated "number 63." Sulzer had utilized this account, kept open until July 15, 1913, to speculate in the market at the very time that he was sponsoring Wall Street reform legislation. Even the committee members who thought the worst of Sulzer were shocked by these disclosures.

In the end, the Frawley Committee found evidence of massive and gross fraud perpetrated by Sulzer. Jacob Friedman, one of those who wrote on Sulzer's impeachment, explained, "The man who had traveled from one end of the state to the other, calling his opponents crooks and grafters, had himself been caught in dishonorable dealings." On 8 August 1913 the Frawley Committee hearings ended, with the chairman declaring that the evidence already heard had proved Sulzer had violated the New York Corrupt Practices Act. Sulzer denied all—and also added that he could not be removed from office for any crime committed prior to his taking office on 1 January 1913. Immediately word leaked that a resolution of impeachment would be introduced in the lower house of the legislature. On 12 August, seventy-two Democrats and seven Republicans voted to impeach, while twenty-six

Democrats, sixteen Republicans, and three Progressives voted against it. A last-ditch confession by his wife that it was she who forged her husband's names on stocks and bank statements did not halt the action. With his impeachment, Sulzer was effectively removed as governor, but he refused to relinquish power to Lieutenant Governor Martin H. Glynn.

Sulzer's impeachment trial opened on 18 September 1913 in front of the New York state senate, presided over by Judge Edgar T. Cullen. There were few "new" revelations—much of the evidence presented was the same that had been examined by the Frawley Committee. Representing Sulzer was criminal attorney Louis Marshall, while the prosecution was presented on behalf of the impeachment managers by Judge Alton B. Parker, who had been the Democrat's presidential candidate in 1904 and was himself a former chief justice of the New York State Court of Appeals. Sulzer's attorneys first argued that because the impeachment vote had been passed during a special session, when only legislation proposed by the governor could be heard, the vote was unconstitutional. When that failed, the defense maintained that the acts alleged occurred before Sulzer took office and were outside the scope of the legislature's authority. One of Sulzer's counsel said, "Was the proceeding instituted because of a desire to accomplish a public good, or was it for the purpose of getting rid of a public official who was performing his duty?" The evidence against Sulzer was damning, and many (including the newspapers, which reported every minute of the trial) speculated he would take the stand in his own defense. Sulzer even said that "amazing revelations" would come from his testimony. In the end, he did not testify, perhaps because his attorneys knew that he could be cross-examined on the bank accounts that damned his case. On 15 October 1913, the Senate voted forty to seventeen to convict Sulzer on three of the eight counts against him, count one being his filing of a false campaign statement, count two that he committed perjury in swearing to that statement's truthfulness, and count four that Sulzer suppressed evidence by threatening witnesses who were to appear before the Frawley Committee. Cullen voted against conviction, but said of Sulzer that his crimes were of "such moral turpitude and delinquency that if they had been committed during the respondent's incumbency of office I think they would require his removal." The following day, the Senate voted forty-three to twelve to remove Sulzer from office, and at that time Lieutenant Governor Glynn was sworn in as the new governor.

Despite becoming the first (and, of this writing, the only) New York governor to be impeached and removed from office, Sulzer was not barred from further public office and in November 1913, just a month after he was convicted, he was elected as an Independent to a seat in the state assembly. The following year he was nominated by both the American Party and the Prohibition Party for governor of New York. Governor Glynn, his successor, was defeated by Charles S. Whitman, a former prosecutor. In 1916 Sulzer refused a nomination for president by the American Party. Sulzer left office and returned to the practice of law, in which he remained until his death. In 1928 he came out against the election of Governor Al Smith for president, and letters from the time show Sulzer to have hated Smith for Roman Catholicism and lack of support for Prohibition.

On 16 September 1941, Sulzer collapsed at his law office, and died in bed on 6 November 1941 at the age of seventy-eight. His obituary was relegated to the back pages of the New York state newspapers.

See also Primary Documents, page 568.

References: "Gov. Sulzer Denies Everything After An All Night Conference, Boldly Declares He Did Not Speculate in Wall Street," *New York Times*, 11 August 1913, 1; Friedman, Jacob Alexis, *The Impeachment of Governor William Sulzer* (New York: Columbia University Press, 1939), 147; Morganthau, Henry, "All in a Life-Time—Chapters from an Autobiography. II. What I Learned From Sulzer and Tammany," *The World's Work*, XLII:5 (September 1921), 465–479; New York State, Court for Trial of Impeachment, *Proceedings of the Court for the Trial of Impeachments. The People of the State of New York, by the Assembly thereof, against William Sulzer as Governor. Held at the Capital in the City of Albany, New York, September 18, 1913, to October 17, 1913* (Albany: J. B. Lyon Company, Printers, 1913); "Sulzer, Guilty on Three Counts, To Be Ousted From Office To-Day, Acquitted of Bribery Charge," *New York Times*, 17 October 1913, 1; "Sulzer, William," in Robert Sobel and John Raimo, eds., *Biographical Directory of the Governors of the United States, 1789$–1978, $4 vols. (Westport, CT: Meckler Books, 1978), III:1097; Weiss, Nancy J., "Sulzer, William," in Allen Johnson and Dumas Malone, et al., eds., *Dictionary of American Biography*, X vols. and 10 supplements (New York: Charles Scribner's Sons, 1930–1995), 3:751–752; Wesser, Robert F., "The Impeachment of a Governor: William Sulzer and the Politics of Excess," *New York History*, LX:4 (October 1979), 407–438; "William Sulzer, Ex-Governor, 78," *New York Times*, 7 November 1941, 23.

## Swartwout-Hoyt Scandal

Nefarious doings in the Port of New York Collectors' Office, exposed in 1841 by President John Tyler. In 1829 President Andrew Jackson appointed Samuel Swartwout as collector for the Port of New York. During his nine years in that position, Swartwout stole millions of dollars and, in 1838, when President Martin Van Buren did not retain him, Swartwout sailed to Europe carrying the money from nine years of corruption. Van Buren ordered an audit of the office, which showed that Swartwout had stolen nearly $2.25 million. Van Buren named an old friend, Jesse D. Hoyt, as Collector of New

York to oversee correcting the problems that allowed Swartwout to get away with such a degree of theft. What Van Buren did not know is that Hoyt saw his own opportunity and began to steal from the office as well.

Rumors of Hoyt's fraud began to surface in 1841, after President John Tyler had taken office following the death of President William Henry Harrison after only a month in office. In May 1841, only a month in office himself, Tyler, without the approval of Congress, established a three-man committee, headed by Senator George Poindexter of Mississippi, to investigate the problems and fraud in the New York Collectors' Office. In addition to Poindexter, Tyler named two Boston manufacturers, Samuel Lawrence and William W. Stone, as private members of the panel. The commission discovered the Hoyt, in addition to Swartwout, had embezzled government funds.

The Whig-dominated House, despite hearing of fraud from two Democratic administrations, felt more slighted that Tyler had named a commission without their authority, and had named two private citizens, to be paid with government funds, to the panel. On 29 April 1842, when Poindexter delivered the report to Tyler, the House demanded to see it. Tyler assented and presented a copy the following day. Again, despite the findings of massive fraud, the House passed a resolution asserting that a president had "no rightful authority" to name a commission to investigate fraud or other corruption, and that the president could not name private citizens to a commission to be compensated "at public expense." The resolution was tabled at the request of Representative John Quincy Adams, the former president, but the final provision of the resolution, that private citizens were not to be paid with public funds to sit on commissions, was added to an appropriations bill enacted in August of that same year.

**References:** *Review of the Communications of Samuel Lawrence and William W. Stone, Manufacturers of Boston: To the Speaker of the House of Representatives, on the Subject of the Investigation at the New York Custom-House, in Two Letters. From the Hon. Geo. Poindexter* (Washington, DC: National Intelligence Office, 1842); Schultz, Jeffrey D., "Presidential Scandals" (Washington, DC: CQ Press, 2000), 71–72, 77; United States Congress, House, Select Committee to Inquire into the Causes and Extent of the Late Defalcations of the Custom-House at New York and Other Places, *Report of the Minority of the Select Committee of the House of Representatives, Appointed on the Seventeenth of January, 1839, to inquire into the Causes and Extent of the Late Defalcations of the Custom-House at New York and Other Places* (Washington, DC: Blair and Rives, 1839).

## Swayne, Charles Henry (1842–1907)

Judge for the Northern District of Florida (1890–1907), impeached but acquitted in the U.S. Senate in 1905 on charges of corruption, which may have been politically motivated. Little is known about Swayne. He was born in Newcastle County, Delaware, on 10 August 1842, the son of Henry and Ann (née Parry) Swayne, and the grandson of Joel Swayne, a Society of Friends (Quaker) missionary to the Seneca Indians at Allegheny, New York. Henry Swayne served as a member of the Delaware legislature (1846–1847, 1880–1881). His son Charles grew up on his family's farm and received his education in public schools and at an academy in Wilmington. Brought up in the Quaker religion, he served as a principal of a Society of Friend's scientific and mathematical school in West Chester, Pennsylvania. In 1869 he moved to Philadelphia, where he studied law under a local attorney, Joseph B. Townsend, and at the University of Pennsylvania, from which he earned a law degree in 1871. He was admitted to the Pennsylvania bar that same year and practiced in that state until he moved to Florida in 1884. In May 1889 President Benjamin Harrison named him a judge of the District Court for the Northern District of Florida.

The state election of 1888 in Florida occasioned many allegations of fraud and corruption, and many of these charges, mainly against Democrats, went before Judge Swayne, a lifelong Republican. Bitterness arose over his alleged handling of the cases, and Democrats swore to avenge his sentencing of Democrats to prison. Starting in 1890, Florida Democrats sent memorials to the U.S. Congress, asking that Swayne be impeached. On 10 December 1903, Representative William Bailey Lamar (D-FL) presented a memorial from the Florida legislature asking for Swayne's impeachment. Lamar asked for an investigation, and the resolution was referred to the House Judiciary Committee. Despite the committee's recommendation of impeachment, Representative Henry Wilbur Palmer of Pennsylvania asked for a delay so that the charges could be further investigated. On 9 December 1904, the Judiciary Committee again submitted a report recommending impeachment. The House adopted the report on 13 December and asked a select committee to draw up impeachment articles. Twelve articles were drawn up, and on 18 January 1905, Swayne was impeached by the U.S. House of Representatives.

On 24 January 1905, only six days later, the first full impeachment trial in the U.S. Senate since that of President Andrew Johnson in 1868 opened. (In 1876 the Senate considered the impeachment of former Secretary of War William Worth Belknap, but did not hold a trial because Belknap had resigned his office.) Representative Palmer served as one of the House managers, along with James Breck Perkins of New York, Henry De Lamar Clayton of Alabama (who was later to serve as a House manager in the impeachment trial of Judge Robert W. Archbald in 1912), David Albaugh

De Armond of Missouri, and David Highbaugh Smith of Kentucky. The charges against Swayne were small: Article I, for instance, charged that as a judge he submitted an expense report for travel in which he charged $230, which the House alleged was false; Article VIII claimed that Swayne "did knowingly and unlawfully" hold an attorney in contempt. In total, he was accused of filing false travel vouchers, improperly traveling on rail cars, and for living outside his district while he looked for a home inside of it. Swayne's attorneys admitted their client was guilty of the offenses, but called each one "inadvertent." The Senate, on 27 February 1905, acquitted Swayne of all charges, holding that none of the crimes advanced to the level of "high crimes and misdemeanors," the standard set for conviction of impeachment. It was decided during the Swayne trial that if an impeachment trial would be held, it should be before a small, established group of Senators sitting as a jury, with their recommendation going to the full Senate. Senator George F. Hoar of Massachusetts recommended the change, and his suggestion is now embodied in Rule XI of the Senate rules.

Swayne returned to the bench, but it appears from all historical evidence that he was physically broken by the impeachment. He died two years later, his name barely known if at all.

See also Primary Documents, page 541, 544.

References: Johnson, Rossiter, ed., *The Twentieth Century Biographical Dictionary of Notable Americans*, 10 vols. (Boston: The Biographical Society, 1904), X; United States Congress, House, *Proceedings in the House of Representatives, Fifty-Eighth Congress, Concerning the Impeachment of Charles Swayne, Judge of the Northern District of Florida* (Washington, DC: Government Printing Office, 1905).

## Symington, John Fife, III (1945– )

Governor of Arizona (1991–1997) who was convicted of fraud and resigned from office, but was later cleared by a federal court and pardoned by President Clinton in 2001. The scion of a famous family, John Fife Symington III was born in New York City on 12 August 1945, a great-grandson of the industrialist and steel magnate Henry Clay Frick, and a cousin of William (Stuart) Symington, a powerful senator from Missouri who nearly became John F. Kennedy's running mate in 1960. He attended the prestigious Gillman Country Day School, and earned a bachelor's degree from Harvard University in 1968. While in Harvard, he became politically active and was a supporter of Arizona Senator Barry Goldwater's presidential run in 1964. After his graduation, Symington went to Arizona, where he was assigned to Luke Air Force Base near Tucson as a U.S. Air Force second lieutenant. He was eventually moved to the 621st Tactical Air Command in Thailand, overseeing air flights over Vietnam. For his service, which ended in 1971, Symington was awarded the Bronze Star for meritorious service.

After returning from Vietnam, Symington settled in Phoenix, Arizona, then a small metropolis with huge potential for growth. He invested in numerous properties, using his name and his reputation to accumulate a small fortune. By 1990 Symington decided to run for governor. Symington ran against Phoenix Mayor Terry Goddard, a Democrat, and defeated him in the November 1990 election, but because neither man had more than 50 percent of the vote a runoff was held. On 26 February 1991, Symington defeated Goddard to become the eighth Republican governor of Arizona since statehood in 1912. He pushed new education reforms, the cleanup of waste from incineration, and tried to put an end to Indian gambling on reservations in Arizona. He was reelected in 1994, easily defeating supermarket magnate Eddie Basha.

Although Symington was never accused of dishonesty in office, his business dealings prior to becoming governor resulted in his undoing. On 13 June 1996, Symington was indicted by an Arizona grand jury on twenty-three counts of making false financial statements, bankruptcy fraud, and wire fraud. The indictment charged that in the 1980s Symington had exaggerated his net worth to obtain bank loans for properties he wanted to buy, and that properties he had purchased had declared bankruptcy. Symington went on trial in 1997, during which he charged that the allegations were politically motivated by a Democratic U.S. attorney, and that any irregularities in his financial statements were due to his tax advisors and not he. Despite this, Symington was convicted on 3 September 1997 on seven counts, and one hour later he resigned as governor, making Jane Dee Hull the second female governor in Arizona history. Symington was sentenced to two and one-half years in prison, five years probation, and a $60,000 fine, all of which were stayed pending appeal.

However, it appeared Symington's conviction was in trouble. A juror had been dismissed prior to the verdict; she claimed that she had been removed because the jurors had made up their minds about Symington's guilt and wanted her removed because she stood for an acquittal. Almost immediately, it became apparent that the dismissal of the single juror was potential reversible error. And on appeal to the U.S. Court of Appeals for the Ninth Circuit, this was one of Symington's motions. On 22 June 1999, that court agreed that the juror should not have been removed and vacated Symington's conviction. Until late 2000, prosecutors were still looking at how they could retry the former governor.

Then, on 20 January 2001, his last day in office, President Bill Clinton gave Symington a full pardon. The reasons behind why a Democratic president would pardon a Republican governor are shadowy, but they are appear to be this: Thomas Caplan, a Baltimore novelist who went to school with Clinton at Georgetown University, was also a friend of Symington's and asked the president to pardon the embattled former governor. What Caplan, nor anyone else, knew was that in college Symington had rescued Clinton from drowning, and Clinton had never forgotten the favor. Whatever the reason, Symington, now a chef at a trendy Scottsdale, Arizona, restaurant, was ecstatic at the prospect that he was freed from future criminal charges. "I'm humbled and gratified," he said in an interview after word of the pardon came out. "I thank the president, and I praise God."

**References:** Flannery, Pat, "Clinton Pardons Symington," *Arizona Republic*, 21 January 2001, A1; "J. Fife Symington III," in Marie Marmo Mullaney, *Biographical Directory of the Governors of the United States, 1988–1994* (Westport, CT: Greenwood Press, 1994), 27–31; Kelly, Charles, and Jerry Kammer, "Symington Conviction Overturned, Court Voids 1997 Verdict," *Arizona Republic*, 23 June 1999, A1; United States Congress, House, Committee on Banking, Finance, and Urban Affairs, Subcommittee on General Oversight and Investigations, *Relationship of Arizona Governor J. Fife Symington III with Southwest Savings and Loan Association: Hearing before the Subcommittee on Oversight and Investigations of the Committee on Banking, Finance, and Urban Affairs, House of Representatives, One Hundred Second Congress, Second Session, February 20, 1992* (Washington, DC: Government Printing Office, 1992).

# T

## Talmadge, Herman Eugene (1913–2002)

Governor of Georgia (1947, 1948–1953) and a U.S. senator from that state (1957–1981), who was denounced by the Senate in 1979 for financial misconduct. Born on his family's farm near McRae, Georgia, on 9 August 1913, he is the son of Eugene Talmadge, a long-time Georgia politician who served as governor from 1933–1937, and from 1941–1943. He studied at local schools in McRae and then went to the University of Georgia at Athens, where he studied law and earned his law degree in 1936. When his father decided to run for governor in 1932, Herman Talmadge left school for a period of time to serve as his father's campaign manager. After earning his law degree, Talmadge was admitted to the state bar in 1936 and commenced the practice of law in Atlanta. In 1941, when World War II broke out, he volunteered for service in the U.S. Navy, and saw major action in the Pacific theater of operations and, by the end of the conflict, when he was discharged, he had attained the rank of lieutenant commander.

It was at this time that Talmadge got caught up in one of the most interesting moments in American political history. Eugene Talmadge, Herman's father, had served two separate terms as governor before leaving office in 1943. In 1946 the elder Talmadge, called the "Wild Man from Sugar Creek," decided to take on Governor Ellis Arnall for another term. But unknown to many, Talmadge was in declining health. Word spread among his supporters to write in his son's name in the Democratic primary, which Eugene Talmadge won, with his son, just home from the war, coming in second. Then Eugene Talmadge suffered a burst blood vessel in his stomach. His health slipped, and on 21 December 1946, after he had been elected governor, Eugene Talmadge died. Governor Arnall announced that he could remain governor for Talmadge's term, but instead would turn the office over to Melvin E. Thompson, the newly-elected lieutenant governor. Talmadge supporters, now led by Herman Talmadge, demanded that the legislature choose the governor from the candidates in the election. On 15 January, the legislature chose Talmadge, and he was sworn into office. When Talmadge went to take over the office, he found Arnall there, refusing to budge and calling the new governor a "pretender." The next day, armed with a gun, Talmadge went to the governor's offices, changed the locks, and named several state officers. Arnall set up a governor's office in downtown Atlanta. On 18 January, Lieutenant Governor Thompson was sworn in as governor, and Arnall "resigned." The two rival governors then took the case to the state supreme court, which held on 19 March that Thompson was the actual governor. Talmadge had served for sixty-seven days. A year later, Talmadge was elected governor in a special election mandated by his father's death and was reelected in 1950, serving until January 1955. He was a popular governor, but stood for segregation of Georgia and Southern society.

In 1956 Senator Walter F. George (D-GA) decided not to run for reelection in the midst of failing health. (He would die on 4 August 1957.) Talmadge, having the year before left the governorship and become a farmer, threw his hat into the ring for the Democratic nomination. In those years the primary *was* the general election, with the Democrat winning the general election with ease. Talmadge won the primary and was elected without opposition. He took his seat in the Senate on 3 January 1957 and would serve until 3 January 1981. During his tenure, Talmadge voted the conservative Southern line, voting against civil rights measures. As the chair of the Agriculture Committee for many years, he worked for farm subsidies for Georgia farmers. He remained chairman when the committee was renamed the Committee on Agriculture and Forestry. He was a member of the Ervin Committee, which heard charges on the Watergate affair in 1973 and 1974.

In August 1978 Talmadge's administrative assistant, Daniel Minchew, told the *Washington Star* that in 1973 and 1974 he had with-drawn, at Talmadge's request, expense money from his congressional expense fund totaling nearly $13,000, for the senator's private use. Secretly, a federal grand jury was assembled to hear the charges, and the Senate Select Committee on Ethics was investigating. In December 1978 the Senate committee issued a report calling for a full-blown investigation, claiming that there was "substantial and credible evidence" of financial misconduct by Talmadge. By a four to one vote, taken on 18 December, the committee decided to enter formal adjudicatory proceedings. On 20 April 1979, Talmadge appeared before the committee, denouncing his accuser (Minchew), and calling the charges "petty" and that they were either untrue or the result of unintended negligence. When the panel questioned Minchew's credibility, Talmadge's ex-wife, Betty, came forward to substantiate the allegations. During a second hearing, Ethics Committee chairman Senator Adlai Stevenson of Illinois noted that Talmadge had never expressed regret for "this whole sordid episode," and asked him if he had any regret now. "I am human," Talmadge answered. "I have made errors, and I am confident I will make errors in the future. I have never used my office for profit and I never will."

On 15 September 1979, after fifteen months of investigation, the Senate Select Committee on Ethics unanimously voted to denounce Talmadge, calling his conduct "reprehensible." The committee distinctly chose not to use the term "censure," despite the fact that most congressional historians equate a senatorial or House "denouncement" with "censure." So stated the committee, "there is no finding of intentional wrongdoing. There is no recommendation of censure." On 11 October 1979, the full Senate voted eighty-one to fifteen to uphold the denouncement of Talmadge. After the vote, Talmadge called it a "victory." "I stand before you firmly criticized," he said on the Senate floor. "But I am not found guilty of intentional, wrongful, unlawful conduct. There is no recommendation of censure."

In 1980, in the midst of the so-called "Reagan landslide," Talmadge won the Democratic primary but lost his seat to Republican Mack Mattingly. Ironically, in the primary he had defeated an up-and-coming politician, Zell Miller, who later served as governor of Georgia and in the U.S. Senate.

Herman Talmadge died at his home in Hampton, Georgia, on 21 March 2002 at the age of eighty-eight.

**References:** Ayres, B. Drummond, Jr., "Senate Denounces Talmadge, 81 to 15, Over His Finances," *New York Times*, 12 October 1979, A1, D12; *Congressional Ethics* (Washington, DC: Congressional Quarterly, 1980), 30–31; Hackbart-Dean, Pamela, "Herman E. Talmadge: From Civil Rights to Watergate," *Georgia Historical Quarterly*, 77 (Spring 1993), 145–157; Talmadge, Herman E., with Mark Royden Winchell, *Talmadge: A Political Legacy, A Politician's Life: A Memoir* (Atlanta: Peachtree Publishers, Ltd., 1987).

# Tammany Hall

Political organization, famed for its control of New York City machine politics and led by a number of politicians either imprisoned or accused of corrupt activities. Also known as the Columbian Order, the Tammany Society was founded in New York City in 1789 by William Mooney, a veteran of the Revolutionary War, whose strident anti-Federalist thinking led him to form a political society with the expressed intent of opposing all Federalist candidates and policies. Mooney chose the name "Tammany" after the Indian chief who allegedly sold the land now known as Pennsylvania to William Penn. Mooney created thirteen "tribes" within Tammany, with one tribe representing each of the thirteen original United States; as well, each of the organization's officers were given Indian denominations—leaders were endowed with the names "sagamore" and "sachem." But Tammany did not become a national organization like the Federalist party. Instead, the party organizations outside of New York City slowly died off, until only the New York City office remained open. It was this group, which became known as "Tammany Hall" or the "Tammany machine," that earned respect for its mobilization of voters in New York City, but also scorn for its incredible amount of corruption that drained untold millions of dollars from city coffers through payoffs and bribes and shoddy bookkeeping. At the same time the organization handled the patronage that kept the city moving.

Although Tammany was involved in several political battles in the first half of the nineteenth century—most notably in the fight between Andrew Jackson and the Congress over the Bank of the United States—it did not achieve any political power until one of its officers, Fernando Wood, was elected mayor of New York City in 1855. Wood utilized the office of mayor to his and Tammany's advantage, doling out patronage and, as many historians suspect, using the city's money for projects that aided Tammany cronies. Following Wood, the machine was commanded by William Magear Tweed, Grand Sachem of Tammany, whose political control of the city was nearly absolute by 1868. Corruption in New York City reached its pinnacle under Tweed, as he and his cronies stole in excess of some $200 million. Tweed was later prosecuted and (after escaping and being caught) later died in prison, but the rest of the "Tweed Ring" escaped harsh punishment.

Tweed's successor, John Kelly, saw the need for reform within Tammany and was able to convince such reformers as Samuel Tilden and Horatio Seymour, leading New York Demo-

*Tammany Hall on 14th Street West in 1914. Tammany Hall was the headquarters of the Tammany Society, a major Democratic political machine in New York City from the mid-nineteenth to mid-twentieth centuries. (Library of Congress, Prints & Photographs Division, LC-USZ62-101734)*

crats, to join. However, Kelly, followed by Richard Croker and Charles F. Murphy, failed to reign in massive corruption. Murphy was investigated by Mayor John P. Mitchel in 1906, but was cleared of wrongdoing.

Following Murphy's death in 1924, Judge George W. Olivany, a district leader for the Democrats, became the titular head of Tammany Hall and, with the assistance of New York Governor Alfred E. Smith, planned a revolution in Tammany to clean it up once and for all. However, the old forces of corruption went to work, and, in March 1929, after only five years in power, Olivany was tossed from the machine in favor of John F. Curry, a student of Croker and Murphy. When the Sea-

bury investigation showed massive corruption in the administration of Mayor James J. Walker, a Tammany protege, Curry was thrown into disfavor, but it took several electoral defeats to dislodge him from control of Tammany. In July 1934 he was succeeded by James J. Dooling. Dooling's reign was marked mostly by the administration of Mayor Fiorello H. LaGuardia, a reformist who distanced himself from Tammany, leaving the organization for the first time not in control of the mayor's office. At the same time, the rise in influence of leaders from the Bronx and Brooklyn also diminished Tammany's power base. Battered by changing times, the Tammany society sold the building where its headquarters had been maintained.

Tammany was not dead yet, however. In the 1945 citywide elections, William O'Dwyer, a Tammany-backed candidate, was elected mayor of New York and dismissed Brooklyn Democratic Party leader Edward Loughlin, replacing him with Tammany crony Frank J. Sampson. Sampson was later ousted by Hugo Rogers, who himself was replaced by Carmine G. De Sapio. De Sapio may have been the most powerful Tammany leader since Tweed, but he could not stem the flow of reform, aimed specifically at Tammany Hall. Robert F. Wagner Jr., son of the former Senator and a reformist in his own right, became the head of an "anti-Tammany" group of politicians. Wagner was elected mayor of New York in 1953, and began an anticorruption campaign that targeted Tammany. Despite De Sapio becoming a Democratic national committeeman, as well as secretary of state for New York, Tammany's days as a power force were numbered. De Sapio was ousted from power in 1961. Later attempts by De Sapio to regain power and to revive Tammany failed. Under the leadership of Mayor John V. Lindsay (1966–1973), New York was able to rid itself at last of the taint of Tammany. With its power gone, the Tammany machine faded from existence.

**See also** Croker, Richard; Seabury, Samuel; Thompson, John Hoffman; Tweed, William Magear

**References:** Allen, Oliver E., *The Tiger: The Rise and Fall of Tammany Hall* (Reading, MA: Addison-Wesley, 1993); Myers, Gustavus, *The History of Tammany Hall* (New York: Boni & Liveright, Inc., 1917); Werner, Morris Robert, *Tammany Hall* (Garden City, NY: Doubleday, Doran & Co., 1928); Riordon, William L., *Plunkitt of Tammany Hall: A Series of Very Plain Talks on Very Practical Politics, delivered by Ex-Senator George Washington Plunkitt, the Tammany Philosopher, from his Rostrum—the New York County Court-House Bootblack Stand—and Recorded by William L. Riordon* (New York: McClure, Phillips, 1905).

# Tate, James Williams (1831–?)

Kentucky state treasurer (1867–1888), known as "Honest Dick" Tate, impeached in absentia after absconding with the entire state treasury—some $247,000. He disappeared from the state and his whereabouts thereafter remained unknown. The grandson of a Revolutionary War soldier, Tate was born near the Forks of Elkhorn, Kentucky, on 2 January 1831. Nothing is known of his early life or education. What is known is that he was heavily involved in property speculation and accumulated a tremendous amount of wealth. In 1854 Governor Lazarus M. Powell named Tate assistant secretary of state, and Governor Beriah Magoffin reappointed Tate to that office in 1859. In 1865 Tate became the assistant clerk of the state house of representatives and, two years later, was named state treasurer. He held this office through a series of reelection victories, due mostly in fact to his alleged honesty, earning him the nickname "Honest Dick" Tate. Historian John J. McAfee wrote in 1886 of Tate, "The secret of this ardent esteem may be traced to the fact that, beyond most men, he adheres strictly to principle in all his dealings with his fellowmen…. In his boyhood he was taught that honesty was the best policy, and he grew up in that belief."

In 1888 questions began to be raised over Tate's oversight of the state treasury. This happened after Tate vanished. On 14 March, he told coworkers that he was going on a trip to Louisville. After staying in Louisville, he took a train to Cincinnati—where he vanished into history. Officials looking into his affairs discovered that Tate had taken in total $247,000 in state funds in gold, silver, and cash with him. Tate was not a poor man—his land investments had kept him in good stead for many years, and he was well paid by the state—so his absconding with these funds surprised everyone. Governor Simon Bolivar Buckner announced that Tate had fled the state with the embezzled state funds. An investigation later showed that for many years Tate had been forging official records to cover up a rampant pattern of fraud. Immediately, a chorus rose to impeach Tate in absentia. He was charged with six offenses: among them abandoning his office, absenting himself without providing for proper administration, "misapplying and perverting, taking and converting" the sum of $197,000—this number representing an initial estimate of how much Tate had stolen. The state house impeached on all six charges quickly, and Tate's trial in the state senate began on 29 March 1888—just two weeks after he vanished. The trial lasted for three days, and Tate was found guilty on four of the six charges. He was removed from office and disqualified from ever holding a state office again.

Of Tate thereafter nothing is known, although some rumors had him in Bremen, Germany, or Toronto, Canada. In 1893, it was reported that he was under arrest in Arizona Territory, but this proved false. In 1897 his daughter came forward to have him declared dead, although she had letters from him from places as far away as China. He was never declared dead, but his date of death, and place of burial, remain a mystery.

Because of the Tate case, Kentucky changed its laws allowing state officials to serve two terms in succession. That did not change until 2000, when several state officials were allowed to run for reelection.

**References:** The author would like to thank Joe Horton, reference librarian at the Department for Libraries and Archives, Frankfort, Kentucky, for his assistance in gathering the information on "Honest Dick" Tate. Bryant, Ron D., "'Honest Dick' Tate," *Kentucky Gazette*, 4 November 1997, 15; Klotter, James C., "Tate, James W.," in John E. Kleber, ed., *Kentucky Encyclopedia* (Lexington, KY: University Press of Kentucky, 1992), 867–868; McAfee, John J., *Kentucky Politicians$—$Sketches of Representatives* (Louisville, KY: The Courier Job Printing Company, 1886), 148; Mittlebeeler, Emmet V., "The Great Kentucky Abscension," *Filson Club History Quarterly*, XXVII (1953), 335–352; "Tate Captured Again. Kentucky's Defaulting Treasurer Said to Have Been Seen On a Cotton Belt Train," *Louisville Courier-Journal*, 26 October 1893, 1.

## Teapot Dome Scandal

Federal scandal (1923–1929) that forced Attorney General Harry Daugherty from office, led to the indictment and conviction of Secretary of the Interior Albert B. Fall, and nearly cost Attorney General Harlan Fiske Stone a seat on the United States Supreme Court. The scandal, in effect, started in 1915, when the administration of President Woodrow Wilson set aside several areas in the nation to be used as strategic oil reserve centers in case of a national emergency. Among these places were Naval Reserve Number One at Elk Hills, California, and Naval Reserve Number Three, located at Salt Creek, Wyoming, but better known as Teapot Dome because of the resemblance of the shape of the land to the top of a teapot. (The third reserve, listed as number two, was located at Buena Vista, California.)

In 1920 Senator Warren G. Harding won the presidency and named U.S. Senator Albert Bacon Fall of New Mexico to be his secretary of the interior. He also named former Representative Edwin Denby of Michigan to be his secretary of the navy. Unknown to Harding, Fall was close friends with two oil men, Harry F. Sinclair, president of the Mammoth Oil Company, and Edward L. Doheny, president of the Pan-American Petroleum and Transport Company. Once in office, Fall persuaded President Harding to transfer control of the reserves from the secretary of the navy to the Interior

Who Says a Watched Pot Never Boils?

Department. Denby, convinced on his own by Fall's arguments, supported Fall's move. Harding then signed an executive order on 31 May 1921, which transferred authority.

Fall then secretly leased Teapot Dome to Sinclair and Elk Hills to Doheny—apparently in exchange for bribes. In November 1921 Doheny made what was later characterized as a "loan" of $100,000 to Fall. In exchange for rights to the oil, Doheny was supposed to erect a refinery in California and construct a pipeline from the reserve to the refinery. For Teapot Dome, Sinclair paid Fall in fourteen animals, including a thoroughbred horse and a bull. On 7 April 1922, Fall, Denby, and Sinclair signed a secret deal allowing full access to Sinclair's company to the Teapot Dome reserves. Historians Morris R. Werner and John Starr wrote, "By the time he was finished leasing the Navy's reserves, Fall had given his two benefactors reserves which each of them estimated roughly to be worth $100 million dollars, and he had collected from them $409,000 in cash and bonds."

Before long, however, the "secret" deal behind the oil reserve leases began to leak out. Oilmen in California and Wyoming began to get suspicious that Doheny was obtaining oil from a government oil lease. Fall was seen to be purchasing new lands around his ranch in New Mexico, as well as showing off the horse and bulls and cows that he received as part of the deal. Soon, newspapermen were hunting for clues. On 14 April 1922, the *Wall Street Journal* reported that Fall, in a secret deal, had illegally leased Teapot Dome to Sinclair. The following day, amid angry voices in the U.S. Senate, that body passed Resolution 277, demanding that the secretary of the navy and the secretary of the interior inform the Senate of any deals involving the leasing of the oil reserves to anyone, and whether there was competitive bidding regarding these leases. The

resolution, submitted by Senator John Benjamin Kendrick (D-WY) read:

> Whereas, there have recently appeared in the public press statements purporting to have been authorized by the Department of the Interior, to the effect that the Secretary of the Interior and the Secretary of the Navy are negotiating with private parties for the operation of lands included in Naval Petroleum Reserve Number 3, Wyoming number 1, withdrawn by Executive order of the President, dated April 30, 1915, known as the Teapot Dome; therefore it is Resolved that the Secretary of the Interior and the Secretary of the Navy are requested to inform the Senate, if not incompatible with the public interests, whether such negotiations are pending, and if so the names of all parties, the terms and conditions of all proposed operating agreements, and whether opportunity will be given the public for competitive bidding for the operation of these lands, or whether it is proposed to award a lease or other operating contract or agreement for the entire area to one person, corporation or association.

Acting Secretary of the Interior Edward Finney, in control of the department while Fall was out of Washington, gave the Senate a copy of the leases on 29 April 1922. Finney also told the Senate that the deals were done in the name of national security, in that the oil in the reserves could not be used in ships and needed to be refined into fuel. This explanation was unacceptable to the Senate, and that body that same day enacted Resolution 282, which established an investigation of the leases in the Committee of Public Lands and Surveys. Senator Miles Poindexter (R-WA) said: "I think Congress ought to know, and that the country ought to know, whether or not the interests of the public are being protected by the terms of the contract or lease which has been made for the extraction of the oil from the Government reserve, and that will be ascertained, I assume, by this investigation."

President Harding stood up for Fall and Denby, telling the Senate in an official letter that he was involved in all of the negotiations regarding the leases. "The policy which has been adopted by the Secretary of the Navy and the Secretary of the Interior in dealing with these matters was submitted to me prior to the adoption thereof, and the policy decided upon and the subsequent acts have at all times had my entire approval," Harding wrote. Senator Reed Smoot (R-UT) was the chairman of the committee, but it included several Republican insurgents who differed with the administration, as well as Senator Thomas J. Walsh (D-MT), who desired to make the hearings part of his attack on the Harding administration.

Walsh's plans changed on 2 August 1923 when Harding, while on a trip to Alaska and California, died in San Francisco. He was succeeded by his vice president, Calvin Coolidge. Hearings on the scandal now known as Teapot Dome opened in the Committee on Public Lands and Surveys on 15 October 1923. Within a week, witnesses started to testify, starting with Secretary of the Interior Fall. Former Secretary Fall, under pressure from the new president, had resigned his office on 4 March 1923. Following Fall was Secretary of the Navy Denby. Walsh dominated the hearings, releasing tidbits of information to reporters behind the scenes and then announcing the stories the following day as important information for the committee to investigate. Fall told the committee that he had borrowed $100,000 in cash from Edward B. McLean, publisher of the *Washington Post*. McLean initially refused to testify, but finally denied that he had never given Fall any funds. Edward Doheny later admitted that he was the source of the payment, having paid it to Fall via Doheny's own son in "a little black bag."

As new allegations appeared on the oil deals, political damage mounted for President Coolidge despite his having no ties to any of part of the scandal. To clear his own administration of any taint, Coolidge decided to name

a special prosecutor to investigate the affair. When it appeared that Coolidge was prepared to name the prosecutor to investigate Teapot Dome, Attorney General Harry M. Daugherty wrote him an impassioned letter, in which he explained:

> May I again urge the desirability that you immediately appoint two outstanding lawyers who as such shall at once take up all phases of the oil leases under investigation of the Senate or others and advise you as to the facts and law justifying legal proceedings of any kind. As you know, I do not desire to evade any responsibility in this or other matters; but considering that Mr. Fall and I served in the Cabinet together, this would be fair to you, to Mr. Fall, and the American people, as well as to the Attorney General, the Department of Justice, and my associates and assistants therein. I do not desire to be consulted as to whom you shall appoint. The only suggestion I have to make in that regard is that those appointed shall be lawyers whom the public will at once recognize as worthy of confidence and who will command the respect of the people by not practicing politics or permitting others to do so in connection with this important public business.

Coolidge disagreed. He wrote:

> It is not for the President to determine criminal guilt or render judgment in civil causes. That is the function of the courts. It is not for him to prejudge. I shall do neither; but when facts are revealed to me that require action for the purpose of insuring the enforcement of either civil or criminal liability, such action will be taken. That is the province of the Executive.
>
> Acting under my direction the Department of Justice has been observing the course of the evidence which has been revealed at the hearings conducted by the senatorial committee investigating certain oil leases made on naval reserves, which I believe warrants action for the purpose of enforcing the law and protecting the rights of the public. This is confirmed by reports made to me from the committee. If there has been any crime, it must be prosecuted. If there has been any property of the United States illegally transferred or leased, it must be recovered.
>
> I feel the public is entitled to know that in the conduct of such action no one is shielded for any party, political or other reason. As I understand, men are involved who belong to both political parties, and having been advised by the Department of Justice that it is in accord with the former precedents, I propose to employ special counsel of high rank drawn from both political parties to bring such

action for the enforcement of the law. Counsel will be instructed to prosecute these cases in the courts so that if there is any guilt it will be punished; if there is civil liability it will be enforced; if there is any fraud it will be revealed; and if there are any contracts which are illegal they will be canceled.

Coolidge picked two lawyers—Republican Silas Strawn and Democrat Thomas Gregory (the latter having served as attorney general in the Woodrow Wilson administration)—but because both had ties to the oil industry, they faced a storm on Capitol Hill. Coolidge withdrew their names when it appeared that neither would be confirmed. On a referral from Senator George Pepper (R-PA), Coolidge selected Philadelphia attorney Owen J. Roberts, a Republican, and attorney Atlee Pomerene, a Democrat and former U.S. senator. Pomerene was confirmed by the Senate by a vote of fifty-nine to thirteen on 16 February 1924, and Roberts was confirmed by a vote of sixty-eight to eight two days later. On the day Roberts was confirmed, 18 February 1924, Secretary of the Navy Edwin Denby handed in his resignation.

Only a month into their inquiry, Roberts and Pomerene indicted Fall, Doheny, and Sinclair. Fall was later convicted of accepting a bribe, although Sinclair and Doheny were acquitted of giving the bribe, a strange and ironic twist. Fall went to prison, the first of two cabinet members ever to be sentenced to a prison term. (The other was Attorney General John Newton Mitchell, implicated in Watergate.) Attorney General Daugherty resigned on 28 March 1924, but he was never tried on any charges relating to Teapot Dome. In all, Roberts and Pomerene indicted eight people, resulting in six criminal trials and two civil trials. Sinclair was later sent to prison for contempt of Congress, and the oil reserves were restored to the control of the U.S. government. Roberts remained on the investigation until

President Herbert Hoover elevated him to a seat on the United States Supreme Court in 1930. Pomerene stayed with the prosecution until he closed it, using his power to exact compensation from Sinclair's and Doheny's oil companies for the oil they stole. Hoover named Pomerene, a Democrat, to head the Reconstruction Finance Corporation in 1932, where he served until Hoover left office the following year.

Teapot Dome remains perhaps one of the most extensive scandals implicating executive branch members and outright bribery and the selling of government assets for bribes. At the time of the scandal Senator Gerald Nye (R-ND) said:

> The investigation has uncovered the slimiest of slimy trails beaten by privilege. The investigation has shown, let us hope, privilege at its worst. The trail is one of dishonesty, greed, violation of law, secrecy, concealment, evasion, falsehood, and cunning. It is a trail of betrayals by trusted and presumably honorable men—betrayals of a government, of certain business interests and the people who trusted and honored them; it is a trail showing a flagrant degree of the exercise of political power and influence, and the power and influence of great wealth upon individuals and political parties; it is the trail of despoilers and schemers, far more dangerous to the well-being of our Nation and our democracy than all those who have been deported from our shores in all time as undesirable citizens. And in the end the story of one of the crushing of brilliant careers when finally the light was played upon those who schemed those unhealthy schemes born in darkness.

**See also** Denby, Edwin; Fall, Albert Bacon

**References:** Busch, Francis X., *Enemies of the State: An Account of the Trials of the Mary Eugenia Surratt Case, the Teapot Dome Cases, the Alphonse Capone Case, the Rosenberg Case* (Indianapolis, IN: Bobbs-Merrill, 1954); Ferrell, Robert H., "Teapot Dome," in Donald C. Bacon, Roger H. Davidson, and Morton Keller, eds., *Encyclopedia of the United States Congress*, 4 vols. (New York: Simon & Schuster, 1995), IV:1935–1937; Noggle, Burl. *Teapot Dome: Oil and Politics in the 1920s* (New York: Norton, 1962); "Normalcy," in David Loth, *Public Plunder: A History of Graft in America* (New York: Carrick & Evans, Inc., 1938),

312–323; Nye, Gerald, senator, comments in United States Senate, *Leases Upon Naval Oil Reserves and Activities of the Continental Trading Co. (Ltd.) of Canada,* Senate Report 1326, 70th Congress, 1st Session (1928), II:2–3; Poindexter, Miles, senator comments in *Congressional Record$—$Proceedings and Debates of the 67th Congress, 2nd Session* (Washington, DC: Government Printing Office, 1922), 6048; Werner, Morris Robert, and John Starr, *Teapot Dome* (New York: Viking Press, 1959), 86.

## Thomas, John Parnell (1895–1970)

United States representative from New Jersey (1937–1950), convicted of fraud and sent to prison for nine months. Thomas was one of the most powerful lawmakers of the late 1940s in his role as chairman of the Committee on Un-American Activities (HUAC). Thomas's fall from grace was perhaps one of the farthest of any politician in American history, although his name is little remembered today. Born in Jersey City, New Jersey, on 16 January 1895, Thomas attended local schools before studying at the University of Pennsylvania. When World War I began, he volunteered for service and served as a second lieutenant in Company B of the 306th Infantry, rising to the rank of first lieutenant and then captain in the Headquarters Regimental Staff of the 50th Infantry. He was discharged in 1919 with the rank of captain. For several years he worked in securities investments and later in the insurance business in New York City.

In 1925, Thomas, a Republican, was elected a member of the borough council of Allendale, New Jersey, and a year later mayor of Allendale. He served in that capacity until 1930. In 1935 he was elected to a seat in the New Jersey House of Assembly, where he served until 1937. In 1936 he ran for a seat in the U.S. House of Representatives, representing the seventh New Jersey district. He defeated Democrat Harold. J. P. Hoffmann, and took his seat in the Seventy-fifth Congress on 3 January 1937. Because of his conservative views, he harshly opposed President Franklin Delano Roosevelt's "New Deal" program of government relief, calling it a threat to the capitalist system. His greatest barbs were aimed at the Federal Theater and Writers Project, a New Deal program that gave stipends to writers and performers. Many of the plays and works that had been created during the program were of a left-wing nature, and conservatives like Thomas objected both to their content and to the donation of government funds to advance them. Thomas stated, "Practically every play presented under the auspices of the project is sheer propaganda for Communism or the New Deal." Despite his stands against the popular Roosevelt, Thomas was reelected in 1938, 1940, 1942, 1944, 1946, and 1948.

In 1947 Thomas was named chairman of the House Committee on Un-American Activities, designed to investigate alleged Communist influences in the United States. Under Thomas, the committee began an investigation into the role of Communists in the motion picture industry. Calling numerous witnesses before the committee, including leading players in motion pictures, several people in the industry were accused of being present or former Communists. Ten men—including writers Dalton Trumbo and Ring Lardner Jr.; directors Herbert Biberman, Edward Dmytryk, John Howard Lawson, and Lester Cole—refused to answer any of the committee's questions and were cited for contempt of Congress. These men became known as "The Hollywood Ten."

Rising anger about Thomas's command over the committee's hearings led to secret investigations of the New Jersey congressman's personal dealings. Unfortunately for Thomas, scandal was ripe for the finding. Soon reports that Thomas had submitted billing statements to Congress for allegedly nonexistent employees and then pocketed the excess payments, brought a grand jury investigation. Appearing before that panel, Thomas ironically took the Fifth Amendment—the same tactic used by witnesses before his own committee. Thomas was indicted for conspiracy to defraud the United States government. He was convicted on all charges and resigned his House seat on 2 January 1950. He was sentenced to prison, serving only nine before he was paroled. Ironically, he served in the same prison with Lester Cole and Ring Lardner Jr., who were still serving out their contempt of Congress citations.

After being released from prison, Thomas worked as the editor and publisher of three daily newspapers in Bergen County, New Jersey; later, he worked as a real estate solicitor and investment adviser. He ran for a U.S. House seat in 1954, but was defeated for the Republican nomination. Thomas moved to St. Petersburg, Florida, where he died on 19 November 1970 at the age of seventy-five.

**References:** *Biographical Directory of the American Congress, 1774–1996* (Alexandria, VA: CQ Staff Directories, Inc., 1996).

## Thompson, Fred Dalton (1942– )

Actor and politician, United States Senator (1995–2002), chairman of the Senate Governmental Affairs Committee's hearings into campaign finance irregularities by the Democratic Party. Born in Sheffield, Alabama, on 19 August 1942, Thompson grew up in Lawrenceburg, Tennessee. He received his undergraduate degree in philosophy from Memphis State University (now the University of Memphis) in 1964 and his law degree from Vanderbilt University in 1967, while working his way through school. Two years after law school, Thompson was named an assistant U.S. attorney and at the age of thirty was appointed minority counsel

to the Senate Watergate Committee, where he served from 1973 to 1974. It was Thompson who asked witness Alexander Butterfield whether the Oval Office had any recording devices, exposing the existence of tapes of the Watergate conspirators admitting to covering up criminal activities and heralding the beginning of the end for the Nixon administration. In 1975 Thompson wrote *At That Point in Time: The Story of the Senate Watergate Committee.*

After leaving Washington in 1974, Thompson defended the chairman of the Tennessee Parole Board after she had been suspiciously fired. Thompson's work helped to expose a cash-for-clemency scheme that ultimately toppled the governor. The scandal became the subject of a best-selling book and later a film, *Marie,* starring Sissy Spacek, in which Thompson played himself. The role exposed the dynamic Thompson to movie audiences, and he began to get more acting opportunities. He went on to act in eighteen motion pictures, including *In the Line of Fire* (1993), *Die Hard II* (1990), and *The Hunt for Red October* (1990).

In 1994 Thompson ran for the remaining two years left in the vacant U.S. Senate seat from Tennessee once held by Vice President Al Gore. Facing Representative Jim Cooper, an establishment Democrat with strong credentials and a large monetary war chest, Thompson portrayed himself as an outsider and won a bitter contest with 61 percent of the vote to Cooper's 39 percent in his first campaign for office. Once in Congress, Thompson quickly established himself as a force for change, making historic progress on the reform of Congress and the balanced budget, working for campaign finance reform, and calling for a smaller federal government. He was returned for a full term by the voters in 1996, winning his second election in two years, each by more than 20 percentage points. In his reelection victory, Senator Thompson received more votes than any candidate for any office in Tennessee history. Presently, Senator Thompson serves as a member of the Senate Judiciary Committee, and in 1997 was elected chairman of the Governmental Affairs Committee, making him the first senator since World War II to serve as chairman of a major Senate committee after only two years of service.

After the 1996 election, reports of large irregularities in Democratic party fundraising, particularly by the Clinton administration, came to light. On 11 March 1997, the Senate voted ninety-nine to zero to direct the Governmental Affairs Committee to investigate illegal or improper activities in connection with the 1996 federal election campaigns, giving Thompson a national spotlight. Thompson's political career seemed on the rise, even though the Republicans were forced into the minority in the Senate in 2001. In 2002, however, Thompson decided not to seek a third term, instead returning to his first love: acting. As the sometimes abrasive but studious DA Arthur Branch on television's *Law & Order*, Thompson put a Republican spin on an office dominated by liberals. In 2007, Thompson left *Law & Order* to run for the Republican nomination for president of the United States.

Although he ran on a mantle of a Reagan Republican, Thompson's campaign never gained traction and, after a series of losses, he resigned from the race in January 2008.

**See also** Senate Finance Committee Hearings

**References:** Duncan, Philip D; and Christine C. Lawrence, *Congressional Quarterly's Politics in America 1996: The 104th Congress* (Washington, DC: Congressional Quarterly Inc., 1995), 1213–1214; Thompson, Fred D., *At That Point in Time: The Inside Story of the Senate Watergate Committee* (New York: Quadrangle/New York Times Book Co., 1975).

## Thompson, William Hale (1869–1944)

Mayor of Chicago (1915–1923, 1927–1931), investigated but never convicted for fraud, which forced him to leave the mayorship in 1923, but his support of the sale of liquor and his backing of known gangsters led to his reelection in 1927. Despite the lack of a conviction, Thompson is figured by historians to have been one of the most corrupt mayors to ever serve in American history. Soon after he was born on 14 May 1869, in Boston, Massachusetts, the son of Colonel William Hale Thompson, a Civil War veteran, he and his family moved to the growing metropolis of Chicago. Colonel Thompson was a member of an affluent New England family—he had served in the New Hampshire state legislature in the late 1870s—and he passed on his wealth to his son William. The younger Thompson attended the prestigious Charles Fessenden Preparatory School in Chicago, after which he decided to head west. His father bought him a 3,800 acre ranch in Nebraska in 1888, but Thompson returned to Chicago in 1891 following his father's death.

In 1899 Thompson entered the political realm after one of his friends told him about an empty aldermanic seat. Thompson ran and won the seat representing Chicago's Second Ward. Although his record was undistinguished, he was noticed by Republican Party boss William Lorimer (later a United States senator), who pushed Thompson to run for a seat on the Cook County (Chicago) Board of Supervisors in 1902. He was elected, but after another two undistinguished years in this position, he felt he had had enough of politics and returned to private life. This would be a short-term move, however.

In 1915 Thompson was again convinced to enter politics, this time with the backing of Lorimer's crony Fred Lundin, and run for mayor of Chicago. With Lundin's backing, he defeated two Republicans in the February 1915 primary, then overcame a massive field of several candidates—including Socialist Seymour Stedman, who would serve as the Socialist vice presidential candidate with Eugene V. Debs in the 1920 election—to be elected Chicago's thirty-third mayor. Although he had never been involved in corruption, Thompson's entire tenure as mayor was marked by massive influence peddling and wholesale bribery. The police department was left in the hands of the criminals who paid for protection; a race riot in July 1919 was ignored as many died; and organized crime figures were allowed to run their illegal businesses, usually involving liquor, as Thompson either didn't care or was actively involved in their crimes. During World War I, he openly espoused the German cause and denounced the British. (He later threatened to punch the king of England in the face if the king ever appeared in Chicago.) The *Chicago Tribune* accused Thompson of stealing $2 million from the city. In 1923, after eight years in office, Thompson backed off running for a third term in exchange for not being prosecuted. (Prior to the election, Fred Lundin and his associates were indicted for stealing more than $1 million from the city's education fund, but Lundin was acquitted, thanks to the tactics of his attorney, Clarence Darrow.) In the 1923 election, a reformer, Democrat William Dever, was elected and began a massive clean-up of the neglect and corruption that had reigned for eight years of "Big Bill" Thompson's tenure. He cracked down on the huge number of speakeasies (illegal bars) that had sprouted up in the city and began wholesale arrests of organized crime figures, including Chicago's Johnny Torrio, and he harassed Alphonse Capone, the leader of Chicago's mafia. He forced prohibition on the city, and threatened police with arrest if liquor was sold in their districts.

After four years, organized crime and the liquor distributors were fed up with Dever's success and sought to toss him out of office. William Thompson was recruited to get his old job back on behalf of these criminal elements. Using strong-arm tactics, Capone initiated a citywide campaign of terror to force people to vote for Thompson, or he used his muscle for massive vote fraud. Thompson also promised an end to prohibition, and a populace more interested in drink than corruption listened intensely. Thompson "defeated" Dever by more than 80,000 votes, and as soon as Thompson took office for his third term, the police crackdown of Capone and organized crime ended. This time, however, Thompson allowed wholesale corruption to reign freely. Historian Jay Robert Nash explained: "Chicago careened out of control between 1927 and 1931 when Thompson left office for the final time. The city was in the hands of the gangsters, and all the civil works projects the mayor had introduced did little to compensate for the sorry record of the city police and the administration which controlled them."

In 1931 Thompson ran for a fourth term, but voters, disgusted with the wholesale corruption, voted in another reformer, Democrat Anton Cermak, who ran on a platform of cleaning up the police and reigning in organized crime. (Cermak was killed in an assassination attempt on the life of President-elect Franklin D. Roosevelt in 1933.) Undaunted, Thompson ran for governor of Illinois in 1936 and 1939, but was defeated both times. He died from heart disease at the Hotel Blackstone in Chicago on 19 March 1944 at the age of seventy-six. Many historians consider him to be the most crooked mayor in American history.

**See also** Small, Lennington "Len"

**References:** Prinz, Andrew K., "Thompson, William
Hale," in Melvin G. Holli and Peter d'A. Jones,
*Biographical Dictionary of American Mayors,
1820$–$1980: Big City Mayors* (Westport, CT:
Greenwood Press, 1981), 362; "Thompson, William
Hale," in Jay Robert Nash, *Encyclopedia of World
Crime: Criminal Justice, Criminology, and Law
Enforcement*, 4 vols. (Wilmette, IL: CrimeBooks, Inc.,
1989), IV:2936–37; Wendt, Lloyd; and Herman Kogan,
*Big Bill of Chicago* (Indianapolis, IN: Bobbs-Merrill
Company, 1953).

## Tillman Act of 1907, 34 Stat. 864 (1907)

Act of Congress, enacted 26 January 1907,
which attempted for the first time to limit
campaign finance spending.

Sponsored by Senator Ben "Pitchfork" Tillman of South Carolina, this legislation for the
first time set out to limit the campaign spending contributions from corporations and banking concerns. It banned corporate gifts to
campaigns, a prohibition that has remained in
effect, despite the proliferation of "soft money" spending.

The act reads:

*An Act to prohibit corporations from making money
contributions in connection with political elections.*

*Be it enacted*, That it shall be unlawful for any national
bank, or any corporation organized by authority of any
laws of Congress, to make a money contribution in
connection with any election to any political office. It
shall also be unlawful for any corporation whatever to
make a money contribution in connection with any
election at which Presidential and Vice Presidential
electors or a Representative in Congress is to be voted for
or any election by any State legislature of a United States
Senator. Every corporation which shall make any
contribution in violation of the foregoing provisions shall
be subject to a fine not exceeding five thousand dollars,
and every officer or director of any corporation who shall
consent to any contribution by the corporation in
violation of the foregoing provisions shall upon
conviction be punished by a fine of not exceeding one
thousand and not less than two hundred and fifty dollars,
or by imprisonment for a term of not more than one year,

or both such fine and imprisonment in the discretion of
the court.

Despite the fact that the Tillman Act was
revolutionary for its time, it was loaded with
loopholes, and within three years Congress
saw fit to revise it. In 1925, as part of the
sweeping law known as the Federal Corrupt
Practices Act, the Tillman Act was repealed.

**See also** Federal Corrupt Practices Act of 1925; Publicity
Act of 1910
**References:** Simkins, Francis Butler, *Pitchfork Ben
Tillman: South Carolinian* (Baton Rouge, LA:
Louisiana State University Press, 1944).

## Tonry, Richard Alvin (1935– )

U.S. Representative from Louisiana (1977),
indicted and convicted of buying votes in his
heavily Democratic district. Tonry served
only four months in the U.S. House. Born in
New Orleans, Louisiana, on 25 June 1935, he
attended local schools, and earned his bachelor's degree from Spring Hill College in Mobile, Alabama, in 1960, and his master's degree from the same institution two years later. After a period of graduate study at
Georgetown University in Washington, D.C.,
Tonry received his law degree from Loyola
University in New Orleans in 1967 and was
admitted to the Louisiana bar that same
year. He then opened a law office in the
towns of Arabi and Chalmette, Louisiana,
where he practiced from 1967 until 1976. In
1976, Tonry was elected as a Democrat to a
seat in the Louisiana state House of Representatives. Before he could serve a single
term, he ran for a seat in the U.S. House of
Representatives, and was elected to the 95th
Congress (1977–79).

Almost as soon as he took the oath of office
for his U.S. House seat on 3 January 1977,
Tonry was in trouble with the law, as it was
soon alleged that he had been involved in a

massive vote-buying and vote-rigging scheme to fix the election in his heavily Democratic district. The focus of the investigation centered on the 2 October 1976 Democratic primary for the party's nomination to run for the seat of Louisiana's 1st Congressional district. The seat had been held by Rep. F. Edward Hebert, the former chairman of the House Armed Services Committee. Tonry defeated his Democratic opponent in the primary, New Orleans City Councilman James A. Moreau, by a slim 184 votes. After the election, Moreau petitioned the state district court to throw out the election because Tonry had won through "widespread vote fraud." A federal grand jury was quickly empaneled, and soon indicted 23 people, charging that some 400 votes were falsified by election commissioners who supported Tonry over Moreau. The grand jury also indicted Tonry associate Donald J. Zimmer for giving a $2,000 illegal contribution to Tonry and trying to cover it up. The House Ethics Committee refused to investigate, saying that any primary election was the subject of state and not federal law. At the same time, if Tonry's election were voided, it meant that his general election victory was to be declared null and void and handed over to the Republican in the race. Tonry, claiming that he was being framed by his political enemies, told reporters on 10 April that he expected to be indicted. "These charges were nothing more than an attempt to smear me. If they can't unseat me, they are going to try to smear me so I can't be re-elected," he said.

On 21 April 1977, Judge Melvin Shortess ruled that at least 229 votes had been fraudulently cast for Tonry, voiding his election victory. "But for the irregularities and fraud, Moreau would have been nominated in the second Democratic primary on Oct. 2, 1976," Shortess wrote in his opinion. However, because the primary election and not the general election was tainted, the House could only act if fraud had been committed in the latter election. Rep. Mendel Davis, Democrat of South Carolina, the chairman of a three-member group in the House Administration Committee looking into the Tonry case, stated that only Congress could punish Tonry for his actions. Tonry agreed, mocking the judge's decision. "I think it was a meaningless decision, just like it was a meaningless trial. Every attorney agrees... that the final decision lies in Congress."

Within a week, however, as the personal cost of the pending indictment rose for him, Tonry decided to throw in the towel. On 4 May 1977 he submitted his resignation to Speaker of the House Thomas P. "Tip" O'Neill. "I just don't have any more to fight the court suits on these charges," Tonry told reporters. At the same time, he wrote to Speaker O'Neill that he intended to run again and win the seat back for the Democrats. "Keep my seat warm and tell my colleagues not to forget me."

A week after his resignation, Tonry was indicted by a federal grand jury in New Orleans on 10 counts of receiving illegal political contributions which totaled more than $54,000, promising jobs and government contracts to three individuals who donated to his campaign, and conspiring to obstruct justice by lying and furnishing false information to the grand jury hearing the case. Also indicted with Tonry was John W. Mumphrey, his law partner, who was charged with conspiracy, obstruction of justice, and lying under oath to the grand jury.

As his trial opened, Tonry ran in the Democratic primary to fill the vacancy created by his resignation. On 24 June 1977, he was defeated in the primary, coming in second to State Rep. Ron Faucheux. Ironically, James A. Moreau, who had alleged that he had been defeated in the 1976 primary because of fraud, ran as a Republican but finished second behind Robert Livingston, Jr., a former prosecutor who won the seat in the general election. Livingston rose to be named Speaker of the U.S. House in 1998 before he was implicated in a sexual scandal involving infidelity and forced to resign.

With his political career shattered and his personal life in ruins, Tonry pled guilty to a reduced number of charges on 1 July 1977. On 28 July 1977 he was sentenced to one year in prison and fined $10,000; he was also placed on three years of probation. As U.S. District Judge Charles Schwartz read the sentence, Tonry showed no emotion.

After serving his sentence, Tonry remained in Arabi, Louisiana, where he resumed the practice of law. In 1983, he was an unsuccessful candidate for a seat in the Louisiana state House of Representatives.

See also Primary Documents, page 614.

References: Tonry biography, courtesy of *The Biographical Directory of the United States Congress*, online at http://bioguide.congress.gov/scripts/biodisplay.pl?index=T000310; Brown, Warren, "New Congressman's Seat Imperiled by Vote-Fraud Charges," *The Washington Post*, 2 February 1977, D1; "Tonry Expects Indictment on Vote Fraud Charges," *The Washington Post*, 13 April 1977, A2; "Tonry Vote Fraud Confirmed in Court; House Still Pending," *The Washington Post*, 22 April 1977, A2; Brown, Warren, "Rep. Tonry Resigns Seat, Cites Voting Fraud Case," *The Washington Post*, 5 April 1977, 1; Goshko, John M., "Ex-Rep. Tonry Is Indicted on Funds Charges," *The Washington Post*, 13 May 1977, A8; "Ex-Representative Tonry Defeated in Louisiana Primary," *The Washington Post*, 26 June 1977, 7; "Tonry Pleads Guilty in Violations Case," *The Washington Post*, 2 July 1977, A2; "Tonry Sentenced to Prison, Fined in Election Fraud," *The Washington Post*, 29 July 1977, A8.

## Torricelli, Robert Guy (1951– )

United States representative (1983–1997) and U.S. senator (1997–2002) from New Jersey, reprimanded by the Senate Ethics Committee for taking illegal gifts and aiding a donor with his influence in obtaining contracts with foreign governments. Torricelli was born in Paterson, New Jersey, on 27 August 1951. He attended local schools in New York, particularly Storm King School in Cornwall-on-the-Hudson, New York, from which he graduated in 1970. He attended Rutgers University in New Brunswick, New Jersey, from which he earned a bachelor's degree in 1974, and Harvard University's Kennedy School of Government, which awarded him a masters in public administration degree in 1980. In 1973 Torricelli went to work on the campaign of Democrat Brendan Byrne, running for governor of New Jersey. Following Byrne's election, Torricelli went to work as his deputy legislative counsel, serving until 1977. Torricelli was admitted to the New Jersey bar in 1978. That same year, Vice President Walter Mondale named Torricelli as the his counsel, a post he held until 1980. Torricelli left the White House to earn his degree from Harvard.

In 1982 Torricelli ran for a seat in the U.S. House of Representatives from New Jersey's Ninth Congressional District. Defeating Republican Harold Hollenbeck, he entered the House on 3 January 1983 and served in the 98th–104th Congresses. In 1996, when Senator Bill Bradley of New Jersey retired, Torricelli announced his candidacy for that seat. He defeated Republican Representative Dick Zimmer and entered the Senate on 2 January 1997.

Torricelli, known as "the Torch" for his antagonistic style, was linked for many years with shady dealings. However, it was not until late in his first term that the Department of Justice looked into these allegations. It was discovered that one of Torricelli's campaign donors, David Chang, a businessman, had given Torricelli improper campaign contributions as well as gifts that violated the gift ban established by the Senate. Chang was arrested and sent to prison; Torricelli, however, decried the charges and maintained his innocence. On 3 January 2002, the Department of Justice announced that it did not have clear and convincing evidence of wrongdoing by Torricelli, but it did hand over all of its materials to the Senate Ethics Committee and asked the panel to make its own findings.

On 30 July 2002, the committee released its report on the Torricelli/Chang investigation. Finding many of Chang's charges to be in fact true, the committee recommended that Torricelli be admonished by the full Senate rather than censured or expelled. In their letter to Torricelli, the committee wrote:

> Your acceptance of a television and stereo CD player upon payment to David Chang of an amount you understood to be the cost to Mr. Chang, rather than fair market retail value, evidenced poor judgment, displayed a lack of due regard for Senate rules....
>
> Your acceptance on loan from Mr. Chang of bronze statues ... for display in your Senate office under your office's policy of accepting the loan of home state artwork was not consistent with Senate rules governing such loans, evidenced poor judgment, displayed a lack of due regard for Senate rules...
>
> Your failure to act to prevent the acceptance of or to pay for gifts of earrings from Mr. Chang to individuals (your sister, an employee, and a friend) in your home at Christmas on the mistaken belief that such items were of little value or were not gifts to you ... evidenced poor judgment, displayed a lack of due regard for Senate rules...
>
> Continuation of a personal and official relationship with Mr. Chang under circumstances where you knew that he was attempting to ingratiate himself, in part through a pattern of attempts to provide you and those around you with gifts over a period of several years when you and your Senate office were taking official actions of benefit to Mr. Chang ... evidenced poor judgment.
>
> After evaluating the extensive body of evidence before it and your testimony, the committee is troubled by incongruities, inconsistencies, and conflicts, particularly concerning actions taken by you which were or could have been of potential benefit to Mr. Chang.

> The Senate Select Committee on Ethics ... expresses its determination that your actions and failure to act led to violations of Senate rules (and related statutes) and created at least the appearance of impropriety, and you are hereby severely admonished.
>
> You must pay Mr. Chang an amount sufficient to bring the total to fair market retail value of the TV and CD player, as well as the fair market retail value of the earrings given to the three individuals at your home, with appropriate interest. The committee understands that you have previously delivered the bronze statues to the Department of Justice, from whence they should be returned to Mr. Chang.

Torricelli, shocked by the findings and punishment by his Senate colleagues, appeared on the Senate floor late that same night and apologized both to his fellow Senators and to the people of New Jersey. "I want my colleagues in the Senate to know I agree with the committee's conclusions, fully accept their findings and take full personal responsibility," he said. "I want to apologize to the people of New Jersey for having placed the seat in the United States Senate they have allowed me to occupy to be placed in this position.... I never stopped fighting for things I believed, I never compromised the struggle to make the lives of the people I love better."

Torricelli was deep in the middle of a tough reelection bid before the Ethics Committee admonished the New Jersey Senator; his work only became harder with this ethics violation on his record just a few months before voters went to the polls. On 26 September 2002, a federal appeals court in Philadelphia held that legal documents regarding Torricelli's case, including a memo produced by investigators in his case, must be released immediately. Polls taken that same week showed that Torricelli's campaign took a large hit from the fresh allegations in the memo—as well as an interview with a local New York television station with Chang—and, on 30 September 2002, just thirty-six days before the election, Torricelli announced his resignation from the race, but not his Senate seat. He was replaced on the ballot by former Senator Frank Lautenberg, who had retired from the U.S. Senate in 2000. Lautenberg won Torricelli's seat on 5 November 2002.

References: *Biographical Directory of the American Congress, 1774–1996* (Alexandria, VA: CQ Staff Directories, Inc., 1996), 1956; Schmidt, Susan, and James V. Grimaldi, "Torricelli and the Money Man: N. J. Senator Had Symbiotic Relationship With Executive," *Washington Post*, 13 May 2001, A1; VandeHei, Jim, and Helen Dewar, "Senate Ethics Panel Rebukes Torricelli; Reprimand Over Gifts Could Have Political Consequences for N.J. Democrat," *Washington Post*, 31 July 2002, A1.

## Traficant, James Anthony, Jr. (1941– )

United States representative from Ohio (1985–2002), convicted in April 2002 of bribery, racketeering, and fraud, and expelled from the House of Representatives, the second such action by the House of Representatives since the end of the Civil War. He was later sentenced to eight years in prison. A colorful and mercurial politician who bucked his party to support ideas he felt deserved backing, many of which were not positions of the Democratic Party, Traficant was born in Youngstown, Ohio, on 8 May 1941. He attended local schools in Youngstown before going to the University of Pittsburgh in Pennsylvania, where he earned a bachelor of science degree in 1963 and in 1973 a master of science degree from the same university. From 1971 to 1981, Traficant served as the executive director of the Mahoning County (Ohio) Drug Program. In 1980 he was elected sheriff of Mahoning County and he earned a reputation as a strong law-and-order officer with a short fuse. In 1983 he was tried on charges relating to taking bribes, but he was acquitted.

In 1984, disgusted with what he felt was a malaise with the national Democratic Party,

Traficant ran as a Democrat for a seat in the U.S. House of Representatives, representing Ohio's Seventeenth District. Elected, he would serve until he was expelled by a vote of Congress on 24 July 2002. During his tenure, he fought his party on tax increases and stood for stronger national security. Always a bane to the party's leaders in Congress, he was nonetheless popular with his blue-collar district where Ronald Reagan earned many votes. In 2000, after he was reelected to his ninth term, he voted to seat Republican Dennis Hastert as Speaker of the House, angering his Democratic colleagues, which led to his being removed from all committee assignments. Appearing on numerous talk shows, he used colorful language to describe his views on important topics. He also used the same language during his speeches on the House floor—one of his favorite phrases was "Beam me up, Scotty!"

On 3 May 2001, Traficant was indicted on ten counts of bribery and conspiracy. Federal prosecutors alleged in the multicount indictment that Traficant had received free labor and materials from construction businesses in Youngstown, Ohio, which was in his district, in exchange for his intervention on behalf of the construction businesses before federal regulators; that he ordered one of his staff to turn over $2,500 from his monthly paycheck; that he tried to get his staff to destroy evidence as well as provide false testimony; that he ordered his staff to do free work on his farm and boat; that he filed false tax returns; and that he committed bribery and mail fraud. Traficant condemned the indictment and the prosecutors, and said he would act as his own attorney (known as a *pro se* appearance). Two of his associates, former Chief of Staff Henry Di-Blasio and contractor Bernard Bucheit were also indicted on federal charges of bribing Traficant and lying to a federal grand jury.

Traficant's trial began on 13 February 2002. Traficant, acting as his own attorney, claimed that he was the victim of prosecutorial misconduct, and that the witnesses called against him were either intimidated or bribed. These witnesses testified that Traficant had received unknown amounts of cash from unknown sources, and that his staff was charged with putting the cash into Traficant's bank accounts. Despite Traficant's protestations about a "vendetta" against him, on 11 April 2002 the jury convicted him of all ten charges after just four days of deliberations. Minutes after the guilty verdicts were announced, leaders of the House of Representatives began an ethics investigation. Representative Richard A. Gephardt (D-MO), the Minority Leader, called on Traficant to resign.

On 23 July 2002, the House Ethics Committee released its report on the Traficant matter—it recommended that the Ohio congressman be expelled if he did not resign his seat. Traficant refused to resign, forcing an expulsion vote for the first time since 1980. On 25 July, following a three-hour debate on the House floor, the House voted 410–1 to expel him—the only vote against expulsion was by Representative Gary Condit (D-CA), who was entangled in his own ethical troubles and had lost in the Democratic primary earlier in the year. Representative Joel Hefley (R-CO), the chairman of the Committee on Standards of Conduct and floor manager of the expulsion proceedings, told the House that there were "1,000 pages" of evidence against Traficant, and that he had to be expelled. "Many of us are very fond of Representative Traficant but at times like this we are required to set aside those feelings," Hefley told a stunned House.

On 30 July 2002, Traficant was sentenced to eight years in federal prison by Judge Lesley Brooks Wells. He maintained his innocence, and ran a 2002 congressional campaign from his prison cell that garnered few votes. Traficant is currently set to be released from prison on or before September 2009.

See also Primary Documents, page 641.

References: *Biographical Directory of the American Congress, 1774–1996* (Alexandria, VA: CQ Staff Directories, Inc., 1996), 1960; Eilperin, Juliet, "Ethics Panel Weighs Traficant Expulsion; Convicted Lawmaker Won't Go Quietly," *Washington Post*, 16 July 2002, A4; Eilperin, Juliet, "House Votes 410 to 1 to Expel Traficant," *Washington Post*, 25 July 2002, A1; Pierre, Robert E., and Juliet Eilperin, "Traficant Is Found Guilty; Ohio Congressman Could Face House Sanctions," *Washington Post*, 12 April 2002, A1.

## Tucker, James Guy, Jr. (1943– )

Governor of Arkansas (1992–1996), implicated along with his predecessor, President Bill Clinton, in the Whitewater affair, for which Tucker was found guilty of bank fraud. Although he rose to serve in some of the highest offices in Arkansas, Tucker was born in Oklahoma City, Oklahoma, on 13 June 1943. However, he moved with his family to Little Rock, Arkansas, as a youngster and attended the public schools of that city. He earned his bachelor's degree from Harvard University in 1964 and his law degree from the University of Arkansas at Fayetteville four years later. In 1964 Tucker volunteered for service in the U.S. Marine Corps Reserve, and served for two tours (1965, 1967) as a free-lance reporter in Vietnam. After finishing these stints, Tucker returned to Little Rock, where in1968 he was admitted to the Arkansas bar. He opened a practice in Little Rock.

Two years after opening his practice, Tucker left to run for the office of prosecuting attorney of the Sixth Judicial District of Arkansas, which he served in from 1971 to 1972. He left that office to run for Arkansas state attorney general. Elected, he served a single term (1973–1977). At that same time, he served as a member of the Arkansas Criminal Code Revision Commission.

In 1976 Tucker was elected to a seat in the U.S. House of Representatives. He only served a single two-year term, declining to run for re-election in 1978, to run instead for a seat in the U.S. Senate. Unsuccessful in that race, he found himself out of politics for the first time in nearly a decade and returned to his law practice. Tucker remained in Little Rock for the entire decade of the 1980s. In 1990 he was selected by the Democrats as their candidate for lieutenant governor. Lieutenant Governor Winston Bryant was stepping down from his position to become a candidate for state attorney general. Bryant had served in the state's second executive position since 1981 under two different governors—William Jefferson "Bill" Clinton, and Frank D. White. Tucker was elected because of the popularity of Clinton, the longest-serving governor of the state. Tucker's two years as lieutenant governor were undistinguished. In 1993, after Clinton left Arkansas to serve as the forty-second president of the United States, Tucker was elevated to become the forty-fifth governor of Arkansas. A special election was held to select Tucker's successor as lieutenant governor, and Republican Mike Huckabee won, making him the highest-ranking Republican in the state.

Tucker would have remained the governor of a small state, barely noticed on the national stage, but for his association with Clinton, whose national administration was racked from its start with scandal and allegations of scandal. The first large affair that struck the administration was Whitewater, a land scheme gone wrong in Arkansas that was financed with money from failing savings and loan institutions. Prosecutors in the Whitewater scandal later accused Tucker of meeting in 1985 with Clinton friend James McDougal, head of the Madison Guaranty Savings &

Loan, and David Hale, head of the Arkansas Small Business Administration (SBA), and scheming to defraud the U.S. government of $3 million through an illegal loan that was procured from the SBA for Susan McDougal, some of which ending up in the Whitewater land deal (which was run by McDougal and his wife, Susan, and Bill and Hillary Clinton), some in Tucker's pocket, and some in Clinton's reelection campaign. In 1993 federal investigators looking into why McDougal's savings & loan bank failed discovered the illegal loan, and charged Hale. He plea-bargained a lesser sentence in exchange for testifying against Tucker, the McDougals, and Clinton (who was never charged), and implicated the president and Tucker in illegalities. On 17 August 1995, Tucker and both McDougals were indicted by a Little Rock grand jury on numerous counts alleging that they conspired to defraud the savings & loan, and thus the government. The conspiracy charge against Susan McDougal was later dismissed. Their trial began in Little Rock on 4 March 1996. Hale testified against the three defendants, and President Clinton likewise testified, via videotaped statement, for the defendants. On 28 May 1996, all three were convicted, Tucker being found guilty on all counts. On 15 July 1996, following the refusal of the judge overseeing the case to set aside the verdict, Tucker resigned as governor, and Lieutenant Governor Mike Huckabee became governor of Arkansas. At the time, Tucker pleaded to have his sentencing put off, as he was diagnosed with liver failure and said he needed a transplant. This operation occurred later in 1996. Because of his medical condition, Tucker was eventually sentenced to eighteen months' home detention. However, when prosecutors pushed in 1998 to have him sentenced to prison, Tucker agreed on 20 February 1998 to plead guilty to charges of defrauding the government. In exchange for not having to go to prison, he appeared before the Whitewater grand jury and cooperated in the investigation against Clinton. Because Clinton was never formally charged with Whitewater crimes, Tucker became the highest-ranking public official to be tried in the scandal.

**See also** Clinton, William Jefferson; Whitewater

**References:** Haddigan, Michael, "Tucker Sentenced to 4 Years' Probation," *Washington Post*, 20 August 1996, A1; "James Guy Tucker, Jr.," in Timothy P. Donovan, Willard B. Gatewood, Jr., and Jeannie M. Whayne, eds. , *The Governors of Arkansas: Essays in Political Biography* (Fayetteville, AR: University of Arkansas Press, 1995), 284–287.

## Turner, George (1750?–1843)

Territorial judge (1789-97/8), whose corruption in his office led to the first serious impeachment inquiry in the U.S. House of Representatives under the new U.S. Constitution. According to Charles Lanman, whose work on the U.S. government remains, more than 120 years after its publication, a major source on the early history of the country, Turner was "born in England in 1750; joined the Revolutionary Army at the breaking out of the war; was a Captain, and commanded in South Carolina; was commissioned, by his personal friend, President Washington, Judge of the Northwest Territory in 1789." Despite his being born in England, the *Oxford Dictionary of National Biography* has no information on Turner. Francis Heitman, compiler of a 1914 work on those who fought for the Continental Army in the American Revolution, noted that Turner served as a second lieutenant in the 1st South Carolina and as a first lieutenant in the same unit. Taken prisoner at Charleston, South Carolina, by the British on 12 May 1780, he was exchanged on an unknown date and served for the remainder of the war as a brevet-major.

The few sources on Turner that exist portray that he was a close friend of General, and later President, George Washington. A history of the state of Ohio noted in 1905 that "President George Washington, in a message to the Senate of the United States, bearing the date of New York, August 18, 1789, nominated to be judges of the Northwest Territory 'in accordance with the law re-establishing the government of the Northwest Territory,' Samuel Holden Parsons, John Cleves Symmes, and William Barton." Barton declined the appointment, and on 8 September 1789 the Senate confirmed Washington's second choice for the seat, George Turner, as an associate justice of the court of the Northwest Territory.

On 5 May 1796, the citizens of St. Clair County in the Northwest Territory sent a petition to the U.S. House of Representatives asking for an investigation into the activities of Turner as a judge. Attorney General Charles Lee examined the letter and its allegations, then wrote to the House four days later explaining the way forward to investigate Turner and the charges against him:

"The Attorney General, in obedience to their resolution bearing date the 5th of this month, referring to him the petition of sundry inhabitants of the county of St. Clair, in the Territory northwest of the river Ohio, relative to the conduct of George Turner, one of the judges of the supreme court of that Territory, most respectfully reports:

That the charges exhibited in the petition against Judge Turner, and especially the first, second, and fifth, are of so serious a nature as to require that a regular and fair examination into the truth of them should be made, in some judicial course of proceeding; and if he be convicted thereof, a removal from office may and ought to be a part of the punishment.

His official tenure is during good behavior: and, consequently, he cannot be removed until he be lawfully convicted of some malversation in office. A judge may be prosecuted in three modes, for official misdemeanors or crimes: by information, or by indictment before an ordinary court, or by impeachment before the Senate of the United States. The last mode, being the most solemn, seems, in general cases, to be best suited to the trial of so high and important an officer; but, in the present instance, it will be found very inconvenient, if not entirely impracticable, on account of the immense distance of the residence of the witnesses from this city. In the prosecution of an impeachment, such rules must be observed as are essential to justice; and, if not exactly the same as those which are practised [sic] in ordinary courts, they must be analogous, and as nearly similar to them as forms will permit."

Lee then presented the petition which outlined the charges alleged against Turner:

"To the Honorable House of Representatives of the United States, in Congress assembled: the humble petition of the inhabitants of the county of St. Clair, in the Territory northwest of the Ohio, humbly showeth:

First, by holding a court unknown to and contrary to the laws of this Territory, and at the extremity of the population of the county, and compelling a great number of the good people of this county to attend thereat, as well suitors as jurors and civil officers of the county, thereby absenting themselves from their abodes, and exposing many families to the ravages of the hostile Indians, and to the great loss and damage of the good people by heavy charges that attended the majority travelling [sic] sixty-six miles to attend that court.

By heavy fines set and levied by the said court; by forfeitures incurred of the property of citizens quietly travelling [sic] on the Ohio; and the people grieved in various other ways,

by suits and prosecutions in the same court, attended with very heavy charges.

By compelling the register to transport the office to the extremity of the population of the county, thereby rendering it unsafe, as well as inconvenient for the people to have recourse to the office.

By denying us, as we conceive, the rights reserved to us by the constitution of the Territory, to wit, the laws and customs heretofore used in regard to the descent and conveyance of property, in which the French and Canadian inhabitants conceive the language as essential.

By taking possession of intestate estates, converting part thereof into ready money, to the great damage of the heirs and creditors, and carrying the same money away with him; the remaining goods left in a loose manner, without any account whatever to satisfy those who have claims.

We therefore pray that your honorable House will take into consideration the injuries we have sustained by the conduct of the honorable George Turner, in this county, and provide us such remedy as you, in your wisdom, may judge expedient; and we shall, as in duty bound, ever pray."

In short, Turner had ruled like a dictator rather than as a judge. He refused to hold court in towns where he had been ordered to by Governor Arthur St. Clair; he held court in places where citizens traveling to them could be attacked by Indians; he had imposed unreasonable fees upon those in his court; and he had used his office to convert intestate estates (those without a will) into his own personal fortune.

Initially, the charges were met with silence in the House: after all, never before had they been asked to act on corruption allegations against a sitting judge under the new U.S. Constitution. They turned the case over to Attorney General Lee, who reported back to the

House that that body should open a formal investigation and hold hearings. The members of the House referred to the matter to a select committee, where it sat for months. No records exist showing that any additional hearings were held; the only notation in the official record shows that on 16 February 1796 Speaker of the House Jonathan Dayton announced that Turner had come to Philadelphia, the then-national capital, to defend himself against the allegations. The House, however, refused to hear Turner's defense. Before the end of February 1796, the House select committee published its report, in which it passed on a federal impeachment and instead opted for a state trial in the Northwest Territory territorial court. Lee had told the House that President Washington had ordered Governor St. Clair to arrest Turner and try him in the territorial court, so the House in effect did nothing of substance and punted the ball to another venue.

What follows is mired in mystery: the history of Ohio notes that "Judge Turner, who had served the territory with distinguished zeal since his appointment... resigned in the winter of 1797-8." Turner's whereabouts for the next 30 years remain a mystery; in 1833, he returned to Philadelphia, where he remained until his death on 16 March 1843.

**References**: Lanman, Charles, *Biographical Annals of the Civil Government of the United States. From Original and Official Sources* (New York: J.M. Morrison, Publisher, 1887), 509; Heitman, Francis B., *Historical Register of Officers of the Continental Army During the War of the Revolution, April 1775, to December, 1783* (Washington, D.C.: The Rare Book Shop Publishing Company, Inc., 1914), 551; *The Biographical Annals of Ohio, 1904-1905. A Handbook of the Government and Institutions of the State of Ohio. Compiled under Authority of the Act of April 19, 1904* (Springfield, Ohio: The Springfield Publishing Company, State Printers, 1905), 144, 662; Turner's appointment in U. S. Congress, Senate, *Journal of the Executive Proceedings of the Senate of the United States of America*" (Washington: Duff Green, 1828), I:25; Carter, Clarence Edwin, ed., *The Territorial Papers of the United States* (Washington, D.C.: Government Printing Office, 1934), II:452, 511-18; III:406-07; for the letter of Charles Lee and the petition against Turner, see *American State Papers. Documents, Legislative and Executive, of the Congress of the United States, from the First Session of the First to the Second Session of the Tenth Congress, Inclusive: Commencing March 3, 1789, and Ending March 3, 1809. Selected and Edited, Under the Authority of Congress, by Walter Lowrie, Secretary of the Senate, and Walter S. Franklin, Clerk of the House of Representatives* (Washington, D. C.: Published by Gales and Seaton; two volumes, 1834), I:151-52; Turner's resignation noted in U.S. Congress, Senate, *Journal of the Executive Proceedings of the Senate of the United States of America* (Washington: Duff Green, 1828), I:261.

## Tweed, William Magear (1823–1878)

New York alderman and powerful politician, indicted and sent to prison for massive corruption, where he died. Born in New York City on 23 April 1823, he was the son of Richard Tweed and Eliza (née Magear) Tweed. Many historians have cited Tweed's middle name as "Marcy," apparently after William Learned Marcy, a Jacksonian Democrat who was elected governor of New York in 1830. But Marcy was unknown when William Tweed was born, and it is biographer Leo Hershkowitz who writes that Tweed's middle name is in fact Magear, his mother's maiden name. He was born at his family's residence of 1 Cherry Street, which has since been demolished to make way for the entrance to the Brooklyn Bridge. Tweed did not attend school for long—he left at age eleven to go to work for his father learning the chair-making trade. Later, he was apprenticed to a saddler and for a time studied bookkeeping and served as a clerk in a mercantile office in New York City. He also became a fireman, joining a volunteer company, Engine Company No. 12, when he was invited by the local assemblyman, John J. Reilly, to firm a new company, No. 6, in 1848. Tweed became the foreman of the company the following year, and it was through this association that he became involved in local municipal politics.

In 1852 Tweed, while running his father's chair-making company, ran for the post of New York City alderman. He was elected and served until 1853. In 1852, as well, he ran as a Democrat for a seat in the U.S. House of Representatives, winning the election and taking his seat in the Thirty-third Congress. However, when he stood for reelection, Tweed was defeated. In 1856 he was appointed to the Board of Education, serving as schools commissioner from 1856 to 1857; that same year, he was elected to the board of supervisors for New York County. By 1858 he had become one of the leading politicians in New York City. Despite this, he was defeated as a candidate for sheriff in 1861.

Starting in 1861, Tweed began to hold a series of positions that took him to the pinnacle of power in the city. Elected deputy street commissioner, serving until 1870, he garnered power by attracting the votes of Catholics and immigrants in his ward. Although he had never studied the law, Tweed was certified by a friend as an attorney and opened a law office at 95 Duane Street in 1860. He was named chairman of the Democratic General Committee of New York County, and, on 1 January 1864 was selected to lead Tammany Hall, the Democratic political machine in the city. When he was named as grand sachem, or leader of Tammany, that April, he earned the nickname "Boss" Tweed.

Over the next decade, Tweed used his position to build a power base that was a first in American politics. Having been influenced by the dictatorial control of New York City Mayor

Fernando Wood, Tweed assembled a group of men in control to rob the city of its wealth. Using the power of Mayor Abraham Oakey Hall, Comptroller Richard B. Connolly, and chief of the Department of Public Works Peter B. Sweeny, Tweed was able to siphon millions of dollars from city coffers. Tweed also controlled the votes of six Democrats on the Board of Supervisors and paid one of the six opposing Republicans, Peter Voorhis, to stay away from the meetings so he could have a majority of the votes. Judges were bought: one, Albert Cardozo, was the father of future Supreme Court Justice Benjamin Cardozo. Another, George G. Barnard, was a former pimp who slept through the trials he was hearing. (Barnard was later the subject of impeachment inquiries in New York State.)

Tweed used every avenue to bleed the city's budget. Historian Robert Jay Nash explained:

William M. Tweed (Library of Congress, Prints & Photographs Division, LC-USZ62-22467)

To control the elections of the late 1860s, Tweed and his fellows took over the naturalization of immigrants who made up almost half of New York's population. Tammany members sold naturalization papers to those who would vote the Tammany ticket. These papers were genuine and issued by Tweed's controlled courts. A man named Rosenberg sold thousands of these papers to immigrants before being arrested by U.S. Marshal Robert Murray, who posed as a foreigner without papers. Said Rosenberg before he was promptly set free by Tweed's hirelings: "Mr. Murray, every certificate that you have purchased from me is genuine, and came out of the courtroom. I am at work for the democratic [sic] party, and paid for this thing[;] I get but very little of the $2 that is paid for these certificates."

The corruption reached new levels in the 1870s. After being named by Tammany to be the commissioner of public works, Tweed pushed for the building of City Hall Park and was paid through back channels; he also purchased benches for $5 each and resold them to the city for $600 each. Tweed controlled all aspects of New York City life for the better part of a decade. It was not until *Harper's Weekly* and the *New York Times* started investigating the city's finances that the massive corruption was uncovered, albeit slowly. On 21 July 1870, the *New York Times* reported on its front page that cronies of Tweed's were being paid massive sums to do ordinary work—for instance, one George Miller, a carpenter with ties to Tweed, was paid more than $360,000 a month for his labor. The governor of New York, Samuel Tilden, and the state attorney general, Charles Fairchild, opened up investigations. Fairchild, figuring Tweed to be a low man on the totem pole, called him in and offered him freedom in exchange for his testimony. Tweed told Fairchild the whole story, but implicated himself as the leader of the crooked gang. Fairchild then backed off his deal and instead charged Tweed, using the evidence Tweed himself had supplied to indict him. Tweed was arrested and his bail set at $6 million, an incredible sum in those days. Using backdoor accounts, Tweed sent his entire family into exile in Europe.

Day after day, Tweed was pilloried in the press—noted journalist/artist Thomas Nast drew Tweed in his popular cartoon as a buffoon, and even drew him with a moneybag for a face. Tweed knew the impact these pictures would have on his case. He told the editor of *Harper's*, "I don't care a straw for your newspaper articles, my constituents don't know how to read, but they can't help seeing them damned pictures." Tweed approached Nast and offered him a bribe of $500,000—far more than his $5,000 annual salary—to stop drawing his cartoons, but Nast refused.

In 1874 Tweed was put on trial and convicted of embezzlement, although the prosecutors did not fully divulge to the jury the vulgar amounts that were stolen. Tweed was sentenced to eight years in prison, and served his time in the New York City prison called "The Tombs." However, in December 1875, he managed to bribe a guard and escaped, catching a ship to Spain. He would have made good his flight but he was recognized in Europe due to Nast's cartoons. Captured, he was sent back on a U.S. man-of-war, and again confined in the Ludlow Street jail. Less than a year and a half after he was returned to America, Tweed, in rapidly declining health, died in prison on 12 April 1878, eleven days shy of his fifty-fifth birthday.

In the years since his death, Tweed has become known as perhaps the greatest single instance of political corruption in American history. Few positive assessments, if any could be found, have ever been published on his reign of financial terror over New York City. Because of his pudgy and scraggly appearance, the cartoons of Thomas Nast, and his seeming lack of remorse for his thievery, Tweed continues to earn popular derision more than a century after his death. Historians even continue to get his middle name wrong.

**References:**Allen, Oliver E., *The Tiger: The Rise and Fall of Tammany Hall* (Reading, MA: Addison-Wesley, 1993); Hershkowitz, Leo, *Tweed's New York: Another Look* (Garden City, NY: Anchor Press-Doubleday, 1977), 5; Lynch, Denis Tilden, *'Boss' Tweed: The Story of a Grim Generation*" (New York: Boni and Liveright, 1927); Roger A. Fischer, *Them Damned Pictures: Explorations in American Cartoon Art* (North Haven, CT: Archon Books, 1996); Share, Allen J., "Tweed, William M(agear) 'Boss,'" Brown, Mary Elizabeth, "Tweed Courthouse," and Mushkat, Jerome, "Tweed Ring," in Kenneth T. Jackson, ed., *The Encyclopedia of New York City* (New Haven: Yale University Press, 1995), 1205–1207; "Tweed, William Marcy," in *The National Cyclopaedia of American Biography*, 57 vols. and supplements A-N (New York: James T. White & Company, 1897–1984), III:389; "Tweed, William Marcy," in Jay Robert Nash, *Encyclopedia of World Crime: Criminal Justice, Criminology, and Law Enforcement*, 4 vols. (Wilmette, IL: CrimeBooks, Inc., 1989), IV:3007–3009.

*James N. Tyner (Library of Congress, Prints & Photographs Division, LC-DIG-cwpbh-04729)*

## Tyner, James Noble (1826–1904)

United States representative (1869–1875), postmaster general in the administration of Ulysses S. Grant (1876–1877), charged but acquitted of massive corruption in the Post Office Department. Tyner was born in the town of Brookville, Indiana, on 17 January 1826 (although the date had been also reported as 7 January 1826), the son of Richard Tyner, a merchant and dry goods store owner. James Tyner studied at local academies before graduating from the Brookville Academy in 1844. He entered private business, working for his father and spending ten years accumulating some wealth, before he studied law and was admitted to the Indiana bar in 1857. He opened a practice in the town of Peru, Indiana.

While studying for the bar, Tyner ran for a seat as a representative in the Indiana General Assembly, representing Miami County, but he was defeated. However, soon after he was admitted to the bar, he was elected secretary of the Indiana state senate, where he served until 1861. He left that position to become a special agent for the United States Post Office Department, starting a career in that government department that would last for most of his life. Five years after starting work there he resigned to return to the practice of law. However, his law practice period was short. In 1868, Tyner decided to reenter the political field. Republican Daniel D. Pratt had been elected to a seat in the U.S. House of Representatives, but when a U.S. Senate seat had opened he was advanced to that position, opening the House seat. Tyner ran as a Republican to fill the vacancy, and was elected in early 1869, taking his seat in the Forty-first Congress. In the House from 4 March 1869 to 3 March 1875, Tyner, as a former member of the U.S. Post Office Department, served as a member of the House Committee on Post Offices and Post Roads. In the Forty-third Congress, the committee's chairman, Representative James A. Garfield, selected Tyner to oversee all congressional activity relating to the appropriations for the Post Office Department. In February 1875 President Ulysses S. Grant named Tyner second assistant postmaster general, making the Indiana Republican the third most powerful man inside the Post Office Department. During his tenure in that office, from 26 February 1875 until 12 July 1876, Tyner was put in charge of the department's contract system with local postmasters.

On 11 July 1876, President Grant fired Postmaster General Marshall Jewell—historians believe that Jewell's investigations into massive corruption by Republican postmasters nationwide caused pressure on Grant to remove him. The following day, Tyner was named as Jewell's replacement. Despite having served under Grant and being named to the department's top position by Grant, Tyner was a close political ally of Ohio Governor Rutherford B. Hayes, who was being pushed by many in his party to challenge Grant's attempts at a third presidential nomination in 1876. Numerous scandals during the eight years of Grant's presidency, including the Whiskey Ring frauds, the Indian Ring frauds, the Sanborn Contract scandal, among others, led many Republicans to become disillusioned with Grant. Tyner secretly worked behind the scenes to aid Hayes, and was rewarded when the Ohioan received the presidential nomination of the party and was elected in a close election. Despite being demoted by Hayes to first assistant postmaster general to make way for a Democrat, David M. Key, Tyner was given control of the day-to-day activities of the department. Many historians believe that it was during this period that Tyner abetted corruption, and may have even been involved in it.

In October 1881, when the massive corruption of the Star Route frauds came to light, Tyner claimed that he had informed Postmaster General Keys in 1878, and then Postmaster

General Thomas L. James in 1879, but was ignored. This half-baked story was believed by no one, and the constant press attention forced Tyner to resign. The *New York Times* dubbed his story "Mr. Tyner's Lame Defense," and editorialized, "Mr. Tyner, by his report of August 1879, shows that he was cognizant of the fraudulent methods being practiced in connection with the postal service, and yet, in February 1880, when the frauds were being exposed in Congress, Mr. Tyner was daily on the floor of the House exerting his influence, to shield [those accused in the frauds] and to secure the passage of a deficiency appropriation of nearly $2,000,000 to continue to perpetuate frauds. It is singular that Mr. Tyner did not produce his report at that time, and thus save the Treasury from further plunder."

Despite this accusation, Tyner was never charged with a crime. And having helped Hayes gain the nomination in 1876, he remained a powerful force in Republican politics. In 1888, when Senator Benjamin Harrison of Indiana was elected president, Tyner was rewarded once again, being named assistant attorney general for the Post Office Department. Again, Tyner allegedly set out and used his position to collect bribes and to look away while corruption went on unabated. He remained in the administration until Harrison left office in 1893. However, in 1896, when Republican William McKinley was elected president, again Tyner was rewarded with the assistant attorney general position and he spend five more years profiting from his position. Finally, in 1902, after years and years of corruption, allegations arose as to his deeds. President Theodore Roosevelt named Fourth Assistant Postmaster General Joseph L. Bristow to investigate. Bristow concluded that Tyner had been taking bribes and kickbacks for much of his tenure. When word leaked what Bristow had concluded as to Tyner's guilt, the seventy-six-year-old Tyner sent his wife and sister-in-law to his Post Office Department office to retrieve and destroy vital documents and other papers. Tyner was indicted nonetheless, but without the key evidence he was acquitted. He then quietly resigned, his three-decade career of graft and corruption put to an end.

Just two years after he was acquitted, on 5 December 1904, Tyner died in Washington, D.C., at the age of seventy-eight, and was buried in that city's Oak Hill Cemetery. Despite his lengthy career of corruption, one of the longest in American history, his name remains unknown today.

**References:** Fowler, Dorothy Ganfield, *The Cabinet Politician: The Postmasters General, 1829–1909* (New York: Columbia University Press, 1943), 156; "James N. Tyner Dead. Was a Member of President Grant's Cabinet. Years in the Service. Was Recently Before the Court on Charges and Was Acquitted by Jury," *Evening Star* (Washington, DC), 5 December 1904, 8; "Mr. Tyner's Lame Defense. His Unavailing Efforts to Retain Office," *New York Times*, 24 October 1881, 1; "Mr. Tyner's Pet Star Route. Costly Postal Service for his Personal Benefit," *New York Times*, 25 October 1881, 1; "Tyner, James Noble," in *The National Cyclopaedia of American Biography*, 57 vols. and supplements A-N (New York: James T. White & Company, 1897–1984), IV:20; Tyner to Chandler, 1 November 1876, in file "Correspondence 1876," *Zachariah Chandler Papers*, Library of Congress.

# U

## United States v. Bramblett, 348 U.S. 503 (1955)

United States Supreme Court decision that "the Disbursing Office of the House of Representatives is a 'department or agency' of the United States within the meaning of 18 U.S.C. 1001, which forbids the willful falsification of a material fact 'in any matter within the jurisdiction of any department or agency of the United States.'" Bramblett, a former Congressman, was found guilty after telling the House Disbursing Office, which pays salaries of House workers, that a particular person known to Bramblett was serving as his clerk, when in fact the person had no official duties in the House. Bramblett was convicted of violating 18 U.S.C. § 1001, which states that "Whoever, in any matter within the jurisdiction of any department or agency of the United States knowingly and willfully falsifies, conceals or covers up by any trick, scheme, or device a material fact, or makes any false, fictitious or fraudulent statements or representations, or makes or uses any false writing or document knowing the same to contain any false, fictitious or fraudulent statement or entry, shall be fined not more than $10,000 or imprisoned not more than five years, or both." Of the eighteen original charges against Bramblett, a trial judgment of acquittal was entered in counts eight to eighteen, and the jury returned with guilty verdicts on the remaining seven counts. The court then granted the defendant's motion that the verdict be arrested, because he claimed that he had not falsified a material fact "within the jurisdiction of any department or agency of the United States," and that the Disbursing Office was not such an office within the meaning of the statute. The United States appealed, and the U.S. Supreme Court granted certiorari (the right to hear the case). Arguments were heard on 7 February 1955.

On 4 April of that same year, Justice Stanley Reed spoke for a six-to-zero majority (Chief Justice Earl Warren, and Associate Justices Harold Burton and John Marshall Harlan did not participate) in holding that the Disbursing Office of the House *was* a "department or agency" of the United States government within the meaning of the relevant statute, 18 U.S.C. § 1001. As Justice Reed explained:

It might be argued that the matter here involved was within the jurisdiction of the Treasury Department, as the appellee's misstatements would require the payment of funds from the United States Treasury. Or, viewing this as a matter within the jurisdiction of the Disbursing Office, it might be argued, as the Government does, that that body is an "authority" within the definition of "agency." We do not rest our decision on either of those interpretations. The context in which this language is used calls for an unrestricted interpretation. This is enforced by its legislative history. It would do violence to the purpose of Congress to limit the section to falsifications made to the executive departments. Congress could not have intended to leave frauds such as this without penalty. The development, scope and purpose of the section shows that "department," as used in this context, was meant to describe the executive, legislative and judicial branches of the Government.

In 1995 the U.S. Supreme Court overruled *Bramblett*, holding it to be a "seriously flawed decision," in the case *Hubbard v. United States*.

> **References:** *Hubbard v. United States*, 514 U.S. 695, 115 S. Ct. 1754 [1995]).

## United States v. Brewster, 408 U.S. 501 (1972)

United States Supreme Court decision holding that the Speech or Debate Clause of the U.S. Constitution does not preclude an inquiry into the alleged conduct of a congressman or a senator apart from his or her actions as a member of Congress. Senator Daniel Brewster (D-MD) was charged with the solicitation and acceptance of bribes in violation of 18 U.S.C. §§ 201(c)(1) and 201(g) (the latter now 18 U.S.C. § 201(c)(1)(B)), which read:

> (c) Whoever (1) otherwise than as provided by law for the proper discharge of official duty (A) directly or indirectly gives, offers, or promises anything of value to any public official, former public official, or person selected to be a public official, for or because of any official act performed or to be performed by such public official, former public official, or person selected to be a public official; or (B) being a public official, former public official, or person selected to be a public official, otherwise than as provided by law for the proper discharge of official duty, directly or indirectly demands, seeks, receives, accepts, or agrees to receive or accept anything of value personally for or because of any official act performed or to be performed by such official or person shall be fined or imprisoned for not more than two years.

Brewster lost his reelection bid in 1968 and in 1969 was indicted on ten counts alleging that, while sitting as a member of the Senate Committee on Post Office and Civil Service, he "directly and indirectly, corruptly asked, solicited, sought, accepted, received and agreed to receive [sums] … in return for being influenced in his performance of official acts in respect to his action, vote, and decision on postage rate legislation which might at any time be pending before him in his official capacity." When the case got to trial, the district court judge threw out five of the counts, holding that they related to the acceptance of bribes in connection with the performance of a legislative function by a senator of the United States, which was protected under the Speech and Debate Clause of the U.S. Constitution. The prosecutor appealed directly to the U.S. Supreme Court; the Court agreed to hear the case, and it was argued—first on 18 October 1971, and again on 20 March 1972.

On 29 June 1972, the Court held six to three that the inquiry into taking bribes in contravention of the law was not protected by the Speech and Debate Clause, and reinstated the five counts that had been dismissed. Holding for the majority, Chief Justice Warren Burger (Justices William O. Douglas, Byron White, and William Brennan dissented) held that bribes were not part of the "performance of a legislative function," and thus inquiry into them were not shielded by the Speech and Debate Clause. Chief Justice Burger explained:

The question is whether it is necessary to inquire into how appellee spoke, how he debated, how he voted, or anything he did in the chamber or in committee in order to make out a violation of this statute. The illegal conduct is taking or agreeing to take money for a promise to act in a certain way. There is no need for the Government to show that appellee fulfilled the alleged illegal bargain; acceptance of the bribe is the violation of the statute, not performance of the illegal promise....

Taking a bribe is, obviously, no part of the legislative process or function; it is not a legislative act. It is not, by any conceivable interpretation, an act performed as a part of or even incidental to the role of a legislator. It is not an "act resulting from the nature, and in the execution, of the office." Nor is it a "thing said or done by him, as a representative, in the exercise of the functions of that office," .... Nor is inquiry into a legislative act or the motivation for a legislative act necessary to a prosecution under this statute or this indictment. When a bribe is taken, it does not matter whether the promise for which the bribe was given was for the performance of a legislative act as here or, as in *Johnson*, for use of a Congressman's influence with the Executive Branch. And an inquiry into the purpose of a bribe "does not draw in question the legislative acts of the defendant member of Congress or his motives for performing them....

Nor does it matter if the Member defaults on his illegal bargain. To make a prima facie case under this indictment, the Government need not show any act of appellee subsequent to the corrupt promise for payment, for it is taking the bribe, not performance of the illicit compact, that is a criminal act. If, for example, there were undisputed evidence that a Member took a bribe in exchange for an agreement to vote for a given bill and if there were also undisputed evidence that he, in fact, voted against the bill, can it be thought that this alters the nature of the bribery or removes it from the area of wrongdoing the Congress sought to make a crime?

With these counts restored, and, having been convicted of the other five counts (which had been reversed), in 1975 Brewster pled guilty to a charge of accepting an illegal gratuity while a United States senator, and served a short prison term.

**See also** Speech and Debate Clause of the U.S. Constitution

**References:** "Former Senator Brewster Charged With Bribery," *News and Observer* (Raleigh, NC), 2 December 1969, 1.

## United States v. Gillock, 445 U.S. 360 (1980)

United States Supreme Court decision that upheld the right of a court to allow the introduction of evidence involving a legislator's legislative career in cases dealing with political corruption. Although not a corruption case per se, the determination nevertheless allowed a widening of latitude in such cases.

Tennessee State Senator Edgar H. Gillock was indicted on 12 August 1976 in the federal District Court for the Western District of Tennessee on five counts of "obtaining money under the color of official right ... one count of using an interstate facility to distribute a bribe ... and one count of participating in an enterprise through a pattern of racketeering activity." The indictment charged Gillock, who was also a practicing attorney, "with accepting money as a fee for using his public office to block the extradition of a defendant from Tennessee to Illinois, and for agreeing to introduce in the State General Assembly legislation which would enable four persons to obtain master electricians' licenses they had been unable to obtain by way of existing examination processes." Before the trial, Gillock asked that the court suppress all evidence relating to his legislative activities under a privilege granted by Rule 501 of the Federal Rules of Evidence, which prohibits courts from allowing the introduction of evidence of one's legislative acts or "underlying motivations." The district court, in granting the motion, held that the ban on such evidence was necessary "to protect the integrity of the [state's] legislative process by insuring the independence of individual legislators" and "to preserve the constitutional relation between our federal and state governments in our federal system." The prosecution appealed, and the ruling was struck down by the United States Court of Appeals for the Sixth Circuit, which vacated the order and remanded back to the district court for additional consideration. (See 559 F.2d 1222 (1977).) In a hearing before the district court judge, the government explained that it intended to use evidence of Gillock's legislative activities to prove that he had violated his office to obtain a bribe and fees for introducing certain legislation. After the hearing, the district court again suppressed this evidence. Again, the government appealed to the Court of Appeals for the Sixth Circuit. In a divided decision, the court upheld the suppression, holding that "the long history and the felt need for protection of legislative speech or debate and the repeated and strong recognition of that history in the cases ... from the Supreme Court, fully justify our affirming [the District Court] in [its] protection of the privilege in this case." (See 587 F.2d 284, 290 (1978).) The government then appealed to the U.S. Supreme Court, which granted certiorari (the right to hear the case). As Chief Justice Warren Burger wrote, "We granted certiorari [in this case] to resolve a conflict in the Circuits over whether the federal courts in a federal criminal prosecution ... should recognize a legislative privilege barring the introduction of evidence of the legislative acts of a state legislator charged with taking bribes or otherwise obtaining money unlawfully through exploitation of his official position."

Arguments were heard on 4 December 1979.

On 19 March 1980 the Court handed down its decision. Speaking for a seven-to-two majority, Chief Justice Burger held that "in the absence of a constitutional limitation on the power of Congress to make state officials, like all other persons, subject to federal criminal sanctions, we discern no basis in these circumstances for a judicially created limitation that handicaps proof of the relevant facts." Finding on the grounds that Congress did not intend for such legislative immunity to be extended to state officials, the Court ordered that evidence of Gillock's legislative activities may be allowed. "We conclude, therefore, that although principles of comity command careful consideration, our cases disclose that where important federal interests are at stake, as in the enforcement of federal criminal statutes, comity yields," Burger went on:

> We recognize that denial of a privilege to a state legislator may have some minimal impact on the exercise of his legislative function; however, similar arguments made to support a claim of executive privilege were found wanting in *United States v. Nixon*, 418 U.S. 683 (1974), when balanced against the need of enforcing federal criminal statutes. There, the genuine risk of inhibiting candor in the internal exchanges at the highest levels of the Executive Branch was held insufficient to justify denying judicial power to secure all relevant evidence in a criminal proceeding. See also *United States v. Burr*, 25 F. Cas. 187 (No. 14,694). Here, we believe that recognition of an evidentiary privilege for state legislators for their legislative acts would impair the legitimate interest of the Federal Government in enforcing its criminal statutes with only speculative benefit to the state legislative process.

**References:** Text of *United States v. Gillock*, 445 U.S. 360 (1980).

## United States v. Helstoski, 442 U.S. 477 (1979)

United States Supreme Court decision holding that the legislative actions of a congressperson that are evidence of political corruption are inadmissible in a court of law. Representative Henry Helstoski (1925–1999) served in the U.S. House of Representatives (1965–1977) as a representative from New Jersey. In 1974 the Department of Justice began investigating reports of political corruption involving Helstoski, including allegations that aliens had paid him for the introduction and processing of private bills that would suspend the application of the immigration laws so as to allow them to remain in the United States. In June 1976 a grand jury returned a twelve-count indictment charging Helstoski and others with numerous criminal acts, including "accepting money in return for Helstoski's 'being influenced in the performance of official acts, to wit: the introduction of private bills in the United States House of Representatives.'" During the grand jury proceedings, Helstoski refused to produce documents that dealt with the controversy, citing the so-called Speech or Debate Clause of the U.S. Constitution. This provision, in Article 1, Section 6, says that "for any Speech or Debate in either House, they [the Senators and Representatives] shall not be questioned in any other Place." On this subject, the trial court held that "The United States may not, during the presentation of its case-in-chief at the trial of [this] Indictment, introduce evidence of the performance of a past legislative act on the part of the defendant, Henry Helstoski, derived from any source and for any purpose." The prosecution appealed to the United States Court of Appeals for the Third Circuit, which rejected both of the government's arguments: (a) that legislative acts could be introduced to show motive; and (b) that legislative acts could be introduced because Helstoski had waived his privilege by testifying before the grand juries. The court relied on *United States v. Brewster*, 408 U.S. 501 (1972), which prohibited "the introduction of evidence as to how a Congressman acted on, voted on, or resolved a legislative issue," reasoning that "to permit evidence of such acts under the guise of showing motive would negate the protection afforded by the Speech or Debate Clause." The government appealed to the United States Supreme Court. Helstoski also sued Judge Meanor, the district judge, for refusing to allow him to quash the indictment with a writ of manda-

mus. The U.S. Supreme Court heard arguments in both of Helstoski's suits on the same day, 27 March 1979.

The Court handed down its decision on 18 June 1979. In *Helstoski v. Meanor*, the court held that a writ of mandamus was an improper way to get a court to throw evidence out. In *United States v. Helstoski*, Chief Justice Burger spoke for a seven-to-one majority (Justice William Brennan dissented, and Justice Lewis Powell did not participate) in refusing to allow the government to introduce evidence of Helstoski's legislative actions. "The Speech or Debate Clause was designed to preclude prosecution of Members for legislative acts," the Chief Justice wrote. "The Clause protects 'against inquiry into acts that occur in the regular course of the legislative process and into the motivation for those acts' ... It 'precludes any showing of how [a legislator] acted, voted, or decided.'" Chief Justice Burger further explained:

The Clause does not simply state, "No proof of a legislative act shall be offered"; the prohibition of the Clause is far broader. It provides that Members "shall not be questioned in any other Place." Indeed, as MR. JUSTICE STEVENS recognizes, the admission of evidence of legislative acts "may reveal [to the jury] some information about the performance of legislative acts and the legislator's motivation in conducting official duties." ... Revealing information as to a legislative act—speaking or debating—to a jury would subject a Member to being "questioned," in a place other than the House or Senate, thereby violating the explicit prohibition of the Speech or Debate Clause.

**See also** *United States v. Johnson*; *United States v. Brewster*

**References:** *Helstoski v. Meanor*, 442 U.S. 500 (1979), 489.

## United States v. Johnson, 383 U.S. 169 (1966)

United States Supreme Court decision that representatives could not be convicted of political corruption on evidence arising from their legislative activities.

Thomas Francis Johnson, a former United States representative from the state of Maryland, was indicted and convicted on seven counts of violating the federal conflict-of-interest statute (18 U.S.C. § 281) and on one count of conspiring to defraud the United States (18 U.S.C. § 371). On appeal, the United States Court of Appeals for the Fourth Circuit set aside Johnson's conviction on the single conspiracy count, holding that the government's allegation that Johnson had conspired to make a speech for compensation on the floor of the House of Representatives was barred by the so-called Speech and Debate Clause of the U.S. Constitution, which says that "for any Speech or Debate in either House, they [Senators and Representatives] shall not be questioned in any other Place." The court then ordered a new trial on the remaining counts, holding that the evidence brought forth to prove conspiracy had "infected the entire prosecution." The United States appealed this ruling to the United States Supreme Court. Arguments were heard on 10 and 15 November 1965.

On 24 February 1965, Justice John Marshall Harlan spoke for a seven-to-zero majority (Justices Hugo Black and Byron White did not participate) in affirming the lower court's decision. Justice Harlan found, in giving a history of the Speech and Debate clause, that it was a fundamental right of representatives to be free from the 'intrusions' of other branches, namely the judicial branch, when discussing their legislative activities, particularly their speeches. He wrote,

> [T]he Government contends that the Speech or Debate Clause was not violated because the gravamen of the count was the alleged conspiracy, not the speech, and because the defendant, not the prosecution, introduced the speech itself. Whatever room the Constitution may

allow for such factors in the context of a different kind of prosecution, we conclude that they cannot serve to save the Government's case under this conspiracy count. It was undisputed that Johnson delivered the speech; it was likewise undisputed that Johnson received the funds; controversy centered upon questions of who first decided that a speech was desirable, who prepared it, and what Johnson's motives were for making it.'

**See also** Johnson, Thomas Francis; Speech or Debate Clause of the U.S. Constitution; *United States v. Brewster*; *United States v. Helstoski*

## United States v. National Treasury Employees Union
*See* Honoraria

## United States v. Salinas (522 U.S. 52 [1997])

U.S. Supreme Court decision, which held that the federal bribery statute is not limited to a bribe which affected federal funds. Brigido Marmolejo was the sheriff of Hidalgo County, Texas; Mario Salinas was one of his deputies. In 1984, the U.S. Marshal's Service entered into a contract with Hidalgo County in which the county would take federal prisoners and the federal government would pay a specific amount to the county for the prisoners and their upkeep. One of the prisoners, Homero Beltran-Aguirre, paid Marmolejo a series of bribes so that he could have conjugal visits with his wife and girlfriend. Salinas also received cash and gifts (including a pickup truck) in exchange for allowing the visits. Marmolejo and Salinas were both indicted and convicted of receiving bribes; however, the Court only heard Salinas's appeal. Salinas appealed his conviction on the grounds that the bribe had to have affected federal funds by either diverting or misappropriating them before the bribe could violate the relevant U.S. statute. On appeal, the

U.S. Court of Appeals for the Fifth Circuit affirmed the convictions; Salinas appealed to the U.S. Supreme Court. Arguments were heard on 8 October 1997, and a decision was delivered on 2 December 1997.

In a unanimous opinion delivered by Justice Anthony Kennedy, the court held that the federal bribery statute was not limited merely to federal funds, or to cases involving federal funds. "Section 666(a)(1)(B) does not require the Government to prove the bribe in question had a demonstrated effect upon federal funds," Kennedy wrote. "The enactment's plain language is expansive and unqualified, both as to the bribes forbidden and the entities covered, demonstrating by its reference to 'any' business or transaction, § 666(a)(1)(B), that it is not confined to transactions affecting federal funds; by its application to all cases in which an 'organization, government, or agency' receives a specified amount of federal benefits, § 666(b), that it reaches the scheme involved here; and by its prohibition on accepting 'anything of value,' § 666(a)(1)(B), that it encompasses the transfers of personal property to petitioner in exchange for his favorable treatment of Beltran. Given the statute's plain and unambiguous meaning, petitioner is not aided by the legislative history."

**Reference**: Text of opinion at 522 U.S. 52 (1997).

## United States v. Shirey, 359 U.S. 255 (1959)

Supreme Court decision holding that a law that prohibits an "offer or promise … of money or thing of value, to any person, firm or corporation in consideration of the use or promise to use any influence to procure any appointive office or place under the United States for any person" includes political parties as well as people not in a legislative seat under the definition of "person." George Donald Shirey was charged with violating this federal law (18 U.S.C. § 214), when he told Congressman S. Walter Stauffer (R-PA) that he would "donate $1,000 a year to the Republican Party to be used as they see fit" in return for Stauffer's help in getting Shirey appointed postmaster of York, Pennsylvania. Stauffer told the authorities, and Shirey was arrested. In federal district court, Shirey asked that the indictment be quashed on the grounds that he was not a "person" covered by the statute, and that offering $1,000 a year to the Republican Party was not offering a bribe to a "person." The district court agreed, and the U.S. government appealed directly to the United States Supreme Court, which agreed to hear the case. Justice Felix Frankfurter wrote, "One sensible reading is to say that even though the Republican Party was to be the ultimate recipient of the money, this was a promise to Stauffer of money (which it plainly was) in consideration of his use of influence." Arguments were heard on 19 January 1959.

Almost exactly three months later, on 20 April 1959, Justice Frankfurter spoke for a unanimous court in reversing the district court's decision and holding that Shirey and the Republican Party could be considered "persons" under the meaning of 18 U.S.C. § 214. Justice Frankfurter explained:

Applying these generalities to the immediate occasion, it is clear that the terms, the history, and the manifest purpose of 18 U.S.C. 214 coalesce in a construction of that statute which validates the information against Shirey. The evil which Congress sought to check and the mischief wrought by what it proscribed are the same when the transaction is triangular as when only two parties are involved. It is incredible to suppose that Congress meant to prohibit Shirey from giving $1,000 to Stauffer, to be passed on by the latter to the Party fund, but that Shirey was outside the congressional prohibition for securing the same influence by a promise to deposit $1,000 directly in the Party's fund. That is not the kind of finessing by which this Court has heretofore allowed penal legislation to be construed.... the judgment is reversed.

## *United States v. Worrall*, 2 U.S. (2 Dall.) 384 (1798)

Important Pennsylvania district case, one of the first to be heard in the United States regarding bribery of federal and state officials, and how such a crime could be charged under the common law. In 1792, Alexander Hamilton, the secretary of the treasury, appointed Tench Coxe commissioner of revenue, a position in which he collected the taxes and tariffs accrued in the nation as a whole.

In 1794 Congress enacted a law calling for the construction of a lighthouse at Cape Hatteras, North Carolina. Coxe, in his position as commissioner of revenue, was put in charge of soliciting proposals for the project and settling on a builder. On 28 September 1797, he received a letter from one Robert Worrall, who was interested in obtaining the contract to build the lighthouse. In his letter, Worrall wrote that he was the right man for the job and, in his closing line, stated:

> If I should be so happy in your recommendation of this work, I should think myself very ungrateful, if I did not offer you one half of the profits as above stated, and would deposit in your hand at receiving the first payment £ 350, and the other £ 350 at the last payment, when the work is finished and completed [sic]. I hope you will not think me troublesome in asking for a line on the business by your next return and will call for it at the Post-Office, or in Third Street. In the mean time I shall subscribe myself to be, your obedient and very humble servt. [sic] to command.

Worrall was promising Coxe a bribe of some £700 pounds, or $1,866.67 at the time. Although Coxe was in dire financial straits when the letter was received, he presented it to authorities, who arrested Worrall and charged him with trying to bribe a federal officer. Worrall was tried and found guilty of both counts. He appealed to the Circuit Court of Pennsylvania's Third Circuit—sitting as judges were Samuel Chase of the U.S. Supreme Court (on circuit duty) and Judge Richard Peters. Two issues were presented: 1) whether a federal common law of crimes existed that prohibited Worrall's conduct, and 2) whether Congress had lawfully passed a statute making it illegal for a federal officer to accept a bribe. Chase argued that under the Tenth Amendment, the federal government could not assume a power not specifically granted to it by the Constitution. Moreover, even if Congress was permitted to enact the law outlawing bribery to certain named federal officials, the commissioner of revenue was not included, so any bribe to him was not covered by the statute. Peters, however, claimed that political corruption went to the heart of a democracy's well being. He wrote:

> Whenever a government has been established, I have always supposed, that a power to preserve itself, was a necessary, and an inseparable, concomitant. But the existence of the Federal government would be precarious, it could no longer be called an independent government, if, for the punishment of offences of this nature, tending to obstruct and pervert the administration of its affairs, an appeal must be made to the State tribunals, or the offenders must escape with absolute impunity. The power to punish misdemeanors, is originally and strictly a common law power; of which, I think, the United States are constitutionally possessed. It might have been exercised by Congress in the form of a Legislative act; but, it may, also, in my opinion be enforced in a course of Judicial proceeding. Whenever an offence aims at the subversion of any Federal institution, or at the corruption of its public officers, it is an offence against the well-being of the United States; from its very nature, it is cognizable under their authority; and, consequently, it is within the jurisdiction of this Court, by virtue of the 11th section of the Judicial act.

Because the court was split, Worrall's conviction was upheld, and, after the two judges consulted with the other Supreme Court justices sitting in Philadelphia, they sentenced Worrall to three month's imprisonment and a fine of $200.

Although little studied today, *United States v. Worrall* was the first case dealing with the impact of political corruption on society and politics, and whether or not it could be punished or should be punished.

**References:** Kawashima, Yasuhide, "Congress Should First Define the Offenses and Apportion the Punishment: Federal Common Law Crimes [*United States v. Worrall*]," in John W. Johnson, ed., *Historic U.S. Court Cases, 1690$–$1990: An Encyclopedia* (New York: Garland Publishing, 1992), 19–22; "Trial of Robert Worrall, For Attempting to Bribe a Commissioner of the Revenue, In the Circuit Court of the United States for the Pennsylvania District, Philadelphia, 1798," in Francis Wharton, ed., *State Trials of the United States During the Administrations of Washington and Adams, With References Historical and Professional and Preliminary Notes on the Politics of the Times* (Philadelphia: Carey & Hart, 1849), 189–199.

# V

## Vare, William Scott (1867–1934)

United States representative (1912–1923, 1923–1927) and U.S. senator-elect (1927–1929), denied his seat because of allegations of fraud in his senatorial election, the legality of which denial was determined in a landmark Supreme Court decision. Vare was born in Philadelphia, Pennsylvania, on 24 December 1867. He attended public schools in Philadelphia, but quit his formal education at the age of fifteen to enter the mercantile business in that city. By 1893 Vare was a successful contractor in the city. In 1898 he entered the political realm, running for and winning a seat on the select council of Philadelphia, where he served until 1901. From 1902 to 1912, he served as the recorder of deeds for the city of Philadelphia and in 1912 was elected to a seat in the Pennsylvania state senate. With his brothers George and Edward, he came to control the political machine in Pennsylvania once run by Simon Cameron and his son James Donald Cameron. Vare later succeeded Senator Boies Penrose as the political "boss" in the state.

Vare did not hold his state senate seat long; following the death of Representative Henry Harrison Bingham on 22 March 1912, a special election was held and Vare won the vacant seat. Vare would ultimately serve in the U.S. House from 24 April 1912 until 2 January 1923, when he resigned. Vare returned to Pennsylvania after his resignation and served for a short time as a member of the state senate. Elected back to the U.S. House of Representatives, he served in the Sixty-eighth and Sixty-ninth Congresses (4 March 1923–3 March 1927).

*Senator William S. Vare (right) and Mayor Kendrick. (Library of Congress, Prints & Photographs Division, LC-DIG-npcc-16496)*

*Ballot boxes in the Vare-Wilson election case arriving at the Capitol on 18 January 1927. (Library of Congress, Prints & Photographs Division, LC-DIG-npcc-16492)*

In 1926 Vare was elected to the United States Senate. At least, at first glance, it *appeared* that he had been elected. Nominated by the Republicans, Vare easily defeated the Democrat and Labor candidate, William B. Wilson (the former secretary of labor (1913–1921) under Woodrow Wilson), by more than 180,000 votes out of some 1.4 million cast. When the new Congress began its session, Vare went to Washington to present his credentials. But Wilson, the defeated candidate, filed an appeal with the Senate, charging massive corruption by Vare during both the Republican primary and the general election. In his petition before Congress, Wilson alleged that Vare and his supporters used padded registration lists, misused campaign expenditures, counted votes for Vare from persons who were dead or never existed, and engaged in intimidation and discouragement of prospective voters. The Senate then voted to refuse Vare his seat until an investigation could be concluded. The Senate Committee on Privileges and Elections began to examine the election controversy. However, they were blocked: Senator David A. Reed (R-PA) filibustered, forcing the investigation to continue into the Seventieth Congress, which convened in December 1927. The Senate's refusal to act left the committee with no jurisdiction for nine full months, until the end of 1927. The Senate had passed, on 11 January 1927, Resolution 324, which empowered the Senate committee to "take ... and preserve all ballot boxes, ... ballots, return sheets ... and other records, books, and documents used in said Senate election." The committee appointed investigator Jerry South to go to Pennsylvania to take control of the materials specified. However, when South went to the commissioners of Delaware County, who had custody of the ballots, they refused to hand them over. Reed, as a member of the Senate committee, demanded the boxes, and when the commissioners refused, he sued in federal court. The case reached the U.S. Supreme Court in 1928. In *Reed v. County Commissioners of Delaware County*, 277 U.S. 376 (1928), the Court held that Reed and the Senate committee did not have standing to sue. The Court held that since the Senate resolution did not allow for senators to sue, they could not even if the Senate Committee was blocked in its investigation. When the Seventieth Congress convened on 5 December 1927, Vare presented his credentials, but was again refused his seat. The Senate committee then began its investigation. Vare and Wilson were able to get the records, and they were presented to the committee for inspection. The Philadelphia district attorney testified that Vare supporters had been involved in election fraud, and that they had been obstructing his own investigation into systematic campaign fraud in the city. In examining the ballots from Philadelphia and Pittsburgh, the committee found that "the fraud pervading the actual count by the division election officers is appalling." Vare was asked for additional testimony before the committee, but he suffered a cerebral hemorrhage, delaying the committee's report. On 22

February 1929, the Committee reported unanimously that because of the corruption, neither Vare nor Wilson was entitled to the seat. On 6 December 1929, the Senate voted by fifty-eight to twenty-two that Vare could not be seated, and by sixty-six to fifteen that Wilson was equally ineligible. On 12 December 1929, the Senate seated Joseph R. Grundy, who had been appointed to the vacancy by Pennsylvania Governor John S. Fisher.

Vare was politically ruined by his failure to capture the Senate seat and returned home to Pennsylvania, where he resumed his business activities. His health declined soon after, and on 7 August 1934, while on a business trip to Atlantic City, New Jersey, he died at the age of sixty-six. He was buried in West Laurel Hill Cemetery in Philadelphia.

Although the name of William Vare is forgotten today, his case ranks as one of the longest contested Senate campaigns in American history. Allegations of excessive campaign expenditures and voter fraud were as big a problem then as they are today.

See also *Barry v. United States ex rel. Cunningham*

**References:** Astorino, Samuel J., "The Contested Senate Election of William Scott Vare," *Pennsylvania History,* 28 (April 1961), 187–201; Salter, John T., *The People's Choice: Philadelphia's William S. Vare* (New York: Exposition Press, 1971); Vare, William S., *My Forty Years in Politics* (Philadelphia: Roland Swain Co., 1933); "William B. Wilson v. William S. Vare," in Anne M. Butler and Wendy Wolff, *United States Senate Election, Expulsion and Censure Cases, 1793–1990* (Washington, DC: Government Printing Office, 1995), 323–329.

## Vermont Right to Life Committee v. Sorrell, 19 F. Supp. 2d 204 (1998), 216 F. 3d 264 (2000)

Federal court of appeals decision holding that federal or state governments may regulate only those political communications that expressly advocate the election, or the defeat, of a clearly identified candidate. In 1997 the state of Vermont enacted a law to reform its campaign financing system. The law, Act No. 64, specifically stated that it was "a response to rising costs of running for state office, the influence of those who make large campaign contributions, and the effect of large campaign expenditures on what the Vermont General Assembly called the '[r]obust debate of issues, candidate interaction with the electorate, and public involvement and confidence in the electoral process.'" The act changed the way Vermont campaigns were financed. It provided for the "public financing of campaigns for the offices of governor and lieutenant governor, limited campaign contributions and expenditures, amended the reporting requirements for candidates and contributors, and imposed disclosure and reporting requirements on, respectively, all 'political advertisements' and 'mass media activities.'" However, in this case, only the political advertising and the mass media activities provisions were at issue. The plaintiff, the Vermont Right to Life Committee (VRLC), charged that the statute was an unconstitutional abridgement on its ability to advertise during an election. The VRLC sued William H. Sorrell, the state attorney general, as well as numerous states' attorneys, to stop the enforcement of three of the provisions of the statute, namely the ones that required that all "political advertisements" disclose the identity of the person or persons or entity paying for the ad, as well as the candidate, party, or political committee on whose behalf it was being aired, and that expenditures for "mass media activities" that were made within thirty days of an election be reported to the state twenty-four hours after they were given.

The VRLC claimed that its activities potentially violated two sections of the act, namely those regarding "political advertisements" and their definitions, and those requiring the name of a candidate to be clearly given on each ad. The U.S. District Court for the District of Vermont gave a summary judgment to the state and to several "intervenor" organizations, among them Common Cause of Vermont, and the League of Women Voters of Vermont. The VRLC appealed to the U.S. Court of Appeals for the Second Circuit.

On 15 June 2000, the court of appeals reversed the district court ruling. Basing its decision on the U.S. Supreme Court decision in *Buckley v. Valeo*, 424 U.S. 1 (1976), the court of appeals held that in order for a state or the federal government to regulate a "communication"—be it an ad in a paper, on television, or on a billboard—"that communication must actually advocate the election, or the defeat, of a clearly identified candidate." Judge Robert D. Sack, appointed to the court of appeals by President Bill Clinton in 1998, spoke for the two-to-one majority (Judge Milton Shadur, a district judge replacing another judge on the Second Circuit, dissented) in holding that issue advocacy was protected by the First Amendment and that the provisions regulating issue advocacy, as well as the disclosure requirements, which infringed on the privacy of association, were unconstitutional. Judge Sack explained:

> There is, meanwhile, reason to think that when the Vermont legislature said "expenditures … for mass media activities" it meant all "expenditures," not only "funds used for communications that expressly advocate the election or defeat of a clearly identified candidate" under *Buckley*. We have seen in the course of our analysis of [the provisions in question] that the General Assembly

was willing to attempt to regulate advertising that "implicitly advocates the success or defeat of a candidate" despite *Buckley*'s clear mandate to the contrary. There is therefore no reason for us to think that when the General Assembly came to consider [that provision], it then intended to follow, rather than test or ignore, principles established by *Buckley*, through the use of the word "expenditure" to exclude expenditures for issue advocacy.

In discussing the law's provision that "communications" such as ads in papers, on television, or on billboards had to clearly show the name of a candidate whom the ad was either supporting or opposing for election, Judge Sack explained:

> In *Virginia Soc'y for Human Life*, 152 F.3d 268 (4th Cir. 1998), the Fourth Circuit considered a Virginia statute that required certain people or organizations that spent money "for the purpose of influencing the outcome of any election," … to … report their expenditures…. The plain language of the statute suggested that it applied to issue advocacy contrary to *Buckley*…. The court of appeals disapproved the district court's narrowing construction of the words "for the purpose of influencing the outcome of any election" to exclude issue advocacy in an effort to conform the statute to the *Buckley* requirements…. The reviewing court reached that conclusion in part because of the limited nature of such a review of a state statute by a federal court—only if such a reading was readily apparent would it survive. But also, "[i]n fact, a de novo review of the text, structure and history of the election laws at issue suggested to [the court] that they did apply to issue advocacy" contrary to *Buckley*…. We likewise find that in light of the text, structure and history of Vermont's [provision in question], the narrowing reading of the provision given to it by the district court was unwarranted…. We conclude that the district court erred in granting summary judgment for the defendants and in failing to enter an injunction forbidding the enforcement by the defendants of the provisions of [the statute].

There is no word as of this writing on whether Vermont will appeal this decision to the U.S. Supreme Court.

**References:** *Vermont Right to Life Committee v. Sorrell*, 216 F. 3d 264 (2000), 270–272.

# W

## Walker, James John (1881–1946)

Mayor of New York City (1925–1932), implicated in, but never formally charged with, massive political corruption. Even though corrupt, Walker was the personification of the "dapper" politician, whose flamboyance was a key to his popularity. The second of nine children, he was born in the Greenwich Village section of New York City on 19 June 1881, the son of an Irish immigrant father and an Irish woman born in America. He attended Catholic schools in New York City, but dropped out. He was allowed to attend the New York Law School, from which he earned a law degree in 1904. Walker did not enter politics immediately. His real calling was songwriting, and he began a career in what was called "The Great White Way." He wrote several songs that became popular and in 1912 married a singer. That same year, he was admitted to the New York state bar.

Walker's father, William Henry Walker, who died in 1916, was a longtime New York City politician who worked under the aegis of Tammany Hall, the preeminent political organization. With the recommendation of his father and an up-and-coming politician named Alfred Emanuel Smith (who would one day serve as governor of New York and the Democrat's presidential candidate in 1928), the younger Walker was allowed to join Tammany Hall, and in 1909 was elected to a seat in the New York state assembly. In 1914 he was elected to a seat in the New York state senate. Hewing to the Democratic Party line, he worked closely with Smith and Tammany to enact progressive legislation. As such he remained in Tammany's good graces, and in 1925 Tammany nominated Walker for mayor of New York City. In New York City in the 1920s, Tammany ruled the Democratic Party machinery, and once Walker won the party's nomination he was a shoe-in to be elected. In his first term, he helped to create a Department of Sanitation, created parks for children, and pushed the Board of Transportation to establish a city-wide train and bus system. In 1929 Walker was overwhelmingly reelected to a second term, defeating the fusion candidate, Fiorello H. La Guardia. His dapper and freewheeling style endeared him to the people of New York City and made him a popular national figure. Walker was so popular that when he marched in a street fair in Philadelphia in November

1926, people cried out that he be the next president of the United States. It seemed that nothing could go wrong for Jimmy Walker.

Within two years of his second electoral victory, however, Walker was under increasing scrutiny for alleged political corruption. In 1931 the New York state legislature established the Hofstadter Committee to investigate allegations of rampant corruption in the Walker administration. The counsel for the committee, Judge Samuel Seabury, was allowed by Governor Franklin Delano Roosevelt complete investigatory powers to find corruption in New York City and root it out. Historian Jay Robert Nash wrote:

> Judge Samuel Seabury ... called on Walker to explain his connection with Russell T. Sherwood, a low-ranking accountant who mysteriously accumulated a fortune of $700,225 and then disappeared. Seabury accused Sherwood of "fronting" for Walker, a charge vigorously denied by the mayor. But it was conclusively shown that on the eve of a cruise Walker took to Europe, Sherwood withdrew $263,838 from the bank for his boss.

Seabury called Walker before the committee and placed him on the stand for lengthy cross-examination. On the stand, Walker admitted that he had put a tremendous amount of money—upwards of nearly half a million dollars—in his own personal bank account, although he said it was from stock speculation on Wall Street. Walker derided Seabury's investigation; he said openly that "Little Boy Blue is going to blow his horn—or his top." Historian Paul Sann noted:

> [Walker] couldn't explain—at least not with any conviction—how he happened to make $26,535.51 in oil stock deals with taxicab impresario J. A. Sisto without having to invest a dime of his own. Nor why J. Allan Smith, contact man for a bus company, staked him to a European jaunt in 1927 with a $10,000 letter of credit and an extra $3,000 to cover an overdraft. Or how he happened to pick up an extra $246,000 bonanza in a joint stock account with Paul Block, Brooklyn financier and publisher.

As the allegations of corruption rose, Governor Roosevelt became more concerned for his party and the appearance of Walker's dishonesty. Roosevelt demanded that Walker resign before Roosevelt, slated to run for President in 1932, was himself tarnished. On 1 September 1932, as Seabury was getting closer to Walker's cronies, Walker resigned as mayor and set sail on a cruise to Europe. No charges were ever brought against him despite the breadth and depth of the corruption tied to him.

Walker returned to New York in 1935 and in 1937 was named assistant counsel to the New York State Transit Commission. Three years later, his successor as mayor, Fiorello La Guardia, named him municipal arbiter of the New York City garment industry. From 1945 until his death, Walker served as the president of Majestic Records in New York. Walker died of a cerebral hemorrhage—a blood clot in the brain—in Doctor's Hospital in New York City on 18 November 1946 at the age of sixty-five. He was buried in the Gate of Heaven Cemetery in Westchester County, New York.

Despite the allegations of corruption against him and the cowardice shown in his forced resignation, Walker remains a popular figure. In 1957 Bob Hope played Walker in the film *Beau James*.

**See also** Seabury, Samuel

**References:** Biles, W. Roger, "Walker, James John," in Melvin G. Holli and Peter d'A. Jones, *Biographical Dictionary of American Mayors, 1820$–$1980: Big City Mayors* (Westport, CT: Greenwood Press, 1981), 380; "[Editorial:] James J. Walker," *New York Times*, 19 November 1946, 30; "Ex-Mayor Walker Succumbs at 65 to Clot on Brain, City Chief for Seven Years Kept Popularity After Resigning Under Seabury Charges," *New York Times*, 19 November 1946, 1; "Hail Mayor Walker as 'Next President'; Philadelphians Line Streets as He Leads New Yorkers' March to Fair Grounds," *New York Times*, 13 November 1926, 1; "Jimmy Walker: The Destruction of 'Beau James'," in George C. Kohn, *Encyclopedia of American Scandal: From ABSCAM to the Zenger Case* (New York: Facts on File, 1989), 346–347; "The Night Mayor of New York," in

Paul Sann, *The Lawless Decade: A Pictorial History of a Great American Transition: From the World War I Armistice and Prohibition to Repeal and the New Deal* (New York: Bonanza Books, 1977), 216; "Walker, James John," in Jay Robert Nash, *Encyclopedia of World Crime: Criminal Justice, Criminology, and Law Enforcement*, 4 vols. (Wilmette, IL: CrimeBooks, Inc., 1989), IV:3076–3077.

## Walsh, Thomas James (1859–1933)

United States senator from Montana (1913–1933), the lead Senate investigator in the Teapot Dome scandal, for which he was considered for the post of U.S. attorney general before his untimely death. He was born in the village of Two Rivers, Wisconsin, on 12 June 1859, and attended the public schools, although he never earned a degree. He taught school for a time and then studied the law. In 1884 he earned a law degree from the University of Wisconsin at Madison and was admitted to the state bar that same year. He immediately left the state, and settled in Redfield, in the Dakota Territory, where he commenced a law practice. Six years later, he relocated again, this time to Helena, Montana, where again he opened a law office. He would be identified with the state of Montana for the remainder of his life.

In 1906 Walsh, a Democrat, ran for a seat in the U.S. House of Representatives, but was unsuccessful. Four years later, he tried for a U.S. Senate seat, but again was defeated, this time by Democrat Henry L. Myers. In 1912, however, when Republican Senator Thomas Henry Carter did not run for reelection, Walsh threw his hat into the ring. Prior to the passage of the Seventeenth Amendment, which allowed for the direct election of senators by the people, legislatures chose senators, and Walsh was able to win because of the Democratic control of the Montana state legislature. He entered the U.S. Senate on 4 March 1913, and remained in that body until his death. He served as the chairman of the Committee on Mines and Mining (Sixty-third to Sixty-fifth Congresses), the Committee on Pensions (Sixty-fifth Congress), and the Committee on the Disposition of Useless Executive Papers (Sixty-fifth Congress).

Early in 1923, rumors surfaced that at least two members of President Warren G. Harding's cabinet were involved in potentially illegal activities, including his attorney general, Harry M. Daugherty. Then Harding died suddenly in San Francisco on 2 August 1923, leaving Vice President Calvin Coolidge as the new president. Congress soon discovered that Harding's secretary of the interior, Albert B. Fall, had leased oil reserves owned by the government in Wyoming and California to two of his cronies. The Senate formed a special committee to investigate the leases and whether any illegalities were involved—Walsh was named chairman of the committee. Using the power of the Senate, Walsh was able to uncover bribes paid to Fall and helped drive both the interior secretary and Attorney General Daugherty from office. He also helped to expose illegal payments to William Gibbs McAdoo, former secretary of the treasury under Woodrow Wilson and a leading Democrat, lending a bipartisan flavor to the scandal. Walsh's skilled oratory and demeanor during the hearings earned him wide praise.

In an article that appeared in *The Forum* in July 1924, Walsh explained:

An all too general view prevails that corruption in high places in the government is not uncommon, but that the operators are ordinarily so clever as to defy detection, or that upon one consideration or another, perhaps in anticipation of reciprocal toleration, even political opponents in a situation to do so refrain from making public official misdeeds or delinquencies. Notwithstanding the startling revelations of the committees inquiring during the recent session of Congress into the conduct of the executive departments, I believe that "crookedness" in Washington is rare, and I am convinced that the notion that it is ever condoned by those who might profit politically by the exposure of it, either through hope or fear, is wholly false. It should be added that I refer to instances in which conduct would be universally, at least generally, condemned as contrary to good morals or plainly involving turpitude. It would seem as though there could be no such thing as degrees of dishonesty, and yet of many acts of public officials varying views are held as to whether they are culpable or as to the degree of culpability which should attach to those concerned in them.

Walsh won considerable praise, both for his handling of the committee hearings and for his steadfast ability to reach across party lines in a fair manner to get to the truth behind the scandal.

In 1932, when New York Governor Franklin D. Roosevelt won the presidency, he turned to Walsh and named the Montana senator his selection for attorney general. Despite his age—Walsh was seventy-two when named—his appointment was hailed. It appeared his confirmation would face no opposition. After the New Year, Walsh and his new wife traveled south for a vacation. He made the train trip back to Washington on 2 March to attend Roosevelt's inauguration, to be held on the fourth. However, as the train neared Wilson, North Carolina, Walsh suffered a fatal heart attack and died before he could be revived. His death stunned Washington, and his funeral was held in the chamber of the U.S. Senate, the body he had served in for nearly twenty years. Walsh's body was taken back to Montana, and he was laid to rest in Resurrection Cemetery in Helena. Today his name is forgotten, but his work in exposing the Teapot Dome frauds shaped the way successful investigations of government corruption are conducted.

**See also** Teapot Dome Scandal
**References:** *Biographical Directory of the American Congress, 1774–1996* (Alexandria, VA: CQ Staff Directories, Inc., 1996); Walsh, Thomas J., "The True Story of Teapot Dome," *The Forum*, LXXII:1 (July 1924), 1–12.

## Walton, John Callaway (1881–1949)

Governor of Oklahoma (1923), impeached and removed from office for suspending the writ of habeas corpus to combat the violence of the Ku Klux Klan. Walton is one of only a handful of governors ever to be impeached and removed from office, but he remains the only one who was accused of violating a state's constitution to combat racial violence. He was born near Indianapolis, Indiana, on 6 March 1881, the son of Louis Walton, a farmer, and Callaway (also spelled Calloway) Walton. In 1885 the family moved to Nebraska, but just four years after that relocated to Arkansas. John Walton was educated in the public schools, completing his secondary education at Fort Smith Commercial College in Fort Smith, Arkansas, in 1898. He volunteered for service in the U.S. Army's field artillery unit during the Spanish-American War, after which he returned to the United States and studied engineering in Mexico. In 1903 he settled in Oklahoma City, Oklahoma. He served in the Engineering Corps of the U.S. Army during World War I with the rank of colonel.

A Democrat, Walton entered the political realm in 1916, when he was elected commissioner of public works for Oklahoma City. Two years later, he ran for and was elected mayor of Oklahoma City, a position he held for four years. Considered honest and reliable (he was nicknamed "Our Jack"), in August 1922 he was nominated for governor by the Democrats and in November 1922 was elected over Republican John Fields by more than 50,000 votes out of some 510,000 cast. Almost from the start of his administration, Walton became unpopular with the members of the state legislature. The early 1920s had seen a revival of the power of the Ku Klux Klan, and many legislative members were either backed by the Klan or were Klan members themselves. Thus when Walton placed Tulsa County under martial law and suspended the writ of habeas corpus, the legislature was up in arms. To stymie the legislature's opposition, Walton used the power of the state National Guard to prevent it from being convened. However, members of the legislature circulated a petition among the state's citizens demanding that a special session of the legislature be convened on the matter. Walton had no choice but to call the legislature into special session. Immediately, the members set about an impeachment inquiry and, on 23 October 1923, impeachment articles were passed. Walton was suspended from office pending the impeachment trial, and Lieutenant Governor Martin Edwin Trapp became acting governor. Walton's critics contended that it was not his opposition to the Klan that was his downfall, but his lavish spending in the state budget and his attacks on the regents of the University of Oklahoma and Oklahoma A&M, whom he removed and replaced with cronies. These university presidents resigned in protest, and there were street protests against Walton's administration. The legislature then met to discuss this situation; however, once they assembled, Walton's conduct was the main focus and he was immediately impeached. Quickly, the state senate voted to convict Walton, and, just ten months after entering office, he was removed. Lieutenant Governor Martin Trapp finished Walton's term.

Walton remained in Oklahoma, but lived the rest of his life in disgrace. He died in Oklahoma City on 25 November 1949 at the age of sixty-eight and was buried in Rose Hill Cemetery in that city.

**References:** Neuringer, Sheldon, "War on the Ku Klux Klan," *Chronicles of Oklahoma,* XLV:2 (Summer 1967); "Walton, John C.," in Robert Sobel and John Raimo, eds., *Biographical Directory of the Governors of the United States, 1789$–1978, $4 vols.* (Westport, CT: Meckler Books, 1978), III:1244–1245.

## Warmoth, Henry Clay (1842–1931)

Governor of Louisiana (1868–1872), impeached but not removed (his term ended before a trial could take place) on charges of massive corruption of which many historians believe him to have been guilty. Warmoth was born in McLeansboro, Illinois, on 9 May 1842, the son of Isaac Sounders Warmoth, a postmaster who worked in New Orleans, and Eleanor (née Lane) Warmoth. The Warmoths apparently named their son after the famous U.S. senator and former secretary of state, Henry Clay, although this fact cannot be completely substantiated. His paternal grandfather, Henry Warmoth, had been an early settler in the American Midwest, settling near Albion, Illinois, in the early 1800s. Eleanor Lane Warmoth was the daughter of an Illinois state senator, Levin Lane. She died around 1853, when her son Henry was eleven, and he moved with his father to Fairfield, Illinois, spending some time with friends of the family. He received his education in the public schools of Fairfield and Salem, and, after completing his primary education, worked in the offices of the *Springfield (Illinois) Journal* while he studied the law. In 1861 he was admitted to practice the law in Lebanon, Missouri. The following year, in the midst of the American Civil War, Warmoth was appointed district attorney for the Eighteenth Judicial District of Missouri, but he soon resigned this office to volunteer for service in the Thirty-second Missouri Infantry, where he was given the rank of lieutenant colonel. He assisted in the

*Henry C. Warmoth (Library of Congress, Prints & Photographs Division, LC-DIG-cwpbh-03726)*

capture of Arkansas Post, after which he was assigned to the staff of Major General John A. McClernand, and saw action at Vicksburg, Mississippi, where he was terribly wounded. In a personal battle for power between McClernand and General Ulysses S. Grant, Warmoth was discharged. However, after a personal appeal to President Abraham Lincoln, he was reinstated to his previous rank and position.

In June 1864 Lincoln assigned Warmoth to the post of judge of the Provost Court for the Gulf of Mexico, with its seat in Louisiana. When the war ended, Warmoth remained in Louisiana, opening a law office in New Orleans. In November 1865 he was elected by a coalition of pro-Unionists in Louisiana to a seat as a "territorial delegate" to Congress (because Louisiana had not be readmitted to the Union, it was not allowed to have congressional representation), but he was denied his seat due not to his own war stance but the state he was

representing. In 1868, when the Republicans in Louisiana met in convention to nominate a gubernatorial candidate, Warmoth was the overwhelming choice for Governor, but because he was only twenty-six years of age, the convention passed a resolution ending the limitation on age (it was thirty at the time) for one to hold the governor's office. On his ticket was Oscar J. Dunn, a black man, nominated for lieutenant governor, the first black in the history of the United States to be nominated for such a high post. Because most whites in Louisiana had their voting rights taken away, no Democrat was nominated for governor, and Warmoth easily defeated Independent James Taliaferro by nearly 30,000 votes out of slightly more than 100,000 votes cast. Joshua Baker had been serving as governor, with General Winfield Scott Hancock serving as district military commander over the state. On 27 June 1868, Hancock was removed from power by President Andrew Johnson, and Johnson named Warmoth to serve as military governor of Louisiana until the state was readmitted to the Union. This occurred on 13 July 1868, and Warmoth was inaugurated as the twenty-third governor of Louisiana. His tenure lasted until 13 January 1873.

From the beginning, Warmoth fought against the Democrats, who did not want civil rights for blacks, and wings of his own party, which wanted more civil rights for blacks. Warmoth explained the hostility against his administration in his 1930 memoir, *War, Politics and Reconstruction: Stormy Days in Louisiana*:

> But, of course, my administration was exceedingly obnoxious to the colored Lieutenant-Governor, Oscar J. Dunn, to the *New York Orleans Tribune*, to United States Marshall Packard, to Senator [William Pitt] Kellogg and the 'Pure Radical' Federal officials, who looked only to negro voters to support the Republican Party. They claimed that in my appointment of conservative white men to office, I was guilty of treason to the negro people.

But Warmoth also gradually dug his own political grave by speculating in railroad and treasury bonds, holding a partnership in the newspaper printing company that was also the state printer, and establishing a State Returning Board, which was instilled with the power to throw out ballots thought to be questionable. Warmoth used this board to have votes from Democrats routinely cast aside, allowing him and his party to keep a firm reign on power. Historians Robert Sobel and John Raimo wrote, "His gubernatorial term was characterized by turbulence, discontent, a wild orgy of speculation in state-aided railroads, a depleted treasury, and bitter strife over the question of black suffrage. He signed the bill which opened the restaurants, railroad coaches, and schools to blacks, but later vetoed a more radical measure." Warmoth's administration saw the state's bond debt rise from $6 million to over $100 million. After Dunn's death early in Warmoth's term, he was replaced by the senate president pro tempore, Pinckney Benton Stewart Pinchback, also a black man.

In 1872, as his term came to an end, Warmoth was passed over for renomination by his party, which then proceeded to break up into three different factions, each nominating different gubernatorial tickets. Democrats and a Reform Party also nominated tickets for governor. After the election, in which there was a dispute over the winner, Warmoth on 4 November 1872 called for an extra session of the state legislature to start on 9 December. The Republicans, in control of the legislature, instead took control over all of state government, impeached Warmoth, and installed Lieutenant Governor Pinckney Benton Stewart Pinchback as acting governor. He was inaugurated on 8 December as the new governor. Warmoth, in the midst of an impeachment inquiry, nonetheless sued to the Louisiana Supreme Court, which held that Pinchback was indeed the true governor. Pinchback then proceeded to sign ten bills into law and make several appointments. Warmoth was not allowed to serve the last thirty-five days of his term. In the meantime Senator William Pitt Kellogg, a Republican but a political nemesis of Warmoth's, had been declared the winner of the 1872 election, and he took office on 13 January 1873 before an impeachment trial could be held on the charges against Warmoth. Historians do believe that the allegations of widespread corruption, both by Warmoth and his allies, were valid, and could have led to his conviction and removal from office. Because he was out of office, Warmoth was considered beyond the reaches of the impeachment inquiry, and it was dropped.

Despite the turbulence of his last days in office, Warmoth remained in Louisiana, and in 1876 was elected to a seat in the lower house of the state legislature, serving for one two-year term. In 1879 he served as a delegate to the state constitutional convention and in 1888 ran for governor, but was defeated badly by Democrat Francis Redding Tillou Nicholls by over 80,000 votes out of nearly 200,000 cast. His last office held was as collector of customs for New Orleans from 1890 to 1893.

In the last years of the nineteenth century and the first years of the twentieth, Warmoth spent his time on his sugar plantation, "Magnolia," south of New Orleans. He outlived all of his contemporaries, and lived long enough to publish his memoirs in 1930. Warmoth died in New Orleans on 30 September 1931 at the age of eighty-nine.

**References:** "The Carpetbagger as Corruptionist: Henry Clay Warmoth," in Richard N. Current, *Three Carpetbag Governors* (Baton Rouge: Louisiana State University Press, 1967), 35–66; "Warmoth, Henry Clay," in Robert Sobel and John Raimo, eds., *Biographical Directory of the Governors of the United States, 1789$–1978, $4 vols. (Westport, CT: Meckler

Books, 1978), II:571–572; Warmoth, Henry Clay, *War, Politics and Reconstruction: Stormy Days in Louisiana* (New York: The Macmillan Company, 1930), 165, 199.

## Watergate

American political scandal that drove President Richard Nixon from office before he could be impeached for obstructing justice. Although no one in power profited financially from the matter, Watergate nonetheless is perhaps the most egregious example of political corruption because of the effect it had in subverting the political process. "Watergate," as the entire affair was called, did not start, as many believe today, with the burglary by five men from the Committee to Reelect the President (ironically called CREEP) at Democratic Committee Headquarters located in the Watergate Hotel Complex in Washington, D.C., in the morning hours of 17 June 1972. From the start of his presidency, faced with growing protests nationwide over the Vietnam War, Richard Nixon initialed the start of a massive use of illegal wiretapping and information gathering to seek out his enemies, political and otherwise, with the approval of his attorney general, John N. Mitchell. This gathered steam on 23 July 1970 when Nixon secretly ordered expanded domestic intelligence gathering by the Federal Bureau of Investigation (FBI), the Central Intelligence Agency (CIA), and other federal government agencies. This approval was rescinded a few days later, but the die had been struck: plans were then undertaken to stem a series of leaks of government plans on the handling of the Vietnam War.

The publication, starting on 13 June 1971, by *New York Times* (and, within a week, *Washington Post*) of the classified Pentagon report later known as "The Pentagon Papers," which was commissioned by President Lyndon Johnson's secretary of defense, Robert McNamara, and detailed the history of how the United States became involved in Vietnam, enraged the administration. Nixon and his administration were determined to find how the report was leaked. A plan, called "Operation Gemstone," was conceived in Attorney General Mitchell's office sometime in 1971, in which a covert White House unit, aptly called "The Plumbers" (in order to "plug" security leaks), was ordered to use any means, including burglary, to find and contain leaks of government secrets on administration policy on Vietnam, and was funded with $250,000 directly from the account of the committee established to aid in Nixon's reelection efforts in 1972. When it was discovered that a former Pentagon worker, Daniel Ellsberg, was responsible for the release of the "Pentagon Papers," the Plumbers, led by attorney George Gordon Liddy, broke into Ellsberg's psychiatrist's office in Los Angeles, California, on 3 September 1971 seeking incriminating material on Ellsberg to destroy his reputation. None was found, but the action set the stage for grander and more dangerous schemes in the future. One of these was an aborted effort to start a fire at the Brookings Institution, a think tank in Washington, D.C., where Plumbers members suspected files on Vietnam War policies were housed.

Sometime in 1972, the Plumbers, backed by men who worked directly for President Nixon, including White House Chief of Staff Harry Robbins ("H.R.") Haldeman and Assistant to the President for Domestic Affairs John Ehrlichman, wanted information on the movement of Democrats running for president in that election year. Ehrlichman was the mastermind behind the Plumbers, and approved of their actions in the Ellsberg break-in. To get information on the Democrats, both Halde-

(a 1973 Herblock Cartoon, copyright by The Herb Block Foundation)

man and Ehrlichman ordered that wiretaps be established on the phone of Larry O'Brien, a former postmaster general and the present chairman of the Democratic National Committee, whose offices were located in the Watergate Hotel Complex in Washington, D.C. Sometime in June 1972 members of the Plumbers broke in and tapped the phones, but some of the taps did not work and much of the material that was collected was inadequate. A return visit was ordered. In the early morning hours of 17 June 1972, five men, among them James McCord, a security official for the Committee to Reelect the President, and E. Howard Hunt, a former CIA official who was the author of several spy novels, broke into O'Brien's office. Unknown to the men, a Watergate security officer found masking tape across a door lock so that it would not close, and began to search for intruders. The men were arrested, and the affair known as Watergate began.

When the men were arraigned the following day, two things were clear: the alleged burglars were connected to the CIA in some way, as well as to Nixon's reelection efforts. In response, the White House called the break-in "a third-rate burglary." On 19 June, *Washington Post* reported McCord's connection with CREEP; former Attorney General Mitchell, who had resigned to head up Nixon's reelection campaign, denied any link between CREEP and the break-in. Two *Post* reporters, Carl Bernstein and Bob Woodward, were placed on the story, and soon traced a cashier's check for $25,000 directly from CREEP accounts into the bank accounts of one of the Watergate burglars. On 29 September, the *Post* reported that John Mitchell, while serving as attorney general, controlled a secret fund from CREEP coffers that was used "to finance widespread intelligence-gathering operations against the Democrats," which included stag-

ing phony events, trailing candidates, and inventing material that was used to destroy the candidacies of Senator Edmund Muskie and former Vice President Hubert Humphrey. By October, just before the 1972 election, the FBI had discovered that Watergate was just a part of "a massive campaign of political spying and sabotage conducted on behalf of the Nixon reelection effort." The next month, even with these allegations swirling, Nixon was reelected over South Dakota Senator George McGovern with over 60 percent of the vote in one of the largest landslides in American political history.

Even after President Nixon was inaugurated for a second term on 20 January 1973, investigators were homing in on officials of his administration. Ten days later, the five Watergate burglars were convicted in a District of Columbia court of conspiracy, burglary, and eavesdropping. After being sentenced, James McCord sent a letter to Judge John J. Sirica, who presided over the trials, alleging that he had taken his orders from high-ranking officers of the Republican Party, including former Attorney General John N. Mitchell (who served as the chairman of CREEP in the 1972 election), and that had they were involved in the cover-up. As a result of McCord's letter, federal investigators in the Department of Justice and Federal Bureau of Investigation open up an investigation into Nixon's aides. Federal grand juries were empaneled, and the U.S. Senate established the Select Committee on Presidential Campaign Activities, better known as the Senate Watergate Committee. Named to chair this panel was Senator Samuel J. Ervin Jr. (D-NC). In hearings that opened on 18 May 1973, held before television cameras that riveted the nation, Ervin's homespun demeanor made him one of the most important persons in the investigation. The *Washington Post* later said of the senator, "With his arching eyebrows and flapping jowls that signaled his moral indignation at much of the testimony before his committee, his half-country, half-courtly demeanor and his predilection for making points by quoting the Bible and Shakespeare and telling folksy stories, Ervin quickly became a hero to many." Numerous witnesses were brought before the committee, including White House counsel John W. Dean III, who told the committee that he had warned Nixon that "a cancer" was on the presidency regarding the coverup of the Watergate break-in. Dean implicated most of the men around the president, and said that Nixon had ordered the payoff of the Watergate burglars to buy their silence. Dean told Nixon that the cost of buying the men off would be $1 million. Dean quoted Nixon as saying, "You could get the money.... You could get a million dollars. And you could get it in cash. I know where it could be gotten."

Allegations that had surfaced prior to the committee hearings led to the resignations of White House Chief of Staff H. R. "Bob" Haldeman and Presidential Adviser on Domestic Affairs John Ehrlichman, and Attorney General Richard Kleindienst on 30 April 1973. White House counsel Dean was fired. To replace Kleindienst, Nixon tapped former cabinet Secretary Eliott Richardson. At the same time that the Senate was investigating the scandal, a special prosecutor, Archibald Cox, who had ties to Senator Edward Kennedy (and had been Richardson's law professor at Harvard), was empowered by the Department of Justice and Attorney General Eliott Richardson to look into any part of the scandal.

On 13 July 1973, Alexander P. Butterfield, the former appointments secretary for President Nixon, told the Senate Watergate Committee that Nixon had been audiotaping Oval Office conversations for several years, and that a taped record of these conversations had been archived. At once, Special Prosecutor Cox demanded access to the White House tapes; the Senate Watergate Committee followed suit. Five days later, according to several sources, Nixon ordered that the Oval office taping system be disconnected. On 23 July, Nixon announced that he would refuse to turn over any taped conversation based upon the president's right to executive privilege. Cox, undeterred, went to court to get a subpoena to force Nixon to turn over the tapes. When Nixon ordered Cox to stop his quest for a subpoena and Cox refused, Nixon ordered Attorney General Richardson to fire the special prosecutor. Richardson refused, and resigned. Nixon then ordered Richardson's assistant, Deputy Attorney General William D. Ruckelshaus, to fire Cox—but Ruckelshaus also refused and likewise resigned. It was left to the number three in the Department of Justice, Solicitor General Robert H. Bork, to assume the office of acting attorney general and fire Cox. This action, on 20 October 1973, became known as the "Saturday Night Massacre." Anger at Nixon exploded—politicians across the political spectrum condemned the firing and demanded that Nixon retract it. Among some, talk of impeachment arose.

To placate the critics, Nixon named a new special prosecutor, attorney Leon Jaworski. Jaworski, armed with confidence in his office that was backed by Congress and the American people, took up Cox's crusade and went to court to get a subpoena to force Nixon to hand over his taped conversations. Jaworski then got indictments against Haldeman, Ehrlichman, White House lawyer Charles Colson, and others for conspiracy, perjury, obstruction of justice, and other crimes. He also revealed that when the five Watergate burglars had been indicted, Nixon had been named as an unindicted coconspirator.

Facing a revolt in Congress, Nixon offered to release transcripts of the taped conversations that Jaworski wanted. Despite Nixon's appearing to deliver some of the tapes, Jaworski was unimpressed and fought to have the actual tapes heard. While preparing the transcript of one tape, presidential secretary Rosemary Woods accidentally "erased" part of it—leaving a gap of eighteen and one-half minutes. Many historians believe that Woods erased evidence showing crimes committed by Nixon, but this has never been proved. On 30 April 1974, Nixon released 1,200 pages of edited transcripts, turning them over to Jaworski and the House Judiciary Committee, now investigating potential impeachment charges against the president. The committee replied that this was not satisfactory, and Jaworski got a subpoena for the tapes. Nixon fought this decision to the U.S. Supreme Court, which held unanimously on 24 July 1974, in *United States v. Nixon*, that the president could not use executive privilege as the basis for withholding the tapes from scrutiny. Three days later, the House Judiciary Committee passed an article of impeachment, charging Nixon with obstruction of justice. Two other articles followed, alleging abuse of power and defiance of congressional subpoenas. Nixon felt that while he would be impeached in the House, he could win the battle in the Senate. However, after he listened to the tapes that would soon be released, he found one, from 23 June 1972, in which he told Chief of Staff Haldeman that he ordered the Federal Bureau of Investigation to stop investigating the Watergate scandal and any ties to the White House. This tape was clear evidence of Nixon's obstruction of justice. It was "the smoking gun." Several senators came to the president and told him that he would be convicted in the Senate and removed from office. On 7 August 1974, Nixon told the American people in a televised speech that he would resign the presidency the following day. Vice President Gerald R. Ford—who had replaced Vice President Spiro T. Agnew when he resigned due to political corruption—was sworn in as the thirty-eighth president on 8 August.

In the end, as many historians and commentators explain, it was not the crime, but the cover-up, that destroyed Richard Nixon. Watergate's effects led to laws increasing the accountability of campaign finance laws and limiting the presidential power of executive privilege. Judge John Sirica, noted for his independence in forcing President Nixon to release the tapes that doomed his presidency, wrote of the scandal in his 1979 work, *To Set the Record Straight: The Break-In, the Tapes, the Conspirators, the Pardon*. He retired from the bench in 1986, and died on 14 August 1992 at the age of eighty-eight. Former White House counsel John W. Dean III, who literally brought down the president, was charged with obstruction of justice and spent four months in prison for his role in the Watergate cover-up. After serving his sentence, he penned the autobiographical *Blind Ambition* (1976), which became a national best seller. His wife, Maureen, known as "Mo," also wrote a Watergate book—*Mo: A Woman's View of Watergate* (1975). John Ehrlichman was convicted of conspiracy to obstruct justice and perjury in Watergate, and of conspiracy in the Ellsberg break-in, and served eighteen months in jail. He wrote *Witness to Power: The Nixon Years* (1982). Senator Sam Ervin retired from the Senate in December 1974, just four months after Nixon resigned, and returned to his home in North Carolina; he wrote, among other works, *The Whole Truth: The Watergate Conspiracy* (1980). Ervin died on 23 April 1985 at the age of eighty-eight. H. R. 'Bob' Haldeman, Nixon's chief of staff, spent eighteen months in prison after he was convicted of conspiracy and obstruction of justice in 1974. After leaving prison, he wrote *The Ends of Power* in 1978. In his later years, Haldeman became a real estate developer in California and an investor in restaurants. He died of cancer in California on 12 November 1993 at the age of sixty-seven. Six months later, *The Haldeman Diaries*, about the initial days of the Watergate crisis, was published. G. Gordon Liddy, the former FBI agent, who was the brains behind the Watergate break-in, and was convicted for his role in that, as well as for conspiracy and contempt of court, spent four and one-half years in prison. When he emerged, unrepentant, he penned *Will* (1980), his explanation of the scandal. Today, he is a conservative radio talk-show host in Virginia, and has assumed an air of respectability more than a quarter century after the break-in.

Watergate and its effects have lasted far longer, and cast a much broader shadow, across the political spectrum of today. Charles Ruff, the fourth and final Watergate special counsel, later served as chief counsel of the White House during the darkest days of the Clinton Administration. Earl Silbert, the U.S. attorney for the District of Columbia in the 1970s who prosecuted many of the Watergate figures, was hired in 1997 as counsel for James Riady, the Indonesia businessman and friend of President Bill Clinton who was implicated in the campaign finance scandal that rocked the Clinton/Gore 1996 reelection campaign. But it is the word "Watergate" that haunts American politics. Today, political scandals routinely append the word "gate" to their names—Travelgate, Irangate, etc. The limits put on presidential power by the U.S. Supreme Court in *United States v. Nixon* have had consequences for the Clinton impeachment in 1998–1999. The use of presidential immunity to shield the testimony of friends and cronies has been given new boundaries. But perhaps Watergate's most lasting effect has been a loss of innocence for the American public as they came to view their government with distrust.

**See also** Federal Election Commission; Mitchell, John Newton; Nixon, Richard Milhaus; Thompson, Fred Dalton

**References:** *The Fall of a President* (New York: Dell Publishing Company, 1974); Dickinson, William B., Jr. , *Watergate: Chronology of a Crisis*, 2 vols. (Washington, DC: Congressional Quarterly, 1974); Mankiewicz, Frank, *United States v. Richard Nixon: The Final Crisis* (New York: Quadrangle/New York Times Book Company, 1975); Meyer, Lawrence, "John N. Mitchell, Principal in Watergate, Dies at 75," *Washington Post*, 10 November 1988, A1; Rosenberg, Kenyon C., and Judith K. Rosenberg, *Watergate: An Annotated Bibliography* (Littleton, CO: Libraries Unlimited, 1975); Saffell, David C., *Watergate: Its Effects on the American Political System* (Cambridge, MA: Winthrop Publishers, 1974); Smith, J. Y., "H.R. Haldeman Dies, Was Nixon Chief of Staff, Watergate Role Led to 18 Months in Prison," *Washington Post*, 13 November 1993, A12; "Watergate," in George C. Kohn, *Encyclopedia of American Scandal: From ABSCAM to the Zenger Case* (New York: Facts on File, 1989), 349–50; Weil, Martin, and Eleanor Randolph, "Richard M. Nixon, 37th President, Dies, Funeral Scheduled for Wednesday for Only Chief Executive Forced From Office," *Washington Post*, 23 April 1994, A1.

# Welch, William Wickham (1818–1892)

United States representative from Connecticut (1855–1857), accused of corruption and the subject of an expulsion hearing in the House in 1857. Welch was a noted physician who happened to run for a seat in Congress and win; little else is known about him. He was born in Norfolk, Connecticut, on 10 December 1818, the son of Benjamin Welch and Louisa (née Guiteau) Welch. Benjamin Welch, one of thirteen children, had studied medicine under a local Norfolk doctor, Ephraim Guiteau, and married his daughter. William Welch was one of ten children, of whom all five sons became physicians. He studied medicine under his father (nothing is noted of his primary school education), graduated from the Yale Medical School in 1839, and began the practice of medicine in Norfolk with his father. He apparently entered the political realm when he ran for and won a seat in the Connecticut state house of representatives, serving from 1848 to 1850. He then won a seat in the state senate, serving in that body in 1851 and 1852. Welch was a member of the American, or "Know Nothing," Party, so named because its platform of excluding Catholics and immigrants was so controversial that its members claimed to "know nothing" if asked about it. In 1855 he ran for a seat in the U.S. House of Representatives under the American Party banner and defeated a Democrat named Noble (no first name has been found) to win the seat representing the Fourth Connecticut District. Welch's time in Washington was limited to one term. Few sources note what occurred, but he was under consideration first for expulsion and/or censure by the House. However, after a thorough investigation by "a committee, consisting of 5 Members, to be appointed by the Speaker, with power to send for persons and papers, to investigate said charges; and that said committee report the evidence taken, and what action, in their judgment, is necessary on the part of the House, without any unnecessary delay," it was held that Welch was not proved guilty and released from further action.

Despite this, Welch did not run for a second term. He resumed the practice of medicine, although he later served as a member of the Connecticut state house in 1869 and 1881. He also served as president of the Norfolk Leather Company, and was one of the incorporators of the Connecticut-Western Railroad and the Norfolk Savings Bank. His biography in the *Dictionary of American Biography* highlights his work as a doctor rather than his congressional career. Welch died in Norfolk on 30 July 1892 at the age of seventy-three and was buried in Center Cemetery in that city.

**References:** Hinds, Asher Crosby, *Hinds' Precedents of the House of Representatives of the United States, including References to Provisions of the Constitution, the Laws, and Decisions of the United States Senate,* 8 vols. (Washington, DC: Government Printing Office, 1907–1908), V:834–836; MacCullum, William G., "Welch, William Wickham," in Allen Johnson and Dumas Malone, et al., eds., *Dictionary of American Biography,* 10 vols. and 10 supplements (New York: Charles Scribner's Sons, 1930–1995), X:624–625; United States Congress, House, Joint Committee on Congressional Operations, *House of Representatives Exclusion, Censure and Expulsion Cases from 1789 to 1973,* 93rd Congress, 1st Session (Washington, DC: Government Printing Office, 1973).

## Whiskey Ring Scandal

National scandal, in which government agents in St. Louis, Missouri, were caught siphoning off tax revenues from the sale of whiskey intended to go into the national treasury. The scandal was exposed in 1875 through the efforts of Secretary of the Treasury Benjamin H. Bristow. Evidence showed that for some years prior to 1875, the United States government had lost at least $1.2 million of tax revenue it should have received from whiskey sales in St. Louis, Missouri, alone. Yet special agents of the Treasury Department sent to investigate from time to time had failed to do more than cause an occasional flurry among the thieves.

The Whiskey Ring was organized in St. Louis when the Liberal Republican Party in that city achieved its first electoral success. Soon after their electoral achievement, it occurred to certain politicians to have revenue officers raise a campaign fund among the many liquor distillers in the city. This idea the

officers later modified, raising money in the same way for themselves and conniving at the grossest thievery. As it became necessary to hide the frauds, newspapers and higher officials were hushed with payoffs, until the ring assumed national dimensions, diverting untold millions from federal coffers. Its headquarters were at St. Louis, but it had branches in Milwaukee, Chicago, Peoria, Cincinnati, and New Orleans, and even had an agent in Washington, D.C. A huge ill-gotten fund was distributed among storekeepers, collectors, and other officials, according to a fixed schedule of prices.

Following an investigation—conducted in secret by Secretary of the Treasury Benjamin Bristow to avoid alerting any of those being targeted—federal agents under the control of Bristow, working without the knowledge of the attorney general or the president, moved on the ring on 10 May 1875 and arrested more than 350 men in raids across the United States. Indictments were handed down by federal grand juries against 152 liquor sellers, as well as 86 persons in the government, including the chief clerk of Bristow's own Treasury Department.

Bristow was widely cheered for his actions, though not by everyone inside the administration. Grant had named Bristow to the Treasury in June 1874 after criticism from reformers, both Republican and otherwise, who saw widespread political corruption as the Achilles' heel of the party for the 1874 midterm elections. Yet Bristow's actions were considered unhelpful by Grant's cronies as exposing the failings of friends of the administration.

Initially, Grant backed Bristow's efforts. However, as the continuing investigation uncovered massive graft and corruption by men tied directly to Grant and the Republican Party, he became less and less interested in getting to the bottom of the scandal. But still

bowing to reformers and embarrassed by press reports regarding the affair, he decided to name a special prosecutor to oversee all of the indictments and trials. This man was General John B. Henderson, a former United States senator from Missouri, who decided that his role required him to prosecute these cases to the fullest extent of the law. As he began trials of Whiskey Ring defendants, evidence was discovered that implicated President Grant's personal secretary, General Orville E. Babcock. The evidence linking Babcock to the graft came from the prosecution of John McDonald, a revenue supervisor in St. Louis, who later wrote a book, *Secrets of the Whiskey Ring; and Eighteen Months in the Penitentiary* (1880), exposing some of the frauds. Letters in code written from Babcock to McDonald were found, with instructions on how to siphon Whiskey Ring funds. When Henderson indicted Babcock, Grant intervened, arguing that as a military officer Babcock must be tried by a military court. This court, with its members named by Grant, asked Henderson for copies of all of his evidence against Babcock. Henderson refused to allow a civilian court to give way to a military one. Grant backed down, and Babcock went on trial in the civilian court. However, when Henderson decried Grant's interference in the Babcock prosecution, Grant fired Henderson—a move mirrored 100 years later when President Richard Nixon fired Special Prosecutor Archibald Cox, a move called "The Saturday Night Massacre." In 1875, though, few took notice of Grant's action, and Henderson left quietly. Grant replaced him with James Broadhead, an attorney with little experience in criminal prosecutions who was unfamiliar with the facts behind the Whiskey Ring trials. In another move to block the trials, Grant wrote a lengthy two-page letter on behalf of Babcock, in which the president declared his secretary's innocence. Babcock was acquitted, and the Whiskey Ring trials ended on a low note. Only a few defendants were ever found guilty, none tying the frauds to Grant or his administration.

Although many historians consider the Whiskey Ring frauds to be one of the worst governmental scandals in American history, few people are familiar with it today, and historical works barely cover it. In October 1876 a lengthy article appeared under the byline of one H. V. Boynton in regards to the Whiskey Ring frauds. Summing up the complexity of the frauds, Boynton explained:

> Congressional investigations and the press have made known, though in somewhat disjointed form, the chief features of the late war upon [the] whiskey thieves and their abettors.... While this movement of Secretary Bristow for the suppression of whiskey frauds was a clearly defined campaign, having a definite beginning, sharp outlines, and a sudden ending, it is yet too early for any one to attempt its full history. Much of it cannot be known, unless the Secretary himself discloses it. The secret machinations by which a formidable array continually excited the President against his Secretary as yet partially appear. For each of the cities where the blow [of prosecution] fell, there is a local history full of interest and illustrative of the political power wielded by the ring, which was not fully known in Washington. Some further developments yet await the ongoing chariot of justice, the wheels of which drag heavily just now.

To this day, the entire story of the Whiskey Ring frauds, their cover-up, and the role of members of the Grant administration in the affair, has yet to be fully told.

See also Henderson, John Brooks

References: Boynton, H. V., "The Whiskey Ring," *North American Review*, CCLII (October 1876), 280–281; Logan, David A., *Historical Uses of a Special Prosecutor: The Administrations of Presidents Grant, Coolidge, and Truman* (Washington, DC: Congressional Research Service, 1973), 13; McDonald, John, *Secrets of the Great Whiskey Ring, Containing a Complete Exposure of the Illicit Whiskey Frauds Culminating in 1875, and the Connection of Grant, Babcock, Douglas, Chester H. Krum, and Other Administration Officers, Established by Positive and Unequivocal Documentary Proofs, Comprising Facsimiles of Confidential Letters and Telegrams Emanating From the White House, Directing the Management of the Ring. Also Photographs of Grant, Babcock, Bristow, Garfield and the Famous Sylph. To Which is Added the Missing Links in the Chain of Evidence of James A. Garfield's Implication with the District of Columbia Ring and Crédit Mobilier Bribery* (Chicago: Belford, Clarke & Co., 1880); Rives, Timothy, "Grant, Babcock, and the Whiskey Ring," *Prologue: Quarterly of the National Archives and Records Administration*, 32:3 (Fall 2000); Seematter, Mary E., "The St. Louis Whiskey Ring," *Gateway Heritage* (Spring 1988), 32–42; "The Whiskey Fraud Trials: General Henderson's Dismissal," *New York Times*, 11 December 1875, 1; "Whisky Trust Bribery," *New York Times*, 9 February 1893, 9.

## Whitewater

Scandal, 1993–2001, that in many ways encapsulated the history of scandal in the administration of President Bill Clinton. The scandal has it roots in land fraud, Southern politics, a rising politician in a small Southern state, and stolen U.S. government funds in the wake of the Savings & Loan scandal of the 1980s. The scandal started in 1978, when an Arkansas land broker, James McDougal, and his wife, Susan, formed a fifty-fifty land partnership with a young up-and-coming Arkansas politician, Bill Clinton, and his wife, Hillary. This land deal encompassed a huge area of forty-two lots of land along the White River in Arkansas. The two couples named the real estate concern the Whitewater Development Corporation, with the intention of selling the land for homes. Clinton and McDougal had become acquainted in 1968, when both men worked for the reelection of Senator William Fulbright of Arkansas. McDougal himself had never entered the political realm, instead becoming the owner of the Madison Guaranty Savings and Loan in Arkansas. He secretly used funds from the S&L to finance the Whitewater land deal. Although it appeared on paper that both the

*James McDougal holds a Whitewater deed. McDougal was convicted of 18 felony counts but received a reduced sentence, from 84 years to 3, after he testified against his ex-wife, Susan, and Arkansas Governor Jim Tucker. McDougal died in prison on 8 March 1998. (© Reuters/CORBIS Jeff J. Mitchell)*

Clintons and the McDougals lost money in the venture, many allegations later appeared that money was indeed earned and hidden from the state and federal government. The attorney for the land deal was Vincent Foster, an Arkansas attorney who was a boyhood friend of Bill Clinton and later served with Hillary Clinton as a member of the Rose Law Firm, one of the most prestigious law firms in Arkansas and the United States. In 1980 Clinton was elected governor of Arkansas, and, although he lost the office in 1982, he won it back in 1984 and held it until 1992. During this period, there were allegations that McDougal used funds from his S&L to finance parts of Clinton's gubernatorial campaigns.

For many years, the McDougals offered the Clintons a buyout of their share of Whitewater, but the Clintons refused until Clinton decided in 1991 to run for president of the United States. After Clinton was elected president, he named Vincent Foster deputy White House counsel. However, during the 1992 campaign, the allegations of financial and other shenanigans involving Whitewater bubbled to the surface, and reporters headed down to Arkansas to look into them. After Clinton took office, demands rose in Washington, D.C., that the land deal be investigated for possible illegalities. The voices rose to a crescendo when Foster was found dead in a Washington park on 20 July 1993—an alleged suicide. Suspicion focused on the White House when White House counsel Bernard Nussbaum ordered that confidential papers, many possibly dealing with Whitewater, be removed from Foster's office after word came that he was found dead. On 12 January 1994, Clinton himself asked that an independent counsel be named, and, on 20 January 1994, Attorney General Janet Reno named New York lawyer and former U.S. attorney Robert B. Fiske Jr., circumventing a court that, under the Independent Counsel Statute, is required to get a recommendation for the naming of an independent counsel and name one of their choosing. Fiske immediately launched an investigation of Foster's death and what he knew of the details of the Whitewater land deal. By August 1994 Fiske had concluded that Foster's death was indeed a suicide, and that the Clintons did not impede an investigation by the Resolution Trust Corporation (RTC), a federal government agency established to investigate potential savings and loans criminality. It appeared that the Clintons were cleared, and that the controversy would die down.

However, on 5 August 1994, when Fiske went to the special three-member judicial panel that had authority to name independent counsels, so that he could close parts of the investigation and get jurisdiction into other areas, the panel instead shocked Washington by removing Fiske from his post, explaining that he had not been properly named by the court initially. Instead, the court named Kenneth Winston Starr Jr., a former federal appeals judge and a former solicitor general under President George H. W. Bush. Immediately, Starr issued subpoenas for documents, such as the Rose Law Firm billing records relating to the land dealings. These records were missing from the firm and they did not turn up for two years, when they were found lying on a table in the White House—eliciting even more suspicion of the Clintons. These records showed that, despite earlier statements that she had done little if any work on behalf of the Whitewater project, Mrs. Clinton in fact had done sixty hours of work on Whitewater. In January 1996 Mrs. Clinton was summoned by Starr before a Washington grand jury to elaborate on the records issue.

The independent counsel's investigation also looked into the role of the Clintons in the collapse of the Madison Guaranty Savings and Loan. After it went under in the mid-1980s, the U.S. government bailed the S&L out at the expense of some $68 million. In 1989 James McDougal was indicted on state charges of bank fraud, but he was acquitted in 1990. However, Starr looked into whether Madison funds were used prior to the bank's demise to bolster the Whitewater land deal. Starr was able to track a 1985 fundraiser by McDougal that assisted in retiring campaign debt from Clinton's 1984 gubernatorial race. The fundraiser raised some $30,000, but $12,000 was traced to checks drawn from Madison. While Starr was investigating, both houses of the U.S. Congress opened investigations. The House Banking Committee, chaired by Repre-

sentative Jim Leach (R-IA) held hearings, which concluded on 10 August 1995, with the finding that no illegalities occurred in Whitewater. The Senate, however, formed the Senate Special Whitewater Committee, chaired by Senator Alfonse D'Amato (R-NY). This latter committee became bogged down in politics between Republicans and Democrats on the panel.

On 17 August 1995, a grand jury in Little Rock, Arkansas, indicted James and Susan McDougal, as well as Arkansas Governor Jim Guy Tucker on charges of bank fraud relating to loans to Whitewater. On 28 May 1996, all three were convicted, despite Clinton testifying for the defense via videotape, the first time a president had testified in a criminal trial. James McDougal made a deal to turn states' evidence against his ex-wife Susan and Jim Tucker. When Susan McDougal was offered a similar deal for her testimony, she refused, and after being held in contempt of court she was sent to prison for two years. She never testified against the Clintons.

In another trial in which Starr brought charges, Arkansas bankers Robert Hill and Herby Branscum Jr., political supporters of Clinton in Arkansas, were tried on charges of using deposits from their Arkansas banks to reimburse themselves for contributions to Clinton's 1990 gubernatorial campaign. However, on 1 August 1996, an Arkansas jury acquitted the two men on four charges and deadlocked on the others.

In all, Starr, and his successor, Robert Ray, who closed the Whitewater investigation in 2001, spent some $52 million under the Independent Counsel Statute, which was not renewed by Congress in 1999. Starr officially ended the Whitewater investigation on 19 November 1998, reporting to the three-member court that while he believed that Clinton himself lied under oath regarding Whitewater, he could not prove the case beyond a reasonable doubt. In 2000 Starr resigned his position and was succeeded by Ray, who issued a report in 2001 that while there were suspicions that the Clintons were involved in illegalities, "this office determined that the evidence was insufficient to prove to a jury beyond a reasonable doubt that either President or Mrs. Clinton knowingly participated in any criminal conduct." The final Whitewater report, issued by Ray's office on 20 March 2002, specifically stated that while there was insufficient evidence to indict either of the Clintons, both had been involved in illegal activity.

Jim McDougal died of a heart attack in prison in Fort Worth, Texas on 8 March 1998, carrying many of the secrets behind the true extent of the political corruption behind the Whitewater affair with him to the grave.

**See also** Clinton, William Jefferson, Tucker, James Guy

**References:** Thompson, Marilyn W., "Whitewater Probe's Insufficient Evidence," *Washington Post*, 20 November 1998, A32; United States Congress, Senate, Special Committee to Investigate Whitewater Development Corporation and Related Matters, *Investigation of Whitewater Development Corporation and Related Matters: Final Report of the Special Committee to Investigate Whitewater Development Corporation and Related Matters, Together with Additional and Minority Views* (Washington: Government Printing Office, 1996).

## Whittemore, Benjamin Franklin (1824–1894)

United States representative from South Carolina (1868–1870), resigned his seat because of allegations that he sold appointments to the U.S. military and naval academies. Born in Malden, Massachusetts, on 18 May 1824, Whittemore attended public schools in nearby Worcester and finished his education at Amherst. (However, Amherst does not have a record of his having attended or graduat-

Benjamin F. Whittemore (Library of Congress, Prints & Photographs Division, LC-DIG-cwpbh-00190)

ing). He then entered private business, engaging in a mercantile concern until 1859, when he studied theology and became a minister in the Methodist Episcopal Church in the New England Conference in 1859. It appeared that he would make the church his life's work.

When the Civil War exploded in 1861, instead of serving as a soldier, Whittemore served the Union Army as a chaplain for the Fifty-third Regiment of the Massachusetts Volunteers, and later with the Thirtieth Regiment of the Veteran Volunteers. There is no record of what kind of action Whittemore may have seen during the war. When the conflict ended, he settled in Darlington, South Carolina, serving as a delegate to the state constitution convention in 1867. Elected president of the Republican state Executive Board that same year, he founded the newspaper the *New Era* in Darlington. In 1868 he served as a member of the South Carolina state senate. When South Carolina was readmitted to the Union under Reconstruction, Whittemore was elected to a seat in the U.S. House of Representatives as a Republican, serving in the Fortieth and Forty-first Congresses from 18 July 1868 to 24 February 1870.

Whittemore apparently got into ethical trouble for selling appointments to West Point and Annapolis for either political favors or cash—which one is not specified. Following a House investigation, it was recommended that Whittemore face expulsion from the House—a sanction not sought since the Civil War. *Hind's Precedents*, which are the proceedings of Congress, reported:

On February 21, 1870, Mr. John A. Logan, of Illinois, from the Committee on Military Affairs, who were instructed to inquire into the alleged sale of appointments to the Military and Naval Academies by Members of Congress, submitted a report, in writing, accompanied by the following resolution, viz:

"Resolved, That B. F. Whittemore, a Representative in Congress from the First Congressional district of South Carolina, be, and is hereby, expelled from his seat as a Member of the House of Representatives in the Forty-first Congress."

On February 23 the Speaker ruled that Mr. Whittemore might, under the resolution, be heard either orally or in writing. So his affidavit was presented and read, in denial of the charge. After it had been read, Mr. Benjamin F. Butler, of Massachusetts, desired to be heard in behalf of the accused Member, having been deputed by him to make his defense.... On February 24, as the House was considering the resolution of expulsion, the Speaker laid before the House a communication from B. F. Whittemore, informing the House that he had transmitted to the governor of South Carolina his resignation of his seat in Congress. The same having been read, Mr. Whittemore was about to address the House, when the Speaker decided that, in view of the communication just read to the House, he could not recognize him as any longer a Member of the House or entitled to address the same. Mr. Whittemore's notice to the Speaker that he had resigned did not reach the desk until after the speech had begun. The Speaker, as soon as he read the notice of resignation, caused Mr. Whittemore to suspend his remarks, and ruled that it was not within the power of the Chair to recognize anyone not a Member of the House. Therefore he ruled that Mr. Whittemore might proceed only by unanimous consent of the House.

After speaking, Whittemore left the House in disgrace. However, no legal or criminal action was ever taken against him. His constituents, angered by his forced resignation, re-elected him to fill the vacancy caused by his resignation, but when Whittemore went to present the credentials of the election to the House he was rebuffed, and the House declined to seat him. Whittemore returned to South Carolina. He later served as a member of the South Carolina state senate in 1877, but after this term, left the state and returned to Massachusetts, where he became the publisher of a small newspaper. Whittemore died in Montvale, Massachusetts, on 25 January 1894 at the age of sixty-nine and was buried in the Salem Street Cemetery in Woburn, Massachusetts.

**References:** *Biographical Directory of the American Congress, 1774–1996 (Alexandria, VA: CQ Staff Directories, Inc., 1996), 2050; Hinds, Asher Crosby, Hinds' Precedents of the House of Representatives of the United States, including References to Provisions of the Constitution, the Laws, and Decisions of the United States Senate, 8 vols. (Washington, DC: Government Printing Office, 1907–1908), V:829–832; Whittemore Amherst information in Robert Fletcher, ed., Amherst College: Biographical Record of the Graduates and Non-Graduates. Centennial Edition, 1821–1921 (Amherst, MA: Published by the College, 1927).*

# Willett, William Forte, Jr. (1869–1938)

United States representative from New York (1907–1911), indicted and convicted for bribery and conspiracy in his attempts to secure a seat on the Queens County (New York) Supreme Court, for which he served more than a year in prison. Willett remains an obscure figure despite being one of only a handful of U.S. representatives to serve time in prison. Born in Brooklyn, New York, on 27 November 1869, he attended the public schools of that city before he received a law degree from New York University in 1895.

*William F. Willett, Jr. (Library of Congress, Prints & Photographs Division, LC-DIG-ggbain-15171)*

He was admitted to the bar the following year and opened a law practice in New York City.

Willett was elected as a Democrat to the U.S. House of Representatives in 1906, taking his seat in the Sixtieth Congress on 4 March 1907. He was reelected in 1908, but was not a candidate for reelection in 1910. Historians who have studied his congressional career note that he is known for doing only two things: delivering a speech on the House floor on 18 January 1909 in which he called outgoing President Theodore Roosevelt "a grinning gargoyle," and the House vote on 27 January 1909 of 126 to 78 expunging that speech from the congressional record. After leaving Congress, Willett returned to New York, where he entered into the business of selling real estate.

In October 1911, according to his indictment, Willett bribed Queens Democratic lead-er "Curley Joe" Cassidy in the amount of $10,000 in order to get a nomination for a seat on the Queens County Supreme Court. The scheme, however, somehow became public: on 1 November 1911, New York City District Attorney Charles Whitman reported that he had proof that Willett paid $37,000 in total bribes to get the Democratic nomination. Tammany Hall leader Charles Murphy told reporters that Tammany Hall did not get any of the money. Whitman went to court and presented evidence against Willett; L. T. Walters Jr., who nominated Willett; Cassidy; and Kings County Democratic Chairman J. H. McCooey; on charges of conspiracy and corrupt practices, including bribery. On 2 November, a Long Island bank where Willett banked revealed that Willett had borrowed $10,000 "for campaign purposes." McCooey denied that he had been involved with Willett or his attempts to get on the ballot. On 20 November, Willett, Walters, and Cassidy were arrested; all three pled not guilty and posted bail. Although a Queens County grand jury refused to indict the men, a grand jury in Kings County opened an investigation, and indicted Walters and Willett on 20 June 1912.

In 1913 all three men went on trial and were convicted on all charges. His appeals exhausted, in 1914 Willett entered Sing Sing prison in upstate New York state. He served fourteen months there, being paroled in 1915. While in prison, Willett became unpopular for enforcing discipline and was beaten up severely.

After leaving prison, Willett quietly worked in real estate ventures, never again surfacing in the political realm. He died in New York City on 12 February 1938 at the age of sixty-eight, and was buried in the Cemetery of the Evergreens in Kings County, New York.

**References:** *Biographical Directory of the American Congress, 1774–1996* (Alexandria, VA: CQ Staff Directories, Inc., 1996), 2058.

# Williams, Harrison Arlington, Jr. (1919–2001)

United States representative (1953–1957) and senator (1959–1982) from New Jersey, the only senator implicated in the ABSCAM scandal, resigned his seat and was convicted of his involvement in the scandal. Born in Plainfield, New Jersey, on 10 December 1919, Williams attended the public schools of New Jersey before attending Oberlin College in Ohio and graduating from that institution in 1941. He then moved to Washington, D.C., where he went to work as a cub reporter for the *Washington Post*. He attended the Georgetown University Foreign Service School until he was called to active duty as a seaman in the United States Naval Reserve. He entered that service as a naval aviator, although it is unknown if he saw any action. When he was discharged in 1945, Williams held the rank of lieutenant, junior grade.

Following the war, Williams went to work in private business in the steel industry. However, he decided to get his law license. He entered Columbia Law School in New York and graduated with a law degree in 1948. He was admitted to the New York bar, but went to New Hampshire for a short time where he opened a law practice. He returned to New Jersey, settled in the town of Plainfield, and opened a law practice there. A Democrat, he entered the political realm in 1951, unsuccessfully running for a seat in the New Jersey House of Assembly. He ran a campaign for the Plainfield city council early the following year, but also lost that race. In late 1952, when Republican Clifford Case left his House seat to run for the U.S. Senate, Williams ran for Case's seat in the U.S. House, representing the sixth district. Elected, he entered the Eighty-third Congress on 3 November 1953 and served in that body until 3 January 1957. He

was reelected in 1954, but defeated in 1956. In 1957 he campaigned for the reelection of New Jersey Governor Robert B. Meyner, a Democrat. Meyner, returning the favor, pushed Williams to run in 1958 for the U.S. Senate against Senator Robert W. Kean, a Republican.

In 1958 Williams defeated Kean and held his Senate seat until his resignation on 11 March 1982. A liberal, he supported Social Security, conservation, and civil rights legislation. He rose to become chairman of the Senate Committee on Labor and Human Resources, losing the chairmanship when the Republicans took control in 1981. He was reelected three times to the Senate.

In the late 1970s, the Federal Bureau of Investigation, acting on rumors that some congressmen and senators were willing to take bribes to aid foreigners to gain citizenship, set up Operation Arab Scam—better known as ABSCAM. An agent of the bureau was dressed as an Arab sheikh, and congressmen and senators who took the bait were invited to speak to the phony sheikh, who offered them bribes in exchange for getting the sheikh and his friends American citizenship. The only senator who decided to take the money and work for the sheikh was Harrison Williams. Videotapes later released showed Williams asking for a loan of $100 million, which he said was to provide for his and his family's security after he left the Senate. The Senate Ethics Committee later called these tapes not just a "smoking gun," but a "smoking machine gun." Williams was indicted on 30 October 1980, and his trial began in Brooklyn, New York, on 1 April 1981. The videotapes were the piece of evidence that nailed Williams. As the *New York Times* stated:

The prosecutors sought to show that Mr. Williams and [his codefendant, Alexander] Feinberg were "predisposed" to commit illegal acts in the immigration and titanium-mining matters. The prosecutors did this by introducing evidence of the defendants' behavior in situations involving an Atlantic City gambling casino and an unsuccessful venture to build a New Jersey garbage-recycling facility—situations that were not part of the charges in the trial.

In the casino matter, the prosecutors played a videotape of a 1979 meeting in which the Senator told the Abscam agents that he had interceded with a New Jersey official to help gain a decision from the state's Casino Control Commission that would have saved a casino-development group $30 million, had its proposed project been carried out. The casino had been proposed by a company in which the controlling interest was held by a second company that employed the Senator's wife as a consultant....

The key prosecution evidence in the titanium-mining and immigration matters were videotapes of two meetings the Senator had with the bogus sheik, played by F.B.I. agent Richard Farhart.

In the first tape, made at a meeting held in an Arlington, Virginia, motel in June 1979, Senator Williams says that there would be "no problem" in using his relationships with the nation's top officials—including President Jimmy Carter—in trying to get the government contract for the mine. In the second tape, made at the Plaza Hotel in January 1980, the Senator gave the phony sheik assurances of help in seeking permanent residency in the United States.

On 1 May 1981, Williams was found guilty of bribery and conspiracy charges. He refused to resign from the Senate, and the Senate Ethics Committee opened an investigation into whether or not Williams should be expelled. Williams continued to assert his innocence, instead decrying FBI tactics in snaring him. Robert S. Bennett, the Washington, D.C., attorney who defended President Bill Clinton, served as special counsel for the Senate Ethics Committee in the Williams investigation. However, the stunning evidence of Williams on tape shaking down the fake Arab sheikhs was his undoing. The Ethics committee recommended on 24 August 1981 that Williams be expelled for his crimes. Debate in the Senate regarding the recommendation began on 3 March 1982. Senator after senator took to the floor to discuss Senate Resolution 204—the expulsion of Harrison Williams. "The unfortu-

nate but unavoidable task of considering Senate Resolution 204 is an arduous responsibility; a disturbing responsibility for every senator, a weighty responsibility for the institution itself," Senator Howard Baker (R-TN), the first speaker, stated. Senator Howell Heflin (D-AL) said, "At any point during this drawn-out, sordid affair, Senator Williams could have said, 'Wait a minute. What you're proposing is wrong. This is not what I had in mind. I can't be involved in this.' But he didn't.... He stayed; he discussed; he agreed; he promised; he pledged to abuse his office, his public trust, for which, now he must be expelled." Senator Daniel Inouye (D-HI) was one of the few voices to speak for Williams. The senator was guilty of nothing "so dastardly, so sinister," but instead had been entrapped "by the FBI, an agency of the executive branch of government.... Who among us has not touted our importance to our constituents? We are here because our egos are immense." Williams spoke to his colleagues for four hours, imploring them not to vote to expel. "It is not only Pete Williams that stands accused or indicted. It is all of us, the entire Senate, that stands accused and intimidated by another branch of government.... The chairman of the Select Committee on Ethics [then-Sen. Malcolm Wallop (R-WY)] ... shelters the FBI and its malcontents from criticism in his prosecution of me. In so doing, I believe he makes the next Abscam easier and more legitimate."

Williams's arguments fell on deaf ears—even his own fellow New Jerseyian, Senator Bill Bradley, supported his expulsion. A move by some Democrats only to censure Williams failed, and, facing an inevitable vote to expel him, the New Jersey senator resigned on 11 March 1982. Williams told his supporters, "I announce my intention to resign. Time, history and Almighty God will vindicate me and the principles for which I fought here in the Senate. I will be vindicated before the people in our land." Williams was sentenced to three years in prison, entering the federal correction facility in Allenwood, Pennsylvania, in 1983, becoming the first senator in eighty years to go to prison. He was paroled in 1986, and returned home to Bedminster, New Jersey.

In his final years, Williams sought the vindication he argued for, asking President Bill Clinton for a pardon in 2000, but Clinton refused. Williams, suffering from cancer and other ailments, died on 20 November 2001, one month shy of his eighty-second birthday.

See also Primary Documents, page 615.

References: Bernstein, Adam, "Harrison A. Williams Jr. Dies, Abscam Ousted N.J. Senator," *Washington Post*, 20 November 2001, B7; *Biographical Directory of the American Congress, 1774–1996* (Alexandria, VA: CQ Staff Directories, Inc., 1996), 2061; Byrd, Robert C., *The Senate, 1789$–$1989: Historical Statistics, 1789–1992* (Washington, DC: Government Printing Office, four volumes, 1993), IV:668; Fried, Joseph P., "Senate Ethics Unit to Consider Action on Williams Verdict," *New York Times*, 3 May 1981, A1; Fried, Joseph P., "Williams Is Guilty on All Nine Counts in Abscam Inquiry, Vows Not to Resign," *New York Times*, 2 May 1981, A1; Sullivan, Joseph F., "Senate Opens Debate on Williams, 'Did Nothing Criminal,' He Insists," *New York Times*, 4 March 1982, A1; Sullivan, Joseph F., "Williams Pleads with Colleagues in 4-Hour Speech on Senate Floor," *New York Times*, 5 March 1982, A1; Sullivan, Joseph F., "Williams Quits Senate Seat as Vote to Expel Him Nears, Still Asserts He Is Innocent," *New York Times*, 12 March 1982, A1.

## Williams, John James (1904–1988)

United States senator (1947–1970) from Delaware, instrumental in numerous investigations into corruption, including the Bobby Baker affair (1964). Born in Bayard, Delaware, on 17 May 1904, the ninth of eleven children of a farming family, he attended local schools before he borrowed some money and established the Millsboro Feed Company in Millsboro, Delaware, with his brother Pre-

ston. This enterprise grew to include the Williams Hatchery, where chickens and turkeys were raised, as well as 2,000 acres of farms and other lands. In 1946 he served in the Millsboro town council.

In late 1946, with little political experience under his belt, Williams decided to run for the United States Senate against Democratic incumbent James M. Tunnell, a popular supporter of President Harry S. Truman. Williams, a Republican who railed against what he perceived to be the slide of the Democratic party toward socialism and who decried Truman's economic and social policies, was given little if any chance to upset the popular Tunnell. Williams easily won the Republican nomination, and, during the campaign, portrayed himself as a small businessman fighting against big government. Tunnell, though only in his first term, was nearly seventy, while Williams was in his early forties. The contrast, and the arguments of Williams, swayed the electorate, and on election day Williams was elected with a nearly 12,000-vote advantage out of 113,500 votes cast.

Williams began his career in the Senate by speaking out against the price supports of the administration, which he felt helped large corporations over the small farmer, the policies of the New Deal Office of Price Administration, and called for a cut in income taxes. In 1947 he was seated on the Committee to Investigate the National Defense, which investigated contracts handed out during World War II to see if there was fraud or waste in any of them. For his work, in 1949 he was named to the prestigious Finance Committee. He eventually rose to become the ranking minority leader on that panel. As a member of the committee, he became skilled in taxation and budgetary issues. A critic of overspending in both Democratic and Republican administrations, in the early 1950s he alleged bookkeeping errors that cost some $350 million at the Commodities Credit Corporation (CCC). As a member of the Agriculture Committee, he worked to expose costly farm programs that he felt benefited a few corporations and not the family farmers the programs were intended to help. For this work, in 1967 he was awarded the American Farm Bureau's highest award for his work on agricultural issues.

Yet Williams's greatest role was in the investigation into Robert G. "Bobby" Baker, the secretary to the former Senate Majority Leader and later Vice President Lyndon Johnson. Starting in 1963, before Johnson became president upon the assassination of John F. Kennedy, Williams was tipped off that Baker had been involved in shady business dealings, and called upon the Senate Rules Committee to open a formal investigation. When the Rules Committee seemed to hesitate to investigate one of their own (the issue could serve to embarrass Johnson, running for a full term on his own in 1964), Williams went public with his accusations. Because of this, in 1964 Johnson spearheaded an effort to defeat him in Delaware, but Williams won, despite the contest being the narrowest of his four victories. Williams was not shy in pointing out corruption within his own party—in 1959 he was one of the first senators to call upon President Eisenhower to fire his chief of staff, Sherman Adams.

In 1960 Williams had been named to the Foreign Relations Committee and when he retired in 1970, he became the last man to serve on both the Senate Finance and Foreign Relations Committees. (A Senate rule passed during Williams's tenure prohibited joint service on two of the "big five" committees, which included Finance and Foreign Relations.) He criticized the misuse of funds from the Agency for International Development (AID), and by the mid-1960s, was a major critic of the war in Vietnam. He opposed continuing the war during both the Johnson and subsequent Nixon administrations. He was, however, considered a leading authority on the issue of honesty in the Senate, and in 1952 and 1968 was considered a leading candidate for vice president, but he refused both times. In 1973, when Vice President Spiro Agnew was forced to resign, Williams's name was floated as a possible replacement. Had he accepted, Williams would have become the thirty-eighth president in 1974.

In 1969, Williams announced that he would retire at the age of sixty-five and not run for a fifth term in 1970. Representative William Roth won the seat that year and held it until 2001. Williams retired with his wife to Millsboro, where he worked in real estate. He died there on 11 January 1988 at the age of eighty-three.

Williams is considered by many historians to have been one of the most honest men ever to serve in the Senate. He was called "The Lonewolf Investigator," "Watchdog of the Treasury," "Honest John," "Mr. Integrity," and "the Conscience of the Senate" by his peers, the press, and his constituents. In 1963 Senator Sam Ervin said of him, he is "the gadfly of the Senate ... on many occasions he has stung the Congress and the executive agencies into righteous conduct."

**See also** Baker, Robert Gene

**References:** *Biographical Directory of the American Congress, 1774–1996* (Alexandria, VA: CQ Staff Directories, Inc., 1996), 2063.

# Williamson, John Newton (1855–1943)

United States representative from Oregon (1903–1907), convicted, with Senator John Hipple Mitchell, of land fraud and forced to leave Congress before he could be stripped of his seat. Because Mitchell was the leading character in that episode, Williamson's name and deeds were largely ignored by the media at the time, and he has slipped into obscurity. Little is known of his life—he was born near Junction City, Oregon, on 8 November 1855, and he attended country schools. He did attend Willamette University in Salem, Oregon, but he apparently never obtained any degree from that institution. Sometime after leaving school, Williamson went into business raising livestock.

A Republican, Williamson was elected sheriff of Cook County, Oregon, in 1886, and served for two years. At the end of that term of office, he was elected to a seat in the Oregon state house of representatives, where he served until 1898. From 1893 until 1896, he owned and edited the *Prineville Review*. In 1900 Williamson was elected to a seat in the state senate, where he served until 1902. In that year Williamson was elected to the U.S. House of Representatives, representing Oregon's Second District. He served in the Fifty-eighth and Fifty-ninth Congresses, from 4 March 1903 until 3 March 1907.

In his time before and during his congressional tenure, Williamson became involved in purchasing land in Oregon. Working closely with Senator John H. Mitchell of Oregon, he bought up homesteads fraudulently from the U.S. government by using fake names and fake documents. Williamson was convicted of the same charges as Mitchell: conspiracy to defraud the United States government. However, a study of Williamson's biography shows no prison term, so the disposition of his case remains unknown. He did not stand for reelection in 1906 and returned to Oregon.

Williamson spent the remainder of his life in Oregon, working on a ranch and engaging in agricultural pursuits; he served as postmaster of Prineville, Oregon, from 1922 until 1934. He died in Prineville on 29 August 1943 and was buried in the Masonic Cemetery in that town.

**See also** Mitchell, John Hipple

**References:** *Biographical Directory of the American Congress, 1774–1996* (Alexandria, VA: CQ Staff Directories, Inc., 1996); Cummings, Hilary Anne, "John H. Mitchell, a Man of His Time: Foundations of His Political Career, 1860–1879," (Ph.D. dissertation, University of Oregon, 1985); O'Callaghan, Jerry A., "Senator John H. Mitchell and the Oregon Land Frauds, 1905." *Pacific Historical Review* 21 (August 1952): 255–261.

## Wilson, Charles Herbert (1917–1984)

United States representative from California (1963–1981), censured by the U.S. House of Representatives in 1980 for financial misconduct, one of only twenty-two House members ever to receive that punishment. Wilson was born in Magna, Utah, on 15 February 1917, but moved with his parents to Los Angeles, California, in 1922. He attended the public schools there and in the nearby town of Inglewood, after which he went to work in a bank starting in 1935. In 1942 he was enlisted in the U.S. Army, and, with the rank of staff sergeant, served from June 1942 to December 1945, seeing limited action in the European theater of operations before he was discharged. Returning to the United States, Wilson established an insurance agency in Los Angeles.

In 1953 Wilson entered the political arena and ran as a Democrat for a seat in the California state legislature. Elected, he served from 1954 to 1962 as an assemblyman from the Sixty-sixth California District. In 1962 he gave up this post to run for a seat in the U.S. House of Representatives, representing the Thirty-first California District. Defeating Republican Gordon Kahn, Wilson took his seat in Congress and ultimately served from 3 January 1963 until 3 January 1981, from the Eighty-eighth through the Ninety-sixth Congresses.

During the 1970s, Wilson was at the forefront of a secret campaign inside the House to advance the influence of the Korean government—and he took gifts and other remuneration from the Korean government for his support. In 1980 the House investigated the role of Wilson in the so-called Koreagate scandal, and found that he had accepted improper gifts, as well as used "ghost" employees in his office (so he could collect additional paychecks), and improperly used campaign funds. However, the House Ethics Committee recommended that Wilson be censured instead of being the subject of an expulsion vote. Wilson was censured by the full House on 6 June 1980, becoming one of only a handful of members to suffer that indignity. Because of his conduct, Wilson lost in the Democratic primary in 1980 and left Congress on 3 January 1981.

In his final years, Wilson lived in Tantallon, Maryland, until his death in Clinton, Maryland, on 21 July 1984 at the age of sixty-seven. His body was returned to California and laid to rest in the Inglewood Park Cemetery in Inglewood, California.

**References:** *Biographical Directory of the American Congress, 1774–1996* (Alexandria, VA: CQ Staff Directories, Inc., 1996).

## Worrall, Robert

*See United States v. Worrall.*

## Wright, James Claude, Jr. (1922– )

United States representative from Texas (1954–1989) and Speaker of the House (1986–1989), forced to step down from the Speakership and his seat after he was accused of violating House rules on financial improprieties and limits on outside earned income. Born in Fort Worth, Texas, on 22 December 1922, James Wright Jr. attended the public schools of Fort Worth and Dallas, before he went to Weatherford College in Texas from 1939 to 1940 and the University of Texas from 1940 to 1941. After the Japanese attack on Pearl Harbor and the entry of the United States into World War II, Wright enlisted in the U.S. Army Air Force. Commissioned in 1942, he was posted to the Pacific theater of operations and flew combat missions in the South Pacific, for which he was awarded the Distinguished Service Cross. After the war, Wright returned home and entered the Texas political arena. He was elected to the Texas state house of representatives in 1946, but was defeated after serving a single term. He then moved to Weatherford, Texas, where he had gone to college, and ran for mayor. He was elected and served from 1950 to 1954. In that latter year, he ran unopposed for a seat in the U.S. House of Representatives, representing Texas's Twelfth District. Wright would be reelected seventeen times. (He ran unsuccessfully for a U.S. Senate seat in 1961.) In 1977, when Majority Leader Thomas P. "Tip" O'Neill was elevated to the Speakership, Wright was named as his replacement for the Majority Leader position. Wright served in this capacity from the Ninety-fifth through the Ninety-ninth congresses. When O'Neill retired from the Speakership and the House in 1985, Wright was elected by the Democrats, then in the majority, to be the Forty-ninth Speaker of the House. Wright would serve as Speaker through the 100th and the 101st Congresses.

Jim Wright got into ethical trouble just as he was becoming one of the most powerful politicians in America. He rented a condominium in Fort Worth from a close friend, real estate developer George Mallick, and paid Mallick for the use of the condo—Mallick's gift of the condo use was in violation of a ban on more than $100 in gifts from any one person. He intervened with federal regulators on behalf of three Texans—a real estate developer, and two executives from a Fort Worth Savings & Loan—in dealings with the Federal Home Loan Bank Board. However, the worst allegation came regarding his memoirs. Wright had penned *Reflections of a Public Man* in 1984; it was a 117-page trifle that was sold in bulk by lobbyists. It had been published by Carlos Moore, whose printing firm had worked for Wright's campaigns for many years. Finally, Wright had gotten 55 percent in royalties from the sales of the book, when normally authors get 10 to 15 percent. In May 1988 Common Cause, a public citizens' action group, called for a congressional inquiry into these allegations. Within days of Common Cause's complaint, Representative Newt Gingrich of Georgia, a firebrand member of the Republican minority in the House, sent a letter, cosigned by seventy-two of his Republican colleagues, to the House Committee on Standards of Official Conduct, the panel which oversees ethics in the House, asking for an investigation of the charges. The Democrat-led committee voted unanimously on 9 June 1988 to conduct a preliminary inquiry; later, a full-blown investigation was ordered, and a special outside counsel, Chicago attorney Richard J. Phelan, was retained. Wright testified for more than five hours before the committee, and on 22 February 1989, Phelan gave his 279-page report to the Committee. It alleged that on sixty-nine separate occasions, Wright had broken congressional rules—specifically regarding the cozy book deal from which he had profited and taking more than $145,000 in gifts from his friend George Mallick. An allegation that Wright was illegally involved in an oil-well

deal that resulted in huge profits for him was never investigated, and, in the end, the House committee dropped more than half of the allegations Phelan disclosed. Wright's attorneys claimed that the committee and Phelan were "misinterpreting" House rules so as to make Wright look guilty and asked for the Speaker to be exonerated. He was not.

On 31 May 1989, Wright took to the floor of the House to deliver his resignation speech and direct a stinging rebuke at the "mindless cannibalism" of ethics investigations. As his voice quivered with emotion, Wright said, "Let me give you back this job you gave to me as a propitiation for all of this season of bad will that has grown up among us.... I don't want to be a party to tearing up this institution. I love it." Wright thus became the first sitting Speaker of the House to resign his post because of scandal. Less than a month later, on 30 June 1989, Wright resigned from the House altogether, ending a forty-four-year congressional career. He and his wife returned to Texas, where he still lives.

Dennis F. Thompson, writing on institutional corruption in American politics, explained in 1995, "The charges against Wright combine in the same case the individual and institutional corruption found, respectively, in the cases of [Senator David] Durenberger and the Keating Five.... The presence of both kinds of corruption in the same case offer an opportunity for a direct comparison. Confronted with a case of both kinds of corruption, the House ethics committee took seriously only the allegations of individual corruption, even though they were arguably less serious than those of institutional corruption."

**See also** Primary Documents, page 629.

**References:** Barry, John M., *The Ambition and the Power* (New York: Viking, 1989); *Congressional Ethics* (Washington, DC: Congressional Quarterly, 1980), 20–21; "Impassioned Wright Quits, Speaker Asks End to Rancor," *Miami Herald*, 1 June 1989, A1; Toner, Robin, "Wright Resigning As Speaker, Defends His Ethics and Urges End of 'Mindless Cannibalism,'" *New York Times*, 1 June 1989, A1, D21; "Transcript of Wright's Address to House of Representatives," *New York Times*, 1 June 1989, D22–23; Thompson, Dennis F., *Ethics in Congress: From Individual to Institutional Corruption* (Washington, DC: The Brookings Institution, 1995), 43–44; United States Congress, *Biographical Directory of the United States Congress, 1774$–$1989: The Continental Congress, September 5, 1774, to October 21, 1788, and the Congress of the United States, from the First through the One Hundredth Congresses, March 4, 1789, to January 3, 1989, inclusive* (Washington, DC: Government Printing Office, 1989); United States Congress, House, Committee on Standards of Official Conduct, *Report of the Special Outside Counsel in the Matter of Speaker James C. Wright, Jr. Committee on Standards of Official Conduct, U.S. House of Representatives, One Hundred First Congress* (Washington, DC: Government Printing Office, 1989).

# Z

## Zenger, John Peter (1697–1746)

Journalist and writer, whose trial for exposing the corruption of the British governor of New York set the stage for the enunciation of the free speech principle in the colonies and later the United States. And although his name belongs to history for his role in standing for free speech, few know of the details of his life or his infamous trial. Zenger was born in what was called the Upper Palatinate (now Bavaria, Germany) sometime in the year 1697, and around 1710 emigrated with his family to New York, then a prosperous English colony. The elder Zenger died en route to the New World, leaving his widow Johanna to care for Peter and his two siblings. The year after he came to the colonies, Zenger went to work as an apprentice for William Bradford, the famed printer who was the royal printer for the New York colony. This apprenticeship ended in 1719, but, six years later, Bradford invited Zenger to become his partner. In 1726 Zenger struck out on his own, starting his own printing establishment. His printing was little noticed except for several theological tracts, but in 1730 he published the first arithmetic book in the colonies.

In 1733 Zenger founded the *New York Weekly Journal*, which would become, in its short history, one of the most important newspapers in American history. The first issue appeared on 5 November 1733. Zenger's enterprise was backed financially by the Popular Party, a group of men in New York colony who opposed the administration of William Cosby, the governor of the colony. One of the leaders of the Popular Party, James Alexander, served as the paper's editor in chief. With each new issue, new editorials and stories called attention to the corruption of Cosby. In these days before any such thing as the First Amendment existed, Zenger and his friends pushed an envelope that really was never opened.

The *New York Weekly Journal* explained in its 25 February 1733 edition:

A Lible [sic] is not the less a Libel for being true, this may seem a Contradiction; but it is neither one in Law, or in common Scope. There are some Truths not fit to be told; where, for Example, the Discovery of a small Fault may do mischief; or where the Discovery of a great fault can do no good, there ought to be no discovery at all, and to make faults where there are none is still worse.... But this Doctrine only holds true as to private and personal failings; and it is quite otherwise when the crimes of Men come to Affect the Publick. Nothing ought to be so dear to us as our Country, and nothing ought to come in Competition with its Interests. Every crime against the Publick, is a great crime, tho there be some greater than others. Ignorance and Folly may be pleaded in Alleviation of private Offenses; but when they come to be publick Offenses, they lose all Benefit of such a Plea; we are no longer to then consider, to what Causes they are owing, but what Evils they may produce, and here we shall readily find, that Folly has overturned States, and private Interest been the parent of Publick Confusion.

Cosby and his friends, angered at the newspaper's growing popularity, established a grand jury that found the editorials to be libelous and seditious, and ordered Zenger's arrest and for the paper to be closed down. On 17 November 1734, Zenger was arrested and imprisoned in Manhattan. Two of the paper's writers, James Alexander and William Smith, condemned the move. They questioned the authority of the Crown to arrest Zenger and condemned the high bail set for him. They wrote a stinging letter to the colonial assembly: "Instead of consulting our law books, and doing what we think consistent therewith, for the benefit of our clients ... [attorneys] must study in great men's causes, and only what will please the judges, and what will most flatter men is power."

Initially finding a lawyer who would oppose the Crown proved difficult (all of those who had acted on behalf of Zenger were disbarred by the colonial authorities), but Scottish attorney Andrew Hamilton (1676?–1741), a leading lawyer in the Pennsylvania colony, stepped forward to defend Zenger on principle despite his sympathy for the royal forces. The trial, taking place in 1735, dealt with whether Zenger's editorials libeled Cosby. Hamilton argued to the jury that the editorials were factually true, and thus could not be libelous. In his classic statement before the jury, Hamilton told them that men had a right "to complain when they are hurt ... publicly to remonstrate the abuses of power in the strongest forms ... and to assert with courage the sense they have of the blessing of liberty, the value they put upon it, and their reputation at all hazards to preserve it." Although the judge instructed the jury that Zenger must be found guilty whether or not his editorials were true, the jury returned with a not guilty verdict, accepting Hamilton's stand that truth is a defense to libel. It was also the first known case of jury nullification. The verdict set the standard for freedom of the press—so much so, that this case was used by the Founding Fathers forty years later as the basis for the First Amendment to the U.S. Constitution.

Zenger was released, but never made an impact in the printing world again. He worked, ironically, as the public printer for the colony of New York in 1737, and in the same position for the colony of New Jersey in 1738. He died quietly in 1746.

**References:** *New-York Weekly Journal, Containing the Frequent Advices, Foreign, and Domestick* (Editorial), 25 February 1733, 1; Morris, Richard B., "Zenger, John Peter," in Allen Johnson and Dumas Malone, et al., eds., *Dictionary of American Biography,* 10 vols. and 10 supplements (New York: Charles Scribner's Sons, 1930–1995), X:648–650; "Trial of John Peter Zenger Before the Supreme Court of New York, For Two Libels on the Government, New York, 1735," in Peleg W. Chandler, *American Criminal Trials,* 2 vols. (Boston: Charles C. Little and James Brown, 841–844), I:154–209; *The Trial of John Peter Zenger, of New York, Printer: Who was Charged with Having Printed and Published a LIBEL against the Government, and Acquitted. With a Narrative of His Case* (London: Printed for J. Almon, Opposite Burlington-House, Piccadilly, 1735); Rutherfurd, Livingston, *John Peter Zenger, His Press, His Trial and a Bibliography of Zenger Imprints, by Livingston Rutherfurd. Also a Reprint of the First Edition of the Trial* (New York: Dodd, Mead, 1904).

# Primary Documents

## Introduction

In 1904, historian James Harvey Robinson wrote in his *Readings in European History*, "It is clear that all our information in regard to past events and conditions must be derived from evidence of some kind. This evidence is called the source. Sometimes there are a number of good and reliable sources for an event, as, for example, for the decapitation of King Charles I of England in 1649, or for the march of Napoleon into Russia. Sometimes there is but a single, unreliable source, as, for instance, in the case of the burial of King Alaric in a river bed. For a great many important matters about which we should like to know there are, unfortunately, no written sources at all, and we can only guess how things were. For example, we do not know what the Germans were doing before Julius Caesar came into contact with them and took the trouble to give a brief account of them. We can learn but little about the bishops of Rome (or popes) before the time of the Emperor Constantine for few references to them have come down to us."

Robinson's two-volume work focuses on specific primary documents and resources to give a view of the event from that time, from that period, by persons who were living at the same time that the event was occurring.

The goal of the Primary Documents section in *Political Corruption in America* is the same as James Harvey Robinson's. Recognizing the important role of media coverage, it includes 58 full-text articles from a variety of newspapers, from 1804 to 2008. These contemporary accounts may not only be more important than modern sources on a particular scandal, but they illustrate how little progress America has made in the political corruption arena.

Discussing actions and feelings that a cold history, written long after the event, cannot hope to capture, these words expose the raw power of the near civil war that erupted in Kentucky following the assassination of Governor William Goebel in 1900, as well as the agony of Senator Thomas J. Dodd pleading his innocence as the US Senate censured him in 1967 for gross political spending violations. You will find the 1804 vote to impeach Judge John Pickering, as commanding as the 2002 vote to expel James A. Traficant, Jr., after he was found guilty of bribery and racketeering. The extensive allegations against President Carter's Management and Budget director Bert Lance in a wide-ranging *Washington Post* editorial is mirrored by a 1876 *New York Times* article documenting the widespread malfeasance of President Grant's Secretary of War William Worth Belknap which led to Belknap's impeachment. The 1963 scandal involving Bobby Baker, Majority Secretary of the US Senate, and his grip over elected members of that body, is interestingly similar to the events surrounding Judge George Washington English's impeachment trial in 1926, the Congressional impeachment of Judges Robert W. Archbald and Charles H. Swayne, and the state impeachment of Governor William Sulzer of New York.

This section of Primary Documents is a chronological examination of the exposure of actions leading up to and involving political corruption, offering first-hand reports of allegations, charges levied, impeachment proceedings and public reactions.

While memories fade and modern researchers and writers attempt to convey the details of an historical action, it is primary documents—such as those on the following 160 pages—that serve to reinforce and in many ways bring to life the episodes that give shape and substance to this work—and to history.

**Source**: Robinson, James Harvey, "The Historical Point of View" in Robinson, ed., "Readings in European History: A Collection of Extracts from the Sources Chosen with the Purpose of Illustrating the Progress of Culture in Western Europe since the German Invasions" (Boston: Ginn and Co.; two volumes, 1904-06), I:1.

# Table of Contents

# IMPEACHMENT OF JOHN PICKERING.

*National Intelligencer*, March 21, 1804.

Friday being the day assigned by the Senate for the commencement of the trial of Judge Pickering, impeached by the House of Representatives, of high crimes and misdemeanors, the Senate formed themselves into a Court of Impeachments, and sent a message to the House of Representatives, informing them that they were ready to receive the managers and proceed with the trial; communicating, at the same time, the following rules entered into by the Senate:

"*Resolved*, That the President of the Senate shall direct all the forms of proceeding, While the Senate are sitting as a court of impeachments, as so opening, adjourning, and all forms, during the session, not otherwise specifically provided for by the Senate.

"And that the president of the Senate be requested to direct the preparations in the Senate chamber, for the accomodation of the Senate while sitting as a court, and for the reception and accomodation of the parties to the impeachment, their counsel, witnesses, etc.

"And that he be authorised to direct the employment of the Marshal or any officer or officers of the district of Columbia, during the session of the court of impeachments, whose services he may think requisite, and which can be obtained for the purpose.

"And all expenses arising under this resolution, after being first allowed by the President of the Senate, shall be paid by the secretary, out of the fund appropriated to defray the contingent expenses of both houses of congress.

"*Resolved*, That on the 2d day of March, in_____ at noon, 2 o'clock, P.M. the legislative and executive business of the Senate, be postponed, and that the court of impeachments shall then be opened—after which the process, which, on the 12th day of January, last, was directed to be issued and served upon John Pickering, and the return thereupon shall be read. And the secretary of the Senate, shall administer an oath to the returning officer, in the following form, viz. I, James Mathews, do solemnly swear, that the return made and subscribed by me, upon the process issued on the 12th day of January, last, by the Senate of the United States, against John Pickering, is truly made, and that I have performed said services, as there described—*So help me God.*

"Which oath shall be entered at large on the records.

"The Secretary shall then give notice to the house of representatives, that the Senate in their capacity of a court of impeachments, are ready to proceed upon the impeachment of John Pickering, in the Senate chamber, (which chamber is prepared with accomodations for the reception of the house of representatives.)

"*Resolved*, That counsel for the parties shall be admitted, to appear and be heard upon said impeachment. And upon attendance of the House of Representatives, their managers, or any person or persons, admitted to appear for the impeachment; the said John Pickering shall be called to appear and answer the articles of impeachment exhibited against him. If he appears or any person for him, the appearance shall be recorded _____ particularly if by himself, or if by agent or attorney, naming the person appearing, and the capacity in which he appears. If he does not appear, either personally, or by agent or attorney, the same shall be recorded. All motions made by the parties or their counsel, shall be addressed to the President of the Senate, and if he shall require it, shall be committed to writing, and read at the secretary's table; and after the parties shall be heard upon such motion, the Senate shall retire to the adjoining committee room, for consideration and decision; which shall be had, as well in such cases, as in all questions to be decided by the Senate, as a court of impeachments, with closed doors.

"All decisions shall be ayes or noes, which shall be entered on the records of the court. After decision, the Senate shall return to their chamber, and the President shall then make known the decision to the parties.

"Witnesses shall be sworn by the secretary in following, form viz. I, A B do swear (or affirm as the case may be) that the evidence I shall give to this court, in the case now depending shall be the truth, the whole truth, and nothing but the truth, so help me God!

"Witnesses shall be examined by the party producing them, and then cross examined in the usual form.

"If a Senator is called as a witness, he shall be sworn and give his testimony standing in his place.

"If a Senator wishes a question to be put to a witness, he shall hand it in writing to the President, who shall put the same."

On motion of Mr. Nicholson the House of Representatives directed the Managers to attend on the trial.

The Managers having accordingly repaired to the Senate chamber, the House of Representatives adjourned with the view, it was understood, of attending the trial.

The Senators were ranged on each side of the chair of the President. The Mangers were placed in front and on the right of the chair; and seats were assigned in the same line on the left for the accused and his counsel. Additional seats on the elevated arae of the Senate were assigned for ladies. Between the Senators and the Managers a seat was allotted to the Speaker of the House.

About half past one o'clock the name of John Pickering was called three times, without any answer being given. The President (Mr. Burr) then stated that he had received a letter from Robert G. Harper, and a petition from—Pickering, son of John Pickering impeached; which were read by the clerk. The petition represents that John Pickering is insane, and could not, from the state of his health, attend without endangering his life, & therefore prays a postponement of the trial. The letter of Mr. Harper contained an offer of his professional services in support of the prayer of the petition.

These papers being read, the President desired Mr. Harper to take the seat assigned for the council of the accused.

Mr. Harper having taken his seat, rose and stated, that he appeared not at the instance of John Pickering, from whom he had received no authority to appear, but from a desire to support the petition offered by his son, to aid the defense of the accused, and in case the Senate, notwithstanding his non-appearance, should proceed to try the articles of impeachment preferred against him, and should permit him to take a part in the proceedings without thereby implicating any acknowledgement, on the part of accused, of their validity.

Mr. Nicholson, on behalf of the Managers, observed, that in his opinion, Mr. Pickering could only appear by himself or by counsel; that Mr. Harper could only, therefore, be admitted to a hearing in the exercise of the right of counsel for the accused; and as he disclaimed all authority from Mr. Pickering, in his opinion, he could not be allowed to take a part in the trial.

Several additional remarks, enforcing the same opinion, were expressed by Messrs. G. W. Campbell, Rodney, Early, and J. Randolph.

Mr. Harper enquired whether it would be regular in him to reply to these remarks.

The President said it would not; and immediately after put the question to the Senate whether Mr. Harper should be heard in support of the prayer of the petition of Pickering.

Whereupon the Senate retired to a private chamber, from which they returned about 3 o'clock, when the President advised the Managers that the Senate would take further time to consider the question before them, and would make them acquainted with their decision.

## THE DISPUTED GOVERNORSHIP OF WISCONSIN

*New York Times*, March 8, 1856

The Legislature, today, received a message from Mr. Barstow, the acting Governor, transmitting a copy of a notice which had been served upon the Supreme Court by the counsel of Mr. Barstow, in the contested election case. The notice protests against the action of the Court, denies its jurisdiction of the case, and recommends that it discharge its legitimate functions, and not arrogate the prerogatives of the Legislature. Finally, the counsel gives notice that they take leave of the Court and its unwarrantable proceedings.

The Governor, in his Message, states that he deems it is his duty to repel, with all the power of the Executive Department, any infringement upon his rights. He declares the proceedings of the Court a dangerous assumption of power, and asks that action be taken on the matter by the Legislature.

The Message was referred to a Special Committee of Five.

The decision of the Court will probably be rendered on Monday.

The Democratic members of the Legislature held a meeting last evening, and determined to sustain Mr. Barstow.

## THE GOVERNORSHIP OF WISCONSIN

*New York Times*, March 26, 1856

### Milwaukee, Tuesday, March 24.

The Supreme Court had issued a writ of ouster against Mr. Barstow, and established Mr. Bashford's claim to the Governorship. The latter has consequently taken the oath, and assumed the duties of the office.

Mr. Bashford took possession of the Executive Chamber this morning, and sent a message to the Senate—the Assembly having previously adjourned to prevent its reception. Mr. McArthur, the Lieutenant Governor, (who assumed the duties of Governor upon the resignation of Mr. Barstow,) refused to give way to Mr. Bashford, and asked the latter if force would be used. Mr. Bashford replied "Yes, if necessary."

# AMES AND BROOKS

*New York Times*, February 28, 1873

## Close of the Debate in the House-Censure Substituted for Expulsion—The Committee Discharged

*Special Dispatch to the New York Times.*

Washington, Feb. 27—THE TIMES dispatches of last night accurately foreshadowed the results of today. The House has refused to expel Brooks and Ames, and has adopted resolutions of severe condemnation instead. The day has been full of the most painful suspense, various phases of facing and action, and has altogether brought into play passions and prejudices which every one hoped would not be felt or known in this contest. There has been less excitement outside of the House, but a great deal more within. The galleries have not been so crowded, but the minds of members have been filled with halting and hesitation, and strange conflicts between duty and sympathy. As your correspondent has maintained from the first, there has never been a chance that the resolutions of expulsion would prevail. The votes of today, although they were not taken squarely on that question, as they ought to have been, nevertheless show that on the direct issue expulsion could command scarce a majority.

The debate on the main question, which had lasted for two whole days and the best part of two whole nights, practically closed at 12 o'clock in an hour's speech from Judge Poland who defended the report, and replied to the arguments of Messrs. Bingham, Butler, and others with unusual ability. He had been lampooned so unmercifully by Butler last night, that he burnished the steel of his lawyer's lance this morning and overturned many of his adversary's best points.

About 12½ o'clock the voting began, but pending the roll-call there was a running fire of parliamentary inquiries to know the effect of this vote or that, in which several members got sharp raps at the hands of the Speaker for interjecting short speeches into their points. It was agreed beforehand that any member should offer such amendments as the House would receive, and accordingly Mr. Sargent prepared a skillful substitute, declaring in effect a want of jurisdiction, then censuring Brooks and Ames, and then discharging the committee from further consideration of the subject matter. Mr. Farnsworth got in the first motion, viz. to lay the whole subject on the table. This was not based on the plea of want of jurisdiction, but all who were that way of thinking voted for the motion. The result showed that that doctrine was not strong in the House, for the yeas were only 59, while the nays were 164, showing 223 members present and voting and only twenty members absent or not voting—a very strong House. The inculpated members, Brooks and Ames, did not vote, nor did Messrs. Dawes, Kelley, Garfield, Schofield, nor Bingham. Mr. Hooper voted nay very emphatically. Of the affirmative vote, 19 were Democrats and 40 were Republicans.

The vote then came on Mr. Sargent's substitute, which put the House on its mettle. It was so adroitly drawn to combine the men who opposed expulsion and those who denied the jurisdiction of the House, with whose favored a milder form of punishment. It proved, in the end, to be a mischievous instrument, and at one time lost the control of affairs to the Republican side. It was adopted by an exceedingly close vote—yeas, 115; nays, 110—the largest vote recorded in this Congress. When the roll-call was completed, and before it was announced, it was beaten by five votes, but three Democrats, Slocum, Eldridge, and Voorhees, and two Republicans, Killinger and Halsey, changed their votes and reversed the decision. The adoption of the resolutions of the substitute condemning the conduct of Ames and Brooks was then a matter of short work. The resolution on Ames was agreed by-ayes, 181; noes, 36. The noes were composed of 13 Democrats and 23 Republicans. The Brooks resolution then followed, and was adopted by –yeas, 174; nays, 32; the latter being divided politically in about the same proportion as on the former vote. On the Ames resolution, Mr. Brooks himself voted noe very emphatically, and Mr. Hooper the same way quite decidedly.

This much having been done, the unfortunate situation in which matters were left became apparent. The Speaker had ruled, as has always been done, that the substitute must be divided, the resolutions on condemnation voted on first, the resolution to discharge next and the preamble last. The Democrats at once began to show their thirst for more victims. Having been compelled to put themselves on record for the condemnation of Brooks, they wheeled into solid party line, and showed their teeth. The next vote was to discharge the committee, which would have ended the matter but the House refused to discharge, by yeas 104, nays 114. Mr. Sargent, seeing where the thing would lead, moved to lay his own preamble on the table to get rid of the whole matter, because that would carry with it all unsettled pending questions. The House refused that also, by yeas 59, nays 171. Next came the vote square on the preamble, which was rejected—yeas, 98; nays 113, probably the fairest test of the sentiment of the House on the question of jurisdiction of any vote taken.

But here the previous question had exhausted itself, and there began a scramble on the Democratic side for the floor, but the Speaker recognized Mr. Eugene Hale, who moved to recommit, but the House would not recommit, the vote by tellers being yeas 77, nays 96.

Then the Democrats got possession of the floor. Fernando Wood was the first man on hand with a resolution censuring all the others, naming them specifically, but he was "bowled out" by the ruling of the Speaker, who declared that the resolutions in regard to the several members must be separate. Mr. Speer, of Pennsylvania, next appeared on the scene with a specific resolution pointed at Mr. Kelley, which, in terms, was quite as severe as the resolutions already passed upon Brooks and Ames. Mr. Dickey sharply objected to its consideration, but the House voted to receive it— yeas 118, nays 82. The only Democrats who voted nay were Messrs. Beck, Eldridge, John T. Harris, Gavett, John Rogers, and Sloss. A shower of substitutes were then offered. One by Sargent, another by Stevenson, and another by J.R. Hawley, but Speer only yielded to hear them read, and they were not received. Having got the floor, Mr. Speer acted as if he had a large-sized elephant on his hands. He was, however, very fair, and yielded successively to Butler and McCrary. Butler at once reminded the House that its chickens had come home to roost, and that there was no end to expulsions or censures under the doctrine which had prevailed. Mr. Speer then arraigned his colleagues for half an hour, and McCrary made a brief strong speech in defense of the action of the committee, which had refused to touch these gentlemen. Mr. Kelley took the floor and moved to recess until 8 o'clock

## THE EVENING SESSION

The House reassembled for the evening session in a state of feverish excitement. Mr. Kelley was granted the floor. He had no bitter words for Mr. Speer, whom he addressed as his "young colleague." He spoke with solemn earnestness for his own name and for the future of his children. He said that his whole life had been a struggle with fortune and that now, in his declining years, it was cruel injustice to charge him with riotous living, and having received a bribe of $329. He demanded a fair trial before sentence was passed, if it was to be passed at all, and gave notice that he should adduce in justification and defense important evidence which had not yet been heard. The evidence would show by the records of Pennsylvania that in June, 1869, he placed a mortgage on certain property for a most pitiful sum, which he never should have done, if it 1868 he had been possessed of the profitable stock alleged by Oakes Ames.

Messrs. Dickey and Stoughton made brief speeches characterizing the resolution and speech of Speer as marked by the grossest partizanship, and the most unfair misrepresentation, and warning the Democrats that if they voted for it these chickens would surely come home to roost.

Gen. Hawley then obtained the floor, and moved to refer the whole matter to the Poland Committee, with an enlargement of its jurisdiction, and instructing it to report to the House whether any further action in relation to any member of the House is demanded by the facts established by the testimony. Then came a sensation. Mr. Dawes rose, and, for the first time in the debate, addressed the House. He said Gen. Hawley wanted to adjourn the Congress with an unfinished investigation hanging over the heads of members of the House. He thought this was cruel and unjust. He was ready, on the evidence here, and now to receive the verdict of his colleagues. Conscious of no impure act or motive since his entrance into Congress, he did not fear the result. If any man on the floor had any further accusation to bring against him he was ready to meet it, and wanted it to be made at once. He had been acquitted by a Select Committee, and he had demanded to know the worst that any man dared to say against his integrity. The effect of this speech was instantaneous. It thrilled the galleries, and brought back the nerve of the Republicans, who shortly afterward showed their suddenly-formed determination to put a summary stop to this miserable farce. The moment Mr. Dawes sat down half the gentlemen on both sides demanded the floor, and, in the midst of great excitement, Mr. Maynard moved to lay the Speer resolution on the table. Hawley's resolution was pushed out of consideration by a point of order raised by Fernando Wood. The yeas and neys were called on Mr. Maynard's motion, and it was carried by 119 to 75. Among those voting for it were a large number of Democrats, who thus recorded in black and white their disgust at the unjust and malicious performance of Speer.

It was now plain that an end to come to this unseemly attempt to force a snap judgement upon those members of the House who had been acquitted by the unanimous report of committee of the charge of being bribed, and had been allowed no opportunity to enter any defense against any other charge. But the rancorous Stevenson would not be still. He sent up a resolution under the cloak of a privileged question, condemning all members of Congress holding stock or bonds in any railroad subject to Congressional action. This was not a privileged question, and Mr. Stevenson was unceremoniously ruled out. But he was not satisfied. He sent up another resolution censuring Samuel Hooper for holding Credit Mobilier stock. This was privileged, and the motion was voted down by the same vote by which the Kelley resolution was tabled.

One more step ended it. Mr. Sargent moved that the Poland Committee be discharged from the further consideration of the subject. This was again carried—114 to 75—and by that vote the whole business of Credit Mobilier, so far as it affects the individual action of Congressmen, was taken out of the reach of the Forty-second Congress. On the Kelley resolution, Oakes Ames, casting his first vote during the day, voted to lay it on the table. All the gentlemen who had been on trial during the past three days voted in the same way.

The House returned immediately from a courtroom back into a legislative body, and the Legislative Appropriation bill was taken up, Mr. Dawes in the chair.

## THE AMES AND BROOKS VOTE

The vote upon the resolution condemning the conduct of Mr. Ames, which was agreed to by 181 yeas to 36 nays, as it follows:

YEAS—Messrs. Acker, Ambler, Archer, Arthur, Banks, Barber, Barnum, Beatty, Beck of Georgia, Bell, Bigby, Biggs, Bird, Blair of Michigan, Boerman, Boles, Braxton, Bright, Buxley, Bunnell, Burchard, Burdett, Caldwell, Campbell, Carroll, Clark, Cobb, Coburn, Conger, Cotton, Cox, Crebs, Critcher, Crocker, Crossland, Darrall, Davis, Dodds, Donnan, Dox, Duboise, Duell, Duke, Dunnell, Eames, Ely, Finkelnburg, Foster of Pennsylvania, Foster of Ohio, Foster of Michigan, Frye, Getz, Giddings, Golladay, Goodrich, Griffith, Haldeman, Hale, Halsey, Hooper, Harris of Mississippi, Havens, Hawley of Illinois, Hawley of Connecticut, Hay, Hazleton of Wisconsin, Hazleton of New Jersey, Hereford, Herndon, Hubbard, Hill, Hoar, Holman, Houghton, Kellogg, Kendall, Ketcham, Killinger, King, Kinsella, Lamison, Lamport, Lansing, Leach, Lewis, Lowe, Lynch, Manson, Marshall, McClelland, McCormick, McCrary, McIntyre, McJunkin, McKee, McKinney, Merriam, Merrick, B.F. Meyers, Mitchell, Monroe, Moore, Morey, Morphis, Myers of Louisiana, Niblack of Florida, Niblack of Indiana, Orr, Packard, Parker of New York, Parker of Missouri, Pendleton, Poland, Porter, Patten, Price, Prindle, Randall, Read, Rice of Illinois, Rice of Kentucky, Ritchie, E. H. Roberts, W.R. Roberts, Robinson, Rogers of New York, Rogers of North Carolina, Roosevelt, Rusk, Sargent, Sessions, Shanks, Shellabarger, Sherwood, Shaler, Shoemaker, Slater, Slocum, Smith of New York, Smith of Ohio, Smith of Kentucky, Speer, Sprague, Stevens, Stevenson, Storm, Stoughton, Stowell, Sutherland, Swann, Terry, Thomas, Townsend of New York, Townsend of Pennsylvania, Turner, Tuthill, Tyner, Upson, Van Trump, Vaughn, Waddell, Wakeman, Walden, Waldron, Wallace, Warren, Wells, Wheeler, Whitley, Whetham, Willard, Williams of Indiana, Wilson of Indiana, Wilson of Ohio, Winchester, Wood, Young—Total 181.

NAYS—Messrs. Adams, Averill, Barry, Beck of Kentucky, Brooks, Buffington, Butler of Massachusetts, Butler of Tennessee, Cornings, Conner, Dickey, Eldridge, Elliott, Esty, Farwell, Garrett, Hayes, Hooker, Maynard, McHenry, Negley, Packer, Peck, Pierce, Perry, Rainy, Sawyer, Seely, Sloss, Snapp, Snyder, St. John, Twitchell, Voorhees, Williams—36.

The vote on the Brooks resolutions was the same.

# THE SECRETARY OF WAR

*New York Times*, March 2, 1876

## PAINFULLY DAMAGING TESTIMONY BEFORE THE COMMITTEE ON EXPENDITURES— ITS TRUTH NOT DENIED NOR ADMITTED BY GEN. BELKNAP.

*Special Dispatch to the New York Times.*

Washington, March 1.—There is a report of a painful disclosure before the Committee on Expenditures in the War Department, which is verified in its main features. A man by the name of Marsh, from New York, testified that he had paid $10,000 to Mrs. Belknap, wife of Secretary Belknap, for the privileges of a post trader for the Army, and has paid her $6,000 a year since the first payment. Secretary Belknap was before the committee to-day, and the testimony was communicated to him. He did not deny the testimony, nor did he admit its truth. The result of the exposure must be followed by the immediate resignation of the Secretary, and more serious consequences would seem unavoidable.

# THE CASE IN THE HOUSE

*New York Times,* March 3, 1876

Presentation of Resolutions of Impeachment–The Previous Question Moved–Debate on the Impeachability of an Officer After Resignation.

Washington, March 2.–In the House today the case of Secretary of War Belknap was brought up by Mr. Clymer, of Pennsylvania, who presented resolutions of impeachment against William W. Belknap, late Secretary of War, for high crimes and misdemeanors in office. In the midst of great excitement and with an unusual stillness in the House, Mr. Clymer rose and said: "I ask permission of the House to make a report from the Committee on Expenditures in the War Department of so grave importance that I am quite certain that when it is heard this House will agree that I am justified in asking that permission at this time." Permission was given, and Mr.. Clymer, taking his position at the Clerk's desk, read the following report" The committee found at the very threshold of its investigation, such unquestioned evidence of the malfeasance of Gen. William W. Belknap, then Secretary of War, that they found it their duty to lay the same before the House. They further report that this day at 11 o'clock a letter of the President of the United States was presented to the committee accepting the resignation of Secretary of War, together with a copy of his letter of resignation, which (the President informed the committee) was accepted about 10:20 this morning. They therefore unanimously report and demand that the said William W. Belknap, late Secretary of War, be dealt with according to the law of the land, and to that end submit herewith the testimony in the case taken, together with the several statements and exhibits thereto attached, and also a report of the proceedings of the committee had during the investigation of this subject, and submit the following resolutions:

## THE RESOLUTIONS OF IMPEACHMENT.

*Resolved,* That William W. Belknap, late secretary of War, be impeached of high crimes and misdemeanors.

*Resolved,* That the testimony in the case of W.W. Belknap, late Secretary of War, be referred to the Judiciary Committee, with instructions to prepare and report without unnecessary delay, suitable articles of impeachment of said W.W. Belknap, late secretary of war.

*Resolved,* that a committee of five members of the House be appointed and instructed to proceed immediately to the bar of the Senate and there impeach William W. Belknap, late secretary of war, in the name of the people of the United Sates, of high crimes and misdemeanors when in office, and to inform that body that formal articles of impeachment will in due time be presented, and to request the Senate to take such order in the premises as they may deem appropriate.

## THE PREVIOUS QUESTION SECONDED.

Mr. Clymer then proceeded to read the testimony of Caleb P. Marsh, taken yesterday before the committee, showing that he had paid Secretary Belknap about twenty thousand dollars in consideration of his appointment as post trader at Fort Sill, Indian Territory. The reading was listened to with intense interest by the members of the House and by a large audience in the galleries. In the more pathetic portions of the narrative Mr. Clymer was frequently forced by his feelings to pause until his voice recovered from its tremulousness and himself from his agitation.

At the close of the reading, after the many members who had taken up positions near the Clerk's desk, the better to hear the testimony and accompanying statements, had returned to their proper seats, Mr. Clymer, who had also gone to his seat again, rose and said with great emotion: "Mr. Speaker, i would not if i could, and could not, in my present condition, if I would, add anything to the facts just reported to the House. Another occasion may be afforded me to do so. They are so plain that everywhere throughout this broad land, and throughout Christendom, whoever the English language is read or spoken, they will for long years constitute a record of official corruption and crimes such as there is no parallel for in our own history or in that of any other country that I know of. If in this hour one sentiment of pity, one word of sympathy, could find utterance from me, it would be because I feel that the late Secretary of War is but the proper outgrowth, the true exponent, of the corruption, the extravagance, the misgovernment that have cursed this land for years past. That being my own reflection, I will discharge my duty best to myself and to this House demanding the previous question on the adoption of the resolutions.

Mr. Kasson, of Iowa, appealed to Mr. Clymer to give an opportunity for some suggestions to be made before asking the previous question on a matter of so grave importance.

Mr. Clymer regretted that he could not oblige his friend, [several Democratic members, "Yes, yes,"] and for the reason that his colleagues on the committee desired to be heard after the previous question was seconded.

Mr. Kasson–Allow me to say that there will not be the slightest opposition to their being all heard.

Mr. Clymer– I decline to yield, and demand the previous question.

Mr. Kasson–Does the gentleman expect the House tonight, after 5 o'clock, and without this report being printed, to vote on these resolutions, when even the impeachability of the officer at present is a point to be considered by the House?

Mr. Clymer–After the previous question has been ordered, I will yield half the hour to the members of the committee who are on the other side of the House.

After some further discussion, the previous question was seconded, and Mr. Clymer yielded the floor to his colleague on the committee, Mr. Robbins, of Maine.

## DEBATE ON THE RESOLUTIONS.

Mr. Robbins, pleaded his mental and physical exhaustion from his continuous service on the committee as the reason why he should not address the House at any length. He spoke of the report as presenting a case of great shame and disgrace to all American citizens. As to the question of impeachability of an officer who had resigned he was not prepared to speak worthily, except to suggest that it could not be true that an officer who was being investigated, and who had been found by evidence to be a criminal, could flee from justice. He alluded to what he called the unseemly acceptance of secretary Belknap's resignation, and referred to the English cases of Warren Hastings and Lord Francis Bacon, both of whom had been impeached after they had ceased to hold offices in which they committed crimes and misdemeanors.

Mr. Bass, of New York, another member of the committee, questioned the statement of the Chairman [Mr. Clymer] as to this case having no parallel and said that he would not have to leave his own borders in order to find not only a parallel for it, but that he could find cases compared with which this case was as white as the driven snow. He admitted that a mere statement of this case as presented by the testimony was sufficient to justify every member to vote for the resolutions presented.

Mr. Lamar, of Mississippi, inquired of Mr. Bass his opinion as to the impeachability of a resigned officer.

Mr. Bass replied that the English authorities seemed to maintain the jurisdiction of impeachment in such cases, but that in this country it was an unadjudicated question, and one that was not free from doubt, but his own best judgement was in favor of the right to impeach and to let the question be adjudicated by the Senate.

Mr. Hoar, of Massachusetts, in reference to the casual remark of some member as to this being a political question, entirely disclaimed and repudiated such an idea. On the point of the impeachability of a person not in office, he referred to the case of Mr. Whittemore, of South Carolina, in which the House had determined that a formal, actual renunciation of an office terminated the office, and that any American citizen could lay down an office held by him without any acceptance of his resignation. Judge Story had laid down the doctrine that it could not be dome in England; but there any citizen could be impeached, and therefore the English cases of Warren Hastings and Lord Bacon did not apply. In America no man could be impeached but a civil officer, and when he ceased to be within the literal description of the Constitution. In this country the only judgement that could be rendered in an impeachment case was removal from office and future disqualification from holding office, but by the statutes a person guilty of such offenses could be indicted, tried, and sentenced by the criminal courts of the country. He protested against hot haste in this matter without having the testimony printed. He thought such haste unworthy of this grave question, and if he stood alone he would still stand here to say so.

Mr. Blackburn, of Kentucky, another member of the committee, expressed his satisfaction that the report which had been read by his colleague, Mr. Clymer, showed to the word that nothing had been left undone by the committee to shield and shelter from dishonor every person except the one whom it was the duty of the committee to investigate and report upon. He would not consent that the gentleman from Massachusetts should make this a political or a partisan question. He would not consent that his side of the House should be placed in the position of prosecutors and the other side should take the position of defenders. It was a question which addressed itself alike to every member of the House. He regarded the case as an unprecedented one in more respects than one. The action of the President in accepting Secretary Belknap's resignation under the circumstances was unprecedented, and this was the first instance in the history of the country where any man, claiming manhood and holding an exalted station, had sought to shelter himself from legitimate investigation by interposing the dishonor of a wife. [Sensation.] Passing to the question of the impeachability of Mr. Belknap, he suggested that that question, as Judge Story had intimated, might properly be left to the decision of the Senate. On such a state of facts, would the House, he asked shrink from the performance of its duty because there might be the mist or shadow of a doubt on that point? The House could not do so. It would not be admissible. He quoted from the impeachment case of Lord Bacon, in which it was stated that where the Lord Chancellor had sought to save himself by a resignation of his high office, the attempt was vain, as the King did not and could not interpose. Was the House to be told that the man in power at the other end of the avenue was able to rob an American Congress of a right and power which a King of Great Britain could not take from parliament? [Sensation and applause.] It used to be the theory that the King could do no wrong, but no man had ever been found bold enough in this country to say that the President can do no wrong. If the man had uttered the memorable sentence "Let no guilty man escape," held it in his power to rob an American Congress of its right to inflict punishment or to pronounce censure on a publicly convicted criminal, where was the barrier to be found beneath whose shelter the liberties of the people could rest secure? [Applause.]

Mr. Hoar—Does the gentleman say that Congress has the power to punish any man in this country?

Mr. Blackburn—I will not submit to interruptions. I am the last man who would introduce one atom of politics in this discussion. It is not admissable here. The Republican members of the committee were as earnest and honest in the prosecution of the inquiry, and in the presentation of this report, as the members representing the majority of this House. We have seen no difference in the committee-room. I appeal to the members of the House that there shall be no difference manifested here. If fraud has been perpetrated; if criminally exists; if corruption has been proved, let the representatives of the people in this house so declare it, and send the issue to the court where it may finally be tried; and if we are unable to punish where guilt is almost openly confessed, let the responsibility for that failure rest on other shoulders than ours.

Mr. Danforth, of Ohio, another member of the committee, expressed it as his judgement that the acceptance of Mr. Belknap's resignation in no manner changed the position of that officer to the country. He disagreed, however, with the statement of the Chairman [Mr. Clymer] that the conduct of this officer was the legitimate outgrowth of the principles of the party in power, and he expressed the hope that there would not be a single vote on the Republican side of the House against the resolutions.

## SENTIMENT OF THE IOWA DELEGATION.

Mr. Kasson, of Iowa, said that a few years ago there had gone from his State a young man, well educated and gallant gentleman to fight the battles of his country. He had gone through the war, and the President afterward had called him to a seat in his Cabinet, placing him at the head of that Army of which he had been a humble but somewhat distinguished member. This morning, for the first time, the delegation from Iowa had heard that that gentleman, who had been so much respected in his own State and so much honored by the nation had been found guilty of receiving a compensation for some act of official duty, and that that compensation had been continuous. The House would judge of the emotion with which the members from that State had listened to the reading of the evidence. He had never heard anything read with greater interest than the report, and when, at the close of the reading, he had made an appeal to his friend from Pennsylvania, [Mr. Clymer,] not for himself alone, but for his colleagues, whose pride and honor were so touched by the character of the report, for a moment's delay, that they might find out whether there might not be in the evidence one extenuating circumstance, he had been met by the demand for the previous question. He did not desire to claim any exemption for Mr. Belknap from all the penalties to which his acts exposed him, but he found the most painful feature disclosed by the evidence to be the fact that not one word of it touched the officer in question until the death which broke a heart had occurred. [Sensation.] Was he to be blamed that he and his colleagues wanted a right to ascertain the extent of that officer's guilt by reading the evidence in point? Was he to be blamed that when he found that the most delicate relations in the human life were involved in this proceeding, (a relation so delicate that he dared not allude to it in detail,) he asked an opportunity to consider whether there was anything to be said in extenuation of so high and so great a misdemeanor? But it was too late to go back to that now. He and his colleagues had been refused that opportunity, and now he only asked the question whether the House did not need more time to ascertain whether this office was impeachable. After quoting from Judge Story on this pint, he argued that the powers of Congress were limited by the Constitution, and that if Mr. Belknap be impeached the Senate could not execute the Constitutional provision which declares that he shall be removed from office. If he were liable to impeachment, let it be understood that they were all without exception for impeachment; but if the House was establishing a precedent which did not rest on the Constitution, and which was dangerous for the future, he thought it right that the House should pause and consider by a report from its Judiciary Committee the question of its right to make this impeachment. If the House could impeach a man not in office, it might go back and impeach Jefferson Davis and John B. Floyd for conspiracy.

Mr. Robbins, of North Carolina, suggested that there was great difference between a conviction on impeachment and a conviction on indictment. In the latter case the man might be pardoned by the Executive, but in the former case it could not be. As to the suggestion of the impeachment of Jefferson Davis, he replied that it had been decided that a Senator could not be impeached, not being an officer of the United States.

The debate being closed, the House proceeded to vote on the resolutions, and they were unanimously adopted.

The Speaker appointed as the committee to notify the Senate of the action of the House, Messrs. Clymer, Robbins, Blackburn, Bass and Danforth, (these members, composing the Committee on the Expenditures of the War Department, making the report.)

Thus ended the most bitterly painful scene that ever took place in this hall, the theatre of so many exciting events. The proceedings not being anticipated nor the facts which led to them generally known, there was at first no very large attendance in the galleries. Mr. Wood was speaking on the Hawaiian treaty in Committee of the Whole, but on an intimation of what was about to take place he left his speech unfinished and gave way to a motion that the committee rise. Mr. Clymer, in making his preliminary remarks to the House, and in subsequently reading from the Clerk's desk the testimony which told in such a plain and convincing manner the guilt of the man who had been so trusted and honored, was visibly affected, and had to exercise a strong mastery over his feelings to suppress the public display of his emotions. He was particularly affected when he came to read the portion of it which described the scene between the witness [Marsh,] Mrs. Belknap, and Mrs. Bowers, [the sister of the then Mrs. Belknap, and now herself holding that name,] in the nursery, where the pecuniary prospects of the innocent child were alluded to, and the other portion which described the efforts made by the wife to screen the husband, and the mental anguish of the witness between the desire to save his friend and resolve not to do so at the expense of his own soul. Mr. Clymer had to pause several times when he came to these passages, and his strong emotion won favor for him from all spectators. During the proceedings, Mr. Kerr occupied the Speaker's chair and beneath him at the Clerk's desk sat his predecessor [Mr. Blaine] evincing a painful interest in the story as told in the testimony of Marsh. Many members whose seats are in the area in front of the Clerk's desk, and all the rest occupied their seats, paying the most marked attention to the reading. Before the scene had closed the galleries had all become crowded, including the Diplomatic Gallery, where the Danish Minister and his wife were among the spectators. There was a feeling of relief experienced by all after the vote was taken and the affair brought to a close.

The committee appointed by the Speaker will tomorrow proceed to the Senate Chamber and communicate to that body the action of the House. The Judiciary Committee tomorrow will also draw up the articles of impeachment and report them to the House. When adopted by the House that body will, headed by its Speaker and high officers, proceed to the Senate Chamber and demand the impeachment of Mr. Belknap. Then the Senate will (in parliamentary phrase) "take order" for the impeachment—that is, arrange the time and manner of conducting the trial—which will be prosecuted on the part of the House by its Judiciary Committee.

# THE DISGRACED SECRETARY

*New York Times*, March 3, 1876

## Gen. Belknap to be Impeached.

### Full report of the testimony affecting the ex-Secretary and of the proceedings in congress thereon—The resignation of Gen. Belknap accepted by the President.

The startling facts in relation to the disgrace of Gen. Belknap, which have already been given in THE TIMES, have received fuller confirmation in the report of the committee investigating the expenditures in the War Department made to the House yesterday; in the proceedings instituted for the impeachment of ex-Secretary, and in the resignation of that officer, which has been accepted by the President. The facts, briefly recapitulated, are that Caleb P. Marsh, of New York, in 1870 was offered the appointment of post trader at Fort Sill, through his intimacy with the family of the Secretary of War. He made a contract with the trader already there, permitting him to continue in consideration of $12,000 of the annual profits, payable in quarterly installments. The money thus received was divided with the Secretary of War for two years by remittances to Mrs. Belknap, and subsequently the reduced amount of $6,000 a year was agreed on with the post trader was similarly divided by remittances direct to the Secretary. These facts, when presented to the House by the committee, resulted, after an hour's debate under the previous question, in a unanimous vote for the impeachment of the ex-Secretary, notwithstanding that his resignation had been accepted by the President. The members of the committee that made the investigation were appointed by the Speaker managers of the proceedings before the Senate.

# ARCHER STOLE HEAVILY

*New York Times*, March 29, 1890

### The State of Maryland Finds Itself Muleted for Over $127,000.
### DISCOVERIES OF THE COMMITTEE
### The Culprit Seems to Have Helped Himself to the Bonds Quite Freely Whenever He Needed Them– Barnes Compton Likely to Become Treasurer.

Annapolis, Md., March 28—The joint committee of the legislature appointed to investigate the defalcations of Stevenson Archer, treasurer of the State, made a report tonight of the result of their investigation in Baltimore as follows:

"In the various sinking funds there should have been, according to the statement furnished by the comptroller, West Virginia and Pittsburg Railroad bonds in the amount of $84,000. We found $75,000, showing a deficit of $9,000.

"Of Frederick City 4 per cent bonds there should have been $133,000; we found $116,000, showing a deficit of $17,000.

"Of Baltimore and Ohio Car Trust bonds there should have been $128,000; we found $91,000, showing a deficit of $37,000.

"Of Piedmont and Cumberland Railroad bonds there should have been $100,000; we found $97,000, showing a deficit of $3,000.

"Of treasury relief loan bonds there should have held a total of $572,000; we found $445,000, showing a deficit of $127,000. This amount is exclusive of coupons on some of these bonds not accounted for, amounting, perhaps, to several thousand dollars more.

"Subsequent investigation may show some change in the figures above given; but that there exists a heavy defalcation there is no room for doubt."

Archer will be removed at once. Little sympathy is felt for the treasurer since the enormity of his shortage became known. The disclosures of the committee proved a great surprise, as it was hoped and believed the deficit would be small. Knowing ones intimate that, when the full truth is known, the loss to the State will foot up $150,000. The talk today has been how to unload Archer and save others who are culpable with him to a great extent.

It is believed Hon. Barnes Compton will become the State treasurer.

# TREASURER ARCHER RESIGNS

*The Washington Post*, April 1, 1890

## A Letter in Which He Admits His Guilt—Nobody Else to Blame

ANNAPOLIS, Md., April 1—The painful silence which State Treasurer Stevenson Archer has maintained ever since the damaging charges against him have been made public has at last been broken. He himself has spoken, and his friends can find little comfort in what he tells them. Today, Mr. Archer's resignation was brought to Annapolis by his son-in-law, Senator Silver. Mr. Archer's letter is as follows:

BELAIR, March 31, 1890
Elihu Jackson, Governor of Maryland:
SIR: I herewith tender you my resignation as treasurer of Maryland. During the four years of the incumbency of the office by me over $18,500,000 have been received and disbursed by my office, every dollar of which has been scrupulously accounted for by the efficient, laborious, and honest employees in my office, so that the books correspond exactly with the charges against me in the comptroller's office. I say this in justice to those officers. The safe deposit boxes in Baltimore, which held the sinking fund belonging to the State, were under my sole and exclusive control, no other person ever having had access to them since I have been in office. Any irregularity in the funds in those boxes is attributable to me alone. If this cannot be explained then I must submit to the majesty of the law.

Respectfully,
Stevenson Archer

# GOVERNOR JACKSON ACTS

*New York Times*, April 16, 1890

## State Treasurer Archer Removed and His Successor Appointed.

ANNAPOLIS, April 15.—Stevenson Archer, treasurer of Maryland, did not appear for trial to-day on the charge of malfeasance in office and embezzlement of the State's securities. He wrote a letter to the governor, saying: "My physical condition is such as to make it impossible for me to present at the time named. I am willing, however, to waive all rights which might result by reason of my non-attendance, and consent that a hearing may take place as if I were personally present. The trial then proceeded before the governor, Attorney General Whyte acting as prosecutor. Messrs. T. Edward Hambleton, C.C. Shriver, Dougne H. Thomas, Fred M. Colston, E.V. Gardner, and John W. Middendorf were questioned as to the correctness of their testimony given before the legislative committee. They replied it was correct. A letter was then read from the counsel of Mr. Archer, saying they neither consented to nor opposed any action of the governor.

The attorney general read a brief statement from the governor saying he had reviewed the testimony and declared the office of treasurer vacant.

Governor Jackson then appointed Edwin H. Brown, of Queen Anne county, State treasurer. He is a lawyer and brother of State Senator John H. Brown.

# HIS FIRST DAY IN PRISON

*The Baltimore Sun*, July 10, 1890

Stevenson Archer was very restless in the penitentiary hospital on the night following his sentence, and remained awake until 4 o'clock yesterday morning. At that hour he fell asleep and slept for an hour and a half. For his first prison breakfast he drank a glass of milk and ate a cracker. For his dinner his only food was a plate of penitentiary soup. He is reticent, and no one is allowed to see him. In accordance with the regulations of the penitentiary regarding new convicts, no one will be allowed to see Archer for thirty days from the time of his admission, unless severe illness or some other dire necessity should arise. Dr. W.W. White, the penitentiary physician, made medical examination of Archer's condition, and found he was suffering from nervous debility. His future occupation has not yet been determined upon, and he will remain as an inmate of the hospital until his health has improved.

---

# GOEBEL SHOT DOWN

*The Washington Post*, January 31, 1900

Physicians Say His Death Is Almost a Certainty.
No Real Clew to Assassin
Harland Whittaker Under Arrest, but He is Probably Innocent
State Militia Called to Frankfort

Great Excitement and Confusion Caused by a Deliberate Attempt Upon the Life of the Gubernatorial Contestant as He Was About to Enter the Capitol Building –

Five Shots Fired from the Upper Window of the Building Occupied by the Governor and Other State Officers—Search for the Guilty Man Hindered by a Number of Armed Mountaineers Who Occupied the Entrances—Belief that the Perpetrator Will Escape Detection—Whittaker Taken to Louisville for Safe Keeping—All Quiet Last Night.

Frankfort, Ky., Jan. 30.—At midnight Mr. Goebel was resting easily, but was very weak. All of the physicians are agreed that if he lives through the night the chances are in his favor, but, with one exception, all of them say that he is almost certain to die before morning.

————

Frankfort, Ky., Jan. 30.—While walking through the capitol grounds on his way to the capitol building at 11:10 o'clock this morning, William Goebel, the Democratic contestant for governor of Kentucky, was shot down and very dangerously wounded.

Harland Whittaker, a farmer from Butler County, the home of Gov. Taylor, is now in jail at Louisville, charged with the crime. There is no direct evidence against Whittaker and he was placed under arrest more because he was caught around the capitol building when the shots were fired than for any other apparent reason. He denies in the most positive manner that he had any connection with the shooting or knew anything about it. He was running toward the scene of the shooting and not away from it when he was arrested.

Senator Goebel was wounded by a rifle ball of small caliber, not over 38, which struck him in the right side, just below the armpit. The ball passed through the back part of the right lung, across the body on a diagonal line, passing out below the left shoulder blade.

## His Condition Hopeless.

In addition to Drs. Hume, Ely, and McCormick, of this place, who are in attendance upon the wounded man, Drs. J.C. McKenzie, N.P. Dundridge, and E.W. Walker were summoned from Cincinnati, and Dr. McMurtry came from Louisville. As soon as the physicians from Louisville and Cincinnati had examined the patient, a consultation was held, at the conclusion of which Dr. Hume announced late tonight that the chances had turned very much against the wounded man and the probability was that he would die before morning. "He has internal hemorrhages," said Dr. Hume, "and we are unable to stop them. Unless we do so, his death is a question of a very short time. We have taken from him over a pint a blood, and there are symptoms of the gravest character. There is hardly a chance that he can live through the night, and practically none that he can recover."

Mr. Goebel was on his way to the senate chamber, in company with Col. Jack Chinn and Warden Eph Lillard, of the Frankfort penitentiary. Mr. Lillard was a few feet in advance of Goebel and Chinn, who were walking side by side, Goebel being on the right and Chinn upon the left.

From the outer edge of the capitol grounds to the step of the capitol building, the distance is about 300 feet. Two-thirds of this had been passed, and the men were walking slowly, when suddenly a shot rang out from a large three-story building which stands fifty feet east of the capitol building. This building is used for offices by nearly all the leading officials of the State, Gov. Taylor and the secretary of state having rooms on the first floor.

## Hit by the First Shot.

As the shot was heard Goebel gave a quick involuntary exclamation of pain and made an effort to draw his own revolver. His strength was unequal to the task, however, and he sank upon the pavement. With great rapidity several more shots were fired, the bullets all striking the brick sidewalk close to where Goebel lay. None of them touched him, however.

Lillard hastily turned around to aid Goebel, who was supported by Chinn, who had his arms about him almost as soon as he touched the pavement.

"Get help," said Chinn to Lillard, and turning to Goebel he asked:

"Are you hurt, Goebel? Did they get you?"

"They have got me this time," said Goebel. "I guess they have killed me."

In less than a minute, a crowd of men was around Goebel. He was losing much blood and was becoming very weak. He was hastily carried to the office of Dr. E.E. Hume, in the basement of the Capitol Hotel, about three hundred yards from the spot where the shooting occurred. Here he was laid on a sofa, where Dr. Hume made a hasty examination, pronouncing the wound to be of a nature that must cause death in a short time.

Goebel, who showed great fortitude and courage throughout, smiled weakly as he heard the verdict, and feebly rolled his head from side to side in token of dissent from the opinion expressed by the physician.

He was then carried to his room on the second floor on the Capitol Hotel, and, in addition to Dr. Hume, Drs. McCormick and Ely were summoned to attend him.

After the wound had been dressed Senator Goebel showed great exhaustion, and it was announced by his physicians that he would in all probability die within a short time. He rallied, however, and under the influence of an opiate sank into a gentle slumber which lasted for several hours.

The bullet which struck Mr. Goebel was fired from a window in the center of the third story of the office building just east of the capitol. The window was raised about eight inches from the sill to permit an unobstructed passage for the bullet when Mr. Goebel should come within range. Both Chinn and Lillard assert that, while the first shot came from the direction of the window in the third story, there were other shots fired from different portions of the same building. Some of those who heard the shorts say that at least one shot was fired from the office of the secretary of state. This, however, is not true, as there were men in the office of the secretary of state, who rushed to the window as soon as the shots were heard, and all of them declare that there was no shot fired at all from that part of the building.

The window in the third story was left open, no effort having been made to close it by the would-be assassin, while not another window in the building was opened, nor were there any places where bullets had been fired through them.

### Arrest of Whittaker.

Whittaker was arrested as he came down the steps on the east side of the State office building, directly below the window from which the shots had been fired. As he reached the sidewalk and was hastening toward the scene of the shooting, he was met by John E. Miles, who is seventy-six years of age. Without hesitation Miles threw himself upon Whittaker, winding his arms around him and calling loudly for help.

It was right at hand; and in an instant Whittaker was surrounded by a group of men, many of them with drawn revolvers. He made no attempt to escape, knowing well that the slightest attempt to do so would have brought a dozen bullets into his body. He submitted quickly to a search, which was quickly made, the proceeds being three revolvers and one big knife. A quick examination of the revolvers showed that none of the cartridges had been used, and there was no powder smut upon any part of his weapons, proving conclusively that he could not have used any of his three revolvers. In addition to this, all those who heard the shots, join in the statement that they were from a rifle and from a smaller weapon.

Whittaker was quickly led away and placed in the jail, while a guard was placed at the outer entrance to keep out all the people who had no direct connection with the institution.

The prisoner is a man slightly over the medium size, with sandy hair and mustache. He was disposed to take things calmly, although he repeated again and again that he knew nothing whatever about the shooting.

### The Prisoner's Statement.

"I was on the first floor of the building," he said, "when I heard Gov. Taylor tell that man Davis, the capitol policeman, to go over at once to see Gen. Collier. I said I would go with him, and that was where I was going. I wanted to know, too, what the shooting was about. When I stepped outside, that man grabbed me, and that's all I know, and that's a fact."

Few people believe that Whittaker is guilty of the crime, but the fact that he was hastily leaving he building from which the shooting was done was enough to make trouble for him. "That man Davis," to whom Whittaker referred, is Col. John Davis, the custodian of the Capitol grounds. His story agrees with that of Whittaker.

"I was just outside of Gov. Taylor's office," said Col. Davis, "when I heard the shots and heard Gov. Taylor say: 'My God, what have they done?' He called to me at once to go over to the office of Adjt. Gen. Collier, and Whittaker went along. I am positive that he could not have done the shooting. We were at the door of the building in too short a time for that."

### Armed Men at the Doors.

As soon as it was known that the bullet which struck down Mr. Goebel had come from the building to the east, a group of men gathered in front of the door on the east side. Others ran around to the door on the west side to prevent the escape of anybody from there. Several men attempted to enter the doors from the outside, but were prevented by groups of mountaineers, who stood in the doorways. Some of these men held Winchesters in their hands and presented an aspect so generally uninviting that no attempt was made to search the building, and nobody gained entrance to it for several minutes after the shooting had been done, and the assassin had ample opportunity to escape.

That the shooting of Mr. Goebel was the result of a carefully laid plan is without question. The man who did the work had evidently taken his stand at the window, which had previously been raised in order to allow the free passage of the bullet, and waited until his victim was in full sight before firing.

Even since the influx of the mountaineers last week a large number of them have been sleeping in the upper part of the State house. It is not known, however, that any of these men did the work or that they had any knowledge of the premeditated crime. There has not, so far, been discovered the slightest direct evidence pointing to any man, and it is not likely now that any will ever be found.

## Used Smokeless Powder.

The man who fired the shots took the precaution to conceal his location by using smokeless powder cartridges. A score of people were where they had a full view of the side of the building from which the firing was done, and all of them declare that not a sign of powder smoke was visible. Both Chinn and Lillard are men of experience in affairs in which powder smoke is a more or less prominent feature, and both declare that while they could tell the general direction from which the bullets came, they could not guess at the spot from which they were fired.

"I tried hard to get a sight of the fellow," said Lillard. "He kept pouring the lead down on us, and I will swear there was not a sign of anything to indicate from where he was shooting. As many shots as he fired would make considerable powder smoke if ordinary cartridges were used, but never a sign of smoke could I see."

"I looked around a mighty brief spell," said Col. Chinn, "but there was nothing for me to look at, so I paid attention to Goebel. The fellow used smokeless powder all right enough, and I guess he was pretty wise to do it. Somebody might have got him if they had known where to look for him. By the time we knew where to look he had gone, and it was time to look somewhere else."

## Denounced by Republicans.

The Republican State officials and members of the legislature without exception denounced the shooting in the most unmeasured terms. Gov. Taylor immediately caused a small address to be published, in which he declared the affair to be a disgrace and an outrage, and calling for the most sober condemnation. He sent orders at once to Adjt. Gen. Collier, directing him to take steps for the preservation of order.

Gen. Collier is a Republican and is opposed to Mr. Goebel. He declared the shooting to be a most cowardly affair and one that upon every consideration was to be regretted. He lost no time in making speeches, however, and before Goebel had been lifted from the ground to be carried to the hotel Gen. Collier had telephoned to the armory, a half mile distant, directing the local infantry company which was stationed there, under command of Capt. Walcott, to proceed at once to the capitol grounds, take possession of them and its approaches, and allow nobody to enter the gates. Twenty minutes after the shooting Capt. Walcott and his men marched across the front of the capitol building and halted at the foot of the steps.

## Militia Called to Frankfort.

Orders were issued to outside companies throughout the State to make ready at once to come to Frankfort, the entire State Guard being called into service. It was feared that the news of the shooting would so inflame the Democrats that they would come to Frankfort in swarms, while the mountaineers would lose no time in coming to the capital for the purpose of upholding their party principles.

"It makes no difference to me," said Gen. Collier, "who starts anything, we will preserve order on both sides."

The excitement among the followers of Mr. Goebel was great, and for a short time immediately following the shooting of their leader there was more than a possibility that some of the hotheads would seek vengeance upon their political enemies. Threats were made against Republican leaders and attorneys during the excitement, but the leading Democratic members of the house and senate soon brought them to calmer talk.

As the news spread through the streets that Goebel had been shot, men began to pour toward the Capitol grounds from all sides, one throng being led by two firemen, one of whom carried a Winchester rifle, which the other finally prevailed upon him to lay aside.

## A Second Tragedy.

A shooting affray occurred in a saloon about this time, Craig Ireland, a sporting man, fatally wounding Ike Williams, a negro. The men were in an altercation when Williams struck Ireland, who promptly sent a bullet through the negro's stomach. Ireland was locked up. This second shooting caused great excitement for a time, as it was thought the long-threatened political shooting in general all along the line had at last been inaugurated. The affair had nothing to do with the political situation.

Senator-elect Blackburn, who was in Washington, was informed of the shooting through the long-distance telephone, and sent back a message urging the Democrats to remain quiet, and take no rash action of any sort.

## Beckham Guarded from Possible Harm.

The Democrats are keeping exceedingly close watch over the person of J.C. W. Beckham, the contestant for the position of lieutenant governor. In the event of the death of Goebel he is their only hope, and they declare, with earnestness, that if Goebel dies there will be no governor but Beckham. He is kept in his room at the Capitol Hotel, and will be guarded very closely until the trouble is over. He declares that he needs no guard, but the Democrats pay no attention to his remonstrances. It was reported at 1 o'clock that Speaker Trimble of the house had declared that the legislature will be removed to Covington, and that Goebel would there be declared governor.

It was reported through the city this afternoon that it was the intention of Lieut. Gov. Marshall to resign his position because of the shooting of Mr. Goebel. Mr. Marshall left for his home in Louisville this afternoon. Before leaving, he said:

"I have not resigned. I do not intend to do so, and never contemplated such a thing. No man could more deeply deplore the shooting of Mr. Goebel than I. It is one of the most horrible things that could possibly have happened. That, however, does not affect my duty. I will not resign under any circumstances."

The house was in session when the shooting occurred, and the Senate was to meet within twenty minutes. The capitol building was, therefore, filled with members of the legislature, and to say that excitement followed is putting it very mildly. From both halls men ran wildly down the steps without hats or coats, and one member of the house came out carrying in his hand a bill on which he had been arguing when the shooting occurred.

By the time the members of the legislature had reached the lower floor, however, Goebel was on his way to the office of Dr. Hume. The members hastily rushed back to their desks, adjourned with the most unceremonious haste, and poured down into the streets again.

## Expected Crowds Did Not Come.

The evening trains did not bring as large a crowd of people as was expected. Word had been received from Covington, the home of Mr. Goebel, that a large crowd would be down, but not over a score of people came in, and they were not of the class that create disturbances. Numberless inquiries were received by members of the legislature from their constituents asking if they were needed. In all cases word was sent back that nobody was needed and that crowds least of all things were needed just now.

Several small places in the neighborhood of Frankfort sent in a man or two to obtain a general idea of the situation and carry reports back. In every case the messenger, whether Democrat or Republican, was sent back with the word that now was a good time to keep out of Frankfort.

## Troops begin to Arrive.

Three hundred men of the Second Kentucky Infantry were camped around the capitol building to-night, and 1,500 more are expected during the night and before to-morrow noon.

Word was received that the Louisville Legion, the First Kentucky Infantry, would bring with it the famous Gatling gun that has figured so extensively in the evidence presented by the Democratic attorney in the gubernatorial contest case. All through the building in which the adjutant general's office is situated lay sleeping soldiers, every man with his cartridge belt still buckled around his waist. Outside the door the rifles were stacked, sentries walking beats beside them. The Gatling gun of the Lexington company was posted just to the west of the capitol steps, and a tall Seargeant who had it in charge had carefully calculated the range to a row of small stores and dwelling houses south of the capitol grounds.

Rumors were thick that armed bodies of men were forming upon the outskirts of town, and that before morning they would pass into the city "just for a little bombardment."

Col. Williams, commanding the troops gathered around the State House to-night, took very little stock in any of these stories, but he was none the less ready to join in the "little bombardment" whenever it proved agreeable to the other side.

## Statement by Dr. Barrow.

Lexington, Ky., Jan. 30.—Dr. David Barrow, of this city, one of the leading surgeons in the South, who was called to attend Senator Goebel, returned from Frankfort late to-night and said: "Senator Goebel is shot through the right lung, and is in a dangerous condition, as some main arteries were severed, and he is bleeding internally. If the bleeding ceases and he lives twenty-four hours, the chances in his favor will be materially increased. There is nothing we can do for him."

# CLARK IS REAPPOINTED

*The Washington Post*, May 16, 1900

## Montana Senator Resigns and Vacancy at Once Filled.

———

## His Friend Acting Governor

———

A Curious Political Drama Enacted Yesterday, One Scene Occurring in Washington and the Other in Montana—The Governor of the State, Who is Clark's Political Enemy, Is Out of the State and the Lieutenant Governor Has Full Power to Appoint.

Helena, Mont., May 15.

Hon. W.A. Clark, Washington, D.C.:

I have the honor to inform you that I have this day appointed you to fill the vacancy of Montana's representative in the Senate of the United States caused by you resignation. I send you certificate by registered mail, and trust you will accept this appointment.

A.E. Spriggs,<br>Governor.

———

Washington, D.C., May 15, 1900.

Hon. A.E. Spriggs, Helena, Mont.:

I have the honor to acknowledge the receipt of your very complimentary message informing me of my appointment to fill the vacancy in the United States Senate caused by my resignation, and to inform you of my acceptance thereof. I fully appreciate the compliment implied by your action, and pledge myself to discharge the duties of the office in the interest of all the people of the State. With assurance of my esteem, yours, sincerely,

W.A. Clark.

Helena, Mont., May 15.—Acting Gov. Spriggs to-night appointed W.A. Clark, of Butte, United States Senator, to serve until the next legislature shall elect his successor. Senator Clark's resignation was filed early in the day with the governor, and to-night he was appointed by Gov. Spriggs to succeed himself. Mr. Clark's reasons for resigning are fully set forth in the speech he delivered to-day in the Senate.

Gov. Spriggs has all along been a friend of Senator Clark, during his candidacy for the Senatorship and since, although he preserved the utmost impartiality in his office as lieutenant governor and president of the senate during the Senatorial campaign. Gov. Smith, a partisan of the Daly people, left the state two weeks ago for California to attend some m___ cases in which he is retained as attorney. At that time there was no thought of Senator Clark resigning. The resignation filed to-day came as a surprise to the people of the State, who had no inkling of the coup prepared. During day Gov. Spriggs received a great many telegrams from all of the State urging him to appoint Senator Clark, alleging that he was the real choice of a large majority of Democrats and a large proportion of Republicans as well. Gov. Spriggs was besieged all day by individuals and by delegations friendly and hostile to Mr. Clark.

Grass Valley, Cal., May 15.—Gov. Smith, of Montana, left here this afternoon for Montana, via Salt Lake, taking the eastbound train at Colfax. His departure was unexpected, and was hastened by news of Senator Clark's resignation and his appointment by Lieut. Gov. Spriggs. Smith left before the news of Senator Clark's resignation was made public and no expression could be secured from him.

In the brief space of a few hours a remarkable political drama was enacted yesterday.

There was a dramatic scene in the Senate early in the afternoon, when, at the close of an intensely earnest defence of his own position, Mr. Clark announced that he had tendered his resignation as a Senator from Montana to the governor of that State. The sensation which this announcement caused, however, was nothing compared with the excitement produced by the intelligence which reached Washington, less than three hours later, that the lieutenant governor of Montana, a friend of Senator Clark, acting in the absence of the governor, who is Clark's political enemy, would appoint Senator Clark to the vacancy.

The maneuver completely outwitted the astute Mr. Chandler. He had received the Senate an agreement to proceed at 1 o'clock yesterday afternoon, to the consideration of the resolution declaring Mr. Clark not entitled to a seat in the Senate. It was Mr. Chandler's intention to press the consideration of this resolution to a vote, his avowed purpose being not to allow Congress to adjourn until he had ousted Mr. Clark. A spirited contest was expected, and every Senator in the city was at his desk. Mr. Clark forestalled Mr. Chandler's programme by announcing his resignation. Mr. Chandler accepted this announcement as an end to the matter, so far as he was concerned. He was asked during the course of the afternoon whether the governor could appoint to the vacancy.

"Of course," said Mr. Chandler. Everybody, including Mr. Chandler, knew that the governor of Montana is a partisan of Marcus Daly, and, therefore, antagonistic to Clark, and so everybody expected that some friend of Daly would be appointed.

## The Vacancy Undoubtedly Exists.

There was no question about the existence of the vacancy. This had been settled by Senator Frye, the President pro tem. of the Senate, who, as soon as Senator Clark had publicly stated the fact of his resignation and had read the letter in which that resignation was tendered, ordered Senator Clark's name to be erased from the rolls of the Senate. He took his action in accordance with precedents which have existed since 1815, a notable case being the Conkling-Platt episode, during Garfield's administration. It has always been held in the Senate that a Senator's announcement of his resignation immediately severed his connection with the body, and that it is not necessary to wait for an official communication from the governor acknowledging the receipt and acceptance of the resignation. In less than an hour after Mr. Clark had made his speech yesterday, a roll call was ordered in the Senate, and when the clerk proceeded to call the names, he omitted all mention of the Senator who had just his dramatic exit from the body.

There is no doubt, therefore, that the vacancy exists, and that it was created by a resignation. The Senate, it should be remembered, had not acted upon the resolution declaring Mr. Clark not entitled to his seat.

## Acting Governor Has Full Power.

Of the power of the acting governor to appoint there is no question, either. The constitution of Montana—a constitution which, curiously enough, was framed by a convention over which Mr. Clark presided—contains a clause which declared that in case the governor dies, resigns, is convicted, or impeached, or "is absent from the State," his "functions, powers, and emoluments" shall devolve upon the lieutenant governor. No clause in any State constitution is so broad, so comprehensive. It became an object of much interest in the Senate late yesterday afternoon, and was examined with especial concern by Senator Carter, the Republican Senator from Montana. Mr. Carter came to the conclusion, as did all other Senators who studied the clause, that it afforded ample authority to the lieutenant governor to make the appointment, nor could the latter be revoked by the governor when he returned to Montana.

Gov. Smith is at present in San Diego, Cal., where he is arguing a law case. Just how he came to go to California and thus open the way for the developments which have occurred cannot be explained by the Daly men who are in the city. Congressman Campbell, who has been the chief counsel for Daly in the prosecution of Senator Clark, was very much cast down last evening. "I have been informed by Senator Chandler," he said, "that the appointment was made at 5 o'clock this afternoon." Mr. Chandler, some time after this talk with Congressman Campbell, announced that he would object to Senator Clark being sworn in on the new credentials. He proposes to have the papers referred to the Committee on Privileges and Elections, and there bury them until the session comes to an end. He hopes by this means to keep Mr. Clark out of the Senate, and thus win the last trick, after all.

The committee will hold a meeting this morning to decide what course to pursue regarding the resolution declaring Mr. Clark not entitled to a seat. This resolution is still on the calendar. If it be decided to press it, Mr. Clark's friends will debate it, and thus prevent a vote until the arrival of the new credentials. These are expected by next Saturday.

## Comments of Senators.

Senator Chandler, chairman of the Committee on Privileges and Elections, would only say when informed of the appointment, "I reckon the trick won't work."

Senator Hoar, second member of the committee in rank, would not consent to express any opinion at all.

Senator McComas, a Republican member of the committee, said, "If the report of the appointment is true, apparently the case would depend upon the fate of the pending resolution reported by the Committee on Privileges and Elections in the Clark case. If that resolution should be passed, it would be a judgment of the Senate to the effect that the seat was vacant from the beginning of the term, and we should then have in the Clark case substantially a repetition of the Quay case. If the resolution should not pass, then the appointment of Mr. Clark would be the filling of a vacancy occasioned by his resignation, and would be quite the ordinary case of filling a vacancy by executive appointment."

Senator Caffery, Democratic member of the committee, heard the statement of Senator McComas and concurred in the conclusion, adding: "If the Senate finds that Clark's election was void by reason of the corrupt use of money, this finding will be equivalent to saying that the vacancy was never filled, and, according to the precedents of the Senate, the vacancy cannot be filled by executive appointment."

Senator Jones, of Arkansas, said the matter would depend upon the action of the Senate upon the action of the Senate upon the resolution of the committee declaring the election void. If it should be adopted, the vacancy created would be the same as in the Quay case, failure of the legislature to elect.

Senator Aldrich, of Rhode Island, said that Senator Clark had made a mistake in getting the appointment. It would possibly revive the whole case in the Senate, and perhaps force action on the report of the committee.

## Thinks Appointment Will Stand.

Senator Allison said: "If the appointment is made under the statutes of Montana I don't think it can be undone by the governor upon his return to Montana. Moreover, my opinion, without having had opportunity to investigate the case closely, is that Senator Clark's resignation takes effect from the time it was tendered. I do not believe that the fact that the resignation is tendered pending an investigation can have any effect. In the Caldwell case, indeed, no further proceedings were taken after Mr. Caldwell tendered his resignation."

Senator Butler (Populist) said: "I don't think that the Senate can refuse to seat Mr. Clark. According to all precedents, vacancies occur when a resignation is tendered, and the fact that such is considered the case in this instance is supported by the immediate elimination of the name of Mr. Clark from the roll-call after he notified the Senate of his resignation. That was sufficient recognition of the vacancy to commit the Senate to it."

When the credentials arrive they will be presented to the Senate, and Mr. Clark will ask to be sworn in. To this programme Senator Frye yesterday stated that he would give his assent, believing that Mr. Clark would be legally entitled to his seat. Senator Chandler, as already stated, will fight to the bitter end, but it is claimed that his motion to refer the credentials to the committee will be defeated in the Senate, as it will have to be voted upon simply upon the merits, and cannot be considered in connection with the investigation recently held.

## Mr. Clark Makes a Speech.

Mr. Clark entered the Senate shortly after the hour of assembling and occupied his usual seat. He waited patiently until the routine business, which was not important, had been transacted and then arose and quietly addressed the chair. He desired, he said, in a low, tense voice, to speak upon the question of privilege personal to himself. Instantly there was a buzz of expectation throughout the chamber. Senators from both sides of main aisle hurried to seats near Mr. Clark, and a hush fell upon the assemblage. The intense interest of the Republicans was evidenced from the fact that almost a score of them crossed to the Democratic side. Senators Allison and Chandler were among the first, and were followed by Messrs. Hale, Simon, Quarles, Ross, Spooner, Clark of Wyoming, Fairbanks, Scott, McBride, Hawley, McCumber, Thurston, and Nelson, while Senators Jones of Nevada, Stewart, and Teller, whose seats are on the Republican side, also left their places and joined the listening throng. All the Senators, Democrats and Republicans alike, turned their faces toward their Montana colleague, who, perfectly calm and composed, stood holding in his hand the manuscript of his address. At first he spoke in tones scarcely audible, but as he proceeded his voice became clear, and while at no time did he speak loudly, the intense earnestness of his utterance carried his words to the remotest part of the chamber.

His address, a full abstract of which is given below, speaks for itself. It was a vigorous and sharp arraignment of the committee's action and report, an analytical discussion of the evidence adduced at the investigation, an explanation of political and business affairs in Montana, a bitter excoriation of Marcus Daly and his friends, who have relentlessly pursued Mr. Clark, and a complete denial of any and all charges which had been made. It was especially severe upon Congressman Campbell, who had deserted to the Daly faction, and who had left his seat in the House to manage the prosecution against Mr. Clark. The entire address was listened to with the closest interest by all the Senators, being accorded a degree of attention rare even in the Senate, though Mr. Chandler, who has been especially prominent in the case, smiled grimly throughout the delivery of the speech.

## Remarkable Demonstration at the Close.

Not until he reached the closing portion of his address did Mr. Clark manifest the slightest emotion. Up to that time there was not a tremor in his voice, while the hand which held the pages of manuscript was as rigid as if carved from marble. When, however, he adverted to his desire to hand down to his children a name untarnished even by the breath of disgrace, tears welled into his eyes and his voice trembled with emotion. The silence in the chamber was impressive, as, for a minute or two, he paused. Then, laying down the manuscript, Senator Clark picked up some additional pages which he had before him, and, bracing himself, announced that he had tendered his resignation. The announcement came like a shock to the Senate, and the stir that it created drowned for several seconds the sound of the Senator's voice. A few minutes later he had finished the reading of the letter of resignation, and had concluded his address with a few gracious words of thanks to the presiding officer for unvarying courtesy and to his colleagues for their consideration.

Then followed a most remarkable scene. Not one or two or a dozen, but more than two score Senators—nearly every member of the body—gathered around Mr. Clark and gave him an ovation the like of which has not been witnessed in the Senate for many a day. The demonstration was not confined to party. Republicans, Democrats, Populists, crowded together to take him by the hand, and to wish him success in his effort to seek vindication in his State. Mr. Carter, his fellow-Senator from Montana, was one of the first to extend his hand, while it was almost pathetic to see the venerable Mr. Vest feebly make his way to Mr. Clark's side to silent press his hand. The demonstration lasted about five minutes, during which time the presiding officer made no effort to check it, and the Senate was only recalled to the routine of business by Mr. Chandler's announcement that the resolution relating to Mr. Clark would go over until to-day. In the meantime, Mr. Clark had withdrawn to the cloak-room, where the ovation to him was renewed.

### The Letter of Resignation.

"Acting upon my own judgment and holding no one responsible for the result," said Senator Clark, in concluding his address, "I have concluded to place my resignation in the hands of the chief executive of Montana, and I here submit a copy of a letter addressed to him, under date of May 11, and which is now in his hands."

The letter follows:

Washington, May 11, 1900.

To His Excellency, the Governor of Montana, Helena, Mont.:

Dear Sir: The sixth legislative assembly, on the 28th day of January, 1899, elected me to represent the State of Montana in the Senate of the United States for the term commencing on the 4th day of March, 1899.

Under the authority of the credentials signed by the governor of the State I entered upon the discharge of the duties of that position on the first Monday of last December, after qualifying by taking the oath of office prescribed by law.

On the 4th day of December, 1899, two memorials were presented to the Senate of the United States praying that my right and title to continue to act as a Senator under the credentials which certified to my election should be investigated. These memorials, with the accompanying papers, were referred to a standing committee of that body.

After a protracted investigation of the allegations of said memorialists, the committee has submitted its conclusion to the Senate, in which it finds that the seat which I now occupy under the credentials issued by authority of the vote taken in the joint assembly of the legislature of the 28th day of January, 1899, should be declared vacant.

### Personal Honor Not Affected.

None of the charges affecting my personal honor, or which alleged that I had been personally guilty of corrupt practices, have been sustained by the finding of the committee.

Conscious of the rectitude of my own conduct, and after a critical examination of all the evidence taken by the committee, convinced that those friends who were so loyal to me during that bitter contest did not resort to dishonorable or corrupt means to influence the action of the members of the legislature in their choice of a Senator, yet I am unwilling to continue to occupy a seat in the Senate of the United States under credentials which its committee has declared rests for their authority upon the action of a legislature which was not free and voluntary in its choice of a Senator.

Self-respect and due regard for the opinion of my associates, and a sense of duty to the people of the State of Montana, demand that I should return the credentials under which I am acting as one of the representatives in the Senate of the United States, leaving the State and her people to take such action as will conserve and promote her best interests in the national council.

Influenced by these conditions, I deem it eminently proper, without unnecessary delay, to resign the position of United States Senator from the State of Montana, to which I was chosen by the sixth legislative assembly of Montana, on the 28th day of January, 1899.

With sentiments of esteem, I remain, respectfully yours,

W.A. Clark.

## Unfair Action of the Committee.

After a brief announcement that he rose to a question of personal privilege, Mr. Clark began by saying:

It is not my desire to cast any aspersions upon the motives which actuated the distinguished Senators composing the committee, and yet, with the most respectful consideration for the learning, legal ability, and eminent standing of these gentlemen, I am forced to the conclusion, which I believe meets with the concurrence of not only a large number of Senators on both sides of this chamber, but also to 80 per cent of my constituency in the State of Montana, regardless of political affiliations, that the methods of procedure in the investigation of this matter were manifestly unfair, non-judicial, and that they resulted in a verdict of the committee entirely opposite to that which would have occurred should the evidence have been confined to that which was admissible and pertinent to the issue.

I contend that an investigation involving a seat in the highest legislative body of this nation, as well as the honor of an individual chosen for that position by the people of one of the sovereign States thereof, should be conducted in a strictly judicial manner, and that in the proceedings the established rules of evidence should be applied. It is well known to everybody that this was not the case. It is true that there was a strong effort made by the honorable Senators from Alabama, Maryland, Kansas, and North Carolina, at the beginning of the investigation, to exclude all the irrelevant testimony, but their efforts were unavailing.

The Senators who filed a minority report expressed in emphatic terms their condemnation of the proceedings in this respect, as well as a denunciation of the character and practices of the principal attorney, and of some of the witnesses who testified for the prosecution.

The result of the admission of all kinds of hearsay, irrelevant, malicious, and perjured testimony was damaging in the extreme to the respondent, as though the medium of both the respectable and the venal press the most widespread publicity was given throughout the land to some of the pernicious falsehoods touching the respondent, and likewise a large number of most eminent and upright legislators who supported him, and who are the peers of the boasted men of any State in this Union.

## Likened to the Dreyfus Case.

Senator Clark said that his case was analogous to that of Dreyfus, in that the committee went on the presumption that the accused was not guilty. He insisted that no proof of personal complicity had been adduced and no charge of that character was made in the committee's report. He also asserted that there had not been proof sufficient to establish the guilt of a single legislator. "On the contrary," he said, "positive evidence has been elicited in every case where the respondent was allowed to introduce testimony that no consideration was given or received or promised, nor any consideration made to secure a vote for the respondent."

The fact that the Daly faction was opposing an honest election law and urging the repeal of the "safety cage" law, accounted, Senator Clark said, for the presence of large sums of money in the legislature. "I submit my belief," he added, "that the conclusions of the committee on the main proposition and those of the majority on all propositions are inferential, incorrect, and are not supported by the evidence, and I confidently believe that after a thorough and fair investigation, the majority report would not be sustained."

## Treacherous Work of Daly.

Mr. Clark took up the detail the findings of the Committee on Privileges and Elections, criticising many of them sharply and at length. He defended his frequent candidacy for office, and said that he had never voluntarily sought to be elected to any office. Speaking of his campaign for Congress in 1888, he attributes his defeat to Mr. Daly, saying: "Treacherous work was done everywhere in the several counties where Daly had men employed, and the result was my defeat by several thousand majority, and from this staggering blow of treachery the party did not recover for many years. There was no provocation for this. There had been no business difficulties, and never an unkind word had been spoken between us. It was simply an envious and diabolical desire on his part to forever destroy my political influence in the Territory."

Mr. Clark asserted that he was not a candidate for election to the Senate until December, 1898; that his business dealings with members of the legislature were honorable, and that his gift to State Representative Daly was not in pursuance of any previous understanding. "Perhaps," he added, "if I had used my influence to create a fat office at the expense of the State or of the government, with which to reward Mr. Daly, as is frequently done, in discharging political liabilities, the incident would not have aroused any criticism."

He defended Mr. Wellcome against the charges affecting Wellcome's integrity, and read an affidavit by George E. McGrath, who testified that Daly told him that the only effective course to pursue was to charge Clark morning, noon, and night with bribery, with the hope of creating a public sentiment which would force him (Clark) to retire. Daly also suggested "letting three or four of our men have a few thousand dollars for the purpose of showing in the legislature, and stating that it is Clark's money. This is the only way I now see to accomplish his defeat," adding that the time had come for "something more than Sunday-school politics."

Mr. Clark added that Mr. McGrath had been in Washington for five weeks during the investigation but had been constantly refused a hearing by the committee. The theory of conspiracy, he thought, was supported by the testimony of State Senator Cullen, Counselor Corbett, and other witnesses whose testimony he quoted.

## Congressman Campbell Criticised.

Senator Clark then explained that the Republican support he received was due to caucus action, which, in turn, was in response to an almost unanimous public sentiment. He referred with evident feeling to Congressman Campbell's part in the prosecution, saying, "Mr. Campbell first appeared as a pretended friend of the cause of co-operation in the interest of good government in Montana, where at a conference he feigned sleep in order to obtain information which he might use to betray his friends. Not then knowing his true character, he received the support of myself and all my friends, which insured his nomination and election. Immediately thereafter he threw off the mask and went to work to encompass my defeat, having been employed, as he stated, as counsel for a mining company belonging to the Anaconda Company, at a salary of $5,000 per annum, ostensibly as a blind, as he could not remember on the witness stand the name of the company for which he pretended to act."

He charged Campbell with neglecting the duties of his office to prosecute this case and referred in many uncomplimentary remarks to the latter's conduct at various stages of the prosecution. "And yet," he closed this part of his speech by saying, "and yet, Mr. President, it appears that there are some members of the committee who have no criticisms to make of the conduct of such a man!"

Mr. Clark said that large expenditure of money had been criticised, but the fact that it covered three campaigns seemed to have been overlooked. The methods of Daly had made the use of money necessary. Mr. Clark uttered a scathing denunciation of the methods of Daly in Montana politics, reviewing his course in elections and in the State capitol fight, where he charged the Anaconda Company with spending a million dollars. After further discussing the methods of Daly, he continued: "How was it possible to attack this un-American despotism without a great effort, which only money could make? I was in a position to aid in this work, and I am proud that I undertook it. It was done legitimately, and with honesty of purpose, and, although here, where the conditions are not fully understood, I have received some censure the honest people of my State approved my action and will accord me grateful recognition."

## Referred to His Own Career.

In a few sentences Mr. Clark then made a brief review of his own career.

"I was born," he said, "amid the humble surroundings of farm life in Pennsylvania. I went to the West when a lad; educated myself as well as I could by my own exertions while working on a farm, and teaching school for a few years, when a spirit of adventure led me to the Rocky Mountains, where I have lived, mostly in Montana, for thirty-eight years. For three years I worked in the mines and then engaged in other pursuits, and my enterprises extend from one ocean to the other. I employ thousands of men, and pay them generously for their labor. I am endeavoring to discharge my duty toward mankind. I have occupied many positions of honor and trust. I was never in all my life charged with a dishonorable act, and I propose to leave to my children a legacy worth more than gold, an unblemished name."

Mr. Clark then read the letter to the governor of Montana, above printed, and in conclusion, said:

"Mr. President, I desire in retiring from the Senate to state that I have here formed some warm friendships, which I regret to leave. I have received from the honorable presiding officer the most courteous attention. I am deeply sensible of the generous sympathy and support of almost all of my Democratic colleagues, and for the cordial good wishes of a great number of Republican friends, I wish to express my profound gratitude."

# CASE AGAINST SWAYNE

*The Washington Post*, January 11, 1905

———

Divided Sentiment Shown in Impeachment Articles.

———

## FORMALLY OFFERED TO HOUSE

Representative Palmer, of Select Committee, Submits Charges Containing Twelve Articles Alleging Corruption–Two Members Dissent, and Mr. Gillett Strongly Opposes Impeachment.

The impeachment charges upon which Judge Charles Swayne will be tried were presented to the House just before adjournment yesterday afternoon, and notice was given by Mr. Palmer, of Pennsylvania, chairman of the select committee of seven which prepared them, that he would call the case up to-morrow. A minority report, dissenting from all articles except that regarding the falsification of expense accounts, was also filed, the latter signed by Representative Gillett, of California, with a note that he dissents from all the articles of impeachment.

There are twelve articles in the document submitted by the majority, embracing charges of obtaining money by false pretenses, using the property of a bankrupt corporation in the hands of a receiver appointed by himself without any compensation, disobeying the laws requiring him to live in his district, "unlawfuly and maliciously" fining and imprisioning E. T. Davis and Simeon Belden, attorneys at law, for an alleged contempt of the circuit court, and "unlawfully committing to prison" W. C. O'Neal for contempt.

The first article as formulated by the majority declares that Judge Charles Swayne on April 20, 1897, at Waco, Tex., presented a false claim against the government in the sum of $230, knowing the claim to be false. The copy of the certificate made by Swayne is given, in which he says that for twenty-three days "my reasonable expenses were $230." On this account he is charged with a high crime and misdemeanor.

## False Expense Account Charged.

Article 2 relates to the charges of $10 a day while at Tyler, Tex., when his expenses were less, and alleges that he obtained money from the government by false pretense.

Article 3 contains similar charges, but cites another occcasion.

Article 4 charges Judge Swayne with appropriating to his own use, without compensation to the owner, a car belonging to Jacksonville, Tampa and Key West Railroad Company to transport himself, family, and friends from Guyencourt, Del., to Jacksonville, Fla., the railroad at the time being in the hands of a receiver on account of necessary expense in operating the road. Wherefore, Judge Swayne is charged with an abuse of official power and a high misdemeanor.

Article 5 charges that he appropriated to his own use the same car for a trip to California, and the same allegation against him is made.

Article 6 charges that Judge Swayne did not acquire a residence in the Northern district of Florida, as provided by the statutes, saying he "totally disregarded his duty" and willfully and knowingly violated the law, and is guilty of a high misdemeanor.

Article 7 alleges nonresidence and carries the period of nonresidence from July 23, 1894, to January 1, 1903, a period of about nine years, and alleges a violation of law and misdemeanor.

Article 8 charges that "on the 12th day of November, 1901, at the city of Pensacola, in the county of Escambia, in the State of Florida, he did maliciously and unlawfully adjudge guilty of contempt of court and impose a fine of $100 upon and commit to prison for a period of ten days E. T. Davis, an attorney and counselor at law, for an alleged contempt of the Circuit Court of the "United States;" and "is guilty of an abuse of judicial power and of a high misdemeanor in office."

## An Abuse of His Judicial Power.

Article 9 is the same as article 8, except that the words "knowingly and unlawfully" are used to characterize his act in fining and imprisoning Mr. Davis.

Article 10 is the same as article 8, except that it relates to Simeon Belden instead of E. T. Davis, and article 11 is the same as article 9, except that it relates to Belden instead of Davis.

The last article alleges an abuse of judicial power in that he committed W. C. O'Neal to prison for sixty days, for an alleged contempt of the District Court at Pensacola, December 9, 1902, which the committee holds to constitute a high misdemeanor in office.

In conclusion the report recites: "And the House of Representatives, by protestation, saving themselves the liberty of exhibiting at any time hereafter, any further articles of accusation of impeachment against the said Charles Swayne, judge of the United States for the Northern district of Florida, and also of replying to his answers, which he shall make, under the articles herein preferred against him and of offering proof of the same and every part thereof, and to all and every other article or accusation or impeachment which shall be exhibited by them as the case shall require, do demand that the said Charles Swayne may be put to answer the high crimes and misdemeanors in office herein charged against him, and that such proceedings, examinations, trials, and judgments may be thereupon had and given as may be agreeable to law and justice."

Representatives Littlefield, of Maine, and Parker, of New Jersey, in dissenting from the report of the committee, say: "The House must establish the truth of these articles by competent testimony beyond reasonable doubt.

## Dissent from All but One Charge.

"The only articles which, in our judgment, the record as it now stands would sustain, are based upon the certificates of expenses. As to these it was claimed in the hearing that other judges have construed the law as it was construed by Judge Swayne, and evidence was offered to establish the claim and was excluded.

"We dissent from all the other articles, and especially as to those based upon the contempt proceedings in the Davis, Belden, and O'Neal cases. These cases clearly involved willful and marked contempt of court, and demanded exemplary and summary punishment from any self-respecting court. The charge as to nonresidence is not supported by such evidence as warrants the adoption of articles in that regard. The use of the private car, which is the proper subject of adverse criticism, taking into account the fact that there is no intimation or claim that any judicial act was influenced thereby or attempted to be influenced thereby, is not of such gravity as to justify impeachment proceedings therefor. The car incident occurred more than ten years ago, and the nonresidence question has existed for more than four years. No statute of limitations can apply, but the great proceeding of impeachment is not to be used as to stale charges not affecting the moral character or fitness of the officer to perform his duty."

## Other Judges in the Same Boat.

"I concur in all that is said in the foregoing views of the minority except as to ther certificates for expenses. At the hearing before the committee Judge Swayne offered to prove the custom and practice of the Federal judges in making certificates for their reasonable expenses for travel and attendance when holding court out of their own districts, the purpose being to show a judicial construction of the statute under which these expenses were allowed.

"While the record is silent upon all these questions for the reason above named still it appears from official records, some of which have been furbished to me by the Treasury Department, that a majority of the district and circuit judges in five circuits, selected at random, make out certificates for $10 a day, and in two of these districts every judge made out such certificates. I am inclined to believe that where a practice has been so general, these judges acted in good faith with an honest belief that a fair construction of the statutes gave them $10 a day as an allowance for travel and attendance while attending court out of their districts, and I also feel that this House would with great reluctance pass a resolution impeaching them all, and if not all, why one? On this article my mind is not satisfied beyond a reasonable doubt that Judge Swayne, in following a practice so well established by so many honorable men, committed a criminal offense for which he should either be prosecuted or impeached, and giving him the benefit if this doubt I cannot consent to any impeachment on that ground."

# SWAYNE NOT GUILTY

*The Washington Post*, February 28, 1905

## So Says the Senate in Impeachment Proceeding.

## Acquitted on Every Count

## Majority in His favor Was Very Decisive, but a Little More Than One-third of the Senators Being Against Him—Verdict Ascertained After Twelve Roll Calls, One for Each Article.

United States District Judge Charles Swayne was yesterday acquitted of high crimes and misdemeanors in office by the Senate. The vote was decisive. On none of the twelve articles of impeachment, preferred by the national House, was there even a majority against the respondent. The highest vote for impeachment was 35, little more than a third of the Senate, where two-thirds would have been necessary to pronounce him guilty.

The impressive and dignified proceeding involved in the final vote occupied one and a half hours. There was a full attendance of the Senate: the galleries were crowded to the doors. The fact that acquittal had long been anticipated did not discount the general interest. The voice of every Senator, as he rose in his seat and pronounced the words "guilty" or "not guilty," according to his conclusions from the evidence, could be distinctly heard throughout the chamber. As roll call followed roll call, the reiteration of the final words sounded weirdly. Even the accents and manners of the Senators in rising were observed by the onlookers in the unusual judicial drama.

In the main the vote was a party vote. A few Republicans found the judge guilty on certain counts, but more Democrats voted him innocent on other counts. His use of the private car of a bankrupt railroad was condemned by only thirteen Senators, all Democrats. The Republican Senators of recognized ability as lawyers all voted for Judge Swayne, except ex-Attorney General Knox. Because of illness and inability to read the voluminous testimony in the case, he asked to be excused from voting.

## Bitter Comments by Members.

The House managers, who, of dejected air, sat mutely during the period of voting, were not, of course, disappointed at the verdict, but they felt none the less keenly the unsuccesful outcome of their efforts. Many of the advocates and opponents of impeachment, when the case was before the House, occupied seats at the rear of the Senate chamber. Among the former there were numerous bitter comments as they wended their way back to the House. On the other hand, those opposed impeachment recalled the prophetic words of Gen. Grosvenor in the course of bitter House debate late in January, when he said:

"We shall see what we shall see, and when our managers come back from the Senate trailing the flag of partisanship and persecution, in the dust of overwhelming defeat, we shall understand then better than we understand now the principles governing this case and the elements of hate that have entered into it."

The chair where Judge Swayne has been seated during the trial was vacant yesterday. He did not enter the chamber, but remained in the president's room, adjoining the rear lobby of the Senate. There the result of each successive ballot was forwarded to him by his attorneys. He remained in the city last night, but goes to Philadelphia today to undergo a surgical operation for a chronic trouble. As the length of his sojourn there for treatment is uncertain, he has not determined yet when he will return to his judicial district in Northern Florida.

## Not Likely to Resign.

There have been rumors that Judge Swayne would forthwith resign from the bench. These are declared to be without foundation. Ex-Senator Thurston, one of his attorneys, said last evening that they certainly did not come from anyone at all connected with the impeachment case. Judge Swayne is now sixty-three years old, and will not be eligible for retirement till he is seventy.

The Senate met shortly before 10 o'clock, and the voting began a few moments after that hour. Senator Platt, of Connecticut, the presiding officer, first announced the rule prohibiting applause, and added that it would be rigidly enforced. Offenders would be promptly removed from the galleries.

The clerk then read the first article of impeachment, charging Judge Swayne with making a false certificate for expense while holding court at Waco, Tex. After this article had been read, and after the reading of each subsequent article, Mr. Platt said:

"Senators, how say you? Is the respondent Charles Swayne, guilty or not guilty as charged in this article?"

The first vote was more interesting than any of the others. As the names were called, all listened intently to ascertain how the trend of Senatorial opinion would be. Senator Alger was the first to vote in each instance. He invariably responded "not guilty." Allison, Allee, and Ankeny, Republicans followed him. Bacon and Bailey were the first Democrats to vote. They nearly always responded "not guilty." On the first article, four Republicans—Bard, Kittridge, McCumber, and Nelson—voted with the Democrats. Senators Dubois and Gibson, Democrats, voted with the Republicans for acquittal. The vote stood 33 to 49 for acquittal on that charge, being as follows:

## The First Roll Call.

Guilty—Bacon, Bailey, Bard, Bate, Berry, Blackburn, Carmack, Clark (Montana), Clay, Cockrell, Culberson, Daniel, Foster (Louisiana), Gorman, Kittredge, Latimer, McCreary, McCumber, McEnery, McLaurin, Mallory, Martin, Money, Morgan, Nelson, Newlands, Overman, Patterson, Pettus, Simmons, Stone, Taliaferro, Teller—33.

Not guilty—Alger, Allee, Allison, Ankeny, Ball, Beveridge, Burnham, Burrows, Clapp, Clark (Wyoming), Crane, Cullom, Depow, Dick, Dietrich, Dillingham, Doiliver, Dryden, Dubois, Elkins, Fairbanks, Foraker, Foster (Washington), Frye, Fulton, Gallinger, Gamble, Gibson, Hale, Hansbrough, Heyburn, Hopkins, Kean, Kearns, Lodge, Long, McComas, Millard, Penrose, Perkins, Platt (Connecticut), Platt of New York, Proctor, Quarles, Scott, Smoot, Spooner, Stewart, Warren—49.

Fifty-five votes in the affirmative would have been necessary to convict. As this vote was almost reversed, Judge Swayne was pronounced to be not guilty. The chair announced this to be the result, saying:

"On article 1 of the impeachment of Charles Swayne 33 Senators have voted 'guilty' and 49 Senators have voted 'not guilty.' Two-thirds not having voted for conviction, Charles Swayne stands acquitted of charges contained in the first article."

The reading and voting upon the other articles followed in rapid succession. The second charge was that of an excessive charge for expenses while holding court at Tyler, Tex. The proceeding in this case was an exact counterpart of that on the first article, and there was only one change in the vote, which was that made by Mr. Clark, of Montana, who, having cast his first vote for conviction, changed on this roll call, and voted for acquittal. The result was 32 for conviction to 50 for acquittal.

## Thirteen Democrats Against Him.

The third charge was also related to excessive charges at Tyler, Tex., and the vote was identical with the vote on the second article, 32 to 50. The fourth and fifth articles related to the use of private cars. There were only 13 votes of guilty on them, as follows:

Bailey, Berry, Blackburn, Carmack, Cockrell, Culberson, Daniel, McLaurin, Martin, Money, Morgan, Newlands, Pettus, all Democrats.

On the sixth charge, that of nonresidence by Judge Swayne in his district, the vote was 31 to 51. On this vote, Mr. Clark, of Montana, changed back to the affirmative side, but Senators Kittredge and McCumber went to the negative. Dubois and Gibson voted for conviction on this charge.

The seventh article, relating to residence, the vote was 19 for conviction to 63 against. The affirmative vote was as follows:

Bate, Berry, Blackburn, Carmack, Clark (Mont.), Cockrell, Daniel, Dubois, Gibson, Lattimer, McCreary, McEnery, McLaurin, Mallory, Martin, Money, Morgan, Pettus, and Taliaferro—19.

The vote on the eighth, ninth, tenth, and eleventh articles, covering the contempt cases of E.T. Davis and Simeon Belden, was 31 to 51. On the articles covering the contempt cases Senators Dubois (Democrat) and Hansbrough (Republican) voted for conviction, and Mr. Bard (Republican) for acquittal. On those articles Senators Hansbrough and McCumber were the only Republicans who voted for conviction, and Stone the only Democrat for acquittal.

## Verdict on a Contempt Case.

The twelfth article was the last. It dealt with the conduct of Judge Swayne in punishing W.C. O'Neal for contempt in assaulting a trustee in bankruptcy appointed by him. The voting was concluded at 11:35 a.m. On the final vote, the result was 35 guilty to 47 not guilty, the largest vote given for conviction. Senators Bard, Hansbrough, Kittredge, McCumber, Nelson, and Quarles (Republican) voted "guilty" with the Democrats, and Senators Gibson and Newlands (Democrats) "not guilty" with the Republicans.

The result on this vote being announced, and with it the entire verdict ascertained, the Chair directed the Secretary to enter and order of acquittal on all the articles. This being done, a motion for final adjournment of the trial was offered by Mr. Fairbanks, and it prevailed. Thus at 11:40 the long and tedious proceeding came to an end.

Ex-Senators Thurston and Higgins, Swayne's attorneys, were congratulated by many Senators: the House managers walked up the center aisle of the chamber and soon took their departure; the galleries were speedily cleared, and the Senate proceeded with its regular business.

## House Learns of Acquittal.

The proceedings of the House were interrupted yesterday afternoon by a message from the Senate announcing the acquittal of Judge Charles Swayne of all the counts against him. There was no demonstration of any kind when the action of the Senate was read.

# BURTON'S SUCCESSOR

*The Washington Post*, June 4, 1906

————

Foster D. Coburn Named as Senator from Kansas.

————

FORMER SENATOR RESIGNED.

————

Conferred with His Advisers at Topeka and Then Sent Brief Notification of His Retirement to Gov. Hoch—Toga Falls to Widely-known Secretary of the State Board of Agriculture.

————

Topeka, Kans. June 4.—Foster Dwight Coburn, of Kansas City, Kans., agriculturist, to-day was appointed United States Senator by Gov. E. W. Hoch to succeed J. Ralph Burton, who resigned earlier in the day. Mr. Coburn has not definately accepted the appointment. Mr. Coburn was not a candidate for the appointment, nor has he been a candidate for election to the Senate.

Mr. Coburn was born in Jefferson County, Wis., in 1846. He served in two Illinois regiments during the civil war, and settled in Kansas in 1867. He has served for the last sixteen years as secretary of the Kansas State board of agriculture. He was a commisionner of live stock exhibits at the St. Louis Exposition in 1904.

### Senator Burton's Resignation.

Senator Burton called upon Gov. Hoch early to-day. After an hour's conference with the governor, Senator Burton returned to his hotel, and immediately entered into conference with his attorneys and friends. After the conference B. P. Waggener and R. P. Hackney, two of the Senator's attorneys, who had been prominent in the trials of the case against the Kansan, went to the executive office. When they emerged a few minutes later, Gov. Hoch informed the waiting newspaper men that he had Senator Burton's resignation in his pocket. The resignation was extremely brief. It read:

"Sir: I hereby resign as a United States Senator for the State of Kansas, to take effect immediately."

Soon after receiving the resignation, Gov. Hoch sent a telegram to Vice President Fairbanks, notifying him as the presiding officer of the Senate of Senator Burton's resignation and acceptance.

# LORIMER OUSTED, FIGHTING TO END

*The Washington Post*, July 12, 1912

————

### Senate Declares Seat Vacated by Vote of 55 to 28.

————

### Thrills With Final Plea.

————

### Assails His Accusers and Says He Will Continue Battle.

————

### No Surprise at Result.

————

Colleagues Listen in Silence to One of Most Eloquent Speeches Delivered in Years—Moved Only by Cullom's Turn Against Him When Balloting Begins—Reviews History of Case and Alleges Conspiracy—In Doubt as to Plan for His Future—Will Return to Chicago for Long Rest—Bailey, Smoot, and Other Friends Escort Him to Cloakroom Door—Walks Away Smiling Wearily—Details of the Day and Vote.

The seat in the United States Senate held by William Lorimer as the representative of Illinois since June 16, 1909, was vacated yesterday at two minutes past 2 o'clock by the decree of that body on a recorded vote of 55 to 28.

The report of the majority of the special investigating committee was overturned, and the minority report, declaring that "corrupt methods and practices were employed in the election" and that Mr. Lorimer's election "was therefore invalid," was adopted.

These are the prosaic facts marking the end of a case that has become historic and about which men forever will differ.

The seven days of debate on the pending resolution, the result of which has been known for weeks to every senator and to Mr. Lorimer, ended a few moments before the vote was cast, in a dramatic and fervid peroration to his three days' defense, during which the Illinois senator held the Senate and crowded galleries spellbound. His denunciation of those whom he believed guilty of traducing him and misrepresenting the facts, will long be remembered, and go down in the history of the Senate as a companion piece to the vitriolic utterances of Ingalls, Vest, and Voorhees, those past masters in invective, sarcasm, and ridicule.

————

## Never Pleaded for Votes.

He never pleaded for votes. His appeal was for the exercise of fair and honest judgment based upon the evidence submitted, and, asserting his innocence, he refused to accept the advice of friends, and in the face of certain defeat, declined to resign. The figure of Mr. Lorimer standing there yesterday in the center of the main aisle, concluding his review of the evidence in his case, fighting with his back to the wall up to the last moment, never will be forgotten by those who witnessed the spectacle.

## Lorimer Would Not Resign.

His appeal was at once pathetic, dramatic, forceful. Pale from the exhaustion of his prolonged defense and the intense heat of the chamber, with hair disheveled and perspiration streaming down his face, he fought gamely to the last, declaring his innocence and his purpose to devote his life to then undoing of the great wrong he said was about to be done him.

"Of, Senators," he cried, "you may cast me out of here, but while I have strength and life I'm going to continue trying to make a reputation and a character of never having been a coward."

"No, I will not resign," he shouted, as if the act had just been suggested to him.

"No, no, no," he exclaimed, as he stepped boldly into the center of the aisle and advanced slightly towards the Vice President's rostrum, holding his hand aloft by way of emphasis. "If I go from this body it will be because more senators vote in favor of that resolution that vote against it. My exit will not be from fear. It will not be because I am a coward. It will be because of the crime of the Senate of the United States."

## Ready for His Fate.

As he uttered these words his arms fell to his side and he bowed his head involuntarily toward the Democratic side, whence came the majority of his opponents. Then he straightened up, looked clearly and calmly over the chamber, and said almost in a whisper:

"I am ready; I am ready, now."

Turning, he walked slowly back to the last row on the Republican side of the chamber and sat down at his own desk—a desk he realized he was not to be permitted to again occupy as a senator of the United States.

And there he sat, with his head resting on his hand while the Senate decided his fate. Calmly and apparently undisturbed, the most self-possessed figure in the chamber, Senator Lorimer awaited the vote he knew would take from him the title to his office. The bells throughout the great building sounded, summoning the few absenters to their seats. Eighty-two senators responded, and a moment or two later the clerk was ordered to call the roll on the resolution.

## Hears Result in Silence.

Senate Ashurst, the first name called, voted "aye," and as the succession of "ayes," with scattering "nays," were recorded, Mr. Lorimer noted the vote without a change of expression. He was the exposure of every eye in the crowded galleries, but he seemed less interested than anybody else. It was only when his aged colleague, Senator Cullom, who voted for him on the previous trial, voted for the resolution, that Mr. Lorimer slightly shifted his position and appeared to notice the character of the vote cast.

And thus it went until, amid the most intense silence, the vote of the Senate was recorded and Mr. Gallinger, in the chair, announced the vote.

"On this resolution the ayes are 55 and the nays are 28," said the presiding officer, "and the resolution is agreed to."

That was all. No other formality was required. The Senate had recorded its judgment.

## Friends Express Sympathy.

As the vote was announced Mr. Lorimer arose from his desk, stood erect, smiled sadly, and walked wearily toward the Republican cloakroom door. He passed through the door and out of the Senate, surrounded by friends, who still believed that the charges against him had not been proved, and that the vote just cast had done an innocent man a grievous wrong.

Senator Bailey met Mr. Lorimer before he reached the door and shook him warmly by the hand. Senator Smoot threw an arm over his shoulder, other senators who had stood loyally by him and a number of members of the House pressed around, grasped his hand in a friendly farewell, and accompanied him within the retreat afforded by the cloakroom.

Always dignified, the Senate solemnly proceeded to other business, and so far as the records of that body are concerned the Lorimer case, over which had fought for more than two years, had passed into history.

Outside the Senate door, as Mr. Lorimer stepped into the corridor, friends greeted him again, and a party of Sisters of Charity pushed forward to express regret at his expulsion. At his office later, when a physician had attended him, he said he would not leave Washington before the first of next week.

Technically, Mr. Lorimer will pass out of the records of the Senate as a member of that body, notwithstanding his more than three years' occupancy of his seat.

## Vote Was No Surprise.

The outcome of the vote was not a surprise, but the leaders of the fight against him had not estimated a greater vote than 50 to 35. Lorimer gained only one of the men who voted against him March 1, 1911, Senator Jones, of Washington, while he lost the votes of his associate, Senator Cullom, and of Senators Curtis, of Kansas; Briggs, of New Jersey; Simmons, of North Carolina; and Watson, of West Virginia.

The moving character of Lorimer's appeal was admitted on every hand. Instead of the pleading defense that had been expected, it was throughout a ringing defiance to those who had opposed him, a declaration of his unfaltering belief in the purity of his election in Illinois, and a promise that he would not give up his fight with his eviction from the Senate.

## Denies Roosevelt Bribe Story.

Only two incidents marked the few minutes between the termination of Lorimer's speech and the taking of the roll call which resulted in his defeat. One was the charge of Senator Dixon, Col. Roosevelt's campaign manager, that the affidavits Lorimer had introduced to show attempted corruption of delegates to the Chicago convention were "malicious and deliberate falsehoods."

The other was the request of Sent Tillman, of South Carolina, feeble from the effects of illness, for permission to have the clerk read a statement from him. It was an affirmation of his belief in Lorimer's innocence and a pathetic statement of his own feebleness. Tillman wept as it was read, and other members of the Senate exhibited deep feeling.

## Senator Tillman Pathetic.

"Since I was stricken with paralysis 30 months ago," said Mr. Tillman's statement, "I have thought often and seriously about death and the hereafter. That I am here at all is in some respects a miracle, and I know I must go hence and meet the Great Judge face to face very soon. I cannot do otherwise than vote as my conscience dictates, and I believe this man is innocent of the charges brought against him."

Senator Tillman expressed the hope that Mr. Lorimer would consecrate the remainder of his life to the purification of politics in Chicago, and to the uplift of his fellow citizens in Illinois.

"I believe if he does bravely fight for a purer and better government in Illinois," he said, "God will strengthen his arm and he will return to the Senate vindicated by the people of that great State."

## Lorimer's Plans in Doubt.

When asked last evening what plans, if any, he had made for the future, Mr. Lorimer said he had not as yet had sufficient time to take that matter into consideration.

"I must think things over and talk with my friends," replied Mr. Lorimer, "before I can say whether I shall go into a political fight for vindication."

"The place for me to make a fight, should I determine on such a course, would be before the people. The candidates for the legislature which will select my successor have already been nominated. Consequently, I can not go into the coming fight. Thus I should have to wait until two years hence. I have not looked that far ahead. Before reaching any decision on that point I want to have full opportunity to talk with the friends back home."

Asked whether he would bring legal action against any of the persons who had preferred specific charges against him, Mr. Lorimer gave the same answer of lack of time to consider the question. He declared, however, that he probably would discuss the feasibility of such a course with Judge Hanecy, who was his counsel in the case before the Senate.

## Going Back to his Business.

"What I must do first of all, however," said Mr. Lorimer, "is to go home and get back into business. I have been away from it for two years. Others have been looking after my affairs. They have been doing their share and mine, too. I must not only hoe my own row, but a double one, to make up for lost time."

Mr. Lorimer announced that he probably would go to his summer home, about 50 miles outside of Chicago, tomorrow. This would depend, however, he added, on whether or not he is called to New York on business.

## Senator Cullom Explains.

In a lengthy statement, explaining why he voted against Senator Lorimer yesterday after having supported him on the former vote on the Lorimer case, Senator Cullom, of Illinois, last night said:

"There was no evidence of this investigation to show that Mr. Lorimer, either personally or through others was guilty of corrupt practices in his election to the Senate. Yet there is evidence, to my mind, of a conclusive character, which shows that corruption did exist in the Forty-sixth general assembly of the State of Illinois, and that the senatorship was connected with and became a part of the program of a certain membership of the legislature which sent Lorimer to the Senate. Whether it was intended that the senatorship should be come a part of this program avails nothing. The fact remains that Senator Lorimer was elected by votes that were tainted, and the testimony of confessed bribe-takers remains, that they were being paid their 'Lorimer money.':

## Senator Lea's Resolution.

The final vote was upon a resolution offered by Senator Luke Lea. It read as follows:

"Resolved, That corrupt methods and practices were employed in the election of William Lorimer to the Senate of the United States from the State of Illinois, and that his election was therefore invalid."

The closing moments of the trial were intensely dramatic. Lorimer holding the floor, making a last defense of his seat, declared he did not appeal for the vote of any senator, but asked for justice. He expressed gratitude for tributes which senators had paid to his private life.

"Every man who had such a life has his own reward—he has it here," he said. "I ask nothing on that account; it has no bearing in the case. I hope it will influence no senator in making up his judgment."

He spoke of his family.

"I have been the happiest of men, living and blessed by God's son," he said. "I ask nothing because of them, or because of my ideal home life.

"It has been said by senators that the worst foes of Lorimer have not impeached his integrity. They have said that his word was good as his bond; that he never turned on a friend; that he had been consistent, right or wrong."

## Points to Record of Forty Years.

"But I ask no consideration for that. When senators are making up their minds, when they are deciding whether they will believe Lorimer or Charles A. White, all I ask is to consider in connection with a record of 40 years my truth and veracity, as stated by my enemies. I ask the consideration of senators, as to whether they will believe the bribe taker, who has lied time and again, or believe me.

"Much has been said about Lorimer resigning," he continued. "If at the beginning of this case I had believed that one man had been bribed to vote for me I would have walked in and laid my resignation on the Vice President's table. But I know the record. I know there was not a corrupt vote cast for me.

"To resign in the face of that knowledge? In the face of that conviction? Why? Because they say the Senate has been canvassed and enough votes have been found to turn Lorimer out. Resign because they defeat stares you in the face? Oh, what an argument! What sort of a man is it that runs in such a case! If the men who founded this country had run when defeat stared them in the face we would have no country, no flag.

"And he who is so cowardly as to run because defeat stares him in the face has no place in this body. This chamber is no place for cowards. It was not built on cowardice.

### Never Intended to Resign.

"Oh, senators, though you all vote to turn me out, though every vote has been canvassed and is against me, yet will I not resign. No, no, no. I'll not resign. If I go from this body it will be because more senators vote for that resolution than against it. My exit will not be for fear; it will not be because I am a coward. It will be because of the crime of the Senate of the United States.

"I am ready," he added, dramatically, as he took his seat.

### The Vote Against Lorimer.

Those who voted to oust Lorimer were Ashurst, Bacon, Borah, Bourne, Briggs, Bristow, Brown, Bryan, Burton, Chamberlain, Clapp, Crawford, Cullom, Cummins, Curtis, Dixon, Fall, Gardner, Gore, Gronna, Hitchcock, Johnson, Kenyon, Kern, La Follette, Lea, Lodge, Martin, Martine, Myers, Nelson, Newlands, O'Gorman, Overman, Page, Poindexter, Pomerene, Rayner, Reed, Root, Sanders, Shively, Simmons, Stone, Sutherland, Swanson, Townsend, Watson, Williams, Works, Clarke (Ark.), Smith (Ariz.), Smith (Ga.), Smith (Mich.), Smith (S.C.)—55.

### For Lorimer and Paired.

Those who voted against the Lea resolution and in favor of Lorimer were Bailey, Bradley, Brandegee, Burnham, Catron, Clark (Wyo.), Crane, Dillingham, Fletcher, Foster, Gallinger, Gamble, Guggenheim, Johnston, Jones, Lippitt, McCumber, Oliver, Paynter, Penrose, Perkins, Richardson, Smith (Md.), Smoot, Stephenson, Thornton, Tillman, Wetmore—28.

Senators paired in favor of the resolution were Chilton, Culberson, Davis, and Owen. Senators paired against it were Bankhead, Du Pont, Heyburn, and Warren.

Senators absent and not paired were Percy and McLean.

Senator Lorimer did not vote.

There being 95 members in the Senate, there being one vacancy from Colorado.

### Work of Conspirators, He Says.

In resuming the floor yesterday to conclude his speech, Mr. Lorimer took up in turn the testimony of the various witnesses against him. He declared that the proceedings had been prosecuted by conspirators.

Lorimer went after Senator Crawford, of South Dakota, who had spoken first and voted against him at the first trial. He referred to charges made against Mr. Crawford, of which the South Dakota senator was fully acquitted, and invited Mr. Crawford out from the cloakroom while he read an affidavit which charged him with having employed a man to file a public land claim in his interest.

"That's supposed to be a sworn affidavit," said Senator Lorimer. "But all the circumstances surrounding it deny the truth. A Federal grand jury cleansed the skirts of this senator."

He declared the affidavit itself had no foundation, and yet appeared to be truthful upon its face.

## Turns to Senator Crawford.

"Has Charles A. White made any statement to your committee stronger that Crawford affidavit?" he demanded. "I think not. And yet Senator Crawford would turn me out of this body on the statement of a man more foul than the man who made this affidavit against him.

"I don't ask for the senator's vote," continued Lorimer. But I am asking you, Senator Crawford, after that awful experience you had, don't you think you ought to weigh carefully, thoughtfully, meditate long and often before you vote to destroy your fellow man on evidence like that?"

## Attacks Burns Detectives.

Senator Lorimer took up the employment of Detective Burns, to whom he referred as the detective who had "driven to his grave a United States senator, whom the people now believe not to have been guilty." The reference was taken by the Senate to apply to the late John H. Mitchell, of Oregon.

Mr. Lorimer declared it had been shown that the Burns detectives had committed perjury, and he made like charges against others. He said White was bought by the Tribune to perjure his soul, that Glavis was bought but lacked the nerve to go through with it, and was then indicted in Washington to close his mouth.

Drawing a parallel from the election of Senator Lea, of Tennessee, Democrat, by 33 Republican and 34 Democratic votes, Mr. Lorimer said these Republicans voted for Lea because of a political condition that made the election of a Republican impossible.

He denied that the "interests" had aided his election.

# ARCHBALD DENIES ALL

*The Washington Post*, January 7, 1913

———

Accused Jurist on Stand in Senate Impeachment Trial.

———

His Wife Also a Witness.

———

Defendant Declares His Official Conduct Has Always Been Free of Corruption—Friendship for His Scranton Associate Attributed as Motive for His Negotiations in Coal Deals.

———

Friendship for his Scranton associates with whom he had lived and worked for years, was the motive that led Judge Robert W. Archbald, of the United States Commerce Court, to negotiate with officials of the Erie and Lehigh Valley railroads over the settlement of coal land matters, and that induced him to indorse certain notes, according to the statements made by the accused jurist yesterday when he took the stand before the impeachment court of the Senate to testify in his own behalf.

Judge Archbald followed his wife upon the witness stand. Led by his attorneys he gave a chronological history of the transactions upon which the House of Representatives had based its impeachment proceedings against him. He repeatedly denied that any improper motives influenced his actions, or that he had sought to corruptly use his powers as a Federal judge to induce the railroad officials to do certain things.

## Mrs. Archbald on Stand.

Mrs. Archbald, an eloquent figure in defense of her husband's integrity as to the trip to Europe, which he enjoyed at the expense of Henry W. Cannon, a director in the Great Northern and other railroads, was under examination but a short time. She said Mr. Cannon was her cousin, that the two families had been intimate for years, and that they had frequently enjoyed pleasure trips together.

The invitation to the Archbalds to go to Europe in 1910 came to Mrs. Archbald personally. She gave the Senate the letter from Mr. Cannon. This and other letters that passed between Mr. Cannon and Judge and Mrs. Archbald were filled with discussion of the trip.

Today the managers for the House will take up cross-examination of the jurist.

---

### Admits Alleged Negotiations.

Judge Archbald admitted his associations with Edward J. Williams, of Scranton, in negotiations for the Katydid refuse coal dump. He admitted that he had talked with Second Vice President Richardson and General Counsel Brownell, on the Erie, in an effort to expedite a decision as to whether the Erie would grant an option on its part of the dump, but he denied that he had tried or intended to influence them to act in his favor.

Judge Archbald declared that he had had no interest whatever in the settlement of the case of the Marian Coal Company, of Scranton, against the Delaware, Lackawanna and Western Railroad. He went to officials of the railroad in that case, he said, as a friend of George M. Watson, the attorney for the coal company, and C.G. Boland, one of the owners of the coal company. He denied that he had tried to get credit from litigants or possible litigants in his courts.

### Questioned by Senators.

Upon one point only was the jurist subjected to much questioning from members of the Senate. This was in reference to the charge that, as a member of the Commerce Court, he had written to Helm Bruce, an attorney for the Louisville and Nashville Railroad, as to the evidence that had been presented in the case of that road against the Interstate Commerce Commission, tried before the Commerce Court.

Judge Archbald declared certain points in the evidence were not clear, and that he had written to Mr. Bruce to clean them up. The points at issue, he said, had no part in the settlement of the case.

Members of the Senate asked if he had shown the correspondence to other members of the Commerce Court, or informed them of it. Judge Archbald said he had not. Senator Reed asked if he thought it proper for a judge, in passing on doubtful points in evidence, to ask the opinion only of the attorney likely to coincide with his own views.

"No, I do not," said Judge Archbald.

### Ignorant of "Silent Party" Agreement.

He declared he had no knowledge of the making of the "silent party" agreement in the office of William P. Boland, in Scranton, through which it appeared that the Katydid dump was controlled by E.J. Williams, W.P. Boland, and a "silent party," known but to a few persons.

Representative Sterling, of the House managers, opposed direct questioning by Judge Archbald's attorneys as to his motive in going to the railroad officials in the various coal-land deals.

### Would Show Motives.

"This jurist is charged with corruptly using his judicial power to influence railroads that might be litigants in his court," said Attorney Worthington, representing Judge Archbald. "The charges against him, if sustained, would forever bar him from public office and disgrace him. We have the right to show by the witness himself whether or not evil intent was present in his mind when he went to these railroad officials."

Senator Bacon, presiding over the impeachment court, ruled direct questioning out as improper, but permitted the attorneys to ask Judge Archbald his motive. In the case of the deal involving the

Erie Railroad, he said it was the desire to expedite a decision as to whether or not the option on the Katydid dump would be given in the Lackawanna case, it was as a friendly act to George M. Watson and C.G. Boland.

# ARCHBALD "GUILTY"

*The Washington Post*, January 14, 1913

———

## Senate Dismisses Judge From Commerce Court Bench.

———

## The Verdict is Unanimous

———

## Charged With Using Judicial Influence for Private Gain.

———

## Jurist Receives News in Guarded Room. Can Never Hold Federal Position—Declares He Is Innocent and No Ballot Can Make Him Otherwise—Chief Justice White Will Designate Judge to Sit in His Place.

———

## THE SENATE'S VERDICT.

———

"The Senate, therefore, do order and decree, and it is hereby adjudged, that the respondent, Robert W. Archbald, circuit judge for the United States for the Third circuit and designated to serve in the Commerce Court, be, and he is hereby removed from office, and that he be, and is hereby forever disqualified to hold and enjoy any office of honor, trust, or profit under the United States."

Amid scenes of the utmost solemnity, the Senate of the United States yesterday afternoon found Robert W. Archbald, judge of the Commerce Court, guilty as charged in five counts of the articles of impeachment upon which the House of Representatives brought him before the bar of the Senate, and acquitted him on eight counts.

Guilty, according to an overwhelming vote of the Senate of "high crimes and misdemeanors," this jurist was stripped of his high office and forever disqualified from holding any position of honor, trust, or profit under the Federal government.

The galleries were crowded, and in the chamber, the walls were lined with representatives, who came over from the House to witness a scene that has been enacted in the Senate only nine times since the foundation of the government.

---

## Situation Is Tense.

The tenseness of the situation finally began to wear upon the nerves of people in the galleries and members on the floor. Here and there a member moved his position; a slight murmur came down from the galleries, and the shuffling of feet, barely heard, as visitors came and went, brought Senator Lodge to his feet with a protest against this interruption of the solemn proceedings then holding the attention of the body. Thereupon, the sergeant-at-arms was instructed to close the galleries, and not until five roll calls had been taken were the occupants given the opportunity to depart and make way for those on the outside who had been clamoring for admission.

## Insists He Is Innocent.

In a little committee room off the gallery floor, behind a guarded door, Judge Archbald, his wife, and son Hugh sat throughout the afternoon as the Senate voted upon the charges against him. The first vote of conviction was carried to him by his son from the gallery. After sentence had been imposed upon him, Judge Archbald and his family left the Capitol, to go at once to the family home at Scranton.

"I have always known that I have done no wrong, and the vote of no one makes it otherwise," was his only comment upon the Senate's action.

Sentence was imposed by Senator Bacon, of Georgia, the presiding officer, after the Senate had, by a vote of 39 to 35, upheld a resolution offered by Senator O'Gorman, of New York, authorizing the full penalty provided by the Constitution.

## Removed From Office.

"The Senate therefore do order and decree," said Senator Bacon, "and it is hereby adjudged, that the respondent, Robert W. Archbald, circuit judge for the United States for the Third judicial circuit and designated to serve in the Commerce Court, be and he is hereby removed from office, and that he be and is hereby forever disqualified to hold and enjoy any office of honor, trust, or profit under the United States."

The sentence of the Senate became operative at once, and directions were given that the President and the House of Representatives be notified of the verdict and the punishment imposed.

## May Extend Life of Court.

Whether a successor to Judge Archbald will be appointed to fill the vacancy for the short time the commerce court will remain in existence is not known. The subcommittee of the Senate committee on appropriations reported in favor of a continuance of this court until June 30, 1914, but the full committee yesterday vetoed that and provided for the continuance of the life of the court until June 30 of this year. Under existing law, the court will go out of existence March 4, but there are a number of pending cases that ought to be disposed of, and it is said this cannot be done unless the court is given further time.

Chief Justice White will designate some circuit judge to sit on this court, and if its life is extended President Taft may nominate some one to succeed the deposed jurist.

The vote on the first charge, that Judge Archbald had corruptly influenced officials of the Erie Railroad to sell him the Katydid coal dump at Scranton, resulted in his conviction by a vote of 68 to 5, a vote that amazed even senators who from the first believed the impeachment of the jurist would be ordered. Conviction of any article carried with it the punishment of removal from the bench.

Senator Hoke Smith moved that the Senate go into secret session, but the Senate insisted upon voting on each article, and the motion was withdrawn.

Following the vote on the thirteenth article, Senator O'Gorman presented an order fixing the punishment as dismissal from his office and forever disqualifying Judge Archbald from holding any office under the Federal government. That the measure of punishment was to be the subject of discussion was recognized when Senator Root moved that the doors be closed for deliberation. During the secret session it was decided that the full punishment should be administered, although there was sharp dissent from that conclusion.

## Removed by Viva Voce.

When the doors were again opened, Senator O'Gorman called for a vote on the order submitted by him. Senator Oliver moved that the order be divided. This was agreed to, and the order providing for dismissal from office was adopted viva voce without a dissenting voice. A yea-and-nay vote was demanded on the disqualification, and it was adopted 39 to 35, thus imposing the full penalty. The detailed vote is as follows:

Yeas–Ashurst, Borah, Bourne, Bristow, Brown, Bryan, Chamberlain, Clapp, Clarke of Arkansas, Crawford, Culberson, Cummins, Dixon, Fletcher, Gore, Gronna, Hitchcock, Johnson, Kenyon, Kern, La Follette, Martin, Martine, Newlands, O'Gorman, Owen, Page, Perky, Poindexter, Pomerene, Reed, Shively, Simmons, Smith of Arizona, Smith of Maryland, Stone, Swanson, Tillman, and Williams.

Nays–Bacon, Bankhead, Brandegee, Burnham, Burton, Catron, Clark of Wyoming, Crane, Cullom, Curtis, du Pont, Foster, Gallinger, Jones, Lippit, Lodge, Mccumber, McLean, Nelson, Oliver, Paynter, Penrose, Perkins, Richardson, Root, Sanders, Smith of Georgia, Smoot, Stephenson, Sutherland, Thornton, Townsend, Warren, Wetmore, and Works.

Voting on the charges began as soon as the impeachment court had been reorganized at 1 o'clock.

As the roll call proceeded, replies of "guilty" came from all parts of the chamber. Each senator, under the rule, rose in his seat and gave his verdict. Robert W. Archbald, Jr., who sat with his father's counsel on the floor of the Senate, exhibited great feeling as it became apparent that the vote was overwhelmingly for conviction.

## Vote on First Article.

The vote in detail on the first charge:

For conviction–Ashurst, Bankhead, Borah, Bourne, Brandegee, Bristow, Brown, Bryan, Burton, Chamberlain, Clapp, Clark, of Wyoming; Clarke, of Arkansas; Crane, Crawford, Culberson, Cullom, Cummins, Curtis, Dixon, Du Pont, Fletcher, Foster, Gallinger, Gore, Gronna, Hitchcock, Johnson, of Maine; Jones, Kenyon, La Follette, Lippitt, Lodge, McCumber, McLean, Martin, Martine, Myers, Nelson, Newlands, O'Gorman, Owen, Page, Perkins, Perky, Poindexter, Pomerene, Reed, Richardson, Root, Sanders, Shively, Simmons, Smith, of Georgia; Smith, of Maryland; Smith, of Arizona; Smoot, Stephenson, Stone, Sutherland, Swanson, Thornton, Tillman, Townsend, Warren, Wetmore, Williams, Works.

Against conviction–Burnham, Catron, Oliver, Paynter, and Penrose.

Absent or not voting–Bacon, Bradley, Briggs, Chilton, Dillingham, Fall, Gamble, Gardner, Guggenheim, Helskell, of Arkansas; Jackson, Johnston, of Alabama; Johnston, of Texas; Kern, Lea, Massey, Overman, Percy, Smith, of South Carolina; Smith, of Michigan; and Watson.

The second charge was not sustained, the vote against Judge Archbald, 46 to 25, being two short of the necessary two-thirds. On the third charge the accused jurist was convicted by a vote of 60 to 11. Senators Brandegee, Clark of Wyoming, Crane, Smoot, Stephenson, and Thornton, who had voted "guilty" on the first article, voted "not guilty" on this charge.

Another verdict of "guilty" came on the fourth charge. The vote was 52 to 20. Additional senators who voted "not guilty" on this charge were: Burton, Cullom, du Pont, Gallinger, Lippitt, McCumber, Root, Sutherland, Swanson, Warren, and Wetmore, while Senator Thornton voted "guilty."

On the fifth charge Judge Archbald received the support of but six senators–Burnham, Catron, Clark of Wyoming, Oliver, Paynter, and Penrose. He was convicted, 66 to 6, on this article.

## Convicted on Last Article.

On the last article many senators asked to be excused from voting, declaring the charges were so general they could not conscientiously vote either way. The final vote resulted in conviction on this article also, 42 to 20.

On this article the detailed vote was:

Guilty–Ashurst, Bourne, Bristow, Brown, Burton, Chamberlain, Clapp, Crawford, Culberson, Cullom, Cummins, Curtis, Dixon, Foster, Gore, Hitchcock, Jones, Kenyon, La Follette, Lodge, McCumber, McLean, Martin, Martine, Myers, O'Gorman, Owen, Perky, Poindexter, Pomerene, Reed, Root, Sanders, Shively, Simmons, Smith, of Arizona; Smith, of Georgia; Smith, of Maryland; Stone, Swanson, Townsend, Williams, and Works–42.

Not guilty–Bankhead, Brandegee, Bryan, Burnham, Catron, Crane, du Pont, Fletcher, Gallinger, Nelson, Oliver, Page, Paynter, Penrose, Perkins, Richardson, Smoot, Stephenson, Thornton, and Wetmore–20.

## Excused From Voting.

Before the first article of impeachment was read, Senator Kern, of Indiana; Senator Dillingham, of Vermont; and Senator Bradley, of Kentucky, asked to be excused from voting because they had not been present throughout the trial. They were excused. Senator Clarke, of Arkansas, was excused from voting on all articles which charged Judge Archbald with wrongful acts before he was elevated to the Commerce Court. Senator Tillman was excused from voting on all articles except the first, and Senators Jackson, of Maryland, Helskell, of Ohio, and Johnston, of Texas, were excused from voting on all articles. They entered the Senate since the trial began.

Judge Archbald received majorities in his favor on seven of the charges against him, besides the acquittal on the second article, where the two-thirds vote against him was not obtained. On the charge that he had wrongfully accepted a purse of $500 raised among Scranton attorneys, the vote was 65 "not guilty" and 1 "guilty," the single vote being cast by Senator Ashurst, of Arizona.

Although no debate was permitted during the progress of the voting, many senators asked to be excused from voting on certain charges, because they did not believe the Senate had authority to take up acts committed by Judge Archbald before he was appointed to the Commerce Court, or because they believed the acts that might be characterized as "misbehavior" were not such as to constitute "high crimes and misdemeanors" involving the extreme penalty of the Constitution.

## Root Explains Vote.

Senator Root, in a statement filed during the voting, in which Senator Lodge, of Massachusetts, partly concurred, said:

"I have voted that the respondent is guilty under articles 1, 2, 3, 5, 6, and 13 because I find that he used the power and influence of his office as judge of the Court of Commerce to secure favors of money value for himself and his friends from railroad companies, some of which were litigants in his court, and all of which were under the regulations of the Interstate Commerce Commission, subject to the review of the Court of Commerce.

"I consider this course of conduct, and each instance of it, to be a high crime and misdemeanor. I have voted not guilty upon the other articles because, while most of them involved improper conduct, I do not consider that the acts proved are high crimes and misdemeanors."

The legal fight before the Senate was in the hands of seven members of the House of Representatives, as the prosecutors, and Judge Archbald's attorneys, who had the personal advice of Judge Archbald throughout the trial. The House managers and attorneys sat throughout the proceedings yesterday, silent witnesses to the Senate decision of the case.

Those who conducted the prosecution for the House were Representatives Clayton, of Alabama; Sterling, of Illinois; Floyd, of Arkansas; Webb, of North Carolina; Davis, of West Virginia; Norris, of Nebraska; and Howland, of Ohio; assisted by Wrisley Brown, of the Department of Justice, who conducted the first investigation of Judge Archbald's conduct.

## Praises Impeachment Process.

At the conclusion of the case yesterday, Representative Clayton gave out the following statement:

"This is the third successful impeachment in the history of the United States. In the other cases, Judge Pickering, who was insane, did not appear at all, and Judge Humphreys had cast his lot with the Confederacy and was within the Confederate lines.

"Today's result proves the efficiency of the process provided by the Constitution for the removal of unfaithful officers and gives life and vitality to the orderly method of impeachment. It also establishes beyond successful future dispute that the scope of impeachment is not limited to criminal acts merely, but that the clause fixing the tenure of Federal judges to during good behavior has a broader significance, in fact, means just what it says. The appointment of Federal judges by the President and their confirmation by the Senate is the exercise of a 'political' power by the Senate representing the States and the people."

A Landmark of Law.

Wrisley Brown said: "The constitutional remedy of the people for the recall of Federal judges has been tested in the balance of the times and found not wanting. In my opinion, the judgment of the Senate in the trial of this impeachment will mark an epoch in American jurisprudence, and the case will go down in history as one of the great landmarks of the law."

Senator Clarence D. Clark, of Wyoming, chairman of the judiciary committee, said: "I do not know what effect the result today will have upon public opinion. Of course, there has never been any doubt of the efficacy of the constitutional provision for the removal of judges by impeachment. There is a demand for impeachment trials to be simplified, so that a committee of the Senate may take testimony as is now done in an election contest."

Tried on Thirteen Charges.

Briefly stated, the thirteen charges brought against Judge Archbald were as follows:

**FIRST–That he influenced officers of the Erie Railroad, then a litigant in his court, to grant option on its share of the Katydid culm dump, near Scranton, Pa.**

Judge Archbald acknowledged his part in the negotiations, but denied he "willfully or unlawfully or corruptly took any advantage of his official position" to influence the railroad officials.

**SECOND–That he attempted to effect a settlement between the Marion Coal Company of Scranton and the Delaware, Lackawanna and Western Railroad of a case then pending before the Interstate Commerce Commission on a basis that would have given him a share of the fee earned by George M. Watson, attorney for the Marion Coal Company.**

Judge Archbald declared he acted in the case only as a friend of the interested parties, and did not expect any compensation for his work.

Sought Coal Property.

**THIRD–That he attempted to influence the Lehigh Valley Railroad Company to relinquish a lease on "Packer No. 3," near Shenandoah, Pa., so that he might lease it on favorable terms from the Girard estate of Philadelphia.**

Judge Archbald claimed his negotiations for this property involved in the exercise of no influence upon the Lehigh officials, but grew out of an attempt to operate on adjoining coal property.

**FOURTH–That Judge Archbald obtained from Attorney Helm Bruce, of the Louisville and Nashville Railroad, private letters and arguments to sustain an opinion in favor of the railroad in a suit before the Commerce Court.**

The jurist answered that his correspondence with Mr. Bruce was only to clear up a disputed bit of testimony, and was not material to the ultimate decision of the case.

Got Note for $500.

**FIFTH–That Judge Archbald influenced officials of the Philadelphia and Reading Coal and Iron Company, owned by the Reading Railroad, to grant a lease on a coal property to Frederick Warnke, for which service Warnke gave him a note of $500.**

Judge Archbald denied that he wrongfully used his influence with the Reading Company, and asserted that the note given him by Warnke was payment for certain other coal properties, in which Judge Archbald had an interest.

**SIXTH–That he tried to influence officials of the Lehigh Valley Railroad to buy an interest in 800 acres of coal land belonging to the "Everhard heirs."**

Judge Archbald denied this.

## Mine Stock No Reward.

**SEVENTH–That he settled an insurance suit in favor of W.W. Rissinger, of Scranton, and accepted certain gold mining stock from Rissinger.**

Judge Archbald declared the stock was not a reward for his decision, but collateral given him to protect him on a note he had signed with Rissinger.

**EIGHTH–That Judge Archbald attempted to have a $500 note discounted by C.G. Boland and W.P. Boland, litigants in his court.**

He denied that he had authorized having the note presented to the Bolands for discount.

**NINTH–That he permitted the same note to be presented to C.H. Van Storch, a Scranton attorney then practicing in his court, who discounted it; and that Judge Archbald had just previously given a decision in Van Storch's favor.**

Judge Archbald denied that his influence as a judge had anything to do with the discounting of this note.

## Accepted Trip to Europe.

**TENTH–That Judge Archbald accepted a trip to Europe at the expense of Henry W. Cannon, of New York, a director in several railroads.**

The defense was that Mr. Cannon was Mrs. Archbald's cousin, and that the trip was an ordinary family courtesy.

**ELEVENTH–That Judge Archbald accepted, at the outset of this trip, a purse of $500 raised by Scranton attorneys practicing in his court.**

He answered that he knew nothing of the collecting of this purse until after it had been presented to him.

**TWELFTH–That Judge Archbald appointed as jury commissioner in the middle district of Pennsylvania J.B. Woodward, a railroad attorney.**

His answer was that Woodward was selected for his fitness for the position, and that the method of jury selection was such that no undue influence could be exerted by a commissioner.

**THIRTEENTH–That Judge Archbald had sought to obtain credit from and through persons interested in suits in his courts; that he had carried on a general business in culm dumps for "speculation and profit" while a judge, and had unlawfully influenced railroad officials.**

All these general charges were denied.

# ARCHBALD IS THIRD JUDGE FOUND GUILTY BY SENATE

*The Washington Post*, January 14, 1913

Judge Robert W. Archbald was the ninth Federal official to be tried by the United States Senate, sitting as an impeachment court, since the adoption of the Federal Constitution. Of the other eight, only two were found guilty. These were John Pickering, 1802-04, and West H. Humphrey, also a Federal judge, whom the Senate removed from office in 1862.

The irregularities of Judge Archbald were first brought to the attention of the government by William P. Boland, president of the Marion Coal Company of Scranton, Pa.

Mr. Boland laid his grievance against Archbald before President Taft. Attorney General Wickersham was directed by the President to make a thorough investigation. He appointed one of his assistants, Wrisley Brown, to make the investigation and to conduct the hearing for the government before the House judicial committee.

On May 7, 1912, the investigation was begun. The hearings were public, and on July 8, 1912, Chairman Clayton, of the House judiciary committee, presented a unanimous report demanding that Judge Archbald be "impeached for misbehavior and for high crimes and misdemeanors."

The House voted the impeachment of Archbald on July 11, and the trial began December 3.

## Boland Accuses Judge.

Perhaps the most sensational witness against Archbald was William P. Boland. He testified that because he had refused to discount a note of Archbald's for $500 which had been "peddled" around Scranton, Pa., the judge overruled a demurrer in his case. He also accused Archbald of being influenced by the railroads of Pennsylvania.

Another serious charge in the impeachment of Archbald was in connection with a trip to Europe taken by Archbald and his wife, all the expenses of which were paid by Henry W. Cannon, a New York banker and a director in a number of railroads companies.

Mrs. Archbald testified that Mr. Cannon was her cousin and that he had given the Archbalds this trip to Europe as a gift to her. Judge Archbald had accepted $500 from some of the attorneys practicing in his court, who raised the money by subscription, to help him on his trip.

## Several Other Charges.

Then there was the matter of his negotiations with the Erie Railroad Company for the purchase of the Katydid coal dump for Edward J. Williams, his business associate.

James H. Rittenhouse, a mining engineer, testified that if the deal had been consummated it would have meant a donation of $30,500 by the Erie to Judge Archbald and his partner. While this deal was under way the Erie had two important cases pending in the Commerce Court.

Some of the other charges against Judge Archbald were:

That he attempted to sell the stock of the Marian Coal Company to the Lackawanna Railroad. The coal company was owned by the Boland brothers, who were at that time litigants against the railroad before the Interstate Commerce Commission. For his efforts in this regard it was testified that he received "a valuable consideration."

## Wrote About Closed Case.

That he wrote to Helm Bruce, attorney for the Louisville and Nashville Railroad, for additional evidence in a case before the Commerce Court which had been closed and given to the judges for decision.

That he figured as the payee of a note for $2,500 by W.W. Reissinger, of Scranton, five days after he had given a decision in an insurance lawsuit in which Reissinger was beneficiary.

Judge Archbald was admitted to the bar in September, 1873, and in 1884 was elected judge of the Lackawanna county courts. President McKinley called him to the Federal bench for the Middle district of Pennsylvania in 1901. He remained in this position until the organization of the Commerce Court, in 1911, at which time President Taft appointed him a member of the new court.

# SULZER, GUILTY ON THREE COUNTS, TO BE OUSTED FROM OFFICE TO-DAY; ACQUITTED OF BRIBERY CHARGE

*New York Times*, October 17, 1913

Not to be Disqualified from Holding Office in the Future

CAMPAIGN CHARGES HOLD

Convicted of Falsifying receipts, of Perjury, and of Trying to Suppress Evidence.

COURT TO CONCLUDE TODAY

Possibly Will Vote Guilty on One of Four Articles Remaining, Not Guilty on Others.

REMOVAL VOTE, 43 TO 14

Take in executive Session and Expected to be Repeated in open Court.

SULZER TAKES NEWS CALMLY

"I Have Just Begun Fighting," He Declares—Judge Cullen Votes for Acquittal.

Special to the *New York Times*

ALBANY, Oct. 16—William Sulzer, the first Governor of the State of New York to be impeached, undoubtedly will be removed from office tomorrow unless he shall resign before the high Court of Impeachment can finish its deliberations. The action of that tribunal today in finding him guilty under three out of four of the eight Articles of Impeachment, on which a vote was taken, clearly foreshadows his removal.

On Article I., charging Mr. Sulzer with filing a false campaign fund statement, the court voted guilty, 39 to 18.

On Article II., alleging that the respondent committed perjury in swearing to that statement, the verdict was guilty by a vote of 39 to 18.

On Article III., charging that Gov. Sulzer bribed witnesses to withhold testimony from Frawley Committee, the respondent was acquitted by unanimous vote.

On Article IV., alleging that the Governor suppressed evidence by means of threats to witnesses summoned by the Frawley Committee, the verdict of guilty was returned by a vote of 43 to 14.

### Court to Conclude Today.

The court will convene again tomorrow to bring its labors to a close. At that time a vote will be taken on the four remaining articles of impeachment. Possibly the verdict will run against Mr. Sulzer on Article VI., in which he is charged with grand larceny in diverting to stock speculation thousands of dollars contributed to his campaign. It is expected that he will be acquitted of the charges made to Articles V., VII., and VIII., probably by a unanimous vote.

The court will stand 43 to 14 on the question of removing the governor from office if the test vote taken at the secret session this forenoon may be accepted as a reliable indication. On the other hand, it is predicted tonight that the decision of the court will be unanimous in favor of not depriving him of the opportunity to hold positions of trust, honor and profit under the State in the future.

## Voting in Secret Session.

According to report, the court voted informally in secret session to remove the Governor from office, by a ballot of 43 to 14. A vote to disqualify him from ever holding another office under the State was lost, it was said. There was not a single vote favorable to his disqualification, it was reported.

The informal vote on the removal of the Governor was reported to have shown the following opposed: Presiding judge Cullen, and Senators Duhamel, Heacock, McKnight, o'Keefe, Palmer, Peckham, Seeley, Silvers, Thomas, Wende, Whecler, Whitney, and one other.

Article VI., which charges that the Governor committed larceny in speculating with his campaign contributions, was said not to have been sustained in the secret session by a vote of fifty declaring the Governor not guilty, to seven against him.

Article V., which charges that he prevented a particular witness, Frederick L. Colwell, from attending the sessions of the Frawley Committee; Article VII., that he threatened to use his office and influences to affect the vote or political action of certain Assemblymen, and Article VIII., that he corruptly used his influence to affect the prices of securities on the Stock Exchange, were also reported to have been decided in favor of the Governor in the secret session by a practically unanimous vote.

Nominally, the failure of the Court of impeachment to cut Mr. Sulzer off from opportunities for future political preferment will leave him a factor to be reckoned with by the Democratic State organization. Mr. Sulzer, according to statements made by some of his friends tonight, intends to make the most of these opportunities and to go on with his fight against Tammany leader Charles F. Murphy. These friends declared that he will be on the firing line again before another week is over, and that he will take an active part in the Assembly campaign this Fall.

But Mr. Sulzer's political foes at the Capitol laugh at these predictions. They believe that the action of the Court of Impeachment and the testimony aduced before the tribunal effectually have barred him from every possibility of success in that direction.

Late tonight it was learned that only stubborn opposition from republican quarters was preventing the disqualification of Mr. Sulzer from holding public office in the future. These Republicans seem to believe that, even though crushed under the adverse decree of the Court of Impeachment, Mr. Sulzer, with this opportunity left open to him, will continue a potent factor for dissention in the party to which he owes all his past political honors and thus be helpful to the Republican opposition.

## Thomas Carries News to Sulzer

Mr. Sulzer was in seclusion in the "People's House" when it became known that the Court of Impeachment had determined to order his removal from office. This was at the close of the morning session at one o'clock. Samuel Bell Thomas, a lawyer who had figured as a prominent member of Mr. Sulzer's "kitchen cabinet," brought him the news.

Mr. Thomas had been about the Capitol corridors all forenoon awaiting news of what the High Court was doing behind closed doors. Just before the forenoon session came to an end his patience gave out and he started back to Mr. Sulzer's official residence.

A newspaper correspondent called up the "People's House" on the telephone and told Mr. Thomas that the Court of Impeachment had taken a tentative vote which indicate that Mr. Sulzer would be found guilty under three or four of the eight Articles of impeachment and that his removal in all probability would be ordered by a vote of 43 to 14, but that he would not be disqualified from holding public office in the future.

"Good!, good!," said Mr. Thomas, enthusiastically referring to the decision not to disqualify. then he hastened to give the news to Mr. Sulzer, who was in his private study on the second floor. Alexander S. Bacon, a Brooklyn lawyer, also prominent in the "kitchen cabinet" was with Mr. Sulzer but was preparing to leave. Mr. Thomas did not give the news to Mr. Sulzer until they were alone together.

"Governor," said Mr. Thomas, so it was learned afterward, "the high Court of Impeachment has voted to find you guilty under Articles I, II, IV. and VI. of the Impeachment and will order your removal from office."

## Sulzer says Fight Will Go On.

"Are you sure that's right?" asked Mr. Sulzer, an intent expression on his face.

"Yes," said Mr. Thomas, giving the source of his information. "I do not think there is the slightest doubt about it Governor."

Mr. Sulzer got up from his chair and began to walk the floor with long, nervous strides. It was a minute or so before Mr. Thomas could tell him that the High Court would not take any action that would prevent him from running for office again.

At this intelligence a wry smile fleeted across the face of Mr. Sulzer. He continued to walk from end to end of the spacious apartment.

"Well," said Mr. Thomas, "will the fight go on?"

"To the limit," said Mr. Sulzer, according to his visitor. "I have just only begun to fight. As soon as the court is finished I shall formulate my plans and call upon all my friends to rally for the fray."

Despite the forecast of an adverse verdict given by the Court of impeachment yesterday, Mr. Sulzer was in good spirits when he awoke this morning. He partook of a hearty breakfast with Mrs. Sulzer and one or two friends. Then he and Samuel Bell Thomas went for a walk. Mr. Sulzer returned to the "People's House" about 11 A.M. and did not again leave his domicile during the day. As for many days past, visitors were turned away with the statement that Mr. Sulzer could not be disturbed.

Shortly after Mr. Sulzer returned from his walk he chanced to look out of a window and espied a newspaper correspondent who for many hours had been keeping lonely vigil in front of the iron gates.

"Can you tell me why they have planted a Pinkerton in front of my home?" Mr. Sulzer sadly asked a friend who happened to be with him. The friend told Mr. Sulzer that the watcher was not a private detective.

"How do you know?" asked Mr. Sulzer. "They have planted them here before."

"I know him, he is a newspaper correspondent," said the visitor.

"Oh, that's too bad," said Mr. Sulzer. "I wish I had known that. i would have asked him to come back on the porch and sit down where he could have been more comfortable."

"The uzzle id off my friends. I would like to be unmuzzled myself, but judge Herrick won't remove it until tomorrow."

This was the message from Mr. Sulzer that Samuel Bell Thomas delivered to newspaper men downtown after he and other members of the "kitchen cabinet" had taken dinner with the impeached Governor.

According to Mr. Thomas, Mr. Sulzer was then in the best of spirits. While newsboys shouted their extras around the executive Mansion tonight. Mr. Sulzer chatted with his dinner guests and calmly outlined his plan of future action.

## Hints at Federal Appeal.

Just what that plan was, Mr. Thomas would not say. He said, however, that when the Court of Impeachment voted today to convict the Governor for acts committed before he assumed office, it violated Section XII of the Federal criminal procedure and thus made the case reviewable by the united States Supreme Court and that the case might be taken to the highest court in the land by means of a writ of prohibition. the Impeachment Managers, however, are of the opinion that there is no appeal from the action of a court of impeachment.

"The Governor has not given up his fight," said one of Mr. Sulzer's callers.

"He will not acknowledge that he will lose his cause in the Court of impeachment, despite the black outlook tonight. That court has done some peculiar things. it is not impossible that it would refuse tomorrow, after voting on the eight articles, to put him out of office.

"The Governor is a fighter. Should he be thrown out of his office he will not give up. He takes the view that he can do more for the people out of office than he can in it, under present conditions, anyhow. As a private citizen he will not be restricted in many ways, as he is now."

Judge Herrick and Mr. Sulzer had a long conference tonight. Mr. Sulzer again urged that he be permitted to issue his 3,500-word statement, it was said, but again Judge Herrick refused to agree to such action.

Mr. Sulzer late tonight told a friend that he would go to New York Monday with a view to entering the fight of the Fusion forces against McCall and the rest of the Tammany ticket.

Up to the moment the court of Impeachment concluded its morning session both Mr. Sulzer and his friends were hopeful that, even thought it seemed a foregone conclusion that he would be held guilty on Article I., his opponents would be unable to muster up the necessary two-thirds majority for his removal. This would have left him secure in his office, despite the adverse judgement of the court on the merits of the charges against him.

## By a Close Margin.

On Article I., in which Mr. Sulzer was charged with violation of the Corrupt Practices act in filing a false statement of campaign receipts and expenditures with the Secretary of State, the vote for guilty was only one in excess of the two-thirds majority required by the constitution. The same was true of Article II., the vote in each case being 30 to 18.

On Article III., which charged Mr. Sulzer with violating Section 2,400 of the penal law in attempting to bribe Louis A. Sarecky, Frederick L. Colwell, and Melville B. Fuller to induce them not to give testimony regarding the administration of Sulzer campaign fund for stock speculation, every member of the high Court voted not guilty.

On Article IV., which charges the respondent with violating Section 814, the penal law in practicing "fraud and deceit, threats and violence," an attempt to prevent the Frawley Committee from procuring true testimony from these witnesses, forty-three members of the high court voted guilty and fourteen not guilty.

Of the Judges of the Court of Appeals, Presiding judge Cullen voted for the acquittal of Mr. Sulzer on all the articles that came before the High Court today. On Articles I and II Judges Bartlett, Cullen, Chase and Werner voted for acquittal and Judges Collin, Cuddeback, Hiscock, Hogan and Miller for a verdict of guilty. On Article IV only Presiding Judge Cullen and Judges Hiscock and Miller voted with Mr. Sulzer.

Presiding Judge Cullen made an elaborate explanation of his vote on Article I. and II., and a briefer explanation of his vote on Article IV. Briefly outlined, his argument, which in more complete form will be filed as part of the record in the case, was that he believed to find Mr. Sulzer guilty of acts committed before he took office would establish a dangerous precedent.

Judges Bartlett, Chase and Werner concurred with the Presiding Judge and on the same ground. Judge Miller, who voted for finding Mr. Sulzer guilt on these two articles, made a vigorous speech in which he dissented from the opinions of three other Judges and held that it was perfectly proper to remove a public official for acts committed after he election and before his incumbency.

On Article IV the presiding Judge explained that he cast his vote against Mr. Sulzer's acquittal on the ground that this article was not broad enough to let in the testimony of Duncan W. Peck and Messrs. Morgenthau and Ryan, and that the Court of Impeachment, by voting affirmatively on its sufficiency for that purpose, had virtually voted to amend the article itself.

"It involves accusing a man of one crime and convicting him on another," said the venerable Presiding Judge.

"Much as I depreciate what the respondent has done, I realize that an observance of the forms of law are important. If they are not observed it will inevitably lead on one hand to oppression and on the other to anarchy.

Judges Hiscock and Miller, who had voted for Mr. Sulzer's conviction on Articles I. and II., switched and voted for his acquittal under Article IV., mainly on the grounds stated by the presiding Judge.

Not only the judges but a majority of the Senate members, some briefly and some more at length, explained their votes orally. Some, too, have written already or are preparing opinions which will be filed with the High Court and printed as part of the record.

## Sulzer Handled Without Gloves.

There was little comfort for Mr. Sulzer even in the speeches of those who stood with him in their vote on the various propositions that came before the High Court today. residing Judge Cullen was unsparing as any in his criticism of conduct of the high respondent, which brought him before the bar of the High Court of Impeachment. All the Judges emphasized the fact that it was their zeal for a strict observance of the letter and the forms of law that made them vote for his acquittal when they did so.

"The acts charged against this respondent display such turpitude and delinquency that if committed after he took the office they would be sufficient ground for removal," said the Presiding Judge of the Court.

"We know that he has committed acts so morally indefensible that they can hardly be described in the language of judicial calm," said Judge Werner, who also voted with Mr. Sulzer on the first two articles.

"He is totally unfit to hold the great office of Governor of this State," said Judge Miller, who voted against Mr. Sulzer on these same articles.

Among the Senators the speech of Senator Sage of Albany was fraught with a biting sarcasm. He referred to the testimony of Allan A. Ryan, where the latter had quoted Mr. Sulzer's terse telephone message, "Tell your father I am still the same old Bill," and added:

"William Sulzer, Governor, is the same old Bill, who, before election, filed a false statement of his expenses: who received Mr. Ryan's $10,000 and the telephone company's $10,000 because he had been useful in Congress. He is the same old useful Bill, indeed, and as such not to be trusted in his present office: and for that reason I vote to find him guilty."

"The respondent had experience in the stock market, and knew something about the market value, and knew something about the market value of securities," said Senator Thompson of Niagara. "He had known the market value of William Sulzer, Congressman, and he knew the value of William Sulzer, nominated for Governor. He went to Schiff and that shrewd financier gave him $2,500. He wanted more, but Mr. Schiff thought he had overplayed himself. He went to Ryan and quoted himself at $7,500. There he underplayed himself and got ten crisp one-thousand dollar bills."

Both houses of the Legislature will meet tomorrow, and possibly Acting Gov. Glynn will communicate with the lawmakers then with regard to necessary appropriation and administrative measures that must be enacted at the very outset of the new administration.

# TRIAL OF ENGLISH TO BE ABANDONED, JURIST RESIGNING

By Norman W. Baxter, *The Washington Post*, November 5, 1926

———

## Managers Decide to Ask House to Dismiss Impeachment.

———

## WILL ADVISE SENATE TO DEFER PROCEDURE

———

## Judge Explains His Usefullness on Bench Has Been Impaired by Charges.

———

The impeachment trial of judge George W. English, of the United States district court for eastern Illinois, scheduled to begin before the Senate on Wednesday, will be abandoned as the result of the accused jurist's resignation, submitted to President Coolidge yesterday.

House managers who had been chosen to serve as prosecuting attorneys in what would have been the tenth such trial in the history of this country announced, following a conference yesterday afternoon, that they would ask the Senate on November 10 to continue the case until the regular December session of Congress in order that the House of Representatives might give them further instructions.

This formal statement, however, did not reveal the whole plan of procedure for the House managers are confident that the chamber which voted impeachment will concur in their unofficial decision that the trial of the Federal jurist should be abandoned and that his resignation will close a chapter of political history such as had been spread before the public only a few times in the life of the nation.

### Five Previous Resignations.

Ample precedent exists for following the course that has been decided upon. In five other instances dating back to 1839, the impeachment of Federal jurists has been ordered and dropped because of the resignation presented by the accused men. The House and Senate have the power to continue the proceedings. They did so in the case of William W. Belknap, Secretary of War under President Grant, even though the vote of impeachment by the House in this case followed the cabinet official's resignation by five hours.

The only thing that could be gained, however, by proceeding with the trial would be that the Senate could, if wished, in connection with a verdict of guilty, disqualify Judge English from holding "any office of honor, trust or profit under the United States." The only other action which the

Senate sitting as a court would take would be to remove the jurist from office, and that has been done already.

Seven of the nine house managers took part in the final deliberations on the case. E. C. Michener, of Michigan; W. E. Boles, of Iowa; I. G. Hersey, of Maine; C. E. Moore, of Ohio; G. R. Stobbs, of Massachusetts; A. J. Montague, of Virginia, and H. W. Summers were those who attended the meeting in the House judiciary room. F. H. Dominick, of South Carolina, and J. N. Tillman, of Arkansas, had not returned from their districts.

## Statement of Managers.

The statement of the managers, issued in their behalf by Representative Michener, chairman, follows:

"The primary purpose of this impeachment proceeding is to remove from office an official whom the House of Representatives has determined to be unfit to further perform the duties of the office. The managers on the part of the House of Representatives are charged with the responsibility of presenting the facts to the Senate. Judge English has tendered his resignation to the President and the resignation has been accepted. He is no longer a United States district judge, and the primary purpose of the impeachment proceeding has been accomplished.

"In consideration of Judge English's resignation and its acceptance, the managers have determined to ask the Senate not to proceed with the impeachment trial on November 10, and will request that the matter be continued before the Senate until the regular session of the Congress, which convenes on the first Monday in December. This request is made in order that the House of Representatives shall have the opportunity to instruct the managers on the part of the House as to the desire of the House in the premises."

The text of Judge English's resignation, made public here and in East St. Louis, follows:

"To His Excellency, the President of the United States:

"I hereby tender my resignation as judge of the district court of the United States for the Eastern district of Illinois, to take effect at once.

"While I am consious of the fact that I have discharged my duties as district judge to the best of my ability, and while I am satisfied that I have the confidence of the law-abiding people of the district, yet I have come to the conclusion on account of the impeachment proceedings instituted against me, regardless of the final result thereof, that my usefulness as a judge has been seriously impaired.

"I, therefore, feel that it is my patriotic duty to resign and let some one who is in nowise hampered be appointed to discharge the duties of the office.

"Your obedient servant. .

"(Signed).

"George W. English."

As matters now stand the Senate will meet on Wednesday, with a quorum drawn from nearby States, and receive the report of the House managers. At the December session the final details necessary to close the record will be taken.

## Appointed by Wilson.

The submission of Judge English's resignation, which came as a dramatic period to the case on the eve of actual trial, was not the only high light in it.

The jurist was elevated to the Federal bench in 1918, during the Wilson administration, through the influence, as it has been established since, of William G. McAdoo.

The investigation of his conduct on the bench was prompted by the St. Louis Post Dispatch, which submitted a list of charges against him through Representative Harry B. Hawes.

These charges included:

Tyranny and oppression; partiality and favoritism; improper and unlawful conduct in connection with a "bankruptcy ring;" manipulation of bankruptcy, himself and his son; a general course of conduct constituting misbehavior and misdemeanor in office.

The first indications were that the accused judge would fight the case trough all stages. In order to do this he employed an impressive array of counsel, which included such figures as J. Hamilton Lewis, former United States senator for Ilinois; W. F. Zumbrunn, revealed since as general counsel of the Ku Klux Klan, and Dan McGlynn, of East St. Louis, wearer of a papal decoration and leader in Catholic lay circles.

## McAdoo Suggests Counsel.

In the preliminary stages of his impeachment English is said to have had the support of some of the same influences that put him on the bench, and the appointment of Zumbrunn as associate counsel is reported to have been suggested by McAdoo.

On the heels of the klan exposures made by Senator James A. Reed, which brought out Zumbrunn's official position with the order, the klan counsel resigned in a brief and curt note, without first giving his client any notice.

Following that it was persistently reported that English would resign, but this was denied until the very last. It is understood that the fact that the House managers had passed the entire summer in the pursuit of new evidence may have had something to do with the abrupt termination of the case.

It was announced yesterday that English is to leave at once for Fort Lauderdale, Fla., where his son now lives, and will make his home there.

# ABSOLVED BY RESOLUTION OF HAVING ACTED WITH CORRUPT MOTIVES.

By Carlisle Bargeron, *The Washington Post*, November 5, 1929

———

### Rebuke is Adopted by 54 to 22 Vote

———

### Norris Complains That Senator Does Not Yet Recognize Guilt.

———

### Object of Action Remains Unmoved

———

### Legislator is Defiant to End on Employment of Eyanson.

———

The Senate pinned Hiram Bingham's shoulders to the ground yesterday, but it could not make him say "uncle." Even when it tired of its strangle hold and offered to let him up, he insisted that he did not want to get up unless the Senate would let his friend, Charles L. Eyanson, up, too.

Whereupon, the Senate gave it up as an impossible job and let the Connecticut senator up anyhow, adopting a modified resolution of censure for his employment of Eyanson as his secretary and taking him into the secret hearings of the Senate finance committee. It did this by a vote of 54 to 22, with Senator Norris, of Nebraska, complaining "He doesn't yet realize that he has done wrong."

As modified, the resolution censured Bingham's act as "contrary to good morals and senatorial ethics," and tending to bring the Senate into "dishonor and disrepute," but that it was not as the result of "corrupt motives on the part of the senator."

## Norris Accepts, But Complains.

The insertion of the corrupt motives absolution, initiated by Senator Glenn, of Illinois, and perfected by Bratton, of New Mexico, was accepted readily by Norris, sponsor of the original resolution, but not uncomplainingly.

"We censure this man," he exclaimed, "for an act which no one has defended and then turn around and say he is the moral genius of the ages."

Bingham, tall of stature and bland of countenance, remained unmoved through it all, sustained in his philosophy that it was all politics, holding to this philosophy, in fact, as even his friends got up and said he had done wrong, even as Senator Reed, of Pennsylvania, perhaps his closest personal senatorial friend, put this serious interpretation upon the resolution:

"I may overrate its importance," said Reed in an obviously friendly effort in Bingham's behalf, "but it that resolution were passed about me I would feel that the rest of my life was to be spent under a cloud."

### Expresses Sorrow for Bingham.

And at another point the Pennsylvania senator, showing how seriously he considered the resolution, declared:

"I feel sorry for the senator (Bingham) from the bottom of my heart."

And in this light Bingham's friends tried twice to modify the resolution, first Smoot, of Utah, and then Edge, of New Jersey, and were successively voted down, 44 to 32 and 43 to 34. Then when Glenn managed to drive an entering wedge into the Senate's belligerent mood and got Norris to accept an amendment that would absolve Bingham of any corrupt motives, the former Yale professor got up and said he did not want this consideration unless it was extended to Eyanson, too.

Senator Bratton, who had perfected Glenn's amendment so as to make the absolution apply to Bingham alone, said he was prepared to make the distinction between the senator and Eyanson, as "I know the senator from Connecticut, and know him to be an honorable man. I know nothing whatsoever about Mr. Eyanson."

"I can say," Bingham replied, "that Mr. Eyanson is absolutely honorable; that his conduct was above reproach."

### Norris Pleads for Understanding.

It was then that Norris, who had already agreed to accept the amendment, declaring that the "regrettable part of this whole matter is that he does not yet realize that he has done wrong." Reiterating that he had no personal feeling in the matter, that he introduced his resolution as a matter of duty, to uphold a principle, he declared: "We would have accomplished something of vast importance if we could just make the senator understand that he has done wrong."

But the Nebraskan and the other senators were willing to give it up by then and despite Bingham's statement that he did not want the modification absolving him of corrupt intentions, went ahead and passed it just the same. Or rather, all except Heflin, who apparently remembered Bingham's attitude on the matter of somebody throwing a beer bottle at him up at Brockton, Mass., not so long ago, were in this mood. Heflin did not want the Senate to relent one bit.

And when it was over, the Connecticut senator walked slowly out of the chamber with the other senators just as he might walk out after the Senate has disposed of any other matter that had brought him from the cloakroom in the first instance and subsequently told inquiring newspapermen that he had no intention of resigning either from the Senate or its finance committee. And that statement, he made known, would be his last on the subject of the whole business, his employment of Eyanson, the $10,000 a year representative of the Connecticut Manufacturers Association, or what further he intended to do about it or anything else concerning the matter at all. To him it is a closed incident.

## The Final Roll Call.

The final roll call follows:

Republicans for the resolution–Allen, Blaine, Borah, Brookhart, Capper, Couzens, Cutting, Frazier, Glenn, Goldsborough, Jones, La Follette, McNary, Norbeck, Norris, Nye, Pine, Robinson, of Indiana; Schall, Stelwer, Thomas, of Idaho; Vandenberg–22.

Democrats–Ashurst, Barkley, Black, Bratton, Brock, Broussard, Caraway, Connally, Copeland, Dill, Fletcher, George, Harris, Harrison, Hayden, Heflin, Kendrick, McKellar, Pittman, Ransdell, Sheppard, Simmons, Smith, Steck, Stephens, Swanson, Thomas, of Oklahoma; Trammell, Tydings, Walsh, of Massachusetts; Walsh, of Montana; Wheeler–32.

Against resolution:

Republicans–Dale, Edge, Fess, Gillette, Golf, Gould, Greene, Hale, Hastings, Hatfield, Hebert, Johnson, Keyes, Metcalf, Moses, Oddie, Phipps, Reed, Shortridge, Smoot, Townsend, Walcott–22.

Paired–Blease, for, Kean against; Hawes for, Sackett unknown; Overman for, Warren unknown.

Bingham voted present.

## Voted With Bingham.

Nine Republicans and two Democrats, Allen, Capper, Goldsborough, Jones, McNary, Schall, Stelwer, Vandenberg and Blease and Walsh, of Massachusetts, voted with Bingham's friends in an effort to modify the blow by adoption of Smoot's substitute, which did not mention Bingham by name and which simply disapproved the principle, and again in favor of Edge's substitute which, while mentioning Bingham and Eyanson, eliminated all reference to good morals and senatorial ethics and merely had the Senate disapproving the practice.

On the Edge proposal, in fact, they were joined by Cutting and Stephens, the latter having just come into the chamber. This group, however, all bolted to the other side on the final vote. Senators Hiram Johnson and Oddie, of Nevada, voted with Bingham all the way through. Otherwise, it was only the waning Old Guard that went down the line for him.

Johnson's vote was, of course, a surprise. In the cynical philosophy that had come to him from such long service in the Senate, however, he refused to become outraged at the Bingham incident and didn't have the heart "to hit a man when he is down."

## Bingham Defends Himself.

Most of the debate turned upon the Smoot substitute. Bingham, unafraid and unchastised, defended himself.

He even brought up the practice of some senators and members of the House employing members of their family in their offices. Norris subsequently replied that he had no criticism of this so long as the members of the family did the work but if there was an instance of where the work was not done he "would not hesitate" to vote a resolution of censure.

As the debate progressed, in fact, the practice of senators censuring one another at all was questioned and there was a vague reference to senatorial "bottle."

"Why, a rumor has it that in the Capitol and in the office building there are bottles that ought not to be there and which members of Congress have there to use," Senator Gillette said, in pointing out that many "improper" things take place, but that the Senate should not be expressing itself except in a "matter of grave importance."

## Gillette Feels for Regulars.

Gillette described Bingham's act, however, as "exceedingly indiscrete and indicates an ingeniousness and a lack of appreciation of results." He complained that there was no reason why the coalition should have any grievance against the Connecticut senator, however.

"We are the ones who will suffer," he said, referring to the regulars. "We're the ones to have a grievance." He explained that those opposed to the tariff hold the manufacturer up as a monster who writes the tariff bill and the Bingham-Eyanson episode will now be cited in support of their claims.

He declared that the Senate should not take the action it was bent upon for "partisan advantage."

"Does the senator think I framed the committee?" asked Norris, referring to his make-up of the subcommittee that made the lobby investigation.

Gillette replied that in naming the committee Norris did not have Bingham in mind, of course, but that he had only put one "anticoalition" man on it, Robinson of Indiana.

"Does the senator deny the Republicanism of the senator from Idaho (Borah) or does he say he was unfair or that there was anything wrong in putting him on the committee?" Norris asked.

## Analyzes Committee Workings.

Gillette replied that "that is not the point at all," but to his way of thinking the committee should have been composed of three coalition members and two anticoalition, instead of four and one as it is. He simply brought this in, he contended, to show that if he were a captious sort he, too, could be criticizing and to point out that the senators should not be too critical of each other.

Norris replied, however, that he presumed the Senate wanted the facts and the accomplishments of his committee justified his naming it. Furthermore, he said, the facts were unchallenged, regardless of what kind of a committee got them. He denied that there was any partisanship in it.

"The senator from Connecticut," he said, "will not accept your apology. He says 'No; what I did was right. I am not apologizing for it.'"

He described Smoot's substitute as an "apology to the country and the speech of the senator from Massachusetts as an apology to the Senate."

## Calls Evidence Undisputed.

"The senator from Connecticut did not tell the committee about that $1,000 check," he said, referring to a check that Bingham sent Eyanson, purportedly for his work with Bingham, but which Eyanson would not cash. "He gave them no information that he did not think was already public, but they had to worm it out of Eyanson until the facts came out."

"It is no defense to say that the chairman of the judiciary committee appointed the wrong subcommittee. The senator from Connecticut has not disputed the evidence, he had not contradicted the facts which were brought out, and yet the answer is that the chairman ought to have appointed stand-pat members on that committee."

Senator Norbeck, of South Dakota, interrupted to observe that he "did not understand why the Republicanism of the senator from Idaho was questioned—the senator who did not only save the West for the party, but went down and rescued Massachusetts when the adjoining States went for Al Smith and the senator from Massachusetts sat on the platform cheering him."

## Criticism Called Premature.

Borah subsequently suggested with a wicked gleam in his eye that it was Bingham's second mistake to charge that the committee was packed against him. "It implies," said Borah, "that if the committee had been made up of regulars they would either have smothered the facts or they would have failed to bring out the facts. We should get off of that proposition."

Reed, when it came his turn, agreed that the "criticism of the committee had been premature."

Bingham's first mistake, Borah said, "was to have employed Eyanson."

"I believe," he said, "that the senator from Connecticut feels in his heart that it was a mistake."

"He didn't indicate any such feeling in his heart by his statement," Senator Dill interjected.

"The senator from Connecticut is under criticism and under fire," Borah replied, "and I can well understand that he may not be conscious of just how he would feel if the situation were different."

When Senator Cole Blease had his turn, he said it was his understanding that the lobby subcommittee had been packed, not against Bingham because it could not have anticipated running across him, but to "make a case against the tariff."

## Caraway After Blease.

When Caraway, of Arkansas, got after him about this, he took a dogged stand:

"Well, that was my impression and I am entitled to my impression. Every senator is entitled to his own views and I will defend mine either on or off the floor."

He warned the Senate that adoption of the resolution would not do anything but solidify Bingham in his State. He recalled the time the Senate censured "Pitchfork" Ben Tillman for fighting on the floor. He kept coming back up here; so, too, did "Pres Brigades," as Blease enunciated it, who resigned from the House while facing a censure for fighting and who was overwhelmingly reelected.

"Nobody can bring disrepute upon me except myself," Blease said referring to the language of the resolution.

## Blease Deprecates Criticism.

Blease made it very feelingly known that he did not like this business of senators criticizing one another.

"I understand that the grand jury will be informed tomorrow about every man who takes a drink," he lamented, referring to Senator Brookhart's forthcoming appearance before the inquisitorial body.

Senator Gould, of Maine, who knows the wrath of the Senate himself, brought down the house, so to speak, when in heated answer to Senator Wheeler's taunts that some member of the Old Guard defend Bingham's act, he exclaimed:

"He made a very fair and square statement just what he done and why he done it."

Wheeler's taunts brought Reed to his feet.

Explaining that he thought Bingham's accusation that the committee was packed was "premature," he said it was "probably based upon the fact that the members of the committee had handled him very roughly, according to the newspapers and without that courtesy that he expected from its membership."

### Terribly Serious, Says Reed.

Bingham's act was "regrettable, unwise and very much to be deplored," Reed said, "but when the Senate collectively finds a verdict of guilty of an act against good morals, of an act against the honor of the Senate, it is a terribly serious thing."

Many unpleasant things occur about the Senate every day, he said. "We hear little sneering remarks, perhaps, from individual colleagues or individual critics," but he contended that to pass such a resolution as was proposed was going too far. He cited Bingham's war record.

All of the senators, foe and friend alike, assured Bingham that no one suspected him of dishonesty, but Senator George, of Georgia, contended that it was necessary to specify him in the resolution because a "public quality" in senators transcends personal considerations.

It was out of these expressions of personal high regard that the modifying note finally came.

### Bingham Strikes Back.

"In the first place," Bingham said in defending himself, "it is claimed that the employment of Mr. Eyanson was contrary to good morals. It is difficult to know exactly what is meant by this expression * * * but if it means anything at all it must mean that there was something in this employment which was immoral in the sense of being dishonorable or corrupt. To this charge, I plead not guilty. There was nothing in his employment which was dishonorable or corrupt. Not one dollar of the public money was wasted. Not a single taxpayer's dollar was employed for any sinister purpose. I did not profit to the extent of one dollar by any part of this transaction. It happens that I have not a single dollar invested in any of the Connecticut companies seeking an increase in tariff rates, which might be presumed to be represented by an official of the Connecticut Manufacturers Association. Not a penny of the public money stuck to my fingers nor to the fingers of Mr. Eyanson. On the contrary, whatever he received while on the Government pay roll was turned over to the clerk who continued to perform the same functions in my office as he had done previously and as he has continued to do since. There was nothing about the transaction that was dishonorable or corrupt. The Connecticut Manufacturers Association did not seek any unfair advantage. In loaning me one of their highly paid officials they did so at my request in order that I might secure that person in Connecticut who was best posted on all sides of the tariff problem. * * *

"Now let us take the second point. It is claimed that his being placed on the rolls of the Senate was contrary to Senatorial ethics. It is fair to assume, Mr. President, that the expression 'Senatorial ethics' relates to what is considered by Senatorial practice to be right or wrong. Every profession has its ethics. There are what is known as newspaper ethics. There are what is known as business ethics. There are what are known as the ethics of the medical profession. This action of mine in placing Mr. Eyanson on the Senatorial rolls is called contrary to Senatorial ethics. Again, Mr. President, I plead not guilty."

He explained that every senator is given four clerkships and that he is permitted to allot them or employ them as he sees fit.

## Cites Employment of Kin.

"There is no restriction," he said, "on who should be appointed or how he or she shall be employed. That is the custom of the Senate. That is the nature of senatorial ethics so far as these positions are concerned. According to senatorial ethics no senator is to be criticized if he chooses to place members of his family in these clerical positions. He is not to be accused of nepotism if he appoints cousins, nephews, nieces, sons or daughters in these positions. He is not to be accused of doing something contrary to senatorial ethics if he uses one of these positions to pay a salary to the wife of his chief clerk, who herself does nothing directly for the Government but indirectly serves the senator and his constituents by helping to keep her husband well and happy and enabling him to give better service to the senator and his constituents. According to business ethics such employment might be regarded askance but it should be remembered that according to Senatorial ethics these four clerical positions have always been considered to be part of the perquisites of a Senator to be used by him in whatever manner he deems to be best for the interest of his constituents.

"The third charge is that my action tends to bring the Senate into dishonor and disrepute, Mr. President. In order for this action to bring the Senate into dishonor and disrespect it must have had some sinister motive and must have been directed against the interest of the people of the United States.

## Sought Information Only.

"Obviously, it is felt by those who favor this resolution that my motives in this action were evil, or else that the action itself resulted in some public calamity, or was adverse to the public interest. Mr. President, I do not believe that those who have done me the honor of listening to, or of reading my previous statements, will accuse me of having had any dishonorable or unpatriotic motives. My sole desire was to secure the best possible information on a difficult and intricate subject, particularly as it related to the people who elected me to the United States Senate."

The resolution that was adopted follows:

"Resolved, That the action of the Senator from Connecticut, Mr. Bingham, in placing Mr. Charles L. Eyanson upon the official rolls of the Senate and his use by Senator Bingham at the time and in the manner set forth in the report of the subcommittee of the committee on the judiciary (Report No. 43, Seventy-first Congress, first session), while not the result of corrupt motives on the part of the senator from Connecticut, is contrary to good morale and senatorial ethics and tends to bring the Senate into dishonor and disrepute, and such conduct is hereby condemned."

# ROWBOTTOM SENTENCED ON 4 BRIBERY COUNTS

Former Representative Given Year and $2,000 Fine.

*The Washington Post*, April 15, 1931

Evansville, Ind., April 15 (A.P.)—Harry E. Rowbottom, former representative in Congress of the First Indiana District, was convicted in Federal court tonight of accepting bribes from persons who sought postoffice appointments.

Rowbottom was sentenced immediately by Judge Charles E. Woodward to serve one year and one day in Leavenworth Penitentiary and was fined $2,000. This sentence was imposed on the first count of the indictment.

Judge Woodward also imposed the same sentence on three other counts on which the jury voted to convict Rowbottom, but he held that the sentences could be served concurrently.

Rowbottom's attorneys indicated that no appeal would be taken. He will remain at liberty under bond of $10,000 until 11 a. m., April 20, when he is to report to the United States marshal at Indianapolis to begin his journey to prison.

The jury returned its verdict after deliberating two hours and five minutes.

The first of the four counts on which the jury found Rowbottom guilty was that he unlawfully agreed to accept from Walter G. Ayer $750 for procuring and aiding to procure for Gresham Ayer, his son, a rural mail carriership at Rockport. The second was that he actually did receive the money.

The third was that he indirectly received $800 for procuring "and aiding to procure" the postmastership at Dale for S. Grant Johnson. The fourth was that he unlawfully received the $800 from Otto A. Weilbrenner for procuring the Dale position.

Before the case was given to the jury one count of the indictment against Rowbottom was dismissed on the motion of District Attorney George R. Jeffrey. This count charged that had conspired with Weilbrenner and William E. Davisson, former Petersburg postmaster, in the matter of accepting bribes.

The jury voted acquittal on four other counts of the indictment.

# IMPEACHMENT OF JUDGE RITTER VOTED BY HOUSE

*The Washington Post,* March 3, 1936

### Finds Member of U. S. Bench Guilty of 'High Crimes' in Office.

The House last night approved a resolution to impeach Federal Judge Halsted L. Ritter, of the Southern District of Florida, on charges of misbehavior, high crimes and misdemeanors in office.

The vote was 181 to 148 for impeachment.

The ballot came after five hours of debate on the case, brought up by the House Judiciary Committee, during which Ritter was characterized as a "tyrant" and a "dictator."

The action sends Ritter's case to the Senate, which will sit as a trial jury to hear the charges as presented by a group of managers from the House. Ritter is charged with granting exorbitant receivership fees to A. L. Rankin, his former law partner, and with accepting $4,500 from Rankin.

## Listens to Debate.

Rittter, a gray-haired main, listened to the debate with his wife from a front-row seat in the gallery.

After the vote was announced, Judge Ritter declined all comment except to say he would "fight the case through." He said he had no immediate plans.

Only 11 times in United States history has the Senate tried impeachment cases. The most recent was the case of Federal Judge Harold Louderback, of the Northern District of California, in 1933. The most celebrated was the impeachment trial of President Andrew Johnson in 1868. Both of these cases resulted in acquittal.

Chairman Hatton W. Sumners (Democrat), Texas, of the House Judiciary Committee, which recommended Ritter's impeachment, brought up the charges against him and explained the case. The committee previously presented a report dealing with his relationship with Rankin in receivership cases.

It alleged that on May 15, 1930, Ritter allowed Rankin an "advance" fee of $2,500 and then asked another Federal judge, Alexander Akerman, to set Rankin's total fee. Akerman, the committee charged, set Rankin's fee at $15,000, but Ritter later fixed what the House group described as an "additional and exorbitant fee of $75,000."

"On December 24, 1930, the judge entered an order for Rankin," Sumners told the House, "who walked out with something like $25,000 in cold cash. It was Christmas Eve, all right.

"He then went down and gave the judge $2,500 in cash. There is not the slightest doubt about it. The judge claimed this was good will for the partnership, but he had not gotten a cent, until Rankin got $75,000 of the people's money."

---

Fail to See "Corruption."

The $25,000 fee was a partial payment on the $75,000 allowed in the Whitehall Building and Operating Co., it was alleged.

Representatives Louis Ludlow (Democrat), Indiana, and John E. Miller (Democrat), Arkansas, both members of the judiciary subcommittee, which investigated the charges, warned the House against impeaching Ritter, and said there was no evidence of "corruption."

Representative J. Mark Wilcox (Democrat), Florida, who comes from Ritter's judicial district, characterized Ritter as "impatient and dictatorial," but added that he did not believe the evidence warranted impeachment.

# RITTER GUILTY; SENATE VOTES HIS REMOVAL AS U.S. JUDGE

By Felix Bruner, *The Washington Post, April 18, 1936*

### Floridian Is Convicted of Misconduct by Margin of One Ballot.

### Confusion Reigns As Austin Protests

### Impeached on 7th Count Combining 6 Charges Dropped Previously

In a tensely dramatic atmosphere, the Senate yesterday found Federal Judge Halstead L. Ritter of Florida guilty of misconduct and removed him from office.

The judge was found not guilty on six counts. On the seventh and last the vote stood 56 for conviction and 28 for acquital, the exact two-thirds necessary for conviction.

For two hours the tall, slender, 65-year-old jurist sat before the bar of the Senate, his arms folded, his face expressionless, but almost as white as his hair as one Senator after another stood in his place on each of seven roll calls and announced his vote as either "guilty" or "not guilty."

As roll call after roll call resulted in acquittal by the slimmest margins—once by only one vote—the expression of the defendent remained unchanged. But when the final vote was announced as for conviction he appeared stunned.

The Senate recessed as a court, but Ritter continued to sit between his lawyers, Frank P. Walsh and Carl T. Hoffman. It was only when Chesley W. Jurney, sergeant at arms of the Senate, beckoned to them that they left the chamber.

## Nothing to Say.

Surrounded by reporters, Ritter said:

"I have nothing to say, God, you can see why I have nothing to say. I'm going back to Florida."

The seventh charge, the one on which Ritter finally was convicted, was a combination of the other six charges plus an accusation that he had brought his court into "scandal and disrepute."

The other charges, with the vote in each instance were:

That he granted A. L. Rankin a former law partner an exhorbitant $75,000 fee in the Whitehall receivership case and corruptly received $4,300. Vote—55 for conviction, 29 for acquittal. The change of one vote from the acquittal to the conviction column would have meant conviction.

That he connived with Rankin and others to bring the Whitehall litigation and then dissipated the hotel's assets. Vote—52 for conviction, 32 for acquittal. That he practiced law for the Mulford Realty Corporation while on the bench. Vote—44 for convivtion, 39 for acquittal.

That he practiced law for the late J.R. Francis of Flint, Mich. Vote–36 for conviction, 48 for acquittal. That he paid no income tax in 1929 on $12,000 he received in addition to his salary. Vote—36 for conviction, 48 for acquittal.

That he paid no income tax in 1930 on $5,300 received in addition to his salary. Vote—46 for conviction, 37 for acquital.

## Appointed by Coolidge.

The vote of the Senate automatically removed Ritter from the office to which he had been appointed for life by President Coolidge in February, 1929. A native of Indiana, he practiced law in Colorado for 30 years, going to Florida in 1925.

In addition to removing the judge, the Senate had the power to bar him forever from holding public office of trust. An order to this effect was presented by Senator Ashurst (Democrat), Arizona, but it was voted down, 76 to 0, Ashurst himself voting against it.

The balloting, conducted before galleries crowded with tourists proceeded quickly until announcement of the vote on the last count. Then the Senate broke into confusion. As Senator Pittman (Democrat), Nevada, president pro tem of the Senate, who was presiding, announced the result of the vote, Senator Austin (Republican), Vermont, jumped to his feet.

The Vermonter insisted that the vote did not consitute a two-thirds majority because one or two Senators in the chamber had not voted. He added that it was "monstrous" to convict a man on a combination of charges of which he had already been acquitted.

The voice of the Senator was drowned by demands of "regular order" and by the voices of Senators insisting on presenting points of order. Adding to the confusion was the noise of spectators leaving the galleries. Pittman overruled Austin's objections and the verdict stood. Then the Senate voted not to bar Ritter from holding office in the future.

The balloting climaxed ten days of hearing and deliberation. For two days the entire Senate discussed the case behind locked doors, reaching a decision Thursday evening to vote yesterday.

On the last vote, three Senators reversed their verdicts on the first count. They were Senator McNary (Republican), of Oregon, who changed his vote from guilty to not guilty, and Senators Minton (Democrat), of Indiana, and Pittman, from not guilty to guilty. That changes clinched the final decision.

It was the twelfth time in United States history that the Senate has gone through the solemn formality of an impeachment vote. It was the fourth time the Senate had found a defendant guilty.

## Two Women Vote.

For the first time in history two women Senators participated in such a vote. Senator Hattie Caraway (Democrat), of Arkansas, voted "not guilty" on most ballots, Senator Rose M. long (Democrat), of Louisiana, voted "guilty" on every count.

The last conviction in a Senate impeachment trial was that of Associate Judge Robert W. Archbald of the United States Commerce Court, in 1913. The last trial was that of Judge Harold Louderback, of California, who was acquitted in 1933.

Most famous of all impeachment trials was that of President Andrew Johnson, who was acquitted by a margin of one vote, in 1868, after a trial lasting three months.

Charges against Ritter, as in all impeachment cases, were brought by the House of Representatives. House managers conducted the prosecution. Members of the Senate sat as a "jury," with the privilege of asking questions presented in writing. Ritter was defended by his own lawyers.

# MANTON'S CONDUCT UNDER U.S. INQUIRY; HE DEFERS DEFENSE

*New York Times,* January 29, 1939

### Murphy Reveals Department of Justice Is Investigating Charges Against Judge

## 'THAT'S GOOD,' SAYS JURIST

### Delays Promised Statement, but Adds, 'Hasn't Judge Right to Buy Stocks?'

The Department of Justice has been investigating charges of misconduct made against Martin T. Manton, senior judge of the United States Circuit Court of Appeals, Attorney General Frank Murphy announced in Washington yesterday.

The following formal statement was issued from Mr. Murphy's office, without elaboration:

"Attorney General Murphy announced to that the Department of Justice has been making an investigation into allegations of misconduct against Martin T. Manton, a Circuit Court judge for the Second Judicial District. This investigation is to determine whether there is basis for action by the Federal authorities."

Judge Manton, who was appointed by President Wilson in 1918, said at the second of two conferences held with reporters in his chambers that he welcomed investigation of his conduct on or off the bench.

"That's good. I'm glad to hear it," he declared, when told of the Attorney General's announcement.

Dwight Brantley, head of the New York office of the Federal Bureau of Investigation, when asked whether his department was investigating the Manton case, replied:

"No comment."

## Judge Defers Statement

Judge Manton's first press interview yesterday came at noon in the anteroom of his chambers on the twenty-fourth floor of the Federal court building in Foley Square. He announced that he had changed his mind about issuing a statement reqarding an article published in *The New York World-Telegram* on Friday, dealing with his alleged business activities while serving on the bench. Because other articles were to follow, he said, he preferred to withhold any statement until all had been published.

"I am not going to issue any statement until after all the articles have been published," he said. "These articles were not shown to me in advance of publication. I do not know what will be published. After all of them have been published I will determine what to say or do, if anything."

After reading the first of the articles Judge Manton said on Friday that he would issue a statement yesterday that would convince the public that there was nothing improper or immoral about his conduct.

Told of rumors that the Department of Justice was interested in the case, Judge Manton said, in response to a direct query, that Attorey General Murphy did not discuss the matter with him when he was in New York earlier in the week.

Judge Manton said that he had read the second of the articles, published yesterday.

The second interview was held in Judge Manton's chambers at 3 o'clock. After he had announced that he welcomed the investigation by the Department of Justice he was asked if he would make any report to Attorney General Murphy in the published charges.

"What charges? What charges?" he exclaimed. "Hasn't a judge the right to buy stocks and bonds?"

Judge Manton invited inspection of his record on the bench which, he said, would show that he had sat in more cases and written more opinions than any other judge in the last fifteen years, indicating that his personal business affairs had not interfered with his judicial duties.

Just before Judge Manton held his first press conference, Louis S. Levy, of the law firm of Stanchfield & Levy, issued a statement denying "without reservation" any possible inference from the published articles that either he or his former firm, Chadbourne, Stanchfield & Levy, "ever had any relations with Judge Manton that were in the slightest degree improper."

The statement was with reference to assertions in *The World-Tele-gram* article of Friday, that Judge manton had sent a business associate, the late James J. Sullivan, to Mr. Levy to seek his aid in obtaining a loan of $250,000 of which some $228,000, according to the article, was used for Judge Manton's business affairs.

"I have not heard of it," Judge Manton said, when told of the lawyer's statement, "but Mr. Levy was never in the seven-cent fare case. The loan was advanced to Mr. Sullivan and not to me, in June, 1932, and the case did not come up until September. Furthermore, he got the money from Lord & Thomas, the advertising agency, and not from Stanchfield & Levy."

Mr. Levy's statement was, specifically, in response to intimations in the article that there was a relationship between the loan and the appearnace of Mr. Levy's former firm as counsel for the receivers for the Interborough Rapid Transit Company, who were appointed in the Fall of 1932. The firm of Chadbourne, Stanchfield & Levy withdrew soon afterward and the present counsel was named by the receiver.

## Ignorant of Judge's Affairs

We never had any matter before Judge Manton or any other judge in which the judge had any interest," Mr. Levy's statement declared. "I know nothing about the judge's financial transactions; neither my firm nor I ever had any financial transactions with him.

"With respect to the loan referred to in the articles as having been made to the late James J. Sullivan, although I had no knowledge at that time that Judge Manton was in any way interested in the loan, and do not know that this was the fact, and although neither I nor any member of my former firm had any inkling or concern as to what Mr. Sullivan intended to do with the proceeds of the loan, and although I had but a very slight connection with the matter, I know of no rule or principle of law or proper conduct which would have prevented my firm from representing Mr. Sullivan legally.

"Mr. Sullivan was a man of affairs and entitled to do business and to have legal representation and advice, regardless of any connection he may have had with Judge Manton or any other judge.

Any New York firm of any standing or size which would have represented Mr. Sullivan was likely to have matters pending before the United States Circuit Court for this circuit, of which Judge Manton was a member.

"There can be no claim of impropriety in the fact that my former partner and myself were the beneficial owners of preferred shares of a corporation in which Judge Manton also held shares. No matter affecting this corporation ever came before Judge Manton." Mr. Levy noted that it was neither unusual nor, in his opinion, improper for friends, co-stockholders or even former law partners of a judge to argue cases before him.

# CURLEY CONVICTION

*The Washington Post*, January 20, 1946

We trust that the conviction of James M. Curley, Representative from Massachusetts and Mayor of Boston for the fourth time, on charges of using the mails to defraud will rouse Bostonians from the chronic state of political apathy and cynicism that is the root cause of rottenness in their municipal government. Mr. Curley's past brushes with the law, and the record of his official misdeeds long ago disqualified him, in the opinion of intelligent men and women, for holding the high offices to which he has been repeatedly elected by his fellow citizens. For that reason we wish that the $10,000 of Federal salary checks hurriedly donated by Representative-Mayor Curley to provide more nursing service for the Boston City Hospital could be used to endow an organization devoted to educating the people of Boston in the duties of citizenship.

The title of public enemy No. 1 is customarily bestowed on some bold gang leader with a long string of robberies and murders to his credit. Yet we doubt whether the criminal activities of such men are anywhere near so deadly in their ultimate effects as the injury done society by lawbreakers of Mr. Curley's type who use political office to feather their nests. For when corrupt politicians escape punishment as a result of their protected position, faith in representative government is undermined and the public is increasingly disposed to endure and ultimately even to condone the illegal practices that yield heavy dividends to crooks.

In the present instance it is matter for congratulation that the Department of Justice resisted political pressure to "lay off" Curley, and persisted in its determination to prosecute him and his partners in a fraudulent war contracts brokerage scheme. The jury's verdict is likewise a blow struck in the cause of good government. Its salutary effects will doubtless be felt not only in Boston, but in numerous other communities that have become subject to political racketeers, because of the inertia of law-abiding citizens.

# DISCLOSES DECISION IN TV TALK

President, Nixon Laud His Record At White House

By Warren Unna, *The Washington Post*, September 23, 1958

Sherman Adams, President Eisenhower's top assistant, announced his resignation last night to a Nationwide TV audience.

"Against my distaste for giving any grounds whatever to the charge of retreating under fire, against my desire to complete my duty during the remaining two years of the term for which President Eisenhower was elected, I must give full consideration to the effect of my continuing presence on the public scene," he declared.

Adams, smiling grimly, enunciating with a terse New England burr and pausing for a gulp only after the word "resignation" had passed his lips, referred to "a campaign of vilification by those who seek personal advantage by my removal from public life."

Immediately after Adams' 12-minute speech, the White House released a "Dear Sherman" letter from the President declaring: "I accept your resignation with sadness."

The President said the work of Adams, his right-hand arm, has been "brilliant" and "unselfish" and that Adams leaves his service with "my complete trust, confidence and respect."

The President made no direct reference to the House investigation this summer which had linked Adams' name with that of Bernard Goldfine, the Boston textile magnate.

Lengthy and explosive hearings brought out that Adams had received gifts and free hotel accommodations from his long-time friend, Goldfine, and that Goldfine, in turn, had asked Adams to make inquiries at the Government regulatory agencies which were giving Goldfine business headaches.

In a second simultaneous announcement, Vice President Richard M. Nixon declared: "Any fair-minded observer who examine his (Adams') whole record will conclude that he made a superb contribution to the efficient operation of the Executive Branch of the Government."

Nixon also declared: "In a position where an indecisive an who tried to please everybody would be a catastrophy, he was a man who had the rare ability to make decisions quickly, fairly and objectively."

## Cites Testimony

In his resignation statement, Adams referred to the sworn testimony that he had given before Congress which "clearly established that I had never influenced nor attempted to influence any agency, or any officer or employe of any agency in any case, decision or matter whatsoever."

He said that when the investigating committee continued its attempts to discredit him, the "easy and obvious way to bring such an attack to an end is to remove the target."

But, said Adams, "It is not—nor has it ever been—-my nature to run in the face of adversity and, in my years of public service—nearly 20 now—I have never once done so."

---

Nevertheless, Adams continued, "I must ask myself whether my retention in office might conceivably delay or retard, even in small degree, the achievements of those goals of President Eisenhower which yet lie ahead... whether the retention of my services might possibly diminish the chances which my Party has of regaining control of the Congress in the November elections."

The defeat for reelection earlier this month of Sen. Frederick G. Payne (R-Me.) has been directly attributed to the Adams-Goldfine case and looked to as a weathervane of Republican chances in the remaining state elections in November.

Payne, like Adams, is also a friend of Goldfine, and also accepted gifts and hospitality from the Boston manufacturer. Payne will be replaced in the Senate by Gov. Edmund S. Muskie, a Democrat.

Adams waited for the final two minutes last night before announcing his decision at 6:43 p.m. in a special appearance at WTOP-TV's Broadcast House.

However, the announcement had been expected ever since early morning when Adams paid a surprise call on the President at his Newport, R.I., vacation headquarters and quickly flew back to Washington accompanied by Presidential Press Secretary James C. Hagerty.

## Chats With Reporters

Arriving at Broadcast House a few minutes ahead of the telecast, Adams smiled and chatted with reporters regarding his Sunday attendance at the Washington Redskins-Chicago Bears football game.

When it came time to go on the air, only Hagerty, Maj. Gen. Wilton D. Persons, Adams' chief assistant, and Gerald D. Morgan, White House counsel, were allowed to remain in the room.

Just before the telecast began, Hagerty removed a prop book from behind Adams' desk. It was entitled: "The Happiest Man in the World."

Upon concluding his speech, and as he walked under the studio's "Exit" sign, Adams told reporters he had no statement regarding future plans and climbed into the driver's seat of his waiting green Pontiac station wagon. A set of golf clubs was in the rear seat, a police lieutenant in the seat next to him.

The Adams-Goldfine investigation occupied the House Special Subcommittee on Legislative Oversight, directly, and the Administration, indirectly, for most of June and July.

Congressional investigators first started airing reports that Adams has accepted expensive gifts and hospitality from his good friend, Goldfine, and that Goldfine's business difficulties had received special treatment from Government regulatory agencies.

Then on June 12, in a letter to Subcommittee Chairman Oren Harris (D-Ark), Adams "categorically" denied as "unwarranted and unfair" the "insinuations" that Goldfine had received "favored treatment" because of his friendship with Adams.

In the same letter, Adams acknowledged that:

- Goldfine had picked up a $2000 bill for putting up Adams and his family at various times from 1953 until this year at Boston's Sheraton-Plaza Hotel. But Adams said he had assumed that Goldfine maintained an apartment at the hotel "on a continuing basis."
- He called Chairman Edward F. Howrey of the Federal Trade Commission twice following inquires from Goldfine. Once was to get a memo regarding the Government's complaint that

Goldfine was mislabeling woolen goods; once to make an appointment for Goldfine to see Howrey.

- Also following an inquiry from Goldfine, he had White House Counsel Morgan check with the Securities and Exchange Commission regarding the Government's case against Goldfine's East Boston real estate investment company.

In none of these instances, Adams declared, did he press the matter beyond routine inquiry, nor did he ask for any special treatment for his friend.

The next day there were reports that, in addition to the hotel suite hospitality, Adams also had received an expensive vicuna coat and an oriental rug from Goldfine.

The Subcommittee then produced vouchers showing that the Adamses had also accepted Goldfine's hospitality at the Hotel Waldorf Astoria in New York City and the Hotel Mayflower in Plymouth, Mass., hospitality which included the paying of long-distance phone calls, bar bills, meals and tips.

White House Press Secretary Hagerty countered that the President "knows of no individual in or out of Government that he has more confidence in that Sherman Adams."

On June 17, Adams took the unprecedented step of voluntary appearing before the Harris Subcommittee.

Adams acknowledged he "may have acted a little imprudently." He then added: "I have no excuses to offer. I did not come up here to make apologies to you (Harris) or to this Committee.

## Called Rug a Loan

Adams then declared:

- The $2400 oriental rug at his 2400 Tilde st. nw. home together with "a couple of small mats," were indeed provided by Goldfine, but only as a loan.
- Goldfine did provide him with a vicuna wool coat and have it tailored for him, but, instead of the rumored $700 price tag, the actual cost of the material at Goldfine's mill was $69.
- It did not occur" to him that the various locations and sizes of Goldfine's Sheraton Plaza Hotel suites would indicate that the accommodations were maintained on anything but a continuing basis.
- As for himself, Adams said he, too, gave gifts, a gold watch to Goldfine, a wedding present for his son, a silver dish, a painting his wife had done for the Goldfine home.

In testimony before the Subcommittee in July, the total of Goldfine's hotel hospitality to the Adamses was raised from the original $2000 to $3096.56.

Following Adams' public testimony, President Eisenhower told his press conference that, while Adams may have been "imprudent," he wanted Adams to stay just where he was as his White House right arm: "I need him."

# TEXT OF ADAMS' RESIGNATION STATEMENT

*The Washington Post*, September 23, 1958

The prepared text of Sherman Adams radio-TV broadcast last night:

Since last June a spirited controversy has taken place in which I, Sherman Adams, Assistant to the President, have found myself cast in a principal role. This controversy has at times unfortunately despleased public consideration of much more important and far reaching problems that directly affect the welfare of our country and its people.

Its quite probable that a great many of you now listening to me have expressed some time in the course of this controversy and as private citizens your views on the matter. It seems to me that nearly everyone active in public life, in one capacity or another, has done so. I am here tonight to express mine.

Several months ago, a committee of the House of Representatives started hearings designed to elicit information as to whether or not any person or persons had exerted improper influence upon the regulatory agencies of the Government. In the course of those hearings, I testified before that committee.

The sworn testimony that I then gave, together with that of every responsible official of whom the Committee made inquiry, clearly established that I had never influenced nor attempted to influence any agency, or any officer or employee of any agency in any case, decision, or matter whatsoever.

Despite the fact that this testimony is wholly undisputed, a calculated and contrived effort has nevertheless been made to attack and discredit me. As part of this effort, the Committee received completely irresponsible testimony and, without conscience, gave ear to rumor, innuendo and even unsubstantiated gossip.

A campaign of vilification by those who seek personal advantage by my removal from public life has continued up to this very moment. These efforts, it is now clear, have been intended to destroy me and in so doing to embarrass the Administration and the President of the United States.

An easy and obvious way to bring such an attack to an end is to remove the target. There were those who thought I should resign because they felt I had been imprudent in not foreseeing the interpretation that could be placed upon my exchanging gifts with a friend, even of some fifteen years standing.

I am sure that many of you have wondered why I have not chosen that course, why—at the very beginning of the controversy—I did not immediately resign. I would like to tell you why.

First it is not—nor has it ever been—my nature to run in the face of adversity and, in my years of public service—nearly twenty now— I have never once done so.

Second, since I have done o wrong, my resigning could have been construed as an admission that I had, in the atmosphere which has surrounded the controversy.

Third, when a man has been afforded the privilege that has been mine of serving a great American, a great humanitarian, and a great President—when a man has come to understand the sel-

---

flessness and the dedication with which that President has served all of our people, regardless of race, creed, religious or political persuasion—it poses a decision, as I am sure you can readily appreciate, difficult in the extreme to make.

Against my distaste for giving any grounds whatever to the charge of retreating under fire, against my desire to complete my duty during the remaining two years of the terms for which President Eisenhower was elected, I must give full consideration to the effect of my continuing presence on the public scene. Under the circumstances and in light of the events of the past three months in which I have been made to be directly concerned. I must ask myself whether my retention in office might conceivably delay or retard, even in small degree, the achievement of those goals of President Eisenhower which yet lie ahead. Another factor that I feel I must consider is whether the retention of my services might possibly diminish the chances which my party has of regaining control of the Congress in the November elections.

Within the past few days I have reached a decision. Early this morning I flew from Washington to the President's vacation headquarters at Newport. I conferred with him and, in the course of that conference, tendered my resignation. This he has accepted, to be effective as soon as an orderly transition can be arranged for the assumption of my duties and responsibilities.

This action of mine is final and unqualified. It is not open to reconsideration.

It is my steadfast belief that the principles and programs for which Dwight Eisenhower stands serve that best interests of our country and, indeed, the people of the Free World.

They deserve to be strengthened through the support of everyone of us. I believe that

I can now best serve my President, and contribute to the support of his objections, by the course that I have undertaken to follow.

I am now about to retire, after nearly six years, from the position in which I have served with pride and which I have given by best efforts to hold with honor.

Now nearly 20 years of public service come to a close, but I can say that it has brought a depth of satisfaction that will always be with me.

Text of President Eisenhower's letter to Sherman Adams on Adams' resignation:
Dear Sherman:

I deeply deplore the circumstances that have decided you to resign at the Assistant to the President.

Your selfless and tireless devotion to the work of the White House and to me personally has been universally recognized. In discharging the responsibilities of your vitally important post, with no hope of reward other than your own satisfaction in knowing that you have served your country well, your total dedication to the Nation's welfare has been of the highest possible order.

Your performance has been brilliant; the public has been the beneficiary of your unselfish work. After our six years of intimate association you have, as you have had throughout, my complete trust, confidence and respect.

I accept your resignation with sadness. You will be sorely missed by your colleagues on the staff and by the departments and agencies of the Government, with which you have worked so efficiently.

With warm regard and highest esteem.
DWIGHT D. EISENHOWER.
As ever.

# BOBBY BAKER MIRRORS THE SENATE HE 'RAN'

By Laurence Stern, *The Washington Post*, October 13, 1963

As much as any one man can epitomize an institution, departed Senate Majority Secretary Robert G. (Bobby) Baker mirrored the personality of the United States Senate.

Within the lofty, marble Senate chamber, to which Bobby Baker first came as a precocious, 14-year-old page, gush the wellsprings of national political power. Within it, too, are engines of personal influence that eternally tempt the ambitious and acquisitive. It is here also–even more than in the diffuse and unruly House of Representatives–that the great national interest groups concentrate their quest for control over national policy.

This is the arena that molded the gangling, bright-eyed lad from Pickens, S.C., into the legendary "boy wonder of the Senate"—the ultimate insider.

"On any issue I have at least 10 Senators in the palm of my hand," Bobby was quoted by the Chicago Daily News last year as having boasted to a group of visiting students. Not many members of the Senate could truthfully make that claim. But Bobby could, and few who know the Senate would be disposed to argue.

## The Establishment

Baker's Models were the men most skilled at manipulating the instruments of power in the Senate, men like Vice President Lyndon B. Johnson, the late Sen. Robert S. Kerr (D-Okla.) and Sen. Richard B. Russell (D-Ga.) These were the men who presided over the inner institution that maverick Pennsylvania Democrat Joseph S. Clark irreverently described as the "Senate Establishment."

As Majority Secretary, Baker commanded a vast army of patronage appointees over whom he held hiring and firing power: page boys, clerks, secretaries, stenographers and committee staffers–the Senate's institutional cement.

To the elected Senators he was the weathervane of leadership attitudes. Poised at the portals to the Senate chamber, it was Bobby who put out the word when votes were needed to shore up the leadership on critical issues.

His nose counts on key votes were regarded by press gallery admirers as close to infallible. But the key to his success was that many Senators voted the way Bobby, as agent of the leadership, told them to vote.

There was no leadership council to which Bobby did not have ready access. And there were few decisions, whether on key senatorial committee assignments, allocation of campaign money or the most secret nuance of legislative strategy, to which he was not privy or on which could not register his influence.

Baker made it his business to study the Senate members intimately–their views on public issues such as cloture, tariff legislation and oil depletion as well as the minutiae of their private attitudes and personal lives.

---

To prominent Senators and to lowly job applicants alike, the password for approaching the Senate power structure was invariably: "See Bobby."

When an experienced Capitol Hill reporter wrote last year that Bobby was, in many respects, a more influential force in the Senate than Majority Leader Mike Mansfield (D-Mont.), it infuriated Mansfield and flustered his Majority Secretary. But many a veteran student of Capitol Hill would agree with the reporter's evaluation.

Baker's authority stemmed from his association with the traditional power centers of the Senate, the senior committee chairmen. His influence was at its apogee when Johnson was Majority Leader and Kerr headed the Public Works Committee, which dealt out pork to the deserving and withheld it from the uncooperative.

With Kerr's death and the passing of the Democratic leadership role to Mansfield, there was a corresponding slippage in Baker's position. Nevertheless, the fact of his entrenchment was accepted as unchanging almost as the Capitol dome.

## An Unlikely Secret

It would be hard to assume that many of Baker's close associates in the Senate were unaware of his extensive private business activities. But once the Majority Secretary's outside works attracted the spotlight of press disclosure, senatorial toleration turned first to privately expressed concern and then to public disapproval.

Baker, after all, had followed the same moral yardstick that many Senators observe in their own public and personal lives. Congress is a stern preacher to the Executive Branch but has traditionally left itself a free hand in combining public and private careers.

Baker had a law practice, an insurance partnership, real estate interests and financial ties to a fast-growing vending machine concern, the Serv-U-Corp. Many members of the Senate could boast an even broader portfolio of private enterprises.

But once the Majority Secretary's outside connections were spotlighted publicly, the self-protective instincts of the politicians in the Senate flashed into play. Also, many Senators like John J. Williams (R-Del.) became deeply concerned about the good name of the Nation's highest legislative forum.

## A Limit on Limits

In its first public reaction to the Baker affair last Thursday, nearly two weeks after the case had burst into public attention, the Senate began speaking openly about a strengthened conflict-of-interest code for its staff. Long after the Federal Bureau of Investigation and the Internal Revenue Service had begun looking into the Baker case, the Senate decided to investigate the matter itself.

It took only 15 minutes to get unanimous Senate approval for the Baker inquiry, proposed by Williams after his one-man investigation into published revelations of Baker's business activities. There were flowery words of tribute for Williams from Democrats and Republicans alike for his "high moral principles" and "crusade for integrity."

But when reform-conscious Senators called upon their colleagues to act on public disclosure and code-of-ethics legislation that would apply to the elected lawmakers themselves, the appeals struck little response.

"The main thing the country wants to hear about," implored Sen. Jacob K. Javits (R-N.Y.), "is not what we are doing about our employes, but what we are doing about ourselves."

And Sen. Wayne Morse (D-Ore.), who year after year has introduced legislation to require disclosure of income sources within all branches of Government, appealed for speedy corrective actions this year. Joining this seemingly hopeless chorus were Sens. Kenneth B. Keating (R-N.Y.) and Joseph S. Clark (D-Pa.).

In the current crop of pending conflict-of-interest legislation is a proposal by Javits and Keating to create a Joint Committee on Ethics to review the conduct of members of Congress and their staffs.

A more modest but possibly more effective proposal has been put forward by Sen. Clifford P. Case (R-N.J.). It would require all Federal employes earning more than $15,000 annually to disclose the sources of their public and private income and would require a public record of all ex parte communications with Federal regulatory agencies.

Similar proposals are drifting in the limbo of congressional apathy in the House, under the sponsorship of a handful of reformers such as Reps. Edith Green (D-Ore.) and John V. Lindsay (R-N.Y.).

The most immediate hope for a sharper congressional consciousness of the dividing line between the trust of public office and private gain would seem to be more vigilant Justice Department enforcement of the conflict-of-interest laws already on the books.

The convictions earlier this year of two former Congressmen, Thomas F. Johnson of Maryland and Frank W. Boykin of Alabama, on conflict-of-interest charges, have had a strong impact on Capitol Hill.

And last Tuesday, a day after Baker's resignation, the congressional newspaper Roll Call published this ominous warning to its readers:

"Congressional staffers must play it 'safe' in any such (outside) dealings. Their interests must not only be legitimate—they must look legitimate. Any operation that smacks of subterfuge or illegality can be quickly blown all out of proportion by news media."

# BAKER DENIES USING HIS INFLUENCE IN VENDING MACHINE FRANCHISES

## Co-Defendants Join in Move

By Jack Landau, *The Washington Post*, October 16, 1963

Robert G. (Bobby) Baker, who resigned last week as Senate Majority Secretary, yesterday formally denied ever using his influence to arrange for vending machine franchises in government contract aerospace plants.

Baker's denial came in answer to a law suit filed in the United States District Court on Sept. 9, by Capitol Vending, Inc. of Washington. The suit asked $300,000 damages for alleged interference in Capitol's vending machine contract at the Falls Church plant of Melpar, Inc.

Two other defendants in the suit also filed across the board denials. They were Ernest C. Tucker, Baker's law partner and chairman of the Board of the Serv-U Corp., and Fred B. Black Jr., a governmental relations consultant for North American Aviation Corp.

Baker left his Senate post last Monday in the wake of a Senate and FBI investigation into his outside business activities.

These include his publicly recorded financial ties to the Serv-U Corp., a vending machine firm which in 18 months has obtained $3.5 million in sales at southern California government aerospace contract plants.

In the Capitol Vending suit the former Senate aide, and his co-defendants, flatly denied that:

- He had accepted $5600 to secure a $100,000 a year vening machine frachise for Capitol at Melpar.
- He had first attempted to buy Capitol out and when that failed, he allegedly persuaded Melpar to cancel its contract with Capitol.
- He is a shareholder in Serv-U.
- He represented to Black that "Baker, as Secretary to the Senate Majority, was in a position to assist in securing contracts for North American."
- North American put ServU into its plants "as a partial return for the services performed" by Black and Baker.
- Black and Baker assisted in securing North American subcontracts for Melpar.
- "In partial return for these services," Melpar agreed to contract with a vending machine firm in which Baker and Black had an interest.

# PANEL URGES SENATE TO CENSURE DODD

### Senator Sits Alone as He Gets Verdict

### Unanimous Report Says Deeds Tend To Dishonor Body

By Richard Harwood, *The Washington Post*, June 24, 1967

The Senate Committee on Standards and Conduct recommended unanimously yesterday that Sen. Thomas J. Dodd (D-Conn.) be "censured" for conduct that "tends to bring the Senate into dishonor and disrepute."

The verdict of the bipartisan Committee had been expected for weeks and was treated by the Senate-and by Dodd-as an anticlimax to an investigation of the Senator's affairs that has been in process for more than a year.

Only a handful of Senators were present at noon when the committee Chairman, Sen. John Stennis (D-Miss.), arose to file the committee's report and announce its verdict. Dodd was in the chamber, sitting all alone.

When Stennis had finished his 5-minute report, Dodd went immediately to the press galleries to announce that he would run for reelection in 1970 and to declare that his "conscience is clear."

He was accused in January, 1966, of having abused his position in the Senate to advance the financial fortunes of foreign agent Julius Klein and of having misused large sums of money given to him for political purposes.

The charges were made by columnists Drew Pearson and Jack Anderson and were based on thousands of documents taken from Dodd's files by a group of former employes that included James P. Boyd, Marjorie Carpenter, Michael V. O'Hare and Terry Golden.

The Committee's judgement was that Dodd's relationship with Klein had been "indiscreet and beyond the responsibilities of a Senator to any citizen." But it found insufficient evidence of "wrongdoing to warrant recommendation of disciplinary action by the Senate."

Dodd's use of political money, however, was strongly condemned by the Committee and was the basis of its censure recommendation.

The committee accused Dodd of using "the influence and power of his office to collect political money for his personal use and of billing both the Government and private organizations for trips he took.

That conduct, said the Committee, "deserves the censure of the Senate"; it "is contrary to accepted morals, derogates from the public trust expected of a Senator, and tends to bring the Senate into dishonor and disrepute."

The censure resolution will be debated and voted on after Dodd has had time to prepare a reply. Dodd said he did not get a copy of the report until 10:45 a.m. yesterday but was eager to answer the Committee's findings.

---

## Definitely a Candidate

What effect a vote of censure would have on Dodd's political career is entirely speculative. Dodd himself said he was optimistic about the judgment of Connecticut's voters when he comes up for reelection three years hence. He will definately be a candidate, he said.

Within the Senate establishment, a censure vote carries no formal penalties — neither a cash fine nor a loss of seniority or committee assignments. Whatever damage results is in the loss of personal standing, reputation and prestige.

The last Senator placed in a similar position was the late Joseph R. McCarthy, whose conduct was "condemned" in 1954. McCarthy's influence in Washington was destroyed by the action. He was an object of pity by the time of his death in 1957.

There has been hair-splitting within the Ethics Committee over the relative impact of a recommendation for "censure" as opposed to "condemnation." The distinction, if any, is purely semantic. The practical effect is the same in both cases.

Dodd's principal problem, in any case, is not the Senate but the Justice Department and the Internal Revenue Service. Both agencies are investigating his financial affairs and his relationships with various political contributors.

## Four Matters Noted

Stennis and his colleagues passed no judgement on some of the more prominent relationships under study by Justice and IRS. But they recommended that the Attorney General take note of four matters:

1. An $8000 contribution to Dodd in 1964 by the International Latex Corp. It was recorded in the company's books as an "industrial relations" expense.

2. Dodd's free use of automobiles supplied by the Dunbar Corp. of Connecticut, a firm interested in Government contracts.

3. The tax status of $203,000 in testimonial contributions received by Dodd in the period 1961 through 1965.

4. The tax status of $246,920 in campaign contributions received by Dodd in the same period.

The Committee also urged the Justice Department to determine whether Boyd and other members of Dodd's staff had violated Federal law by removing documents from his office.

## No Emotion Displayed

The Committee said the Senate could take no action against the employees because "they are no longer in the empoly of the Senate."

Dodd seemed resigned weeks ago to the Committee's verdict and displayed no emotion or loss of composure when it was rendered. Stennis went to Dodd's office at 11:15 a.m. to make a formal announcement of the recommendation that would be made.

Dodd emerged from the office at noon in a freshly pressed dark blue suit. His face was powdered, perhaps in anticipation of the television appearance he made immediately after the Stennis report to the Senate.

He had not contested any of the facts on which the report was based. At the Committee's hearings last summer, he admitted that he hoped to help foreign agent Klein mend fences with German clients in the course of a trip to Germany by Dodd, ostensibly on Senate business, in 1964.

The extent to which Dodd pleaded Klein's case with German government officials was impossible to determine, the Committee said.

## Admits Use of Funds

Dodd also admitted at Committee hearings last month that thousands of dollars contributed at campaign and testmonial functions had been used to underwrite his personal standard of living. In some cases, these functions had been advertised as fundraisers for Dodd's 1964 reelection campaign; others were advertised as "testimonals" to the Senator.

They produced $450,273. At least $116,083 of the total was converted to Dodd's personal use, the Committee said. He used the money to pay income taxes, to repay personal loans, finance trips for his family, pay household and club bills and other family living expenses.

Dodd's defense was that he considered the money as a personal, tax-free gift that he could use in any way he saw fit.

The Committee, however, said it was unable to find "one solicitation letter, invitation, ticket, program or other written communication" that said the money was to be used for Dodd's personal living expenses.

"I still maintain I have done nothing wrong," Dodd said yesterday. The Committee report does not change his mind on that, he said.

## Could Have Been Harsher

Of the Committee's censure recommendation, Dodd said: "I don't see how it could have been harsher."

He was incorrect. The Committee could have recommended that Dodd be expelled from the Senate.

But the Committee Vice Chairman, Republican Sen. Wallace F. Bennett of Utah, told the Senate that "expulsion from the Senate was too severe" a punishment. "Complete exoneration was unsound," he said. "The use of the word 'censure,' which has a traditional meaning in the Senate, and which has been used before, was the next strongest alternative open to us."

Another committee member, Sen. Eugene J. McMarthy (D-Minn.) said "each member of the Committee had some reservations about some aspects of the report or about some of the language."

# SENATE CENSURES DODD BY 92-TO-5 VOTE

By Andrew J. Glass, *The Washington Post*, June 24, 1967

## 2d Charge Is Rejected In Voting

### Senator Found Guilty Of Using Donations; Will Keep Seat, Rights

Thomas Joseph Dodd, in his ninth year as a United States Senator, was censured by his peers yesterday for spending political funds to pay his personal expenses.

By a vote of 92 to 5, the Senate upheld the unanimous finding of its Ethics Committee that Dodd, a Connecticut Democrat, employed "the influence and power of his office... to obtain and use for his personal benefit" at least $116,083 that he raised through testimonials and in contributions to his 1964 political campaign.

The Senate censured Dodd for conduct "which is contrary to accepted morals, derogates from the public trust expected of a Senator and tends to bring the Senate into dishonor and disrepute."

Censure carries no other penalties; Dodd will retain all of the privileges and seniority of his office. After the vote, he again said he will run for a third term in 1970.

After censuring Dodd, the Senate, by a vote of 51 to 45, absolved him of a second charge lodged by the Ethics Committee, that he requested and accepted reimbursements from both Senate and private groups for identical travel expenses.

Dodd was the first legislator in the 179-year history of the Senate to be censured for personal financial misconduct and the first to vote against his own censure, the others absenting themselves.

It was the sixth censure case in the Senate annals. The Senate last voted to punish one of its members in 1954, when the late Sen. Joseph R. McCarthy (R-Wis.) was condemned for abusive behavior toward his colleagues.

The Senators who voted with Dodd in a futile effort to clear him of wrongdoing were: Democratic Whip Russell B. Long (La.), who acted as his chief defender throughout the nine-day debate; Abraham Ribicoff, Dodd's Democratic colleague from Connecticut, and two Republicans, John G. Tower (Tex.) and Strom Thurmond (S.C.).

Dodd left the chamber during the roll call, then returned at 3:30 p.m. and met with his lawyers as the tally clerk read the long list of Senators who had voted for the censure resolution. Moving to his own seat, Dodd rose, was recognized by Vice President Humphrey and shouted his own vote—a defiant "No"! The clerk then announced the 92 to 5 result.

The censured Senator remained standing to address the chamber. "I'm grateful to those who have expressed some confidence in my character," he said. "I'm not bitter toward anyone," even the six members of the Ethics Committee who, Dodd said, "are all honorable men."

His voice cracked and there were tears in his eyes as he continued to speak: "I think a grave mistake has been made. And I'm the one who has to bear the scars of that for the rest of my life."

## Thanks Sen. Long

Momentarily bracing himself Dodd thanked Russell Long for his help. He also thanked the Republicans who had supported him in the debate, singling out Sen. Edward W. Brooke (Mass.). "I wish," he said, "there were more on my side of the aisle. But that's the way of life and politics."

His voice faltered once more and he seemed to be weeping softly when he said: "Without the wonderful support of my wife, I don't think I could have carried on for the last 18 months.

"I want to tell the Senate that I'll do the best I can. I'll be here tomorrow. I'll be here everyday. It won't be easy. But that's my job.

"I can do that," Dodd went on," because in here [clutching a fist against his heart], I don't have any feeling of wrongdoing. If I did, I would resign tomorrow. I love the Senate and I like all of you and I hope you'll find it within your power to do toward me as I would do toward you."

Dodd grasped the rails of his desk and swayed slightly. "I hope my honor is not diminished in your eyes. And so I bid you all farewell for today." He left by a rear door, pausing only to shake hands with Sen. Wayne Morse (D-Ore.), who had voted against him on both counts.

Sen. John C. Stennis, the courtly Mississippian whom Humphrey named in 1965 to head the newly formed ethics panel, said the outcome marked "a new start in a way for the Senate. I believe and I hope that it's a new start for Sen. Dodd as well. And I say too with all emphasis that all of us have a lot of sympathy for him.

"There's not victory here for anyone," Stennis continued. "I think the Senate realized that it had to face this matter and it did to a great degree and that means a new start."

## Will Frame New Code

Stennis's group—formally known as the Select Committee on Standards and Conduct—will now proceed to frame a formal code of ethics for the Senate that will be ready in time to be voted upon during the current session.

It was Dodd himself who initially requested the Stennis panel to investigate his conduct, thus giving the committee its first case. The inquiry took 14 months.

It stemmed from a series of columns about Dodd written by Drew Pearson and Jack Anderson that began to appear in January, 1966. Anderson had received about 6000 documents from Dodd's files that were taken, copied and returned by four of the Senator's employes.

The four defectors were James P. Boyd Jr., his former $22,000-a-year administrative assistant; Mrs. Marjorie Carpenter, his personal secretary, whom Dodd fired abruptly in December, 1964; Michael V. O'Hare, his former bookkeeper and office manager, who resigned in January, 1966, and Terry Golden, O'Hare's girlfriend, who was employed in the Dodd office as a clerk.

Dodd still faces possible action by the Internal Revenue Service over his tax returns. The Justice Department is also investigating other allegations against him based on material gathered by the Ethics Committee and turned over to the Department.

In the wake of Thursday's parliamentary convolutions, an air of finality descended over the Senate when the legislators resumed their deliberations on the Dodd case at noon yesterday.

The 60-year-old Dodd was in his seat, his shoulders hunched, his white hair appearing to be thinner than before his troubles began. Behind him lay a 30-year career in Connecticut and national politics, including service as an FBI agent, a district attorney, an assistant prosecutor at the War Crimes Trials in Nuremberg and a two-year term in the House.

## New Somber Mood

Majority Leader Mike Mansfield (Mont.), who had adjourned the Senate Thursday in despair over its seeming inability to come to grips with the Dodd case, reflected the new somber mood which had jelled overnight.

"To sit in judgment over a fellow Senator," Mansfield said, "is one of the most distasteful tasks any member of this body can face—with the exception of sitting now where Sen. Dodd sits. . . It is time to bring this question to an orderly close."

From a rear-row seat on the Republican side, Sen. Tower tried once more to mitigate the punishment. Working in concert with Long, Tower proposed an amendment stating that Dodd's actions were "contrary to accepted standards of conduct," instead of "accepted morals," as the Ethics Committee had charged.

When the Tower amendment was defeated, 78 to 18, the pro-Dodd forces realized that they could make no further headway on the campaign finances matter. All that was left was for Dodd to speak once more in his defence.

"Whatever fate befalls me," Dodd said in summation, "I am satisfied that history will justify me. Only time will tell. For now my fate and my future are in your hands. You know me well enough to let your consciences be your guide."

Long put his arm around Dodd's shoulder and led him into the well of the chamber. He turned Dodd over to Mansfield. Together, they stepped up to the brown marble rostrum where the tally clerk was preparing to read the roll. Dodd voted in his own behalf and Mansfield led him out by a rear door.

The 92-to-5 vote nailed censure on the campaign finance charge into resolution. Two hours later, after Dodd was cleared on the companion charge, the resolution of censure itself was passed by the same 92-to-5 margin.

Between the two identical votes, Sen. Carl T. Curtis (R-Neb.) launched an effort to impugn the Committee's handling of Boyd and Mrs. Carpenter, both of whom testified against Dodd.

"Was there any particular reason why they were granted a sanctuary of silence against barring their misdeeds before the world?" Curtis asked. ". . . I've heard of the unsworn testimony of a young lady who quit because of the (employes') goings on. As a matter of fact, the Committee knew there was something wrong in Denmark."

Long passed Curtis what he said was an "FBI note" and remarked: "I don't think the Senator would like to put that in the record." The "note" was a memorandum that Dodd had written to the FBI. Long also read part of a December, 1964, letter to Dodd from Mrs. Carpenter that said: "I know that you and Mrs. Dodd have long found Jim's conduct and mine intolerable."

Boyd issued a statement reporting that he had agreed upon "an amicable divorce" from his wife in December, 1963, and that the Senator was informed in February, 1964.

The former Dodd aide said the charge that Dodd's discovery of "my relationship with Marjorie Carpenter in November, 1964," led to dismissal "is a calculated falsehood, invented to create a diversion from his own public misconduct."

# VICE PRESIDENT AGNEW RESIGNS, FINED FOR INCOME TAX EVASION

By Laurence Stern, *The Washington Post*, October 11, 1973

In a stunning and historic finale to his two-month public ordeal, Spiro T. Agnew resigned the vice presidency yesterday and accepted a criminal sentence for federal tax evasion.

The sentence—three years of unsupervised probation and a $10,000 fine—was imposed by U.S. District Court Judge Walter E. Hoffman, who called the affair "a tragic event in history."

The resignation was accepted by President Nixon in the form of a "Dear Ted" letter which paid tribute to Agnew's decision to resign rather than bring on "a protracted period of national division and uncertainty" through extended battle in the courts and Congress.

The President immediately launched the search for a successor to serve out the remaining three years of his administration. He asked Republican politicians—congressional leaders, governors, state chairmen and Republican National Committee members—to submit suggestions today.

The dramatic news of Agnew's resignation reverberated quickly through Congress. It was received with reactions of shock and compassion.

"Everything is so unreal. I've got to go straighten myself out," said Sen. Daniel K. Inouye (D-Hawaii). Republican National Chairman George Bush praised Agnew for his "great personal courage," but said the action was "in the best interest of the country."

In the great national guessing game over Agnew's successor, speculation centered most heavily on former Treasury Secretary and Texas Gov. John B. Connally, New York Gov. Nelson A. Rockefeller and former Secretary of State William P. Rogers. The three men were non-commital on the question.

For Agnew the paramount event of the day was when he stood erect and expressionless before Judge Hoffman to enter his "no contest" plea on the tax evasion charge.

That plea, which the judge declared to be the "full equivalent of a plea of guilty," was the result of days of plea bargaining between Agnew's lawyers and top Justice Department officials.

In return for the plea and his resignation the government agreed not to prosecute Agnew for alleged acts of extortion and bribery stretching over a 10-year period and involving at least $87,500. The charges were spelled out in a 40-page Justice Department "exposition of evidence" submitted to Judge Hoffman.

Attorney General Elliot L. Richardson defended the compromise and also asked for leniency in the sentencing of the former Vice President. The alternative, he said, would have been prolonged trial or impeachment proceedings.

"It is unthinkable that this nation should have been required to endure the anguish and uncertainty of a prolonged period in which the man next in line of succession to the presidency was fighting the charges brought against him by his own government," Richardson said.

The Attorney General asked that Agnew not be jailed "out of compassion for the man, out of respect for the office he has held, and out of appreciation for the fact that by his resignation he has spared the nation the prolonged agony that would have attended upon his trial."

And so Spiro Agnew became the first Vice President of the United States to be driven from office by a cloud of personal scandal.

# REP. BRASCO CONVICTED IN BRIBERY CASE

*The Washington Post*, July 19, 1974

NEW YORK, July 19 (UPI)—Brooklyn Democratic Rep. Frank Brasco was found guilty tonight of bribery and conspiracy in a scheme to obtain Post Office contracts for a reputed mobster-run trucking firm.

The jury received the case about noon and returned a guilty verdict shortly before 9 p.m. The trial began June 20.

There was shock in the courtroom as the verdict was announced.

"They must be stupid people," one spectator shouted, rising to his feet. Brasco, 41, buried his head in his hands as his wife put her arms around his shoulders. He refused to comment to reporters, but his lawyer said an appeal would be filed.

Brasco, a four-term congressman and member of the House Post Office Committee, was accused of peddling his political influence for a $27,500 payoff in exchange for helping reputed mobster John (Gentlemen John) Masiello obtain valuable Post Office tucking contracts for Masiello's ANR leasing corp.

Brasco testified that he was unaware of Masiello's reputed underworld background during 1967 and 1968, the time covered by the indictment.

# REP. PODELL PLEADS GUILTY TO CONSPIRACY

*The Washington Post,* October 1, 1974

NEW YORK. Oct. 1 (AP)—Rep. Bertram L. Podell (D-N.Y.) interrupted his trial in U.S. District Court today to plead guilty to charges of conspiracy and conflict of interest.

The 48-year-old Brooklyn congressman changed his plea on the ninth day of his trial on charges of using his influence to help a small airline in return for $41,350.

Sentencing was set for Jan. 9. Podell could get up to seven years in prison and a $20,000 fine.

After some two hours of discussions with the prosecutor, the graying congressman reappeared in the courtroom, seeming slightly shaken. He bumped against a courtroom railing before he took his seat and his lawyer entered the guilty plea.

"Are you in fact guilty?" asked Judge Robert L. Carter.

"Yes, your honor." Podell replied.

Podell who was elected to Congress in a special election in February, 1968, was defeated in the Sept. 10 primary.

He was accused of taking the money in return for trying to help the now-defunct Florida Atlantic Airlines get a Miami-Bahamas franchise. He had maintained that the money was for legitimate legal fees.

The congressman said a $29,000 check payable to the "Citizens' Committee for B.L. Podell" on May 1, 1969, was: personal donation from Martin Miller, a Miami business man, who was a co-defendant.

Miller, who was president of the parent firm of the airline, also pleaded guilty to a single conspiracy count.

Podell acknowledged that he was "indirectly compensated through my law firm" for his efforts on behalf of Florida Atlantic.

"I did not at that time know I was violating any law …," Podell told the judge.

# THE ALLEGATIONS AGAINST LANCE

*The Washington Post*, September 22, 1977

During the Lance affair, more than a dozen allegations of wrongdoing were made against the former director of the Office of Management and Budget. He successfully refuted several of them, but others could not be dismissed. Among them:

- Overdrafts. The comptroller of the currency found that Lance and his wife—whose financial affairs, according to both of them, were handled by Lance—overdrew personal checking accounts by as much as $100,000 and more. For years these overdrafts—amounting to loans—were permitted to them with no interest or service charge.

Moreover, Lance helped finance his campaign for governor of Georgia in 1974 with overdrafts, which were high as $152,000, from the Calhoun bank that he ran.

The comptroller said both the personal and campaign overdrafts appeared to violate banking laws and regulations, which severely limit how much a bank officer can borrow from his bank.

- Improper use of corporate aircraft. When he became president of the National Bank of Georgia (NBG) in 1975, Lance sold that bank and executive aircraft he had previously purchased for $80,000. The bank paid $120,000 for it. Lance then used the plane on banking trips and on other trips whose business purposes are being questioned. He has acknowledged, for example, flying the plane to University of Georgia football games, the Mardi Gras, and to several political events. Apparently, the bank deducted the cost of these trips as business expenses, while Lance did not report their value as personal income.

The Justice Department, Internal Revenue Service, Securities and Exchange Commission and Federal Election Commission are investigating Lance's use of the plane for possible criminal prosecution.

- Double pledging of the same collateral. According to the terms of a note he had signed with the Manufacturers Hanover Bank in New York, Lance should have turned over to that bank "forthwith" a stock dividend of nearly 15,000 NBG shares he had received in December, 1975. But instead, he pledged those shares as collateral on another loan note he signed with the Chemical Bank of New York.

- Improper use of influence. Two potentially embarrassing federal actions involving Lance were dropped within days of his appointment to head the OMB. One was a cease-and-desist agreement with his Calhoun bank. The second was a criminal investigation of his campaign overdrafts.

Testimony showed that Lance lunched with and visited with the federal officials who decided to drop those actions. Although Lance denied it, other testimony charged that he specifically asked that the bank agreement be dropped. Lance's lawyer acknowledged that he asked the U.S. attorney in Atlanta to drop the criminal investigation.

---

- Compensating balances. Bank examiners found a pattern of cases in which banks made large personal loans to Lance soon after banks he ran had established "correspondent" relationships with them. The comptroller said that there was no clear proof of wrongdoing, but that this pattern raised serious questions about what was proper banking practice.

Charges were also made that Lance failed to report his personal borrowings to fellow bank directors as required by law and that he filed incomplete financial statements with the Senate before his confirmation in January.

It was also revealed during the course of the Lance affair that some federal bank examiners had a poor opinion of him as a bank administrator. One called him a "very weak" administrator.

# REP. LEACH INDICTED ON FEDERAL VOTE-BUYING CHARGES IN '78 ELECTION

By Charles R. Babcock, *The Washington Post*, July 21, 1979

Rep. Claude (Buddy) Leach (D-La.) was indicted by a federal grand jury in Louisiana yesterday on charges of buying votes in both the primary and general elections that sent him to Congress this year.

Leach, 46, was accused of initiating a campaign to buy the "commercial black vote" in his hometown of Leesville. Votes in the primary cost $10 and those in the general election $5, the indictment alleged.

Leach won the seat to succeed longtime representative Joe Waggonner by 266 votes last November over Republican Jimmy Wilson. He won the primary by an even narrower margin, 169 votes.

Twin indictments charge he bought more than enough votes to make the margins of victory—440 in the general and 397 in the primary. Several individuals have pleaded guilty in the case, including two men to whom Leach is accused of making vote payoffs.

Leach could not be reached for comment yesterday but he has denied the vote-buying charges in earlier statements.

Opponent Wilson has asked that Leach be un seated by the house because of charges made public during the investigation.

Another Louisiana House Democrat, representative Richard A. Tonry was indicted on similar charges in 1977. He later pleaded guilty to accepting illegal campaign contributions and was sentenced to a year in prison.

Leach also was charged in the indictment with violations of the campaign finance laws to fund the alleged vote-buying scheme.

According to the indictment, Leach allies hired drivers to pick up voters and deliver them to the polls. Each voter was given a slip of paper telling him how to vote and after leaving the polls was driven to a nearby home. There his name would be checked off a list and he would be paid in cash, the charges said.

The mayor of Leesville and the town marshal have been convicted in the case. Yesterday's indictment also included charges against a state district judge, a state district attorney and two assistants, a U.S. magistrate and three others.

J. Randall Keene, the U.S. attorney in Shreveport said the investigation is continuing. Leach, if convicted, faces up to five years in prison and a $10,000 fine on the conspiracy and vote-buying charges and a year in prison and a $25,000 fine on the alleged campaign finance violations.

The indictment alleges 14 specific instances of vote buying.

# FBI 'STING' SNARES SEVERAL IN CONGRESS

By Charles R. Babcock, *Washington Post*, February 3, 1980

An FBI undercover "sting" operation, set up to catch organized crime figures selling stolen securities and art objects, has snared several members of Congress on potential bribery charges, according to sources.

The sources said the FBI has videotapes of several transactions in which different members of Congress discuss their willingness to help FBI undercover agents with legislation or other favors. The FBI agents were posing as representatives of Arab businessmen.

The investigation is described as the largest ever involving members of Congress. More than $400,000 in cash has been paid out to some congressmen and some state officials over the past year, sources said.

One of the videotaped transactions was as recent as mid-January, sources said.

Sources said the subjects of the investigation include Sen. Harrison A. Williams Jr. (D-N.J.), chairman of the Senate Labor Committee; Reps. John M. Murphy (D-N.Y.), chairman of the House Administration Committee; John Murtha (D-Pa.) a member of the House Ethics Committee; John W. Jenrette Jr. (D-S.C.) and Richard Kelly (R-Fla.)

The Long Island paper *Newsday* reported last night that Reps. Michael Myers and Raymond F. Lederer, both Pennsylvania Democrats, also are subjects of the inquiry.

Several state and local officials in New Jersey and Pennsylvania are also said to be involved. These include the mayor of Camden, N.J., and a New Jersey state gambling official, according to sources.

The political fallout from the investigation could be immense because of the number of members of Congress involved, including three committee chairmen, and the apparent quality of the evidence.

It seems certain the case will provide new energy to the dormant debate about congressional ethics. The last major scandal involving Congress was the South Korean influencingbuying scheme, which produced major congressional hearings but few criminal charges and little disciplinary action against House members by their peers.

In one case, for example, a videotape shows Murphy discussing with the undercover agents how to help their "Arab" clients get permanent residency if they entered the United States, the sources said. A briefcase containing $50,000 was handed to a Murphy associate after the discussion, they added.

Murphy said through an aide last night that he had "no idea of any [bribery] allegations."

The Camden mayor, Angelo J. Errichetti, was a key figure early in the investigation, sources said.

Staff writers Spencer Rich, Timothy S. Robinson, Chip Brown and Tom Sherwood contributed to this article.

He offered help in getting an Atlantic City casino license for the "Arab." A state gaming commission official was later paid $100,000, the sources added.

An even more central figure was Howard Criden, a Philadelphia lawyer, who was the go-between in transactions involving Reps. Murpy, Thompson, Lederer and Myers, sources said.

Criden, a former assistant district attorney, allegedly told the undercover agents he could introduce them to members of Congress who would help their "Arab" client for cash.

Sources said Crideri was questioned by FBI agents yesterday and began to cooperate, opening the door to confronting the four House members with whom he dealt.

In each case, Criden or the member is alleged to have accepted about $50,000 in cash in return for promises the help the "Arab oil shiek" with any problems he might have entering the United States or settling here.

Jenrette of South Carolina also reportedly was recorded as talking about accepting $50,000 for an immigration bill, and the money was later picked up by an associate, sources said.

Sen. Williams was implicated when he agreed to help in obtaining military contracts for a titanium mine for which he received stock, the sources said.

Sources cautioned that indictments might not result from all the cases.

Thompson said last night that he was questioned by the FBI yesterday, and acknowledged months ago talking to two men in Washington who said they represented an investor with a large amount of money. Criden made the introductions, he said.

Thompson emphatically denied ever taking money for help with legislation. He said he did suggest the names of some New Jersey banks in his district as possible places to invest the money.

Williams, in a statement issued by his office, said, "Nobody from the Department of Justice has talked to me at all about this. In fact, not one soul has talked to me. Honestly, I can say I don't have any comment on this."

The other members of Congress under investigation could not be reached for comment.

A focal point of this investigation was a large house in northwest Washington where the undercover agents entertained some of their congressional guests.

NBC-TV last night showed film it took of the house where the FBI filmed members. Reporter Brian Ross noted that the lights in the house were unusually bright to accommodate the secret FBI videotaping equipment.

More than 100 FBI agents were involved yesterday in trying to reach the members of Congress and others in the case because word of the investigation had begun to leak out to several news organizations.

A federal grand jury in Washington is expected to begin hearing evidence this week, though any move for indictments is considered weeks or months away, sources said.

Sources gave this account of the case: the investigation began in the summer of 1978 when FBI agents set up a "sting" operation in the hope of luring organized crime members to sell stolen government securities and other valuables, starting on Long Island. That investigation, too, has been highly successful, though it has not been publicized yet.

The undercover agents solicited business by letting the underworld sources know they represented "Arab businessmen" with millions of dollars to "invest." The FBI calls the operation AB-SCAM—for Arab scam.

By that fall, associates of some of the members of Congress made contact with the "sting" operation and allegedly began arranging meetings, in Washington and New York, between the undercover agents and the federal officials.

In one videotaped transaction, a member of Congress and his companion are shown fighting over a briefcase full of cash as they leave the room.

On another occasion, another member of Congress flatly refused to take part in the discussion when it turned to money-forlegislation and stalked out of the room.

One source who has viewed some of the tapes said he was "sickened" by the sight of members of Congress nodding in agreement and saying "no problem" when the undercover agents mentioned giving them money for legislative favors.

In a copyrighted story by its Washington bureau chief, Anthony Marro, *Newsday* reported that in one transaction caught on videotape, a member of Congress is seen stuffing greenbacks into his trouser and jacket pockets.

To establish their "covers" as representatives of "rich Arabs," the FBI undercover agents were provided with a large yacht, a condominium at an ocean resort, the house here, and private planes in addition to the hundreds of thousands of dollars in cash, *Newsday* said.

The investigation is being coordinated from New York by Thomas Puccio, head of the Justice Department's organized crime strike force in Brooklyn according to sources. Other prosecuters in New Jersey, Philadelphia, and Florida also are working on the case.

Sources said that middlemen, who claimed they could influence state and federal officials were attracted to the "sting" when they heard of the millions in Arab money.

Thompson said the FBI agents who questioned him yesterday asked him about his association with the attorney, whom he described as "a constituent, as far as I know a reputable person."

He said he met with the lawyer and two Men—who introduced themselves as Weinstein or Weintraub and DeVito—last October at the Foxhall Road area home. The two men, according to Thompson, said they had "some principal with a considerable amount of money he wants to spread around" in investments.

"I suggested names of some banks in New Jersey where he [the attorney] could ask his clients to put money in," Thompson said. "As far as I know, nothing ever happened."

Thompson added that the FBI agents who interviewed him yesterday implied he was under suspicion and left him with the impression he might have been recorded at the meeting.

No one at the Justice Department would make any official comment on the investigation yesterday, but some officials said they were concerned that future defendants in the case would complain about the publicity.

It also is clear, they said, that any defendants would try to say they were entrapped by the undercover agents.

Sources said they were startled by the increasing number of members of Congress who became involved in the investigation as it continued. When word of the "Arab" money circulated, "it was like drawing sharks to blood in the water," one source said.

Some powerful and prominent men in congress are among those said to be involved in the investigation.

Sen. Williams, 60, a Democrat of Bedminnter, N.J., was first elected to the U.S. Senate in 1958 after spending five years in the House. With his 21 years of seniority, his strong labor backing, his reputation as a leading liberal, he has become a power baron.

He is chairman of the Labor and Human Resources Committee, which has jurisdiction over labor law, education and the arts and many of the health and welfare programs that make up the greatest focus of attention for organized labor and liberal groups nationwide.

Since there is no separate subcommittee for labor law matters, Williams as full committee chairman is in effect chairman for labor law, which the full committee handles by itself.

Williams is second-ranking Democrat on the Senate Banking Committee and chairman of the housing and urban affairs subcommittee with enormous influence over the housing industry, the cities and housing for the poor.

Williams' House colleague from New Jersey, Thompson, 61, a Democrat from Trenton, was first elected to Congress in 1954. As secondranking Democrat on the House Education and Labor Committee and chairman of its labor-management relations subcommittee, he has had the same power over labor unions, the same pro-labor and liberal records on labor matters and most other domestic legislation as Williams has in the Senate. Together, the two men are the dominant Democrats on each side of Capitol Hill on labor matters.

Thompson, however, is also chairman of the House Administration committee, a minor-sounding but extremely influential unit which has some of the same housekeeping functions as Senate Rules. Thompson's committee helped write the campaign funding laws and restrictions in the past. Many of the little benefits of office—the staff privileges and rules of operation—are under this committee's jurisdiction. As chairman of Administration, Thompson succeeded former representative Wayne Hays (D-Ohio), who left Congress after a sex scandal.

Murphy has been chairman of the Merchant Marine Committee since 1976.

The 53-year-old representative from Staten Island is a West point graduate who was a staunch supporter of former strongmen Park Chung Hee of South Korea, the shah of Iran and Anastasio Somoza of Nicaragua.

Jenrette, 43, from North Myrtle Beach, was elected in 1974 to the House seat from the 6th District of South Carolina. He was won a reputation as a flamboyant personality. Two years ago, the press reported he held a fund-raiser at his home here, and for $100 a person, gave his guests all the homemade grape wine, liquor and "chicken bog" they could down raising $20,000. Jenrette is a member of the House Appropriations Committee.

Murtha, 47, was elected in 1974 in a special election to fill a seat left vacant by the death of an incumbent. He is a member of the Appropriations and Ethics committees. Murtha was one those named to probe phantom house votes last year. Murtha comes from Johnstown, Pa., was a marine in Vietnam, car wash owner and rated high in voting record compilations put together by labor.

Kelly, 55, of Zephyrhills, Fla., was first elected in 1974 and is a member of the Agriculture and Banking committees. Last year it was reported that while he had made a point in his career of attacking the big spenders in government, he himself had run $11,500 over his office allowance for 1978.

In 1976, he spearheaded an effort to get strikers disqualified from the food stamp program unless they were on it before a strike started. Disney World is in his district. In 1978 his labor rating was zero, his Americans for Democratic Action rating 5 percent, his Americans for Constitutional Action 100 percent.

Lederer, 41, from Philadelphia's Third District, was elected in 1976. He comes from a family long active in city politics. His older brother is a judge, and another brother was once chief of detectives. Lederer, a member of the powerful Ways and Means Committee, was once reported to have ambitions to become chairman of the Democratic committee of the city but his name disappeared from the contenders.

Michael (Ozzie) Myers, 36, was elected in 1976 as Democratic congressman from Philadelphia's First District. Myers, a former longshoreman, pleaded no-contest to one charge of disorderly conduct last April 10 after originally having been charged with assault and battery for allegedly participating in a brawl in a rooftop bar in an Arlington, Va., motel, Myers denied there was any punching and said "we were just doing a little partying… I'm a gentle guy." Myers, who is on the Education and Labor Merchant Marine Committees, reportedly was part of the Frank Rizzo organization when Rizzo was mayor of Philadelphia.

# EX-REP. KELLY, 2 OTHERS GUILTY IN ABSCAM TRIAL

By Laura A. Kiernan, *The Washington Post*, January 27, 1981

Former Florida congressman Richard Kelly and two codefendants were convicted in U.S. District Court here yesterday of conspiracy and bribery charges stemming from the FBI's controversial Abscam undercover "sting" operation.

The jury's verdict closed out the government's prosecution of six House members—of which Kelly was the only Republican—and an assortment of middlemen who were captured on FBI video and audio tapes in an elaborate hoax in which agents posed as front men for fictitious Arab sheiks willing to pay for legislative favors. All the congressmen were convicted of federal criminal charges; only one, Rep. Raymond Lederer (D-Pa.) is still in the House.

The seventh and final Abscam criminal case against a member of Congress is pending against Sen. Harrison A. Williams (D-N.J.), who was indicted last October on bribery and conspiracy charges. All of the Abscam convictions face legal challenges, as attorneys for the defendants contend that their clients were lured into the operation and trapped.

Foreman David W.K. Peacock Jr., wearing a yellow ribbon in his jacket lapel in commemoration of the release of the American hostages, delivered the jury's verdict after about 5 ½ hours of deliberation.

Kelly, 56, a former federal presecutor and state court judge before he was elected to Congress in 1974, stood expressionless, his hands clasped in front of him as the verdict was announced.

Outside the courthouse, Kelly said he was disappointed but not surprised at the verdict. He said he knew he had to live with the public's perception that all politicians "are a notorious group of liars."

But, he aded, "I'm not whining." Asked if he would appeal the verdict, Kelly responded, "The war goes on."

The jury's decision followed a seven-week trial before Chief Judge William B. Bryant during which the government played a videotape that showed Kelly stuffing $25,000 into his pockets during a meeting with an FBI undercover agent at a Washington townhouse in January 1980.

Kelly has maintained that he took the money — which he returned to the government when the Abscam operation became public — as part of his own secret investigation into suspicious characters who he thought had infiltrated his congressional office. Kelly, who was soundly defeated in his bid for reelection in the primary last fall contended that these characters were out to destroy him politically.

A codefendant, New York accountant Stanley Weisz, was shown on tape taking a $50,000 payoff, which he said he regarded as a legal finder's fee for introducing Kelly to the fictitious sheik's representatives. The other codefendant, Robert (Gino) Ciuzio, a Longwood, Fla., businessman, said he took part because he was trying to outwit the sheik's "con men."

Assistant U.S. Attorney Roger M. Adelman called Kelly's defense "a sham" and told the jury that any "honest politician" would have turned aside the bribe immediately. Assistant U.S. Attorney Stephen R. Spivack also represented the government in the case.

Kelly's lawyer, Anthony Battaglia, argued that the government had let "a pack of crooks" loose on Kelly and subjected him to "mind-boggling temptation" to get Kelly to take the bribe. Kelly accepted the $25,000 because he thought it was the only way to get the information he needed for his investigation, Battaglia told the jury.

Commenting after the jury's verdict, Kelly said that he thought that the government during the trial had succeeded in showing that "there were an awful lot of crooks around" who were worth investigating. He said he plans to continue his own investigation and plans to add the government as a target.

Asked by a reporter if he was one of those crooks uncovered during the trial, Kelly responded, "The story of my life has been that I have not been a crook."

Bryant scheduled sentencing for Kelly, Weisz and Ciuzio for Feb. 23. Each faces a maximum of 25 years in jail and more then $40,000 in fines for their convictions of conspiracy and bribery and of a charge of interstate travel in aid of the bribery conspiracy.

## REP. LEDERER RESIGNS SEAT OVER ABSCAM CONVICTION

*The Washington Post*, April 29, 1981

PHILADELPHIA, April 29 (AP)—Rep. Raymond F. Lederer (D-Pa.), the only congressman indicted in the Abscam bribery scandel who won reelection last November, announced today he will resign his house seat Tuesday because of the "time and energy" needed to fight his conviction."

The 42-year-old Lederer, one of six House members convicted of accpeting bribes from FBI agents masquerading as representatives of a fictitious Arab sheik, said in a statement read by his lawyer that his constituents need a full-time representative.

"It is in the best interests of the people of the 3rd District for me to resign my seat," Lederer's attorney, James Binns, quoted him as saying.

"This was a difficult decision for me because I believe that the mandate the voters gave me in November is something that must be taken seriously. On the other hand, those same voters have the right to a congressman who can devote his full energies to their service."

Lederer's resignation, submitted in letters delivered this morning to house Speaker Thomas P. (Tip) O'Neill Jr., Chairman Louis Stokes of the House ethics committee and Pennsylvania Gov. Richard L. Thornburgh, followed by a day the 10-to-2 recommendation by the ethics panel that the third-term congressman be expelled.

Last year, another Philadelphia Democrat, Michael Myers, became the first congressman to be thrown out of the House since Civil War days. Myers, like Lederer, was convicted of accepting $50,000 from an undercover FBI agent in exchange for official favors.

# IDAHO CONGRESSMAN IS CONVICTED OF HIDING FINANCIAL TRANSACTIONS

*New York Times*, April 3, 1984

AP

Representative George Hansen was found guilty today of failing to report $333,978 in personal loans and other transactions on financial disclosure documents.

A jury in Federal District Court here deliberated for three-and-a-half hours before finding the Idaho Republican guilty of four counts of filing false disclosure documents.

Mr. Hansen, 53 years old, is the first elected public official to be charged with violating the Ethics in Government Act of 1978. Under the law, virtually all major Government officials are required to disclose annually their financial holdings, liabilities and transactions, including gifts, loans and profits for themselves and members of their immediate families. Each count carries a maximum penalty of five years' imprisonment and a $10,000 fine.

The Congressman said he was disappointed by the verdict and would appeal it, saying Government prosecutors "made a lot of smokescreen that obscured the facts for the jury."

## Defense Has 30 Days

"A man has a right to rely on the law," said Mr. Hansen, who contended that he was not required to report the omitted information. "It is a sad commentary where the District of Columbia is trying to decide who should represent the people of a state two thousand miles away."

Judge Joyce Hens Green said she would not set a date for sentencing until after the defense filed motions for a judgment of acquittal and a new trial. She gave defense attorneys until April 30 to file their motions.

Nathan Lewin, chief lawyer for the seven-term Congressman, said the charges were a result of "personal ambition," apparently a reference to the prosecutor in the case, and were based on "absolutely nothing."

Mr. Lewin's main argument was that Mr. Hansen omitted certain loans and transactions from his financial disclosure forms for 1978 through 1981 because his lawyers advised him to do so.

Three of the counts against Mr. Hansen charged that he failed to report loans and transactions made in the name of his wife, Connie Hansen, with the help of the Texas oilman Nelson Bunker Hunt. The fourth count said he did not report three loans from three men in southern Virginia.

## Legal Advice an Issue

Mr. Lewin said the Congressman's lawyers told him he did not have to report his wife's financial transactions because the couple had signed a property separation agreement and she was an independent individual. The other loans were not reported, the lawyer said, because the funds went to the Association of Concerned Taxpayers, a nonprofit organization Mr. Hansen founded, and not to him personally.

"The question is not whether it is right or wrong," Mr. Lewin said of the advice, "but whether he relied on it. Even if the lawyers were wrong, he was entitled to rely on it."

Mr. Weingarten said Mr. Hansen did not report the transactions because he did not want to disclose them to other Congressmen, voters in Idaho, the press, the general public and law.

"Congressman Hansen calls himself a populist," he told the jury. "How would it look to the people in Idaho if it were disclosed that this populist was getting money from a Texas oilman and some men in Virginia, none of whom were his constituents?"

# HOUSE PANEL ASKS REPRIMAND OF IDAHO LAWMAKER

By Steven V. Roberts, *New York Times*, June 21, 1984

The House Committee on Standards of Official Conduct recommended today that the House reprimand Representative George Hansen for failing to disclose complete details of his complicated financial affairs.

In an unusual public hearing before the vote, the Idaho Republican vehemently denied the charges and said, "If you can tell me I covered up anything, I'll eat your hat."

Mr. Hansen was convicted by a Federal District Court in April on four felony charges relating to his financial records. Specifically, he was charged with failing to file information on four transactions as required under the Ethics in Government Act. Mr. Hansen was the first person prosecuted for failing to comply with the act, which was enacted in 1978.

Earlier this month the lawmaker was sentenced to serve 5 to 15 months in jail and pay a $40,000 fine. His case is now on appeal, but he has relinquished his right to vote on the House floor since the conviction was handed down.

Under House rules, a "reprimand" is justified by a "serious" violation of ethical standards. It is not as serious as a censure, which requires the member to stand in the well of the House while the judgment against him is read by the Speaker. Only 19 Congressmen have ever been censured, and only four have been expelled.

A reprimand involves no loss of pay or privileges, and the Congressman is not required to be present when the judgment is read.

The special counsels to the Committee on Standards of Official Conduct, Stanley M. Brand and Abbe David Lowell, had suggested that a $10,000 fine also be imposed on Mr. Hansen, but the committee rejected that.

## Renominated to 8th Term

Mr. Hansen, who won renomination last month to an eighth term, had urged the committee to vote no penalty, or simply report his violation to the House without additional comment.

Mr. Hansen's tangled financial dealings began in 1977, when he devised a way to raise money from the public to help pay off his debts. When House experts said the plan was inappropriate, he transferred the debts to his wife, who then pursued various ways of raising money.

The four financial transactions that Mr. Hansen did not disclose mainly related to his wife's debt-reduction efforts. He contends that he was advised not to reveal them by his attorneys, but the special counsel argued that the requirements for disclosure were clear.

In an emotional appeal to the committee, Mr. Hansen said he was being penalized for his attempts to do an honorable thing and meet his debts. Others, he said, including Presidential candidates, do not pay off their debts in full and are not subject to the same kind of treatment.

"It is no fun," he said, "trying to be responsible in the irresponsible atmosphere of the nation's capital."

He suggested that the special counsel to the committee was motivated by politics and a desire to help his Democratic opponent this fall. The committee, headed by Representative Louis Stokes, an Ohio Democrat, is composed of six members from each party.

Frustrated and angry, Mr. Hansen shouted at one point: "I should have robbed a bank. I would have had the money, and not as big a penalty as for screwing up a Government form."

The Idaho Republican warned that now that he has been successfully prosecuted for such an act, other members of Congress could now be vulnerable to similar charges. "Who is going to be next?" he asked the committee.

# HOUSE REPRIMANDS IDAHO REPUBLICAN IN FINANCIAL DISCLOSURE CASE

By Steven V. Roberts, *New York Times*, August 1, 1984

The House of Representatives voted overwhelmingly today to reprimand Representative George Hansen, an Idaho Republican, for failing to comply with Federal law that requires public officials to disclose their financial holdings.

Mr. Hansen has been convicted of four felony counts in the matter.

The vote on the reprimand was 354 to 52, with six representatives voting "present." Ten Democrats joined 42 Republicans in opposing the recommendation of the Committee on Standards of Official Conduct, usually known as the ethics committee.

In defending himself today, Representative Hansen charged that he was not the only official "who has a problem" with the disclosure law. Among those who have not fully complied, he said, is Representative Geraldine A. Ferraro of New York, the Democratic candidate for Vice President. Lott Says Questions Remain

Representative Trent Lott of Mississippi, the Republican whip, said later that there were still "unanswered questions" about Mrs. Ferraro's financial dealings. If the Democratic candidate does not answer them promptly, he added, Republicans might ask for an investigation by the ethics committee.

In her six years in Congress, Mrs. Ferraro has always completed her financial disclosure forms, but she has not included information about her husband, John A. Zaccaro, a New York real estate broker. It was the failure to include her husband's activities that raised questions, Mr. Lott said.

A spokesman in Mrs. Ferraro's office here said she would make a complete disclosure of her financial picture in the next two weeks.

The key distinction between the Hansen and Ferraro cases lies in the requirements of the Ethics in Government Act of 1978. That statute says that a public official is exempt from having to disclose any financial asset of a spouse as long as the official does not control that asset or derive any benefit from it.

## Their Responses Different

When signing the disclosure form required by the law, the official is asked whether he or she is withholding information about assets that fall under the exemption rule. Mr. Hansen said he was not withholding information, even though his wife was involved in tangled transactions designed to help the Hansens out of debt.

In the judgment of the jury that tried Mr. Hansen, and of the ethics committee that studied his case, he did derive a benefit from his wife's dealings and should have disclosed them.

In contrast, Mrs. Ferraro said she was withholding information about the financial activities of her husband.

In comparing the Hansen and Ferraro cases, Representative Nick J. Rahall of West Virginia, a Democrat who serves on the Ethics Committee, said, "It's the difference between disclosing, and trying to hide something."

However, Mr. Lott says that even though Mrs. Ferraro claimed an exemption, she might not have been entitled to one. The Mississippi Republican pointed out that to qualify for the exemption, she could not have derived any benefit from her husband's activities.

## 'Hard to Believe,' He Says

"I find it hard to believe," he said, that Mrs. Ferraro received no benefits.

Under Federal election law, Mrs. Ferraro is required to disclose her financial assets within a month after her nomination. She said in a recent statement that this disclosure would include information about her husband because the couple had decided that it was "in the public interest to do so."

Representative Hansen was the first public official prosecuted under the Ethics in Government Act, although a Federal judge in Nevada was subsequently indicted under it. Mr. Hansen has been renominated by Idaho Republicans for an eighth term but faces tough opposition in November.

Mr. Hansen is the fifth Congressman in history to receive a reprimand, the mildest penalty the House could have administered. Twenty-three others have been censured and four expelled.

In laying out the case against Mr. Hansen, Representative Louis Stokes of Ohio charged that his colleague had deliberately hidden data about his complex financial dealings with Nelson Bunker Hunt, the Texas oil man, and a group of Virginia businessmen. "He simply didn't want these transactions known," said Mr. Stokes, who heads the ethics panel.

Mr. Hansen argued he was not trying to hide anything and did not report his wife's activities because she was "absolutely independent of me."

"I view myself as a victim of a horrendously unfair process," he said.

# WRIGHT TO RESIGN SPEAKER'S POST, HOUSE SEAT

By Tom Kenworthy, *The Washington Post*, June 1, 1989

## Texan Again Rebuts Charges, Decries Conflict Over Ethics

House Speaker Jim Wright (D-Tex.), portraying himself as the victim of an ethics feeding frenzy, said yesterday that he will resign his office and congressional seat as "total payment for the anger and hostility" that has accompanied a yearlong investigation into his personal finances.

"I don't want to be a party to tearing up the institution; I love it," Wright told his House colleagues in an emotional farewell speech that climaxed a 51-week investigation into his finances and extraordinary drama that has transfixed Congress for months.

Wright, who has represented his Fort Worth district for 34 years, said he will relinquish the speaker's gavel upon the election of his successor Tuesday and that he will give up his congressional seat before the end of this month. His almost certain successor, Majority Leader Thomas S. Foley (D-Wash.), presided during the dramatic, hour-long resignation speech.

Wright will be the fourth House speaker in history to resign, but the first to be forced from office under an ethical cloud.

The 66-year-old Texan faced almost certain conviction by the House on charges that he broke House rules in his financial dealings. His resignation had come to seem inevitable in recent weeks. It came after the House ethics committee charged him with repeated violations of House rules, as new charges of wrongdoing surfaced in the news media and as other members of his party came under ethical attack.

Referring to this heated atmosphere over ethics charges that has consumed and paralyzed the House this year, Wright emotionally urged his colleagues to "bring this mindless cannibalism to an end."

Democrats and most Republicans—many of the Republicans at first with apparent reluctance—gave Wright a standing ovation at that point, a graphic demonstration of the House's weariness with the turmoil of the Wright affair and its bewildering entry into a new era of ethical standards in which few understand the shifting ground rules.

Wright announced his resignation at the end of the speech, portraying the action as a sacrifice he is making to spare the House and its members further political and personal agony. Wright characterized his resignation as "a propitiation," a seldom used word that means a gesture that appeases a deity.

"Let me give you back this job you gave to me as a propitiation for all of this season of bad will that has grown up among us," he said.

Foley, the House's second-ranking Democratic leader, is expected to be nominated Tuesday as the new speaker by the House Democratic Caucus without opposition. The full House is expected to ratify that decision in a party-line vote later that day.

Elections to fill Foley's office and the third-ranking whip's position—becoming vacant June 15 through the announced resignation of Rep. Tony Coelho (D-Calif.) in the face of questions about his financial dealings—will follow.

The Democrats' wholesale leadership changes—Rep. David R. Obey (D-Wis.) called it a generational shift that is bringing a "reform generation" to power—come just 2½ years after the team of Wright, Foley, and Coelho took control of the House and pushed through a thoroughly Democratic legislative program in the waning years of the Reagan era.

Although Wright had been bitterly criticized even within his party in recent weeks for prolonging the House's agony, Democrats and Republicans alike largely put such thoughts aside yesterday and praised his exit.

"It was a testament to his character," said Rep. Jack Brooks (D-Tex.), one of Wright's most vociferous defenders.

"He's going out on as high a note as possible," said Rep. Vin Weber (R-Minn.), a frequent critic. "No one likes to see a man who's given his life in service to his country go down this way."

During a speech largely devoted to a point-by-point defense against the charges leveled against him by the 12-man ethics committee on April 17, Wright made a plea that Republicans and Democrats strike a truce in the escalating warfare over alleged ethical violations and return to addressing the nation's problems.

"Let us not to try to get even with each other," said Wright, alluding to the vows of some in his party that they will exact retribution on Wright's principal accuser, Minority Whip Newt Gingrich (R-Ga.). "We ought to be more mature than that. Let's restore to this institution the rightful priorities of what is good for this country."

But it was clear that it will take more than a personal plea from a departing speaker to persuade embittered members of both parties to put away their long knives.

"There's an evil wind blowing in the halls of Congress today that's reminiscent of the Spanish inquisition," said Brooks, a crusty Texan who doesn't take even mild slights with equanimity. "We've replaced comity and compassion with hatred and malice."

Brooks, in a broadside at the news media, said Wright had been "lynched by leaks... Fleet Street never had so much competition for the most unfounded headline."

In his speech, Wright also proposed sweeping changes in the way the House regulates the behavior of its members, including creation of a House counsel to offer advice and splitting the ethics panel into separate investigative and trial bodies.

The speaker also asked that the current ethics committee, formally known as the Committee on Standards of Official Conduct, rule on pending motions by his attorneys to dismiss the most serious charges against him. "I think it is important for the motions to be ruled upon, and I earnestly hope the committee will look at it from that standpoint and grant our motions," Wright said.

That contained echoes of attempts last week by attorneys for Wright and the ethics committee to negotiate an orderly withdrawal by the speaker in exchange for the dropping of charges that Wright broke House rules by accepting $145,000 in what it termed "gifts" from his Fort Worth business partner, George A. Mallick. That was a particular concern to Wright because the charges involved his wife, Betty, whom the ethics committee's special counsel characterized as a conduit for the gifts in the form of an $18,000-a-year salary and use of a car and condominium apartment.

The ethics committee had been scheduled to rule on those motions today, but now will not meet until next Thursday, after Wright's resignation.

There was no immediate indication what the committee will do with those charges, but prior to Wright's speech there were seven solid votes against the speaker's motions to dismiss.

That was conveyed to Wright's lawyers last week. According to one knowledgeable Democrat, the speaker made up his mind at that point to resign his position.

"He had no choice," said the lawmaker.

"I think there was a raging debate, but it was all in his own mind," said Rep. Robert G. Torricelli (D-N.J.), one of Wright's legal advisors. "He had a deep desire to establish his own integrity, but he also recognized the institution needed this final act of service."

Although Wright proclaimed his innocence throughout yesterday's speech before a packed House chamber and a gallery audience that included his wife, he also acknowledged errors of judgment.

"Have I made mistakes—oh boy how many?" Wright said. "Mistake in judgment. I'll make some more."

During the speech ending his political career, Wright also made an emotional defense of his hiring of John P. Mack, a convicted felon who rose to become the highest-ranking members of the speaker's staff. Mack recently resigned following publication in *The Washington Post* of a graphic account of a savage beating he inflicted on a young woman 16 years ago that sparked a public uproar that had a dramatic impact on Wright's political fortunes.

"I do not think it is bad judgment to try to give a young man a second chance," Wright said.

But Wright conceded that during his 29 months as speaker he might have been "too partisan," "too insistent" and "too abrasive."

"If I have offended anybody in the other party, I am sorry," he said.

Proclaiming his love for the House, Wright said that he would never "knowingly or intentionally do or say anything to violate its rules or detract from its standards."

Rep. Henry J. Hyde (Ill.) was among the Republicans who spoke of ending the partisan attacks. "I hope his advice that we stop turning this place into Beirut and run this like a Congress will be adopted by all sides," he told CBS News.

"Frankly, if the Republican Party was in control of the House for 35 years, the shoe might be on the other foot," said Republican National Committee Chairman Lee Atwater.

Former House speaker Thomas P. "Tip" O'Neill (D-Mass.) said that if the attacks on those with political power continue, "You'll have nothing but the imbecilic sons and daughters of wealthy families who want to send their children to Congress... "

Wright's decision to resign came amid increasing evidence that the ethics committee had run out of patience and preparing to force his hand. The committee was fully prepared, said some members, to continue investigating two issues not addressed in its original charges of April 17: a controversial oil and gas deal that netted Wright a quick $170,000 profit last year, and a failed $100,000 investment in a nursing home operation during which Wright appeared to receive more favorable treatment than other investors before the company went bankrupt.

The committee's resolve may have tipped the balance for Wright, who had been getting conflicting advice from what was dubbed his "war party" and his "peace party." Some of Wright's attorneys, including Stephen D. Susman of Houston and Democratic elder Clark M. Clifford of Washington, as well as Wright's wife, were reported to be urging him to press on with the fight, forcing the issue to a vote by the full House.

Others, however, argued to Wright that he must face the inevitable, that his situation was untenable and that he should resign in the interest of the House he reveres. Their argument was bolstered by the sudden resignation announcement Friday of Coelho, who said he wanted to spare the House another tortuous ethics probe involving a $100,000 "junk bond" purchase.

"What's the point of getting humiliated?" asked one Wright advisor yesterday morning as he reported that the speaker was wavering. "They [ethics committee members] are going to line him up like that guy in Saigon with a gun to his head who ended up with his picture in *Life* magazine."

# SENATE REMOVES HASTINGS

By Ruth Marcus, *The Washington Post*, October 21, 1989

## U.S. Judge Convicted Of Extortion Plan, Despite Jury Acquittal

U.S. District Judge Alcee L. Hastings was convicted by the Senate yesterday of engaging in a "corrupt conspiracy" to extort a $150,000 bribe in a case before him, marking the first time a federal official has been impeached and removed from office for a crime he had been acquitted of by a jury.

In a solemn and tense session, the Senate voted 69 to 26—five votes more than needed for conviction—to find Hastings guilty of the major charge against him and strip the 53-year-old jurist of his lifetime, $89,500-a-year position.

Hastings, Florida's first black federal trial judge, sat facing the senators as the lawmakers rose, one by one, to render their verdicts on the charge that he conspired with disbarred Washington lawyer William A. Borders Jr. to obtain the bribe.

The outcome of the proceedings—eight years after Hastings was first accused and five years after a jury found him not guilty—was unclear until nearly the end of the roll call. Both the chairman, Sen. Jeff Bingaman (D-N.M.), and the vice chairman, Sen. Arlen Specter (R-Pa.), of the 12-member panel that heard the evidence in the case voted for acquittal. The 12 members of the panel voted 7 to 5 for conviction.

When he left the Senate after the vote on the second article of impeachment, Hastings, besieged by reporters on the Capitol steps, said, "I have no choice but to accept their judgment." But, he said, "I'm in thorough disagreement with their decision and that's all."

He said his conviction violates the constitutional prohibition against double jeopardy. And he criticized the process under which only 12 of the 100 senators heard the witnesses against him. Hastings also announced his plans to open a private law practice and to run as a Democratic candidate for governor of Florida next year.

"My momma had a man," Hastings, who was named to the bench by President Jimmy Carter in 1979, said of his plans to remain in the public eye. "She did not have anybody that was afraid of the system."

The Senate, in two hours of roll calls, voted on 11 of the 17 articles of impeachment. It convicted Hastings of eight of the 11 articles, finding that he engaged in the bribery conspiracy and repeatedly lied under oath at his trial and forged letters in order to win acquittal.

Hastings was acquitted on one of the perjury charges and an umbrella count that accused him of "bringing disrepute on the federal courts" through his actions. He was unanimously cleared, by 95 to 0, of a separate charge of leaking confidential information from a wiretap that he had authorized as a judge. The Senate did not vote on six of the 17 articles because it had already decided to remove Hastings from office.

Four senators did not vote yesterday because they were members of the House when it voted 413 to 3 in August 1988 to impeach Hastings. Sen. Pete Wilson (R-Calif.) was not present. Under the Constitution, conviction required the votes of two-thirds of the senators present, or at least 64 in this case.

Shortly after noon yesterday, Senate President Pro Tempore Robert C. Byrd (D-W.Va.) announced the result. With Hastings convicted of eight high crimes and misdemeanors, Byrd said, "it is therefore ordered and adjudged that said Alcee J. Hastings be and he is hereby removed from office."

The vote on Hastings did not break down along ideological, regional, or other identifiable lines.

The 26 senators—21 Democrats and five Republicans—who voted to acquit him of the major charge included some of the Senate's most conservative members—William L. Armstrong (R-Colo.) and Orrin G. Hatch (R-Utah)—and some of its most liberal—Howard M. Metzenbaum (D-Ohio) and Alan Cranston (D-Calif.).

Sen. Warren B. Rudman (R-N.H.), a former prosecutor on the trial committee, voted for conviction and Specter, another former prosecutor on the panel, voted to acquit.

Hastings is the sixth federal official, all judges, impeached by the House and removed from office after conviction by the Senate. The case proved a particularly anguishing decision for the senators, who deliberated behind closed doors for 7½ hours Thursday, because of the circumstantial nature of the evidence, the earlier jury verdict to acquit and the charges of racism.

In an eloquent plea for acquittal on the floor Wednesday, Hastings said that he did not think race was a factor in the case, and Rep. John Conyers Jr. (D-Mich.), a member of the House prosecution team, agreed. However, a number of Hastings supporters have cast the case in those terms.

The Senate found that Hastings had arranged with Borders, his close friend and a prominent Washington lawyer, to solicit a bribe from an FBI undercover agent posing as one of two brothers who were defendants in a racketeering case before Hastings. In return for $150,000—$25,000 of which was given to Borders as a down payment—Hastings was to sentence the Romano brothers to probation rather than prison and to return $845,000 in forfeited property.

There was circumstantial evidence that Hastings was part of the scheme, including a pattern of telephone calls between Hastings and Borders at key junctures in the Roman case, Borders' successful promise to an FBI agent to have Hastings turn up for dinner at the Fontainbleau Hotel at a specified time and a key, cryptic telephone conversation between Borders and Hastings that prosecutors contended was a coded discussions of the bribe arrangements.

But Hastings' lawyers argued that these actions, while seemingly suspicious, had other, innocuous explanations, and portrayed Hastings as the innocent victim of a scam perpetrated by Borders. There was no direct evidence of Hastings' participation in the conspiracy because the Federal Bureau of Investigation arrested Borders before money could be traced to Hastings.

Borders, who was convicted of the bribery conspiracy charges in a separate trial in 1982, refused to testify—despite a grant of immunity—before the grand jury or the House and Senate panels. He was jailed on contempt charges from Aug. 22 until yesterday for refusing to testify before the Senate committee.

Some senators said after the verdict that they found the evidence insufficient and were troubled by the earlier jury acquittal, while others took the opposite view. Senators could choose whatever standard of proof—beyond a reasonable doubt, clear and convincing, or another measure—they deemed appropriate.

"The facts simply led me to the inference that Judge Hastings quite clearly was involved in a scheme with Bill Borders," said Sen. Slade Gorton (R-Wash.), a member of the trial panel.

But committee Chairman Bingaman said that "the evidence, although furnishing grounds for investigation and trial, does not provide a sound basis upon which I can vote for conviction."

## GORE SAYS HE DID NOTHING ILLEGAL IN SOLICITING FROM WHITE HOUSE

By Alison Mitchell, *New York Times*, March 4, 1997

Vice President Al Gore acknowledged today that "on a few occasions" he had made telephone calls from his White House office seeking Democratic campaign contributions. Insisting he had not done "anything wrong, much less illegal," he said he would nevertheless refrain from making such solicitations in the future.

Mr. Gore answered questions about his aggressive fund-raising role in the last Presidential race in a rare solo appearance in the White House briefing room, one in which he was making his own case instead of playing his usual role of promoting President Clinton's initiatives.

"I am proud of what I did," Mr. Gore said. "I do not feel like I did anything wrong, much less illegal. I am proud to have done everything I possibly could to help support the re-election of this President and to help move his agenda forward. It is helping this country."

The Vice President spoke calmly and remained cool under questioning after a weekend in which news reports that he had made phone calls for campaign contributions in 1995 and 1996 drew criticism even from some Democrats.

The reports at least temporarily complicated Mr. Gore's unannounced campaign for his party's Presidential nomination in 2000.

Mr. Gore said the Vice President, like the President, is exempt from the Federal Hatch Act, which makes it illegal for most other Federal officials to raise money for campaigns. And he used legalistic language, which he repeated verbatim several times, to say he had not violated another law that prohibits anybody from raising campaign money in the White House.

"My counsel advises me that there is no controlling legal authority or case that says there was any violation of law whatsoever," Mr. Gore said.

Ever since their re-election, President Clinton and Mr. Gore have come under increasing scrutiny for carrying out an aggressive fund-raising campaign of unprecedented scope in 1995 and 1996, using all the perquisites of incumbency to woo donors. The Democratic Party has also returned more than $3 million in contributions because the sources were thought to be either questionable or unlawful. Today for the first time, the Clinton-Gore re-election campaign announced that it had refunded six campaign contributions of from $200 to $1,000 from five individuals deemed to be "inappropriate contributors."

The scrutiny of the Democrats has turned both on the legality of some of the donations they received and on the seemliness of Mr. Clinton's use of his incumbency to raise money.

Documents turned over to Congressional investigators last week showed that Mr. Clinton approved a plan under which the Democratic Party rewarded some top donors and fund-raisers with coffees, meals, golf outings and jogs with the President and overnight stays in the White House.

As Vice President, Mr. Gore not only played the traditional role of attending numerous fund-raising dinners and receptions across the nation, but he also personally worked the phones for campaign cash in some instances. Until now, he had turned down requests for interviews about his role.

At his news conference, Mr. Gore said that the "vast majority" of the campaign money he raised had come from conventional fund-raising events that featured him as a speaker. But he said that "on a few occasions," in December of 1995 and the spring of 1996, he had telephoned potential contributors from his White House office to seek campaign contributions. He said he had billed the calls to a credit card issued by the Democratic National Committee.

On another occasion in 1994, Mr. Gore said, he went to the Democratic National Committee's offices to make fund-raising calls.

Mr. Gore said that President Clinton had never asked him to make any fund-raising calls and that he had not been aware that the President himself refused to make such calls. But the Vice President sidestepped questions about how much money he had sought in such solicitations or how potential donors had been singled out for his attention.

Mr. Gore insisted that he had done nothing to make those he telephoned feel that they were being forced to give. "I never ever said or did anything that would have given rise to a feeling like that on the part of someone who was asked to support our campaign," he said. "I never did that, and I never would do that." Nor, the Vice President said, had he ever asked any Federal employee or anyone who was on Federal property for a donation.

Mr. Gore, a former Senator from Tennessee whose father was also a Senator, has long had a reputation for integrity. He was clearly working to make sure today that the ongoing scrutiny about the Democrats' 1996 fund raising did nothing to tarnish his image in 2000, when he is expected to seek the Presidency himself.

Even though he said he was proud of his role in the campaign, Mr. Gore said he was ruling out further fund-raising calls "because it's aroused a great deal of concern and comment."

Mr. Gore refused to discuss any Presidential ambitions. "I've made no decision about that whatsoever," he said.

In his defense of his phone calls and insistence that they raised no legal issue, Mr. Gore referred today to a statute that makes it unlawful for "any person to solicit or receive any contribution" "in any room or building occupied in the discharge of official duties," such as the offices in the White House.

The statute, Section 607 of Title 18 of the United States Code, has its roots in an 1876 law intended to discourage "political assessments": the collection from Government employees of part of their salary to support the incumbent party. The statute carries a maximum penalty of $5,000 and three years' imprisonment.

Unlike the Hatch Act, Section 607 makes no exceptions for any officials—including the President or Vice President. And on its face, it is broadly worded, seeming to apply to any official who asks for a donation.

But the law has rarely been enforced. Legal experts said that it was debatable whether the law applied to Mr. Gore's calls because it was originally enacted as part of legislation intended to prevent Federal officials from soliciting money from other officials or from people doing business with the Government.

An earlier version of the provision was last interpreted by the Justice Department in 1979, when the department was deciding whether to begin an investigation of the Carter Administration for a White House luncheon where political contributions were solicited.

That inquiry was closed when the department decided that because the luncheon had been in the Family Dining Room of the White House, it was not covered by the law. But the 1979 opinion also made clear that "areas routinely used in connection with the discharge of official duties," such as the Vice resident's office, would come under the statute. The 1979 opinion did not resolve the question of whether the law is violated when the person being solicited is not a Federal officer or employee.

# SENATORS ENDORSE CAMPAIGN INQUIRY WITH WIDER SCOPE

By Eric Schmitt, *New York Times*, March 12, 1997

In an abrupt change of course, the Senate today unanimously approved a much broader investigation into White House and Congressional campaign fund-raising practices than most Senate Republicans had originally wanted.

Under pressure from Democrats and facing rebellious moderate Republicans, Senator Trent Lott of Mississippi, the Senate Republican leader, bowed to demands to expand the inquiry to include "illegal and improper activities" in the 1996 elections. The Senate Rules Committee voted along party lines last week for a plan, brokered by Mr. Lott, that would have limited the inquiry's scope to "illegal activities" only.

The change may seem like a minor distinction. But today's vote will allow Senate investigators to examine some of the most criticized legal fund-raising practices, like unregulated "soft money" contributions, the fund-raising coffees and sleep overs that President Clinton held at the White House and unrestricted political spending by tax-exempt groups.

"We didn't want the scope so narrow as to look like we were protecting ourselves or trying not to embarrass ourselves," said Senator Fred Thompson, Republican of Tennessee. He heads the Governmental Affairs Committee, which is leading the main Senate inquiry.

The committee has already issued 52 subpoenas, and it will set a schedule for hearings soon.

The Senate vote today restores the scope to the broader form that Mr. Thompson's committee approved last month, before a handful of Republicans on the Rules Committee vowed to water it down. Mr. Lott negotiated the scaled-back plan, and Mr. Thompson went along reluctantly, viewing it as the only one that could pass.

But that was also before some of the most jarring fund-raising accusations surfaced. Several senators said today that the seemingly daily disclosures of questionable fund-raising practices, whether Vice President Al Gore's soliciting contributions from his White House office or reports that China sought to buy influence in the 1996 elections, exposed the limits of an inquiry that scrutinized only illegal activities.

"There'll be an argument over what will be legal and what will be illegal," Senator Arlen Specter, Republican of Pennsylvania, said.

Indeed, Mr. Thompson had told Senate colleagues recently that he feared Democrats would deliberately tie up hearings with time-consuming procedural questions over what was legal and what was not. That would steal precious time from the actual business of investigating, Republicans said.

"One of the most important things you get out of this is comity with the Democrats," said Senator John McCain, Republican of Arizona, who is a sponsor of legislation to revamp the campaign finance process.

---

The turning point came today at a spirited two-hour lunch that Senate Republicans held in a private caucus room. At least eight senators, including Mr. Thompson and Mr. McCain, urged their colleagues to broaden investigators' jurisdiction—enough to deny Mr. Lott the votes he needed to approve the narrower inquiry.

"There are a number of allegations that may or may not be illegal, but they may be improper," Senator Susan Collins, Republican of Maine, said after the lunch meeting.

Senator Sam Brownback, Republican of Kansas, said the expanded inquiry "goes to the integrity of the process at this point—is the process trustworthy?"

The deal-making moved to the Senate floor after lunch. In an extraordinary scene, a knot of Democratic and Republican senators huddled privately on the Senate floor for more than 30 minutes. Mr. Lott and Senator Carl Levin, Democrat of Michigan, seemed to lead the negotiations, along with Mr. Thompson.

In an indication of where the talks were heading, two of the most outspoken Republican opponents of expanding the scope, Senator Mitch McConnell of Kentucky and Senator Rick Santorum of Pennsylvania, stood outside the huddle, looking glum. The Democrats were smiling.

Before and after the vote to expand the scope, Senate critics sought to put the best face on the situation. "I think it's fine," Mr. McConnell said tersely on his way to vote.

Mr. Santorum said, "Obviously, I preferred the other one, but I'm voting for this."

Only Senator Christopher Dodd, Democrat of Connecticut, declined to go along with the plan, citing his two years as general chairman of the Democratic National Committee, which has figured prominently in the fund-raising furor. In the end, he voted "present," in effect abstaining.

Republicans said the broader definition will empower investigators to delve into the hundreds of fund-raising coffees and sleepovers that President Clinton and his top aides held for large donors at the White House.

"We're getting what we can all live with to get the job done," Mr. Lott said.

He denied that moderate Republicans had broken ranks and dealt him a personal rebuke, and he said it was more important to get the investigation under way and "quit fiddling while Washington burns."

Under the compromise worked out in the Rules Committee, the inquiry will have a $4.35 million budget, scaled back from Mr. Thompson's original request of $6.5 million.

In a bow to Democrats, the plan calls for the inquiry to be completed by Dec. 31, as opposed to the open-ended investigation that Mr. Thompson had wanted. The committee will have until Jan. 31, 1998, to finish its report.

As part of the bargaining on the Senate floor, Democrats won pledges from Mr. Thompson to insure that the Governmental Affairs Committee uses fair procedures.

Mr. Levin demanded and received assurances of bipartisan access to documents, bipartisan notice to take witness statements and bipartisan consideration of subpoenas.

Although most Republicans argue that correcting the system of campaign financing is enough, Senate Democrats expressed optimism that an expanded inquiry will find serious flaws needing legislative remedies.

"We believe this will allow us to show that current campaign finance laws are inadequate," said Senator Tom Daschle of South Dakota, the Senate Democratic leader.

# HOUSE VOTES, WITH LONE DISSENT FROM CONDIT, TO EXPEL TRAFICANT FROM RANKS

By Alison Mitchell, *New York Times*, July 25, 2002

In a near unanimous vote, a grim and subdued House tonight expelled Representative James A. Traficant Jr. a maverick Ohio Democrat who was convicted in April on 10 counts of bribery, racketeering and corruption.

In the end, after nine terms in the House, Mr. Traficant, 61, could barely muster any support and was removed from office by a vote of 420 to 1, with 9 lawmakers voting present. It was only the second time since the Civil War and fifth time in its 213-year history that the House chose to impose the ultimate penalty for unethical conduct and strip a member of office.

The lone lawmaker voting against Mr. Traficant's expulsion was Representative Gary A. Condit, Democrat of California, who was defeated in a primary after he became known for a relationship with a missing intern, Chandra Ann Levy, whose remains were recently found in a Washington park.

Known for his bombastic, sometimes erratic, one-minute speeches on the House floor, Mr. Traficant had promised the performance of his life when the House moved against him.

"When I walk on the floor for the final execution I'll wear a denim suit," he proclaimed recently, "I'll walk in there like Willie Nelson, John Wayne, Will Smith, 'Men in Black,' James Brown. Maybe do a Michael Jackson moon walk."

In fact, Mr. Traficant showed up in a dark jacket and tie, not the denim he had threatened. While for the most part he kept his mordant humor in check, he did joke that he styled his unruly gray hair with a weed whacker.

Expecting quite a show, House staff members started lining up for seats in the gallery a full two hours before the evening debate. Speaker J. Dennis Hastert took the rostrum as the debate opened, and firmly reminded the chamber that rules prohibit use of abusive, "profane, vulgar or obscene" language.

For all his threats to be unruly, Mr. Traficant was subdued, arguing in a rambling defense that one of the witnesses against him had "lied through his teeth" and that the government had been out to get him and had pressured witnesses to turn on him. "I'll go to jail," he thundered, waving his arms. "But I'll be damned that I'll be pressured by a government that pressured these witnesses to death."

---

**Correction:** August 3, 2002, Saturday An article on July 25 about the expulsion of James A. Traficant Jr. from the House misstated a word in a comment from Representative Kenny Hulshof, Republican of Missouri, who reminded his colleagues that in recent years they had reprimanded the House speaker, Newt Gingrich, and had voted to impeach President Bill Clinton. He said, "Here we are again tonight with the lens of history trained upon us"—not "the winds of history."

With a crack of the gavel, the presiding officer told him to avoid profane language. After this rebuke, Mr. Traficant went on to repeat his frequent accusation that former Attorney General Janet Reno was a traitor, and he attacked the Democratic Party.

"Vote your conscience," he finally said. "Nothing personal."

Lawmakers from the House ethics committee, Republicans and Democrats alike, argued that his conduct had been egregious and that he had brought disgrace upon the House.

Representative Howard L. Berman of California, the ranking Democrat on the ethics committee, said that to believe Mr. Traficant's assertion that he was a victim of a government vendetta, "you would have to accept the gentleman's notion of a vast unparalleled conspiracy" that involved "the office of the U.S. attorney, the I.R.S., the F.B.I. and a respected U.S. district judge."

Representative Kenny Hulshof, Republican of Missouri, reminded many of his colleagues that in recent, turbulent years they had reprimanded a speaker, Newt Gingrich, and voted to impeach a president, Bill Clinton.

"Here we are again tonight with the winds of history trained upon us," Mr. Hulshof said. "I believe that tonight will be one of this institution's finest hours."

One of Mr. Traficant's colleagues in the Ohio delegation, Representative Steven C. LaTourette, a Republican and former prosecutor, made a last plea for the House to delay its decision until September, after Mr. Traficant's expected sentencing next week and after courts could hear some of his legal motions seeking a new trial and other relief.

Mr. LaTourette, an ethics committee member who had joined other committee members in calling for Mr. Traficant's expulsion, warned his colleagues that otherwise the decision they would make would be "the political death penalty."

"You can't put the toothpaste back in the tube," he said.

The request for delay won an unexpectedly large amount of support, mostly from Republicans, but was defeated, 146 to 285. Mr. Traficant himself voted for delay.

Other members of the ethics committee said the House's task was sad but had to go ahead.

"Tonight is the night that we need to do this business," said Representative Joel Hefley, the low-key Colorado Republican who is chairman of the House ethics committee. "This is no rush to judgment."

Only rarely does the House take the grave step of expelling someone, a sanction that requires a two-thirds vote. Three representatives were voted out in 1861 on charges of treason at the start of the Civil War. A fourth, Michael J. Myers, Democrat of Pennsylvania, was expelled after he was caught on videotape accepting a bribe from the F.B.I. in a sting operation, known as Abscam, in which agents posed as Arab sheiks.

Other disgraced lawmakers had done what Mr. Traficant refused to do and resigned before the House could expel them.

The House action brought Mr. Traficant's flamboyant political career full-circle. When he was a local sheriff in 1982, the government accused him of taking bribes from mobsters, having caught him on tape. Acting as his own lawyer, Mr. Traficant convinced a jury that he had been running a sting operation. Riding a wave of publicity, he was elected to Congress in 1984.

When he was indicted again last year, he argued that the Justice Department had a vendetta against him because he had beat the government and because he had been sharply critical of Attorney General Reno.

But this time a jury convicted him after a two-month trial on charges that he had run his Congressional office as a racketeering enterprise, seeking bribes from business executives for government favors and demanding salary kickbacks and manual labor from his staff.

A former Congressional employee testified that Mr. Traficant had demanded half his salary, $2,500 a month, as a kickback for being hired. Other staff members told of long hours of having to work with pitchforks in barns on Mr. Traficant's family farm. The congressman insisted the witnesses against him were lying under government pressure or immunity agreements.

This evening he repeated the rants against the government that had led tourists to seek his autograph during breaks in his ethics hearing last week and prompted callers to C-Span to speak out in his defense.

But his fellow lawmakers were clearly weary of his theatrics. For three hours the House was unusually packed and silent except for the speakers. Four senior Republican leaders sat side by side near the front watching. Representative Richard A. Gephardt, the minority leader, refused to attend the session. His aides said he was watching it on television at home. He returned to vote for Mr. Traficant's expulsion.

As Mr. Traficant's legal problems mounted in recent years, he became increasingly estranged from his own party, which backed a primary challenger against him. He crossed party lines to vote for Mr. Hastert, an Illinois Republican, for speaker, a vote that made him a pariah in the Democratic caucus and left him without any committee assignments.

On Tuesday, Republican leaders briefly debated whether to delay Mr. Traficant's expulsion until after the August recess. But Democrats said that they would force the House to take the expulsion vote this week if the Republicans tried to delay.

Mr. Traficant's district was cut apart in redistricting, but he still plans to seek re-election, threatening to serve in office from prison.

"I'm running as an independent," he told his colleagues. "Don't be surprised if I win behind bars."

## OPERATION OPEN DOORS

*The Washington Post*, December 3, 2004

When his name surfaced in connection with the Senate Indian Affairs Committee investigation of lobbyists Jack Abramoff and Michael Scanlon, Rep. Robert W. Ney (R-Ohio) presented himself as another victim of the rapacious duo, who collected $66 million from casino-operating Indian tribes that sought their help to stay in business. Like the tribes, Mr. Ney said, he was duped by Mr. Abramoff when the lobbyist sought his help in getting a tribal casino reopened.

Maybe so. But Mr. Ney also pocketed large campaign contributions from the Tigua tribe of El Paso—contributions steered his way by Mr. Abramoff—and then pushed the tribe's cause in Congress. And he continued to embrace that cause well beyond the time he claims to have lost interest.

According to e-mails uncovered by Sen. John McCain (R-Ariz.), Mr. Abramoff enlisted Mr. Ney in the Tigua cause in March 2002. Mr. Ney was the lead House sponsor of a pending election reform bill, and the plan was to slip a casino-reopening provision into that unrelated measure. "Just met with Ney!!! We're f'ing gold!!!! He's going to do Tigua," Mr. Abramoff e-mailed Mr. Scanlon on March 20. Six days later Mr. Abramoff told the tribe it needed to come up with contributions for the congressman.

The tribe anted up, becoming by far Mr. Ney's biggest contributor that election cycle. It gave $3,000 to his campaign committee ($2,000 more than permitted at the time), $5,000 to his leadership political action committee and $25,000 to the PAC's "soft money" arm, which was set up just in time to take the Tiguas' check. The soft-money PAC was established on April 30, 2002, the day after the Tiguas' $5,000 check was deposited in the federal PAC, and the $25,000 from the tribe was, other than a lone $1,000 donation, the only contribution the soft-money arm received. Meanwhile, the two lobbyists contributed $5,500 to Mr. Ney's campaign and PAC, and other tribes they represented gave $9,000. Total take: $47,500.

In addition, the week that Mr. Ney's involvement in the Tigua matter was revealed at a Senate hearing, his campaign belatedly amended its campaign finance reports for 2002 and 2003 to reflect in-kind contributions for events at MCI Center, where Mr. Abramoff had a box. The contributions, which totaled $1,470, came from Neil Volz, a former top Ney staffer who had gone to work with Mr. Abramoff at his law firm. Did the money talk? Mr. Ney acknowledges that he raised the Tigua issue with Sen. Christopher J. Dodd (D-Conn.), who was leading the election reform bill in the Senate. Mr. Ney says he acted because Mr. Abramoff had assured him that Mr. Dodd wanted the provision in the bill. When Mr. Dodd said he knew nothing of it, Mr. Ney says he felt betrayed and dropped the issue. "The matter was then closed from my perspective," Mr. Ney said in a statement.

If so, why, the following month, did Mr. Ney meet with Tigua representatives in his Capitol office, pledging to help them, according to those who attended, and heaping praise on Mr. Abramoff? "So he was giving you assurances that he was on board, he was working to solve this problem for you?" Sen. Byron L. Dorgan (D-N.D.) asked Marc Schwartz, a Tigua consultant, at a Senate Indian Affairs Committee hearing last month. "Absolutely," Mr. Schwartz replied.

Meanwhile, Mr. Ney's staff continued to try to get the provision inserted in the election reform bill, according to a statement from Mr. Dodd. Ney staff members approached his office "during the waning hours of negotiations over the ... legislation to inquire whether recognition provisions for the Tigua tribe could be included in the bill," the statement says. "The suggestion was summarily rejected." After the measure passed without the Tigua provision, Mr. Ney held a conference call with the tribal council. According to Mr. Schwartz, he "told them about his disbelief that Senator Dodd had gone back on his word. He further reported that he would continue to work on the issue and believed that the tribe was entitled to their gaming operation."

Mr. Ney's spokesman, Brian Walsh, says that Mr. Ney has a different recollection of his conversations with the tribe and that his support for their provision had nothing to do with the contributions. "Not at any point ever was the issue of any donations brought up," he said. But what explains Mr. Ney's devotion to the Tigua cause? The tribe isn't from Mr. Ney's state, let alone his district. The committees he sits on have nothing to do with the subject. (In fact, he chairs the committee that oversees campaign finance laws.) Early on, Messrs. Abramoff and Scanlon told the Tigua that they would have to pay $300,000 in campaign contributions to underwrite what the lobbyists called "Operation Open Doors." At least in Mr. Ney's case the operation may have been a success.

# BRAZEN CONSPIRACY

*The Washington Post*, November 29, 2005

Yesterday's guilty plea by Rep. Randy "Duke" Cunningham—make that former representative, since he resigned after entering the plea—reveals the most brazen bribery conspiracy in modern congressional history. A San Diego Republican and Vietnam War veteran who served on the House Appropriations defense subcommittee and the intelligence committee, Mr. Cunningham admitted taking $2.4 million in bribes from two defense contractors angling for government contracts and from two other co-conspirators.

The bribes are breathtaking in their scope, audacity and sheer greed: Payments for Mr. Cunningham's yacht and his Rolls Royce. Silver candelabras. A leather sofa. Two Laser Shot shooting simulators for $9,200. A graduation party for the congressman's daughter (for only $2,000).

Mr. Cunningham not only sold his Del Mar, Calif., home to a defense contractor at an inflated price of $1.5 million; he then jacked up the price an additional $175,000, hid the defense contractor's participation by removing his name from the sales agreement, took a $115,100 check to cover the capital gains taxes and had the defense contractor pick up $11,000 in moving fees. Then the two defense contractors paid more than $1 million toward the mortgage on Mr. Cunningham's new home.

The defense contractors and other conspirators aren't named in court papers, but one of them is apparently Mitchell J. Wade of D.C.-based MZM Inc. Though MZM was created in 1993, its business didn't begin to take off until about 2002—after Mr. Cunningham started taking the bribes. Since then, it has received $163 million in government contracts since 2002 for vaguely worded intelligence programs.

The court papers filed in the case, jaw-dropping as they are, don't address a critical question: How could this happen? To some extent, it's hard to guard against out-and-out corruption and criminality by someone bent on breaking the law; as the court papers describe it, the congressman and his co-conspirators worked to "conceal and disguise" their activities "by directing payments through multi-layered transactions involving corporate entities and bank accounts." Mr. Cunningham also lied on his financial disclosure forms and filed false tax returns.

But there are also indications that the system failed. Mr. Cunningham's ability to pull off this caper was helped by the fact that lawmakers don't need to list their homes or mortgage debt on financial disclosure forms; such a listing might have provided an earlier clue to the wrongdoing. More fundamentally, the papers say that Mr. Cunningham used his influence in the congressional appropriations process to benefit the contractors and "took other official action to pressure and influence" Defense Department personnel to give contracts to his co-conspirators. This case ought to spur an overhaul of the congressional appropriations process, which has become infected with the kind of earmarks that breed corruption. The Pentagon, in its turn, may need to strengthen its processes to withstand the pressure of an influential congressional appropriator.

---

# ABRAMOFF PLEADS GUILTY TO 3 COUNTS; LOBBYIST TO TESTIFY ABOUT LAWMAKERS IN CORRUPTION PROBE

By Susan Schmidt and James V. Grimaldi, *The Washington Post*, January 4, 2006

Jack Abramoff, the once-powerful lobbyist at the center of a wide-ranging public corruption investigation, pleaded guilty yesterday to fraud, tax evasion and conspiracy to bribe public officials in a deal that requires him to provide evidence about members of Congress.

The plea deal could have enormous legal and political consequences for the lawmakers on whom Abramoff lavished luxury trips, skybox fundraisers, campaign contributions, jobs for their spouses, and meals at Signatures, the lobbyist's upscale restaurant.

In court papers, prosecutors refer to only one congressman: Rep. Robert W. Ney (R-Ohio). But Abramoff, who built a political alliance with House Republicans, including former majority leader Tom DeLay of Texas, has agreed to provide information and testimony about half a dozen House and Senate members, officials familiar with the inquiry said. He also is to provide evidence about congressional staffers, Interior Department workers and other executive branch officials, and other lobbyists.

"The corruption scheme with Mr. Abramoff is very extensive," Alice S. Fisher, head of the Justice Department's criminal division, said at a news conference with other high-ranking officials of the Internal Revenue Service and the FBI. "We're going to follow this wherever it goes."

Fisher declined to identify the officials under scrutiny. "We name people in indictments," she said, adding: "We are moving very quickly."

Among the allegations in the court documents is that Abramoff arranged for payments totaling $50,000 for the wife of an unnamed congressional staffer in return for the staffer's help in killing an Internet gambling measure. The Washington Post has previously reported that Tony Rudy, a former top aide to DeLay, worked with Abramoff to kill such a bill in 2000 before going to work for Abramoff.

Abramoff's appearance in U.S. District Court came nearly two years after his lobbying practices gained public notice because of the enormous payments—eventually tallied at $82 million—that he and a public relations partner received from casino-rich Indian tribes. Yesterday, he admitted defrauding four of those tribal clients out of millions of dollars. He also pleaded guilty to evading taxes, to conspiring to bribe lawmakers, and to conspiring to induce former Capitol Hill staffers to violate the one-year ban on lobbying their former bosses.

Under terms of his plea agreement, Abramoff can expect to receive a jail sentence of 9 1/2 to 11 years, and he is required to make restitution of $26.7 million to the IRS and to the Indian tribes he defrauded. Today he is to plead guilty to fraud and conspiracy counts in a related case in Florida involving his purchase of a casino cruise line.

Standing before U.S. District Judge Ellen Segal Huvelle in Washington yesterday, Abramoff looked sheepish and sad. "Your Honor, words will not be able to ever express how sorry I am for this, and I have profound regret and sorrow for the multitude of mistakes and harm I have caused," he said softly. "All of my remaining days, I will feel tremendous sadness and regret for my conduct and for what I have done. I only hope that I can merit forgiveness from the Almighty and from those I have wronged or caused to suffer."

Abramoff has been in extensive discussions with government lawyers for months leading up to yesterday's plea.

Ney, chairman of the House Administration Committee, is among the first of those expected to feel the fallout. In the court documents—which identify him only as "Representative #1"—Ney is accused of meeting with one of Abramoff's clients in Russia in 2003 to "influence the process for obtaining a [U.S.] visa" for one of the client's relatives and of agreeing to aid a California tribe represented by Abramoff on tax and post office issues.

Ney also placed comments in the Congressional Record backing Abramoff's efforts to gain control of the Florida gambling company, SunCruz Casinos, and offered legislative language sought by Abramoff that would have reopened a Texas tribe's shuttered casino.

The court papers said Ney advanced the prospects of an Abramoff client, a telecommunications company that won a contract to wire the House.

Two of Abramoff's former partners have already pleaded guilty and have promised to cooperate in the ongoing investigation of congressional corruption and are prepared to testify against Ney in connection with his aid in the SunCruz purchase. Prosecutors in Florida and Washington are in discussions about where a case against Ney should be brought, officials said.

Ney reiterated yesterday that he had done nothing wrong and said he was misled by Abramoff.

One of Abramoff's former associates, Michael Scanlon, a onetime press aide to DeLay, was a secret partner in Abramoff's Indian tribal scheme. Abramoff not only charged the tribes lobbying fees but also urged them to hire Scanlon's public relations firm at hugely inflated prices. Scanlon, in turn, kicked back half of the money to Abramoff, who was thus able to conceal the funds from public disclosure and even from the lobbyist's law firm.

They spread tribal money around and sought legislative favors in return. Abramoff and Scanlon "offered and provided a stream of things of value to public officials in exchange for official acts and influence and agreements to provide official action and influence," a statement of facts attached to the plea agreement said. "These things of value included, but are not limited to, foreign and domestic travel, golf fees, frequent meals, entertainment, election support for candidates for government office, employment for relatives of officials and campaign contributions."

Among the things of interest to investigators are payments made by Abramoff and his colleagues to the wives of some lawmakers and actions taken by Rudy and other senior Capitol Hill aides, some of whom went to work for Abramoff at the law firm Greenberg Traurig LLP, lawyers and others familiar with the probe said.

Another person under scrutiny, sources said, is DeLay, who is facing separate campaign finance charges in his home state of Texas.

"Tom DeLay is not concerned that Mr. Abramoff is cooperating," said Richard Cullen, his attorney. "He urges everyone involved to cooperate in the investigation and to tell the truth." Cullen had no comment on allegations involving former DeLay aides Rudy and Scanlon.

Among the trips under scrutiny is a golf excursion to Scotland that DeLay and aides took with Abramoff in 2000 and a similar trip Ney took two years later.

DeLay has taken three overseas trips with Abramoff since 1997—to the Mariana Islands, Russia and Scotland—and received more than $70,000 from Abramoff, his associates and tribal clients for his campaign committees.

Investigating DeLay, who is facing campaign finance charges in Texas, could take up to a year and require the cooperation of other witnesses before issues surrounding the Texas Republican are resolved, according to people familiar with the case.

Sen. Conrad Burns (R-Mont.), Rep. John T. Doolittle (R-Calif.) and other legislators involved with Indian issues are among those being investigated, sources said.

A spokesman for Doolittle, whose wife received payments from Abramoff's lobbying firm, has previously said there was no connection with her husband's work. Burns's office has said his actions on behalf of Abramoff's tribal clients were in sync with his support for improving the lot of Indian tribes.

Also of interest to prosecutors is former deputy interior secretary J. Steven Griles, who held the job from 2001 to 2004. He has said he never tried to intercede on behalf of Abramoff's clients, but e-mails released by a Senate committee show more than half a dozen contacts Griles had with Abramoff or with a woman working as the lobbyist's go-between.

Prosecutors are continuing to investigate two of DeLay's top former deputies, Rudy and Edwin A. Buckham. Rudy is under investigation for assistance he allegedly provided Abramoff's lobbying clients while he was working for DeLay. Payments from Abramoff clients and associates to Liberty Consulting—a political firm founded by Rudy's wife, Lisa—are also under review by the Justice Department. Rudy did not return calls seeking comment yesterday.

Abramoff maintained a business relationship with Buckham, who runs the Alexander Strategy Group with Rudy. Among the areas of interest to prosecutors is client business directed to the Alexander Strategy Group when the firm was hiring the spouses of members of Congress, including DeLay's wife, Christine.

Christine DeLay was paid about $115,000 over three years while performing a special project—contacting members of Congress to find out their favorite charity, according to her attorney.

Fisher, offering the Justice Department's first public comments on an inquiry that began in spring 2004, said that the Abramoff case is "very active and ongoing." She said the department is committed to making sure that people know "government is not for sale."

# THE SORRY STATE OF ILLINOIS

By Dennis Byrne, *Chicago Tribune*, April 23, 2006

Why was there even mild surprise last week when a jury convicted former Illinois Gov. George Ryan of corruption? When Illinois juries get their hands on a governor, they tend to put him away.

Of our seven prior governors, three now have been convicted. In Illinois, jurors are batting .750. So, give jurors a chance and they'll take down corrupt governors. Which makes me wonder about any bewilderment that this jury convicted Ryan on all counts. Look at history: just three governors before Republican Ryan was Democrat Dan Walker, who served 17 months for fraudulently obtaining bank loans. But that was after he left office, so maybe he doesn't count; the governorship was only training camp.

Five years before Walker was Democrat Otto Kerner who was convicted in 1973 on charges of bribery, conspiracy, mail fraud, tax evasion and perjury. He was paroled after serving a year. Immediately before him was Republican William Stratton, who was indicted for federal tax evasion. He was acquitted. Not to worry; while the governor's suite at the federal pen is unoccupied, other top state officers often keep it warm.

Has any other Illinois office harbored such a high proportion of serial offenders? (Chicago aldermen, maybe, but doing the math gives me a headache.) In the face of such gubernatorial recidivism, you'd think that at least a few Illinois politicians might recognize the dangers and run the other way. How to explain such recklessness?

I think I know one reason, but obviously not the only reason. Once elected to high office, their lordships begin sharing the same rarified air that the rich and powerful heads of the town's big national and international corporations breathe. It's a long way from the humble work of hustling votes by ringing doorbells or holding someone's fedora. On MRI brain scans, it shows up as metastasizing clumps of self-importance. Governors, mayors, agency chairmen, department heads and even aldermen all display the symptoms. It makes them feel untouchable.

In fact, their egos are tolerated, if not cultivated, by the corporate power structure. It never hurts to have a few gofers who can change a law, ease a regulation or smooth over certain misunderstandings. Pols don't get it; they're grubby street urchins who are allowed into the ball to serve hors d'oeuvres.

But the corporate community also has large quantities of things that the Ryans and Daleys desperately want: power, access to money, endorsement, legitimization, to name a few. In this game of favor doing, the business leadership holds the high cards.

So, the corporate denizens are just the people to put the corrupt pols in their place. 'George, we're running global businesses bigger than yours; don't hand us the same crap you give the voters about your pure heart and clean hands. We and this town can't take it any more. Cut it out, or we'll cut you out.' 'Richie, your joke about not knowing about all the graft going on right under your nose makes us laugh. If we were running our businesses the way you run City Hall, we'd be out on our butts. Or, on trial, like those guys from Enron. You're through.'

Instead, this town's corporate leadership gathers in well-upholstered clubs, patting themselves on their backs for their 'civic involvement' with various booster projects. Or they issue studies telling us what the Chicago area ought to look like in 2020. They jabber on by 'decaying infrastructure' and pony up millions for lakefront parks. And gratify themselves with their roles as community leaders whose names appear on the letterheads of visible do-gooder groups.

But get their hands dirty to clean up the swill—our state's most pressing problem—and where are they? Yes, they support such efforts as the Better Government Association and the Chicago Crime Commission, which carry on the fight, with quixotic-like determination. But the unwavering silence of the corporate suites about the costly and destructive system of graft inescapably suggests acquiescence, approval or even complicity.

This is meant to be a broad brush and harsh attack; it wouldn't be necessary if Chicago's and Illinois' business community were united in shutting down career criminals like George Ryan and some in Mayor Daley's inner circle. I don't mean that we should turn government over to a corporate junta. But the 12 honest jurors who convict the likes of Ryan sure could use some help.

# GOV. BLAGOJEVICH AND OPERATION BOARD GAMES: 'IT'S "PAY-TO-PLAY... ON STEROIDS"

Gov in spotlight as feds indict top fund-raiser in shakedown scheme

By Natasha Korecki, Chris Fusco, Dave McKinney, Steve Warmbir, *The Chicago Sun-Times*, October 12, 2006

A member of Gov. Blagojevich's inner circle was hit with wide-ranging public corruption charges Wednesday, and now the feds want to know what the governor knew about his friend's actions.

The 24-count indictment against Antoin "Tony" Rezko, a top fund-raiser for Blagojevich and a former business associate of the governor's wife, outlines a "pay-to-play scheme on steroids," U.S. Attorney Patrick Fitzgerald said.

Rezko, 51, is accused of trying to collect nearly $6 million in kickbacks from government deals and trying to shake down a Hollywood producer for $1.5 million in campaign contributions to Blagojevich.

Sources said the feds are looking closely at the alleged shakedown, first reported by the *Chicago Sun-Times* last month, and whether Blagojevich knew Rezko was trying to extort cash for the governor.

Investigators also have found strong relationships between the Rezko and Blagojevich families and continue to investigate their dealings, sources close to the investigation said. Illinois first lady Patti Blagojevich made nearly $39,000 off real estate deals involving Rezko, she disclosed on 2004 tax forms.

Blagojevich told the *Sun-Times* on Wednesday night he was shocked by the indictment and would feel "a tremendous sense of personal betrayal" if the allegations are proven.

"I pray that this isn't true," Blagojevich said. "I pray that he didn't do these things."

Blagojevich said he never authorized any shakedown, hasn't engaged in pay-to-play politics and that the indictment "had absolutely nothing to do with Patti's real estate business."

Lawyers for Rezko called the indictment "sensational" and said it "contains no specifics as to how any money benefited Mr. Rezko."

But Fitzgerald said there was a "feeding frenzy" by Rezko and associates, including Teachers' Retirement System board member Stuart Levine, who was indicted on corruption charges last year and is expected to plead guilty later this month.

"The amounts of money that were being shaken down in one... eight-week span was in the millions," Fitzgerald said. But Rezko and Levine collected only about $250,000 because federal investigators tripped up their plans.

Chicago FBI chief Robert Grant called those named in the indictment "parasites that have plagued our public institutions."

---

Rezko and others allegedly demanded the kickbacks under the guise of consulting fees from companies seeking business with TRS. Levine was able to control TRS business by working with Rezko to have two other people appointed by the governor who would vote with Levine, Fitzgerald said.

Two other political insiders allegedly were part of one of the schemes: to shake down Capri/Capital Advisors and Hollywood producer Tom Rosenberg, who co-owned the firm until recently.

### 'Individual A,' 'Individual B'

One is Christopher G. Kelly, a close Blagojevich friend and top fund-raiser. The second is Springfield powerbroker William Cellini, a Republican who has helped direct $86,000 in campaign cash to the Democratic governor and whose family's firm has secured $340 million in pension business under Blagojevich.

Cellini and Kelly were identified as "Individual A" and "Individual B" in the indictment, but sources confirmed their identities.

Rosenberg's firm was slated to get a $220 million deal from TRS in February 2004, but Levine helped stall approval, according to the indictment. Three months later, Capri and Rosenberg allegedly were told to cough up $2 million to a financial consultant of Rezko's and Levine's choosing or arrange for $1.5 million to be contributed "to a certain public official."

That official is Blagojevich, sources said.

On May 8, 2004, Rosenberg told Cellini "he would not be extorted," the indictment says. Two days later, Rezko, Levine, Cellini and Kelly agreed that "it was too risky to continue demanding money from [Capri]."

Rosenberg's firm ended up getting the TRS deal on May 25, 2004, and no contributions to Blagojevich's campaign were made.

Many of the allegations against Rezko are based on what the feds have gathered from Levine, who began cooperating with them early this year. Rezko, who also was charged Wednesday with swindling General Electric Capital Corp. out of $10.5 million in loans to a pizza restaurant business is to appear in court Friday, but the feds said they're not sure where he is. If he doesn't appear, prosecutors said he may be considered a fugitive.

Authorities have been tracking Rezko's movements and knew he checked out of a hotel in the Middle East last week and paid in cash.

Some investigators said they feared Rezko wouldn't return to the country because he's in substantial debt, sources said. The indictment was returned last week but kept under seal in anticipation of his return this weekend.

On Wednesday, Rezko's lawyers said efforts were under way to get him back to the United States. FBI agents were still looking for him. They visited Rezko's North Shore home Wednesday afternoon with an arrest warrant.

# HONORABLE EXPLANATION? CHOOSE ONE

By James Gill, *The Times-Picayune* (New Orleans), June 6, 2007

Congressman William Jefferson, D-New Orleans, has so far been too modest to reveal the "honorable explanation" he promised for the behavior that has finally led to his indictment.

Some cynics say there can be none, pointing out that the feds taped his shakedowns and found marked moolah in his freezer. Several former associates have agreed to testify against him and there is abundant documentary evidence of dirty deals on two continents.

What can Jefferson possibly say to get out of this jam? Here are a few possibilities.

Honorable Explanation 1:

"I was just trying to help the poor people of Africa by bringing them the benefits of high-speed telecommunications. Unfortunately, Nigeria has a reputation as the most corrupt country in Africa, and I could do nothing for the masses without winning the confidence of high-ranking public officials.

"I wanted to make them think I was a man they could trust, so I posed as a congressman on the take. Distasteful though this was, I had no other way to achieve my ends. As you can see, I sure had everyone fooled. They thought I fit right in."

Honorable Explanation 2:

"One of the great constitutional questions of recent years has been whether the legislative branch has ceded too much power to the Bush administration.

"As a keen student of constitutional law, I was eager to obtain a definitive ruling regarding the separation of powers. After much careful thought, I hit on the idea of precipitating an FBI raid on my congressional office. I lured the feds in by pretending to use my official powers for personal gain.

"It was not easy, since never in the history of the republic have the G-Men rifled through the official papers of a sitting congressman. But the hoax worked, and my reward was to see the courts wrestling with the speech and debate clause, as I had always hoped they would. I acted out of patriotism, pure and simple."

Honorable Explanation 3:

"I was conducting my own investigation. Frankly, I had long entertained doubts about my aide, Brent Pfeffer, and businessman Vernon Jackson, a businessman looking to flog telecommunications gizmos to Africa.

"Unfortunately, they figured out I was on their tail before I had a chance to expose them. Now they have confessed and gone to prison, which is where they belong.

"They have falsely fingered me as some kind of criminal mastermind, but who you gonna believe—a couple of felons or good old Dollar Bill?

"During my investigation Lori Mody, who was proposing to invest in technology projects, took the bait when I suggested bribing the Nigerian vice president. I was horrified at her willingness to break the law, but did not let on.

"I took custody of a briefcase full of cash without, of course, any intention of making the drop. My only concern was to preserve the evidence, so I made sure it was not exposed to the summer heat. I planned to turn the money over to the FBI later, but it slipped my mind and was still there when agents raided my house.

"I can see how that might create an unfortunate impression, but what's a little embarrassment when the integrity of public life is at stake?"

Honorable Explanation 4:

"This is the best of them all. I'll tell you what it is as soon as you make a hefty deposit in my family's bank account, hire one of my daughters and give me a 10 percent stake in your company."

# MR ROWLAND'S RETURN

*Hartford Courant*, January 24, 2008

We have to swallow hard to accept Waterbury Mayor Michael Jarjura's choice of convicted former Gov. John G. Rowland as the city's economic development coordinator. But Mr. Rowland has served his time, the city needs a financial boost and Mr. Rowland has expertise in revitalizing urban centers.

He has done penance for taking more than $100,000 in gifts and services from people doing business with his administration. After he was forced to resign, Mr. Rowland served 10 months in a federal prison, then traveled about the state giving lectures and interviews on the arrogance of power, in which he took responsibility for his crimes.

Society owes former felons a second chance to prove that they have been rehabilitated. Mr. Rowland is no exception.

As an ex-governor who, despite his illegalities, did much to revitalize Connecticut's cities, Mr. Rowland appears qualified to be his hometown's economic development coordinator, a job in which he is expected to attract new businesses and help existing ones expand. The relationships he developed while in office could prove helpful to the city. He is now painfully aware of the boundaries between public and private benefit and should be trusted to observe them.

Waterbury's Regional Chamber of Commerce, which will pay a share of Mr. Rowland's salary, has endorsed his appointment.

The job does carry liabilities. Mr. Rowland's administration set the standard for political corruption in Connecticut. He will be scrutinized for signs that he has returned to his old unethical ways.

Mr. Rowland has a second chance. We hope he uses it wisely and well.

# U.S. DEPARTMENT OF JUSTICE NEWS RELEASE ON THE CONVICTION OF FORMER ALABAMA GOVERNOR DON SIEGELMAN, JUNE 29, 2006

*June 29, 2006*

## Former Alabama Governor Don Siegelman, Former HealthSouth CEO Richard Scrushy Convicted of Bribery, Conspiracy and Fraud

WASHINGTON—A jury in Montgomery, Ala. convicted former Alabama Governor Don Eugene Siegelman and former HealthSouth Chief Executive Officer Richard Scrushy of conspiracy, bribery and fraud, Assistant Attorney General Alice S. Fisher for the Criminal Division and Acting U.S. Attorney Louis V. Franklin, Sr. of the Middle District of Alabama announced today.

Siegelman, 60, was convicted on seven of the 33 counts against him: one count of bribery, one count of conspiracy to commit honest services mail fraud, four counts of honest services mail fraud and one count of obstruction of justice. Siegelman was acquitted on charges of racketeering, honest services wire fraud, extortion, obstruction of justice, and 16 counts of honest services mail fraud. Scrushy, 53, was convicted on all of the six counts with which he was charged: one count of bribery, one count of conspiracy to commit honest services mail fraud, and four counts of honest services mail fraud. Siegelman's former Chief of Staff Paul Hamrick and his former Highway Director Gary "Mac" Roberts were acquitted on all charges.

Maximum penalties for the charges are as follows: conspiracy to commit honest services mail fraud, 5 years in prison; bribery, 10 years in prison and a $250,000 fine; honest services mail fraud, 20 years in prison and a $250,000 fine; obstruction of justice, 10 years in prison.

"With today's verdict, this jury sends the message that Americans will not tolerate the bribery of our public officials. Bribery of this sort—between a sitting governor and a corporate chief executive officer—has a devastating impact on public confidence in our government," said Assistant Attorney General Fisher. "The Justice Department will continue to aggressively investigate and prosecute corrupt public officials and those who conspire to corrupt them."

Siegelman was convicted of mail fraud arising from a pay-for-play scheme in which he exchanged official acts and influence for cash, property, and services from Alabama businessman and consultant Clayton "Lanny" Young. The jury found that Siegelman took thousands of dollars in bribes from Young to aid Young's business interests, including the awarding of contracts to companies controlled by Young. The jury also found Siegelman and Scrushy guilty of crimes arising from a bribery scheme in which Scrushy paid Siegelman $500,000 in laundered funds to obtain a seat on a state regulatory board governing HealthSouth.

"We know the jury worked hard to decide this case and we are pleased with their verdict," said Acting U.S. Attorney Franklin. "Their verdict today sends a clear message that the integrity of Alabama's government is not for sale."

The case was prosecuted by Acting U.S. Attorney for the Middle District of Alabama Louis V. Franklin, Sr., and Assistant U.S. Attorneys Stephen P. Feaga and J.B. Perrine, Middle District of Alabama; Trial Attorney Richard Pilger of the Public Integrity Section of the Criminal Division; and Assistant Attorneys General Joseph Fitzpatrick and Jenny Garrett for the State of Alabama.

The investigation was conducted jointly by the Federal Bureau of Investigation, agents from the Alabama Attorney General's Office, and the U.S. Department of Transportation's Office of Inspector General.

# APPENDIX ONE

## Cases of Expulsion, Censure, and Condemnation in the U.S. House of Representatives and U.S. Senate, 1798–Present

Under Article I, Section 5 of the United States Constitution, each house of Congress may determine the rules of its proceedings and set the rules for punishing members as it sees fit—and whether to reprimand, condemn, censure, or, in the most egregious examples, expel a member. Since 1789 the House has expelled only four men (three of these for supporting the Confederacy), and the Senate has expelled fifteen men, fourteen of whom were charged with supporting the Confederacy. Thus, despite a history of many members being accused of corrupt acts, only two have been formally removed because of political corruption: Representatives Michael J. "Ozzie" Myers (D-PA), implicated in the famed ABSCAM scandal, and James A. Traficant (D-OH), who was convicted of several crimes relating to corruption. In the Senate, only four members in total have been convicted in a courtroom of criminal acts: Republicans Joseph R. Burton (1905), John H. Mitchell (1905), and Truman H. Newberry (1920), and Democrat Harrison Williams (1981). Newberry resigned, but his conviction was later overturned; Mitchell died before he could be expelled from the Senate, and Burton and Williams resigned before they, too, could be expelled.

### Cases of Expulsion in the House

| Year | Member | Grounds | Disposition |
|------|--------|---------|-------------|
| 1798 | Matthew Lyon (AF–Vermont) | Assault on another representative | Not expelled |
| 1798 | Roger Griswold (F–Connecticut) | Assault on another representative | Not expelled |
| 1799 | Matthew Lyon (AF–Vermont) | Sedition | Not expelled |
| 1838 | William J. Graves (W–Kentucky) | Killing of another representative in a duel | Not expelled |
| 1839 | Alexander Duncan (W–Ohio) | Offensive publication | Not expelled |
| 1856 | Preston S. Brooks (SRD–S.C.) | Assault on U.S. senator[1] | Not expelled |
| 1857 | Orsamus B. Matteson (W–New York) | Corruption | Not expelled |
| 1857 | William A. Gilbert (W–New York) | Corruption | Not expelled |
| 1857 | William W. Welch (Am–Connecticut) | Corruption | Not expelled |
| 1857 | Francis S. Edwards (Am–New York) | Corruption | Not expelled |
| 1858 | Orsamus B. Matteson (W–New York) | Corruption | Not expelled |
| 1861 | John B. Clark (D–Missouri) | Support of rebellion | Expelled |
| 1861 | Henry C. Burnett (D–Kentucky) | Support of rebellion | Expelled |
| 1861 | John W. Reid (D–Missouri) | Support of rebellion | Expelled |
| 1864 | Alexander Long (D–Ohio) | Treasonable utterance | Not expelled[2] |
| 1864 | Benjamin G. Harris (D–Maryland) | Treasonable utterance | Not expelled[2] |
| 1866 | Lovell H. Rousseau (R–Kentucky) | Assault on another representative | Not expelled[2] |
| 1870 | Benjamin F. Whittemore (R–South Carolina) | Corruption | Not expelled[2] |
|  | Roderick R. Butler (R–Tennessee) | Corruption | Not expelled[2] |
| 1873 | Oakes Ames (R–Massachusetts) | Corruption | Not expelled[2] |
| 1873 | James Brooks (D–New York) | Corruption | Not expelled[2] |
| 1875 | John Y. Brown (D–Kentucky) | Insult to representative | Not expelled[2] |
| 1875 | William S. King (R–Minnesota) | Corruption | Not expelled |

*(continues)*

## Cases of Expulsion in the House (continued)

| Year | Member | Grounds | Disposition |
|---|---|---|---|
| 1875 | John D. Schumaker (D–New York) | Corruption | Not expelled |
| 1884 | William P. Kellogg (R–Louisiana) | Corruption | Not expelled |
| 1921 | Thomas R. Blanton (D–Texas) | Abuse of Leave to Print | Not expelled[2] |
| 1979 | Charles C. Diggs, Jr. (D–Michigan) | Misuse of clerk funds | Not expelled[2] |
| 1980 | Michael J. Myers (D–Pennsylvania) | Corruption | Expelled |
| 1988 | Mario Biaggi (D–New York) | Corruption | Not expelled[3] |
| 1990 | Barney Frank (D–Massachusetts) | Discrediting House | Not expelled[4] |

## Cases of Expulsion in the Senate

| Year | Member | Grounds | Disposition |
|---|---|---|---|
| 1797 | William Blount (R–Tennessee) | Anti–Spanish conspiracy | Expelled |
| 1808 | John Smith (R–Ohio)[5] | Disloyalty/Treason | Not expelled |
| 1858 | Henry M. Rice (D–Minnesota) | Corruption | Not expelled |
| 1861 | James M. Mason (D–Virginia) | Support of rebellion | Expelled |
| 1861 | Robert M. T. Hunter (D–Virginia) | Support of rebellion | Expelled |
| 1861 | Thomas L. Clingman (D–N.C.) | Support of rebellion | Expelled |
| 1861 | Thomas Bragg (D–N.C.) | Support of rebellion | Expelled |
| 1861 | James Chesnut, Jr. (D–S.C.) | Support of rebellion | Expelled |
| 1861 | Alfred O. P. Nicholson (D–TN) | Support of rebellion | Expelled |
| 1861 | William K. Sebastion (D–AR)[6] | Support of rebellion | Expelled |
| 1861 | Charles B. Mitchel (D–AR) | Support of rebellion | Expelled |
| 1861 | John Hemphill (D–TX) | Support of rebellion | Expelled |
| 1861 | Louis T. Wigfall (D–TX)[7] | Support of rebellion | Expelled |
| 1861 | John C. Breckinridge (D–KY) | Support of rebellion | Expelled |
| 1862 | Lazarus W. Powell (D–KY) | Support of rebellion | Not expelled |
| 1862 | Trusten Polk (D–MO) | Support of rebellion | Expelled |
| 1862 | Jesse D. Bright (D–IN) | Support of rebellion | Expelled |
| 1862 | Waldo P. Johnson (D–MO) | Support of rebellion | Expelled |
| 1862 | James F. Simmons (R–RI)[8] | Corruption | Resigned |
| 1873 | James W. Patterson (R–NH)[9] | Corruption | Term Expired |
| 1893 | William N. Roach (D–ND)[10] | Embezzlement | Not expelled |
| 1905 | John H. Mitchell (R–OR)[11] | Corruption | Not expelled |
| 1906 | Joseph R. Burton (R–KS)[12] | Corruption | Resigned |
| 1907 | Reed Smoot (R–UT)[13] | Mormonism | Not expelled |
| 1919 | Robert M. LaFollette (R–WI)[14] | Disloyalty | Not expelled |
| 1922 | Truman H. Newberry (R–MI)[15] | Election fraud | Resigned |
| 1924 | Burton K. Wheeler (D–MT)[16] | Conflict of interest | Not expelled |
| 1934 | John H. Overton (D–LA)[17] | Election fraud | No Senate action |
|  | Huey P. Long (D–LA)[18] | Election fraud | No Senate action |
| 1942 | William Langer (R–ND)[19] | Corruption | Not expelled |
| 1982 | Harrison A. Williams, Jr. (D–NJ)[20] | Corruption | Resigned |
| 1995 | Robert W. Packwood (D–OR)[21] | Misconduct | Resigned |

## Cases of Censure in the House

| Year | Member | Grounds | Disposition |
|------|--------|---------|-------------|
| 1798 | Matthew Lyons (AF–Vermont) | Assault on another representative | Not censured |
| 1798 | Roger Griswold (F–Connecticut) | Assault on another representative | Not censured |
| 1832 | William Stanbery (JD–Ohio) | Insult to speaker | Censured |
| 1836 | Sherrod Williams (W–Kentucky) | Insult to speaker | Not censured |
| 1838 | Henry A. Wise (TD–Virginia) | Acted as Second in Duel | Not censured |
| 1839 | Alexander Duncan (W–Ohio) | Offensive Publication | Not censured |
| 1842 | John Quincy Adams (W–Mass.) | Treasonable Petition | Not censured |
|  | Joshua R. Giddings (W–Ohio) | Offensive Paper | Censured |
| 1856 | Henry A. Edmundson (D–Virginia) | Complicity in Assault on a U.S. senator | Not censured |
|  | Laurence M. Keitt (D–S.C.)[1] | Complicity in Assault on a U.S. senator | Censured |
| 1860 | George S. Houston (D–Alabama) | Insult to representative | Not censured |
| 1864 | Alexander Long (D–Ohio) | Treasonable utterance | Censured |
|  | Benjamin G. Harris (D–Maryland) | Treasonable utterance | Censured |
| 1866 | John W. Chanler (D–New York) | Insult to House | Censured |
|  | Lovell H. Rousseau (R–Kentucky) | Assault on another representative | Censured |
| 1867 | John W. Hunter (I–New York) | Insult to representative | Censured |
| 1868 | Fernando Wood (D–New York) | Offensive utterance | Censured |
|  | E. D. Holbrook (D–Idaho)[22] | Offensive utterance | Censured |
| 1870 | Benjamin F. Whittemore (R–S.C.) | Corruption | Censured |
|  | Roderick R. Butler (R–Tennessee) | Corruption | Censured |
|  | John T. Deweese (D–North Carolina) | Corruption | Censured |
| 1873 | Oakes Ames (R–Massachusetts) | Corruption | Censured |
|  | James Brooks (D–New York) | Corruption | Censured |
| 1875 | John Y. Brown (D–Kentucky) | Insult to representative | Censured[23] |
| 1876 | James G. Blaine (R–Maine) | Corruption | Not censured |
| 1882 | William D. Kelley (R–Pennsylvania) | Offensive utterance | Not censured |
|  | John D. White (R–Kentucky) | Offensive utterance | Not censured |
| 1882 | John Van Voorhis (R–New York) | Offensive utterance | Not censured |
| 1890 | William D. Bynum (D–Indiana) | Offensive utterance | Censured |
| 1921 | Thomas L. Blanton (D–Texas) | Abuse of leave to print | Censured |
| 1978 | Edward R. Roybal (D–California) | Lying to House committee | Not censured[24] |
| 1979 | Charles C. Diggs, Jr. (D–Michigan) | Misuse of clerk funds | Censured |
| 1980 | Charles H. Wilson (D–California) | Financial misconduct | Censured |
| 1983 | Gerry E. Studds (D–Massachusetts) | Sexual misconduct | Censured |
|  | Daniel B. Crane (R–Illinois) | Sexual misconduct | Censured |
| 1990 | Barney Frank (D–Massachusetts) | Discrediting House | Not censured[4] |

## Cases of Censure in the Senate

| Year | Member | Grounds | Disposition |
|------|--------|---------|-------------|
| 1811 | Timothy Pickering (F–Massachusetts) | Reading confidential documents; "breach of confidence" | Censured |
| 1844 | Benjamin Tappan (D–Ohio) | Releasing confidential documents; "breach of confidence" | Censured |
| 1850 | Thomas H. Benton (D–Missouri) | Disorderly conduct | Not censured |
|  | Henry S. Foote (U–Mississippi) | Disorderly conduct | Not censured |

## Cases of Censure in the Senate *(continued)*

| Year | Member | Grounds | Disposition |
|---|---|---|---|
| 1902 | Benjamin R. Tillman (D–S.C.) | Fighting in Senate chamber | Censured |
| | John L. McLaurin (D–S.C.) | Fighting in Senate chamber | Censured |
| 1929 | Hiram Bingham (R–Connecticut) | "Bringing Senate into Disrepute" | Condemned[25] |
| 1954 | Joseph R. McCarthy (R–Wisconsin) | Obstruction of legislative process | Condemned[25] |
| 1967 | Thomas J. Dodd (D–Connecticut) | Financial misconduct; Corruption | Censured |
| 1979 | Herman E. Talmadge (D–Georgia) | Financial misconduct | Denounced[26] |
| 1990 | David F. Durenberger (R–Minnesota) | Financial misconduct | Denounced[26] |
| 1991 | Alan Cranston (D–California) | Improper conduct | Reprimanded[27] |

*Key to Party Affiliation:*
AF = Anti-Federalist
Am = American
F = Federalist
I = Independent
JD = Jacksonian Democrat
R = Republican
S = Socialist
SRD = States' Rights Democrat
TD = Tyler Democrat
U = Unionist
W = Whig

*Footnotes:*

1. Brooks was threatened with expulsion for physically attacking Senator Charles Sumner (R-MA), who had made a speech attacking Brooks's cousin, Senator Andrew Pickens Butter (SC). Representatives Henry A. Edmundson (D-VA) and Laurence M. Keitt (D-SC) were threatened with censure proceedings because of their complicity in Brooks's attack. Keitt was censured, Edmundson was not.

2. Censured after expulsion move failed or was withdrawn.

3. Facing probable expulsion, Biaggi resigned from Congress on 8 August 1988.

4. Reprimanded after expulsion and censure moves failed.

5. Expulsion failed on a vote of nineteen to ten, less than the necessary two-thirds majority. At the request of the Ohio legislature, Smith resigned two weeks after the vote. (His counsel was Francis Scott Key.)

6. On 3 March 1877, the Senate reversed its decision to expel Sebastian. Because Sebastian had died in 1865, his children were paid an amount equal to his Senate salary between the time of his expulsion and the date of his death.

7. In March 1861, the Senate took no action on an initial resolution expelling Wigfall because he represented a state that had seceded from the Union. Three months later, on 10 July 1861, he was expelled for supporting the Confederacy.

8. On 14 July 1862, the Judiciary Committee reported that the charges against Simmons were essentially correct. The Senate adjourned three days later, and Simmons resigned on 15 August before the Senate could take action.

9. A Senate select committee recommended expulsion on 27 February. On 1 March, a Republican caucus decided that there was insufficient time remaining in the session to deliberate the matter. Patterson's term expired 3 March, and no further action was taken.

10. After extensive deliberation, the Senate took no action, assuming that it lacked jurisdiction over members' behavior before their election to the Senate. The alleged embezzlement had occurred thirteen years earlier.

11. Mitchell was indicted on 1 January 1905, and convicted on 5 July of that same year, during a Senate recess. Mitchell died on 8 December while his case was still on appeal and before the Senate, which had convened on 4 December, could take any action against him.

12. Burton was indicted and convicted of receiving compensation for intervening with a federal agency. When the Supreme Court upheld his conviction, he resigned rather than face expulsion.

13. After an investigation spanning two years, the Committee on Privileges and Elections reported that Smoot was not entitled to his seat because he was a leader in a religion that advocated polygamy and a union of church and state, contrary to the U.S. Constitution. By a vote of twenty-seven to forty-three, however, the Senate failed to expel him, finding that he satisfied the constitutional requirements for serving as a senator.

14. The Committee on Privileges and Elections recommended that the Senate take no action as the speech in question (a 1917 speech opposing U.S. entry into World War I) did not warrant it. The Senate agreed fifty to twenty-one.

15. On 20 March 1920, Newberry was convicted on charges of spending $3,750 to secure his Senate election. The U.S. Supreme Court overturned this decision (2 May 1921) on the grounds that the U.S. Senate exceeded its powers in attempting to regulate primary elections. By a vote of forty-six to forty-one (12 January 1922), the Senate declared Newberry to have been duly elected in 1918. On 18 November, two days before the start of the third session of the Sixty-seventh Congress, Newberry resigned as certain members resumed their efforts to unseat him.

16. Wheeler was indicted for serving while a senator in matters in which the United States was a party. A Senate committee, however, found that his dealings related to litigation before state courts and that he received no compensation for any service before federal departments. The Senate exonerated him by a vote of fifty-six to five.

17. The Committee on Privileges and Elections concluded that the charges and evidence were insufficient to warrant further consideration.

18. The Privileges and Elections Committee considered this case in conjunction with that against Senator Overton (see footnote 17) and reached the same conclusion.

19. Recommending that this case was properly one of exclusion, not expulsion, the Committee on Privileges and Elections declared Langer guilty of moral turpitude and voted, thirteen to two, to deny him his seat. The Senate disagreed, fifty-two to thirty, arguing that the evidence was hearsay and inconclusive. Langer retained his seat.

20. The Committee on Ethics recommended that Williams be expelled because of his ethically repugnant conduct in the ABSCAM scandal, for which he was convicted of conspiracy, bribery, and conflict of interest. Prior to a Senate vote on his expulsion, Williams resigned on 11 March 1982.

21. The Committee on Ethics recommended that Packwood be expelled for abuse of his power as a senator by repeatedly committing sexual misconduct and by engaging in a deliberate plan to enhance his personal financial position by seeking favors from persons who had a particular interest in legislation or issues that he could influence, as well as for seeking to obstruct and impede the committee's inquiries by withholding, altering, and destroying relevant evidence. On 7 September 1995, the day after the committee issued its recommendation, Packwood announced his resignation without specifying an effective date. On 8 September he indicated that he would resign effective 1 October 1995.

22. Holbrook was a territorial delegate, not a representative.

23. The House later rescinded part of the censure resolution against Brown.

24. Roybal was reprimanded after the censure motion failed and was withdrawn.

25. In the cases of Bingham and McCarthy, "condemned" carries the same weight as "censured."

26. In the cases of Talmadge and Durenberger, "denounced" carries the same weight as "censured."

27. The Senate Ethics Committee reprimanded Cranston on behalf of the full Senate, after determining that it lacked the authority to issue a censure order in the same manner. The reprimand was delivered on the floor of the U.S. Senate by committee leaders, but there was not vote or formal action by the full Senate. It is the first use of the punishment of "reprimand" in the U.S. Senate's history.

*References:* U.S. Congress, Senate, Committee on Rules and Administration, *Senate Election, Expulsion and Censure Cases from 1793 to 1972,* Senate Document No. 92–7, 92nd Congress, 1st Session, 1972; *Congress A to Z: CQ's Encyclopedia of American Government* (Washington, DC: Congressional Quarterly, 1993), 462–465.

# APPENDIX TWO

## Senate Cases Involving Qualifications for Membership

According to the rules of the U.S. House and Senate, the members themselves may establish regulations for who may sit in those bodies. Over the 200-year history of the U.S. Congress, several members have had their qualifications for membership questioned and investigated. The following table lists these members, with the grounds for potential disqualification, and the disposition of their cases.

| Congress | Year | Member-elect | Grounds | Disposition |
|----------|------|--------------|---------|-------------|
| 3rd | 1793 | Albert Gallatin (D-Penn.) | Questioned Citizenship | Excluded |
| 11th | 1809 | Stanley Griswold (D-Ohio) | Questioned Residence | Admitted |
| 28th | 1844 | John M. Niles (D-Conn.) | Sanity | Admitted |
| 31st | 1849 | James Shields (D-Illinois) | Citizenship | Excluded |
| 37th | 1861 | Benjamin Stark (D-Oregon) | Loyalty | Admitted |
| 40th | 1867 | Philip F. Thomas (D-Maryland) | Loyalty | Excluded |
| 41st | 1870 | Hiram R. Revels (D-Mississippi) | Citizenship | Admitted |
| 41st | 1870 | Adelbert Ames (R-Mississippi) | Residence | Admitted |
| 59th | 1907 | Reed Smoot (R-Utah) | Mormonism | Admitted[1] |
| 69th | 1926 | Arthur R. Gould (R-Maine) | Character | Admitted |
| 74th | 1935 | Rush D. Holt (D-West Virginia) | Age | Admitted |
| 75th | 1937 | George L. Berry (D-Tennessee) | Character | Admitted |
| 77th | 1942 | William Langer (R-North Dakota) | Character | Admitted |
| 80th | 1947 | Theodore G. Bilbo (D-Miss.) | Character | None[2] |

*Footnotes:*

1. The Senate decided that a 2/3rds majority, as in expulsion cases, would be required to exclude a senator from being seated in this case.
2. Bilbo died before the Senate could act.

*References:* U.S. Congress, Senate, Committee on Rules and Administration, Subcommittee on Privileges and Elections, *Senate Election, Expulsion and Censure Cases from 1793 to 1972* (Washington, DC: Government Printing Office, 1972); Congressional Quarterly, *Congressional Ethics* (Washington, D.C.: Congressional Quarterly, 1980), 152.

# APPENDIX THREE

## Independent Counsel Investigations, 1979–1999

| Independent Counsel | Subject(s) | Result(s) | Cost |
|---|---|---|---|
| Arthur H. Christy (29 November 1979) | Hamilton Jordan | No charges | $182,000 |
| Gerard J. Gallinghouse (9 September 1980) | Timothy Kraft | No charges | $3,300 |
| Leon Silverman (29 December 1981) | Raymond Donovan | No charges | $326,000 |
| Jacob A. Stein (2 April 1984) | Edwin Meese III | No charges | $312,000 |
| James C. McKay (23 April 1986) Alexia Morrison (29 May 1986) | Theodore B. Olson | No charges | $2.1 million |
| Whitney N. Seymour, Jr. (29 May 1986) | Michael K. Deaver | 1 Guilty plea | $1.6 million |
| Lawrence E. Walsh (19 December 1986)—(Iran Contra Scandal) | Elliott Abrams, Carl Channell, Alan Fiers, Albert Hakim, Robert McFarland, Richard Miller, Richard Secord, Thomas Clines, John Poindexter, Oliver North, Clair George, Duane Clarridge, Joseph Fernandez, Caspar Weinberger | 7 Guilty pleas, 4 Convictions (2 Overturned on Appeal) 6 Presidential pardons | $47.4 million |
| James C. McKay (2 February 1987) | Lyn Nofziger, Edwin Meese III | 1 Conviction, (Overturned on appeal), 1 Acquittal | $2.8 million |
| Carl Rauh (19 December 1986) James R. Harper (17 August 1987) | Investigated finances of former Assistant Attorney General W. Lawrence Wallace | No charges | $50,000 |
| Sealed (31 May 1989) | Confidential | Confidential | $15,000 |
| Arlin M. Adams (1 March 1990)—(HUD Scandal) Larry D. Thompson (3 July 1995) | Samuel Pierce, Deborah Dean, Tom Demery, Phillip Winn, S. DeBartolomeis, Lance Wilson, Carlos Figueroa, J. Queenan, Ronald Mahon, Catalina Villapando, Robert Olson, Len Briscoe, Maurice Steier, Elaine Richardson, Sam Singletary, Victor Cruise | 7 Guilty pleas, 11 Convictions, 1 Acquittal | $27.1 million |

*(continues)*

| Independent Counsel | Subject(s) | Result(s) | Cost |
|---|---|---|---|
| Sealed (19 April 1991) | Confidential | Confidential | $93,000 |
| Joseph diGenova (14 December 1992), Michael F. Zeldin (11 January 1996) | Janet Mullins, Margaret Tutwiler | No charges | $3.2 million |
| Robert B. Fiske, Jr. (21 January 1994) | William Clinton et al. | 3 Guilty pleas | $6.1 million |
| Kenneth W. Starr (5 August 1994) Robert Ray | William Clinton et al. | 6 Guilty pleas, 3 Convictions 2 Acquittals, Impeachment Report sent to Congress | $52 million |
| Donald C. Smaltz (9 September 1994) | Michael Espy | 1 Guilty plea, 2 Convictions, 2 Acquittals, | $11.9 million |
| David M. Barrett (24 May 1995) | Henry G. Cisneros et al. | Presidential pardon | $3.8 million |
| Daniel S. Pearson (6 July 1995) | Ronald H. Brown | Terminated (subject deceased) | $3.2 million |
| Sealed (27 November 1996) | Confidential | Confidential | $48,784 |
| Carol Elder Bruce (19 March 1998) | Bruce Babbitt | No charges | Unknown or Not Released |
| Ralph I. Lancaster, Jr. (1998) | Alexis Herman | No charges | Not Released |
| John C. Danforth (9 September 1999)* | Government Assault on Branch Davidian Compound in Waco, Texas | No charges | Not Released |

Footnote:
*Because the Independent Counsel Act had expired, Attorney General Janet Reno herself named Danforth "special counsel," and not an independent counsel.

References: Office of the Independent Counsel, Washington, D.C.; "Clinton Probes Cost $60 Million; Total Counsel Costs for Administration Top $110 Million," *The Washington Post*, 31 March 2001, A10.

# APPENDIX FOUR

## House Cases Involving Qualifications for Membership

Just like the Senate, the House of Representatives has had many cases in which members' qualifications to hold their seats have been challenged. The following table highlights these cases, with the year, the member, the grounds, and what happened to that member's case.

| Congress | Year | Member–elect | Grounds | Disposition |
|---|---|---|---|---|
| 1st | 1789 | William L. Smith (Fed.–S.C.) | Questionable citizenship | Admitted |
| 10th | 1807 | Philip B. Key (Fed.–Maryland) | Questionable residence | Admitted |
| 10th | 1807 | William McCreery (R–Md.) | Questionable residence | Admitted |
| 18th | 1823 | Gabriel Richard (I–Mich. Terr.) | Questionable citizenship | Admitted |
| 18th | 1823 | John Bailey (I–Massachusetts) | Questionable residence | Excluded |
| 18th | 1823 | John Forsyth (D–Georgia) | Questionable residence | Admitted |
| 27th | 1841 | David Y. Levy (R–Fla. Terr.) | Questionable citizenship | Admitted |
| 36th | 1857 | John Y. Brown (D–Kentucky) | Age | Admitted |
| 40th | 1867 | William H. Hooper (D–Utah Terr.) | Mormonism | Admitted |
| 40th | 1867 | Lawrence S. Trimble (D–Kentucky) | Loyalty | Admitted |
| 40th | 1867 | John Y. Brown (D–Kentucky) | Loyalty | Excluded |
| 40th | 1867 | John D. Young (D–Kentucky) | Loyalty | Excluded |
| 40th | 1867 | Roderick R. Butler (R–Tennessee) | Loyalty | Admitted |
| 40th | 1867 | John A. Wimpy (I–Georgia) | Loyalty | Excluded |
| 40th | 1867 | W.D. Simpson (I–S.C.) | Loyalty | Excluded |
| 41st | 1869 | John M. Rice (D–Kentucky) | Loyalty | Admitted |
| 41st | 1870 | Lewis McKenzie (U–Virginia) | Loyalty | Admitted |
| 41st | 1870 | George W. Booker (C–Virginia) | Loyalty | Admitted |
| 41st | 1870 | Benjamin F. Whittemore (R–S.C.) | Malfeasance | Excluded |
| 41st | 1870 | John C. Connor (D–Texas) | Misconduct | Admitted |
| 43rd | 1873 | George Q. Cannon (R–Utah Terr.) | Mormonism | Admitted |
| 43rd | 1873 | George Q. Cannon (R–Utah Terr.) | Polygamy | Admitted |
| 47th | 1881 | John S. Barbour (D–Virginia) | Questionable residence | Admitted |
| 47th | 1881 | George Q. Cannon (R–Utah Terr.) | Polygamy | Seat Vacated[1] |
| 50th | 1887 | James B. White (R–Indiana) | Questionable citizenship | Admitted |
| 56th | 1899 | Robert W. Wilcox (I–Hawaii Terr.) | Bigamy, Treason | Admitted |
| 56th | 1900 | Brigham H. Roberts (D–Utah) | Polygamy | Excluded |
| 59th | 1905 | Anthony Michalek (R–Illinois) | Questionable citizenship | Admitted |
| 66th | 1919 | Victor L. Berger (Soc.–Wisconsin) | Sedition | Excluded |
| 66th | 1919 | Victor L. Berger (Soc.–Wisconsin) | Sedition | Excluded |

(continues)

| Congress | Year | Member–elect | Grounds | Disposition |
|----------|------|--------------|---------|-------------|
| 69th | 1926 | John W. Langley (R–Kentucky) | Criminal misconduct | Resigned |
| 70th | 1927 | James M. Beck (R–Pennsylvania) | Questionable residence | Admitted |
| 70th | 1929 | Ruth B. Owen (D–Florida) | Questionable residence | Admitted |
| 90th | 1967 | Adam Clayton Powell, Jr. (D–N.Y.) | Misconduct | Excluded[2] |
| 96th | 1979 | Richard A. Tonry (D–Louisiana) | Vote fraud | Resigned |

*Footnotes:*

1. Discussions on Mormonism and polygamy led to a debate and to a declaration that Cannon's seat was vacant.

2. The U.S. Supreme Court held in *Powell v. McCormack* that the House had improperly excluded Powell, and ordered his reinstatement.

*References:* Hinds, Asher Crosby, *Hinds' Precedents of the House of Representatives of the United States, Including References to Provisions of the Constitution, the Laws, and Decisions of the United States Senate*, 8 vols. (Washington, DC: Government Printing Office, 1907); *Congressional Ethics* (Washington, DC: Congressional Quarterly, 1980), 18–19.

# APPENDIX FIVE

## United States Senators Tried and Convicted and Tried and Acquitted, 1806–1981

The following listing examines the cases of those U.S. Senators who were tried in criminal courts for crimes, some relating to corruption, others not. The table shows the name of the member, the date of conviction or acquittal, and the resolution of his case.

| Senator | Date Acquitted | Date Convicted | Resolution of Case |
|---|---|---|---|
| John Smith (D–Ohio) | 1806 | | Later subject of Senate Expulsion action, which failed. Resigned seat on 25 April 1808. |
| Charles H. Dietrich (R–Nebraska) | 1904[1] | | Left the Senate 3 March 1905 at end of term. |
| John H. Mitchell (R–Oregon) | | 1905 | Died 8 December 1905, pending appeal. |
| Joseph R. Burton (R–Kansas) | | 1905 | Resigned seat in June 1906 after the U.S. Supreme Court upheld his conviction. |
| Truman Newberry (R–Michigan) | | 1920 | U.S. Supreme Court reversed conviction, May 1921, but Newberry resigned from Senate November 1922. |
| Burton K. Wheeler (D–Montana) | 1924 | | Acquitted of bribery charge. Returned to Senate seat. |
| Edward J. Gurney (R–Florida) | 1975/76[2] | | Had resigned seat 31 December 1974. |
| Harrison A. Williams (D–New Jersey) | | 1981 | Resigned his seat, 11 March 1982, after it appeared that he would be expelled. |

*Footnotes:*

1. Charges were dropped on a technicality.

2. Gurney was indicted in April 1974 for election law violations. This indictment was dismissed in May 1974. He was indicted in July 1974 on charges of bribery and perjury, and Gurney resigned his Senate seat. He was acquitted of the bribery solicitation charge in August 1975, and on the perjury charge in October 1976.

*Reference: Congressional Ethics* (Washington, DC: Congressional Quarterly, 1980), 18–19.

# APPENDIX SIX

## United States Governors in Ethical Trouble— Impeachments, Crimes, and Convictions, 1851–Present

Governors have also had a long record of criminal mischief no different from their counterparts in the U.S. Congress. Although previous appendices examined only those members of Congress who were actually tried for their crimes, this specific appendix broadly examines all sitting or former governors who were merely accused of criminal activity. It includes the state they served, whether they were impeached, whether they were criminally charged in a court of law, and the disposition of their cases.

| Governor | State | Year | State Action | Criminally Charged? | Outcome |
|---|---|---|---|---|---|
| John A. Quitman | Mississippi | 1851 | None | Yes | Resigned[1] |
| Charles Robinson | Kansas | 1862 | Impeached | No | Acquitted |
| Harrison Reed | Florida | 1868 | Impeached | No | Acquitted |
| William W. Holden | North Carolina | 1870 | Impeached | No | Convicted and removed |
| Powell Clayton | Arkansas | 1871 | Impeached | No | Acquitted |
| David C. Butler | Nebraska | 1871 | Impeached | No | Convicted and removed |
| Henry C. Warmoth | Louisiana | 1872 | Impeached | No | Term Ended |
| Harrison Reed | Florida | 1872 | Impeached | No | Acquitted |
| Adelbert Ames | Mississippi | 1876 | Impeached | No | Resigned |
| Alexander Davis | Mississippi | 1876 | Impeached | No | Convicted and removed |
| William P. Kellogg | Louisiana | 1876 | Impeached | No | Acquitted |
| William Sulzer | New York | 1913 | Impeached | No | Convicted and removed |
| James Ferguson | Texas | 1917 | Impeached | No | Convicted and Resigned |
| Lynn J. Frazier | North Dakota | 1921 | Not impeached | No | Recalled by voters |
| John C. Walton | Oklahoma | 1923 | Impeached | No | Convicted and removed |
| Warren T. McCray | Indiana | 1924 | Not impeached | Yes | Resigned[2] |
| Edward F. Jackson | Indiana | 1928 | Not impeached | Yes | Finished term[3] |
| Henry S. Johnston | Oklahoma | 1928 | Impeached | No | Acquitted |
| Henry S. Johnston | Oklahoma | 1929 | Impeached | No | Convicted and removed |
| Huey P. Long | Louisiana | 1929 | Impeached | No | Acquitted |
| Henry Horton | Tennessee | 1931 | Impeached | No | Acquitted |
| William L. Langer | North Dakota | 1934 | Not impeached | Yes | Removed from office[4] |
| Thomas L. Moodie | North Dakota | 1935 | Not impeached | No | Removed from office[5] |
| Richard Leche | Louisiana | 1939 | Not impeached | No | Resigned[6] |
| J. Howard Pyle | Arizona | 1955 | Not impeached | No | Term ended[7] |
| Arch A. Moore, Jr. | West Virginia | 1975 | Not impeached | Yes | Acquitted[8] |
| Marvin Mandel | Maryland | 1979 | Not impeached | Yes | Removed from office[9] |
| Edwin Edwards | Louisiana | 1985 | Not impeached | Yes | |
| Evan Mecham | Arizona | 1988 | Impeached | Yes | Convicted and removed[10] |
| Guy Hunt | Alabama | 1992 | Not impeached | Yes | Resigned[11] |
| David Walters | Oklahoma | 1993 | Not impeached | Yes | |
| J. Fife Symington | Arizona | 1997 | Not impeached | Yes | Resigned[12] |
| Edwin Edwards | Louisiana | 2000 | Not impeached[13] | Yes | Out of office[14] |
| George Ryan | Illinois | 2003 | None | Yes | Convicted[15] |
| Don Siegelman | Alabama | 2004 | None | Yes | Convicted[16] |
| Ernie Fletcher | Kentucky | 2006 | None | Yes | Not Tried[17] |
| Eliot Spitzer | New York | 2008 | None | No[18] | Resigned[19] |
| Anibal Acevedo-Vila | Puerto Rico | 2008 | Federal | Yes | [20] |

*Footnotes:*

1. Quitman resigned on 3 February 1851 after he was indicted on charges of violating U.S. neutrality laws by collaborating with a Cuban insurrection against Spain. He was later acquitted of all charges.

2. McCray resigned following his conviction for mail fraud.

3. Jackson was tried after leaving office on charges of conspiracy to bribe an official, but was cleared only because the statute of limitations had expired.

4. Langer was removed from office by the North Dakota state supreme court after he was indicted for various crimes, including soliciting funds from federal employees which he then used for his personal spending. He was tried four times with three hung juries before being acquitted on all charges in 1936. He later ran again for governor in 1936 as an Independent and was elected.

5. Moodie was found to have been a citizen of another state when he ran for governor of North Dakota. He was removed from office by the North Dakota state supreme court after serving just thirteen months in office.

6. Leche was threatened with impeachment, forcing his resignation.

7. A recall petition against Pyle was certified, but Pyle's term expired before a recall election could be held.

8. Moore was indicted in 1975 on charges of extortion, but acquitted in 1976. He pled guilty in 1990 to federal corruption charges.

9. Mandel was removed after he was tried and convicted on charges of federal mail fraud and bribery.

10. Mecham was impeached on charges that he accepted a loan for his business, charges unrelated to his term in office, but he was convicted and removed. He stood trial in 1988 and, with his brother Willard, was acquitted on all charges.

11. Indicted on 28 December 1992, on charges of taking more than $200,000 from his 1987 inaugural fund for personal uses, Hunt was convicted in April 1993. He then resigned his office.

12. Symington was convicted in 1997 on charges that prior to becoming governor he had used his influence to get loans that he should have been denied. He resigned the same day of his conviction. An appeals court later overturned his conviction, and in January 2001 Symington was pardoned by President Bill Clinton.

13. Edwards had already left office when he was indicted and tried.

14. Edwards was convicted of nine charges relating to kickbacks on 9 May 2000, and sentenced to ten years in prison.

15. Ryan was convicted in 2006, and in November 2007 entered a federal prison to begin serving a 6 ½ year sentence.

16. Siegelman was indicted in 2004 and convicted in 2006 after a multi-year federal investigation.

17. Fletcher was defeated for re-election in 2007, but his 2006 indictment was eventually dismissed. As of this writing, he has not been re-indicted.

18. Spitzer was investigated nearly from the start of his administration in January 2007 until March 2008 for several criminal offenses, including using state funds to investigate his political opponents. By March 2008, none of these investigations had concluded in any criminal charges against Spitzer.

19. Despite allegations of criminal activity while Governor, Spitzer resigned in March 2008 after it was discovered that he had solicited prostitutes in New York State and Washington, D.C. among other places. As of this writing, he has not been charged with a crime relating to that allegation, nor has he been charged and/or indicted for the alledged crimes for which he was being investigated for up until his resignation from the governorship.

20. Acevedo-Vila was indicted by a federal grand jury in San Juan, Puerto Rico, on 28 March 2008 on charges of conspiracy to violate campaign finance laws, wire fraud, conspiracy to defraud the Internal Revenue Severice (IRS) and filing a false tax return. Indicted with him were four Democrats in Philadelphia, including prominent party fundraiser Robert M. Feldman, who was charged with aiding Acevedo-Vila raise more than $100,000 in illegal campaign donations.

# APPENDIX SEVEN

## Impeachments of Federal Officials, 1799–1999

The Senate has sat as a court of impeachment in the following cases:

William Blount, senator from Tennessee; charges dismissed for want of jurisdiction, 14 January 1799.

John Pickering, judge of the U.S. District Court for New Hampshire; removed from office 12 March 1804.

Samuel Chase, associate justice of the Supreme Court; acquitted 1 March 1805.

James H. Peck, judge of the U.S. District Court for Missouri; acquitted 31 January 1831.

West H. Humphreys, judge of the U.S. District Court for the Middle, Eastern, and Western Districts of Tennessee; removed from office 26 June 1862.

Andrew Johnson, president of the United States; acquitted 26 May 1868.

William W. Belknap, secretary of war; acquitted 1 August 1876.

Charles Swayne, judge of the U.S. District Court for the Northern District of Florida; acquitted 27 February 1905.

Robert W. Archbald, associate judge of the U.S. Commerce Court; removed 13 January 1913.

George W. English, judge of the U.S. District Court for the Eastern District of Illinois; resigned 4 November 1926, proceedings dismissed.

Harold Louderback, judge of the U.S. District Court for the Northern District of California; acquitted 24 May 1933.

Halsted L. Ritter, judge of the U.S. District Court for the Southern District of Florida; removed from office 17 April 1936.

Harry E. Claiborne, judge of the U.S. District Court for the District of Nevada; removed from office 9 October 1986.

Alcee L. Hastings, judge of the U.S. District Court for the Southern District of Florida; removed from office 20 October 1989.

Walter L. Nixon, judge of the U.S. District Court for Mississippi; removed from office 3 November 1989.

William Jefferson Clinton, president of the United States; acquitted 12 February 1999.

*Footnote:*
The procedure for the impeachment of Federal officials is detailed in Article I, Section 3, of the Constitution.

# APPENDIX EIGHT

## Rules of Procedure and Practice in the Senate when Sitting on Impeachment Trials

[Revised pursuant to Senate Resolution 479, 99–2, 16 August 1986.]

I.Whensoever the Senate shall receive notice from the House of Representatives that managers are appointed on their part to conduct an impeachment against any person and are directed to carry articles of impeachment to the Senate, the Secretary of the Senate shall immediately inform the House of Representatives that the Senate is ready to receive the managers for the purpose of exhibiting such articles of impeachment, agreeably to such notice.

II.When the managers of an impeachment shall be introduced at the bar of the Senate and shall signify that they are ready to exhibit articles of impeachment against any person, the Presiding Officer of the Senate shall direct the Sergeant at Arms to make proclamation, who shall, after making proclamation, repeat the following words, viz: "All persons are commanded to keep silence, on pain of imprisonment, while the House of Representatives is exhibiting to the Senate of the United States articles of impeachment against_____ "; after which the articles shall be exhibited, and then the Presiding Officer of the Senate shall inform the managers that the Senate will take proper order on the subject of the impeachment, of which due notice shall be given to the House of Representatives.

III.Upon such articles being presented to the Senate, the Senate shall, at 1 o'clock afternoon of the day (Sunday excepted) following such presentation, or sooner if ordered by the Senate, proceed to the consideration of such articles and shall continue in session from day to day (Sundays excepted) after the trial shall commence (unless otherwise ordered by the Senate) until final judgment shall be rendered, and so much longer as may, in its judgment, be needful. Before proceeding to the consideration of the articles of impeachment, the Presiding Officer shall administer the oath hereinafter provided to the members of the Senate then present and to the other members of the Senate as they shall appear, whose duty it shall be to take the same.

IV.When the President of the United States or the Vice President of the United States, upon whom the powers and duties of the Office of President shall have devolved, shall be impeached, the Chief Justice of the United States shall preside; and in a case requiring the said Chief Justice to preside notice shall be given to him by the Presiding Officer of the Senate of the time and place fixed for the consideration of the articles of impeachment, as aforesaid, with a request to attend; and the said Chief Justice shall be administered the oath by the Presiding Officer of the Senate and shall preside over the Senate during the consideration of said articles and upon the trial of the person impeached therein.

V.The Presiding Officer shall have power to make and issue, by himself or by the Secretary of the Senate, all orders, mandates, writs, and precepts authorized by these rules or by the Senate, and to make and enforce such other regulations and orders in the premises as the Senate may authorize or provide.

VI.The Senate shall have power to compel the attendance of witnesses, to enforce obedience to its orders, mandates, writs, precepts, and judgments, to preserve order, and to punish in a summary way contempts of, and disobedience to, its authority, orders, mandates, writs, precepts, or judgments, and to make all lawful orders, rules, and regulations which it may deem essential or conducive to the ends of justice. And the Sergeant at Arms, under the direction of the Senate, may employ such aid and assistance as may be necessary to enforce, execute, and carry into effect the lawful orders, mandates, writs, and precepts of the Senate.

VII.The Presiding Officer of the Senate shall direct all necessary preparations in the Senate Chamber, and the Presiding Officer on the trial shall direct all the forms of proceedings while the Senate is sitting for the purpose of trying an impeachment, and all forms during the trial not otherwise specially provided for. And the Presiding Officer on the trial may rule on all questions of evidence including, but not limited to, questions of relevancy, materiality, and redundancy of evidence and incidental questions, which ruling shall stand as the judgment of the Senate, unless some Member of the Senate shall ask that a formal vote be taken thereon, in which case it shall be submitted to the Senate for decision without debate; or he may at his option, in the first instance, submit any such question to a vote of the Members of the Senate. Upon all such questions the vote shall be taken in accordance with the Standing Rules of the Senate.

VIII.Upon the presentation of articles of impeachment and the organization of the Senate as hereinbefore provided, a writ of summons shall issue to the person impeached, reciting said articles, and notifying him to appear before the Senate upon a day and at a place to be fixed by the Senate and named in such writ, and file his answer to said articles of impeachment, and to stand to and abide the orders and judgments of the Senate thereon; which writ shall be served by such officer or person as shall be named in the precept thereof, such number of days prior to the day fixed for such appearance as shall be named in such precept, either by the delivery of an attested copy thereof to the person impeached, or if that can not conveniently be done, by leaving such copy at the last known place of abode of such person, or at his usual place of business in some conspicuous place therein; or if such service shall be, in the judgment of the Senate, impracticable, notice to the person impeached to appear shall be given in such other manner, by publication or otherwise, as shall be deemed just; and if the writ aforesaid shall fail of service in the manner aforesaid, the proceedings shall not thereby abate, but further service may be made in such manner as the Senate shall direct. If the person impeached, after service, shall fail to appear, either in person or by attorney, on the day so fixed therefor as aforesaid, or, appearing, shall fail to file his answer to such articles of impeachment, the trial shall proceed, nevertheless, as upon a plea of not guilty. If a plea of guilty shall be entered, judgment may be entered thereon without further proceedings.

IX.At 12:30 o'clock afternoon of the day appointed for the return of the summons against the person impeached, the legislative and executive business of the Senate shall be suspended, and the Secretary of the Senate shall administer an oath to the returning officer in the form following, viz:

"I,_____ , do solemnly swear that the return made by me upon the process issued on the ____ day of ____ , by the Senate of the United States, against _____ , is truly made, and that I have performed such service as therein described: So help me God." Which oath shall be entered at large on the records.

X.The person impeached shall then be called to appear and answer the articles of impeachment against him. If he appears, or any person for him, the appearance shall be recorded, stating particularly if by himself, or by agent or attorney, naming the person appearing and the capacity in which he appears. If he does not appear, either personally or by agent or attorney, the same shall be recorded.

XI.That in the trial of any impeachment the Presiding Officer of the Senate, if the Senate so orders, shall appoint a committee of Senators to receive evidence and take testimony at such times and places as the committee may determine, and for such purpose the committee so appointed and the chairman thereof, to be elected by the committee, shall unless otherwise ordered by the Senate, exercise all the powers and functions conferred upon the Senate and the Presiding Officer of the Senate, respectively, under the rules of procedure and practice in the Senate when sitting on impeachment trials. Unless otherwise ordered by the Senate, the rules of procedure and practice in the Senate when sitting on impeachment trials shall govern the procedure and practice of the committee so appointed. The committee so appointed shall report to the Senate in writing a certified copy of the transcript of the proceedings and testimony had and given before such committee, and such report shall be received by the Senate and the evidence so received and the testimony so taken shall be considered to all intents and purposes, subject to the right of the Senate to determine competency, relevancy, and materiality, as having been received and taken before the Senate, but nothing herein shall prevent the Senate from sending for any witness and hearing his testimony in open Senate, or by order of the Senate having the entire trial in open Senate.

XII.At 12:30 o'clock afternoon, or at such other hour as the Senate may order, of the day appointed for the trial of an impeachment, the legislative and executive business of the Senate shall be suspended, and the Secretary shall give notice to the House of Representatives that the Senate is ready to proceed upon the impeachment of _____ , in the Senate Chamber.

XIII.The hour of the day at which the Senate shall sit upon the trial of an impeachment shall be (unless otherwise ordered) 12 o'clock m.; and when the hour shall arrive, the Presiding Officer upon such trial shall cause proclamation to be made, and the business of the trial shall proceed. The adjournment of the Senate sitting in said trial shall not operate as an adjournment of the Senate; but on such adjournment the Senate shall resume the consideration of its legislative and executive business.

XIV.The Secretary of the Senate shall record the proceedings in cases of impeachment as in the case of legislative proceedings, and the same shall be reported in the same manner as the legislative proceedings of the Senate.

XV.Counsel for the parties shall be admitted to appear and be heard upon an impeachment.

XVI.All motions, objections, requests, or applications whether relating to the procedure of the Senate or relating immediately to the trial (including questions with respect to admission of evidence or other questions arising during the trial) made by the parties or their counsel shall be addressed to the Presiding Officer only, and if he, or any Senator, shall require it, they shall be committed to writing, and read at the Secretary's table.

XVII.Witnesses shall be examined by one person on behalf of the party producing them, and then cross-examined by one person on the other side.

XVIII.If a Senator is called as a witness, he shall be sworn, and give his testimony standing in his place.

XIX.If a Senator wishes a question to be put to a witness, or to a manager, or to counsel of the person impeached, or to offer a motion or order (except a motion to adjourn), it shall be reduced to writing, and put by the Presiding Officer. The parties or their counsel may interpose objections to witnesses answering questions propounded at the request of any Senator and the merits of any such objection may be argued by the parties or their counsel. Ruling on any such objection shall be made as provided in Rule VII. It shall not be in order for any Senator to engage in colloquy.

XX. At all times while the Senate is sitting upon the trial of an impeachment the doors of the Senate shall be kept open, unless the Senate shall direct the doors to be closed while deliberating upon its decisions. A motion to close the doors may be acted upon without objection, or, if objection is heard, the motion shall be voted on without debate by the yeas and nays, which shall be entered on the record.

XXI. All preliminary or interlocutory questions, and all motions, shall be argued for not exceeding one hour (unless the Senate otherwise orders) on each side.

XXII. The case, on each side, shall be opened by one person. The final argument on the merits may be made by two persons on each side (unless otherwise ordered by the Senate upon application for that purpose), and the argument shall be opened and closed on the part of the House of Representatives.

XXIII. An article of impeachment shall not be divisible for the purpose of voting thereon at any time during the trial. Once voting has commenced on an article of impeachment, voting shall be continued until voting has been completed on all articles of impeachment unless the Senate adjourns for a period not to exceed one day or adjourns sine die. On the final question whether the impeachment is sustained, the yeas and nays shall be taken on each article of impeachment separately; and if the impeachment shall not, upon any of the articles presented, be sustained by the votes of two-thirds of the Members present, a judgment of acquittal shall be entered; but if the person impeached shall be convicted upon any such article by the votes of two-thirds of the Members present, the Senate shall proceed to the consideration of such other matters as may be determined to be appropriate prior to pronouncing judgment. Upon pronouncing judgment, a certified copy of such judgment shall be deposited in the office of the Secretary of State. A motion to reconsider the vote by which any article of impeachment is sustained or rejected shall not be in order.

FORM OF PUTTING THE QUESTION ON EACH ARTICLE OF IMPEACHMENT.

The Presiding Officer shall first state the question; thereafter each Senator, as his name is called, shall rise in his place and answer: guilty or not guilty.

XXIV. All the orders and decisions may be acted upon without objection, or, if objection is heard, the orders and decisions shall be voted on without debate by yeas and nays, which shall be entered on the record, subject, however, to the operation of Rule VII, except when the doors shall be closed for deliberation, and in that case no member shall speak more than once on one question, and for not more than ten minutes on an interlocutory question, and for not more than fifteen minutes on the final question, unless by consent of the Senate, to be had without debate; but a motion to adjourn may be decided without the yeas and nays, unless they be demanded by one-fifth of the members present. The fifteen minutes herein allowed shall be for the whole deliberation on the final question, and not on the final question on each article of impeachment.

XXV. Witnesses shall be sworn in the following form, viz: "You,_____ , do swear (or affirm, as the case may be) that the evidence you shall give in the case now pending between the United States and_____ , shall be the truth, the whole truth, and nothing but the truth: So help you God." Which oath shall be administered by the Secretary, or any other duly authorized person.

FORM OF A SUBPOENA BE ISSUED ON THE APPLICATION OF THE MANAGERS OF THE IMPEACHMENT, OR OF THE PARTY IMPEACHED, OR OF HIS COUNSEL.

To_____ , greeting:

You and each of you are hereby commanded to appear before the Senate of the United States, on the____ day of____ , at the Senate Chamber in the city of Washington, then and there to testify your knowledge in the cause which is before the Senate in which the House of Representatives have impeached_____ .

Fail not.

Witness_____ , and Presiding Officer of the Senate, at the city of Washington, this____ day of____ , in the year of our Lord_____ , and of the Independence of the United States the_____ .

_____ ,[signed]

Presiding Officer of the Senate.

FORM OF DIRECTION FOR THE SERVICE OF SAID SUBPOENA

The Senate of the United States to_____ , greeting: You are hereby commanded to serve and return the within subpoena according to law.

Dated at Washington, this____ day of____ , in the year of our Lord____ , and of the Independence of the United States the_____ .

_____ ,[signed]

Secretary of the Senate.

FORM OF OATH TO BE ADMINISTERED TO THE MEMBERS OF THE SENATE AND THE PRESIDING OFFICER SITTING IN THE TRIAL OF IMPEACHMENTS

"I solemnly swear (or affirm, as the case may be) that in all things appertaining to the trial of the impeachment of_____ , now pending, I will do impartial justice according to the Constitution and laws: So help me God."

FORM OF SUMMONS TO BE ISSUED AND SERVED UPON THE PERSON IMPEACHED

The United States of America, ss:

The Senate of the United States to_____ , greeting:

Whereas the House of Representatives of the United States of America did, on the____ day of____ , exhibit to the Senate articles of impeachment against you, the said_____ , in the words following:

[Here insert the articles]

And demand that you, the said_____ , should be put to answer the accusations as set forth in said articles, and that such proceedings, examinations, trials, and judgments might be thereupon had as are agreeable to law and justice. You, the said_____ , are therefore hereby summoned to be and appear before the Senate of the United States of America, at their Chamber in the city of Washington, on the____ day of____ , at____ o'clock____ , then and there to answer to the said articles of impeachment, and then and there to abide by, obey, and perform such orders, directions, and judgments as the Senate of the United States shall make in the premises according to the Constitution and laws of the United States.

Hereof you are not to fail.

Witness_____ , and Presiding Officer of the said Senate, at the city of Washington, this____ day of____ , in the year of our Lord_____ , and of the Independence of the United States the_____ .

_____ ,[signed]

Presiding Officer of the Senate.

FORM OF PRECEPT TO BE INDORSED ON SAID WRIT OF SUMMONS

The United States of America, ss:

The Senate of the United States to_____ , greeting:

You are hereby commanded to deliver to and leave with_____ , if conveniently to be found, or if not, to leave at his usual place of abode, or at his usual place of business in some conspicuous place, a true and attested copy of the within writ of summons, together with a like copy of this precept; and in whichsoever way you perform the service, let it be done at least____ days before the appearance day mentioned in the said writ of summons.

Fail not, and make return of this writ of summons and precept, with your proceedings thereon indorsed, on or before the appearance day mentioned in the said writ of summons.

Witness_____ , and Presiding Officer of the Senate, at the city of Washington, this____ day of____ , in the year of our Lord_____ , and of the Independence of the United States the_____ .

_____ ,[signed]

Presiding Officer of the Senate.

All process shall be served by the Sergeant at Arms of the Senate, unless otherwise ordered by the Senate.

XXVI. If the Senate shall at any time fail to sit for the consideration of articles of impeachment on the day or hour fixed therefor, the Senate may, by an order to be adopted without debate, fix a day and hour for resuming such consideration.

# APPENDIX NINE

## United States Mayors Involved in Political Corruption

While the corruption of US representatives, US Senators, and Governors are big news, the corruption involving mayors of big and small cities is usually overlooked or forgotten. The following is just a small listing of some of the mayors of American cities implicated in corrupt activities. The list is not exhaustive, however; many names do not appear here because they were never charged with a crime despite allegations of corruption. Two cases in point: William Hale "Big Bill" Thompson, Mayor of Chicago (1915–23, 1927–31), whose administration is considered by most historians of that city to be one of the most corrupt in American history. Nevertheless, Thompson was never formally charged with a crime, and he never served any time in prison. Another, James John "Jimmy" Walker of New York City, was implicated by Samuel Seabury in corruption, but he also was never charged with a crime and never went to prison. The following mayors were charged with a crime in a criminal proceeding.

| Mayor | City | Allegation | Trial Held? | Outcome |
|---|---|---|---|---|
| A. Oakey Hall | New York, NY | Rampant corruption | 1872 | Acquitted |
| Thomas Coman | New York, NY | Rampant corruption | 1875 | [1] |
| William M. Tweed | New York, NY | Rampant corruption | 1874 | Prison[2] |
| Eugene Schmitz | San Francisco, CA | Extortion | 1907 | [3] |
| Hiram C. Gill | Seattle, WA | Rampant corruption | No | Recalled[4] |
| John L. Duvall | Indianapolis, IN | Bribery | 1929 | Jail[5] |
| James J. Walker | New York, NY | Financial irregularities | No | Resigned |
| James M. Curley | Boston, MA | Influence Peddling | | |
| S. Davis Wilson | Philadelphia, PA | Extortion, Bribery | No | Died in Office[6] |
| T. Frank Hayes | Waterbury, CT | Fraud | Yes | Prison[7] |
| Frank L. Shaw | Los Angeles, CA | Protection of Gambling | No[8] | |
| Hugh J. Addonizio | Newark, NJ | Bribery | 1970 | Prison |
| Thomas J. Whelan | Jersey City, NJ | Conspiracy, Extortion | 1971 | Prison |
| Richard W. Reading | Detroit, MI | Bribery | Yes | Prison |
| Angelo Errichetti | Camden, NJ | ABSCAM involvement | 1981 | Prison |
| Roger Hedgecock | San Diego, CA | Conspiracy, Perjury | 1985 | No |
| Michael A. Traficante | Cranston, RI | Violating campaign finance laws | 1991 | Probation |
| Brian J. Sarault | Pawtucket, RI | Extortion | 1991 | Prison |
| Milton Milan | Camden, NJ | Bribery | 2000 | Prison |
| Vincent A. Cianci, Jr. | Providence, RI | Conspiracy | 2002 | Prison |
| Martin Barnes | Paterson, NJ | Acceptance of Gifts | 2003 | Prison |
| Sara Bost | Irvington, NJ | Bribery | 2003 | Prison |
| Philip Giordano | Waterbury, CT | Unknown | 2003 | [9] |
| Paul H. Richards II | Lynwood, CA | Fraud in city contracts | 2005 | Prison[10] |
| Joseph Ganim | Bridgeport, CT | Accepting kickbacks | 2003 | Prison |
| Matthew Scannapieco | Marlboro, NJ | Bribery | 2005 | Prison |
| Michael Zucchet[11] | San Diego, CA | Conspiracy | 2005 | Prison |
| Bill Campbell | Atlanta, GA | Bribery[12] | 2006 | Prison |

*continues*

| Mayor | City | Allegation | Trial Held? | Outcome |
|-------|------|-----------|-------------|---------|
| Leonis Malburg | Vernon, CA | Illegal voting registration | ? | [13] |
| Samuel Rivera | Passaic, NJ | Acceptance of illegal payments | ? | [14] |
| Jim Hayes | Fairbanks, AK | Conspiracy, Money Laundering | 2008 | |
| Sharpe James | Newark, NJ | Sale of city property to friend | 2008 | [15] |
| Kwame Kilpatrick | Detroit, MI | Perjury, Obstruction of Justice | | [16] |

Footnotes:

1. Coman was implicated in the ring involving William M. Tweed. Despite being convicted of his connection to the massive corruption of the period, Coman's conviction was thrown out by an appeals court and he was never retried.

2. Tweed was sentenced to eight years in prison in 1874. However, he bribed a guard in 1875 and escaped to Spain. He was captured and returned to the United States, and died in prison in 1878.

3. Schmitz was convicted of extortion on 13 June 1907, and was sentenced to five years in prison. Held in county jail while his appeal was heard, on 9 January 1908 the District Court of Appeals struck down Schmitz's conviction. He was tried in 1912 on a bribery indictment, but because of a lack of witnesses he was acquitted. He was never retried on the extortion charges, and never served any time in prison.

4. Gill, a former city councilman, allowed during his term as mayor to let gambling saloons and brothels to operate openly. In 1911, he was recalled after women were given the right to vote in Washington State. Despite the recall, in 1914 he ran again for mayor and was elected. Again, his administration was mired in rampant and abusive corruption. In 1918, when he ran for re-election, he finished third in the Republican primary and left office.

5. Duvall was sentenced to only 3 days in the Marion County jail, a $1,000 fine, and had his voting privileges removed until November 1929. He was convicted of accepting a $14,500 bribe in exchange for naming three friends of a gambler to city positions.

6. Mayor Samuel Davis Wilson was indicted in 1938 on 30 counts of extortion and bribery while mayor of Philadelphia. He was still in office, and had not yet gone to trial, when he died on 19 August 1939 at the age of 57.

7. Hayes and 22 other city officials were found guilty of a massive scheme to defraud the city of more than $1,000,000. He was sentenced to 10-15 years in prison, but served only six.

8. Shaw became the first mayor in the history of the United States to be recalled when he was thrown out of office in 1938.

9. Giordano was in the midst of a massive political corruption investigation when phone taps revealed that he had been molesting 8 and 10 year old girls as well as other charges relating to pedophilia. The corruption investigation was ended, and in 2003 he was convicted instead of molesting several children.

10. Richards was convicted of a scheme that funneled city business to a company controlled by his family in 2005, and sentenced in 2006 to 188 months in prison, one of the longest sentences relating to a federal political corruption case. His sister, Paula Cameo Harris, was sentenced to 72 months for her role in the scheme.

11. Zucchet, convicted with Councilman Ralph Inzunza, was the acting Mayor of San Diego.

12. Campbell was found guilty of tax evasion, but was cleared by a federal jury of all of the other charges against him.

13. Malburg ran Vernon for 50 years. He was indicted in November 2006 on seven counts of aiding illegal votes and fraudulently voting, assisting an unqualified voter, and false voter registration. Also indicted were Malburg's wife Dominica and his son John Leonis Malburg. Their trials had not yet begun when the second edition of this book was going to press.

14. Rivera, along with 11 other politicians, was arrested in a wide sweep in September 2007. Their trials had not yet begun when the second edition of this book was going to press.

15. The first of two corruption trials against James were just beginning as the second edition of this book was going to press in March 2008.

16. Kilpatrick was indicted along with a former aide, Christine Beatty, on 24 March 2008 for perjury and obstruction of justice along with other counts of official misconduct in a city scandal in which Kilpatrick used his office to fire several police officers investigating corruption in the mayor's office, a case later settled by the city for millions of dollars.

# CHRONOLOGY

## 1635

April   The first impeachment in the English colonies occurs. Governor John Harvey of Virginia is informed by the House of Burgesses that he is being impeached according to provisions established by Parliament in London for his Indian, land-grant, and trade policies. No corruption is alleged, but this "petition of grievances" leads to Harvey's departure from the colony and return to London in disgrace. No impeachment trial is ever held.

## 1649

22 May   The first fraudulent campaign law in the British colonies is passed. The General Court in Warwick, Rhode Island, enacts the law, which provides that "no one should bring into any votes that he did not receive from the voter's own hands, and that all votes should be filed by the Recorder in the presence of the Assembly."

## 1685

Nicolas More, chief justice of Philadelphia, is impeached by the Pennsylvania Assembly on ten charges, among them "assuming himself an unlimited and arbitrary power in office." He is convicted and removed from office on 2 June 1685, but the council in London overseeing the colony refuses to sanction the proceedings or the removal.

## 1757

During his race for a seat in the Virginia House of Burgesses, George Washington is questioned about the spending of money by his campaign. Washington reportedly bought wine and spirits for the few hundred constituents in his district.

## 1795

28 December   Robert Randall and Charles Whitney are taken into custody for attempting to bribe several congressmen. Whitney would be discharged on 7 January 1796, before he could stand trial; however, on 6 January, Randall is tried in Congress and found guilty of contempt and breach of the privileges of Congress, reprimanded by the Speaker of the House, Jonathan Dayton of New Jersey, and committed to the custody of the sergeant at arms. On 13 January his petition to be discharged is granted, after he pays a fine.

## 1795–1796

The U.S. House of Representatives is asked to investigate Judge George Turner of St. Clair, in the Ohio Territory, for unspecified crimes.

## 1797

The House committee investigating Judge George Turner recommends further proceedings, but Turner resigns. A new judge, Jonathan Return Meigs, is named to his vacant post on 12 February 1798.

July   President John Adams sends a message to the U.S. Senate, describing in detail alleged charges against Senator William Blount of Tennessee. Based on Adams's letter, the Senate votes to expel Blount by a vote of twenty-five to one.

## 1798

29 January   Former U.S. Senator William Blount of Tennessee is impeached by the U.S. House of Representatives for assisting in a "military expedition against Spanish Florida and [the] Louisiana Territories, [and] interference with [an] Indian agent," among other crimes.

## 1799

11 January   The U.S. Senate votes fourteen to eleven that U.S. Senator William Blount of Tennessee is not a civil officer of the government subject to the impeachment power and dismisses all charges against him.

## 1800

The U.S. House of Representatives debates a measure of censure against President John Adams, criticizing him for communicating with a judge, which is found to be a "dangerous interference of the Executive with Judicial decisions," but the censure motion is not passed.

**1803**
30 December    The U.S. House of Representatives votes to impeach John Pickering, judge for the federal district of New Hampshire, for tyrannical conduct and drunkenness.

**1804**
The U.S. House of Representatives investigates whether to bring impeachment articles against Judge Richard Peters for misconduct in the so-called Sedition Trials. In the end, the House finds that such articles are not warranted.

12 March    The U.S. Senate votes nineteen to seven to convict Judge John Pickering of all four impeachment articles against him, and then votes twenty to six to remove him from office. Pickering becomes the first federal judge in the United States to be impeached and removed from office.

4 December    The U.S. House of Representatives votes to impeach Samuel Chase, associate justice of the Supreme Court of the United States, for "conduct[ing] himself in a manner highly arbitrary, oppressive, and unjust" during a trial he sat on, and for other crimes, totaling eight articles.

**1805**
1 March    The U.S. Senate fails to reach a two-thirds vote on any of the impeachment articles against Associate Justice Samuel Chase, leading to Chase's acquittal.

**1807–1808**
The U.S. House of Representatives investigates whether Judge Harry Innis plotted with Spain "to seduce Kentucky from the Union," but absolves Innis of all charges.

**1808**
11 April    A resolution of the U.S. House of Representatives orders Delegate George Poindexter, from the Mississippi Territory, to investigate allegations against Judge Peter B. Bruin, presiding judge of the territory.

**1809**
7 March    The investigation against Judge Peter B. Bruin ends when Francis Xavier Martin is named to replace Bruin on the bench. No explanation is found in the records whether Bruin died or resigned.

**1811**
16 December    The Speaker of the Mississippi House of Representatives, Cowles Mead, sends a letter to the U.S. House, asking for Judge Harry Toulmin, judge of the superior court for the Washington District of Mississippi, to be impeached and removed from office, after a grand jury in

Mississippi brings an indictment against Toulmin for alleged malfeasance in office. Delegate George Poindexter, from the Mississippi Territory, is asked to head up a panel to look into potential impeachment proceedings.

**1812**
21 May    The panel headed up by Delegate George Poindexter finds no impeachable offenses committed by Judge Harry Toulmin, and asks that the House investigation into the judge be closed.

**1818**
The U.S. House of Representatives opens an inquiry into the conduct of Judges William P. Van Ness and Mathias B. Tallmadge of the district court of New York, and William Stephens, judge of the district court of Georgia. Under pressure, Stephens resigns, and he is dismissed from any further proceedings. Representative John C. Spencer of New York is ordered to make an inquiry into potential impeachable offenses. Immediately, Spencer finds that the complaints against Van Ness relate to his judicial opinions, and it is agreed that any inquiry into his case should be dismissed immediately.

**1819**
17 February    Representative John C. Spencer of New York reports that while Judge Mathias B. Tallmadge of New York had not held court on the dates he was instructed to by law, this was not an impeachable offense, and asks for and end to the inquiry against Tallmadge.

**1822–1823**
The U.S. House of Representatives investigates charges of improper court conduct against Judge Charles Tait. Tait is ultimately exonerated.

**1825**
The U.S. House is asked to investigate the conduct of Judge Buckner Thurston, associate judge of the Circuit Court of the United States for the District of Columbia. Representative William Plumer Jr. of the House Judiciary Committee finds no reason for an inquiry, and the case is closed.

**1825–1826**
The U.S. House opens a series of three inquiries into Judge Joseph L. Smith, judge of the Supreme Court of the Territory of Florida, calling attention to alleged "dictatorial powers" he wielded in court. All inquiries are ended with no impeachment proceedings.

**1829–1830**
The U.S. House of Representatives investigates potential impeachment charges against Judge Alfred Conkling for

"unjudicial conduct, malice, and partiality, but tables the investigation.

**1830**

The "citizens of East Florida" send a memorial to the U.S. House of Representatives asking for Judge Joseph L. Smith to be removed because of "tyrannical and oppressive conduct," but a motion to open an impeachment inquiry is tabled.

1 May    The U.S. House of Representatives votes to impeach James H. Peck, judge of the District of Missouri, for a "misuse of powers."

**1831**

21 January    The U.S. Senate acquits Judge James H. Peck by a vote of twenty-one to twenty-two.

**1833**

In *United States v. Wilson*, 32 U.S. (7 Pet.) 150, at 160, Chief Justice Marshall of the U.S. Supreme Court defines a presidential pardon as "an act of grace, proceeding from the power intrusted [sic] with the execution of the laws, which exempts the individual, on whom it is bestowed, from the punishment the law inflicts for a crime he has committed." The U.S. House of Representatives investigates potential impeachment charges against Judge Benjamin Johnson for "favoritism and drunkenness." The investigation is ultimately tabled.

**1837**

31 January    The House is asked to investigate Judge Buckner Thurston, associate judge of the District Court for the District of Columbia, for the second time (the first was in 1825). Evidence is eventually taken, including that from Judge Thurston. There is no record relating to the case, but the House later chooses not to impeach the judge. He remains on the court until his death in 1845.

**1839**

The U.S. House of Representatives investigates potential impeachment charges against Judge Philip K. Lawrence for "abuse of power and drunkenness." The investigation is tabled when Judge Lawrence resigns.

**1841**

Charles Franklin Mitchell, a U.S. Representative from New York (1837–1841) is sent to prison for forgery.

**1845**

22 September    After it is revealed that he gave a speech that had been plagiarized from one delivered by former Vice President Aaron Burr, former Representative and Speaker of the House of Representatives John White takes his own life.

**1849**

The U.S. House of Representatives investigates, for the second time (the first was in 1829), charges against Judge Alfred Conkling. Again, the investigation is tabled.

**1852–1853**

A major investigation by the U.S. House of Representatives into charges against Judge John C. Watrous begins. He is accused of validating fraudulent land certificates. The investigation will ultimately last eight years. Initially, it is tabled.

**1857**

The investigation by the U.S. House of Representatives into Judge John C. Watrous reaches a higher stage when the House Judiciary Committee recommends against impeachment.

**1859**

The U.S. House of Representatives investigates potential impeachment charges against Judge Thomas Irwin; the investigation concludes when Irwin resigns his seat.

**1860**

The U.S. House of Representatives adopts a resolution of "reproof," similar to that of censure or a rebuke, by a vote of 106 to 61, against President James Buchanan and Secretary of the Navy Isaac Toucey, accusing the two men of "receiving and considering the party relations of bidders for contracts with the United States, and the effect of awarding contracts upon pending elections" which was "dangerous to the public safety."

**1860–1861**

The House Judiciary Committee, investigating the case against Judge John C. Watrous for the third time in eight years, recommends that impeachment charges be brought, but reverses the action when Watrous resigns his seat.

**1862**

The U.S. House of Representatives debates, and then tables, a resolution of censure against former President James Buchanan for not taking proper actions to prevent the secession of the Southern states from the Union.

19 May    The U.S. House of Representatives votes to impeach West H. Humphreys, judge for the District of Tennessee, for siding with the Confederate revolt.

26 June    The U.S. Senate votes to convict Judge West H. Humphreys of six of the seven articles of impeachment against him, and then votes thirty-eight to zero to remove him from office, and thirty-six to zero to disqualify him from holding any future office under the United States.

15 August   Senator James Fowler Simmons of Rhode Island resigns his seat rather than face expulsion for helping a contractor from his home state gain a federal contract in exchange for a payoff of $50,000.

**1866**
26 March   Governor Frederick Low of California signs into law the first state fraudulent election law. Entitled "an Act to protect the elections of voluntary political associations, and to punish frauds therein," it becomes a landmark in state election law.

11 July   Senator James Henry Lane (R–KS) takes his own life after being implicated in the sale of illegal contracts that provide services to Indian reservations.

**1867**
Congress enacts, as part of the Naval Appropriations Bill, the first congressional attempt to regulate campaign finance spending. An impeachment investigation against Charles Francis Adams, U.S. minister to Great Britain, for "neglect of American citizens in England and Ireland," is initiated, but no action is taken. A second impeachment investigation is begun against William West, American consul in Ireland, for "failure to aid American prisoners in Ireland." No action is ever taken on the charges.

**1868**
An impeachment investigation is begin in the U.S. House of Representatives regarding Henry A. Smythe, the collector of customs in New York, for "maladministration of New York Custom House receipts and other charges." No action is taken on the charges.

2 March   The U.S. House of Representatives votes to impeach President Andrew Johnson for violating the Tenure of Office Act.

16 May   The U.S. Senate votes thirty-five to nineteen to sustain Article 11 of the impeachment charges against President Johnson, falling short of conviction by one vote. The Senate then adjourns.

26 May   The U.S. Senate reconvenes then votes thirty-five to nineteen to convict President Johnson on Articles 2 and 3, again falling one vote shy of the two-thirds needed to convict. The Senate then votes to adjourn the impeachment trial, and Chief Justice Salmon P. Chase, sitting as the trial judge, announces Johnson's acquittal.

**1869–1877**
During the eight years of the administration of President Ulysses S. Grant, Congress undertakes thirty-seven separate inquiries into maladministration in the executive and legislative branches—a record.

**1871**
22 March   Governor William Woods Holden of North Carolina becomes the first state governor to be impeached and removed from office. Charged in 1870 with eight separate articles, he is convicted of six.

**1872**
2 December   The U.S. House of Representatives appoints a select committee, headed by Representative Luke P. Poland (R–VT), to investigate the allegations involved in the Crédit Mobilier scandal.

**1873**
The Judiciary Committee of the U.S. House of Representatives recommends that Judge Mark H. Delahay be impeached for "intoxication and other corrupt dealings," but Delahay resigns before an impeachment vote can be taken. Vice President Schuyler Colfax is investigated for his role in the Crédit Mobilier railroad scandal, but because he has left office as of 4 March, no action is taken. The House investigates charges of alleged influence peddling by Judge Charles T. Sherman, but before it can vote on potential impeachment charges Sherman resigns his seat.

6 January   The U.S. House of Representatives forms a second select committee to investigate the Crédit Mobilier affair, this time to investigate the financial relationship between the company and the Union Pacific Railroad. This committee is headed by Representative Jeremiah M. Wilson (R–IN).

4 February   The U.S. Senate establishes its own select committee to investigate the Crédit Mobilier affair, headed by Senator Lot M. Morrill (R–ME).

18 February   The Poland Committee files its report with the House, clearing Speaker of the House James G. Blaine of complicity in the Crédit Mobilier scandal, but recommending that Representatives Oakes Ames and James Brooks be expelled.

27 February   The U.S. House of Representatives condemns Representatives James Brooks and Oakes Ames for their roles in the Crédit Mobilier railroad scandal, passing over a chance to expel them.

1 March   The Morrill Committee releases its report, saying that of all the senators alleged to have been involved, Senator James W. Patterson (R–NH), was found to be liable, and asked for his expulsion from the Senate. Due to Patterson having lost his reelection attempt in November

1872, and his leaving the Senate on 3 March, the Senate holds off action and allows Patterson to simply retire.

3 March    The Wilson Committee releases its report, saying that the financial relationship between the Crédit Mobilier and the Union Pacific Railroad was too cozy, and that some officers of both companies had held bonds illegally. Court action is recommended.

24 March    Senator Alexander Caldwell of Kansas resigns his seat to avoid being expelled, after he is accused of using bribes to get elected to the Senate.

### 1874
The U.S. House of Representatives investigates charges of irregularities in court funds lodged against Judge William F. Story. The House decides to pass on impeaching Story, instead passing the evidence on to the attorney general, who closes the case with no further proceedings ordered. Kansas State Treasurer Josiah Hayes is impeached for financial irregularities; however, when his trial opens in Topeka on 12 May, his resignation is announced, and the impeachment is abandoned.

### 1875
The Judiciary Committee of the U.S. House of Representatives recommends that Judge Richard Busteed be impeached for "non-residence, failure to hold court, and [the] improper use of [his] official position,' but the vote is tabled when Busteed resigns his seat. The House also investigates Judge Edward H. Durell for drunkenness and improper business transactions. The inquiry ends when Durell resigns his seat.

### 1876
The U.S. House of Representatives investigates charges of court administration irregularities against Judge Andrew Wylie of the Supreme Court of the District of Columbia. The inquiry ends when Wylie resigns his seat.

2 March    Secretary of War William Worth Belknap resigns his office amid allegations of massive financial misconduct.

3 April    Despite Belknap's resignation, the U.S. House of Representatives impeaches him on five articles accusing him of taking bribes.

1 August    Belknap appears at his Senate trial, but refuses to enter a plea, saying that as a private citizen he could not be impeached. The Senate agrees, voting on this date by a vote of thirty-seven to twenty-five to find Belknap guilty, but short of the two-thirds necessary to convict. Twenty-two of the senators who voted to acquit, as well as two who voted

to convict, later report that they agreed that the Senate lacked jurisdiction over the case.

### 1878
The U.S. House of Representatives investigates Consul-General Oliver B. Bradford on charges of corruption, but no action is taken after the matter is referred to the Judiciary Committee.

### 1879
The U.S. House of Representatives investigates Consul-General George F. Seward on charges of "corruptly receiv[ing] monies in the settlement of estates, and appropriat[ing] U.S. funds for [his] own use." No further action is ever taken on the ensuing investigation. Judge Henry W. Blodgett is also investigated by the House for allegedly "defrauding creditors, enriching friends in bankruptcy proceedings, and exceeding jurisdiction" in cases, but the investigation is tabled for lack of evidence.

### 1880
The United States Supreme Court, in *Kilbourn v. Thompson*, 103 U.S. 168, holds that the Congress may not hold persons outside of members of Congress in contempt and thus may not jail them for such contempt.

### 1883
Congress enacts the Pendleton Act, which outlaws the collection of campaign contributions on federal property. This ends the practice of forcing government workers to contribute money to campaigns to keep their jobs.

### 1884
The U.S. House of Representatives investigates Judge James W. Locke on charges of interfering in elections, but exonerates him. Judge Samuel B. Axtell is also investigated on charges of incompetence and misconduct while in office, but a House committee finds that the charges do not merit an impeachment vote.

23 May    Speaker of the U.S. House of Representatives John G. Carlisle tells the House that no member of that body should ever be punished for any offense alleged to have been committed previous to their congressional service and adds that "that has been so frequently decided by the House that it is no longer a matter of dispute."

### 1890
Maryland state Treasurer Stevenson Archer is charged with embezzlement after an investigation finds some $132,000 in state funds under his control missing. He pleads guilty to the charge, telling the court that he spent the money and had only $1 of it left. Sentenced to five years in prison, by 1894 he is in failing health and is pardoned by Governor

Frank Brown. He dies in August 1898, having never divulged where he spent the money.

**1892**

Judge Aleck Boardman is investigated by the U.S. House of Representatives on charges of the misuse of court funds and is censured by the subcommittee hearing the evidence rather than face an impeachment trial.

**1894**

May   Responding to published charges that senators had taken bribes to support tariff schedules favorable to the sugar industry, the U.S. Senate establishes the Special Investigative Committee. Uncertain as to the scope of its investigative powers, the Senate in August orders a comprehensive survey of all other congressional investigations. The resulting thousand-page compilation, "Decisions and Precedents of the Senate and House of Representatives Relating to Their Powers and Privileges Respecting Their Members and Officers," usefully documents Congress's institutional development throughout its first century.

**1895**

Delegate Robert William Wilcox from Hawaii is tried by a jury for his role in the Hawaiian Rebellion of 1895 and sentenced to death; his sentenced is commuted to thirty-five years in prison, and he is pardoned by the Hawaiian president in 1898. He dies in 1903.

**1901**

Eugene Schmitz, a bandleader, is elected Mayor of San Francisco, California, and begins an era rife with graft and corruption.

**1903**

20 September   In San Francisco, a deputy U.S. Marshall takes his own life, and three deputy sheriffs from the city are arrested on charges of taking bribes to allow Chinese immigrants into the country in violation of the Exclusion Act, which placed a barrier on immigration.

**1904**

Theodore Roosevelt campaigns for a full term as president on a platform of campaign reform and control of the so-called trusts—despite the fact that many of these same trusts are funding his campaign. Democratic presidential candidate Judge Alton B. Parker alleges that corporations are funding Roosevelt's campaign. Roosevelt initially denies this, only to admit to the charge after the election. Representative William Bourke Cochran of New York calls for federal financing of elections. *San Francisco Bulletin* publisher R. A. Crothers is mugged by an unknown assailant, after the *Bulletin* charges the administration of Mayor Eugene

Schmitz, and Schmitz's political leader Abe Ruef, with graft and corruption.

**1905**

In his annual message, President Theodore Roosevelt calls for campaign finance reform. This move, building on a second call in his 1906 annual message, leads to the establishment of the National Publicity Law Organization (NPLO), which lobbies for national campaign finance reform.

**1906**

24 October   San Francisco District Attorney William H. Langdon names Francis J. Heney, the special counsel in the Oregon land frauds cases, to assist him in prosecuting fraud and corruption in San Francisco. Heney is appointed assistant district attorney.

25 October   Acting Mayor James L. Gallagher of San Francisco suspends District Attorney William H. Langdon for "neglect of duty" and appoints political boss Abe Ruef in his place. Assistant District Attorney Francis J. Heney says that he does not recognize Ruef as district attorney.

26 October   A local San Francisco judge signs a temporary restraining order barring Ruef from becoming district attorney. District Attorney Langdon has guards protect his office from Ruef or his cronies to prevent them from taking control.

31 October   A demonstration held in San Francisco by Ruef protests graft inquiries against the Schmitz administration.

15 November   A grand jury empaneled by District Attorney Langdon hands down indictments against Mayor Eugene Schmitz, "Boss" Abe Ruef, and Police Chief Jeremiah Dinan.

**1907**

26 January   Congress enacts the Tillman Act, which bans direct contributions from corporations to individuals, but leaves a loophole allowing the heads of corporations to continue to contribute unlimited amounts of money.

4 March   "Boss" Abraham Ruef surrenders and is arraigned. He posts bond, then vanishes.

8 March   The judge overseeing the Ruef prosecution orders his arrest and names William J. Biggy to find him. Two hours later, Ruef is found at the Trocadero House, a hotel in Stern Grove, California, near San Francisco. Biggy is later named to replace Jeremiah Dinan as chief of police.

13 June   Mayor Eugene Schmitz is convicted by a San Francisco jury of extortion.

**1908**

16 November    Assistant District Attorney Francis J. Heney is shot in court by Morris Haas, whose criminal activity had been revealed by Heney some months earlier. Heney survives, but must be replaced by Hiram W. Johnson. Haas is a bagman for "Boss" Ruef. He is later found dead in his jail cell, a potential suicide from a smuggled gun. In the aftermath of the shooting of Heney and the death of Haas, Chief of Police Biggy is suspected of being in the pay of "Boss" Ruef.

1 December    Police Chief Biggy disappears off a police boat in San Francisco Bay.

10 December    "Boss" Ruef is found guilty of bribing a supervisor to vote to build the United Railroad, and is sentenced to fourteen years in prison.

15 December    The body of Police Chief Biggy is found near Angel Island in San Francisco Bay. The coroner rules that his was an accidental death. The circumstances of his death are never revealed, and the case goes unsolved.

**1909**

After Theodore Roosevelt leaves the White House, it is discovered that his 1904 campaign was funded by railroads, oil companies, and other businesses on which he was cracking down at the time as monopolies. For instance, J. P. Morgan alone gave $150,000.

**1910**

25 June    Congress enacts the Federal Corrupt Practices Act (also called the Publicity Act), requiring all U.S. House candidates—and, later, all U.S. Senate candidates when such candidates are directly elected by the people—to fully disclose all campaign contributions and spending.

**1911**

11 August    Congress enacts amendments to the Publicity Act of 1910, which established firm spending limits for federal campaigns. The amendments are designed to improve disclosure requirements.

**1912**

13 July    The U.S. Senate declares the election of William Lorimer (R–IL) to be invalid after it hears allegations that he won the seat in the Illinois legislature through bribery.

**1913**

Colonel Martin M. Mulhall, a lobbyist for the National Association of Manufacturers (NAM), implicates Representative James T. McDermott (D–IL) in bribe taking. Mulhall states that he had paid McDermott approximately $2,000 for "legislative favors." A congressional investigation leads to disciplinary charges against McDermott by the full House, but he is not expelled or censured. McDermott resigns his seat in 1914, but is reelected in November to his old seat.

**1921**

Senator Truman H. Newberry (R–MI) is indicted by a grand jury and later convicted of violating campaign spending limits in his 1918 Senate race against Democrat Henry Ford. The U.S. Supreme Court, in *Newberry v. United States*, 256 U.S. 232, holds that congressional authority to regulate elections does not extend to party primaries and election activities, and strikes down the spending limits Newberry had been convicted of violating.

**1922**

Secretary of the Interior Albert B. Fall leases the Teapot Dome oil reserves in Wyoming to cronies to pay them back for the campaign contributions they gave to President Warren G. Harding in his 1920 presidential campaign.

**1923**

22 October    The first hearing on the Teapot Dome allegations takes place.

**1924**

Representative John Wesley Langley (R-KY) is convicted of violating the National Prohibition Act.

**1925**

28 February    Congress revises the 1910 Federal Corrupt Practices Act, putting a cap on spending for senatorial campaigns at $25,000 and congressional campaigns at $5,000. Passed in response to the burgeoning Teapot Dome scandal, the law does not cover primary campaigns. Despite flagrant violations of this law and its revisions, only two men—Republicans William S. Vare of Pennsylvania and Frank L. Smith of Virginia—are ever prosecuted for violating it. They are excluded from Congress.

**1926**

District of Columbia Commissioner Frederick A. Fenning is impeached for "acting as an attorney while commissioner, champerty [a sharing in the proceeds of a lawsuit by an outside party who has promoted the litigation], exorbitant remuneration for guardianship of lunatics, among other charges." Fenning is later censured and forced to resign under pressure from President Calvin Coolidge.

12 April    In a stunning move, the U.S. Senate votes along party lines, forty-five to forty-one, to seat Democrat Daniel Steck over Republican Smith Brookhart, after Steck alleges voting irregularities.

## 1928

Representative Edgar Howard (D–NE) proposes a bill that would mandate a prison sentence for any former member of Congress who remains in Washington after his term of office to lobby his former colleagues.

## 1929

Representative Frederick N. Zihlman (R–MD) offers not to run for re-election and resigns as chairman of the House Committee on the District of Columbia, after he is indicted on charges of corruption.

## 1931

Representative Harry E. Rowbottom (R-IN) is convicted of bribery.

## 1934

Two members of the "Anti-Smith Committee of Virginia," James Cannon Jr. and Ada L. Burroughs, are acquitted of using campaign funds to defeat former Governor Al Smith of New York in violation of the Federal Corrupt Practices Act.

Representative George E. Foulkes (D-MI) is convicted of conspiracy to try to force postmasters in his district to pay political contributions.

## 1936

President Franklin Delano Roosevelt receives a $250,000 contribution from the head of the Congress of Industrial Organizations (CIO), the first major donation from a union to a political candidate.

Donn M. Roberts, mayor of Terre Haute, Indiana, who had been convicted in 1915 of bribery and served three and one-half years in prison, is convicted of embezzlement and sentenced to prison a second time; however, following a heart attack, he is released from prison and dies on 3 August 1936.

## 1939

Responding to allegations that the administration of President Franklin Delano Roosevelt has forced federal government workers to donate to his presidential campaign, Congress enacts the Hatch Act, which prohibits federal employees from contributing to, or participating in, federal campaigns.

25 June   Roy E. Brownmiller, Pennsylvania secretary of highways, is convicted of using state payroll funds to finance the 1938 election campaign of Governor George Howard Earle III, who lost. Brownmiller eventually serves prison time, but is released after one year due to declining health.

## 1940

19 July   Congress enacts amendments to the Hatch Act, imposing a limit of $5,000 a year on individual contributions to federal candidates or national party committees.

## 1941

In *United States v. Classic*, 31 U.S. 299, the U.S. Supreme Court reverses its 1921 ruling in *Newberry v. United States* and holds that Congress does have the authority to regulate spending limits for primaries and election activities.

## 1943

Congress enacts, over President Franklin Delano Roosevelt's veto, the Smith-Connally Anti-Strike Act (also known as the War Labor Disputes Act) to prevent labor unions from making political contributions. It is passed as a war measure only, and expires six months after the end of the war in 1945.

16 September   A Federal grand jury indicts Representative James M. Curley (D–MA) on charges of using the mail to defraud companies.

1 November   A federal court voids the indictment against Representative James M. Curley, stating that the grand jury was "illegally summoned."

## 1944

18 January   Another federal grand jury in Washington, D.C., indicts Representative James M. Curley.

## 1946

18 January   Representative James M. Curley is convicted by a federal jury in Washington of using the mail to defraud companies of mail contracts during the Second World War.

## 1947

13 January   The U.S. Court of Appeals for the D.C. Circuit upholds the conviction of Representative James M. Curley.

23 January   A federal grand jury in Washington, D.C., indicts Representative Andrew J. May (D–KY) for accepting funds to influence war contracts during the Second World War.

18 February   Representative James M. Curley is sentenced to six to eighteen months in prison and fined $1,000 for mail fraud.

2 June   The U.S. Supreme Court upholds Curley's conviction.

23 June   Congress reenacts the provisions against campaign spending by labor unions as part of the Labor

Management Relations Act of 1947, also called the Taft-Hartley Act.

26 June    Representative James M. Curley enters a prison to begin serving his sentence.

3 July    Representative Andrew J. May is convicted on charges of bribery and conspiracy.

26 November    President Harry S. Truman commutes the remainder of Curley's jail sentence.

**1948**
8 November    Representative J. Parnell Thomas (R–NJ) is indicted on charges of defrauding the government by padding his congressional payroll and taking kickbacks from his staff.

**1949**
14 November    The U.S. Supreme Court refuses to review the conviction of Representative Andrew J. May (D–KY).

30 November    Representative J. Parnell Thomas pleads no contest to charges that he took illicit payoffs from his staff.

5 December    Representative Andrew J. May begins serving his prison sentence.

9 December    Representative J. Parnell Thomas is sentenced to six to eighteen months in prison and fined $10,000.

**1950**
10 September    Representative J. Parnell Thomas is paroled from prison after serving eight and one-half months in prison.

18 September    Representative Andrew J. May is paroled after serving nine months of his prison sentence.

20 December    Representative Walter E. Brehm (R–OH) is indicted for accepting contributions from his congressional staff.

24 December    President Harry S. Truman pardons Representative Andrew J. May.

**1951**
In the wake of charges that supporters of Taiwan's Nationalist Party (called "The China Lobby") have been trying to influence Congress, Senator Wayne Morse (R–OR) calls for an investigation into lobbying by foreign governments to influence U.S. foreign policy. Representative Charles Bennett (D–FL) introduces a resolution calling on

"all Government employees, including officeholders" to adhere to a congressional ethics code.

30 April    Representative Walter E. Brehm is convicted of accepting campaign contributions from one of his employees.

8 June    Representative Theodore Leonard Irving (D–MO) is indicted by a federal grand jury in Washington, D.C., for violating the Corrupt Practices Act and the Taft-Hartley Act for misusing funds when he served as the head of a labor union during his 1948 campaign for Congress.

11 June    Representative Walter E. Brehm is sentenced to five to fifteen months in prison and fined $5,000. His sentence is summarily suspended by the judge, and Brehm never serves any time in prison.

28 December    Representative Theodore Leonard Irving is acquitted by a federal jury of all charges.

**1953**
14 January    Representative John L. McMillan (D–SC) is indicted for violating a law barring members of Congress from making contracts with the government when he leased oil and gas properties in Utah from the Department of the Interior.

16 May    Representative John L. McMillan is acquitted of all charges.

17 June    Representative Ernest K. Bramblett (R–CA) is indicted for making false statements in connection with a kickback investigation involving congressional aides and staff.

**1954**
9 February    Representative Ernest K. Bramblett is convicted of charges that he lied during a House kickback investigation.

14 April    Bramblett's sentencing is stayed pending an appeal to the United States Supreme Court.

**1955**
4 April    The U.S. Supreme Court upholds the conviction of Representative Ernest K. Bramblett.

15 June    Bramblett is sentenced to four to twelve months in prison and fined $5,000. The judge suspends the sentence, and Bramblett does not serve any jail time.

**1956**

5 March   Representative Thomas J. Lane (D–MA) is indicted for federal income tax evasion for the years 1949–1951.

20 April   Representative Lane pleads guilty to income tax evasion and is sentenced to four months in prison and fined $10,000.

14 December   Representative William J. Green (D–PA) is indicted with six others for conspiracy to defraud the government when he accepted business for his personal company in exchange for working to gain a contract with the U.S. Army Signal Corps for a contributor.

**1958**

8 May   Representative Adam Clayton Powell (D–NY) is indicted for federal income tax evasion.

**1959**

27 February   Representative William J. Green is acquitted of all charges.

**1960**

5 and 7 April   A federal judge dismisses two of the three charges against Representative Adam Clayton Powell.

22 April   Representative Adam Clayton Powell's trial on a single charge of income tax evasion is declared a mistrial due to a hung jury.

23 May   The judge overseeing the trial of Representative Adam Clayton Powell refuses to dismiss the indictment against him.

**1961**

13 April   The U.S. attorney overseeing the trial of Representative Adam Clayton Powell asks to have the single charge still against him dismissed.

**1962**

16 October   Representative Thomas F. Johnson (D–MD) is indicted with Representative Frank W. Boykin (D–AL) and two others for conspiracy to defraud the government by trying to influence a Department of Justice inquiry into fraud at a Maryland savings & loan bank.

**1963**

13 June   Representative Thomas F. Johnson is convicted on all charges relating to his attempt to end an investigation of a Maryland savings & loan bank. Also convicted is Representative Frank Boykin on charges of conflict of interest and conspiracy to defraud the government.

7 October   Representative Frank Boykin is sentenced to probation for six months and fined $40,000.

**1964**

24 July   The U.S. Senate Committee on Rules and Administration rules on the Bobby Baker case, holding that the Senate aide had used his office for personal gain. However, he is not charged with any crime.

16 September   The U.S. Court of Appeals for the Fourth Circuit strikes down the conviction of Representative Thomas F. Johnson on the grounds that the conviction arose from a speech he gave on behalf of a Maryland savings & loan bank; the court holds that such speech is protected by the Speech and Debate clause of the U.S. Constitution. The court does order a new trial on other charges relating to a conflict of interest.

**1965**

9 July   A year after it was established, the first members of the Senate Committee on Standards and Conduct are named. John Stennis (D–MS) is named chairman.

17 December   President Lyndon Baines Johnson pardons Representative Frank Boykin of Alabama.

**1966**

24 February   The U.S. Supreme Court affirms the striking down of the conviction of Representative Thomas F. Johnson, sustaining the Speech and Debate clause of the U.S. Constitution.

**1967**

29 January   A former congressman, W. Pat Jennings, becomes the first Clerk of the House to actually collect campaign finance reports and to report violators to the Department of Justice, as directed by the 1925 Federal Corrupt Practices Act. The United States Senate opens an investigation into the dealings of Senator Edward V. Long (D–MO) for allegedly accepting legal fees from a lawyer representing James R. Hoffa, the head of the Teamsters union, at the same time that Long was conducting a Senate investigation of government wiretapping and electronic eavesdropping of officials under FBI investigation, which included Hoffa. The Senate later clears Long of any wrongdoing.

Former Senate Majority Leader Secretary Bobby Baker is convicted on seven counts of income tax invasion, theft, and conspiracy to defraud the Government. On 7 April he is sentenced to at least one year in prison.

23 June   Senator Thomas J. Dodd (D–CT) is censured by the Senate for using campaign funds for personal use, setting off a new wave of campaign finance reform efforts.

## 1968

26 January   Representative Thomas F. Johnson is convicted of conflict of interest charges relating to his work to hinder the investigation of a Maryland savings & loan bank.

30 January   Representative Thomas F. Johnson is sentenced to six months in prison.

4 October   President Lyndon B. Johnson withdraws the name of Justice Abe Fortas for the position of chief justice after allegations of corruption against him are aired.

## 1969

18 December   Representative Hugh J. Addonizio (D–NJ) is indicted on charges of extortion, conspiracy, and income tax evasion relating to crimes he allegedly committed while serving as mayor of Newark, New Jersey.

## 1970

31 March   Representative John V. Dowdy (D–TX) is indicted on charges of bribery, conspiracy, and perjury relating to his receipt of money from a Maryland company under investigation for fraud.

22 July   Representative Hugh J. Addonizio is convicted of sixty-four counts of extortion, conspiracy, and income tax evasion.

23 July   President Nixon secretly approves a plan to expand domestic wiretapping and other intelligence gathering activities by the FBI, the CIA, and other federal agencies. A few days later, after having second thoughts, he rescinds the order. Former Secretary of Health, Education, and Welfare John Gardner founds Common Cause, a citizen lobbying and reform group.

22 September   Representative Hugh J. Addonizio is sentenced to ten years in prison and fined $25,000.

16 December   Representative Martin B. McKneally (R–NY) is indicted for failure to file federal income taxes for the years 1964–1967.

## 1971

Speaker of the House of Representatives John McCormack (D–MA) retires after one of his top aides, Martin Sweig, is accused of using the Speaker's office and name for dishonest purposes.

3 September   A unit is formed inside the White House to plug leaks inside administration offices. The group is called "The Plumbers."

18 October   Representative Martin B. McKneally pleads guilty to federal income tax evasion.

20 December   Representative McKneally is sentenced to one year in prison and one year on probation and fined $5,000. The judge suspends the prison sentence, and McKneally does not serve any jail time.

30 December   Representative John Dowdy is convicted of all charges relating to bribery and perjury.

## 1972

7 February   President Nixon signs the Federal Election Campaign Act, establishing spending limits on both presidential and congressional candidates and requiring the reporting of campaign contributions.

15 February   Attorney General John N. Mitchell resigns from his post to serve as the chairman of President Nixon's 1972 reelection campaign.

23 February   Representative John Dowdy is sentenced to eighteen months in prison and fined $25,000.

7 April   Representative Cornelius Gallagher (D–NJ) is indicted for federal income tax evasion for the years 1966–1967, perjury, and conspiracy for his work in assisting two other people to evade income tax payment.

28 May   Unknown to all but the small group called "The Plumbers," electronic surveillance equipment is installed at Democratic National Committee headquarters in the Watergate building in Washington, D.C.

17 June   Five men break into the office of the Democratic National Committee in the Watergate Hotel in Washington, D.C., in an attempt to fix a broken bug that has been installed a few weeks earlier. All five are arrested.

19 June   The Washington Post reports that a Republican security aide, James W. McCord Jr., is one of the Watergate burglars.

1 August   The Washington Post reports that a $25,000 check, made out to the Nixon 1972 campaign reelection committee, wound up in the bank account of one of the Watergate burglars.

30 August   President Nixon reports that an investigation of potential White House involvement in the Watergate break-

in, conducted by White House counsel John Dean, shows no White House involvement.

**15 September**   E. Howard Hunt, G. Gordon Liddy, and the five Watergate burglars, Bernard Barker, Virgilio Gonzalez, Eugenio Martinez, James W. McCord Jr., and Frank Sturgis—are indicted by a federal grand jury in the burgeoning Watergate scandal.

**29 September**   *The Washington Post* reports that while serving as attorney general, John Mitchell controlled a secret slush fund that he used to finance secret bugging and other intelligence-gathering activities, much of which was illegal.

**10 October**   *The Washington Post* reports that the FBI has concluded that the Watergate break-in was part of a massive campaign of political spying and espionage by the Nixon reelection committee.

**21 December**   Representative Cornelius Gallagher pleads guilty to income tax evasion.

**1973**
**8 January**   The trial of the Watergate defendants begins.

**11 January**   Watergate defendant E. Howard Hunt pleads guilty.

**15 January**   Watergate defendants Barker, Gonzalez, Martinez, and Sturgis plead guilty.

**30 January**   G. Gordon Liddy and James W. McCord Jr. are convicted of conspiracy, burglary, and wiretapping for their roles in the Watergate break-in.

**7 February**   Amid growing questions over the role of high Nixon administration officials in the Watergate break-in, the U.S. Senate establishes the Select Committee on Presidential Campaign Activities, also known as the Senate Watergate Committee. Senator Sam Ervin (D–NC) is named the committee's chairman, while Senator Howard H. Baker (R–TN) is named vice chairman.

**13 March**   The U.S. Court of Appeals for the Fourth Circuit strikes down the bribery and conspiracy convictions of Representative John V. Dowdy; however, the court does uphold the perjury conviction.

**19 March**   Convicted Watergate defendant James W. McCord Jr. writes a letter to Judge John Sirica, overseeing the Watergate trials, and tells him that the five Watergate defendants who pled guilty shortly before the start of their trial were pressured into doing so, that perjury was

committed in the trial, and that other people were involved in the break-in.

**29 March**   *The Los Angeles Times* and *The Washington Post* both report that James McCord told Samuel Dash, chief counsel to the Senate Watergate Committee, that former Nixon aide Jeb Stuart Magruder and White House counsel John Dean knew of the plan to break in to Democratic headquarters and bug the phones. *The Post* states that Liddy had told McCord that the operation had the backing and approval of former Attorney General John Mitchell and Charles Colson, former special counsel to Nixon.

**6 April**   White House counsel John Dean begins to cooperate with Watergate investigators.

**30 April**   Nixon aides H. R. Haldeman and John Ehrlichman, as well as Attorney General Richard Kleindienst, resign in the midst of the growing Watergate scandal. President Nixon fires White House counsel John Dean.

**18 May**   The Senate Watergate Committee begins televised hearings, capturing the nation's attention. Attorney General-designate Elliot Richardson names former Solicitor General Archibald Cox as the Department of Justice special prosecutor on Watergate.

**3 June**   *The Washington Post* reports that John Dean told Watergate investigators that he discussed the Watergate scandal with President Nixon at least thirty-five times.

**13 June**   Watergate investigators discover a memo addressed to former Nixon aide John Ehrlichman outlining a plan to burglarize the office of the psychiatrist of former Department of Defense official Daniel Ellsberg, who had released the so-called Pentagon Papers.

**15 June**   Representative Cornelius Gallagher is sentenced to two years in prison and fined $10,000.

**25 June**   In televised hearings before the Senate Watergate Committee, former White House counsel John Dean tells the committee under oath that the White House had a major plan for domestic espionage of the president's political enemies, and that Nixon planned the cover-up of the Watergate burglary within days of the occurrence of the break-in.

**7 July**   President Nixon tells the Senate Watergate Committee that he will not appear in person before the committee or grant the committee access to any presidential papers.

13 July Former presidential appointments secretary Alexander Butterfield tells the Senate Watergate Committee that President Nixon had been taping all White House conversations since 1971. The Committee concludes that the Nixon campaign was involved in domestic spying, abuse of campaign funds, favors for the milk industry in return for campaign contributions, and that President Nixon had hampered the investigation, although no charge of obstruction of justice was put forward.

23 July Following a request from the Senate Watergate Committee and Special Watergate Prosecutor Archibald Cox for any and all tapes regarding Oval Office conversations, President Nixon refuses to turn over any tapes, citing executive privilege.

25 July Nixon refuses to comply with a subpoena from Cox.

26 July The Senate Watergate Committee votes to subpoena the Nixon tapes.

2 August Vice President Spiro Agnew is notified that he is under investigation by the U.S. Attorney's Office in Baltimore, Maryland, for his role in a milk bribery scheme while he served as governor of that state.

9 August The Senate Watergate Committee sues President Nixon for access to the White House tapes.

29 August Judge John Sirica orders President Nixon to deliver nine Oval Office tapes for the judge to privately review.

26 September Vice President Spiro Agnew's request for a congressional investigation in his alleged role in a milk bribery scheme while he served as governor of Maryland is refused by Speaker of the U.S. House of Representatives Carl Albert (D–OK).

27 September A federal in grand jury in Baltimore begins to hear evidence in the bribery investigation of Vice President Spiro Agnew.

9 October The U.S. Supreme Court upholds the perjury conviction of Representative John V. Dowdy.

10 October Vice President Spiro Agnew resigns, becoming the second vice president to resign his office, the first being John Calhoun, who resigned in 1832 over political differences with President Andrew Jackson.

19 October President Nixon tries to broker a deal over the White House tapes with Senator John Stennis (D–MS),

under which Stennis would be allowed to hear the actual tapes while Nixon would provide a detailed summary to special prosecutor Cox.

20 October Special prosecutor Cox refuses to accept the Stennis compromise and demands additional tapes from Nixon. President Nixon then orders Attorney General Elliot Richardson to fire Cox. Richardson refuses and resigns. Deputy Attorney General William D. Ruckelshaus also refuses and also resigns. It is left up to Solicitor General Robert H. Bork to fire Cox. The event is known as the Saturday Night Massacre.

23 October Nixon agrees to comply with a subpoena to hand over certain White House taped conversations.

1 November Under increasing pressure in Congress, President Nixon names attorney Leon Jaworski as the new Watergate special prosecutor.

12 November Nixon decides to hand over several unsubpoenaed recordings and portions of his diary for inspection.

17 November In a press conference, Nixon tells reporters that he is innocent of any crimes in the Watergate scandal. "I am not a crook," Nixon says with fervor.

7 December Officials of the Nixon administration cannot explain why there is a gap of eighteen and one-half minutes on one of the subpoenaed Watergate tapes.

**1974**
28 January Representative John V. Dowdy enters prison to serve a six-month sentence after the U.S. Supreme Court upholds his perjury conviction.

6 February The U.S. House of Representatives votes to authorize the House Judiciary Committee to hold hearings on possible impeachment charges being brought against President Nixon.

1 March Seven former aides of President Nixon are indicted for various offenses relating to Watergate; Nixon is named as an unindicted coconspirator.

6 April Senator Edward R. Gurney (R–FL) is indicted by a Florida grand jury on charges that he violated state campaign finance laws.

16 April Watergate special prosecutor Leon Jaworski demands access to sixty-four White House tapes.

30 April    The White House releases 1,200 pages of transcripts edited from Oval Office tapes, but the Senate Watergate Committee continues to demand the tapes themselves.

9 May    The House Judiciary Committee begins hearings on possible impeachment charges against President Nixon.

17 May    The indictment against Senator Edward R. Gurney is dismissed.

10 July    A federal grand jury indicts Senator Edward R. Gurney and six other defendants for conspiracy, perjury, and soliciting bribes in the form of campaign contributions from Florida construction concerns.

19 July    Representative Frank J. Brasco (D–NY) is convicted of conspiracy to receive bribes and conspiracy involving a scheme to get government Post Office contracts for a trucking firm with ties to the Mafia.

23 July    Representative Lawrence Hogan (R–MD) becomes the first Republican in the Congress to call for President Nixon's resignation.

24 July    The U.S. Supreme Court, in *Nixon v. United States*, 418 U.S. 683, holds that Nixon must turn over tapes from sixty-four White House conversations, and that these conversations are not protected by executive privilege.

27 July    The House Judiciary Committee votes for an article of impeachment, charging President Nixon with obstruction of justice.

29 July    The House Judiciary Committee votes a second article of impeachment, charging President Nixon with misuse of presidential powers and violation of his oath of office.

30 July    The House Judiciary Committee adopts a third article of impeachment, charging President Nixon with a failure to comply with House subpoenas for White House tapes.

5 August    Nixon releases the transcript of a conversation with H. R. Haldeman from 23 June 1972, six days after the Watergate break-in, in which Nixon orders the Federal Bureau of Investigation to abandon its inquiry into the burglary. This tape is considered the 'smoking gun' implicating Nixon in obstruction of justice.

7 August    Republican leaders meet with Nixon, telling him that impeachment was assured in the House, and that he

was quickly losing support in the Senate to forestall conviction.

8 August    Nixon tells the nation in a televised address that he will resign the following day.

9 August    Nixon resigns, becoming the first American president to do so. Vice President Gerald R. Ford becomes the thirty-eighth president of the United States.

8 September    One month after becoming president, Gerald Ford pardons former President Richard Nixon for any and all crimes he may have committee during his presidency.

1 October    Representative Bertram L. Podell (D–NY) halts his trial on charges of conspiracy and conflict of interest to plead guilty. Podell later admits that a $29,000 check payable to the "Citizens' Committee for B.L. Podell" was a bribe to obtain a government contract for Florida Atlantic Airtlines.

## 1975
The Senate resolves one of the most corrupt elections in American history. Senator Henry Bellmon (R–OK) was challenged by Democrat Ed Edmondson. In a close race, Bellmon won, but Edmondson challenged the result. After a Senate investigation, which held that Oklahoma election rules were violated, but that it was unable to determine which side would have won the election if the violations had not occurred, the full Senate voted forty-seven to forty-six that Bellmon would be seated and Edmonson's challenge be thrown out.

26 June    Jack L. Chestnut, a former aide to Senator and former Vice President Hubert H. Humphrey, is sentenced to four months in prison and fined $5,000 for accepting an illegal campaign contribution during Humphrey's 1970 U.S. Senate campaign.

6 August    Senator Edward R. Gurney is acquitted of the bribery charge, but the jury fails to reach a verdict on the other counts.

## 1976
26 January    Representative Andrew Jackson Hinshaw (R–CA) is convicted by a jury in California on two counts of bribery stemming from his first run for Congress in 1972.

29 January    Representative James R. Jones (D–OK) pleads guilty to a misdemeanor on the allegation that he failed to report a cash contribution in 1972 from the Gulf Oil Corporation.

24 February   Representative Andrew Jackson Hinshaw is sentenced to concurrent one-to-fourteen-year prison sentences.

2 June   Representative Henry Helstoski (D–NJ) is indicted by a federal grand jury in New Jersey on charges that he solicited and accepted bribes from Chilean and Argentinean immigrants in exchange for introducing bills in Congress designed to block their extradition from the United States. Helstoski, along with three aides, were charged with bribery, conspiracy, obstruction of justice, and lying to a federal grand jury.

21 September   Former Representative James F. Hastings (R–NY), who had served in the House from 1965 to 1975, is indicted by a federal grand jury in Washington, D.C., on charges that he operated a kickback scheme out of his congressional office with members of his congressional staff. Despite pleading not guilty to the charges, Hastings is convicted on twenty-eight counts on 17 December and sentenced to serve twenty months to five years in federal prison.

24 October   *The Washington Post* breaks the "Koreagate" story, leading to the largest congressional scandal in decades.

27 October   The Justice Department announces that it is dropping its civil suit against Representative William "Bill" Clay (D–MO), after Clay agrees to reimburse the U.S. government $1,754 he overcharged on travel expenses. Senator Edward R. Gurney (R–FL) is acquitted by a federal jury of lying to a federal grand jury.

**1977**
April   Former Representative Hugh J. Addonizio is released from prison after serving five years of a ten-year sentence.

11 April   William Cahn, district attorney of Nassau County, New York, is convicted of forty-five counts of mail fraud arising from the embezzlement of travel expenses. A first trial in February 1976 had ended with a hung jury.

4 May   Representative Richard A. Tonry (D–LA) resigns his seat in the U.S. House of Representatives, held just four months, as he faced probable indictment of vote-rigging in the 1976 Democratic primary.

12 May   A federal grand jury in New Orleans indicts former Representative Richard A. Tonry on charges of obstructing justice by lying to a federal grand jury, and receiving illegal campaign contributions.

1 July   Former Representative Richard A. Tonry pleads guilty to reduced charges involving obstruction of justice and lying under oath; he is later sentenced to one year in prison and fined $10,000.

**1978**
20 January   Judge Herbert Allen Fogel of the Eastern District of Pennsylvania writes to President Jimmy Carter that he will resign from the bench, effective 1 May, after the Department of Justice threatens to prosecute him for numerous offenses.

October   Representative Charles C. Diggs Jr. (D–MI) is convicted by a jury for illegally diverting more than $60,000 of his employees' salaries for his personal use. On 20 November, he is sentenced to three years in prison.

21 November   James Y. Carter, the Chicago taxi commissioner since 1960, is convicted of nine counts of extortion, racketeering, and income tax evasion.

**1979**
Congress amends the Federal Election Campaign Act so that "soft money" is exempt from 1971 limitations. This allows the explosion of "soft money" advertising and spending that is to dominate elections over the next twenty years.

January   House leaders convince Representative Charles C. Diggs Jr. to resign as chairman of the House Foreign Affairs Subcommittee on Africa after he is convicted of financial misconduct.

18 July   Cleveland City Council President George L. Forbes, the city's top black leader, is acquitted by a jury of eleven counts of bribery, theft in office, and extortion, all tied to an alleged gambling kickback scheme.

20 July   Representative Claude "Buddy" Leach (D–LA) is indicted on federal charges of buying votes in the 1978 general election. He is later acquitted of all the charges, although 23 people tied to Leach are convicted of rigging votes in that election.

31 July   The U.S. House of Representatives censures Representative Charles C. Diggs Jr., by a vote of 414–0, for the misuse of his clerk-hire funds. This is only the second time in the twentieth century that a sitting member has been censured. (The first, Representative Thomas L. Blanton (D–TX), was censured for using objectionable language that was printed in *The Congressional Record*.)

**1980**
29 May   The House Democratic Caucus passes a rule to automatically remove a committee or subcommittee

chairmanship from any party member who is censured by the House or indicted or convicted of a felony with a sentence lasting more than two years.

## 1981

24 August    The Senate Ethics Committee votes unanimously to expel Senator Harrison Williams for his role in the ABSCAM scandal.

## 1982

3 March    The Senate begins debate on the punishment for Senator Harrison Williams of New Jersey.

11 March    Senator Harrison Williams resigns after it appears he will be expelled from the Senate for his conviction in the ABSCAM case.

## 1984

2 April    Representative George Hansen (R–ID) becomes the first person convicted of violating the Ethics in Government Act of 1978, when he is found guilty by a federal jury in Washington, D.C., of four counts of filing incorrect financial statements. On 25 June, Hansen is sentenced to five to fifteen months in prison, and fined $40,000. On 31 July, the U.S. House of Representatives votes 354–42 to reprimand Hansen. Hansen loses his seat in the election in November.

## 1986

10 January    Queens (New York) Borough President Donald R. Manes is discovered by police driving erratically; upon closer examination, he is found with his wrists slashed in a failed suicide attempt. It is soon discovered that Manes is in the middle of a vast financial scandal.

11 February    Queens Borough President Donald R. Manes resigns his office.

13 March    Donald R. Manes commits suicide by shoving a knife into his heart.

25 November    Bronx Democratic Party Chairman Stanley M. Friedman is convicted by a federal jury of racketeering, conspiracy, and mail fraud. The U.S. attorney, Rudolph W. Guiliani, calls the scheme that Friedman was involved in an "enterprise for illegal plunder."

19 December    A court in Washington, D.C., names attorney Lawrence Walsh to investigate potential violations of law in the Iran-Contra Affair.

## 1987

January    William Sterling Anderson, a former Speaker of the South Carolina House of Representatives pro tem, is

sentenced to fourteen months in prison for falsifying the customer credit records of his mobile home business.

21 January    The U.S. Parole Commission votes eight to zero against an appeal for early release by impeached Judge Harry E. Claiborne, convicted of tax fraud. The commission states that Claiborne had "seriously breached the public's trust."

22 January    At a news conference prior to his sentencing for taking a $300,000 kickback, former Pennsylvania Treasurer R. Budd Dwyer shoots himself in the mouth with a pistol in front of the television cameras in Harrisburg, Pennsylvania.

## 1988

18 May    The public affairs group Common Cause calls for an investigation of House Speaker Jim Wright, alleging that Wright may have broken the law in his financial arrangement surrounding the publication of his book, *Reflections of a Public Man*, and that Wright intervened with federal bank regulators regarding a Texas savings & loan bank.

26 May    Representative Newt Gingrich of Georgia, backed by seventy-two Republican members of the U.S. House of Representatives, files a complaint with the House Committee on Standards of Official Conduct regarding Speaker of the House Jim Wright.

9 June    The House Committee on Standards of Official Conduct votes unanimously to conduct an inquiry into the Wright matter, including other allegations of wrongdoing.

26 July    The House Committee on Standards of Official Conduct hires attorney Richard J. Phelan of Chicago as special outside counsel to investigate House Speaker Jim Wright.

4 August    Representative Mario Biaggi (D–NY) resigns from the House when he faces an almost certain expulsion vote for his role in the Wedtech scandal.

14 September    Speaker Jim Wright testifies before the House Committee on Standards of Official Conduct for five hours.

21 November    Representative Robert Garcia (D–NY) is indicted on charges of influence peddling in the Wedtech case.

**1989**

22 February    Richard Phelan, special outside counsel to the House Committee on Standards of Official Conduct, submits a 279-page report on the Jim Wright investigation.

13 April    Speaker Wright goes before television cameras to call for fairness, as word leaks out that special outside counsel Phelan has found evidence of serious crimes committed by Wright. The Speaker is emotional as he tries to rebut the accusations lodged against him.

17 April    The House Committee on Standards of Official Conduct releases its report on Wright, detailing that it has "reason to believe" that the Speaker has violated the rules of congressional conduct sixty-nine separate times. These sixty-nine charges fall into two categories: that Wright conspired to use the sales of his book to hide income from House-imposed limits, and that he accepted $145,000 in improper gifts from George Mallick, a Fort Worth developer and real estate businessman who was a friend of Wright's.

23 May    Lawyers for Speaker Wright appear before the House Committee on Standards of Official Conduct and claim that the panel has misinterpreted House rules and ask that the charges against Wright be thrown out.

31 May    Taking to the floor of the U.S. House, Speaker Jim Wright tells the members that he will resign as Speaker, and offers to vacate his House seat as well.

30 June    Former Speaker Jim Wright resigns his House seat.

20 October    Representative Robert Garcia (D–NY) and his wife are convicted on charges of extortion and influence peddling in the Wedtech scandal.

**1990**

7 January    Representative Robert Garcia resigns from the House. Twelve days later he is sentenced to three years in prison for his role in the Wedtech case.

29 June    The convictions of former Representative Robert Garcia and his wife in the Wedtech scandal are struck down by a federal appeals court.

**1992**

24 December    In a controversial move, President George H. W. Bush, in his last days in office, pardons former Secretary of Defense Caspar Weinberger and five others—Elliott Abrams, a former assistant secretary of state for inter-American affairs; former National Security Adviser Robert McFarlane; and Duane Clarridge, Alan Fiers, and Clair George, all former employees of the Central Intelligence Agency—for their roles in the Iran-Contra scandal. Weinberger had been indicted shortly before the 1992 election and was scheduled to go on trial 5 January 1993.

**1993**

19 May    Several longtime employees of the White House Travel Office are fired. Controversy erupts when it is discovered that several of President Clinton's friends—including a cousin, Catherine Cornelius—were behind the firings, allegedly so that they could get the business.

25 May    Following a wave of protest and anger, five workers from the White House Travel Office who were fired on 19 May are reinstated.

19 July    Senator Robert J. Dole (R–KS) calls for the appointment of a special counsel to investigate the White House Travel Office firings.

**1994**

9 January    Senator Daniel Patrick Moynihan (D–NY) calls for the appointment of a special counsel to investigate the allegations against President Clinton and his wife regarding the Whitewater land deal in Arkansas.

12 January    Amid calls from other Democrats, President Clinton agrees to ask the attorney general to name an independent counsel to investigate the Whitewater land deal.

February    Jay Stephens, a Republican attorney, is named to investigate the Resolution Trust Corporation's investigation of the Clinton's ties to the failure of Little Rock-based Madison Guaranty Bank.

14 March    Following allegations that he was involved in misconduct at his law firm in Arkansas, Associate Attorney General Webster Hubbell resigns.

26 July    The U.S. House of Representatives opens hearings on the Whitewater allegations.

5 August    A panel of three federal judges names former Solicitor General Kenneth W. Starr to be the independent counsel overseeing the Whitewater investigation, replacing Robert B. Fiske, who had been on the job since January 1994.

3 October    Secretary of Agriculture Mike Espy resigns after he is implicated in accepting gifts from companies over which his department had jurisdiction.

15 December    Former Associate Attorney General Webster Hubbell, a former law partner of First Lady Hillary Rodham Clinton, pleads guilty in Arkansas to charges of mail fraud

and tax evasion, and is sentenced to twenty-one months in prison.

**1995**
3 January   The Senate Banking Committee holding hearings on the Whitewater land deal finds that no laws were broken and closes the investigation.

17 May   The U.S. Senate votes ninety-six to three to establish the Special Committee to Investigate Whitewater Development Corporation and Related Matters, also known as the Senate Whitewater Committee, chaired by Senator Alphonse D'Amato (R–NY).

9 June   The U.S. Court of Appeals for the Seventh Circuit upholds the conviction of Judge Adam Stillo Sr., who had been convicted, along with his nephew, of conspiracy to commit extortion under the color of official right, in violation of the Hobbs Act.

10 August   The House Banking Committee closes hearings on the Madison Guaranty Bank allegations, finding no illegalities.

17 August   A grand jury in Little Rock, Arkansas, indicts Governor Jim Guy Tucker and James and Susan McDougal on charges of bank fraud related to the Whitewater land scheme.

26 October   The Senate Whitewater Committee issues forty-nine subpoenas to the White House and other agencies for documents.

19 December   Congress enacts the Lobbying Disclosure Act of 1995, which requires the semiannual disclosure of the hiring of lobbyists, the areas of legislation they specialize in, and whether a certain lobbyist has worked for the government in the past year.

**1996**
4 January   First Lady Hillary Rodham Clinton's billing records from the Rose law firm in Little Rock are found on a table in the White House residence book room; it is unknown how they got there, two years after being subpoenaed.

22 January   Independent Counsel Kenneth Starr subpoenas Hillary Rodham Clinton to appear before a federal grand jury on the Rose law firm billing records.

26 January   First Lady Hillary Rodham Clinton appears before a Washington, D.C., federal grand jury, the first such case in the American history.

22 April   David Hale, a former chief of a government lending agency, testifies at the trial of Governor Jim Guy Tucker that then-Governor Bill Clinton pressured him to make a fraudulent $300,000 loan to Susan McDougal.

26 April   Vice President Al Gore attends a fundraising event at the Hsi Lai Buddhist temple in Los Angeles. Initially billed as "community outreach," it is later discovered that money was raised from the monks for the Clinton/Gore 1996 campaign in violation of campaign finance laws.

29 May   A jury convicts Whitewater defendants James and Susan McDougal. James is convicted of eighteen counts, while his wife is convicted of four.

14 June   The FBI issues a report on the "Filegate" scandal stating that the White House had requested specific files.

17 June   White House security chief Craig Livingston is questioned by the House Committee on Government Reform and Oversight on the "Filegate" scandal.

20 June   Attorney General Janet Reno asks Independent Counsel Kenneth Starr to take over the "Filegate" investigation.

15 July   Arkansas Governor Jim Guy Tucker resigns after he is threatened with impeachment by Lieutenant Governor Mike Huckabee. Tucker resigns and Huckabee is sworn in as governor.

20 August   Facing ten-years imprisonment for his Whitewater crimes, former Arkansas Governor Jim Guy Tucker, suffering from a failing liver, receives mercy and is given four-years' probation.

17 October   *The Wall Street Journal* reports that monks from the Hsi Lai Buddhist temple visited by Vice President Al Gore in April had contributed some $50,000 to the Democratic National Committee.

18 October   Following the story on the Hsi Lai Buddhist temple in *The Wall Street Journal*, the Democratic National Committee announces it will reimburse the temple $15,000 for Gore's fundraiser.

28 October   The Democratic National Committee, stung by reports of alleged massive campaign finance law violations, announces that it will not file a preelection spending report with the Federal Election Commission.

30 October   After forty-eight hours of denunciations, the Democratic National Committee reverses course and releases a partial list of DNC donors. John Huang, an agent of the

People's Republic of China, is shown to have visited the White House seventy-eight times in the year before.

8 November   In his first postelection news conference, Clinton says contributions from Indonesian sources had 'absolutely not' influenced his foreign policy. The president calls for campaign finance reform and endorses the so-called McCain-Feingold campaign finance bill.

13 November   Attorney General Janet Reno turns down a request from Senator John McCain (R–AZ) to appoint an independent counsel to investigate President Clinton and Vice President Gore and their 1996 campaign fundraising activities.

15 November   The Democratic National Committee announces that it will investigate tens of thousands of dollars in contributions made to the party by Thai businesswoman Pauline Kanchanalak and her American company, Ben Chang International.

23 November   The Democratic National Committee announces that it will return a $450,000 donation from Arief and Soraya Wiriadinata, former U.S. residents who had ties to the Lippo Group. This is the largest donation returned by the Democratic National Committee in the burgeoning financial scandal.

17 December   The legal defense fund founded to aid President and Mrs. Clinton during their legal difficulties while in office divulges that some $640,000 in questionable donations had been returned; much of these funds had come from Clinton's friend Yah Lin "Charlie" Trie, an Arkansas businessman. An additional $122,000 is later returned to Trie.

19 December   The Department of Justice announces that its investigation into Democratic National Committee fundraising is being expanded to examine the Clintons' legal defense fund. Department attorneys issue subpoenas to the Presidential Legal Expense Trust demanding documents on the funds returned to Yah Lin "Charlie" Trie.

20 December   The White House admits that Yah Lin "Charlie" Trie had helped Wang Jun, a Chinese arms dealer with connections to the Communist government in Beijing, get into the White House for a reception in which Wang met with President Clinton. White House Press Secretary Mike McCurry says that Clinton had no idea who Wang was when he met him.

28 December   The Democratic National Committee releases documents showing that the party put together a program called the National Asia Pacific American Campaign Plan, established to raise some $7 million from Asians and Asian Americans. The documents show that John Huang, aided by Doris Matsui, a deputy assistant to President Clinton, put together the plan with officials from the Democratic National Committee and the Clinton/Gore 1996 campaign.

**1997**

January   The White House releases documents showing that the Democratic National Committee sponsored thirty-one "coffees" at the White House, with an unknown number attended personally by President Clinton and Vice President Gore.

24 January   Documents released by the White House show that approximately 100 "coffees," arranged by the Democratic National Committee, were held at the White House, with President Clinton at most of them and Vice President Al Gore at several. In an interview, Gore admits to "mistakes" in raising contributions, especially the controversial 29 April 1996 Buddhist Temple event, of which Gore says, "I knew it was a political event and I knew there were finance people who were going to be present."

28 January   In his first press conference since being inaugurated, President Clinton admits that "mistakes were made" in his 1996 fundraising effort but denies that any policies were made because of the donations.

29 January   Senator Fred Thompson (R–TN), in a speech on the U.S. Senate floor, calls for an investigation of the burgeoning White House fundraising scandal with a staff of some eighty people and a budget of $6.5 million.

12 February   Allegations surface that the Democratic National Committee has accepted contributions from the Chinese government in Beijing.

13 February   In a press conference, President Clinton calls for a "vigorous" and "thorough" investigation into allegations that people from the government of the People's Republic of China used contributions to the Democratic National Committee to influence American foreign policy.

14 February   The White House releases documents showing that the National Security Council warned the Clinton administration that Democratic National Committee fundraising trips to Asia could endanger American policy there. The documents focused on DNC official Johnny Chung, who gave some $366,000 to the party in exchange for influence and contacts. The documents from the National Security Council called Chung a "hustler" and denounced his trips to China, where he was flouting his ties to the White House, as "very troubling."

16 February   Representative Dan Burton (R–IN), chairman of the House Government Reform and Oversight Committee issues twenty subpoenas in the growing DNC fundraising scandal, and tells reporters he plans to interview some 500 people before the committee.

20 February   News reports show that several Asian American businessmen told investigators that John Huang pressured them to provide some $250,000 in donations to the Democratic National Committee and the Clinton/Gore campaign, and asked that the money be masked to show it came from their lobbying group. Huang denies the charge.

21 February   John Huang and former Assistant Attorney General Webster Hubbell both take the Fifth Amendment and refuse to provide congressional investigators with documents relating to the Democratic National Committee fundraising scandal. Huang reportedly demands partial immunity in exchange for the documents. Democratic National Committee chairman Roy Romer admits that an additional $1 million in donations to the party would have to be returned due to questionable circumstances.

26 February   In a press conference, President Clinton admits that large donors to the Democratic National Committee were rewarded with overnight stays in the Lincoln Bedroom. Figures later reveal that these donors gave the Clinton/Gore campaign and/or the Democratic National Committee some $5.4 million.

28 February   The Democratic National Committee discloses that it will return an additional $1.5 million in improper donations that it received from seventy-seven donors in the 1996 election year. Documents released by the White House show that former Deputy Chief of Staff Harold Ickes planned a program to reward large donors with "better coordination on appointments to boards and commissions."

2 March   *The Washington Post* reports that Vice President Al Gore made numerous fundraising calls from his White House office in violation of the law.

3 March   Former Clinton advisor George Stephanopoulos tells reporters that Vice President Al Gore did make fundraising calls from his office in the White House in violation of campaign donation law. Gore, in a press conference, says his calls were within the law and that he had used a Democratic National Committee credit card to make the calls. It is later revealed that Gore had used a Clinton/Gore 1996 credit card.

7 March   The Senate Rules Committee approves funding of $4.3 million to probe the White House/Democratic National Committee fundraising scandal, specifying that the investigation must end by 31 December 1997 and a report turned in by January 1998.

9 March   *The Washington Post* reports that the FBI warned six unnamed members of Congress that the Communist Chinese government was using Asian donors to buy influence in Congress and the administration. In a press conference, President Clinton says that he had never received this warning.

10 March   Senator Dianne Feinstein (D–CA) reports that she will return some $12,000 in donations from the Lippo Group.

11 March   The U.S. Senate votes unanimously to authorize the Senate Governmental Affairs Committee to conduct "an investigation of illegal and improper activities in connection with 1996 Federal election campaigns" in an effort to get to the bottom of the Democrats' potential illegal fundraising.

12 March   The Democratic National Committee reports that it will return a donation of $107,000 from an American Indian tribe after it is reported that the tribe may have taken the funds from a tribal welfare account.

13 March   White House Press Secretary Mike McCurry reports that no further White House coffees will be held.

17 March   Clinton Central Intelligence Agency nominee Anthony Lake withdraws his nomination in the face of allegations over his finances and his contacts with controversial Democratic National Committee donors.

18 March   U.S. House of Representatives Minority Leader Richard Gephardt (D–MO) reports that he will return donations totaling $22,000 given by the Lippo Group.

23 March   White House documents released show that White House coffees were estimated to raise $400,000 each time they were held, despite earlier White House statements that their main reason to was discuss policy and government issues.

25 April   *The Washington Post* reports that Department of Justice and other investigators have discovered a Chinese plan to spend up to $2 million to buy influence in the Clinton administration and Congress.

29 April   Visiting Washington, Chinese foreign minister Qian Qichen denies the report on the Chinese government plan to use money to buy influence in the U.S. government.

8 May    The Republican National Committee reports that it has found donations of more than $110,000 from Asian sources it could not properly identify.

9 May    Chinese President Jiang Zemin denies that the Chinese government contributed to American politicians to gain influence in the United States.

30 May    The Federal Election Commission fines the Clinton/Gore 1992 campaign $15,000 for illegal loans.

9 June    Documents released by the Republican National Committee show that the party raised some $1.6 million from Asian donors in Hong Kong.

8 July    Hearings begin before Senator Fred Thompson's committee. In his introduction, Thompson reports that he has discovered links between the Chinese government and the attempts to influence the 1996 U.S. election.

13 July    The Justice Department tells reporters that Senator Thompson's assertion that the Chinese government was behind the fundraising scandal has not been proved.

15 July    Senator Joseph I. Lieberman (D–CT) backs Senator Thompson's claim that the Chinese government was behind the fundraising scandal.

24 July    The first Republican to testify before the Thompson Committee, former Republican National Committee chairman Haley Barbour, testifies that the repayment of a loan from Asian sources was "legal and proper." He says that the money was not used for the 1994 elections, and that he did not discover it came from foreign sources until the 1996 election.

25 July    Lobbyist Richard Richards disputes Barbour's testimony, claiming that the Asian loan was in fact to elect new congressmen in 1994, and that Barbour was told in mid-1994 of the loan's source.

5 August    President Clinton tells reporters that he is "sick at heart" that the Democratic National Committee may have accepted foreign donations. He calls for an end to soft money in American elections.

11 August    Representative Jay Kim (R–CA) pleads guilty to charges that he accepted illegal foreign donations to his congressional campaigns.

20 August    NBC News airs an interview with Johnny Huang in which he says that he funneled a $25,000 donation from the Chinese government to the Democratic National

Committee to obtain a meeting between a Chinese chemical official and then-Secretary of Energy Hazel O'Leary.

24 October    *The Washington Post* reports that the Republicans gave some $1 million to independent groups for the 1996 election.

11 December    Former Secretary of Housing and Urban Development Henry Cisneros is indicted by a federal grand jury in Washington, D.C., on charges that he lied to the FBI regarding hush payments to a mistress.

**1998**
18 March    Ronald Blackley, the former chief of staff to former Secretary of Agriculture Mike Espy, is sentenced to twenty-seven months in prison for lying to federal investigators in the Espy investigation.

19 March    A three-judge panel names Washington, D.C., attorney Carol Elder Bruce as the independent counsel to investigate Secretary of the Interior Bruce Babbitt and his potential ties to illegal fundraising from Native Americans.

8 October    The U.S. House of Representatives votes to start an impeachment investigation of President Bill Clinton on charges of perjury and obstruction of justice stemming from his testimony in a lawsuit brought by former Arkansas government employee Paula Jones who alleged that Clinton sexually harassed her when he was governor of the state. Clinton's denials that he had a sexual relationship with White House intern Monica Lewinsky when he testified in the Jones case were found to be untrue and are the basis of the impeachment charges.

19 December    The U.S. House of Representatives votes to impeach President Clinton.

**1999**
12 February    The U.S. Senate acquits Clinton of both impeachment articles.

7 September    Former Secretary of Housing and Urban Development Henry Cisneros pleads guilty to a misdemeanor after a four-year, $9 million probe into charges he lied about payments to a former mistress.

**2000**
20 September    Independent Counsel Robert Ray clears both Clintons of criminal wrongdoing in the Whitewater land deal.

28 December    President Clinton ends a five-year ban on the lobbying of government appointees after they have left government.

## 2001

**20 January**   In the final hours of his presidency, President Bill Clinton offers 140 pardons and 36 clemencies and commutations, many to controversial figures, including Marc Rich, a fugitive from American justice for 18 years; Carlos Vignali, a convicted drug dealer; Glenn Braswell, convicted of selling vitamins as a cure for diseases in the 1980s; and John Hemmingson, convicted in 1996 of laundering money to cover a campaign loan for the brother of former Agriculture Secretary Mike Espy.

**15 June**   A federal judge sentences former Mayor Milton Milan of Camden, New Jersey, to seven years, three months in prison for his convictions on fourteen counts of bribery, racketeering and money laundering, linked to his acceptance of bribes from undercover world figures. The judge tells Milan that he made his city "a laughingstock."

**21 June**   The House Ethics Committee unanimously rebukes Representative Earl Hilliard (D–AL) for numerous campaign finance violations, but gives him the mildest punishment because Hilliard admits to the wrongdoing and asks for leniency from the committee.

## 2002

**11 April**   Representative James A. Traficant Jr. (D–OH) is convicted in a federal court in Cleveland of ten counts of racketeering, bribery and fraud.

**27 September**   Former Representative Edward Mezvinsky (D–IA) pleads guilty to thirty-one counts of fraud after admitting to bilking investors in one of his companies of more than $10 million.

**7 November**   The U.S. government files a lawsuit for Medicare and Medicaid fraud against Dr. Steve Henry, the lieutenant governor of Kentucky, claiming that he was involved in fraud while running for office in 1995 and even while serving as lieutenant governor of the state.

## 2003

The FBI sets up Operation Tennessee Waltz, a probe to investigate political corruption in Tennessee.

**6 March**   A federal grand jury in Austin, Texas, indicts former state Attorney General Dan Morales on charges of misusing state tobacco fund money and campaign funds. Morales, who had once been the Democratic candidate for governor of Texas, was also charged with mail fraud, conspiracy, filing a false tax return, and making false statements on a loan application.

## 2004

**27 May**   Former Alabama Governor Don Siegelman is indicted by a federal grand jury on charges of bribery, racketeering, and mail fraud. He is later acquitted of all of these charges.

## 2005

**26 May**   Tennessee state Senator John N. Ford is indicted along with several other Tennessee politicians for their roles in accepting bribes from a fake company set up by the FBI.

**26 October**   Former Alabama Governor Don Siegelman, along with Richard M. Scrushy, the former CEO of HealthSouth, a health care provider, are indicted by a federal grand jury of charges of bribery and mail fraud.

## 2006

**28 February**   The National Legal and Policy Center (NLPC) files an ethics complaint against Representative Allan Mollohan (D-WV) for allegedly steering earmarks to companies that did business with his family charity.

**9 June**   Kentucky Governor Ernie Fletcher pleads not guilty to charges of illegal state hiring practices.

**20 June**   Former Office of Federal Procurement Policy in the Office of Management and Budget David H. Safavian is convicted by a federal jury in Washington, D.C. for lying to federal investigators about his ties to former lobbyist Jack Abramoff.

**29 June**   Former Alabama Governor Don Siegelman and Richard Scrushy are found guilty by a federal jury of bribery and mail fraud.

**13 October**   Representative Bob Ney (R-OH) pleads guilty to influence peddling relating to the Jack Abramoff investigation. Ney told the court that he had accepted campaign contributions, luxury travel, meals, and sports tickets in exchange for performing official acts to aid Abramoff's lobbying activities.

**18 December**   While on trial for his role in the Operation Tennessee Waltz scandal, former Tennessee State Senator John N. Ford is indicted by a second federal grand jury for money stolen from TennCare, the Tennessee State health care system.

**31 December**   *The New York Post* reports that New York State Public Integrity Commission Executive Director Herbert Teitelbaum has taken a 2 ½ week vacation in Argentina in the middle of the investigation of whether or not Governor Eliot Spitzer and his aides broke state laws by using police to politically damage New York state Senate

Majority Leader Joseph Bruno. The vacation comes just days after one of Spitzer's aides secretly okayed a $15,000 pay raise for Teitelbaum.

## 2007

**27 April**    Former Tennessee State Senator John N. Ford is convicted of taking bribes from federal agents and threatening to kill any federal agent who exposed him. Ford is later sentenced to 5 ½ years in prison.

## 2008

**4 January**    Democratic campaign contributor Norman Hsu is ordered to prison after being a fugitive from justice since 1992.

**8 January**    A Washington, D.C. watchdog group files a complaint against U.S. Senator Mary Landrieu (D-LA), accusing her of pushing a $2 million earmark for a company which days earlier gave her a $30,000 campaign contribution. Citizens for Responsibility and Ethics called on the U.S. Department of Justice to investigate whether Landrieu broke federal law in 2001 by pushing for the earmark, just days after lobbyists for the company threw a fundraiser and raised cash for her campaign fund.

**19 January**    The *Chicago Sun-Times* reports that the name of U.S. Senator Barack Obama (D-IL) has surfaced in a document as a "political candidate" which outlines the case against Obama crony and indicted real-estate developer Antoin "Tony" Rezko. The paper reports that Obama's name appears in one paragraph of the 78-page document laying out the case against Rezko, a major fundraiser for Obama and fellow Democrat Illinois Governor Rod Blagojevich.

**20 January**    Facing increasing scrutiny over his connections to indicted "slumlord" Tony Rezko, U.S. Senator Barack Obama (D-IL) announces that he will donate $40,000 that was given to Obama's 2004 US Senate campaign by seven individuals linked to Rezko to charity.

**24 January**    Governor Rod Blagojevich (D–IL) refuses to answer reporters' questions why his campaign had racked up more than $2 million in legal bills and expenses. Blagojevich is under investigation for corruption in the hiring of workers in his administration, and federal prosecutors have subpoenaed records from his campaign fund to discover if his campaign exchanged campaign donations for jobs and political support.

**28 January**    Antoin "Tony" Rezko, the indicted fundraiser tied to Illinois Governor Rod Blagojevich and U.S. Senator Barack Obama, is arrested by federal agents and taken to prison after a federal judge revokes his $2 million bail.

**29 January**    The *Chicago Sun-Times* reports that Senator Barack Obama (D-IL) will donate to charity all remaining contributions from indicted fundraiser and friend Antoin "Tony" Rezko. Obama initially gave $44,000 of Rezko's money to charity, then announced in early January 2008 that an additional $40,000 would be given away. The paper further reports that a fund of $72, 650 from persons tied to Rezko, including employees of companies he ran, would also be given to charity, making the total given by Rezko to Obama's 2004 U.S. Senate campaign at least $156, 650.

**11 February**    A federal grand jury in Alaska convicts former Fairbanks Mayor Jim Hayes of 16 counts of corruption involving the abuse and misuse of some $450,000 in US government grants given to an Alaska social services agency. Hayes was acquitted of four additional counts and the jury hung on seven other counts. In all, Hayes was found guilty of conspiracy, theft, fraud, money laundering, and filing false tax returns.

**21 February**    Rep. Rick Renzi, Republican of Arizona, is indicted by a federal grand jury in Phoenix on 35 total charges including money laundering, extortion and conspiracy regarding payments made to his family business in Arizona. Also indicted with Renzi are James Sandlin, a real estate investor and a Renzi backer, and Andrew Beardall, an attorney for Renzi's family's insurance business. Diane J. Humetewa, the US Attorney for Arizona, told reporters, "Congressman Renzi misused his public office by forcing a land sale that would financially benefit himself and a business associate, and in so doing, he betrayed the trust of the citizens of Arizona."

**28 February**    In response to the indictment of Rep. Rick Renzi, the House Ethics Committee announces that it will open an investigation on him and his actions.

**4 March**    Rep. Rick Renzi of Arizona pleads not guilty in district court in Tucson, Arizona, to charges of money laundering and extortion, among other charges.

**19 March**    The Detroit, Michigan, city council demands the resignation of Mayor Kwame Kilpatrick, embroiled in a scandal over whether or not he committed perjury before a civil trial involving police officers challenging their firing by the mayor. Kilpatrick refuses to resign.

**24 March**    Detroit, Michigan, Mayor Kwame Kilpatrick is indicted by a state grand jury on 8 counts of perjury, conspiracy, obstruction of justice, and misconduct in office. Kilpatrick, indicted along with his aide and mistress Christine Beatty, pleads not guilty.

27 March    Governor Anibal Acevedo-Vila, Democrat of Puerto Rico, is indicted on charges of conspiracy to violate campaign finance laws, wire fraud, conspiracy to defraud the Internal Revenue Service (IRS) and filing a false tax return. Indicted along with Acevedo-Vila are four persons from Philadelphia, including prominent Democratic fundraiser Robert M. Feldman, charged with violating campaign finance laws in aiding the governor to raise money illegally for his campaigns.

**References:** Hoffer, Peter C., and N. E. H. Hull, "The First American Impeachments," The William and Mary Quarterly, Third Series, XXXV:4 (October 1978), 653–667; "Congressional Ethics: History, Facts, and Controversy" (Washington, D.C.: Congressional Quarterly, 1992); *Chicago Sun-Times; The New York Times; The Wall Street Journal; The Washington Post*

# BIBLIOGRAPHY

## Books

Abbott, Richard H., "The Republican Party Press in Reconstruction Georgia, 1867–1874," *Journal of Southern History* 61, 4 (November 1995), 725–760.

Abels, Jules, *The Truman Scandals* (Chicago: Regnery, 1956).

Abernathy, Thomas Perkins, *The Burr Conspiracy* (New York: Oxford University Press, 1954).

*An Account of the Impeachment and Trial of the Late Francis Hopkinson, Esquire, Judge of the Court of Admiralty for the Commonwealth of Pennsylvania* (Philadelphia: Printed by Francis Bailey, at Yorick's Head, 1795).

Adams, George Burton, and H. Morse Stephens, eds., *Select Documents of English Constitutional History* (New York: Macmillan, 1927).

Adams, Samuel Hopkins, *Incredible Era: The Life and Times of Warren Gamaliel Harding* (Boston: Houghton Mifflin, 1939).

Adams, Sherman, *Firsthand Report: The Story of the Eisenhower Administration* (New York: Harper, 1961).

Agnew, Spiro T., *Go Quietly... Or Else* (New York: Morrow, 1980).

Albright, Joseph, *What Makes Spiro Run: The Life and Times of Spiro Agnew* (New York: Dodd, Mead, 1972).

Allen, Oliver E., *The Tiger: The Rise and Fall of Tammany Hall* (Reading, MA: Addison-Wesley, 1993).

Amer, Mildred, *The Senate Select Committee on Ethics: A Brief History of Its Evolution and Jurisdiction* (Washington, DC: Congressional Research Service, 1993).

Ames, Blanche Ames, *Adelbert Ames, 1835–1933: General, Senator, Governor* (New York: Argosy-Antiquarian, 1964).

Amick, George, *The American Way of Graft: A Study of Corruption in State and Local Government, How It Happens, and What Can Be Done About It* (Princeton, NJ: Center for Analysis of Public Issues, 1976).

Andrews, James De Witt, ed., *The Works of James Wilson: Associate Justice of the Supreme Court of the United States and Professor of Law in the College of Philadelphia, Being his Public Discourses Upon Jurisprudence and the Political Science, Including Lectures and Professor of Law, 1790–92*, 2 vols. (Chicago: Callaghan, 1896).

Angle, Paul M., "The Recollections of William Pitt Kellogg," *Abraham Lincoln Quarterly* 3 (September 1945), 319–339.

Anhalt, Walter C., and Glenn H. Smith, "He Saved the Farm? Governor Langer and the Mortgage Moratoria," *North Dakota Quarterly* 44 (Autumn 1976), 5–17.

Anyon, Jean, *Ghetto Schooling: A Political Economy of Urban Educational Reform* (New York: Teachers College Press, 1997).

Astorino, Samuel J., "The Contested Senate Election of William Scott Vare," *Pennsylvania History* 28 (April 1961), 187–201.

Bacon, Donald C., Roger H. Davidson, and Morton Keller, eds., *The Encyclopedia of the United States Congress*, 3 vols. (New York: Simon and Schuster, 1995).

Baker, Bobby, with Larry King, *Wheeling and Dealing: Confessions of a Capitol Hill Operator* (New York: W. W. Norton, 1978).

Baker, Peter, *The Breach: Inside the Impeachment and Trial of William Jefferson Clinton* (New York: Scribner, 2000).

Baker, Ross K., *The New Fat Cats: Members of Congress as Political Benefactors* (New York: Priority Press, 1989).

Balch, William Ralston, *The Life of James Abram Garfield, Late President of the United States. The Record of a Wonderful Career* (New York: William H. Shepard, 1881).

Baltimore Reform League, *Special Report of the Executive Committee of Baltimore Reform League as to the Statements of Candidates and Others, Filed under Provisions of the Corrupt Practices Act subsequently to the Primary Election for Representatives in Congress, held August 30, 1910* (Baltimore, MD: The League, 1910).

Barber, Charles M., "A Diamond in the Rough: William Langer Reexamined," *North Dakota History* 64 (Fall 1998), 2–18.

Barnhart, Bill, and Gene Schickman, *Kerner: The Conflict of Intangible Rights* (Urbana: University of Illinois Press, 1999).

Barry, John M., *The Ambition and the Power* (New York: Viking, 1989).

Barth, Alan, *Government by Investigation* (New York: Viking, 1955).

Bates, J. Leonard, "Walsh of Montana in Dakota Territory: Political Beginnings, 1884–90," *Pacific Northwest Quarterly* 56 (July 1965), 114–124.

———, "Politics and Ideology: Thomas J. Walsh and the Rise of Populism," *Pacific Northwest Quarterly* 65 (April 1974), 49–56.

———, *Senator Thomas J. Walsh of Montana: Law and Public Affairs, from TR to FDR* (Urbana: University of Illinois Press, 1999).

Bean, Walton, *Boss Ruef's San Francisco: The Story of the Union Labor Party, Big Business, and the Graft Prosecution* (Berkeley: University of California Press, 1952).

Beatty, Jack, *The Rascal King: The Life and Times of James Michael Curley* (Reading, MA: Addison-Wesley, 1993).

Bell, William Gardner, *Secretaries of War and Secretaries of the Army: Portraits and Biographical Sketches* (Washington, DC: United States Army Center of Military History, 1982).

Benson, George Charles Sumner, *Political Corruption in America* (Lexington, MA: Lexington Books, 1978).

Berg, Larry L., *Corruption in the American Political System* (Morristown, NJ: General Learning Press, 1976).

Berger, Raoul, *Impeachment: The Constitutional Problems* (Cambridge, MA: Harvard University Press, 1973).

———, *Executive Privilege: A Constitutional Myth* (Cambridge, MA: Harvard University Press, 1974).

Bernard, George S., *Civil Service Reform versus the Spoils System. The Merit Plan for the Filling of Public Offices Advocated in a Series of Articles Originally Published in a Virginia Journal* (New York: J. B. Alden, 1885).

Bingham, Alfred M., "Raiders of the Lost City," *American Heritage*, 38 (July/August 1987), 54–64.

———, *Portrait of an Explorer: Hiram Bingham, Discover of Machu Picchu* (Ames: Iowa State University Press, 1989).

Bingham, Hiram, *An Explorer in the Air Service* (New Haven, CT: Yale University Press, 1920).

Bingham, Woodbridge, *Hiram Bingham: A Personal History* (Boulder, CO: Bin Lan Zhen, 1989).

Binning, William C., Larry Esterly, and Paul A. Sracic, *Encyclopedia of American Parties, Campaigns, and Elections* (Westport, CT: Greenwood Press, 1999).

Binstein, Michael, *Trust Me: Charles Keating and the Missing Billions* (New York: Random House, 1993).

*The Biographical Annals of Ohio, 1904-1905. A Handbook of the Government and Institutions of the State of Ohio. Compiled under Authority of the Act of April 19, 1904* (Springfield, Ohio: The Springfield Publishing Company, State Printers, 1905).

*Biographical Directory of the American Congress, 1774–1996* (Alexandria, VA: CQ Staff Directories, 1996).

Birnbaum, Jeffrey H. *The Lobbyists: How Influence Peddlers Get Their Way in Washington* (New York: Times Books, 1992).

———, "The Influence Merchants," *Fortune* 138, 11 (7 December 1998), 134–138.

Black, Charles L., Jr., *Impeachment: A Handbook* (New Haven, CT: Yale University Press, 1974).

Blackmar, Frank Wilson, *The Life of Charles Robinson, the First State Governor of Kansas* (Topeka, KS: Crane & Company, 1901).

*Black's Law Dictionary*, 6th ed. (St. Paul, MN: West, 1990).

Blodgett, Geoffrey T., "The Mind of the Boston Mugwumps," *Mississippi Valley Historical Review* 48, 4 (March 1962), 614–634.

Bloss, George, *Life and Speeches of George H. Pendleton* (Cincinnati, OH: Miami Printing and Publishing Co., 1868).

Bodenhamer, David J., and Robert G. Barrows, eds., *The Encyclopedia of Indianapolis* (Bloomington: Indiana University Press, 1994).

Boettcher, Robert, *Gifts of Deceit: Sun Myung Moon, Tongsun Park, and the Korean Scandal* (New York: Holt, Rinehart and Winston, 1980).

Bollens, John Constantinus, *Political Corruption: Power, Money, and Sex* (Pacific Palisades, CA: Palisades Publishers, 1979).

Boomhower, Ray, *Jacob Piatt Dunn, Jr.: A Life in History and Politics* (Indianapolis: Indiana University Press, 1998).

Borkin, Joseph, *The Corrupt Judge: An Inquiry into Bribery and Other High Crimes and Misdemeanors in the Federal Courts* (New York: Clarkson N. Potter, 1962).

Bouvier, John, *A Law Dictionary, Adapted to the Constitution and Laws of the United States of America, and of the Several States of the American Union: with References to the Civil and other Systems of Foreign Law*, Daniel Angell Gleason, ed. (Philadelphia: G. W. Childs, Printer, 1868).

Boynton, H. V., "The Whiskey Ring," *North American Review* 252 (October 1876), 280–327.

Bridges, Tyler, *Bad Bet on the Bayou: The Rise of Gambling in Louisiana and the Fall of Governor Edwin Edwards* (New York: Farrar, Straus & Giroux, 2001).

Brown, Canter, Jr., "Carpetbagger Intrigues, Black Leadership, and a Southern Loyalist Triumph: Florida's Gubernatorial Election of 1872," *Florida Historical Quarterly* 72, 3 (1994), 275–301.

Buice, S. David, "The Military Career of Adelbert Ames," *Southern Quarterly* 2 (April 1964), 236–246.

Burnham, David, *Above the Law: Secret Deals, Political Fixes and Other Misadventures of the U.S. Department of Justice* (New York: Charles Scribner's Sons, 1996).

Busch, Francis X., *Enemies of the State: An Account of the Trials of the Mary Eugenia Surratt Case, the Teapot Dome Cases, the Alphonse Capone Case, the Rosenberg Case* (Indianapolis, IN: Bobbs-Merrill, 1954).

Bushnell, Eleanore, "The Impeachment and Trial of James H. Peck," *Missouri Historical Review* 74 (January 1980), 137–165.

——, "One of Twelve: The Nevada Impeachment Connection," *Nevada Historical Society Quarterly* 26, 4 (Winter 1983), 2–12.

——, "Judge Harry E. Claiborne and the Federal Impeachment Process," *Nevada Historical Society Quarterly* XXXII:32, 4 (Winter 1989), 3–12.

——, *Crimes, Follies, and Misfortunes: The Federal Impeachment Trials* (Urbana and Chicago: University of Illinois Press, 1992).

Butler, Anne M., *United States Senate Election, Expulsion, and Censure Cases, 1793–1990* (Washington, DC: Government Printing Office, 1995).

Butler, Anne M., and Wendy Wolff, *United States Senate Election, Expulsion and Censure Cases, 1793–1990* (Washington, DC: Government Printing Office, 1995).

Byrd, Robert C., *The Senate, 1789–1989: Historical Statistics, 1789–1992,* 4 vols. (Washington, DC: Government Printing Office, 1993).

*Calendar of State Papers: Domestic Series, of the Reign of William and Mary,* 5 vols. William John Hardy, ed. (London: Printed for His Majesty's Stationery Office by Eyre and Spottiswoode, 1895–1906).

Calkins, Hiram, and Dewitt Van Buren, *Biographical Sketches of John T. Hoffman and Allen C. Beach: The Democratic Nominees for Governor and Lieutenant-Governor of the State of New York. Also, a Record of the Events in the Lives of Oliver Bascom, David B. McNeil, and Edwin O. Perrin, the Other Candidates on the Same Ticket* (New York: New York Printing Company, 1868).

Caperton, Thomas J., *Rogue! Being an Account of the Life and High Times of Stephen W. Dorsey, United States Senator and New Mexico Cattle Baron* (Santa Fe, NM: Museum of New Mexico Press, 1978).

Caplan, Lincoln, *The Tenth Justice: The Solicitor General and the Rule of Law* (New York: Alfred A. Knopf, 1987).

Caro, Robert A., *Lyndon Johnson: Master of the Senate* (New York: Alfred A. Knopf, 2002).

Cary, Edward, *George William Curtis* (Boston: Houghton, Mifflin, 1894).

Chandler, Peleg W., *American Criminal Trials,* 2 vols. (Boston: Charles C. Little and James Brown, 1841–1844).

Charlton, Thomas Usher Pulaski, *The Life of Major General James Jackson* (Augusta, GA: Geo. F. Randolph & Co., 1809).

Chase, Harold, et al., comps., *Biographical Dictionary of the Federal Judiciary* (Detroit, MI: Gale Research Company, 1976).

Chester, Edward W., "The Impact of the Covode Congressional Investigation," *Western Pennsylvania Historical Magazine* 42 (December 1959), 343–350.

Clark, John G., "Mark W. Delahay: Peripatetic Politician," *Kansas Historical Quarterly* 25, 3 (Autumn 1959), 301–312.

Clarke, Mary Patterson, *Parliamentary Privilege in the American Colonies: Essays in Colonial History Presented to Charles McLean Andrews* (New Haven, CT: Yale University Press, 1943).

Clayton, Powell, *The Aftermath of the Civil War, in Arkansas* (New York: Neale Publishing, 1915).

Clinton, Henry Lauren, *Celebrated Trials* (New York: Harper & Brothers, 1897).

Clopton, John, *Mr. Clopton's Motion Proposing an Amendment to the Constitution of the United States* (Washington, DC: A. & G. Way, 1808).

Cockburn, Alexander, *Al Gore: A User's Manual* (London: Verso, 2000).

Cohen, Richard E., *Rostenkowski: The Pursuit of Power and the End of the Old Politics* (Chicago: Ivan R. Dee, 1999).

——, "Rosty Revisited," *National Journal* 31, 42 (16 October 1999), 2956–2965.

Cohen, Richard M., and Jules Witcover, *A Heartbeat Away: The Investigation and Resignation of Vice President Spiro T. Agnew* (New York: Viking, 1974).

Cohen, William S., and George J. Mitchell, *Men of Zeal: A Candid Inside Story of the Iran-Contra Hearings* (New York: Viking, 1988).

*A Collection of Some Memorable and Weighty Transactions in Parliament; in the Year 1678, and Afterwards; In Relation to the Impeachment of Thomas Earl of Danby* (London: Privately Published, 1695).

*Congressional Ethics* (Washington, DC: Congressional Quarterly, 1980).

*Congressional Ethics: History, Facts, and Controversy* (Washington, DC: Congressional Quarterly, 1992).

Connally, John B., with Mickey Herskowitz, *In History's Shadow: An American Odyssey* (New York: Hyperion, 1993).

Conrad, Barnaby, *San Francisco: A Profile with Pictures* (New York: Bramhall House, 1959).

Cook, James F., *The Governors of Georgia, 1754–1995* (Macon, GA: Mercer University Press, 1995).

Costello, William, *The Facts about Nixon: An Unauthorized Biography* (New York: Viking, 1960).

Cramer, Clarence Henley, *Royal Bob: The Life of Robert G. Ingersoll* (Indianapolis, IN: Bobbs-Merrill, 1952).

Crawford, Jay Boyd, *The Crédit Mobilier of America–Its Origin and History, Its Work of Constructing the Union Pacific Railroad and the Relation of Members of Congress Therewith* (Boston: C. W. Calkins & Co., 1880).

Croker, Richard, "Tammany Hall and the Democracy," *North American Review* 154, 423 (February 1892), 225–230.

Cumming, Hiram, *Secret History of the Perfidies, Intrigues, and Corruptions of the Tyler Dynasty, with the Mysteries of Washington City, Connected with that Vile Administration, in a Series of Letters to the Ex-acting President, by One most Familiar with the Subject* (Washington and New York: [Published by] The Author, 1845).

Cunningham, Randy, and Jeffrey L. Ethell, *Fox Two: The Story of America's First Ace in Vietnam* (Mesa, Arizona: Champlin Fighter Museum, 1989).

Curley, James Michael, *I'd Do It Again: A Record of All My Uproarious Years* (Englewood Cliffs, NJ: Prentice-Hall, 1957).

Current, Richard N., *Three Carpetbag Governors* (Baton Rouge: Louisiana State University Press, 1967).

Curtis, George William, *Orations and Addresses of George William Curtis*, Charles Eliot Norton, ed. (New York: Harper & Brothers, 1894).

Czitrom, Daniel, "Underworlds and Underdogs: Big Time Sullivan and Metropolitan Politics in New York, 1889-1913," *Journal of American History* 78, :2 (September 1991), 536–558.

Daugherty, Harry M., and Thomas Dixon, *The Inside Story of the Harding Tragedy* (New York: Churchill Company, 1932).

Davidson, Roger H., and Walter J. Oleszek, *Congress and Its Members* (Washington, DC: CQ Press, 1994).

Davis, Charles B., "Judge James Hawkins Peck," *Missouri Historical Review* 27, 1 (October 1932), 3–20.

Davis, Joseph Stancliffe, *Essays in the Earlier History of American Corporations* (Cambridge, MA: Harvard University Press, 1917).

Davis, William Watson, *The Civil War and Reconstruction in Florida* (New York: Columbia University, 1913).

DeShields, James T., *They Sat in High Places: The Presidents and Governors of Texas* (San Antonio: Naylor Company, 1940).

Dewey, John, ed., *New York and the Seabury Investigation: A Digest and Interpretation of the Reports by Samuel Seabury concerning the Government of New York City, Prepared by a Committee of Educators and Civic Workers under the Chairmanship of John Dewey* (New York: City Affairs Committee of New York, 1933).

Dewey, Thomas E., *Twenty against the Underworld* (New York: Doubleday, 1974).

Dickinson, William B., Jr., comp., *Watergate: Chronology of a Crisis* (Washington, DC: Congressional Quarterly, 1973).

*Dictionary of American History*, 7 vols. (New York: Charles Scribner's Sons, 1976–1978).

Dimock, Marshall Edward, *Congressional Investigating Committees* (Baltimore, MD: Johns Hopkins University Press, 1929).

Dinneen, Joseph F., *The Purple Shamrock: The Honorable James Michael Curley of Boston* (New York: W. W. Norton, 1949).

Dionisopoulos, P. Allan, *Rebellion, Racism and Representation: The Adam Clayton Powell Case and Its Antecedents* (DeKalb: Northern Illinois University Press, 1970).

Dionne, E. J., and William Kristol, eds., *Bush v. Gore: The Court Cases and the Commentary* (Washington, DC: Brookings Institution Press, 2001).

Donovan, Timothy P., Willard B. Gatewood Jr., and Jeannie M. Whayne, eds., *The Governors of Arkansas: Essays in Political Biography* (Fayetteville: University of Arkansas Press, 1995).

*Dorman B. Eaton: 1823–1899* (New York: Privately Published, 1900).

Draper, Robert, "Elegy for Edwin Edwards, Man of the People," *GQ* (July 2000), 160–167, 184–186.

Driggs, Orval Truman, Jr., "The Issues of the Powell Clayton Regime, 1868–1871," *Arkansas Historical Quarterly* 8 (Spring 1949), 1–75.

Duker, William F., "The Presidential Power to Pardon: A Constitutional History," *William and Mary Law Review* 18 (1977), 475–538.

Dunar, Andrew J., *The Truman Scandals and the Politics of Morality* (Columbia MO: University of Missouri Press, 1984).

Duncan, Philip D. and Christine C. Lawrence, *Congressional Quarterly's Politics in America 1996: The 104th Congress* (Washington, DC: Congressional Quarterly, 1995).

Duran, Tobias, "Francisco Chalvez, Thomas B. Catron, and Organized Political Violence in Santa Fe in the 1890s," *New Mexico Historical Review* 59 (July 1984), 291–310.

Dwight, Theodore, "Trial by Impeachment," *American Law Register* (University of Pennsylvania Law Review) 6 (November 1866-November 1867), 257–283.

Easby-Smith, J. S., *The Department of Justice: Its History and Functions* (Washington, DC: W. H. Lowdermilk & Co., 1904).

Eberling, Ernest J., *Congressional Investigation: A Study of the Origin and Development of the Power of Congress to Investigate and Punish for Contempt* (New York: Columbia University Press, 1928).

Elkin, Steven L., "Contempt of Congress: The Iran-Contra Affair and the American Constitution," *Congress and the Presidency* 18, 1 (Spring 1991), 1–16.

Elliot, Jonathan, ed., *The Debates in the Several State Conventions on the Adoption of the Federal Constitution, as Recommended by the General Convention at Philadelphia in 1787. Together with the Journal of the Federal Convention, Luther Martin's letter, Yates's Minutes, Congressional Opinions, Virginia and Kentucky Resolutions of '98–'99, and other Illustrations of the Constitution. Collected and Revised from Contemporary Publications, by Jonathan Elliott. Published under the Sanction of Congress*, 5 vols. (Washington, DC: Printed for the editor, 1836–1845).

*Essays in the History of New York City: A Memorial to Sidney Pomerantz* (Port Washington, NY: Kennikat Press, 1978).

Etzioni, Amitai, *Capital Corruption: The New Attack on American Democracy* (New Brunswick: Transaction Books, 1988).

Evans, C. Lawrence, *Leadership in Committee: A Comparative Analysis of Leadership Behavior in the U.S. Senate* (Ann Arbor: University of Michigan Press, 1991).

Ewing, Cortez A. M., "Early Kansas Impeachments," *Kansas Historical Quarterly* 1, 4 (August 1932), 307–325.

———, "Two Reconstruction Impeachments," *North Carolina Historical Review* 15, 3 (July 1938), 204–225.

———, "Notes on Two Kansas Impeachments," *Kansas Historical Quarterly* 23, 3 (Autumn 1957), 281–297.

*The Fall of a President by the Staff of the Washington Post* (New York: Dell, 1974).

Farrand, Max, *Records from the Federal Convention* (New Haven, CT: Yale University Press, 1911).

Faust, Patricia L., ed., *Historical Times Illustrated Encyclopedia of the Civil War* (New York: Harper & Row, 1986).

Federal Election Commission, *Campaign Guide for Congressional Candidates and Committees* (Washington, DC: Government Printing Office, 1995).

Feerick, John, "Impeaching Federal Judges: A Study of the Constitutional Provisions," *Fordham Law Review* 39 (1970–1971), 1–58.

Fischer, Roger A., *Them Damned Pictures: Explorations in American Cartoon Art* (North Haven, CT: Archon Books, 1996).

Fisher, Louis, *Constitutional Conflicts Between Congress and the President* (Lawrence: University Press of Kansas, 1997).

Fletcher, Robert, ed., *Amherst College: Biographical Record of the Graduates and Non-Graduates. Centennial Edition, 1821–1921* (Amherst, MA: Published by the College, 1927).

Foley, Michael, *The New Senate: Liberal Influence on a Conservative Institution, 1959–1972* (New Haven, CT: Yale University Press, 1980).

Forward, Ross, *Political Reform. An Exposition of the Causes which Have Produced Political Corruption in the United States, and a Presentation of the Only Reform Now Adequate to Save Our Present Form of Government* (Cincinnati, OH: Printed by James Barclay, 1886).

Foster, William, *James Jackson: Duelist and Militant Statesman* (Athens: University of Georgia Press, 1960).

Fowle, Eleanor, *Cranston, the Senator from California* (San Rafael, CA: Presidio Press, 1980).

Fowler, Dorothy Ganfield, *The Cabinet Politician: The Postmasters General, 1829–1909* (New York: Columbia University Press, 1943).

———, "Precursors of the Hatch Act," *Mississippi Valley Historical Review* 47, 2 (September 1960), 247–262.

Foxe, Fanne, *Fanne Foxe, by Annabel "Fanne Foxe" Battistella with Yvonne Dunleavy* (New York: Pinnacle Books, 1975).

Frankfurter, Felix, and James Landis, *The Business of the Supreme Court: A Study in the Federal Judicial System* (New York: Macmillan, 1928).

Friedman, Jacob Alexis, *The Impeachment of Governor William Sulzer* (New York: Columbia University Press, 1939).

Fuller, Hubert Bruce, *The Speakers of the House* (Boston: Little, Brown, 1909).

Galloway, George Barnes, *History of the House of Representatives* (New York: Crowell, 1962).

Garment, Suzanne, *Scandal: The Crisis of Mistrust in American Politics* (New York: Times Books, 1991).

Garraty, John A., and Mark C. Carnes, gen. eds., *American National Biography*, 24 vols. (New York: Oxford University Press, 1999).

Geelan, Agnes, *The Dakota Maverick: The Political Life of William Langer, also Known as "Wild Bill" Langer* (Fargo, ND: Privately Published, 1975).

Gershman, Bennett L., "Abscam, the Judiciary, and the Ethics of Entrapment," *The Yale Law Journal*, 91:8 (July 1982), 1565–91.

Gertz, Bill, *Betrayal: How the Clinton Administration Undermined American Security* (Washington, DC: Regnery Publishing, 1999).

Gianos, Phillip L., *Politics and Politicians in American Film* (Westport, CT: Praeger, 1999).

Giglio, James N., *H. M. Daugherty and the Politics of Expediency* (Kent, OH: Kent State University Press, 1978).

Goehlert, Robert, *Political Corruption: A Selected Bibliography* (Monticello, IL: Vance Bibliographies, 1985).

Golden, David A., "The Ethics Reform Act of 1987: Why the Taxman Can't Be a Paperback Writer," *Brigham Young University Law Review* 1991 (1991), 1025–1051.

Goodpasture, Albert V., "William Blount and the Southwest Territory," *American Historical Magazine and Tennessee Historical Society Quarterly* 8 (January 1903), 1–13.

"Götterdämmerung in Topeka: The Downfall of Senator Pomeroy," *Kansas Historical Quarterly* 18, 3 (Autumn 1950), 243–278.

Grabow, John C., *Congressional Investigations: Law and Practice* (Clifton, NJ: Prentice Hall Law & Business, 1988).

Grant, Marilyn, "Judge Levi Hubbell: A Man Impeached," *Wisconsin Magazine of History* 64, 1 (Autumn 1980), 28–39.

Griffin, Appleton Prentiss Clark, *Selected List of References on Impeachment* (Washington, DC: Government Printing Office, 1905).

Grossman, Mark, *The ABC-CLIO Companion to the Native American Rights Movement* (Santa Barbara, CA: ABC-CLIO, 1996).

——, *Encyclopedia of the United States Cabinet*, 3 vols. (Santa Barbara, CA: ABC-CLIO, 2000).

Guenther, Nancy Anderman, *United States Supreme Court Decisions: An Index to Excerpts, Reprints, and Discussions* (Metuchen, NJ: Scarecrow Press, 1983).

Hackbart-Dean, Pamela, "Herman E. Talmadge: From Civil Rights to Watergate," *Georgia Historical Quarterly* 77 (Spring 1993), 145–157.

Hall, Kermit L., "West H. Humphreys and the Crisis of the Union," *Tennessee Historical Quarterly* 34, 1 (Spring 1975), 48–69.

Hallam, Elizabeth, ed., *Medieval Monarchs* (London: Tiger Books International, 1996).

Hamilton, Charles V., *Adam Clayton Powell, Jr.: The Political Biography of an American Dilemma* (New York: Atheneum, 1991).

Hamilton, James, *The Power to Probe: A Study of Congressional Investigations* (New York: Random House, 1976).

Hansen, Gladys, *San Francisco Almanac: Everything You Want to Know about the City* (San Francisco: Chronicle Books, 1975).

Harriger, Katy Jean, *Independent Justice: The Federal Special Prosecutor in American Politics* (Lawrence: University Press of Kansas, 1992).

Hazard, Rowland, "The Crédit Mobilier of America: A Paper Read Before the Rhode Island Historical Society, Tuesday Evening, February 22, 1881, by Rowland Hazard," (Providence, RI: S. S. Rider, 1881).

Heidenheimer, Arnold, Michael Johnston, and Victor LeVine, eds., *Political Corruption: A Handbook* (New Brunswick, NJ: Transaction Publishers, 1990).

Heitman, Francis B., *Historical Register of Officers of the Continental Army During the War of the Revolution, April 1775, to December, 1783* (Washington, D.C.: The Rare Book Shop Publishing Company, Inc., 1914).

Herbert, Edward, *The Impeachment of Sir Edward Harbert, Knight, His Maiesties Attourney Generall, by the Commons Assembled in Parliament* (London: Printed for Iohn Burroughes, and Iohn Franke, 1641).

Hershkowitz, Leo, *Tweed's New York: Another Look* (Garden City, NY: Anchor Press/Doubleday, 1977).

Hettena, Scott, *Feasting on the Spoils: The Life and Times of Randy 'Duke' Cunningham, History's Most Corrupt Congressman* (New York: St. Martin's Press, 2007).

Hichborn, Franklin, *"The System" as Uncovered by the San Francisco Graft Prosecution* (San Francisco: Press of the James H. Barry Company, 1915).

Hildreth, Richard, *The History of the United States of America, from the Discovery of the Continent to the Organization of Government under the Federal Constitution*, 6 vols. (New York: Harper & Brothers, 1880).

Hillin, Hank, *FBI Codename TENNPAR: Tennessee's Ray Blanton Years* (Nashville, TN: Pine Hall Press, 1985).

Hinds, Asher Crosby, *Hinds' Precedents of the House of Representatives of the United States, including References to Provisions of the Constitution, the Laws, and Decisions of the United States Senate*, 8 vols. (Washington, DC: Government Printing Office, 1907–1908).

Hodder, Alfred, *A Fight for the City* (New York: Macmillan, 1903).

Hoffer, Peter C., and N. E. H. Hull, "The First American Impeachments," *William and Mary Quarterly*, 3d Series, 35, 4 (October 1978), 653–667.

——, *Impeachment in America, 1635–1805* (New Haven, CT: Yale University Press, 1984).

Hoffman, John Thompson, *Law and Order* (New York: United States Publishing Company, 1876).

Holden, William Woods, *Memoirs of W. W. Holden* (Durham, NC: Seeman Printery, 1911).

Holli, Melvin G., and Peter d'A. Jones, eds., *Biographical Dictionary of American Mayors, 1820–1980* (Westport, CT: Greenwood Press, 1981).

Holzworth, John M., *The Fighting Governor: The Story of William Langer and the State of North Dakota* (Chicago: Pointer Press, 1938).

Hoogenboom, Ari, "The Pendleton Act and Civil Service," *American Historical Review* 64, 2 (January 1959), 301–318.

——, "Thomas A. Jenckes and Civil Service Reform," *Mississippi Valley Historical Review* 47 (March 1961), 636–658.

——, *Outlawing the Spoils: A History of the Civil Service Reform Movement, 1865–1883* (Urbana: University of Illinois Press, 1961).

Hoogenboom, Ari, and Olive Hoogenboom, *A History of the ICC: From Panacea to Palliative* (New York: W. W. Norton, 1976).

Howard, Thomas W., "Peter G. Van Winkle's Vote in the Impeachment of President Andrew Johnson: A West Virginian as a Profile in Courage," *West Virginia History* 35, 4 (1974), 290–295.

Humbert, W. H., *The Pardoning Power of the President* (Washington, DC: American Council on Public Affairs, 1941).

"Impeachment of the President," *Law Reporter* 7 (August 1844), 161–169.

*Impeachment Trial of David Butler, Governor of Nebraska, at Lincoln. Messrs. Bell, Hall and Brown, Official Reporters* (Omaha, NE: Tribune Steam Book and Job Printing House, 1871).

Ingersoll, Lurton D., *A History of the War Department of the United States, with Biographical Sketches of the Secretaries* (Washington, DC: Francis B. Mohun, 1879).

Jackley, John L., *Below the Beltway: Money, Power, and Sex in Bill Clinton's Washington* (Washington, DC: Regnery Publishing, 1996).

Jackson, Brooks, *Honest Graft: Big Money and the American Political Process* (Washington, DC: Farragut Publishing, 1990).

Jackson, Kenneth T., ed., *The Encyclopedia of New York City* (New Haven, CT: Yale University Press, 1995).

Jacobs, Bradford, *Thimbleriggers: The Law v. Governor Marvin Mandel* (Baltimore, MD: Johns Hopkins University Press, 1984).

Jacobsen, Joel K. "An Excess of Law in Lincoln County: Thomas Catron, Samuel Axtell, and the Lincoln County War," *New Mexico Historical Review* 68 (April 1993), 133–151.

Jefferson, Thomas, *The Writings of Thomas Jefferson*, 10 vols. Collected and edited by Paul Leicester Ford (New York: G. P. Putnam's Sons, 1892–1899).

Jenkins, Sammy S, *Mecham, Arizona's Fighting Governor: A Constitutional Conflict, "Freedom of the Press" or Political Assassination* (Albuquerque, NM: All States Publishing, 1988).

Jennewein, J. Leonard, and Jane Boorman, eds., *Dakota Panorama* (Bismarck: Dakota Territory Centennial Commission, 1961).

Johnson, Allen, and Dumas Malone, et al., eds., *Dictionary of American Biography*, X vols. and 10 supplements (New York: Charles Scribner's Sons, 1930–1995).

Johnson, John W., ed., *Historic U.S. Court Cases, 1690–1990: An Encyclopedia* (New York: Garland, 1992), 19–22.

Johnson, Loch K., Erna Gelles, and John C. Kuzenski, "The Study of Congressional Investigations: Research Strategies," *Congress and the Presidency* 19, 2 (Autumn 1992), 137–156.

Johnson, Rossiter, ed., *The Twentieth Century Biographical Dictionary of Notable Americans: Brief Biographies of Authors, Administrators, Clergymen, Commanders, Editors, Engineers, Jurists, Merchants, Officials, Philanthropists, Scientists, Statesman, and Others Who Are Making American History*, 10 vols. (Boston: Biographical Society, 1897–1904).

Jones, Robert F., "William Duer and the Business of Government in the Era of the American Revolution," *William and Mary Quarterly* 32, 3 (July 1975), 393–416.

Joyner, Fred B., "Robert Cumming Schenck, First Citizen and Statesman of the Miami Valley," *Ohio State Archaeological and Historical Quarterly* 58 (July 1949), 286–297.

Kelley, Colleen E., "The 1984 Campaign Rhetoric of Representative George Hansen: A Pentadic Analysis," *Western Journal of Speech Communication*, 51:2 (Spring 1987), 204-17.

Kleber, John E., ed., *The Kentucky Encyclopedia* (Lexington: University Press of Kentucky, 1992).

Klotsche, J. Martin, "The Star Route Cases," *Mississippi Valley Historical Review* 22, 3 (December 1935), 405–418.

Klotter, James C., *William Goebel: The Politics of Wrath* (Lexington: University Press of Kentucky, 1977).

Knapperman, Edward W., ed., *Great American Trials* (Detroit, MI: Visible Ink Press, 1994).

Kohn, George C., *Encyclopedia of American Scandal: From ABSCAM to the Zenger Case* (New York: Facts on File, 1989).

Kvasnicka, Robert M., and Herman J. Viola, *The Commissioners of Indian Affairs, 1824–1977* (Lincoln: University of Nebraska Press, 1979).

Lacayo, Richard, and Adam Cohen, "Inside Starr and His Operation," *Time*, 9 February 1998, 42–48.

LaForte, Robert S., "Gilded Age Senator: The Election, Investigation, and Resignation of Alexander Caldwell, 1871–1873," *Kansas History* 21, 4 (Winter 1998–1999), 234–255.

Lamplugh, George R. "'Oh The Colossus! The Colossus!': James Jackson and the Jeffersonian Republican Party in Georgia, 1796–1806," *Journal of the Early Republic* 9 (Fall 1989), 315–334.

Lance, Bert, *The Truth of the Matter: My Life in and out of Politics* (New York: Summit Books, 1991).

Lanman, Charles, *Biographical Annals of the Civil Government of the United States. From Original and Official Sources* (New York: J.M. Morrison, Publisher, 1887).

Larsen, Lawrence H., "William Langer: A Maverick in the Senate," *Wisconsin Magazine of History* 44 (Spring 1961), 189–198.

Larsen, Lawrence H., and Nancy J. Hulston, *Pendergast!* (Columbia: University of Missouri Press, 1997).

Lawrence, Alexander A., "James Jackson: Passionate Patriot," *Georgia Historical Quarterly* 34 (June 1950), 75–86.

Lawrence, William, "The Law of Impeachment," *American Law Register* 6 (1867), 641–680.

Lederkramer, David M., "A Statutory Proposal for Case-by-Case Congressional Waiver of the Speech or Debate Privilege in Bribery Cases," *Cardozo Law Review* 3, 3 (Spring 1982), 465–518.

Lee, David D. "The Attempt to Impeach Governor Horton," *Tennessee Historical Quarterly*, XXXIV:2 (Summer 1975), 188–201.

Levey, Peter B., *Encyclopedia of the Reagan-Bush Years* (Westport, CT: Greenwood Press, 1996).

Lewis, Alfred Henry, *Richard Croker* (New York: Life Publishing, 1901).

Lindgren, James, "The Theory, History, and Practice of the Bribery-Extortion Distinction," *University of Pennsylvania Law Review*, 141:5 (May 1993), 1695-1740.

Littlefield, Charles E., "The Impeachment of Judge Swayne," *Green Bag* 17 (April 1905), 193–207.

Logan, David A., *Historical Uses of a Special Prosecutor: The Administrations of Presidents Grant, Coolidge, and Truman* (Washington, DC: Congressional Research Service, 1973).

Lord, Stuart B., "Adelbert Ames, Soldier Politician: A Reevaluation," *Maine Historical Society Quarterly* 13 (Fall 1973), 81–97.

Loth, David, *Public Plunder: A History of Graft in America* (New York: Carrick & Evans, 1938).

Lowell, John, *Remarks on the Hon. John Quincy Adams's Review of Mr. Ames's Works, with Some Strictures on the Views of the Author* (Boston: Printed by T.B. Wait and Co., 1809).

Lowry, Sharon K., "Mirrors and Blue Smoke: Stephen Dorsey and the Santa Fe Ring in the 1880s," *New Mexico Historical Review* 59 (October 1984), 395–409.

Lucas, Jim Griffing, *Agnew: Profile in Conflict* (New York: Award Books, 1970).

Lynch, Denis Tilden, *"Boss" Tweed: The Story of a Grim Generation* (New York: Boni and Liveright, 1927).

Mach, Thomas Stuart, "George Hunt Pendleton, The Ohio Idea and Political Continuity in Reconstruction America," *Ohio History* 108 (Summer–Autumn 1999), 125–144.

Majeske, Andrew, "The Greylord Investigation Guidelines: Protection for Greylord Attorneys," *Loyola University Chicago Law Journal*, 16:3 (Spring 1985), 641-64.

Makinson, Larry, and Joshua Goldstein, *Open Secrets: The Encyclopedia of Congressional Money and Politics* (Washington, DC: Congressional Quarterly, 1992).

Malone, Michael P., "Midas of the West: The Incredible Career of William Andrews Clark," *Montana: Magazine of Western History* 33 (Autumn 1983), 2–17.

Mankiewicz, Frank, *U.S. v. Richard Nixon: The Final Crisis* (New York: Quadrangle/New York Times Book Company, 1975).

Manley, John F., *The Politics of Finance: the House Committee on Ways and Means* (Boston: Little, Brown, 1970).

Marsh, Robert, *Agnew: The Unexamined Man–A Political Profile* (New York: M. Evans, 1971).

Marshall, James V., *The United States Manual of Biography and History* (Philadelphia: James B. Smith & Co., 1856).

Marshall, Prince J. *The Impeachment of Warren Hastings* (London: Oxford University Press, 1965).

Martin, Edward Sandford, *The Life of Joseph Hodges Choate, As Gathered Chiefly from His Letters*, 2 vols. (New York: Charles Scribner's Sons, 1920).

Martin, Edward Winslow, *The Life and Public Services of Schuyler Colfax, Together with His Most Important Speeches* (New York: United States Publishing Company, 1868).

May, Thomas Erskine, Lord Farnborough, *A Treatise on the Law, Privileges, Proceedings and Usage of Parliament* (London: Butterworths, 1873).

Mazo, Earl, *Nixon: A Political Portrait* (New York: Harper & Row, 1968).

McAfee, John J., *Kentucky Politicians–Sketches of Representatives* (Louisville, KY: Courier Job Printing Company, 1886).

McDonald, John, *Secrets of the Great Whiskey Ring, Containing a Complete Exposure of the Illicit Whiskey Frauds Culminating in 1875, and the Connection of Grant, Babcock, Douglas, Chester H. Krum, and Other Administration Officers, Established by Positive and Unequivocal Documentary Proofs, Comprising Facsimiles of Confidential Letters and Telegrams Emanating From the White House, Directing the Management of the Ring. Also Photographs of Grant, Babcock, Bristow, Garfield and the Famous Sylph. To Which is Added the Missing Links in the Chain of Evidence of James A. Garfield's Implication with the District of Columbia Ring and Crédit Mobilier Bribery* (Chicago: Belford, Clarke & Co., 1880).

McFarland, Gerald W., *Mugwumps, Morals & Politics, 1884–1920* (Amherst: University of Massachusetts Press, 1975).

McGeary, Nelson, *The Developments of Congressional Investigative Power* (New York: Columbia University Press, 1940).

McGinnis, Patrick J., "A Case of Judicial Misconduct: The Impeachment and Trial of Robert W. Archbald," *Pennsylvania Magazine of History and Biography* 101 (1977), 506–520.

McMullin, Thomas A., and David Walker, *Biographical Directory of American Territorial Governors* (Westport, CT: Meckler Publishing, 1984).

McMurray, Carl D., *The Impeachment of Circuit Judge Richard Kelly* (Tallahassee: Florida State University, 1964).

Mecham, Evan, *Impeachment: The Arizona Conspiracy* (Glendale, AZ: MP Press, 1988).

Meier, Kenneth, and Thomas M. Holbrook, "'I Seen My Opportunities and I Took 'Em:' Political Corruption in the American States," *The Journal of Politics*, 54:1 (February 1992), 135-55.

Melton, Buckner F., Jr., *The First Impeachment: The Constitution's Framers and the Case of Senator William Blount* (Macon, GA: Mercer University Press, 1998).

Merriner, James L., *Mr. Chairman: Power in Dan Rostenkowski's America* (Carbondale: Southern Illinois University Press, 1999).

Messick, Hank, *The Politics of Prosecution: Jim Thompson, Marje Everett, Richard Nixon and the Trial of Otto Kerner* (Ottawa, IL: Caroline House Books, 1978).

Miller, Lillian B., et al., *"If Elected... ": Unsuccessful Candidates for the Presidency, 1796–1968* (Washington, DC: Smithsonian Institution Press, 1972).

Milne, Gordon, *George William Curtis and the Genteel Tradition* (Bloomington: Indiana University Press, 1956).

Mitchell, Jack, *Executive Privilege: Two Centuries of White House Scandals* (New York: Hippocrene Books, 1992).

Mitgang, Herbert, *The Man Who Rode the Tiger: The Life of Judge Samuel Seabury and the Story of the Greatest Investigation of City Corruption in this Century* (New York: W. W. Norton, 1979).

———, *Once Upon a Time in New York: Jimmy Walker, Franklin Roosevelt, and the Last Great Battle of the Jazz Age* (New York: Free Press, 2000).

Mittlebeeler, Emmet V., "The Great Kentucky Absconsion," *Filson Club History Quarterly* 27 (1953), 335–352.

Moore, Kathleen Dean, *Pardons: Justice, Mercy, and the Public Interest* (New York: Oxford University Press, 1997).

Morgan, Chester, *Redneck Liberal: Theodore G. Bilbo and the New Deal* (Baton Rouge: Louisiana State University Press, 1985).

Morgenthau, Henry, "All in a Life-Time—Chapters from an Autobiography. II. What I Learned From Sulzer and Tammany," *World's Work* 42, 5 (September 1921), 465–479.

Moritz, Charles, ed., *Current Biography 1977* (New York: H. W. Wilson & Co., 1977).

Morris, Newbold, *Let the Chips Fall: My Battles with Corruption* (New York: Appleton-Century-Crofts, 1955).

Mullaney, Marie Marmo, *Biographical Directory of the Governors of the United States, 1983–1988* (Westport, CT: Greenwood Press, 1988).

———, *Biographical Directory of the Governors of the United States, 1988–1994* (Westport, CT: Greenwood Press, 1994).

Munro, William Bennett, *The Initiative, Referendum and Recall* (New York: Appleton, 1912).

Muzzey, David Saville, *James G. Blaine: A Political Idol of Other Days* (New York: Dodd, Mead, 1935).

Myers, Gustavus, *The History of Tammany Hall* (New York: Boni and Liveright, 1917).

Nalle, Ouida Ferguson, *The Fergusons of Texas; Or, "Two Governors for the Price of One": A Biography of James Edward Ferguson and his wife, Miriam Amanda Ferguson, ex-Governors of the State of Texas* (San Antonio, TX: Naylor Company, 1946).

Nash, Jay Robert, *Encyclopedia of World Crime: Criminal Justice, Criminology, and Law Enforcement*, 4 vols. (Wilmette, IL: CrimeBooks, 1989).

*The National Cyclopaedia of American Biography*, 57 vols. and supplements A-N (New York: James T. White & Company, 1897–1984).

Noggle, Burl, *Teapot Dome: Oil and Politics in the 1920s* (Baton Rouge: Louisiana State University Press, 1962).

Northrop, William Bacot, *The Insolence of Office: The Story of the Seabury Investigations* (New York and London: G. P. Putnam's Sons, 1932).

O'Callaghan, Jerry A. "Senator John H. Mitchell and the Oregon Land Frauds, 1905," *Pacific Historical Review* 21 (August 1952): 255–261.

O'Connor, Richard, *Courtroom Warrior: The Combative Career of William Travers Jerome* (Boston: Little, Brown, 1963).

Omrcanin, Margaret Stewart, *The Novel and Political Insurgency* (Philadelphia: Dorrance & Company, 1973).

Paine, Albert Bigelow, *Mark Twain: A Biography* (New York: Harper & Brothers, 1912).

Peskin, Allan, *Garfield: A Biography* (Kent, OH: Kent State University Press, 1999).

Peters, John G., and Susan Welch, "Political Corruption in America: A Search for Definitions and a Theory, or If Political Corruption Is in the Mainstream of American Politics Why Is it Not in the Mainstream of American Politics Research?," *The American Political Science Review*, 72:3 (September 1978), 974-84.

Phillips, Cabell B. H., *The Truman Presidency: The History of a Triumphant Succession* (New York: Macmillan, 1962).

Phillips, David Graham, "The Treason of the Senate," *Cosmopolitan* 40, 5 (March 1906), 487–502.

Pink, Louis Heaton, *Gaynor, the Tammany Mayor Who Swallowed the Tiger: Lawyer, Judge, Philosopher* (New York: International Press, 1931).

Pitcher, M. Avis, "John Smith, First Senator from Ohio and his Connections with Aaron Burr," *Archaeological and Historical Society Quarterly* 45 (1936), 68–75.

Plucknett, Theodore Frank Thomas, *Studies in English History* (London: Hambledon Press, 1983).

Plummer, Mark A., "Profile in Courage? Edmund G. Ross and the Impeachment Trial," *Midwest Quarterly*, 27 (1985), 30–48.

Plungis, Jeff, "The Driving Force of Bud Shuster," *CQ Weekly*, 7 August 1999, 1914–1919.

Pollock, Sir Frederick, Bart., and Frederic William Maitland, *The History of English Law Before the Time of Edward I*, 2 vols. (Cambridge, UK: Cambridge University Press, 1899).

Porter, David, "Senator Carl Hatch and the Hatch Act of 1939," *New Mexico Historical Review*, 48 (April 1973), 151–161.

Posner, Richard A., *An Affair of State: The Investigation, Impeachment, and Trial of President Clinton* (Cambridge, MA: Harvard University Press, 1999).

Powell, Adam Clayton, *Adam by Adam* (New York: Dial Press, 1971).

Powers, Caleb, *My Own Story: An Account of the Conditions in Kentucky Leading to the Assassination of William Goebel, Who Was Declared Governor of the State, and My Indictment and Conviction on the Charge of Complicity in His Murder, by Caleb Powers* (Indianapolis, IN: Bobbs-Merrill, 1905).

Prickett, Robert C., "The Malfeasance of William Worth Belknap, Secretary of War, October 13, 1869 to March 2,

1876," *North Dakota History*, 17:1 (January 1950), 5–51, and 17:2 (April 1950), 97–134.

Priest, Loring B., *Uncle Sam's Stepchildren* (New Brunswick, NJ: Rutgers University Press, 1975).

*Proceeding in the Second Trial of the Case of the United States v. John W. Dorsey, John R. Miner, John M. Peck, Stephen W. Dorsey, Harvey M. Vaile, Montfort C. Rerdell, and Thomas J. Brady, for Conspiracy*, 4 vols. (Washington, DC: Government Printing Office, 1883).

Quisenberry, Anderson Chenault, *The Life and Times of Hon. Humphrey Marshall: Sometime an Officer in the Revolutionary War, Senator in Congress from 1795 to 1801* (Winchester, KY: Sun Publishing, 1892).

Ragsdale, Bruce A., and Joel D. Treese, *Black Americans in Congress, 1870–1989* (Washington, DC: Government Printing Office, 1990).

Reams, Bernard D., Jr., and Carol J. Gray, *The Congressional Impeachment Process and the Judiciary: Documents and Materials on the Removal of Federal District Judge Harry E. Claiborne* (Buffalo, NY: W. S. Hein, 1987).

*Record of the Proceedings of the High Court of Impeachment on the Trial of Calvin Pease: Consisting of the Senate of the State of Ohio as is Provided by the Constitution and in Pursuance of a Resolution of the Senate* (Chillicothe, OH: Nashee & Denny for Collins, 1809).

Reeves, Miriam G., *The Governors of Louisiana* (Gretna, LA: Pelican Publishing, 1972).

*Remarks on the Trial of John Peter Zenger, Printer of the New-York Weekly Journal, who was Lately Try'd and Acquitted for Printing and Publishing Two Libels against the Government of That Province* (London: Printed by J. Roberts, 1738).

*Report of the Trial of the Hon. Samuel Chase: One of the Associate Justices of the Supreme Court of the United States, before the High Court of Impeachment, Composed of the Senate of the United States, for Charges Exhibited against Him by the House of Representatives, in the Name of Themselves and of all the People of the United States, for High Crimes and Misdemeanors Supposed to Have Been by Him Committed, with the Necessary Documents and Official Papers from his Impeachment to Final Acquittal … Taken in Short Hand by Charles Evans, and the Arguments of Counsel Revised by Them from his Manuscript* (Baltimore, MD: Printed for Samuel Butler and George Keatinge, 1805).

Reston, James, *The Lone Star: The Life of John Connally* (New York: Harper & Row, 1989).

*Review of the Communications of Samuel Lawrence and William W. Stone, Manufacturers of Boston: To the Speaker of the House of Representatives, on the Subject of the Investigation at the New York Custom-House, in Two Letters. From the Hon. Geo. Poindexter* (Washington, DC: Printed at the National Intelligence Office, 1842).

Richardson, James D., ed., *A Compilation of the Messages and Papers of the Presidents, 1789–1907*, 9 vols. and 1 appendix (Washington, DC: Government Printing Office, 1896–1900).

Riordon, William L., *Plunkitt of Tammany Hall: A Series of Very Plain Talks on Very Practical Politics, delivered by Ex-Senator George Washington Plunkitt, the Tammany Philosopher, from his Rostrum–the New York County Court-House Bootblack Stand–and Recorded by William L. Riordon* (New York: McClure, Phillips, 1905).

Rogers, Cameron, *Colonel Bob Ingersoll: A Biographical Narrative of the Great American Orator and Agnostic* (Garden City, NY: Doubleday, Page, 1927).

Rosenberg, Kenyon C., and Judith K. Rosenberg, *Watergate: An Annotated Bibliography* (Littleton, CO: Libraries Unlimited, 1975).

Rosenbloom, David H., ed. (with the assistance of Mark A. Emmert), *Centenary Issues of the Pendleton Act of 1883: The Problematic Legacy of Civil Service Reform* (New York: M. Dekker, 1982).

Roske, Ralph J. "The Seven Martyrs?" *American Historical Review*, 64 (January 1959), 323–330.

Rozell, Mark J., *In Contempt of Congress: Postwar Press Coverage on Capitol Hill* (Westport, CT: Praeger, 1996).

Rudnick, Sharon A., "Speech or Debate Clause Immunity for Congressional Hiring Practices: Its Necessity and Its Implications," *UCLA Law Review* 28, 2 (December 1980), 217–251.

Ruegamer, Lana, *Biographies of the Governors* (Indianapolis, IN: Indiana Historical Society, 1978).

Russell, Francis, *The Shadow of Blooming Grove: Warren G. Harding in His Times* (New York: McGraw-Hill, 1968).

Rutherford, Bruce, *The Impeachment of Jim Ferguson* (Austin, TX: Eakin Press, 1983).

Rutherfurd, Livingston, *John Peter Zenger, His Press, His Trial and a Bibliography of Zenger Imprints, by Livingston Rutherfurd. Also a Reprint of the First Edition of the Trial* (New York: Dodd, Mead, 1904).

Saffell, David C., *Watergate: Its Effects on the American Political System* (Cambridge, MA: Winthrop Publishers, 1974).

Salokar, Rebecca Mae, *The Solicitor General: The Politics of Law* (Philadelphia: Temple University Press, 1992).

Salter, John T., *The People's Choice: Philadelphia's William S. Vare* (New York: Exposition Press, 1971).

Sann, Paul, *The Lawless Decade: A Pictorial History of a Great American Transition: From the World War I Armistice and Prohibition to Repeal and the New Deal* (New York: Bonanza Books, 1977).

Schell, Herbert S., *History of South Dakota* (Lincoln: University of Nebraska Press, 1975).

Schlup, Leonard C., "William N. Roach: North Dakota Isolationist and Gilded Age Senator," *North Dakota History* 57 (Fall 1990), 2–11.

Schmidt, John R., *The Mayor Who Cleaned Up Chicago: A Political Biography of William E. Dever* (DeKalb: Northern Illinois University Press, 1989).

Schultz, Jeffrey D., *Presidential Scandals* (Washington, DC: CQ Press, 2000).

Sears, Edward I., "The Impeachment Trial and its Results," *National Quarterly Review* 17 (June 1868), 144–156.

Seghetti, Michael R., "Speech or Debate Immunity: Preserving Legislative Independence while Cutting Costs of Congressional Immunity," *Notre Dame Law Review* 60, 3 (1985), 589–602.

Shapansky, Jay R., "Congress' Contempt Power," Congressional Research Service Report No. 86–83A, 28 February 1986.

Shofner, Jerrell H., *Nor Is It Over Yet: Florida in the Era of Reconstruction, 1863–1877* (Gainesville: University Presses of Florida, 1974).

Short, Jim, *Caleb Powers and the Mountain Army: The Story of a Statesman from Eastern Kentucky* (Olive Hill, KY: Jessica Publications, 1997).

Sikes, Bob, *He-Coon: The Bob Sikes Story* (Pensacola, FL: Perdido Bay Press, 1984).

Simkins, Francis Butler, *Pitchfork Ben Tillman: South Carolinian* (Baton Rouge: Louisiana State University Press, 1944).

Simpson, Alexander, Jr., *A Treatise on Federal Impeachments, With an Appendix Containing, Inter Alia, an Abstract of the Articles of Impeachment in all of the Federal Impeachments in this Country and in England* (Philadelphia: Law Association of Philadelphia, 1916).

Smith, Gaddis, *Impeachment: What Are Its Origins, History and the Process by which It Is Carried Out?* (Washington, DC: Center for Information on America, 1973).

Smith, Glenn H., *Langer of North Dakota: A Study in Isolationism, 1940–1959* (New York: Garland, 1979.)

Smith, Mortimer Brewster, *William Jay Gaynor, Mayor of New York* (Chicago: H. Regnery Co. 1951).

Smith, Steven S., and Christopher J. Deering, *Committees in Congress* (Washington, DC: CQ Press, 1990).

Smith, W. Calvin, "The Reconstruction 'Triumph' of Rufus B. Bullock," *Georgia Historical Quarterly* 52, 4 (December 1968), 414–425.

Sobel, Robert, and John Raimo, eds., *Biographical Directory of the Governors of the United States, 1789–1978*, 4 vols. (Westport, CT: Meckler Books, 1978).

*Speech of Mr. Black, of Georgia, on the Right of Members to Their Seats in the House of Representatives. Delivered in the House of Representatives, February 12, 1844* (Washington, DC: Printed at the Globe Office, 1844).

Stansbury, Arthur J., *Report of the Trial of James H. Peck, Judge of the United States District Court for the District of Missouri, Before the Senate of the United States, on an Impeachment Preferred by the House of Representatives Against Him for High Misdemeanors in Office* (Boston: Hilliard, Gray & Co., 1833).

*Statement of the Measure of the Contemplates Against Samuel Bryan, Esquire, Register-General of the Commonwealth of Pennsylvania* (Philadelphia: Printed by Francis and Robert Bailey, 1800).

Steffens, Lincoln, *The Struggle for Self-Government: Being an Attempt to Trace American Political Corruption to its Sources in Six States of the United States* (New York: McClure, Phillips, 1906).

Stephen, Sir James Fitz-James, Bart., *A History of the Criminal Law of England*, 3 vols. (London: Macmillan, 1883).

Stoddard, Lothrop, *Master of Manhattan: The Life of Richard Croker* (New York: Longmans, Green, 1931).

Stolberg, Mary M., *Fighting Organized Crime: Politics, Justice, and the Legacy of Thomas E. Dewey* (Boston: Northeastern University Press, 1995).

Stratton, David H., "Two Western Senators and Teapot Dome: Thomas J. Walsh and Albert B. Fall," *Pacific Northwest Quarterly* 65 (April 1974), 57–65.

Strong, Theron George, *Joseph Choate, New Englander, New Yorker, Lawyer, Ambassador* (New York: Dodd, Mead, 1917).

Stroud, Richard H., ed., *National Leaders of American Conservation* (Washington, DC: Smithsonian Institution Press, 1985).

Sullivan, Thomas P., *The Trial of My Life: Behind the Scenes at Operation Greylord* (Chicago: American Bar Association Division for Public Education, 1999).

Swindler, William F., "High Court of Congress: Impeachment Trials, 1797–1936," *American Bar Association Journal* 60 (1974), 420–428.

Swinney, Everette, "*United States v. Powell Clayton*: Use of the Federal Enforcement Acts in Arkansas," *Arkansas Historical Quarterly* 26 (Summer 1967), 143–154.

Taft, George S., *Compilation of Senate Election Cases from 1789 to 1885* (Washington, DC: Government Printing Office, 1885).

Talmadge, Herman E., with Mark Royden Winchell, *Talmadge: A Political Legacy, A Politician's Life: A Memoir* (Atlanta, GA: Peachtree Publishers, 1987).

Tarr, Joel Arthur, *A Study in Boss Politics: William Lorimer of Chicago* (Urbana: University of Illinois Press, 1971).

Taylor, Hannis, "The American Law of Impeachment," *North American Review*, 180 (January-June 1905), 502–512.

Taylor, Telford, *Grand Inquest: The Story of Congressional Investigations* (New York: Simon and Schuster, 1955).

*The Testimony in the Impeachment of Adelbert Ames, As Governor of Mississippi* (Jackson: Power & Barksdale, 1877).

Thayer, George, *Who Shakes the Money Tree? American Campaign Financing Practices from 1789 to the Present* (New York: Simon and Schuster, 1974).

Thayer, William Makepeace, *From Log-Cabin to the White House* (Boston: J. H. Earle, 1881).

Theoharis, Athan G., ed. et al., *The FBI: A Comprehensive Reference Guide* (Phoenix, AZ: Oryx Press, 1999).

Thomas, David Y., "The Law of Impeachment in the United States," *American Political Science Review* 2 (1908), 378–395.

Thomas, Lately, *A Debonair Scoundrel: An Episode in the Moral History of San Francisco* (New York: Holt, Rinehart and Winston, 1962).

Thompson, Clifford, ed., *Current Biography 1998* (New York: H. W. Wilson, 1998).

——, *Current Biography 1999* (New York: H. W. Wilson, 2000).

Thompson, Dennis F., *Ethics in Congress: From Individual to Institutional Corruption* (Washington, DC: Brookings Institution, 1995).

Thompson, Fred Dalton, *At That Point in Time: The Story of the Senate Watergate Committee* (New York: Quadrangle/New York Times Book Company, 1975).

Thurber, James A., and Roger H. Davidson, *Remaking Congress: Change and Stability in the 1990s* (Washington, DC: CQ Press, 1995).

Tilden, Samuel J., *The Writings and Speeches of Samuel J. Tilden* (New York: Harper & Brothers, 1885).

Timperlake, Edward, and William C. Triplett II, *Year of the Rat: How Bill Clinton Compromised U.S. Security for Chinese Cash* (Washington, DC: Regnery, 1998).

Trefousse, Hans L., "Ben Wade and the Failure of the Impeachment of Johnson," *Historical and Philosophical Society of Ohio Bulletin* 18 (October 1960), 241–252.

Trefousse, Hans L., Abraham Eisenstadt, and Ari Hoogenboom, eds., *Before Watergate: Problems of Corruption in American Society* (New York: Columbia University Press, 1978).

Trevelyan, George Macaulay, *History of England* (New York: Longmans, Green, 1927).

*The Trial in the Supreme Court, of the Information in the Nature of a Quo Warranto filed by the Attorney General on the Relation of Coles Bashford vs. Wm. A. Barstow, Contesting the Right to the Office of Governor of Wisconsin* (Madison, WI: Calkins & Proudfit, and Atwood and Rublee, 1856).

*The Trial of John Peter Zenger, of New York, Printer: Who was Charged with Having Printed and Published a LIBEL against the Government, and Acquitted. With a Narrative of His Case* (London: Printed for J. Almon 1735).

Tucker, David M., *Mugwumps: Public Moralists of the Gilded Age* (Columbia: University of Missouri Press, 1998).

Tuohy, James, and Rob Warden, *Greylord: Justice, Chicago Style* (New York: Putnam, 1989).

Turner, Frederick Jackson, ed., "Documents on the Blount Conspiracy, 1795–1797," *American Historical Review* 10 (April 1905), 574–606.

Turner, Lynn W., "The Impeachment of John Pickering," *American Historical Review* 54 (April 1949), 485–507.

*The United States Government Manual, 2000/2001* (Washington, DC: Government Printing Office, 2001).

Utter, Glenn H., and Ruth Ann Strickland, *Campaign and Election Reform: A Reference Handbook* (Santa Barbara, CA: ABC-CLIO, 1997).

Van Nest, G. Willet, "Impeachable Offences under the Constitution of the United States," *American Legal Review* 16 (1882), 798–817.

Van Riper, Paul P., *History of the United States Civil Service* (Evanston, IL: Row, Peterson, 1958).

Van Tassel, Emily Field, and Paul Finkelman, *Impeachable Offenses: A Documentary History from 1787 to the Present* (Washington, DC: Congressional Quarterly, 1999).

Vare, William S., *My Forty Years in Politics* (Philadelphia: Roland Swain Co., 1933).

Volcansek, Mary L., *Judicial Impeachment: None Called for Justice* (Urbana, IL: University of Illinois Press, 1993).

Walden, Gregory S., *On Best Behavior: The Clinton Administration and Ethics in Government* (Indianapolis, IN: Hudson Institute, 1996).

Walsh, Thomas J., "The True Story of Teapot Dome," *Forum* 72, 1 (July 1924), 1–12.

Ward, Sir Adolphus William, et al., eds., *The Cambridge History of English and American Literature*, 18 vols. (New York: G. P. Putnam's Sons, 1907–1921).

Warmoth, Henry Clay, *War, Politics and Reconstruction: Stormy Days in Louisiana* (New York: Macmillan, 1930).

Weeks, Kent M., *Adam Clayton Powell and the Supreme Court* (New York: Dunellen, 1971).

Wendt, Lloyd; and Herman Kogan, *Lords of the Levee: The Story of Bathhouse John & Hinky Dink* (Indianapolis, IN: Bobbs-Merrill, 1943).

——, *Big Bill of Chicago* (Indianapolis, IN: Bobbs-Merrill, 1953).

Werner, Morris Robert, *Tammany Hall* (Garden City, NY: Doubleday, Doran, 1928).

Werner, Morris Robert, and John Starr, *Teapot Dome* (Clifton, NJ: A. M. Kelley, 1950).

Wesser, Robert F., "The Impeachment of a Governor: William Sulzer and the Politics of Excess," *New York History* 60, :4 (October 1979), 407–438.

Westphall, Victor, *Thomas Benton Catron and His Era* (Tucson, AZ: University of Arizona Press, 1973).

Westwood, Howard C. "The Federals' Cold Shoulder to Arkansas' Powell Clayton," *Civil War History* 26 (September 1980), 240–256.

Wharton, Francis, ed., *State Trials of the United States during the Administrations of Washington and Adams, with References Historical and Professional and Preliminary*

*Notes on the Politics of the Times* (Philadelphia: Carey & Hart, 1849).

White, Theodore H., *Breach of Faith: The Fall of Richard Nixon* (New York: Atheneum, 1975).

Wilhelmy, Robert W., "Senator John Smith and the Aaron Burr Conspiracy," *Cincinnati Historical Society Bulletin* 28 (Spring 1970), 39–60.

Williston, Samuel, "Does a Pardon Blot Out Guilt?," *Harvard Law Review* 28 (1915), 647–654.

Wolff, Wendy, ed., *Vice Presidents of the United States, 1789–1993* (Washington, DC: Government Printing Office, 1997).

Wooddy, Carroll Hill, *The Case of Frank L. Smith: A Study in Representative Government* (Chicago: University of Chicago Press, 1931).

Woodward, C. Vann, *Responses of the Presidents to Charges of Misconduct* (New York: Delacorte Press, 1974).

Wright, Marcus J., *Some Account of the Life and Services of William Blount* (Washington, DC: E. J. Gray, 1884).

Zelizer, Julian E., *Taxing America: Wilbur D. Mills, Congress, and the State, 1945–1975* (Cambridge, UK: Cambridge University Press, 1999).

Zelnick, Bob, *Gore: A Political Life* (Washington, DC: Regnery, 1999).

Zink, Harold, *City Bosses in the United States* (Durham, NC: Duke University Press, 1930).

Zuber, Richard L., *North Carolina during Reconstruction* (Raleigh, NC: State Department of Archives and History, 1996).

**Dissertations and Theses**

Bates, J. Leonard, "Senator Walsh of Montana, 1918–1924: A Liberal under Pressure" (Ph.D. dissertation, University of North Carolina at Chapel Hill, 1952).

Benson, Harry King, "The Public Career of Adelbert Ames, 1861–1876" (Ph.D. dissertation, University of Virginia, 1975).

Beyer, Barry K., "Thomas E. Dewey, 1937–1947: A Study in Political Leadership" (Master's thesis, University of Rochester [New York], 1962).

Brammer, Clarence Lee, "Thomas J. Walsh: Spokesman for Montana" (Ph.D. dissertation, University of Missouri, Columbia, 1972).

Byler, Charles A., "Trial by Congress: The Controversy over the Powers and Procedures of Congressional Investigations, 1945–1954" (Ph.D. dissertation, Yale University, 1990).

Cognac, Robert Earl, "The Senatorial Career of Henry Fountain Ashurst" (Master's thesis, Arizona State University, 1953).

Cummings, Hilary Anne, "John H. Mitchell, a Man of His Time: Foundations of His Political Career, 1860–1879" (Ph.D. dissertation, University of Oregon, 1985).

Dodds, Archibald J., "'Honest John' Covode" (Master's thesis, University of Pittsburgh, 1933).

Dunar, Andrew J., "All Honorable Men: The Truman Scandals and the Politics of Morality" (Ph.D. dissertation, University of Southern California, 1981).

Dunnington, Miles W., "Senator Thomas J. Walsh, Independent Democrat in the Wilson Years" (Ph.D. dissertation, University of Chicago, 1941).

Foot, Forrest L., 'The Senatorial Aspirations of William A. Clark, 1898–1901: A Study In Montana Politics" (Ph.D. dissertation, University of California, 1941).

Forth, William S., "Wesley L. Jones: A Political Biography" (Ph.D. dissertation, University of Washington, 1962).

Giglio, James M., "The Political Career of Harry M. Daugherty" (Ph.D. dissertation, Ohio State University, 1968).

Gregg, Leigh E., "The First Amendment in the Nineteenth Century: Journalists' Privilege and Congressional Investigations" (Ph.D. dissertation, University of Wisconsin, 1984).

Hill, Janellen, "Spiro T. Agnew: Tactics of Self-Defense, August 1 to October 15, 1974" (Master's thesis, Arizona State University, 1974).

Hjalmervik, Gary L., "William Langer's First Administration, 1932–1934" (Master's thesis, University of North Dakota, 1966).

Horne, Robert M., "The Controversy over the Seating of William Langer, 1940–1942" (Master's thesis, University of North Dakota, 1964).

Johnson, Gordon W., "William Langer's Resurgence to Political Power in 1932" (Master's thesis, University of North Dakota, 1970).

Jones, Robert F. "The Public Career of William Duer: Rebel, Federalist Politician, Entrepreneur and Speculator 1775–1792" (Ph.D. dissertation, University of Notre Dame, 1967).

Keighton, Robert Laurie, "The Executive Privilege and the Congressional Right to Know: A Study of the Investigating Powers of Congressional Committees" (Master's thesis, University of Pennsylvania, 1961).

Lowry, Sharon K., "Portrait of an Age: The Political Career of Stephen W. Dorsey, 1868–1889" (Ph.D. dissertation, North Texas State University, 1980).

Mach, Thomas Stuart, "'Gentleman George' Hunt Pendleton: A Study in Political Continuity" (Ph.D. dissertation, University of Akron, 1996).

Martin, Jennie McKee, "The Administration of Governor Barstow" (Bachelor's thesis, University of Wisconsin, 1921).

Mattingly, Arthur H., "Senator John Brooks Henderson, United States Senator from Missouri" (Ph.D. dissertation, Kansas State University, 1971).

Miller, Frank L., "Fathers and Sons: The Binghams and American Reform, 1790–1970" (Ph.D. dissertation, Johns Hopkins University, 1970).

Raper, Horace Wilson, "William Woods Holden: A Political Biography" (Ph.D. dissertation, University of North Carolina, Chapel Hill, 1951).

Sherman, Robert Lindsay, "Public Officials and Land Fraud in Arizona" (Master's thesis, Arizona State University, 1978).

Sinow, David Martin, "The Foreign Corrupt Practices Act of 1977" (Master's thesis, University of Illinois, Urbana-Champaign, 1982).

Smith, Charles P., "Theodore G. Bilbo's Senatorial Career: The Final Years, 1941–1947" (Ph.D. dissertation, University of Southern Mississippi, 1983).

Smith, Willard Harvey, "The Political Career of Schuyler Colfax to His Election as Vice President in 1868" (Ph.D. dissertation, Indiana University, 1939).

Thompson, Margaret S., "The 'Spider Web': Congress and Lobbying in the Age of Grant" (Ph.D. dissertation, University of Wisconsin, 1979).

## Government Documents, United States Government

Bazan, Elizabeth B., and Jay R. Shampansky, *Compendium of Precedents Involving Evidentiary Rulings and Applications of Evidentiary Principles from Selected Impeachment Trials*, Congressional Research Service (CRS) Report for Congress, 3 July 1989.

District of Columbia, Supreme Court, *Title United States v. Harry F. Sinclair and Albert B. Fall. Indictment: Violation Section 37, Penal code, Conspiracy to defraud the United States. (Presented May 27, 1925.) Atlee Pomerene, Owen J. Roberts, Special Counsel of the United States* (Washington, DC: Government Printing Office, 1925).

Doyle, Charles, *Impeachment Grounds: A Collection of Selected Materials*, Congressional Research Service (CRS) Report to Congress, 29 October 1998.

*Final Report of the Independent Counsel for Iran/Contra Matters. Lawrence E. Walsh, Independent Counsel*, 3 vols. (Washington, DC: U.S. Court of Appeals for the District of Columbia Circuit, Division for the Purpose of Appointing Independent Counsel, 1993).

*Final Report of the Independent Counsel in re: Bruce Edward Babbitt. Before: Sentelle, Senior Circuit Judge, Presiding, Cudahy, Senior Circuit Judge, and Fay, Senior Circuit Judge. Carol Elder Bruce, Independent Counsel* (Washington, DC: U.S. Court of Appeals for the District of Columbia Circuit, Division for the Purpose of Appointing Independent Counsel, 2000).

*Final Report of the Independent Counsel in re: Eli J. Segal. Curtis Emery Von Kahn, Independent Counsel* (Washington, DC: U.S. Court of Appeals for the District of Columbia Circuit, Division for the Purpose of Appointing Independent Counsels, 1997).

*Final Report of the Independent Counsel in re: Janet G. Mullins. Joseph E. diGenova, Independent Counsel* (Washington, DC: U.S. Court of Appeals for the District of Columbia Circuit, 1995).

*Final Report of the Independent Counsel in re: Madison Guaranty Savings & Loan Association. Kenneth W. Starr, Independent Counsel* (Washington, DC: Office of Independent Counsel, 2000).

*Final Report of the Independent Counsel in re: Madison Guaranty Savings & Loan Association: in re: William David Watkins and in re: Hillary Rodham Clinton. Robert W. Ray, Independent Counsel* (Washington, DC: U.S. Court of Appeals for the District of Columbia Circuit, Division for the Purpose of Appointing Independent Counsels, Division no. 94–1, 2000).

*Final Report of the Independent Counsel in re: Ronald H. Brown. Daniel S. Pearson, Independent Counsel* (Washington, DC: U.S. Court of Appeals for the District of Columbia Circuit, Division for the Purpose of Appointing Independent Counsel, 1996).

*Final Report of the Independent Counsel in re: Samuel R. Pierce, Jr., Arlin M. Adams, Larry D. Thompson, Independent Counsels*, 6 vols. (Washington, DC: U.S. Court of Appeals for the District of Columbia Circuit, Division for the Purpose of Appointing Independent Counsels, 1998).

*History of the Committee on the Judiciary of the House of Representatives*, House Committee Print, 97th Cong., 2d Sess. (1982).

*House Rules Manual*, House Document No. 106–320, 107th Cong. (Washington, DC: Government Printing Office, 1999).

*Memorial Address of the Life and Character of Michael Crawford Kerr (Speaker of the House of Representatives of the United States). Delivered in the House of Representatives December 16, 1876, and in the Senate February 27, 1877. Published by Order of Congress* (Washington, DC: Government Printing Office, 1877).

*Report of the Select Committee of the House of Representatives, Appointed Under the Resolution of January 6, 1873, to Make Inquiry In Relation to the Affairs of the Union Pacific Railroad Company, the Crédit Mobilier of America, and Other Matters Specified in Said Resolution and in Other Resolutions Referred to Said Committee* (Washington, DC: Government Printing Office, 1873).

Shapansky, Jay R., *Congress' Contempt Power*, Congressional Research Service (CRS) Report No. 86–83A, 28 February 1986.

*Speech of Mr. Black, of Georgia, on the Right of Members to Their Seats in the House of Representatives. Delivered in the House of Representatives, February 12, 1844* (Washington, DC: Printed at the Globe Office, 1844).

United States Information Agency, Office of Inspector General. *Report of Audit, Review of Planning and Management of Lisbon Expo 98* (Washington, DC: Government Printing Office, 1999).

U.S. Congress, Joint Committee on Congressional Operations, *House of Representatives Exclusion, Censure and Expulsion Cases from 1789 to 1973*, 93d Cong., 1st Sess. (Washington, DC: Government Printing Office, 1973).

U.S. House, *Conduct of George W. English, United States District Judge, Eastern District of Illinois: Hearing Before the Special Committee of the House of Representatives Pursuant to House Joint Resolution 347*, 2 vols. (Washington, DC: Government Printing Office, 1925).

———, *Conduct of Harold Louderback, United States District Judge, Northern District of California. Hearing Before the Special Committee of the House of Representatives, Seventy-second Congress, Pursuant to H[ouse] Res[olution] 239, September 6 to September 12, 1932*, 3 vols. (Washington, DC: Government Printing Office, 1933).

———, *Conduct of Judge George W. English: Report on the Report of the Special Committee of the House of Representatives Authorized to Inquire into the Official Conduct of George W. English [House Report 69-653]* (Washington, DC: Government Printing Office, 1926).

———, *Conduct of Judge Harold Louderback. Report to Accompany H[ouse] Res[olution] 387*, House Report 72-2065, (Washington, DC: Government Printing Office, 1933).

———, *Impeachment of Halsted L. Ritter. [House Report 74-2025]* (Washington, DC: Government Printing Office, 1936).

———, *Impeachment of Judge Alcee L. Hastings: Report of the Committee on the Judiciary to Accompany H[ouse] Res[olution] 499*, House Report 100-810, (Washington, DC: Government Printing Office, 1988).

———, *Impeachment of Judge Harry E. Claiborne: Report to Accompany H[ouse] Res[olution] 461*, House Report 99-668, (Washington, DC: Government Printing Office, 1986).

———, *Impeachment of the President: Articles of Impeachment Exhibited by the House of Representatives Against Andrew Johnson, President of the United States*, House Miscellaneous Documents 40-91, (Washington, DC: Government Printing Office, 1868).

———, *Impeachment of the President: [Report] from the Judiciary Committee*, House Report 40-7, (Washington, DC: Government Printing Office, 1868).

———, *Impeachment of Richard M. Nixon*, House Report 93-1305, 93rd Cong., 2d Sess., 1974.

———, *Impeachment of Walter L. Nixon, Jr.: Report To Accompany H. Res. 87*, House Report 101-36, (Washington, DC: Government Printing Office, 1989).

———, *Impeachment of West H. Humphreys, Judge of the United States District Court of Tennessee*, House Report 37-44, (Washington, DC: Government Printing Office, 1862).

———, *Impeachment of William W. Belknap, Late Secretary of War*, House Report 41-345, (Washington, DC: Government Printing Office, 1876).

———, *In the Matter of Representative E. G. "Bud" Shuster: Report*, House Report 106-979, (Washington, DC: Government Printing Office, 2000).

———, *In the Matter of Representative John W. Jenrette, Jr.*, House Report 96-1537, 96th Cong., 2d Sess. (Washington. D.C.: Government Printing Office, 1980).

———, *In the Matter of Representative Mario Biaggi*, House Report 100-506, 100th Cong., 2d Sess. (Washington, DC: Government Printing Office, 1988).

———, *In the Matter of Representative Michael J. Myers*, House Report 96-1387, 96th Cong., 2d Sess. (Washington, DC: Government Printing Office, 1980).

———, *In the Matter of Representative Raymond F. Lederer*, House Report 97-110, 97th Cong., 1st Sess. (Washington, DC: Government Printing Office, 1981).

———, *Investigatory Powers of Committee on the Judiciary with Respect to Its Impeachment Inquiry: Report Together with Additional, Supplemental, and Separate Views (To Accompany a Resolution (H. Res. 803) Providing Appropriate Power to the Committee on the Judiciary to Conduct an Investigation of Whether Sufficient Grounds Exist to Impeach Richard M. Nixon, President of the United States, and for Other Purposes)*, House Report 93-774, (Washington, DC: Government Printing Office, 1974).

———, *Judge Walter L. Nixon, Jr., Impeachment Inquiry: Hearings Before the Subcommittee on Civil and Constitutional Rights of the Committee of the Judiciary* (Washington, DC: Government Printing Office, 1989).

———, *Judge Walter L. Nixon, Jr., Impeachment Inquiry Transcript of Proceedings U.S.A. v. Walter L. Nixon, Jr.*, 2 vols. Criminal Action No. H85-00012(L) (Washington, DC: Government Printing Office, 1989).

———, *Memorial Services Held in the House of Representatives of the United States, Together with Remarks Presented in Eulogy of Thomas J. Walsh, Late a Senator from Montana* (Washington: Government Printing Office, 1934).

———, *Memorial Services in the Congress of the United States and Tributes in Eulogy of Richard M. Nixon, Late a President of the United States* (Washington, DC: U.S. Government Printing Office, 1996).

———, *Proceedings in the House of Representatives, Fifty-Eighth Congress, Concerning the Impeachment of Charles Swayne* (Washington, DC: Government Printing Office, 1912).

———, *Report of the House Managers on the Impeachment of W. W. Belknap, Late Secretary of War*, House Report 44–791, (Washington, DC: Government Printing Office, 1876).

———, *Star Route Transportation of Mails*, House Report 1701, 47th Cong., 1st Sess. (Washington, DC: Government Printing Office, 1882).

———, *Testimony Relating to Expenditures in the Department of Justice: The Star Route Cases*, House Miscellaneous Document No. 38, Part II, 48th Cong., 1st Sess. (Washington, DC: Government Printing Office, 1884).

U.S. House, Committee on Banking, Finance, and Urban Affairs, Subcommittee on General Oversight and Investigations, *Relationship of Arizona Governor J. Fife Symington III with Southwest Savings and Loan Association: Hearing Before the Subcommittee on Oversight and Investigations of the Committee on Banking, Finance, and Urban Affairs*, 102nd Cong., 2d Sess., February 20, 1992.

U.S. House, Committee on Government Reform and Oversight, *Report of the FBI General Counsel on the Dissemination of FBI File Information to the White House, issued on June 14, 1996, by FBI General Counsel Howard M. Shapiro; Investigation into the White House and Department of Justice on Security of FBI Background Investigation Files*, House Report 104–862, 104th Cong., 2d Sess., 28 September 1996.

U.S. House, Committee on Post Office and Civil Service, *Display of Code of Ethics for Government Service: Report to Accompany H.R. 5997*, (Washington, DC: Government Printing Office, 1980).

U.S. House, Committee on Rules, *Congressional Gift Reform: Hearings before the Committee on Rules, House of Representatives, on H. Res. 250*, 104th Cong., 1st Sess., November 2 and 7, 1995.

U.S. House, Committee on Standards of Official Conduct, *Ethics Manual for Members and Employees of the U.S. House of Representatives*, 96th Cong., 1st Sess. (Washington, DC: U.S. Government Printing Office, 1979).

———, *In the Matter of Representative Charles C. Diggs, Jr.: Report, Together with Supplemental Views to Accompany H. Res. 378*, 2 vols. (Washington, DC: Government Printing Office, 1979).

———, *In the Matter of Representative Raymond F. Lederer*, House Report No. 110, 97th Congress, 1st Session (Washington, D.C.: Government Printing Office, 1981).

———, *Inquiry into the Operation of the Bank of the Sergeant-at-Arms of the House of Representatives, Together with Minority Views (to accompany H. Res. 393)* (Washington, DC: Government Printing Office, 1992).

———, *Manual of Offenses and Procedures: Korean Influence Investigation, Pursuant to House Resolution 252*, (Washington, D.C.: Government Printing Office, 1977).

———, *Report of the Special Outside Counsel in the Matter of Speaker James C. Wright, Jr.*, 101st Cong., (Washington, DC: Government Printing Office, 1989).

———, *Rules of Procedure: Committee on Standards of Official Conduct* (Washington, DC: Government Printing Office, 1987).

———, *Summary of Activities* 101st Congress, House Report No. 101–995, 101st Cong., 2d Sess. (Washington, DC: Government Printing Office, 1990)

U.S. House, Committee on the Judiciary, *Impeachment: Evidence on the Resolution Concerning Charles Swayne, Judge of the United States District Court for the Northern District of Florida*, March 21, 1904, (Washington, DC: Government Printing Office, 1904).

———, *Hearings of the Committee on the Judiciary (Impeachment of President Richard M. Nixon)*, 93rd Cong., 2d Sess., 1974.

———, *Constitutional Grounds for Presidential Impeachment: Report by the Staff of the Impeachment Inquiry* House Committee Report, 93rd Cong., 2d Sess., February 1974.

———, *Markup of House Resolution 461, Impeachment of Judge Harry E. Claiborne*, 99th Cong., 2d Sess. (Washington, DC: Government Printing Office, 1986).

U.S. House, Select Committee on U.S. National Security and Military/Commercial Concerns with the People's Republic of China, *U.S. National Security and Military/Commercial Concerns with the People's Republic of China. Submitted by Mr. Cox of California*, 3 vols. (Washington, DC: Government Printing Office, 1999).

U.S. House, Select Committee to Inquire into the Causes and Extent of the Late Defalcations of the Custom-House at New York and Other Places, *Report of the Minority of the Select Committee of the House of Representatives, Appointed on the Seventeenth of January, 1839, to inquire into the Causes and Extent of the Late Defalcations of the Custom-House at New York and other Places* (Washington: Printed by Blair and Rives, 1839).

U.S. House, Select Committee to Investigate Covert Arms Transactions with Iran [with the U.S. Senate Committee on Secret Military Assistance to Iran and the Nicaraguan Opposition], *Report of the Congressional Committees Investigating the Iran-Contra Affair, With Supplemental, Minority, and Additional Views*, 3 vols. (Washington, DC: Government Printing Office; three volumes, 1987).

U.S. Senate, *Answer of George W. English, District Judge of the United States for the Eastern District of Illinois: To the Articles of Impeachment Against Him by the House of Representatives of the United States*, Senate Document 104, 69th Cong., 1st Sess. (Washington, DC: Government Printing Office, 1926).

——, *The Senate, 1789–1989: Addresses on the History of the United States Senate, by Robert C. Byrd*, 3 vols. Senate Doc. 100–20, 100th Cong., 1st Sess. (Washington, DC: Government Printing Office, 1991).

——, *Extracts from the Journal of the United States Senate in all Cases of Impeachment Presented by the House of Representatives: 1798–1904*, Senate Document 876, 62nd Cong., 2nd Sess. (Washington, DC: Government Printing Office, 1912).

——, *Final Report of the Investigation of Illegal or Improper Activities in Connection With 1996 Federal Election Campaigns, Together With Additional and Minority Views*, 10 vols. Senate Report 105–167, 105th Cong., 2d Sess. (Washington, DC: Government Printing Office, 1999).

——, *Final Report of the Senate Select Committee to Study Undercover Activities of Components of the Department of Justice*, Senate Report 682, 97th Cong., 2d Sess. (Washington, DC: Government Printing Office, 1982)

——, *Journal of the Executive Proceedings of the Senate of the United States of America* (Washington: Duff Green, 1828).

——, *Law Enforcement Undercover Activities: Hearings Before the Senate Select Committee to Study Law Enforcement Undercover Activities of Components of the Department of Justice*, 97th Cong., 2d Sess. (Washington, DC: Government Printing Office, 1982).

——, *Leases Upon Naval Oil Reserves and Activities of the Continental Trading Co. (Ltd.) of Canada*, Senate Report 1326, 70th Cong., 1st Sess. (Washington, DC: Government Printing Office, 1928).

——, *Proceedings of the Senate Sitting for the Trial of William W. Belknap, Late Secretary of War, on the Articles of Impeachment Exhibited by the House of Representatives*, 4 vols. 44th Cong., 1st Sess. (Washington, DC: Government Printing Office, 1876).

——, *Proceedings of the United States Senate in the Trial of Impeachment of George W. English, District Judge of the United States for the Eastern District of Illinois*, Senate Document No. 177, 69th Cong., 2d Sess., 1926.

——, *Proceedings of the United States Senate and the House of Representatives in the Trial of Impeachment of Robert W. Archbald, Additional Circuit Judge of the United States from the Third Judicial Circuit and designated a Judge of the Commerce Court*, 3 vols. Senate Document 1140, 62nd Cong., 3d Sess. (Washington, DC: Government Printing Office, 1913).

——, *Proceedings of the United States Senate in the Impeachment Trial of President William Jefferson Clinton*, Senate Document 4, 106th Cong., 1st Sess. (Washington, DC: Government Printing Office, 2000).

——, *Report [of] the Committee Appointed to investigate the Charges of Bribery in the Recent Senatorial Election of Kansas, Preferred against Senator Pomeroy by A. M. York and B. F. Simpson*, Senate Report No. 523, 42nd Cong., 3rd Sess. (Washington, DC: Government Printing Office, 1873).

——, *Report of the Senate Impeachment Trial Committee on the Impeachment of Harry E. Claiborne, Judge of the United States District Court for the District of Nevada, of High Crimes and Misdemeanors*, Senate Document 99–812, 99th Cong., 2d Sess., August 15 to September 23, 1986. (Washington, DC: Government Printing Office, 1989).

U.S. Senate, Committee on Governmental Affairs, *Hearings on the Nomination of Thomas B. Lance to be Director of the Office of Management and Budget, and Nomination of James T. McIntyre, Jr., to be Deputy Director of the Office of Management and Budget*, 95th Cong., 1st Sess., January 17 and 18, 1977, and March 4, 1977.

——, *Investigation of Illegal or Improper Activities in Connection with 1996 Federal Election Campaigns–Final Report of the Committee on Governmental Affairs*, 6 vols. Senate Report 105–167, 105th Cong., 2d Sess., 10 March 1998 (Washington, DC: Government Printing Office; 6 volumes, 1998).

——, *Matters Relating to T. Bertram Lance: Hearings Before the Committee on Governmental Affairs*, 3 vols. 95th Cong., 1st Sess. (Washington, DC: Government Printing Office, 1977).

U.S. Senate, Select Committee on Ethics, *Investigation of Senator Alan Cranston*, 2 vols. (Washington, DC: Government Printing Office, 1991).

——, *Investigation of Senator David F. Durenberger: Report of the Select Committee on Ethics and the Report of Special Counsel on S. Res. 311*, (Washington, DC: Government Printing Office, 1990).

——, *Preliminary Inquiry into Allegations Regarding Senators Cranston, DeConcini, Glenn, McCain, and Riegle, and Lincoln Savings and Loan: Open Session Hearings*, 101st Cong., 2d Sess., November 15, 1990, through January 16, 1991.

U.S. Senate, Select Committee on Investigation of the Attorney General, *Investigation of Hon. Harry M. Daugherty, Formerly Attorney General of the United States. Hearings pursuant to S. Res. 157, directing a Committee to investigate the Failure of the Attorney General to Prosecute or Defend Certain Criminal and Civil Actions, wherein the Government is Interested*, 68th Cong., 1st Sess. (Washington, DC: Government Printing Office, 1924).

U.S. Senate, Select Committee on Standards and Conduct, *Hearings, on Allegations Against Senator Thomas J. Dodd, Pursuant to Senate Resolution 338*, 2 vols. 89th Cong. 2d Sess. (Washington, DC: Government Printing Office, 1966–1967).

U.S. Senate, Special Committee on Official Conduct, *Senate Code of Official Conduct: Report of the Special Committee on Official Conduct, United States Senate, to Accompany S.*

*Res. 110*, (Washington, DC: Government Printing Office, 1977).

U.S. Senate, Special Committee to Investigate Whitewater Development Corporation and Related Matters, *Investigation of Whitewater Development Corporation and Related Matters: Final Report of the Special Committee to Investigate Whitewater Development Corporation and Related Matters, Together with Additional and Minority Views*, (Washington, DC: Government Printing Office, 1996).

**Government Documents—Individual States**

[Arizona], *Record of Proceedings of the Court of Impeachment: In the Trail of Honorable Evan Mecham, Governor, State of Arizona. Arizona State Senate, Sitting as a Court of Impeachment* (St. Paul, MN: West Publishing Company, 1991).

[California], San Francisco Municipal Government, *Report on the Causes of Municipal Corruption in San Francisco, as Disclosed by the Investigations of the Oliver Grand Jury, and the Prosecution of Certain Persons for Bribery and Other Offenses Against the State; William Denman, Chairman. Committee Appointed by the Mayor, October 12, 1908. Reprinted with a Preface and Index of Names and Subjects by the California Weekly* (San Francisco: Rincon Publishing Co., 1910).

[Kansas], *Proceedings in the Cases of the Impeachment of Charles Robinson, Governor, John W. Robinson, Secretary of State, George S. Hillyer, Auditor of State, of Kansas* (Lawrence: Kansas State Journal Steam Press, 1862).

[Massachusetts]. *Report of the Trial by Impeachment of James Prescott, Judge of the Probate of Wills, & C. for the County of Middlesex for Misconduct and Maladministration in Office, before the Senate of Massachusetts in the Year 1821. with an Appendix, Containing an Account of Former Impeachments in the Same State. by Octavius Pickering and William Howard Gardiner, of the Suffolk Bar* (Boston: Office of the Daily Advertiser, 1821).

[New Jersey] New Jersey, Department of Law and Public Safety, *Final Report on the Investigation of the Division of Employment Security, Department of Labor and Industry to Robert B. Meyner, Governor, State of New Jersey. With Foreword* (Trenton: State of New Jersey Official Report, 1955).

[New York] *By His Excellency William Cosby, Captain General and Governour [Sic] in Chief of the Provinces New-York, New-Jersey ... a Proclamation: Whereas by the Contrivance of Some Evil Disposed and Disaffected Persons, Divers Journals or Printed News Papers (Entitled, the New-York Weekly Journal... Have Been Caused to Be Printed and Published by John Peter Zenger... I Have Thought Fit... Issue This Proclamation, Hereby Promising a Reward of Fifty Pounds to Such Person or Persons Who Shall Discover the Author or Authors of the Said ... Journals or Printed News-Papers ... Given Under My Hand and Seal at Fort-George in New-York This Sixth Day of November ... in the Year of Our Lord 1734* (New York: Printed by William Bradford, 1734).

[New York] Court for Trial of Impeachment, *Proceedings of the Court for the Trial of Impeachments. The People of the State of New York, by the Assembly thereof, against William Sulzer as Governor. Held at the Capital in the City of Albany, New York, September 18, 1913, to October 17, 1913* (Albany: J.B. Lyon Company, Printers, 1913).

[New York] Legislature, Senate, Standing Committee on Judiciary, *New York's Impeachment Law and the Trial of Governor Sulzer: A Case for Reform. Prepared by the Staff of the New York State Senate Judiciary Committee* (Albany: The Committee [on the Judiciary], 1986).

[New York] *The Trial of the Hon. John C. Mather, One of the Canal Commissioners of the State of New York, in the Court for the Trial of Impeachments, Held at the Capitol in the City of Albany, Commencing Wednesday, July 27th, 1853 ... Richard Sutton, Short Hand Writer to the Court of Impeachments* (Albany: H. H. Van Dyck, Printer—Atlas Steam Press, 1853).

[New York] State Supreme Court, Appellate Division, *The Investigation of the Magistrates Courts in the First Judicial Department and the Magistrates Thereof, and of Attorneys-at-Law Practicing in Said Courts: Final Report of Samuel Seabury, Referee* (New York: The City Club of New York, 1932).

[North Carolina] Legislature, *Articles Against William W. Holden*, Document No. 18, 1870–1871 Session (Raleigh: James H. Moore, State Printer, 1871).

[Ohio], *Record of the Proceedings of the High Court of Impeachment on the Trial of William Irvin: Consisting of the Senate of the State of Ohio* (Chillicothe: Printed by Thomas G. Bradford & Co., Printers for the State, 1806).

[Pennsylvania]. *The Trial of Alexander Addison, esq.: President of the Courts of Common Pleas, in the Circuit consisting of the Counties of Westmoreland, Fayette, Washington and Allegheny: On an Impeachment, by the House of Representatives, before the Senate of the Commonwealth of Pennsylvania ... Taken in Short Hand by Thomas Lloyd* (Lancaster: Printed by George Helmbold, Junior, for Lloyd and Helmbold, 1803).

[Texas] *Record of Proceedings of the High Court of Impeachment on the Trial of Hon. James E. Ferguson, Governor, Before the Senate of the State of Texas, Pursuant to the State Constitution and Rules Provided by the Senate during the Second and Third Called Sessions of the 35th Legislature. Convened in the City of Austin, August 1, 1917, and Adjourned Without Day, September 29, 1917. Published by Authority of the Legislature, T.H. Yarbrough, Journal Clerk, Senate* (Austin: A.O. Baldwin & Sons, State Printers, 1917).

[Virginia] *Debates and Other Proceedings of the Convention of Virginia, Convened at Richmond, on Monday the Second of June, 1788, for the Purpose of Deliberating on the Constitution Recommended by the Grand Federal Convention. to Which Is Prefixed the Federal Constitution. Taken in Short Hand, by David Robertson of Petersburg*, 3 vols. (Petersburg: Printed by Hunter and Prentis, 1788–1789).

[Wisconsin] State Senate, *Trial of Impeachment of Levi Hubbell, Judge of the Second Judicial Circuit, by the Senate of the State of Wisconsin, June 1853. Reported by T. C. Leland* (Madison: B. Brown, 1853).

[Wisconsin] State Senate, *Trial of Impeachment of Levi Hubbell, Judge of the Second Judicial Circuit, by the Senate of the State of Wisconsin, June 1853. Reported by T. C. Leland* (Madison, WI: B. Brown, 1853).

## Manuscript Collections

Henry S. Johnston Collection, Special Collections and University Archives, Edmon Low Library, Oklahoma State University, Stillwater, Oklahoma.

James Buchanan Papers, Historical Society of Pennsylvania, Philadelphia [Papers regarding the impeachment of Judge James Hawkins Peck].

Letters to and from Senator Burton K. Wheeler, American Civil Liberties Papers, Princeton University, Princeton, New Jersey.

Matthew J. Connelly Official File, Harry S. Truman Library, Independence, Missouri.

Official records of the Impeachment of George W. English, File 69B-A1 in Records of Impeachment Proceedings, 1st–90th Congress (1789–1968), General Records of the United States House of Representatives, 1789–1988, RG 233, National Archives, Washington, D.C.

Official Records of the Impeachment of Judge James H. Peck, File 21B-B1, in Records of Impeachment Proceedings, 1st–90th Congresses (1789–1968), General Records of the U.S. House of Representatives, 1789–1968, RG 233, National Archives, Washington, D.C.

State Governors' Incoming Correspondence, 1857–1888, Series 577, Florida Department of State, Division of Library & Information Services, Bureau of Archives & RecordsManagement, Tallahassee, Florida.

Warren Hastings Papers (minutes and related papers related to his impeachment in Parliament in 1787), Add[itional] MSS 17061–62, 16261–67, Add[itional] MSS 17066–082, 24222–268, British Library (London).

William Dudley Foulke Papers, Library of Congress, Washington, D.C.

William Wirt Papers, Maryland Historical Society, Baltimore, Maryland [Papers regarding the impeachment of Judge James Hawkins Peck].

Zachariah Chandler Papers, Library of Congress, Washington, D.C.

## Oral Histories

Abe Fortas Oral History Interview, 14 August 1969, Lyndon Baines Johnson Library, Austin, Texas.

Charles S. Murphy Oral History Interview, 25 July 1969, Harry S. Truman Presidential Library, Independence, Missouri.

Matthew J. Connelly Oral History Interview, 28 November 1967, Courtesy Harry S. Truman Library, Independence, Missouri.

"Memoirs of Thomas Woodnut Miller, a Public Spirited Citizen of Delaware and Nevada. An Oral History Conducted by Mary Ellen Glass" (University of Nevada at Reno Oral History Program, 1966).

Wilbur D. Mills Oral History Interview I, 2 November 1971, Lyndon Baines Johnson Library, Austin, Texas.

## Court Cases

*Addonizio v. United States*, 405 U.S. 936 (1972)

*Austin v. Michigan Chamber of Commerce*, 494 U.S. 652 (1990)

*Barry v. United States*, 865 F.2d 1317 (D.C. Cir. 1989)

*Barry v. United States ex rel. Cunningham*, 297 U.S. 597 (1929)

*Buckley v. Valeo*, 424 U.S. 1 (1976)

*Burton v. United States*, 196 U.S. 283 (1905)

*Burton v. United States*, 202 U.S. 344 (1906)

*Claiborne v. United States*, 727 F.2d 842 (1984)

*Claiborne v. United States*, 465 U.S. 1305 (1984)

*Colorado Republican Federal Campaign Committee v. Federal Election Commission*, 116 S. Ct. 2309 (1996)

*Federal Election Commission v. Massachusetts Citizens for Life, Inc.*, 479 U.S. 238 (1986)

*Federal Election Commission v. National Conservative Political Action Committee*, 470 U.S. 480 (1985)

*Federal Election Commission v. National Right to Work Committee*, 459 U.S. 197 (1982)

*Finn v. Schiller*, 72 F.3d 1182 (4th Cir. 1996)

*Flanagan v. United States*, 465 U.S. 259 (1984)

*Florida Right to Life, Inc. v. Lamar*, (11th Cir. 2001)

*Hastings v. United States*, 802 F. Supp. 490 (D.D.C. 1992)

*Helstoski v. United States*, 442 U.S. 477 (1979)

*Hubbard v. United States*, 514 U.S. 695, 115 S. Ct. 1754 (1995)

*In re Grand Jury Investigation [Bert Lance]*, 610 F.2d 202 (5th Cir. 1980)

*In re Grand Jury Investigation Into Possible Violations of Title 18*, 587 F.2d 589 (3d Cir. 1978)

*In re Sealed Case*, 267 U.S. Appeals Court D.C. 178 (1988)

*In re Secretary of Labor Raymond J. Donovan*, 838 F.2d 476, 1986 U.S. App. LEXIS 29829 (D.C. Cir. Special Division, 1986)

*In the Matter of the Search of: Rayburn House Office Bldg. Room Number 2113*, Case No. 06-231-M-01 (30 May 2006).

*Jurney v. MacCracken*, 294 U.S. 125 (1935)

*Kilbourn v. Thompson*, 103 U.S. 168 (1881)

*McCormick v. United States*, 500 U.S. 257 (1991)

*McGrain v. Daugherty*, 273 U.S. 135 (1927)

*Morrison v. Olson*, 487 U.S. 654 (1988)

*Newberry v. United States*, 256 U.S. 232 (1921)

*Nixon v. Shrink Missouri PAC*, 528 U.S. 528 U.S. 377 (2000)

*Nixon v. United States*, 506 U.S. 224 (1993)

*Pan American Petroleum & Transport Co. v. United States*, 273 U.S. 456 (1927)

*Pendergast v. United States*, 317 U.S. 412 (1943)

*Powell v. McCormack*, 395 U.S. 486 (1969)

*Tenney v. Brandhove*, 341 U.S. 367 (1951)

*United States v. National Treasury Employees Union*, 513 U.S. 454, 115 S. Ct. 1103 (1995)

*United States v. Addonizio*, 442 U.S. 178 (1979).

*United States v. Bramblett*, 348 U.S. 503 (1955)

*United States v. Brewster*, 408 U.S. 501 (1972)

*United States v. Eilberg*, 465 F. Supp. 1080 (E.D. Pa. 1979)

*United States v. Eilberg*, 507 F. Supp. 267 (E.D. Pa. 1980)

*United States v. Eilberg*, 536 F. Supp. 514 (E.D. Pa. 1982)

*United States v. Eisenberg*, 711 F.2d 959 (11th Cir. 1983)

*United States v. Gillock*, 445 U.S. 360 (1980)

*United States v. Helstoski*, 442 U.S. 477 (1979)

*United States v. Jefferson*, Criminal indictment 1:07CR209 (E. D. Va. 2007).

*United States v. Johnson*, 383 U.S. 169 (1966)

*United States v. Mandel*, 591 F.2d 1347, *vacated*, 602 F.2d 653 (4th Cir. 1979) (en banc), *second rehearing denied*, 609 F.2d 1076 (4th Cir. 1979), *cert. denied*, 445 U.S. 961 (1980)

*United States v. Nixon*, 418 U.S. 683 (1974)

*United States v. Oakar*, (No. 96–3084A), U.S. Court of Appeals for the DC Circuit, 1997

*United States v. Rostenkowski*, 59 F.3d 1291 (D.C. Cir. 1995)

*United States v. Shirey*, 359 U.S. 255 (1959)

*United States v. Worrall*, 2 U.S. (2 Dall.) 384 (1798)

*Vermont Right to Life Committee v. Sorrell*, (No. 98–9325), 19 F.2d 204 (1998)

# INDEX

Rep. James Brooks, 47–49
*Buckley v. Valeo* (1976), 49
Attorney Joseph H. Choate, 71
Mayor Thomas Coman, 92–93
Gov. Thomas E. Dewey, 129–130
Rep. Francis S. Edwards, 146–147
Rep. Robert Garcia, 185
Mayor William J. Gaynor, 187–189
Rep. William A. Gilbert, 190–191
Mayor A. Oakey Hall, 201–202
Comptroller Alan G. Hevesi, 214–215
Mayor John T. Hoffman, 218–220
Rep. Thomas Downey, 225
Impeachment proceedings in, 240
Gov. William Sulzer, 240–241, 416–419
William Travers Jerome, 259–260
Rep. Caleb Lyon, 287
Judge Martin T. Manton, 291–292
Rep. Orsamus B. Matteson, 294–295
Rep. Adam C. Powell, Jr., 356–359
Rep. Frederick W. Richmond, 369
Deputy Assistant Secretary of Defense Robert Tripp, 376–377
Rep. John G. Schumaker, 389
Samuel Seabury, 390–391
Political boss Timothy Sullivan, 414–416
Swartwout-Hoyt Scandal, 419–420
Tammany Hall, 427–429
"Boss" Richard Croker, 71–72, 111–113, 428
Mayor William Tweed, 71, 118, 201–202, 218–220, 350, 427, 448–451
Mayor Jimmy Walker, 390–391, 469–470
Rep. William F. Willett, Jr., 489–490
Mayor Fernando Wood, 427
John Peter Zenger, 499–500
New York City, 138–139, 143, 182, 242, 248, 287, 291, 356, 369, 372
corrupt mayors of, 10, 92–93, 201–202, 352
corruption fighters in, 71–73, 188, 390–391
Committee of Thirty, 72
Mazet Committee, 112
Tweed Ring, 201, 218–219, 448–452
Mayor Hoffman, 218–220
Lexow Committee, 259–260
Committee of Seventy, 260
Queens Borough president, 352
Mayor Walker, 390, 469–471
*See also* Tammany Hall
New York Collector's Office, 419–420
*New York Times*, 9, 24, 32, 92, 112, 136, 146, 174, 202, 210, 227, 388, 292, 451, 453, 476, 491
*New York Weekly Journal*, 499
*Newberry v. United States*, **321–322**
Newberry, Truman, 158, 321–322
Ney, Robert William, 3, 5, **322–323**
Nez Perce Indians, 74, 287
Niblack, William E., 110
Nicaragua. *See* Iran-Contra Affair
Nicholson, Joseph Hopper, 348
*Nixon v. Shrink Missouri PAC*, 50, 168, **327–328**
*Nixon v. United States*, 207, **328–330**
Nixon, Jeremiah, 328
Nixon, Richard Milhaus, **323–327**
and Vicuna Coat scandal, 9
and Spiro Agnew, 13
and use of Executive Privilege, 155–156

and John N. Mitchell, 310–313
and Watergate, 476–481
Nixon, Walter L., Jr., 239–240
Nixon, Walter, 329
*Nixon*, 352
Noe, James Albert, 281
Norris, George W., 38
North Carolina
Rep. John T. Deweese, 128–129
Gov. William W. Holden, 220–223
North Dakota
Gov. William Langer, 279–280
Senator William N. Roach, 370–372
North, Oliver, 250
NTEU. *See* National Treasury Employees Union
Nunan, Josef, 242
Nussbaum, Bernard, 174, 486
Nussle, James, 226
Nye, Gerald, 280, 434

O'Brien, Larry, 478
O'Connor, Edwin G., 117, 354
O'Connor, Sandra Day, 23, 91, 224, 300, 410
O'Hare, Michael, 133
O'Rourke, Joanna G., 227
Oakar, Mary Rose, 225–226
Obama, Barack Hussein, 39–40
Oberholtzer, Madge, 254
Obstruction of Justice, **331**
Office of Alien Property Custodian, 306
Office of Management and Budget, 277–278
Office of the Pardon Attorney, 337
Ohio
Rep. Bob Ney, 3–4, 322–323
Rep. Walter E. Brehm, 46
Attorney General Harry M. Daugherty, 121–123, 302
Rep. James A. Traficant, Jr., 158–159, 443–444
Rep. James A. Garfield, 186–187
Rep. Wayne L. Hays, 208–210
Rep. Mary Rose Oakar, 225
Rep. George H. Pendleton, 342–345
Rep. Robert C. Schenck, 385–386
Senator John Smith, 407–408
Judge George Turner, 446–448
Oil reserves. *See* Teapot Dome Scandal
Oklahoma
Gov. John C. Walton, 472
Older, Fremont, 387–388
Olin, Abram B., 101
Oliphant, Charles, 242, 274
Olivany, George W., 428
Olson, Theodore, 316–318
*On the Waterfront*, 351
Operation Board Games, 40
Operation Gemstone, 311–313, 476
Operation Greylord, **332**
Operation Plunder Dome, 73
Opper, Frederick, 350
Ordway, Nehemiah George, **332–334**
Oregon
Gov. La Fayette Grover, 196–197
Impeachment proceedings in, 240
Senator John H. Mitchell, 308–310
Use of Recall, 363

# Business Information • Ratings Guides • General Reference • Education • Statistics • Demographics • Health Information • Canadian Information

## The Directory of Business Information Resources, 2008

With 100% verification, over 1,000 new listings and more than 12,000 updates, *The Directory of Business Information Resources* is the most up-to-date source for contacts in over 98 business areas – from advertising and agriculture to utilities and wholesalers. This carefully researched volume details: the Associations representing each industry; the Newsletters that keep members current; the Magazines and Journals - with their "Special Issues" - that are important to the trade, the Conventions that are "must attends," Databases, Directories and Industry Web Sites that provide access to must-have marketing resources. Includes contact names, phone & fax numbers, web sites and e-mail addresses. This one-volume resource is a gold mine of information and would be a welcome addition to any reference collection.

*"This is a most useful and easy-to-use addition to any researcher's library." –The Information Professionals Institute*

Softcover ISBN 978-1-59237-193-8, 2,500 pages, $195.00 | Online Database $495.00

## Hudson's Washington News Media Contacts Directory, 2008

With 100% verification of data, Hudson's Washington News Media Contacts Directory is the most accurate, most up-to-date source for media contacts in our nation's capital. With the largest concentration of news media in the world, having access to Washington's news media will get your message heard by these key media outlets. Published for over 40 years, Hudson's Washington News Media Contacts Directory brings you immediate access to: News Services & Newspapers, News Service Syndicates, DC Newspapers, Foreign Newspapers, Radio & TV, Magazines & Newsletters, and Freelance Writers & Photographers. The easy-to-read entries include contact names, phone & fax numbers, web sites and e-mail and more. For easy navigation, Hudson's Washington News Media Contacts Directory contains two indexes: Entry Index and Executive Index. This kind of comprehensive and up-to-date information would cost thousands of dollars to replicate or countless hours of searching to find. Don't miss this opportunity to have this important resource in your collection, and start saving time and money today. Hudson's Washington News Media Contacts Directory is the perfect research tool for Public Relations, Marketing, Networking and so much more. This resource is a gold mine of information and would be a welcome addition to any reference collection.

Softcover ISBN 978-1-59237-393-2, 800 pages, $289.00

## Nations of the World, 2007/08  A Political, Economic and Business Handbook

This completely revised edition covers all the nations of the world in an easy-to-use, single volume. Each nation is profiled in a single chapter that includes Key Facts, Political & Economic Issues, a Country Profile and Business Information. In this fast-changing world, it is extremely important to make sure that the most up-to-date information is included in your reference collection. This edition is just the answer. Each of the 200+ country chapters have been carefully reviewed by a political expert to make sure that the text reflects the most current information on Politics, Travel Advisories, Economics and more. You'll find such vital information as a Country Map, Population Characteristics, Inflation, Agricultural Production, Foreign Debt, Political History, Foreign Policy, Regional Insecurity, Economics, Trade & Tourism, Historical Profile, Political Systems, Ethnicity, Languages, Media, Climate, Hotels, Chambers of Commerce, Banking, Travel Information and more. Five Regional Chapters follow the main text and include a Regional Map, an Introductory Article, Key Indicators and Currencies for the Region. As an added bonus, an all-inclusive CD-ROM is available as a companion to the printed text. Noted for its sophisticated, up-to-date and reliable compilation of political, economic and business information, this brand new edition will be an important acquisition to any public, academic or special library reference collection.

*"A useful addition to both general reference collections and business collections." –RUSQ*

Softcover ISBN 978-1-59237-177-8, 1,700 pages, $155.00

## The Directory of Venture Capital & Private Equity Firms, 2008

This edition has been extensively updated and broadly expanded to offer direct access to over 2,800 Domestic and International Venture Capital Firms, including address, phone & fax numbers, e-mail addresses and web sites for both primary and branch locations. Entries include details on the firm's Mission Statement, Industry Group Preferences, Geographic Preferences, Average and Minimum Investments and Investment Criteria. You'll also find details that are available nowhere else, including the Firm's Portfolio Companies and extensive information on each of the firm's Managing Partners, such as Education, Professional Background and Directorships held, along with the Partner's E-mail Address. *The Directory of Venture Capital & Private Equity Firms* offers five important indexes: Geographic Index, Executive Name Index, Portfolio Company Index, Industry Preference Index and College & University Index. With its comprehensive coverage and detailed, extensive information on each company, The Directory of Venture Capital & Private Equity Firms is an important addition to any finance collection.

*"The sheer number of listings, the descriptive information and the outstanding indexing make this directory a better value than ...Pratt's Guide to Venture Capital Sources. Recommended for business collections in large public, academic and business libraries." –Choice*

Softcover ISBN 978-1-59237-272-0, 1,300 pages, $565/$450 Library | Online Database $889.00

## The Encyclopedia of Emerging Industries

*Published under an exclusive license from the Gale Group, Inc.

The fifth edition of the *Encyclopedia of Emerging Industries* details the inception, emergence, and current status of nearly 120 flourishing U.S. industries and industry segments. These focused essays unearth for users a wealth of relevant, current, factual data previously accessible only through a diverse variety of sources. This volume provides broad-based, highly-readable, industry information under such headings as Industry Snapshot, Organization & Structure, Background & Development, Industry Leaders, Current Conditions, America and the World, Pioneers, and Research & Technology. Essays in this new edition, arranged alphabetically for easy use, have been completely revised, with updated statistics and the most current information on industry trends and developments. In addition, there are new essays on some of the most interesting and influential new business fields, including Application Service Providers, Concierge Services, Entrepreneurial Training, Fuel Cells, Logistics Outsourcing Services, Pharmacogenomics, and Tissue Engineering. Two indexes, General and Industry, provide immediate access to this wealth of information. Plus, two conversion tables for SIC and NAICS codes, along with Suggested Further Readings, are provided to aid the user. *The Encyclopedia of Emerging Industries* pinpoints emerging industries while they are still in the spotlight. This important resource will be an important acquisition to any business reference collection.

*"This well-designed source...should become another standard business source, nicely complementing Standard & Poor's Industry Surveys. It contains more information on each industry than Hoover's Handbook of Emerging Companies, is broader in scope than The Almanac of American Employers 1998-1999, but is less expansive than the Encyclopedia of Careers & Vocational Guidance. Highly recommended for all academic libraries and specialized business collections."* –Library Journal

Hardcover ISBN 978-1-59237-242-3, 1,400 pages, $325.00

## Encyclopedia of American Industries

*Published under an exclusive license from the Gale Group, Inc.

*The Encyclopedia of American Industries* is a major business reference tool that provides detailed, comprehensive information on a wide range of industries in every realm of American business. A two volume set, Volume I provides separate coverage of nearly 500 manufacturing industries, while Volume II presents nearly 600 essays covering the vast array of services and other non-manufacturing industries in the United States. Combined, these two volumes provide individual essays on every industry recognized by the U.S. Standard Industrial Classification (SIC) system. Both volumes are arranged numerically by SIC code, for easy use. Additionally, each entry includes the corresponding NAICS code(s). The *Encyclopedia's* business coverage includes information on historical events of consequence, as well as current trends and statistics. Essays include an Industry Snapshot, Organization & Structure, Background & Development, Current Conditions, Industry Leaders, Workforce, America and the World, Research & Technology along with Suggested Further Readings. Both SIC and NAICS code conversion tables and an all-encompassing Subject Index, with cross-references, complete the text. With its detailed, comprehensive information on a wide range of industries, this resource will be an important tool for both the industry newcomer and the seasoned professional.

*"Encyclopedia of American Industries contains detailed, signed essays on virtually every industry in contemporary society. ... Highly recommended for all but the smallest libraries."* -American Reference Books Annual

Two Volumes, Hardcover ISBN 978-1-59237-244-7, 3,000 pages, $650.00

## Encyclopedia of Global Industries

*Published under an exclusive license from the Gale Group, Inc.

This fourth edition of the acclaimed *Encyclopedia of Global Industries* presents a thoroughly revised and expanded look at more than 125 business sectors of global significance. Detailed, insightful articles discuss the origins, development, trends, key statistics and current international character of the world's most lucrative, dynamic and widely researched industries – including hundreds of profiles of leading international corporations. Beginning researchers will gain from this book a solid understanding of how each industry operates and which countries and companies are significant participants, while experienced researchers will glean current and historical figures for comparison and analysis. The industries profiled in previous editions have been updated, and in some cases, expanded to reflect recent industry trends. Additionally, this edition provides both SIC and NAICS codes for all industries profiled. As in the original volumes, *The Encyclopedia of Global Industries* offers thorough studies of some of the biggest and most frequently researched industry sectors, including Aircraft, Biotechnology, Computers, Internet Services, Motor Vehicles, Pharmaceuticals, Semiconductors, Software and Telecommunications. An SIC and NAICS conversion table and an all-encompassing Subject Index, with cross-references, are provided to ensure easy access to this wealth of information. These and many others make the *Encyclopedia of Global Industries* the authoritative reference for studies of international industries.

*"Provides detailed coverage of the history, development, and current status of 115 of "the world's most lucrative and high-profile industries." It far surpasses the Department of Commerce's U.S. Global Trade Outlook 1995-2000 (GPO, 1995) in scope and coverage. Recommended for comprehensive public and academic library business collections."* -Booklist

Hardcover ISBN 978-1-59237-243-0, 1,400 pages, $495.00

# Business Information ◆ Ratings Guides ◆ General Reference ◆ Education ◆
## Statistics ◆ Demographics ◆ Health Information ◆ Canadian Information

## The Directory of Mail Order Catalogs, 2008

Published since 1981, *The Directory of Mail Order Catalogs* is the premier source of information on the mail order catalog industry. It is the source that business professionals and librarians have come to rely on for the thousands of catalog companies in the US. Since the 2007 edition, *The Directory of Mail Order Catalogs* has been combined with its companion volume, *The Directory of Business to Business Catalogs*, to offer all 13,000 catalog companies in one easy-to-use volume. Section I: Consumer Catalogs, covers over 9,000 consumer catalog companies in 44 different product chapters from Animals to Toys & Games. Section II: Business to Business Catalogs, details 5,000 business catalogs, everything from computers to laboratory supplies, building construction and much more. Listings contain detailed contact information including mailing address, phone & fax numbers, web sites, e-mail addresses and key contacts along with important business details such as product descriptions, employee size, years in business, sales volume, catalog size, number of catalogs mailed and more. Three indexes are included for easy access to information: Catalog & Company Name Index, Geographic Index and Product Index. *The Directory of Mail Order Catalogs*, now with its expanded business to business catalogs, is the largest and most comprehensive resource covering this billion-dollar industry. It is the standard in its field. This important resource is a useful tool for entrepreneurs searching for catalogs to pick up their product, vendors looking to expand their customer base in the catalog industry, market researchers, small businesses investigating new supply vendors, along with the library patron who is exploring the available catalogs in their areas of interest.

*"This is a godsend for those looking for information."* –Reference Book Review

**Softcover ISBN 978-1-59237-202-7, 1,700 pages, $350/$250 Library | Online Database $495.00**

## Sports Market Place Directory, 2008

For over 20 years, this comprehensive, up-to-date directory has offered direct access to the Who, What, When & Where of the Sports Industry. With over 20,000 updates and enhancements, the *Sports Market Place Directory* is the most detailed, comprehensive and current sports business reference source available. In 1,800 information-packed pages, *Sports Market Place Directory* profiles contact information and key executives for: Single Sport Organizations, Professional Leagues, Multi-Sport Organizations, Disabled Sports, High School & Youth Sports, Military Sports, Olympic Organizations, Media, Sponsors, Sponsorship & Marketing Event Agencies, Event & Meeting Calendars, Professional Services, College Sports, Manufacturers & Retailers, Facilities and much more. The Sports Market Place Directory provides organization's contact information with detailed descriptions including: Key Contacts, physical, mailing, email and web addresses plus phone and fax numbers. *Sports Market Place Directory* provides a one-stop resources for this billion-dollar industry. This will be an important resource for large public libraries, university libraries, university athletic programs, career services or job placement organizations, and is a must for anyone doing research on or marketing to the US and Canadian sports industry.

*"Grey House is the new publisher and has produced an excellent edition...highly recommended for public libraries and academic libraries with sports management programs or strong interest in athletics."* -Booklist

Softcover ISBN 978-1-59237-348-2, 1,800 pages, $225.00 | Online Database $479.00

## Food and Beverage Market Place, 2008

*Food and Beverage Market Place* is bigger and better than ever with thousands of new companies, thousands of updates to existing companies and two revised and enhanced product category indexes. This comprehensive directory profiles over 18,000 Food & Beverage Manufacturers, 12,000 Equipment & Supply Companies, 2,200 Transportation & Warehouse Companies, 2,000 Brokers & Wholesalers, 8,000 Importers & Exporters, 900 Industry Resources and hundreds of Mail Order Catalogs. Listings include detailed Contact Information, Sales Volumes, Key Contacts, Brand & Product Information, Packaging Details and much more. *Food and Beverage Market Place* is available as a three-volume printed set, a subscription-based Online Database via the Internet, on CD-ROM, as well as mailing lists and a licensable database.

*"An essential purchase for those in the food industry but will also be useful in public libraries where needed. Much of the information will be difficult and time consuming to locate without this handy three-volume ready-reference source."* –ARBA

3 Vol Set, Softcover ISBN 978-1-59237-198-3, 8,500 pages, $595 | Online Database $795 | Online Database & 3 Vol Set Combo, $995

## The Grey House Performing Arts Directory, 2007

*The Grey House Performing Arts Directory* is the most comprehensive resource covering the Performing Arts. This important directory provides current information on over 8,500 Dance Companies, Instrumental Music Programs, Opera Companies, Choral Groups, Theater Companies, Performing Arts Series and Performing Arts Facilities. Plus, this edition now contains a brand new section on Artist Management Groups. In addition to mailing address, phone & fax numbers, e-mail addresses and web sites, dozens of other fields of available information include mission statement, key contacts, facilities, seating capacity, season, attendance and more. This directory also provides an important Information Resources section that covers hundreds of Performing Arts Associations, Magazines, Newsletters, Trade Shows, Directories, Databases and Industry Web Sites. Five indexes provide immediate access to this wealth of information: Entry Name, Executive Name, Performance Facilities, Geographic and Information Resources. *The Grey House Performing Arts Directory* pulls together thousands of Performing Arts Organizations, Facilities and Information Resources into an easy-to-use source – this kind of comprehensiveness and extensive detail is not available in any resource on the market place today.

*"Immensely useful and user-friendly ... recommended for public, academic and certain special library reference collections."* –Booklist

## To preview any of our Directories Risk-Free for 30 days, call (800) 562-2139 or fax (518) 789-0556
## www.greyhouse.com   books@greyhouse.com

Softcover ISBN 978-1-59237-138-9, 1,500 pages, $185.00 | Online Database $335.00

## New York State Directory, 2007/08

*The New York State Directory*, published annually since 1983, is a comprehensive and easy-to-use guide to accessing public officials and private sector organizations and individuals who influence public policy in the state of New York. *The New York State Directory* includes important information on all New York state legislators and congressional representatives, including biographies and key committee assignments. It also includes staff rosters for all branches of New York state government and for federal agencies and departments that impact the state policy process. Following the state government section are 25 chapters covering policy areas from agriculture through veterans' affairs. Each chapter identifies the state, local and federal agencies and officials that formulate or implement policy. In addition, each chapter contains a roster of private sector experts and advocates who influence the policy process. The directory also offers appendices that include statewide party officials; chambers of commerce; lobbying organizations; public and private universities and colleges; television, radio and print media; and local government agencies and officials.

*"This comprehensive directory covers not only New York State government offices and key personnel but pertinent U.S. government agencies and non-governmental entities. This directory is all encompassing... recommended." -Choice*

*New York State Directory* - Softcover ISBN 978-1-59237-190-7, 800 pages, $145.00
*New York State Directory* with *Profiles of New York* – 2 Volumes, Softcover ISBN 978-1-59237-191-4, 1,600 pages, $225.00

## The Grey House Homeland Security Directory, 2008

This updated edition features the latest contact information for government and private organizations involved with Homeland Security along with the latest product information and provides detailed profiles of nearly 1,000 Federal & State Organizations & Agencies and over 3,000 Officials and Key Executives involved with Homeland Security. These listings are incredibly detailed and include Mailing Address, Phone & Fax Numbers, Email Addresses & Web Sites, a complete Description of the Agency and a complete list of the Officials and Key Executives associated with the Agency. Next, *The Grey House Homeland Security Directory* provides the go-to source for Homeland Security Products & Services. This section features over 2,000 Companies that provide Consulting, Products or Services. With this Buyer's Guide at their fingertips, users can locate suppliers of everything from Training Materials to Access Controls, from Perimeter Security to BioTerrorism Countermeasures and everything in between – complete with contact information and product descriptions. A handy Product Locator Index is provided to quickly and easily locate suppliers of a particular product. This comprehensive, information-packed resource will be a welcome tool for any company or agency that is in need of Homeland Security information and will be a necessary acquisition for the reference collection of all public libraries and large school districts.

*"Compiles this information in one place and is discerning in content. A useful purchase for public and academic libraries." –Booklist*

Softcover ISBN 978-1-59237-196-6, 800 pages, $195.00 | Online Database $385.00

## The Grey House Safety & Security Directory, 2008

*The Grey House Safety & Security Directory* is the most comprehensive reference tool and buyer's guide for the safety and security industry. Arranged by safety topic, each chapter begins with OSHA regulations for the topic, followed by Training Articles written by top professionals in the field and Self-Inspection Checklists. Next, each topic contains Buyer's Guide sections that feature related products and services. Topics include Administration, Insurance, Loss Control & Consulting, Protective Equipment & Apparel, Noise & Vibration, Facilities Monitoring & Maintenance, Employee Health Maintenance & Ergonomics, Retail Food Services, Machine Guards, Process Guidelines & Tool Handling, Ordinary Materials Handling, Hazardous Materials Handling, Workplace Preparation & Maintenance, Electrical Lighting & Safety, Fire & Rescue and Security. Six important indexes make finding information and product manufacturers quick and easy: Geographical Index of Manufacturers and Distributors, Company Profile Index, Brand Name Index, Product Index, Index of Web Sites and Index of Advertisers. This comprehensive, up-to-date reference will provide every tool necessary to make sure a business is in compliance with OSHA regulations and locate the products and services needed to meet those regulations.

*"Presents industrial safety information for engineers, plant managers, risk managers, and construction site supervisors..." –Choice*

Softcover ISBN 978-1-59237-205-8, 1,500 pages, $165.00

## Business Information ◆ Ratings Guides ◆ General Reference ◆ Education ◆ Statistics ◆ Demographics ◆ Health Information ◆ Canadian Information

### The Grey House Transportation Security Directory & Handbook

This is the only reference of its kind that brings together current data on Transportation Security. With information on everything from Regulatory Authorities to Security Equipment, this top-flight database brings together the relevant information necessary for creating and maintaining a security plan for a wide range of transportation facilities. With this current, comprehensive directory at the ready you'll have immediate access to: Regulatory Authorities & Legislation; Information Resources; Sample Security Plans & Checklists; Contact Data for Major Airports, Seaports, Railroads, Trucking Companies and Oil Pipelines; Security Service Providers; Recommended Equipment & Product Information and more. Using the *Grey House Transportation Security Directory & Handbook*, managers will be able to quickly and easily assess their current security plans; develop contacts to create and maintain new security procedures; and source the products and services necessary to adequately maintain a secure environment. This valuable resource is a must for all Security Managers at Airports, Seaports, Railroads, Trucking Companies and Oil Pipelines.

*"Highly recommended. Library collections that support all levels of readers, including professionals/practitioners; and schools/organizations offering education and training in transportation security." -Choice*

Softcover ISBN 978-1-59237-075-7, 800 pages, $195.00

### The Grey House Biometric Information Directory

This edition offers a complete, current overview of biometric companies and products – one of the fastest growing industries in today's economy. Detailed profiles of manufacturers of the latest biometric technology, including Finger, Voice, Face, Hand, Signature, Iris, Vein and Palm Identification systems. Data on the companies include key executives, company size and a detailed, indexed description of their product line. Information in the directory includes: Editorial on Advancements in Biometrics; Profiles of 700+ companies listed with contact information; Organizations, Trade & Educational Associations, Publications, Conferences, Trade Shows and Expositions Worldwide; Web Site Index; Biometric & Vendors Services Index by Types of Biometrics; and a Glossary of Biometric Terms. This resource will be an important source for anyone who is considering the use of a biometric product, investing in the development of biometric technology, support existing marketing and sales efforts and will be an important acquisition for the business reference collection for large public and business libraries.

*"This book should prove useful to agencies or businesses seeking companies that deal with biometric technology. Summing Up: Recommended. Specialized collections serving researchers/faculty and professionals/practitioners." -Choice*

Softcover ISBN 978-1-59237-121-1, 800 pages, $225.00

### The Environmental Resource Handbook, 2007/08

*The Environmental Resource Handbook* is the most up-to-date and comprehensive source for Environmental Resources and Statistics. Section I: Resources provides detailed contact information for thousands of information sources, including Associations & Organizations, Awards & Honors, Conferences, Foundations & Grants, Environmental Health, Government Agencies, National Parks & Wildlife Refuges, Publications, Research Centers, Educational Programs, Green Product Catalogs, Consultants and much more. Section II: Statistics, provides statistics and rankings on hundreds of important topics, including Children's Environmental Index, Municipal Finances, Toxic Chemicals, Recycling, Climate, Air & Water Quality and more. This kind of up-to-date environmental data, all in one place, is not available anywhere else on the market place today. This vast compilation of resources and statistics is a must-have for all public and academic libraries as well as any organization with a primary focus on the environment.

*"...the intrinsic value of the information make it worth consideration by libraries with environmental collections and environmentally concerned users." –Booklist*

Softcover ISBN 978-1-59237-195-2, 1,000 pages, $155.00 | Online Database $300.00

**To preview any of our Directories Risk-Free for 30 days, call (800) 562-2139 or fax (518) 789-0556**
**www.greyhouse.com  books@greyhouse.com**

## The Rauch Guide to the US Adhesives & Sealants, Cosmetics & Toiletries, Ink, Paint, Plastics, Pulp & Paper and Rubber Industries

*The Rauch Guides* save time and money by organizing widely scattered information and providing estimates for important business decisions, some of which are available nowhere else. Within each Guide, after a brief introduction, the ECONOMICS section provides data on industry shipments; long-term growth and forecasts; prices; company performance; employment, expenditures, and productivity; transportation and geographical patterns; packaging; foreign trade; and government regulations. Next, TECHNOLOGY & RAW MATERIALS provide market, technical, and raw material information for chemicals, equipment and related materials, including market size and leading suppliers, prices, end uses, and trends. PRODUCTS & MARKETS provide information for each major industry product, including market size and historical trends, leading suppliers, five-year forecasts, industry structure, and major end uses. Next, the COMPANY DIRECTORY profiles major industry companies, both public and private. Information includes complete contact information, web address, estimated total and domestic sales, product description, and recent mergers and acquisitions. *The Rauch Guides* will prove to be an invaluable source of market information, company data, trends and forecasts that anyone in these fast-paced industries.

*"An invaluable and affordable publication. The comprehensive nature of the data and text offers considerable insights into the industry, market sizes, company activities, and applications of the products of the industry. The additions that have been made have certainly enhanced the value of the Guide." –Adhesives & Sealants Newsletter of the Rauch Guide to the US Adhesives & Sealants Industry*

Paint Industry: Softcover ISBN 978-1-59237-127-3 $595 | Plastics Industry: Softcover ISBN 978-1-59237-128-0 $595 | Adhesives and Sealants Industry: Softcover ISBN 978-1-59237-129-7 $595 | Ink Industry: Softcover ISBN 978-1-59237-126-6 $595 | Rubber Industry: Softcover ISBN 978-1-59237-130-3 $595 | Pulp and Paper Industry: Softcover ISBN 978-1-59237-131-0 $595 | Cosmetic & Toiletries Industry: Softcover ISBN 978-1-59237-132-7 $895

## Research Services Directory: Commercial & Corporate Research Centers

This ninth edition provides access to well over 8,000 independent Commercial Research Firms, Corporate Research Centers and Laboratories offering contract services for hands-on, basic or applied research. Research Services Directory covers the thousands of types of research companies, including Biotechnology & Pharmaceutical Developers, Consumer Product Research, Defense Contractors, Electronics & Software Engineers, Think Tanks, Forensic Investigators, Independent Commercial Laboratories, Information Brokers, Market & Survey Research Companies, Medical Diagnostic Facilities, Product Research & Development Firms and more. Each entry provides the company's name, mailing address, phone & fax numbers, key contacts, web site, e-mail address, as well as a company description and research and technical fields served. Four indexes provide immediate access to this wealth of information: Research Firms Index, Geographic Index, Personnel Name Index and Subject Index.

*"An important source for organizations in need of information about laboratories, individuals and other facilities." –ARBA*

Softcover ISBN 978-1-59237-003-0, 1,400 pages, $465.00

## International Business and Trade Directories

Completely updated, the Third Edition of *International Business and Trade Directories* now contains more than 10,000 entries, over 2,000 more than the last edition, making this directory the most comprehensive resource of the worlds business and trade directories. Entries include content descriptions, price, publisher's name and address, web site and e-mail addresses, phone and fax numbers and editorial staff. Organized by industry group, and then by region, this resource puts over 10,000 industry-specific business and trade directories at the reader's fingertips. Three indexes are included for quick access to information: Geographic Index, Publisher Index and Title Index. Public, college and corporate libraries, as well as individuals and corporations seeking critical market information will want to add this directory to their marketing collection.

*"Reasonably priced for a work of this type, this directory should appeal to larger academic, public and corporate libraries with an international focus." –Library Journal*

Softcover ISBN 978-1-930956-63-6, 1,800 pages, $225.00

## TheStreet.com Ratings Guide to Health Insurers

*TheStreet.com Ratings Guide to Health Insurers* is the first and only source to cover the financial stability of the nation's health care system, rating the financial safety of more than 6,000 health insurance providers, health maintenance organizations (HMOs) and all of the Blue Cross Blue Shield plans – updated quarterly to ensure the most accurate information. The Guide also provides a complete listing of all the major health insurers, including all Long-Term Care and Medigap insurers. Our *Guide to Health Insurers* includes comprehensive, timely coverage on the financial stability of HMOs and health insurers; the most accurate insurance company ratings available–the same quality ratings heralded by the U.S. General Accounting Office; separate listings for those companies offering Medigap and long-term care policies; the number of serious consumer complaints filed against most HMOs so you can see who is actually providing the best (or worst) service and more. The easy-to-use layout gives you a one-line summary analysis for each company that we track, followed by an in-depth, detailed analysis of all HMOs and the largest health insurers. The guide also includes a list of TheStreet.com Ratings Recommended Companies with information on how to contact them, and the reasoning behind any rating upgrades or downgrades.

*"With 20 years behind its insurance-advocacy research [the rating guide] continues to offer a wealth of information that helps consumers weigh their healthcare options now and in the future." -Today's Librarian*

Issues published quarterly, Softcover, 550 pages, $499.00 for four quarterly issues, $249.00 for a single issue

## TheStreet.com Ratings Guide to Life & Annuity Insurers

TheStreet.com Safety Ratings are the most reliable source for evaluating an insurer's financial solvency risk. Consequently, policyholders have come to rely on TheStreet.com's flagship publication, *TheStreet.com Ratings Guide to Life & Annuity Insurers*, to help them identify the safest companies to do business with. Each easy-to-use edition delivers TheStreet.com's independent ratings and analyses on more than 1,100 insurers, updated every quarter. Plus, your patrons will find a complete list of TheStreet.com Recommended Companies, including contact information, and the reasoning behind any rating upgrades or downgrades. This guide is perfect for those who are considering the purchase of a life insurance policy, placing money in an annuity, or advising clients about insurance and annuities. A life or health insurance policy or annuity is only as secure as the insurance company issuing it. Therefore, make sure your patrons have what they need to periodically monitor the financial condition of the companies with whom they have an investment. The TheStreet.com Ratings product line is designed to help them in their evaluations.

*"Weiss has an excellent reputation and this title is held by hundreds of libraries. This guide is recommended for public and academic libraries." -ARBA*

Issues published quarterly, Softcover, 360 pages, $499.00 for four quarterly issues, $249.00 for a single issue

## TheStreet.com Ratings Guide to Property & Casualty Insurers

*TheStreet.com Ratings Guide to Property and Casualty Insurers* provides the most extensive coverage of insurers writing policies, helping consumers and businesses avoid financial headaches. Updated quarterly, this easy-to-use publication delivers the independent, unbiased TheStreet.com Safety Ratings and supporting analyses on more than 2,800 U.S. insurance companies, offering auto & homeowners insurance, business insurance, worker's compensation insurance, product liability insurance, medical malpractice and other professional liability insurance. Each edition includes a list of TheStreet.com Recommended Companies by type of insurance, including a contact number, plus helpful information about the coverage provided by the State Guarantee Associations.

*"In contrast to the other major insurance rating agencies...Weiss does not have a financial relationship worth the companies it rates. A GAO study found that Weiss identified financial vulnerability earlier than the other rating agencies." -ARBA*

Issues published quarterly, Softcover, 455 pages, $499.00 for four quarterly issues, $249.00 for a single issue

## TheStreet.com Ratings Consumer Box Set

Deliver the critical information your patrons need to safeguard their personal finances with *TheStreet.com Ratings' Consumer Guide Box Set*. Each of the eight guides is packed with accurate, unbiased information and recommendations to help your patrons make sound financial decisions. TheStreet.com Ratings Consumer Guide Box Set provides your patrons with easy to understand guidance on important personal finance topics, including: *Consumer Guide to Variable Annuities, Consumer Guide to Medicare Supplement Insurance, Consumer Guide to Elder Care Choices, Consumer Guide to Automobile Insurance, Consumer Guide to Long-Term Care Insurance, Consumer Guide to Homeowners Insurance, Consumer Guide to Term Life Insurance, and Consumer Guide to Medicare Prescription Drug Coverage*. Each guide provides an easy-to-read overview of the topic, what to look out for when selecting a company or insurance plan to do business with, who are the recommended companies to work with and how to navigate through these often-times difficult decisions. Custom worksheets and step-by-step directions make these resources accessible to all types of users. Packaged in a handy custom display box, these helpful guides will prove to be a much-used addition to any reference collection.

Issues published twice per year, Softcover, 600 pages, $499.00 for two biennial issues

**To preview any of our Directories Risk-Free for 30 days, call (800) 562-2139 or fax (518) 789-0556
www.greyhouse.com  books@greyhouse.com**

## TheStreet.com Ratings Guide to Stock Mutual Funds

*TheStreet.com Ratings Guide to Stock Mutual Funds* offers ratings and analyses on more than 8,800 equity mutual funds – more than any other publication. The exclusive TheStreet.com Investment Ratings combine an objective evaluation of each fund's performance and risk to provide a single, user-friendly, composite rating, giving your patrons a better handle on a mutual fund's risk-adjusted performance. Each edition identifies the top-performing mutual funds based on risk category, type of fund, and overall risk-adjusted performance. TheStreet.com's unique investment rating system makes it easy to see exactly which stocks are on the rise and which ones should be avoided. For those investors looking to tailor their mutual fund selections based on age, income, and tolerance for risk, we've also assigned two component ratings to each fund: a performance rating and a risk rating. With these, you can identify those funds that are best suited to meet your - or your client's – individual needs and goals. Plus, we include a handy Risk Profile Quiz to help you assess your personal tolerance for risk. So whether you're an investing novice or professional, the *Guide to Stock Mutual Funds* gives you everything you need to find a mutual fund that is right for you.

> *"There is tremendous need for information such as that provided by this Weiss publication. This reasonably priced guide is recommended for public and academic libraries serving investors." -ARBA*

Issues published quarterly, Softcover, 655 pages, $499 for four quarterly issues, $249 for a single issue

## TheStreet.com Ratings Guide to Exchange-Traded Funds

TheStreet.com Ratings editors analyze hundreds of mutual funds each quarter, condensing all of the available data into a single composite opinion of each fund's risk-adjusted performance. The intuitive, consumer-friendly ratings allow investors to instantly identify those funds that have historically done well and those that have under-performed the market. Each quarterly edition identifies the top-performing exchange-traded funds based on risk category, type of fund, and overall risk-adjusted performance. The rating scale, A through F, gives you a better handle on an exchange-traded fund's risk-adjusted performance. Other features include Top & Bottom 200 Exchange-Traded Funds; Performance and Risk: 100 Best and Worst Exchange- Traded Funds; Investor Profile Quiz; Performance Benchmarks and Fund Type Descriptions. With the growing popularity of mutual fund investing, consumers need a reliable source to help them track and evaluate the performance of their mutual fund holdings. Plus, they need a way of identifying and monitoring other funds as potential new investments. Unfortunately, the hundreds of performance and risk measures available, multiplied by the vast number of mutual fund investments on the market today, can make this a daunting task for even the most sophisticated investor. This Guide will serve as a useful tool for both the first-time and seasoned investor.

Editions published quarterly, Softcover, 440 pages, $499.00 for four quarterly issues, $249.00 for a single issue

## TheStreet.com Ratings Guide to Bond & Money Market Mutual Funds

*TheStreet.com Ratings Guide to Bond & Money Market Mutual Funds* has everything your patrons need to easily identify the top-performing fixed income funds on the market today. Each quarterly edition contains TheStreet.com's independent ratings and analyses on more than 4,600 fixed income funds – more than any other publication, including corporate bond funds, high-yield bond funds, municipal bond funds, mortgage security funds, money market funds, global bond funds and government bond funds. In addition, the fund's risk rating is combined with its three-year performance rating to get an overall picture of the fund's risk-adjusted performance. The resulting TheStreet.com Investment Rating gives a single, user-friendly, objective evaluation that makes it easy to compare one fund to another and select the right fund based on the level of risk tolerance. Most investors think of fixed income mutual funds as "safe" investments. That's not always the case, however, depending on the credit risk, interest rate risk, and prepayment risk of the securities owned by the fund. TheStreet.com Ratings assesses each of these risks and assigns each fund a risk rating to help investors quickly evaluate the fund's risk component. Plus, we include a handy Risk Profile Quiz to help you assess your personal tolerance for risk. So whether you're an investing novice or professional, the *Guide to Bond and Money Market Mutual Funds* gives you everything you need to find a mutual fund that is right for you.

> *"Comprehensive... It is easy to use and consumer-oriented, and can be recommended for larger public and academic libraries." -ARBA*

Issues published quarterly, Softcover, 470 pages, $499.00 for four quarterly issues, $249.00 for a single issue

## TheStreet.com Ratings Guide to Banks & Thrifts

Updated quarterly, for the most up-to-date information, *TheStreet.com Ratings Guide to Banks and Thrifts* offers accurate, intuitive safety ratings your patrons can trust; supporting ratios and analyses that show an institution's strong & weak points; identification of the TheStreet.com Recommended Companies with branches in your area; a complete list of institutions receiving upgrades/downgrades; and comprehensive coverage of every bank and thrift in the nation – more than 9,000. TheStreet.com Safety Ratings are then based on the analysts' review of publicly available information collected by the federal banking regulators. The easy-to-use layout gives you: the institution's TheStreet.com Safety Rating for the last 3 years; the five key indexes used to evaluate each institution; along with the primary ratios and statistics used in determining the company's rating. *TheStreet.com Ratings Guide to Banks & Thrifts* will be a must for individuals who are concerned about the safety of their CD or savings account; need to be sure that an existing line of credit will be there when they need it; or simply want to avoid the hassles of dealing with a failing or troubled institution.

> *"Large public and academic libraries most definitely need to acquire the work. Likewise, special libraries in large corporations will find this title indispensable." -ARBA*

Issues published quarterly, Softcover, 370 pages, $499.00 for four quarterly issues, $249.00 for a single issue

**To preview any of our Directories Risk-Free for 30 days, call (800) 562-2139 or fax (518) 789-0556
www.greyhouse.com   books@greyhouse.com**

## TheStreet.com Ratings Guide to Common Stocks

*TheStreet.com Ratings Guide to Common Stocks* gives your patrons reliable insight into the risk-adjusted performance of common stocks listed on the NYSE, AMEX, and Nasdaq – over 5,800 stocks in all – more than any other publication. TheStreet.com's unique investment rating system makes it easy to see exactly which stocks are on the rise and which ones should be avoided. In addition, your patrons also get supporting analysis showing growth trends, profitability, debt levels, valuation levels, the top-rated stocks within each industry, and more. Plus, each stock is ranked with the easy-to-use buy-hold-sell equivalents commonly used by Wall Street. Whether they're selecting their own investments or checking up on a broker's recommendation, TheStreet.com Ratings can help them in their evaluations.

*"Users... will find the information succinct and the explanations readable, easy to understand, and helpful to a novice." -Library Journal*

Issues published quarterly, Softcover, 440 pages, $499.00 for four quarterly issues, $249.00 for a single issue

## TheStreet.com Ratings Ultimate Guided Tour of Stock Investing

This important reference guide from TheStreet.com Ratings is just what librarians around the country have asked for: a step-by-step introduction to stock investing for the beginning to intermediate investor. This easy-to-navigate guide explores the basics of stock investing and includes the intuitive TheStreet.com Investment Rating on more than 5,800 stocks, complete with real-world investing information that can be put to use immediately with stocks that fit the concepts discussed in the guide; informative charts, graphs and worksheets; easy-to-understand explanations on topics like P/E, compound interest, marked indices, diversifications, brokers, and much more; along with financial safety ratings for every stock on the NYSE, American Stock Exchange and the Nasdaq. This consumer-friendly guide offers complete how-to information on stock investing that can be put to use right away; a friendly format complete with our "Wise Guide" who leads the reader on a safari to learn about the investing jungle; helpful charts, graphs and simple worksheets; the intuitive TheStreet.com Investment rating on over 6,000 stocks — every stock found on the NYSE, American Stock Exchange and the NASDAQ; and much more.

*"Provides investors with an alternative to stock broker recommendations, which recently have been tarnished by conflicts of interest. In summary, the guide serves as a welcome addition for all public library collections." -ARBA*

Issues published quarterly, Softcover, 370 pages, $499.00 for four quarterly issues, $249.00 for a single issue

## TheStreet.com Ratings' Reports & Services

- Ratings Online — An on-line summary covering an individual company's TheStreet.com Financial Strength Rating or an investment's unique TheStreet.com Investment Rating with the factors contributing to that rating; available 24 hours a day by visiting www.thestreet.com/tscratings or calling (800) 289-9222.
- Unlimited Ratings Research — The ultimate research tool providing fast, easy online access to the very latest TheStreet.com Financial Strength Ratings and Investment Ratings. Price: $559 per industry.

Contact TheStreet.com for more information about Reports & Services at www.thestreet.com/tscratings or call (800) 289-9222

## TheStreet.com Ratings' Custom Reports

TheStreet.com Ratings is pleased to offer two customized options for receiving ratings data. Each taps into TheStreet.com's vast data repositories and is designed to provide exactly the data you need. Choose from a variety of industries, companies, data variables, and delivery formats including print, Excel, SQL, Text or Access.

- Customized Reports - get right to the heart of your company's research and data needs with a report customized to your specifications.
- Complete Database Download – TheStreet.com will design and deliver the database; from there you can sort it, recalculate it, and format your results to suit your specific needs.

Contact TheStreet.com for more information about Custom Reports at www.thestreet.com/tscratings or call (800) 289-9222

## The Value of a Dollar 1600-1859, The Colonial Era to The Civil War

Following the format of the widely acclaimed, *The Value of a Dollar, 1860-2004*, *The Value of a Dollar 1600-1859, The Colonial Era to The Civil War* records the actual prices of thousands of items that consumers purchased from the Colonial Era to the Civil War. Our editorial department had been flooded with requests from users of our *Value of a Dollar* for the same type of information, just from an earlier time period. This new volume is just the answer – with pricing data from 1600 to 1859. Arranged into five-year chapters, each 5-year chapter includes a Historical Snapshot, Consumer Expenditures, Investments, Selected Income, Income/Standard Jobs, Food Basket, Standard Prices and Miscellany. There is also a section on Trends. This informative section charts the change in price over time and provides added detail on the reasons prices changed within the time period, including industry developments, changes in consumer attitudes and important historical facts. This fascinating survey will serve a wide range of research needs and will be useful in all high school, public and academic library reference collections.

*"The Value of a Dollar: Colonial Era to the Civil War, 1600-1865 will find a happy audience among students, researchers, and general browsers. It offers a fascinating and detailed look at early American history from the viewpoint of everyday people trying to make ends meet. This title and the earlier publication, The Value of a Dollar, 1860-2004, complement each other very well, and readers will appreciate finding them side-by-side on the shelf." -Booklist*

Hardcover ISBN 978-1-59237-094-8, 600 pages, $145.00 | Ebook ISBN 978-1-59237-169-3 www.gale.com/gvrl/partners/grey.htm

## The Value of a Dollar 1860-2004, Third Edition

A guide to practical economy, *The Value of a Dollar* records the actual prices of thousands of items that consumers purchased from the Civil War to the present, along with facts about investment options and income opportunities. This brand new Third Edition boasts a brand new addition to each five-year chapter, a section on Trends. This informative section charts the change in price over time and provides added detail on the reasons prices changed within the time period, including industry developments, changes in consumer attitudes and important historical facts. Plus, a brand new chapter for 2000-2004 has been added. Each 5-year chapter includes a Historical Snapshot, Consumer Expenditures, Investments, Selected Income, Income/Standard Jobs, Food Basket, Standard Prices and Miscellany. This interesting and useful publication will be widely used in any reference collection.

*"Business historians, reporters, writers and students will find this source... very helpful for historical research. Libraries will want to purchase it." –ARBA*

Hardcover ISBN 978-1-59237-074-0, 600 pages, $145.00 | Ebook ISBN 978-1-59237-173-0 www.gale.com/gvrl/partners/grey.htm

## Working Americans 1880-1999
## Volume I: The Working Class, Volume II: The Middle Class, Volume III: The Upper Class

Each of the volumes in the *Working Americans* series focuses on a particular class of Americans, The Working Class, The Middle Class and The Upper Class over the last 120 years. Chapters in each volume focus on one decade and profile three to five families. Family Profiles include real data on Income & Job Descriptions, Selected Prices of the Times, Annual Income, Annual Budgets, Family Finances, Life at Work, Life at Home, Life in the Community, Working Conditions, Cost of Living, Amusements and much more. Each chapter also contains an Economic Profile with Average Wages of other Professions, a selection of Typical Pricing, Key Events & Inventions, News Profiles, Articles from Local Media and Illustrations. The *Working Americans* series captures the lifestyles of each of the classes from the last twelve decades, covers a vast array of occupations and ethnic backgrounds and travels the entire nation. These interesting and useful compilations of portraits of the American Working, Middle and Upper Classes during the last 120 years will be an important addition to any high school, public or academic library reference collection.

*"These interesting, unique compilations of economic and social facts, figures and graphs will support multiple research needs. They will engage and enlighten patrons in high school, public and academic library collections." –Booklist*

Volume I: The Working Class Hardcover ISBN 978-1-891482-81-6, 558 pages, $145.00 | Volume II: The Middle Class Hardcover ISBN 978-1-891482-72-4, 591 pages, $145.00 | Volume III: The Upper Class Hardcover ISBN 978-1-930956-38-4, 567 pages, $145.00 | Ebooks www.gale.com/gvrl/partners/grey.htm

## Working Americans 1880-1999  Volume IV: Their Children

This Fourth Volume in the highly successful *Working Americans* series focuses on American children, decade by decade from 1880 to 1999. This interesting and useful volume introduces the reader to three children in each decade, one from each of the Working, Middle and Upper classes. Like the first three volumes in the series, the individual profiles are created from interviews, diaries, statistical studies, biographies and news reports. Profiles cover a broad range of ethnic backgrounds, geographic area and lifestyles – everything from an orphan in Memphis in 1882, following the Yellow Fever epidemic of 1878 to an eleven-year-old nephew of a beer baron and owner of the New York Yankees in New York City in 1921. Chapters also contain important supplementary materials including News Features as well as information on everything from Schools to Parks, Infectious Diseases to Childhood Fears along with Entertainment, Family Life and much more to provide an informative overview of the lifestyles of children from each decade. This interesting account of what life was like for Children in the Working, Middle and Upper Classes will be a welcome addition to the reference collection of any high school, public or academic library.

Hardcover ISBN 978-1-930956-35-3, 600 pages, $145.00 | Ebook ISBN 978-1-59237-166-2 www.gale.com/gvrl/partners/grey.htm

**To preview any of our Directories Risk-Free for 30 days, call (800) 562-2139 or fax (518) 789-0556**
**www.greyhouse.com  books@greyhouse.com**

## Working Americans 1880-2003 Volume V: Americans At War

*Working Americans 1880-2003 Volume V: Americans At War* is divided into 11 chapters, each covering a decade from 1880-2003 and examines the lives of Americans during the time of war, including declared conflicts, one-time military actions, protests, and preparations for war. Each decade includes several personal profiles, whether on the battlefield or on the homefront, that tell the stories of civilians, soldiers, and officers during the decade. The profiles examine: Life at Home; Life at Work; and Life in the Community. Each decade also includes an Economic Profile with statistical comparisons, a Historical Snapshot, News Profiles, local News Articles, and Illustrations that provide a solid historical background to the decade being examined. Profiles range widely not only geographically, but also emotionally, from that of a girl whose leg was torn off in a blast during WWI, to the boredom of being stationed in the Dakotas as the Indian Wars were drawing to a close. As in previous volumes of the *Working Americans* series, information is presented in narrative form, but hard facts and real-life situations back up each story. The basis of the profiles come from diaries, private print books, personal interviews, family histories, estate documents and magazine articles. For easy reference, *Working Americans 1880-2003 Volume V: Americans At War* includes an in-depth Subject Index. The Working Americans series has become an important reference for public libraries, academic libraries and high school libraries. This fifth volume will be a welcome addition to all of these types of reference collections.

Hardcover ISBN 978-1-59237-024-5, 600 pages, $145.00 | Ebook ISBN 978-1-59237-167-9 www.gale.com/gvrl/partners/grey.htm

## Working Americans 1880-2005 Volume VI: Women at Work

Unlike any other volume in the *Working Americans* series, this Sixth Volume, is the first to focus on a particular gender of Americans. *Volume VI: Women at Work*, traces what life was like for working women from the 1860's to the present time. Beginning with the life of a maid in 1890 and a store clerk in 1900 and ending with the life and times of the modern working women, this text captures the struggle, strengths and changing perception of the American woman at work. Each chapter focuses on one decade and profiles three to five women with real data on Income & Job Descriptions, Selected Prices of the Times, Annual Income, Annual Budgets, Family Finances, Life at Work, Life at Home, Life in the Community, Working Conditions, Cost of Living, Amusements and much more. For even broader access to the events, economics and attitude towards women throughout the past 130 years, each chapter is supplemented with News Profiles, Articles from Local Media, Illustrations, Economic Profiles, Typical Pricing, Key Events, Inventions and more. This important volume illustrates what life was like for working women over time and allows the reader to develop an understanding of the changing role of women at work. These interesting and useful compilations of portraits of women at work will be an important addition to any high school, public or academic library reference collection.

Hardcover ISBN 978-1-59237-063-4, 600 pages, $145.00 | Ebook ISBN 978-1-59237-168-6 www.gale.com/gvrl/partners/grey.htm

## Working Americans 1880-2005 Volume VII: Social Movements

*Working Americans series, Volume VII: Social Movements* explores how Americans sought and fought for change from the 1880s to the present time. Following the format of previous volumes in the Working Americans series, the text examines the lives of 34 individuals who have worked -- often behind the scenes --- to bring about change. Issues include topics as diverse as the Anti-smoking movement of 1901 to efforts by Native Americans to reassert their long lost rights. Along the way, the book will profile individuals brave enough to demand suffrage for Kansas women in 1912 or demand an end to lynching during a March on Washington in 1923. Each profile is enriched with real data on Income & Job Descriptions, Selected Prices of the Times, Annual Incomes & Budgets, Life at Work, Life at Home, Life in the Community, along with News Features, Key Events, and Illustrations. The depth of information contained in each profile allow the user to explore the private, financial and public lives of these subjects, deepening our understanding of how calls for change took place in our society. A must-purchase for the reference collections of high school libraries, public libraries and academic libraries.

Hardcover ISBN 978-1-59237-101-3, 600 pages, $145.00 | Ebook ISBN 978-1-59237-174-7 www.gale.com/gvrl/partners/grey.htm

## Working Americans 1880-2005 Volume VIII: Immigrants

*Working Americans 1880-2007 Volume VIII: Immigrants* illustrates what life was like for families leaving their homeland and creating a new life in the United States. Each chapter covers one decade and introduces the reader to three immigrant families. Family profiles cover what life was like in their homeland, in their community in the United States, their home life, working conditions and so much more. As the reader moves through these pages, the families and individuals come to life, painting a picture of why they left their homeland, their experiences in setting roots in a new country, their struggles and triumphs, stretching from the 1800s to the present time. Profiles include a seven-year-old Swedish girl who meets her father for the first time at Ellis Island; a Chinese photographer's assistant; an Armenian who flees the genocide of his country to build Ford automobiles in Detroit; a 38-year-old German bachelor cigar maker who settles in Newark NJ, but contemplates tobacco farming in Virginia; a 19-year-old Irish domestic servant who is amazed at the easy life of American dogs; a 19-year-old Filipino who came to Hawaii against his parent's wishes to farm sugar cane; a French-Canadian who finds success as a boxer in Maine and many more. As in previous volumes, information is presented in narrative form, but hard facts and real-life situations back up each story. With the topic of immigration being so hotly debated in this country, this timely resource will prove to be a useful source for students, researchers, historians and library patrons to discover the issues facing immigrants in the United States. This title will be a useful addition to reference collections of public libraries, university libraries and high schools.

Hardcover ISBN 978-1-59237-197-6, 600 pages, $145.00 | Ebook ISBN 978-1-59237-232-4 www.gale.com/gvrl/partners/grey.htm

## The Encyclopedia of Warrior Peoples & Fighting Groups

Many military groups throughout the world have excelled in their craft either by fortuitous circumstances, outstanding leadership, or intense training. This new second edition of *The Encyclopedia of Warrior Peoples and Fighting Groups* explores the origins and leadership of these outstanding combat forces, chronicles their conquests and accomplishments, examines the circumstances surrounding their decline or disbanding, and assesses their influence on the groups and methods of warfare that followed. Readers will encounter ferocious tribes, charismatic leaders, and daring militias, from ancient times to the present, including Amazons, Buffalo Soldiers, Green Berets, Iron Brigade, Kamikazes, Peoples of the Sea, Polish Winged Hussars, Teutonic Knights, and Texas Rangers. With over 100 alphabetical entries, numerous cross-references and illustrations, a comprehensive bibliography, and index, the *Encyclopedia of Warrior Peoples and Fighting Groups* is a valuable resource for readers seeking insight into the bold history of distinguished fighting forces.

*"Especially useful for high school students, undergraduates, and general readers with an interest in military history." –Library Journal*

Hardcover ISBN 978-1-59237-116-7, 660 pages, $135.00 | Ebook ISBN 978-1-59237-172-3 www.gale.com/gvrl/partners/grey.htm

## The Encyclopedia of Invasions & Conquests, From the Ancient Times to the Present

This second edition of the popular *Encyclopedia of Invasions & Conquests*, a comprehensive guide to over 150 invasions, conquests, battles and occupations from ancient times to the present, takes readers on a journey that includes the Roman conquest of Britain, the Portuguese colonization of Brazil, and the Iraqi invasion of Kuwait, to name a few. New articles will explore the late 20th and 21st centuries, with a specific focus on recent conflicts in Afghanistan, Kuwait, Iraq, Yugoslavia, Grenada and Chechnya. In addition to covering the military aspects of invasions and conquests, entries cover some of the political, economic, and cultural aspects, for example, the effects of a conquest on the invade country's political and monetary system and in its language and religion. The entries on leaders – among them Sargon, Alexander the Great, William the Conqueror, and Adolf Hitler – deal with the people who sought to gain control, expand power, or exert religious or political influence over others through military means. Revised and updated for this second edition, entries are arranged alphabetically within historical periods. Each chapter provides a map to help readers locate key areas and geographical features, and bibliographical references appear at the end of each entry. Other useful features include cross-references, a cumulative bibliography and a comprehensive subject index. This authoritative, well-organized, lucidly written volume will prove invaluable for a variety of readers, including high school students, military historians, members of the armed forces, history buffs and hobbyists.

*"Engaging writing, sensible organization, nice illustrations, interesting and obscure facts, and useful maps make this book a pleasure to read." –ARBA*

Hardcover ISBN 978-1-59237-114-3, 598 pages, $135.00 | Ebook ISBN 978-1-59237-171-6 www.gale.com/gvrl/partners/grey.htm

## Encyclopedia of Prisoners of War & Internment

This authoritative second edition provides a valuable overview of the history of prisoners of war and interned civilians, from earliest times to the present. Written by an international team of experts in the field of POW studies, this fascinating and thought-provoking volume includes entries on a wide range of subjects including the Crusades, Plains Indian Warfare, concentration camps, the two world wars, and famous POWs throughout history, as well as atrocities, escapes, and much more. Written in a clear and easily understandable style, this informative reference details over 350 entries, 30% larger than the first edition, that survey the history of prisoners of war and interned civilians from the earliest times to the present, with emphasis on the 19th and 20th centuries. Medical conditions, international law, exchanges of prisoners, organizations working on behalf of POWs, and trials associated with the treatment of captives are just some of the themes explored. Entries are arranged alphabetically, plus illustrations and maps are provided for easy reference. The text also includes an introduction, bibliography, appendix of selected documents, and end-of-entry reading suggestions. This one-of-a-kind reference will be a helpful addition to the reference collections of all public libraries, high schools, and university libraries and will prove invaluable to historians and military enthusiasts.

*"Thorough and detailed yet accessible to the lay reader. Of special interest to subject specialists and historians; recommended for public and academic libraries." - Library Journal*

Hardcover ISBN 978-1-59237-120-4, 676 pages, $135.00 | Ebook ISBN 978-1-59237-170-9 www.gale.com/gvrl/partners/grey.htm

## The Encyclopedia of Rural America: the Land & People

History, sociology, anthropology, and public policy are combined to deliver the encyclopedia destined to become the standard reference work in American rural studies. From irrigation and marriage to games and mental health, this encyclopedia is the first to explore the contemporary landscape of rural America, placed in historical perspective. With over 300 articles prepared by leading experts from across the nation, this timely encyclopedia documents and explains the major themes, concepts, industries, concerns, and everyday life of the people and land who make up rural America. Entries range from the industrial sector and government policy to arts and humanities and social and family concerns. Articles explore every aspect of life in rural America. *Encyclopedia of Rural America*, with its broad range of coverage, will appeal to high school and college students as well as graduate students, faculty, scholars, and people whose work pertains to rural areas.

*"This exemplary encyclopedia is guaranteed to educate our highly urban society about the uniqueness of rural America. Recommended for public and academic libraries." -Library Journal*

Two Volumes, Hardcover, ISBN 978-1-59237-115-0, 800 pages, $195.00

**To preview any of our Directories Risk-Free for 30 days, call (800) 562-2139 or fax (518) 789-0556
www.greyhouse.com  books@greyhouse.com**

## The Religious Right, A Reference Handbook

Timely and unbiased, this third edition updates and expands its examination of the religious right and its influence on our government, citizens, society, and politics. From the fight to outlaw the teaching of Darwin's theory of evolution to the struggle to outlaw abortion, the religious right is continually exerting an influence on public policy. This text explores the influence of religion on legislation and society, while examining the alignment of the religious right with the political right. A historical survey of the movement highlights the shift to "hands-on" approach to politics and the struggle to present a unified front. The coverage offers a critical historical survey of the religious right movement, focusing on its increased involvement in the political arena, attempts to forge coalitions, and notable successes and failures. The text offers complete coverage of biographies of the men and women who have advanced the cause and an up to date chronology illuminate the movement's goals, including their accomplishments and failures. This edition offers an extensive update to all sections along with several brand new entries. Two new sections complement this third edition, a chapter on legal issues and court decisions and a chapter on demographic statistics and electoral patterns. To aid in further research, *The Religious Right*, offers an entire section of annotated listings of print and non-print resources, as well as of organizations affiliated with the religious right, and those opposing it. Comprehensive in its scope, this work offers easy-to-read, pertinent information for those seeking to understand the religious right and its evolving role in American society. A must for libraries of all sizes, university religion departments, activists, high schools and for those interested in the evolving role of the religious right.

*" Recommended for all public and academic libraries." - Library Journal*

Hardcover ISBN 978-1-59237-113-6, 600 pages, $135.00 | Ebook ISBN 978-1-59237-226-3 www.gale.com/gvrl/partners/grey.htm

## From Suffrage to the Senate, America's Political Women

*From Suffrage to the Senate* is a comprehensive and valuable compendium of biographies of leading women in U.S. politics, past and present, and an examination of the wide range of women's movements. Up to date through 2006, this dynamically illustrated reference work explores American women's path to political power and social equality from the struggle for the right to vote and the abolition of slavery to the first African American woman in the U.S. Senate and beyond. This new edition includes over 150 new entries and a brand new section on trends and demographics of women in politics. The in-depth coverage also traces the political heritage of the abolition, labor, suffrage, temperance, and reproductive rights movements. The alphabetically arranged entries include biographies of every woman from across the political spectrum who has served in the U.S. House and Senate, along with women in the Judiciary and the U.S. Cabinet and, new to this edition, biographies of activists and political consultants. Bibliographical references follow each entry. For easy reference, a handy chronology is provided detailing 150 years of women's history. This up-to-date reference will be a must-purchase for women's studies departments, high schools and public libraries and will be a handy resource for those researching the key players in women's politics, past and present.

*"An engaging tool that would be useful in high school, public, and academic libraries looking for an overview of the political history of women in the US." –Booklist*

Two Volumes, Hardcover ISBN 978-1-59237-117-4, 1,160 pages, $195.00 | Ebook ISBN 978-1-59237-227-0 www.gale.com/gvrl/partners/grey.htm

## An African Biographical Dictionary

This landmark second edition is the only biographical dictionary to bring together, in one volume, cultural, social and political leaders – both historical and contemporary – of the sub-Saharan region. Over 800 biographical sketches of prominent Africans, as well as foreigners who have affected the continent's history, are featured, 150 more than the previous edition. The wide spectrum of leaders includes religious figures, writers, politicians, scientists, entertainers, sports personalities and more. Access to these fascinating individuals is provided in a user-friendly format. The biographies are arranged alphabetically, cross-referenced and indexed. Entries include the country or countries in which the person was significant and the commonly accepted dates of birth and death. Each biographical sketch is chronologically written; entries for cultural personalities add an evaluation of their work. This information is followed by a selection of references often found in university and public libraries, including autobiographies and principal biographical works. Appendixes list each individual by country and by field of accomplishment – rulers, musicians, explorers, missionaries, businessmen, physicists – nearly thirty categories in all. Another convenient appendix lists heads of state since independence by country. Up-to-date and representative of African societies as a whole, An African Biographical Dictionary provides a wealth of vital information for students of African culture and is an indispensable reference guide for anyone interested in African affairs.

*"An unquestionable convenience to have these concise, informative biographies gathered into one source, indexed, and analyzed by appendixes listing entrants by nation and occupational field." –Wilson Library Bulletin*

Hardcover ISBN 978-1-59237-112-9, 667 pages, $135.00 | Ebook ISBN 978-1-59237-229-4 www.gale.com/gvrl/partners/grey.htm

## American Environmental Leaders, From Colonial Times to the Present

A comprehensive and diverse award winning collection of biographies of the most important figures in American environmentalism. Few subjects arouse the passions the way the environment does. How will we feed an ever-increasing population and how can that food be made safe for consumption? Who decides how land is developed? How can environmental policies be made fair for everyone, including multiethnic groups, women, children, and the poor? *American Environmental Leaders* presents more than 350 biographies of men and women who have devoted their lives to studying, debating, and organizing these and other controversial issues over the last 200 years. In addition to the scientists who have analyzed how human actions affect nature, we are introduced to poets, landscape architects, presidents, painters, activists, even sanitation engineers, and others who have forever altered how we think about the environment. The easy to use A–Z format provides instant access to these fascinating individuals, and frequent cross references indicate others with whom individuals worked (and sometimes clashed). End of entry references provide users with a starting point for further research.

*"Highly recommended for high school, academic, and public libraries needing environmental biographical information." –Library Journal/Starred Review*

Two Volumes, Hardcover ISBN 978-1-59237-119-8, 900 pages $195.00 | Ebook ISBN 978-1-59237-230-0
www.gale.com/gvrl/partners/grey.htm

## World Cultural Leaders of the Twentieth & Twenty-First Centuries

*World Cultural Leaders of the Twentieth & Twenty-First Centuries* is a window into the arts, performances, movements, and music that shaped the world's cultural development since 1900. A remarkable around-the-world look at one-hundred-plus years of cultural development through the eyes of those that set the stage and stayed to play. This second edition offers over 120 new biographies along with a complete update of existing biographies. To further aid the reader, a handy fold-out timeline traces important events in all six cultural categories from 1900 through the present time. Plus, a new section of detailed material and resources for 100 selected individuals is also new to this edition, with further data on museums, homesteads, websites, artwork and more. This remarkable compilation will answer a wide range of questions. Who was the originator of the term "documentary"? Which poet married the daughter of the famed novelist Thomas Mann in order to help her escape Nazi Germany? Which British writer served as an agent in Russia against the Bolsheviks before the 1917 revolution? A handy two-volume set that makes it easy to look up 450 worldwide cultural icons: novelists, poets, playwrights, painters, sculptors, architects, dancers, choreographers, actors, directors, filmmakers, singers, composers, and musicians. *World Cultural Leaders of the Twentieth & Twenty-First Centuries* provides entries (many of them illustrated) covering the person's works, achievements, and professional career in a thorough essay and offers interesting facts and statistics. Entries are fully cross-referenced so that readers can learn how various individuals influenced others. An index of leaders by occupation, a useful glossary and a thorough general index complete the coverage. This remarkable resource will be an important acquisition for the reference collections of public libraries, university libraries and high schools.

*"Fills a need for handy, concise information on a wide array of international cultural figures."-ARBA*

Two Volumes, Hardcover ISBN 978-1-59237-118-1, 900 pages, $195.00 | Ebook ISBN 978-1-59237-231-7
www.gale.com/gvrl/partners/grey.htm

## Political Corruption in America: An Encyclopedia of Scandals, Power, and Greed

The complete scandal-filled history of American political corruption, focusing on the infamous people and cases, as well as society's electoral and judicial reactions. Since colonial times, there has been no shortage of politicians willing to take a bribe, skirt campaign finance laws, or act in their own interests. Corruption like the Whiskey Ring, Watergate, and Whitewater cases dominate American life, making political scandal a leading U.S. industry. From judges to senators, presidents to mayors, *Political Corruption in America* discusses the infamous people throughout history who have been accused of and implicated in crooked behavior. In this new second edition, more than 250 A–Z entries explore the people, crimes, investigations, and court cases behind 200 years of American political scandals. This unbiased volume also delves into the issues surrounding Koreagate, the Chinese campaign scandal, and other ethical lapses. Relevant statutes and terms, including the Independent Counsel Statute and impeachment as a tool of political punishment, are examined as well. Students, scholars, and other readers interested in American history, political science, and ethics will appreciate this survey of a wide range of corrupting influences. This title focuses on how politicians from all parties have fallen because of their greed and hubris, and how society has used electoral and judicial means against those who tested the accepted standards of political conduct. A full range of illustrations including political cartoons, photos of key figures such as Abe Fortas and Archibald Cox, graphs of presidential pardons, and tables showing the number of expulsions and censures in both the House and Senate round out the text. In addition, a comprehensive chronology of major political scandals in U.S. history from colonial times until the present. For further reading, an extensive bibliography lists sources including archival letters, newspapers, and private manuscript collections from the United States and Great Britain. With its comprehensive coverage of this interesting topic, *Political Corruption in America: An Encyclopedia of Scandals, Power, and Greed* will prove to be a useful addition to the reference collections of all public libraries, university libraries, history collections, political science collections and high schools.

*"...this encyclopedia is a useful contribution to the field. Highly recommended." - CHOICE*
*"Political Corruption should be useful in most academic, high school, and public libraries." Booklist*

Hardcover ISBN 978-1-59237-297-3, 500 pages, $135.00

**To preview any of our Directories Risk-Free for 30 days, call (800) 562-2139 or fax (518) 789-0556**
**www.greyhouse.com  books@greyhouse.com**

## Religion and Law: A Dictionary

This informative, easy-to-use reference work covers a wide range of legal issues that affect the roles of religion and law in American society. Extensive A–Z entries provide coverage of key court decisions, case studies, concepts, individuals, religious groups, organizations, and agencies shaping religion and law in today's society. This *Dictionary* focuses on topics involved with the constitutional theory and interpretation of religion and the law; terms providing a historical explanation of the ways in which America's ever increasing ethnic and religious diversity contributed to our current understanding of the mandates of the First and Fourteenth Amendments; terms and concepts describing the development of religion clause jurisprudence; an analytical examination of the distinct vocabulary used in this area of the law; the means by which American courts have attempted to balance religious liberty against other important individual and social interests in a wide variety of physical and regulatory environments, including the classroom, the workplace, the courtroom, religious group organization and structure, taxation, the clash of "secular" and "religious" values, and the relationship of the generalized idea of individual autonomy of the specific concept of religious liberty. Important legislation and legal cases affecting religion and society are thoroughly covered in this timely volume, including a detailed Table of Cases and Table of Statutes for more detailed research. A guide to further reading and an index are also included. This useful resource will be an important acquisition for the reference collections of all public libraries, university libraries, religion reference collections and high schools.

Hardcover ISBN 978-1-59237-298-0, 500 pages, $135.00

## Human Rights in the United States: A Dictionary and Documents

This two volume set offers easy to grasp explanations of the basic concepts, laws, and case law in the field, with emphasis on human rights in the historical, political, and legal experience of the United States. Human rights is a term not fully understood by many Americans. Addressing this gap, the new second edition of *Human Rights in the United States: A Dictionary and Documents* offers a comprehensive introduction that places the history of human rights in the United States in an international context. It surveys the legal protection of human dignity in the United States, examines the sources of human rights norms, cites key legal cases, explains the role of international governmental and non-governmental organizations, and charts global, regional, and U.N. human rights measures. Over 240 dictionary entries of human rights terms are detailed—ranging from asylum and cultural relativism to hate crimes and torture. Each entry discusses the significance of the term, gives examples, and cites appropriate documents and court decisions. In addition, a Documents section is provided that contains 59 conventions, treaties, and protocols related to the most up to date international action on ethnic cleansing; freedom of expression and religion; violence against women; and much more. A bibliography, extensive glossary, and comprehensive index round out this indispensable volume. This comprehensive, timely volume is a must for large public libraries, university libraries and social science departments, along with high school libraries.

> "...invaluable for anyone interested in human rights issues ... highly recommended for all reference collections."
> - American Reference Books Annual

Two Volumes, Hardcover ISBN 978-1-59237-290-4, 750 pages, $225.00

**Business Information ◆ Ratings Guides ◆ General Reference ◆ <u>Education</u> ◆
Statistics ◆ Demographics ◆ Health Information ◆ Canadian Information**

## The Comparative Guide to American Elementary & Secondary Schools, 2008

The only guide of its kind, this award winning compilation offers a snapshot profile of every public school district in the United States serving 1,500 or more students – more than 5,900 districts are covered. Organized alphabetically by district within state, each chapter begins with a Statistical Overview of the state. Each district listing includes contact information (name, address, phone number and web site) plus Grades Served, the Numbers of Students and Teachers and the Number of Regular, Special Education, Alternative and Vocational Schools in the district along with statistics on Student/Classroom Teacher Ratios, Drop Out Rates, Ethnicity, the Numbers of Librarians and Guidance Counselors and District Expenditures per student. As an added bonus, *The Comparative Guide to American Elementary and Secondary Schools* provides important ranking tables, both by state and nationally, for each data element. For easy navigation through this wealth of information, this handbook contains a useful City Index that lists all districts that operate schools within a city. These important comparative statistics are necessary for anyone considering relocation or doing comparative research on their own district and would be a perfect acquisition for any public library or school district library.

*"This straightforward guide is an easy way to find general information.
Valuable for academic and large public library collections." –ARBA*

Softcover ISBN 978-1-59237-223-2, 2,400 pages, $125.00 | Ebook ISBN 978-1-59237-238-6 www.gale.com/gvrl/partners/grey.htm

## The Complete Learning Disabilities Directory, 2008

*The Complete Learning Disabilities Directory* is the most comprehensive database of Programs, Services, Curriculum Materials, Professional Meetings & Resources, Camps, Newsletters and Support Groups for teachers, students and families concerned with learning disabilities. This information-packed directory includes information about Associations & Organizations, Schools, Colleges & Testing Materials, Government Agencies, Legal Resources and much more. For quick, easy access to information, this directory contains four indexes: Entry Name Index, Subject Index and Geographic Index. With every passing year, the field of learning disabilities attracts more attention and the network of caring, committed and knowledgeable professionals grows every day. This directory is an invaluable research tool for these parents, students and professionals.

*"Due to its wealth and depth of coverage, parents, teachers and others… should find this an invaluable resource." -Booklist*

Softcover ISBN 978-1-59237-207-2, 900 pages, $145.00 | Online Database $195.00 | Online Database & Directory Combo $280.00

## Educators Resource Directory, 2007/08

*Educators Resource Directory* is a comprehensive resource that provides the educational professional with thousands of resources and statistical data for professional development. This directory saves hours of research time by providing immediate access to Associations & Organizations, Conferences & Trade Shows, Educational Research Centers, Employment Opportunities & Teaching Abroad, School Library Services, Scholarships, Financial Resources, Professional Consultants, Computer Software & Testing Resources and much more. Plus, this comprehensive directory also includes a section on Statistics and Rankings with over 100 tables, including statistics on Average Teacher Salaries, SAT/ACT scores, Revenues & Expenditures and more. These important statistics will allow the user to see how their school rates among others, make relocation decisions and so much more. For quick access to information, this directory contains four indexes: Entry & Publisher Index, Geographic Index, a Subject & Grade Index and Web Sites Index. *Educators Resource Directory* will be a well-used addition to the reference collection of any school district, education department or public library.

*"Recommended for all collections that serve elementary and secondary school professionals." –Choice*

Softcover ISBN 978-1-59237-179-2, 800 pages, $145.00 | Online Database $195.00 | Online Database & Directory Combo $280.00

## Profiles of New York | Profiles of Florida | Profiles of Texas | Profiles of Illinois | Profiles of Michigan | Profiles of Ohio | Profiles of New Jersey | Profiles of Massachusetts | Profiles of Pennsylvania | Profiles of Wisconsin | Profiles of Connecticut & Rhode Island | Profiles of Indiana | Profiles of North Carolina & South Carolina | Profiles of Virginia | Profiles of California

The careful layout gives the user an easy-to-read snapshot of every single place and county in the state, from the biggest metropolis to the smallest unincorporated hamlet. The richness of each place or county profile is astounding in its depth, from history to weather, all packed in an easy-to-navigate, compact format. Each profile contains data on History, Geography, Climate, Population, Vital Statistics, Economy, Income, Taxes, Education, Housing, Health & Environment, Public Safety, Newspapers, Transportation, Presidential Election Results, Information Contacts and Chambers of Commerce. As an added bonus, there is a section on Selected Statistics, where data from the 100 largest towns and cities is arranged into easy-to-use charts. Each of 22 different data points has its own two-page spread with the cities listed in alpha order so researchers can easily compare and rank cities. A remarkable compilation that offers overviews and insights into each corner of the state, each volume goes beyond Census statistics, beyond metro area coverage, beyond the 100 best places to live. Drawn from official census information, other government statistics and original research, you will have at your fingertips data that's available nowhere else in one single source.

*"The publisher claims that this is the 'most comprehensive portrait of the state of Florida ever published,' and this reviewer is inclined to believe it...Recommended. All levels." –Choice on Profiles of Florida*

Each Profiles of... title ranges from 400-800 pages, priced at $149.00 each

## America's Top-Rated Cities, 2008

*America's Top-Rated Cities* provides current, comprehensive statistical information and other essential data in one easy-to-use source on the 100 "top" cities that have been cited as the best for business and living in the U.S. This handbook allows readers to see, at a glance, a concise social, business, economic, demographic and environmental profile of each city, including brief evaluative comments. In addition to detailed data on Cost of Living, Finances, Real Estate, Education, Major Employers, Media, Crime and Climate, city reports now include Housing Vacancies, Tax Audits, Bankruptcy, Presidential Election Results and more. This outstanding source of information will be widely used in any reference collection.

*"The only source of its kind that brings together all of this information into one easy-to-use source. It will be beneficial to many business and public libraries." –ARBA*

Four Volumes, Softcover ISBN 978-1-59237-349-9, 2,500 pages, $195.00 | Ebook ISBN 978-1-59237-233-1
www.gale.com/gvrl/partners/grey.htm

## America's Top-Rated Smaller Cities, 2008/09

A perfect companion to *America's Top-Rated Cities*, *America's Top-Rated Smaller Cities* provides current, comprehensive business and living profiles of smaller cities (population 25,000-99,999) that have been cited as the best for business and living in the United States. Sixty cities make up this 2004 edition of America's Top-Rated Smaller Cities, all are top-ranked by Population Growth, Median Income, Unemployment Rate and Crime Rate. City reports reflect the most current data available on a wide-range of statistics, including Employment & Earnings, Household Income, Unemployment Rate, Population Characteristics, Taxes, Cost of Living, Education, Health Care, Public Safety, Recreation, Media, Air & Water Quality and much more. Plus, each city report contains a Background of the City, and an Overview of the State Finances. *America's Top-Rated Smaller Cities* offers a reliable, one-stop source for statistical data that, before now, could only be found scattered in hundreds of sources. This volume is designed for a wide range of readers: individuals considering relocating a residence or business; professionals considering expanding their business or changing careers; general and market researchers; real estate consultants; human resource personnel; urban planners and investors.

*"Provides current, comprehensive statistical information in one easy-to-use source...
Recommended for public and academic libraries and specialized collections." –Library Journal*

Two Volumes, Softcover ISBN 978-1-59237-284-3, 1,100 pages, $195.00 | Ebook ISBN 978-1-59237-234-8
www.gale.com/gvrl/partners/grey.htm

## Profiles of America: Facts, Figures & Statistics for Every Populated Place in the United States

*Profiles of America* is the only source that pulls together, in one place, statistical, historical and descriptive information about every place in the United States in an easy-to-use format. This award winning reference set, now in its second edition, compiles statistics and data from over 20 different sources – the latest census information has been included along with more than nine brand new statistical topics. This Four-Volume Set details over 40,000 places, from the biggest metropolis to the smallest unincorporated hamlet, and provides statistical details and information on over 50 different topics including Geography, Climate, Population, Vital Statistics, Economy, Income, Taxes, Education, Housing, Health & Environment, Public Safety, Newspapers, Transportation, Presidential Election Results and Information Contacts or Chambers of Commerce. Profiles are arranged, for ease-of-use, by state and then by county. Each county begins with a County-Wide Overview and is followed by information for each Community in that particular county. The Community Profiles within the county are arranged alphabetically. *Profiles of America* is a virtual snapshot of America at your fingertips and a unique compilation of information that will be widely used in any reference collection.

*A Library Journal Best Reference Book "An outstanding compilation." –Library Journal*

Four Volumes, Softcover ISBN 978-1-891482-80-9, 10,000 pages, $595.00

**To preview any of our Directories Risk-Free for 30 days, call (800) 562-2139 or fax (518) 789-0556**
**www.greyhouse.com   books@greyhouse.com**

## The Comparative Guide to American Suburbs, 2007/08

*The Comparative Guide to American Suburbs* is a one-stop source for Statistics on the 2,000+ suburban communities surrounding the 50 largest metropolitan areas – their population characteristics, income levels, economy, school system and important data on how they compare to one another. Organized into 50 Metropolitan Area chapters, each chapter contains an overview of the Metropolitan Area, a detailed Map followed by a comprehensive Statistical Profile of each Suburban Community, including Contact Information, Physical Characteristics, Population Characteristics, Income, Economy, Unemployment Rate, Cost of Living, Education, Chambers of Commerce and more. Next, statistical data is sorted into Ranking Tables that rank the suburbs by twenty different criteria, including Population, Per Capita Income, Unemployment Rate, Crime Rate, Cost of Living and more. *The Comparative Guide to American Suburbs* is the best source for locating data on suburbs. Those looking to relocate, as well as those doing preliminary market research, will find this an invaluable timesaving resource.

> *"Public and academic libraries will find this compilation useful…The work draws together figures from many sources and will be especially helpful for job relocation decisions." – Booklist*

Softcover ISBN 978-1-59237-180-8, 1,700 pages, $130.00 | Ebook ISBN 978-1-59237-235-5 www.gale.com/gvrl/partners/grey.htm

## The American Tally: Statistics & Comparative Rankings for U.S. Cities with Populations over 10,000

This important statistical handbook compiles, all in one place, comparative statistics on all U.S. cities and towns with a 10,000+ population. *The American Tally* provides statistical details on over 4,000 cities and towns and profiles how they compare with one another in Population Characteristics, Education, Language & Immigration, Income & Employment and Housing. Each section begins with an alphabetical listing of cities by state, allowing for quick access to both the statistics and relative rankings of any city. Next, the highest and lowest cities are listed in each statistic. These important, informative lists provide quick reference to which cities are at both extremes of the spectrum for each statistic. Unlike any other reference, *The American Tally* provides quick, easy access to comparative statistics – a must-have for any reference collection.

> *"A solid library reference." -Bookwatch*

Softcover ISBN 978-1-930956-29-2, 500 pages, $125.00 | Ebook ISBN 978-1-59237-241-6 www.gale.com/gvrl/partners/grey.htm

## The Asian Databook: Statistics for all US Counties & Cities with Over 10,000 Population

This is the first-ever resource that compiles statistics and rankings on the US Asian population. *The Asian Databook* presents over 20 statistical data points for each city and county, arranged alphabetically by state, then alphabetically by place name. Data reported for each place includes Population, Languages Spoken at Home, Foreign-Born, Educational Attainment, Income Figures, Poverty Status, Homeownership, Home Values & Rent, and more. Next, in the Rankings Section, the top 75 places are listed for each data element. These easy-to-access ranking tables allow the user to quickly determine trends and population characteristics. This kind of comparative data can not be found elsewhere, in print or on the web, in a format that's as easy-to-use or more concise. A useful resource for those searching for demographics data, career search and relocation information and also for market research. With data ranging from Ancestry to Education, *The Asian Databook* presents a useful compilation of information that will be a much-needed resource in the reference collection of any public or academic library along with the marketing collection of any company whose primary focus in on the Asian population.

> *"This useful resource will help those searching for demographics data, and market research or relocation information… Accurate and clearly laid out, the publication is recommended for large public library and research collections." -Booklist*

Softcover ISBN 978-1-59237-044-3, 1,000 pages, $150.00

## The Hispanic Databook: Statistics for all US Counties & Cities with Over 10,000 Population

Previously published by Toucan Valley Publications, this second edition has been completely updated with figures from the latest census and has been broadly expanded to include dozens of new data elements and a brand new Rankings section. The Hispanic population in the United States has increased over 42% in the last 10 years and accounts for 12.5% of the total US population. For ease-of-use, *The Hispanic Databook* presents over 20 statistical data points for each city and county, arranged alphabetically by state, then alphabetically by place name. Data reported for each place includes Population, Languages Spoken at Home, Foreign-Born, Educational Attainment, Income Figures, Poverty Status, Homeownership, Home Values & Rent, and more. Next, in the Rankings Section, the top 75 places are listed for each data element. These easy-to-access ranking tables allow the user to quickly determine trends and population characteristics. This kind of comparative data can not be found elsewhere, in print or on the web, in a format that's as easy-to-use or more concise. A useful resource for those searching for demographics data, career search and relocation information and also for market research. With data ranging from Ancestry to Education, *The Hispanic Databook* presents a useful compilation of information that will be a much-needed resource in the reference collection of any public or academic library along with the marketing collection of any company whose primary focus in on the Hispanic population.

> *"This accurate, clearly presented volume of selected Hispanic demographics is recommended for large public libraries and research collections."-Library Journal*

Softcover ISBN 978-1-59237-008-5, 1,000 pages, $150.00

Business Information ◆ Ratings Guides ◆ General Reference ◆ Education ◆
**Statistics** ◆ **Demographics** ◆ Health Information ◆ Canadian Information

## Ancestry in America: A Comparative Guide to Over 200 Ethnic Backgrounds

This brand new reference work pulls together thousands of comparative statistics on the Ethnic Backgrounds of all populated places in the United States with populations over 10,000. Never before has this kind of information been reported in a single volume. Section One, Statistics by Place, is made up of a list of over 200 ancestry and race categories arranged alphabetically by each of the 5,000 different places with populations over 10,000. The population number of the ancestry group in that city or town is provided along with the percent that group represents of the total population. This informative city-by-city section allows the user to quickly and easily explore the ethnic makeup of all major population bases in the United States. Section Two, Comparative Rankings, contains three tables for each ethnicity and race. In the first table, the top 150 populated places are ranked by population number for that particular ancestry group, regardless of population. In the second table, the top 150 populated places are ranked by the percent of the total population for that ancestry group. In the third table, those top 150 populated places with 10,000 population are ranked by population number for each ancestry group. These easy-to-navigate tables allow users to see ancestry population patterns and make city-by-city comparisons as well. This brand new, information-packed resource will serve a wide-range or research requests for demographics, population characteristics, relocation information and much more. *Ancestry in America: A Comparative Guide to Over 200 Ethnic Backgrounds* will be an important acquisition to all reference collections.

*"This compilation will serve a wide range of research requests for population characteristics … it offers much more detail than other sources." –Booklist*

Softcover ISBN 978-1-59237-029-0, 1,500 pages, $225.00

## Weather America, A Thirty-Year Summary of Statistical Weather Data and Rankings

This valuable resource provides extensive climatological data for over 4,000 National and Cooperative Weather Stations throughout the United States. Weather America begins with a new Major Storms section that details major storm events of the nation and a National Rankings section that details rankings for several data elements, such as Maximum Temperature and Precipitation. The main body of Weather America is organized into 50 state sections. Each section provides a Data Table on each Weather Station, organized alphabetically, that provides statistics on Maximum and Minimum Temperatures, Precipitation, Snowfall, Extreme Temperatures, Foggy Days, Humidity and more. State sections contain two brand new features in this edition – a City Index and a narrative Description of the climatic conditions of the state. Each section also includes a revised Map of the State that includes not only weather stations, but cities and towns.

*"Best Reference Book of the Year." –Library Journal*

Softcover ISBN 978-1-891482-29-8, 2,013 pages, $175.00 | Ebook ISBN 978-1-59237-237-9 www.gale.com/gvrl/partners/grey.htm

## Crime in America's Top-Rated Cities

This volume includes over 20 years of crime statistics in all major crime categories: violent crimes, property crimes and total crime. *Crime in America's Top-Rated Cities* is conveniently arranged by city and covers 76 top-rated cities. Crime in America's Top-Rated Cities offers details that compare the number of crimes and crime rates for the city, suburbs and metro area along with national crime trends for violent, property and total crimes. Also, this handbook contains important information and statistics on Anti-Crime Programs, Crime Risk, Hate Crimes, Illegal Drugs, Law Enforcement, Correctional Facilities, Death Penalty Laws and much more. A much-needed resource for people who are relocating, business professionals, general researchers, the press, law enforcement officials and students of criminal justice.

*"Data is easy to access and will save hours of searching." –Global Enforcement Review*

Softcover ISBN 978-1-891482-84-7, 832 pages, $155.00

## The Complete Directory for People with Disabilities, 2008

A wealth of information, now in one comprehensive sourcebook. Completely updated, this edition contains more information than ever before, including thousands of new entries and enhancements to existing entries and thousands of additional web sites and e-mail addresses. This up-to-date directory is the most comprehensive resource available for people with disabilities, detailing Independent Living Centers, Rehabilitation Facilities, State & Federal Agencies, Associations, Support Groups, Periodicals & Books, Assistive Devices, Employment & Education Programs, Camps and Travel Groups. Each year, more libraries, schools, colleges, hospitals, rehabilitation centers and individuals add *The Complete Directory for People with Disabilities* to their collections, making sure that this information is readily available to the families, individuals and professionals who can benefit most from the amazing wealth of resources cataloged here.

*"No other reference tool exists to meet the special needs of the disabled in one convenient resource for information." –Library Journal*

Softcover ISBN 978-1-59237-194-5, 1,200 pages, $165.00 | Online Database $215.00 | Online Database & Directory Combo $300.00

## The Complete Learning Disabilities Directory, 2008

*The Complete Learning Disabilities Directory* is the most comprehensive database of Programs, Services, Curriculum Materials, Professional Meetings & Resources, Camps, Newsletters and Support Groups for teachers, students and families concerned with learning disabilities. This information-packed directory includes information about Associations & Organizations, Schools, Colleges & Testing Materials, Government Agencies, Legal Resources and much more. For quick, easy access to information, this directory contains four indexes: Entry Name Index, Subject Index and Geographic Index. With every passing year, the field of learning disabilities attracts more attention and the network of caring, committed and knowledgeable professionals grows every day. This directory is an invaluable research tool for these parents, students and professionals.

*"Due to its wealth and depth of coverage, parents, teachers and others… should find this an invaluable resource." -Booklist*

Softcover ISBN 978-1-59237-207-2, 900 pages, $145.00 | Online Database $195.00 | Online Database & Directory Combo $280.00

## The Complete Directory for People with Chronic Illness, 2007/08

Thousands of hours of research have gone into this completely updated edition – several new chapters have been added along with thousands of new entries and enhancements to existing entries. Plus, each chronic illness chapter has been reviewed by a medical expert in the field. This widely-hailed directory is structured around the 90 most prevalent chronic illnesses – from Asthma to Cancer to Wilson's Disease – and provides a comprehensive overview of the support services and information resources available for people diagnosed with a chronic illness. Each chronic illness has its own chapter and contains a brief description in layman's language, followed by important resources for National & Local Organizations, State Agencies, Newsletters, Books & Periodicals, Libraries & Research Centers, Support Groups & Hotlines, Web Sites and much more. This directory is an important resource for health care professionals, the collections of hospital and health care libraries, as well as an invaluable tool for people with a chronic illness and their support network.

*"A must purchase for all hospital and health care libraries and is strongly recommended for all public library reference departments." –ARBA*

Softcover ISBN 978-1-59237-183-9, 1,200 pages, $165.00 | Online Database $215.00 | Online Database & Directory Combo $300.00

## The Complete Mental Health Directory, 2008/09

This is the most comprehensive resource covering the field of behavioral health, with critical information for both the layman and the mental health professional. For the layman, this directory offers understandable descriptions of 25 Mental Health Disorders as well as detailed information on Associations, Media, Support Groups and Mental Health Facilities. For the professional, The Complete Mental Health Directory offers critical and comprehensive information on Managed Care Organizations, Information Systems, Government Agencies and Provider Organizations. This comprehensive volume of needed information will be widely used in any reference collection.

*"… the strength of this directory is that it consolidates widely dispersed information into a single volume." –Booklist*

Softcover ISBN 978-1-59237-285-0, 800 pages, $165.00 | Online Database $215.00 | Online & Directory Combo $300.00

**Business Information ◆ Ratings Guides ◆ General Reference ◆ Education ◆
Statistics ◆ Demographics ◆ <u>Health Information</u> ◆ Canadian Information**

## The Comparative Guide to American Hospitals, Second Edition

This new second edition compares all of the nation's hospitals by 24 measures of quality in the treatment of heart attack, heart failure, pneumonia, and, new to this edition, surgical procedures and pregnancy care. Plus, this second edition is now available in regional volumes, to make locating information about hospitals in your area quicker and easier than ever before. The Comparative Guide to American Hospitals provides a snapshot profile of each of the nations 4,200+ hospitals. These informative profiles illustrate how the hospital rates when providing 24 different treatments within four broad categories: Heart Attack Care, Heart Failure Care, Surgical Infection Prevention (NEW), and Pregnancy Care measures (NEW). Each profile includes the raw percentage for that hospital, the state average, the US average and data on the top hospital. For easy access to contact information, each profile includes the hospital's address, phone and fax numbers, email and web addresses, type and accreditation along with 5 top key administrations. These profiles will allow the user to quickly identify the quality of the hospital and have the necessary information at their fingertips to make contact with that hospital. Most importantly, *The Comparative Guide to American Hospitals* provides easy-to-use Regional State by State Statistical Summary Tables for each of the data elements to allow the user to quickly locate hospitals with the best level of service. Plus, a new 30-Day Mortality Chart, Glossary of Terms and Regional Hospital Profile Index make this a must-have source. This new, expanded edition will be a must for the reference collection at all public, medical and academic libraries.

*"These data will help those with heart conditions and pneumonia make informed decisions about their healthcare and encourage hospitals to improve the quality of care they provide. Large medical, hospital, and public libraries are most likely to benefit from this weighty resource."-Library Journal*

Four Volumes Softcover ISBN 978-1-59237-182-2, 3,500 pages, $325.00 | Regional Volumes $135.00 |
Ebook ISBN 978-1-59237-239-3 www.gale.com/gvrl/partners/grey.htm

## Older Americans Information Directory, 2007

Completely updated for 2007, this sixth edition has been completely revised and now contains 1,000 new listings, over 8,000 updates to existing listings and over 3,000 brand new e-mail addresses and web sites. You'll find important resources for Older Americans including National, Regional, State & Local Organizations, Government Agencies, Research Centers, Libraries & Information Centers, Legal Resources, Discount Travel Information, Continuing Education Programs, Disability Aids & Assistive Devices, Health, Print Media and Electronic Media. Three indexes: Entry Index, Subject Index and Geographic Index make it easy to find just the right source of information. This comprehensive guide to resources for Older Americans will be a welcome addition to any reference collection.

*"Highly recommended for academic, public, health science and consumer libraries..." –Choice*

1,200 pages; Softcover ISBN 978-1-59237-136-5, $165.00 | Online Database $215.00 | Online Database & Directory Combo $300.00

## The Complete Directory for Pediatric Disorders, 2008

This important directory provides parents and caregivers with information about Pediatric Conditions, Disorders, Diseases and Disabilities, including Blood Disorders, Bone & Spinal Disorders, Brain Defects & Abnormalities, Chromosomal Disorders, Congenital Heart Defects, Movement Disorders, Neuromuscular Disorders and Pediatric Tumors & Cancers. This carefully written directory offers: understandable Descriptions of 15 major bodily systems; Descriptions of more than 200 Disorders and a Resources Section, detailing National Agencies & Associations, State Associations, Online Services, Libraries & Resource Centers, Research Centers, Support Groups & Hotlines, Camps, Books and Periodicals. This resource will provide immediate access to information crucial to families and caregivers when coping with children's illnesses.

*"Recommended for public and consumer health libraries." –Library Journal*

Softcover ISBN 978-1-59237-150-1, 1,200 pages, $165.00 | Online Database $215.00 | Online Database & Directory Combo $300.00

## The Directory of Drug & Alcohol Residential Rehabilitation Facilities

This brand new directory is the first-ever resource to bring together, all in one place, data on the thousands of drug and alcohol residential rehabilitation facilities in the United States. The Directory of Drug & Alcohol Residential Rehabilitation Facilities covers over 1,000 facilities, with detailed contact information for each one, including mailing address, phone and fax numbers, email addresses and web sites, mission statement, type of treatment programs, cost, average length of stay, numbers of residents and counselors, accreditation, insurance plans accepted, type of environment, religious affiliation, education components and much more. It also contains a helpful chapter on General Resources that provides contact information for Associations, Print & Electronic Media, Support Groups and Conferences. Multiple indexes allow the user to pinpoint the facilities that meet very specific criteria. This time-saving tool is what so many counselors, parents and medical professionals have been asking for. The Directory of Drug & Alcohol Residential Rehabilitation Facilities will be a helpful tool in locating the right source for treatment for a wide range of individuals. This comprehensive directory will be an important acquisition for all reference collections: public and academic libraries, case managers, social workers, state agencies and many more.

*"This is an excellent, much needed directory that fills an important gap..." –Booklist*

Softcover ISBN 978-1-59237-031-3, 300 pages, $135.00

**To preview any of our Directories Risk-Free for 30 days, call (800) 562-2139 or fax (518) 789-0556
www.greyhouse.com  books@greyhouse.com**

### The Directory of Hospital Personnel, 2008

*The Directory of Hospital Personnel* is the best resource you can have at your fingertips when researching or marketing a product or service to the hospital market. A "Who's Who" of the hospital universe, this directory puts you in touch with over 150,000 key decision-makers. With 100% verification of data you can rest assured that you will reach the right person with just one call. Every hospital in the U.S. is profiled, listed alphabetically by city within state. Plus, three easy-to-use, cross-referenced indexes put the facts at your fingertips faster and more easily than any other directory: Hospital Name Index, Bed Size Index and Personnel Index. *The Directory of Hospital Personnel* is the only complete source for key hospital decision-makers by name. Whether you want to define or restructure sales territories… locate hospitals with the purchasing power to accept your proposals… keep track of important contacts or colleagues… or find information on which insurance plans are accepted, *The Directory of Hospital Personnel* gives you the information you need – easily, efficiently, effectively and accurately.

*"Recommended for college, university and medical libraries." -ARBA*

Softcover ISBN 978-1-59237-286-7, 2,500 pages, $325.00 | Online Database $545.00 | Online Database & Directory Combo, $650.00

### The Directory of Health Care Group Purchasing Organizations, 2008

This comprehensive directory provides the important data you need to get in touch with over 800 Group Purchasing Organizations. By providing in-depth information on this growing market and its members, *The Directory of Health Care Group Purchasing Organizations* fills a major need for the most accurate and comprehensive information on over 800 GPOs – Mailing Address, Phone & Fax Numbers, E-mail Addresses, Key Contacts, Purchasing Agents, Group Descriptions, Membership Categorization, Standard Vendor Proposal Requirements, Membership Fees & Terms, Expanded Services, Total Member Beds & Outpatient Visits represented and more. Five Indexes provide a number of ways to locate the right GPO: Alphabetical Index, Expanded Services Index, Organization Type Index, Geographic Index and Member Institution Index. With its comprehensive and detailed information on each purchasing organization, *The Directory of Health Care Group Purchasing Organizations* is the go-to source for anyone looking to target this market.

*"The information is clearly arranged and easy to access…recommended for those needing this very specialized information." –ARBA*

1,000 pages; Softcover ISBN 978-1-59237-287-4, $325.00 | Online Database, $650.00 | Online Database & Directory Combo, $750.00

### The HMO/PPO Directory, 2008

*The HMO/PPO Directory* is a comprehensive source that provides detailed information about Health Maintenance Organizations and Preferred Provider Organizations nationwide. This comprehensive directory details more information about more managed health care organizations than ever before. Over 1,100 HMOs, PPOs, Medicare Advantage Plans and affiliated companies are listed, arranged alphabetically by state. Detailed listings include Key Contact Information, Prescription Drug Benefits, Enrollment, Geographical Areas served, Affiliated Physicians & Hospitals, Federal Qualifications, Status, Year Founded, Managed Care Partners, Employer References, Fees & Payment Information and more. Plus, five years of historical information is included related to Revenues, Net Income, Medical Loss Ratios, Membership Enrollment and Number of Patient Complaints. Five easy-to-use, cross-referenced indexes will put this vast array of information at your fingertips immediately: HMO Index, PPO Index, Other Providers Index, Personnel Index and Enrollment Index. *The HMO/PPO Directory* provides the most comprehensive data on the most companies available on the market place today.

*"Helpful to individuals requesting certain HMO/PPO issues such as co-payment costs, subscription costs and patient complaints. Individuals concerned (or those with questions) about their insurance may find this text to be of use to them." -ARBA*

Softcover ISBN 978-1-59237-204-1, 600 pages, $325.00 | Online Database, $495.00 | Online Database & Directory Combo, $600.00

### Medical Device Register, 2008

The only one-stop resource of every medical supplier licensed to sell products in the US. This award-winning directory offers immediate access to over 13,000 companies - and more than 65,000 products – in two information-packed volumes. This comprehensive resource saves hours of time and trouble when searching for medical equipment and supplies and the manufacturers who provide them. Volume I: The Product Directory, provides essential information for purchasing or specifying medical supplies for every medical device, supply, and diagnostic available in the US. Listings provide FDA codes & Federal Procurement Eligibility, Contact information for every manufacturer of the product along with Prices and Product Specifications. Volume 2 - Supplier Profiles, offers the most complete and important data about Suppliers, Manufacturers and Distributors. Company Profiles detail the number of employees, ownership, method of distribution, sales volume, net income, key executives detailed contact information medical products the company supplies, plus the medical specialties they cover. Four indexes provide immediate access to this wealth of information: Keyword Index, Trade Name Index, Supplier Geographical Index and OEM (Original Equipment Manufacturer) Index. *Medical Device Register* is the only one-stop source for locating suppliers and products; looking for new manufacturers or hard-to-find medical devices; comparing products and companies; know who's selling what and who to buy from cost effectively. This directory has become the standard in its field and will be a welcome addition to the reference collection of any medical library, large public library, university library along with the collections that serve the medical community.

*"A wealth of information on medical devices, medical device companies… and key personnel in the industry is provide in this comprehensive reference work… A valuable reference work, one of the best hardcopy compilations available." -Doody Publishing*

Two Volumes, Hardcover ISBN 978-1-59237-206-5, 3,000 pages, $325.00

**To preview any of our Directories Risk-Free for 30 days, call (800) 562-2139 or fax (518) 789-0556**
**www.greyhouse.com  books@greyhouse.com**

### Canadian Almanac & Directory, 2008

*The Canadian Almanac & Directory* contains sixteen directories in one – giving you all the facts and figures you will ever need about Canada. No other single source provides users with the quality and depth of up-to-date information for all types of research. This national directory and guide gives you access to statistics, images and over 100,000 names and addresses for everything from Airlines to Zoos - updated every year. It's Ten Directories in One! Each section is a directory in itself, providing robust information on business and finance, communications, government, associations, arts and culture (museums, zoos, libraries, etc.), health, transportation, law, education, and more.  Government information includes federal, provincial and territorial - and includes an easy-to-use quick index to find key information. A separate municipal government section includes every municipality in Canada, with full profiles of Canada's largest urban centers. A complete legal directory lists judges and judicial officials, court locations and law firms across the country. A wealth of general information, the *Canadian Almanac & Directory* also includes national statistics on population, employment, imports and exports, and more. National awards and honors are presented, along with forms of address, Commonwealth information and full color photos of Canadian symbols. Postal information, weights, measures, distances and other useful charts are also incorporated. Complete almanac information includes perpetual calendars, five-year holiday planners and astronomical information. Published continuously for 160 years, *The Canadian Almanac & Directory* is the best single reference source for business executives, managers and assistants; government and public affairs executives; lawyers; marketing, sales and advertising executives; researchers, editors and journalists.

Hardcover ISBN 978-1-59237-220-1, 1,600 pages, $315.00

### Associations Canada, 2008

The Most Powerful Fact-Finder to Business, Trade, Professional and Consumer Organizations
*Associations Canada* covers Canadian organizations and international groups including industry, commercial and professional associations, registered charities, special interest and common interest organizations. This annually revised compendium provides detailed listings and abstracts for nearly 20,000 regional, national and international organizations.  This popular volume provides the most comprehensive picture of Canada's non-profit sector. Detailed listings enable users to identify an organization's budget, founding date, scope of activity, licensing body, sources of funding, executive information, full address and complete contact information, just to name a few. Powerful indexes help researchers find information quickly and easily. The following indexes are included: subject, acronym, geographic, budget, executive name, conferences & conventions, mailing list, defunct and unreachable associations and registered charitable organizations. In addition to annual spending of over $1 billion on transportation and conventions alone, Canadian associations account for many millions more in pursuit of membership interests. *Associations Canada* provides complete access to this highly lucrative market.  *Associations Canada* is a strong source of prospects for sales and marketing executives, tourism and convention officials, researchers, government officials - anyone who wants to locate non-profit interest groups and trade associations.

Hardcover ISBN 978-1-59237-277-5, 1,600 pages, $315.00

### Financial Services Canada, 2008/09

*Financial Services Canada* is the only master file of current contacts and information that serves the needs of the entire financial services industry in Canada.  With over 18,000 organizations and hard-to-find business information, Financial Services Canada is the most up-to-date source for names and contact numbers of industry professionals, senior executives, portfolio managers, financial advisors, agency bureaucrats and elected representatives.  Financial Services Canada incorporates the latest changes in the industry to provide you with the most current details on each company, including: name, title, organization, telephone and fax numbers, e-mail and web addresses. *Financial Services Canada* also includes private company listings never before compiled, government agencies, association and consultant services - to ensure that you'll never miss a client or a contact. Current listings include: banks and branches, non-depository institutions, stock exchanges and brokers, investment management firms, insurance companies, major accounting and law firms, government agencies and financial associations.  Powerful indexes assist researchers with locating the vital financial information they need. The following indexes are included: alphabetic, geographic, executive name, corporate web site/e-mail, government quick reference and subject. *Financial Services Canada* is a valuable resource for financial executives, bankers, financial planners, sales and marketing professionals, lawyers and chartered accountants, government officials, investment dealers, journalists, librarians and reference specialists.

Hardcover ISBN 978-1-59237-278-2, 900 pages, $315.00

### Directory of Libraries in Canada, 2008/09

*The Directory of Libraries in Canada* brings together almost 7,000 listings including libraries and their branches, information resource centers, archives and library associations and learning centers. The directory offers complete and comprehensive information on Canadian libraries, resource centers, business information centers, professional associations, regional library systems, archives, library schools and library technical programs. *The Directory of Libraries in Canada* includes important features of each library and service, including library information; personnel details, including contact names and e-mail addresses; collection information; services available to users; acquisitions budgets; and computers and automated systems.  Useful information on each library's electronic access is also included, such as Internet browser, connectivity and public Internet/CD-ROM/subscription database access. The directory also provides powerful indexes for subject, location, personal name and Web site/e-mail to assist researchers with locating the crucial information they need. *The Directory of Libraries in Canada* is a vital reference tool for publishers, advocacy groups, students, research institutions, computer hardware suppliers, and other diverse groups that provide products and services to this unique market.

Hardcover ISBN 978-1-59237-279-9, 850 pages, $315.00

**To preview any of our Directories Risk-Free for 30 days, call (800) 562-2139 or fax (518) 789-0556**
**www.greyhouse.com  books@greyhouse.com**

## Canadian Environmental Directory, 2008 /09

*The Canadian Environmental Directory* is Canada's most complete and only national listing of environmental associations and organizations, government regulators and purchasing groups, product and service companies, special libraries, and more! The extensive Products and Services section provides detailed listings enabling users to identify the company name, address, phone, fax, e-mail, Web address, firm type, contact names (and titles), product and service information, affiliations, trade information, branch and affiliate data. The Government section gives you all the contact information you need at every government level – federal, provincial and municipal. We also include descriptions of current environmental initiatives, programs and agreements, names of environment-related acts administered by each ministry or department PLUS information and tips on who to contact and how to sell to governments in Canada. The Associations section provides complete contact information and a brief description of activities. Included are Canadian environmental organizations and international groups including industry, commercial and professional associations, registered charities, special interest and common interest organizations. All the Information you need about the Canadian environmental industry: directory of products and services, special libraries and resource, conferences, seminars and tradeshows, chronology of environmental events, law firms and major Canadian companies, *The Canadian Environmental Directory* is ideal for business, government, engineers and anyone conducting research on the environment.

Softcover ISBN 978-1-59237-224-9, 900 pages, $315.00

## Canadian Parliamentary Guide, 2008

An indispensable guide to government in Canada, the annual *Canadian Parliamentary Guide* provides information on both federal and provincial governments, courts, and their elected and appointed members. The Guide is completely bilingual, with each record appearing both in English and then in French. The Guide contains biographical sketches of members of the Governor General's Household, the Privy Council, members of Canadian legislatures (federal, including both the House of Commons and the Senate, provincial and territorial), members of the federal superior courts (Supreme, Federal, Federal Appeal, Court Martial Appeal and Tax Courts) and the senior staff for these institutions. Biographies cover personal data, political career, private career and contact information. In addition, the Guide provides descriptions of each of the institutions, including brief historical information in text and chart format and significant facts (i.e. number of members and their salaries). The Guide covers the results of all federal general elections and by-elections from Confederations to the present and the results of the most recent provincial elections. A complete name index rounds out the text, making information easy to find. No other resources presents a more up-to-date, more complete picture of Canadian government and her political leaders. A must-have resource for all Canadian reference collections.

Hardcover ISBN 978-1-59237-310-9, 800 pages, $184.00